THE GOLDEN SHAKESPEARE

also by Logan Pearsall Smith

ALL TRIVIA

ON READING SHAKESPEARE

A TREASURY OF ENGLISH APHORISMS

A TREASURY OF ENGLISH PROSE

WORDS AND IDIOMS

The Golden Shakespeare

AN ANTHOLOGY
compiled by
Logan Pearsall Smith

CONSTABLE & CO LTD
London W.C.2

LONDON
PUBLISHED BY
Constable and Company Ltd
10–12 ORANGE STREET, W.C.2

INDIA *and* PAKISTAN
Orient Longmans Ltd
BOMBAY   CALCUTTA   MADRAS

CANADA
Longmans, Green and Company
TORONTO

Nov. 1953

First published 1949

PRINTED IN GREAT BRITAIN
BY R. & R. CLARK, LTD., EDINBURGH

PREFACE

LOGAN PEARSALL SMITH told me on one occasion (not without a little natural and human gratification) that he had once been described as the man who first raised the compiling of anthologies to the level of an art. Although this eminence could alone have excused a short account of his methods at work, there is another reason for giving such an account, and perhaps, in the circumstances, a more pressing one.

My old friend, as will be found in his introduction, thanked me in anticipation for performing the task I have now completed. The undertaking of it was not as I had anticipated, when he first read aloud to me a draft of that introduction. I had expected only to save him the preparation of the copy, some tedium of proof-correcting, and the answering of such questions as printers and publishers are bound to ask. Instead, after his death, I have had to deal with a selection of extracts which, although he had perused and corrected it many times, he had not yet come to look upon as utterly complete and perfect.

Pearsall Smith's book, *On Reading Shakespeare*, had a notable success when it was published in 1933 (indeed, when in 1932, as a contribution to *Life and Letters*, the essay first appeared before being enlarged, it had a wider success than is usual on such occasions). The most noticeable consequence was the request for an anthology of passages from Shakespeare. For various reasons of no great interest or importance, he never came to a final agreement with the original proposer. The cause of his never entirely completing the selection was his own exquisitely fastidious taste. ' I have worked on it a good deal at various times . . . ' he once wrote to me about another anthology of his, ' and then put it by, as I like to put my books by to mellow.' *The Golden Shakespeare* was put away in the cellar, so to speak, and taken out and held to the light, and put back again a great many times during a period of some twelve years. I assisted at many of these re-examinations, and I shared in all the labour of the first selection.

For him, this was no new task, since all of his reading was in part anthologizing, and his marked volume of Shakespeare was already a garland of splendid passages. It wasn't even his first attempt at collecting together such passages. In Florence, about the turn of the century, he with his sister and brother-in-law, Mr. and Mrs. Berenson, in their private beautiful magazine, *The Golden Urn*, had anthologized Milton, Keats, and Shakespeare. The work was so exquisitely—so over-exquisitely—done that it became, in this case, perhaps too precious, too refinedly fastidious, and giving some justification to those austere readers and opponents of garlanding, whom he referred to as ' whole-hoggers '. These pages of *The Golden Urn* look a little like transcriptions from a damaged papyrus, in which, miraculously, only fine phrases have survived the worms and the weather. His later task was a larger and soberer one, for which he demanded my help, and the foil of my less experienced opinion.

We both read the works of Shakespeare through from beginning to end, in a probably chronological order, marking all hopeful, possible, likely, or certainly golden passages. From my clumsier diggings, he did obtain some shining dust and a few nuggets of fine gold which he himself had missed. The passages decided on, I cut out and stuck on to sheets of paper, making a sort of unbound scrap-book. This selection itself was then subjected to much the same process as the complete works, a process which entailed remaking large parts of the original. From the resulting collection of papers the text of the present volume was prepared. Before it reached the condition in which I used it, Pearsall Smith had revised it very considerably, both by subtraction and addition ; the copy is full of crossings-out, and also of passages added in manuscript, some in his hand-writing, but mostly in my own.

During about three years of the war, *The Golden Shake-*

speare, with various papers and letters of his, was sheltering in my country home. When I had the opportunity, I looked through the copy (I also, to make extra sure of preserving the selection, marked the chosen passages in a copy of Shakespeare's works). In addition to his latest alterations, he had put marks of query against some passages. Where I had doubts about the wisdom of his tentative changes, I made a note in the margin. In 1943 he thought of publishing the book, and I returned the copy to him. Once again, however, after working through the selection, he put it away to mellow. When I went over it for publication, I discovered that he had silently accepted some of my suggestions, and had rejected others; over some he had come to no decision. One play, *Troilus and Cressida*, was marked ' unrevised '.

My hardest task, therefore, has been to decide on which passages to retain from this particular play, and the result, in this book, is, in effect, my own choice from Pearsall Smith's unperfected selection. With other plays I have, in a few cases, followed my own suggestions where I had expressed doubt of his undecided plans, and where he had evidently not made up his mind. In all this work I consulted the friend who had been so fully consulted over the original work, Sir Trevor Bigham; and for the trouble he took I must add my own warm tribute of admiration and gratitude. The final responsibility, of course, has been my own; but in almost every case I have followed his advice. It must be understood that with these passages I have never included anything that had not been accepted at one time by Pearsall Smith, or which had been finally and decisively discarded by him : never, that is, except for three songs.

He included a short Shakespearean extract from *The Two Noble Kinsmen*; and from *Henry VIII* he took, among other passages more probably authentic, Wolsey's famous speech, which has often been attributed to Fletcher. Having done so much, I cannot think he would have gravely objected to my adding, as I have done, those lovely songs, *Orpheus with his lute* from the latter, and from the former *Roses their sharp spines being gone*, and *Urns and odours bring away*. These are surely authentic gold, though whether Shakespearean or not, remains and, I surmise, will always remain a question beyond the decisive powers of any critical touchstone.

His introduction presented much the same problems,— though less complicated,—as the rest of the book. There were two typescripts, in a state of not quite finished correction. At some time, in a mood of depression, he had evidently considered the cutting out of certain passages ; since these were often passages of characteristic and most excellent writing, I have shamelessly and without hesitation restored most of them.

There was also to be considered a series of preliminary notes to a few of the poems and plays. I remember his discussing his plan of writing these notes ; nothing was resolved on, but I think his final intention was to write a series of short illuminating observations for the beginning of each section. Unluckily, no more was achieved of this plan than notes to the early poems and plays, together with an introduction to the first section, *The Dawn*. These are admittedly unfinished ; however, since they are, in my opinion, too interesting to be lost, I have printed them as an appendix.

Among some of the detached passages which did not seem to fit very happily into the introduction was this : ' The text of this *Golden Shakespeare* is the Cambridge text—that of the Globe edition [1]—which is generally admitted to be the nearest approach to a standard text of Shakespeare which we possess. I do not accept every one of its readings, but mark with a note any variations from it.'

These variations do not require the elaborate apparatus of special notes, for they are only three. In *Twelfth Night*, Pope's emendation of ' sound ' to ' south ', in Act I, Scene i, line 5, has been accepted,

> O, it came o'er my ear like the sweet south
> That breathes upon a bank of violets.

[1] References are to the edition of 1928.

In *Antony and Cleopatra*, Act IV, Scene xv, line 11, he accepted the amendment of ' shore ' to ' star ', first suggested by Staunton in 1873,

> Darkling stand
> The varying star o' the world.

In early editions, the first two lines of Sonnet CXLVI are printed,

> Poor soul the centre of my sinful earth,
> My sinful earth these rebel powers that thee array. . . .

In many modern editions a conjectureless blank is left for the first three words of line 2. Pearsall Smith has used the commonly accepted emendation,

> Fooled by these rebel powers that thee array.

In one respect his observation as to the text requires correcting. For the extracts from *The Two Noble Kinsmen*, a play which, although Shakespeare assuredly had a hand in it, is not printed with the regular Shakespearean canon, the text of the 1679 folio of Beaumont and Fletcher has been used.

The device on the binding is reproduced from the famous golden medal struck to commemorate the defeat of the Armada; it has, I believe, been sometimes ascribed to Nicholas Hilliard, the miniaturist, who engraved the Great Seal in 1586. Pearsall Smith used to declare that it seemed to contain all the distillation and essence of the Elizabethan period; and it was his wish that it should adorn the cover of his *Golden Shakespeare*.

ROBERT GATHORNE-HARDY

CONTENTS

CONTENTS

POEMS

Contents

INTRODUCTION

I

IF it be ever permissible to make a book of selections from the works of an old author, surely Shakespeare's works will profit as much as any by such a process of sifting. They have come down to us, as we know, more encumbered perhaps than those of any great writer with alien or dead matter. As modern investigation has shown, Shakespeare was at first a cobbler and patcher-up of old plays, which, when he had retouched them, however slightly, were pitchforked bodily, as being wholly of his composition, into the folio of works.

Research [as Dr Mackail says] has done away with the old careless belief that the body of work passing under Shakespeare's name is all his. . . . The amount of non-Shakespearean work in what is called Shakespeare is large : alike in the earlier period when he was adapting and piecing out older men's plays, in the later period when younger men were doing the same with his, and even between the two, where the stage-text that has reached us was made up in a hurry by putting several hands to work on it, or had been altered for performance by stage-managers or by irresponsible actors.[1]

The battle between the 'accepters' of the Folio, who attempt to swallow that compilation whole, and the 'disintegrators' who assign large portions of it to other writers, is raging fiercely at present ; what will be its outcome no one can yet foretell, but it becomes apparent that even the most orthodox are coming to reject more than they are always quite willing to admit.

II

Besides this work of other and inferior playwrights, all critics are forced to agree that there is no small amount of

[1] *Studies of English Poets*, p. 15.

inferior stuff even in Shakespeare's admittedly authentic work. While on one side of him he was the greatest of the world's poets, he was also, on another side, a most generous purveyor to the taste of his audience and of his time. That element which pleased his own age, but is wearisome to ours, consists partly in the verbal trifling and intolerable smart talk in which the fashionables of the Court delighted, partly in the crude horror and bloody bones, the buffoonery, horse-play, and scurrility which rejoiced the vulgar. Robert Bridges held that Shakespeare deliberately played false to his artistic ideals in order to gratify ' those wretched creatures ', as he calls the Elizabethan audience, ' who can never be forgiven for their shame in preventing the greatest poet and dramatist of the world from being the greatest artist '. But what proof is there that Shakespeare possessed the artistic ideals which Bridges attributes to him ? His work shows no sign of that love of perfection which was unsought for in our literature before the time of Milton. Shakespeare's advance in power is prodigious, is overwhelming ; but towards those heights where perfection dwells, there is no evidence of progress. His negligence, indeed, seems to grow upon him, and his latest plays are more carelessly composed than all the others. Even in the Sonnets, so choicely indited for his private friends, we find the same mingling of gold and rubbish which surprises us in the plays, the same magic of enchanting poetry along with dull ribaldry and dull conceits and quibbles. Shakespeare had a genuine relish for ribaldry ; and puns and quibbles he loved with an even greater passion. A quibble was for him, as Dr. Johnson said, ' the fatal Cleopatra for which he lost the world, and was content to lose it '.

Shakespeare often, moreover, falls, as Dryden remarked, into a ' carelessness, and, as I may call it, a lethargy of thought, for whole scenes together ', and is then content to turn out hackneyed stuff, or tamely to versify whole speeches from the chronicles or romances in front of him. Many of his plays are pot-boilers, and, as Sir Walter Raleigh bluntly puts it, they are ' bad plays ; poor and confused in structure, or defaced with feeble writing. Some of them contain whole scenes written in Shakespeare's most splendid manner, and fully conceived characters drawn with all his vigour, while other scenes and characters in the same play pass the bounds of inanity.'

III

Another element of inferior quality in the plays consists of the merely scenic business,—the bag of old theatrical tricks,— disguises, recognitions, patched-up matings and happy endings, which Shakespeare makes use of again and again without scruple. These theatricalities are features of the old, foolish plots which he accepts as he finds them. Not only in the historical dramas were his incidents and characters fixed be- forehand ; in the comedies and tragedies also, the stories he dramatized were often too familiar for him to alter them, even had he wished to do so.

Recent criticism, especially in America, has been largely concerned with the historical aspect of Shakespeare's achieve- ment, the close relation of his plays to those of his fellow dramatists,—how he, like them, inherited the old conventions of the English stage, the stock characters, the stock themes for declamation ; and how he also followed, as they did, the changes of fashionable taste, being indeed quite as sensitive as the others to these changes, and quite as ready to satisfy them by imitating and adapting, and (being no innovator himself) by making use of other men's inventions. But it is not the Elizabethan element in Shakespeare's work which claims the anthologist's interest ; his aim indeed is to discard it, and fix his attention only on that portion of Shakespeare's work which remains significant after the conditions which actually produced it are past. It is when Shakespeare trans- forms what he inherits, or what other men invent, into vital creations of his own, that we find the gold we seek for. Granted that his plots are for the most part inherited or borrowed, that they are often so full of old story-book, even fairy-tale business, as to be frankly absurd : and that the characters in them, the deep-dyed villains, the braggart cowards, the buffoons, the musical, mad girls, and the heroines in doublet and hose, are the stock characters of the Elizabethan drama, it is his transformation of these puppets into living and breathing human creatures which claims our attention : the way he endows his clowns and buffoons with an independent and individual existence of their own, and creates heroes who are so superior to their actions that we quite forget, in our sense of what they are, the absurdity, the incongruity, and sometimes the baseness of the things they do. Shakespeare's plays are seldom, therefore, as earnest thinkers have tried to make out, perfect and well-rounded wholes, inspired by, and expressive of some great conception ; they are remodellings of old, traditional plots in which the characters who carry on the action are conceived with an intensity of imagination which is unsurpassed in the literature of the world. Such plays oscillate, therefore, as it has been well said, between an extreme psychological truth and an equally extreme disregard of truth and human nature,—and also, it must be added, a deliberate and not infrequent sacrifice of truth to theatrical effect.

Certainly it is best to read Shakespeare's plays as they have come down to us, encumbered though they be with interpolations, absurdities, and tiresome and unpleasing elements, which after all do not matter very much. It is thus that his true lovers read him ; and no meagre books of selections can ever take for them the place of their complete editions. But there are dainty and less strenuous moments in the moods of many readers, when all they want is the perfection of some great writer's achievement : when it pleases them to feed, so to speak, on his purer essence, and have presented to them his imperfect masterpieces (and all masterpieces are imperfect in this imperfect world) disengaged from all that is of inferior quality and obsolete interest in them. This pruning away of

alien and dead matter is what, greatly daring, I have under-
taken in this book. And with the dull rhetoric, the dull
scurrility, the puns and quibbles, I have also eliminated,—
save when transmuted by the magic of style,—that gnomic
element of sententious reflection with which Shakespeare
edified and pleased his contemporaries,—and pleased, it would
seem, eighteenth- and nineteenth-century readers as well,
since so many of their Selections and Birthday Books and
Calendars are full of moralizings of this kind.

IV

What then remains ? Well, simply all the opulence of
Shakespeare's authentic gold,—all that he coined in his own
mint, all that he wrote when the inspiration of his genius was
upon him. This treasure consists first of all in the poetry of
this greatest of all the world's poets,—poetry found sometimes
in the splendid speeches which develop the action of his
dramas, and sometimes too in passages of pure poetry which
have little or no relation to the play into which he interpolates
them, but which, like Mercutio's discourse on Queen Mab, or
Oberon's vision, read as if they had not been cast originally
in the dramatic mould, but were extracts from a poet's note-
book, or from some cherished, unpublished book of verse.

These lyrical passages appear most frequently in the earlier
plays ; in the later ones we find speeches in which Shakespeare
seems to appear himself before the footlights and give utterance to his own deepest meditations, as if intent only on the
creation of a spiritual reality of his own. These cadenzas, if
I may so borrow the musical term, are sometimes, like Orsino's
discourse on music, not incongruous with the character which
speaks them ; but they are often quite out of place, if not of
character, like for instance the Duke's great speech on death
in *Measure for Measure*, a speech which seems so cruel and
callous (which the Duke was not) when addressed to a youth
condemned to execution. And now and then Shakespeare's

personages seem to put their masks entirely aside to utter great soliloquies like those of Macbeth, in which this savage murderer of a savage age reveals a visage pale with thought like that of Hamlet, like that, we cannot but believe, of Shakespeare himself; and it is in these great passages (all of which are included in this volume) that we find much of the purest gold of Shakespeare's poetry.

In a finely-wrought epigram, Sir William Watson has drawn a fine distinction between ' the gong and cymbals' din ' of Marlowe's verse, and ' the long slow slopes, and vast curves of Shakespeare's violin '. There is in Shakespeare's plays much of the resounding brass of Elizabethan music: the disintegrators assign it to Kyd and Peele and Greene and Chapman and Marlowe and other dramatists of the time, rejecting, for instance, the whole of *Richard III*,—that magnificent performance on the brass,—and even that greatest piece of the world's rhetoric, Mark Antony's oration over the corpse of Caesar. But surely Shakespeare could play gloriously on the trumpets and the trombones when he wanted; and I cannot omit (I only wish I had room for more) the finest of these fanfares which the disintegrators so ruthlessly discard. What they listen for, what they regard as alone authentic, is the tone, the tamber, the accent of Shakespeare's violin, in which they find the very echo and resonance of his soul. For this I listen also, for this music above all other music; and even more than in the great cadenzas of musing and meditation, I find its most delicate and spontaneous out-trilling in the magic and enchantment of his plays. How magically the strains of ' Take, O take those lips away ', fall on our ears in that little remote, romantic scene of Mariana's deserted grange, or Ariel's unearthly songs in the enchanted island, or the songs of Autolycus by the shepherd's cottage, or Feste's almost nonsensical verses, when the golden light goes out at the end of *Twelfth Night*, and in the wind and the rain the curtain falls !

It is in songs like these, where absurd touches of everyday

life and common words are often mingled with gushes of incomparable sweetness, and irrelevant little melodies appear and falter, that we seem to hear the soul of Shakespeare nightingaling to itself its most magical and enchanting song.

V

' Magic ', ' enchantment ',—I feel that I have already overworked these outworn words ; but I must (such is the poverty of our vocabulary) make use of them again to speak of another aspect of the evocative power of this greatest of all the world's magicians. This power, which is generally looked upon as the most supreme of all Shakespeare's gifts, is his unparalleled gift for character-creation, for filling his stage with the real people I have spoken of, who live and breathe in their own right.

By what art Shakespeare performed these miracles of creation is beyond our comprehension ; but whenever the sense of the theatre is replaced by the illusion of real life,— whenever we catch the eye of a real person, or hear a real voice speaking, I have included all such scenes. They are rare at first ; but sometimes amid the puppets of his early plays, a minor character will interrupt the upholstered dummies with a real remark ; and, little by little, preposterous persons begin to rush forward and entertain us with their own irrelevant affairs. This introduction of realistic characters, and often groups of outrageous reprobates whom the dramatist for the most part invents himself (since there is seldom a trace of them in the authorities he draws on), and who, like the low-life characters in Dickens, have little or no relation to the story he relates, is a common feature of the Elizabethan drama, and one which, in Shakespeare's hands, produces a truly astonishing effect. The historical narratives and artificial plots of the earlier plays are made real for us by vital and absurd creatures like Cade and Launce and Sly and Bottom, by Lancelot Gobbo and by Juliet's Nurse. The Henry IV plays largely consist of realistic and irrelevant scenes and characters; and as the great artist in him grows in power, more and more Shakespeare links these comic scenes to the main subject of his plays, causing them to strengthen rather than to interrupt their dramatic and tragic effect. How the buffoonery of Lear's Fool, of the Porter in *Macbeth*, of the Gravediggers in *Hamlet*,—all of which seemed to Voltaire and the refined taste of his time so outrageous,—heighten and enrich our sense of the strangeness and splendour of those great plays!

This encroachment of reality on artificial drama and romance shows itself still more strikingly in the way by which Shakespeare comes to transform the main characters of his farces and melodramas into beings with a depth, a complexity, a splendour, or a depravity of soul such as he alone could imagine and create. Greatest of all are those Michelangelesque heroes of his later tragedies, whose struggles with each other, or with themselves, or with the stream of fate which bears them to their doom, are portrayed in the passages which fill the greater portion of this book. For it is in scenes like these that the true Shakespearean drama consists: drama which does not depend on the weaving and unweaving of plots, or rhetoric or declamation or theatrical surprises, but rather on the struggles of heroic and passionate beings in their conflicts with circumstance and fate. To penetrate to the very centre of a great soul, to touch those deepest springs of impulse and passion which decide the issues of life and death, to develop these with flawless strength and subtlety and truth,—it is in achieving this that Shakespeare gives the vast meaning and import to his greatest plays. And with his growing mastery of this great art, in which he has no equal, he develops also an unparalleled mastery of his instrument of expression, until, with its compass, its flexibility, its variety of modulation, it becomes the richest, most subtle, and the grandest utterance which has ever fallen on mortal ears.

This book, then, is a book of talk,—the talk of a myriad of

eloquent creatures, endowed with a genius for rhetorical, poetical, and imaginative expression, and almost every one of them endowed with an intense individuality of speech, a tone of voice, a choice of image, an idiom, a syntax, a rhythm, a cadence, and a kind of sing-song which gives it an inalienable reality that is all its own.

The method of making characters talk themselves alive is perhaps Shakespeare's supreme invention, since it was hardly known before his time, and it is certainly his greatest legacy to the dramatists (or rather to the novelists, since the great English drama died with Shakespeare) who succeeded him, and who learnt from him the art (now also dead) of making characters come to life in the words they speak.

And in what a wealth of words these outspoken beings of Shakespeare's creation express themselves to each other, or clothe their meditations in the radiance of speech! Shakespeare possessed, as Hazlitt said, a magic power over words; they came wingéd at his bidding; and to the vocables that flocked to him from all regions of heaven and earth and hell, from the talk of the exquisite, euphuistic court, from the dialects of upland villages, and the scurrility of stews and bawdy-houses,—to all this wealth of speech he added almost countless expressive terms of his own invention. Being, indeed, the greatest word-creator of the world, he has done more to enrich our language than all our other poets put together, thus pouring on the English language a Danaë shower of expressive sound which has made that Low-Dutch dialect into the richest and most far-spoken language of the earth.

VI

The growth in Shakespeare's mastery of language, of poetry, and of character-creation, becomes most clearly apparent to us when we read his plays in the chronological order in which he wrote them. It is only thus indeed that we can appreciate his achievement as an organic whole, and watch the progress and development of his powers from promise to performance,—from bungling experiment to masterly achievement.

Discarding, therefore, the chaotic order and arrangement of the Folio, which is one of the greatest hindrances to a true appreciation of Shakespeare's genius, I have arranged in this volume my extracts from the plays more or less in that chronological order of their composition, the approximate ascertainment of which is perhaps the most important of the many achievements of modern Shakespeare scholarship. Only the Sonnets, whose dating is still disputed, and that strange poem, *The Phoenix and the Turtle*, have been placed out of chronological sequence at the end.

I am aware (since the dating of some of them is still disputed) of the lack of certainty in any rigid chronological arrangement of Shakespeare's plays; and I am still more aware,—especially since I have read Professor Lawrence's *Shakespeare's Problem Comedies*,—of the risk of dividing his achievements into definite and clear-cut periods.

Such a division gives indeed an air of system and finality; but, as Professor Lawrence says, it

leads easily to the false assumption that Shakespeare's creative activity followed a succession of well-marked stages, each different from the preceding, and each containing within it plays set apart by distinctive characteristics. It neglects the obvious possibility that a literary artist, and still more a busy dramatist, may turn quickly from one style of writing to another, and back again, that relaxation from the strain of tragedy may be found in light comedy, and that external conditions, such as literary fashion and theatrical supply and demand, may be more potent than personal interests and artistic preoccupations.[1]

And yet the development of Shakespeare's gifts keeps pace in so accurate a manner with the ascertained dating of almost all his plays, and his genius seems to move so definitely from

[1] *Shakespeare's Problem Comedies*, W. W. Lawrence (Macmillan, 1931), p. 230.

one to another of the five great stages of his progress, that I have divided the selection in this volume into five sections, which I designate, in perhaps too banal a fashion (but on the whole I like it), by the names *Dawn*, *Sunrise*, *Noon*, stormy *Afternoon*, and *Sunset*.

I include in the first section the few lines and fragments of the early plays and poems which show, as through the twilight of dawn, the first glimmerings cast by the sun of his genius while still below the Elizabethan horizon.

Then comes the sunburst of Shakespeare's first masterpieces, and real and great successes, *Romeo and Juliet*, *Richard II*, *The Merchant of Venice*, and the great luminous flood of poetry in *A Midsummer-Night's Dream*. Noon swiftly follows this sunrise; the full noon of the three golden comedies, *Much Ado*, *As You Like It*, and *Twelfth Night*, and the two great Falstaff plays.

As in a sudden storm in the Tropics, the skies begin to blacken, and what is called the Dark Period follows,—the period of Shakespeare's most sublime achievement, until, after the seven great tragedies from *Julius Caesar* through *Hamlet*, *Othello*, *Lear*, *Macbeth*, *Antony and Cleopatra*, *Coriolanus*, and the almost incoherent outburst of *Timon* (and with these the bitter and dark comedies, *Measure for Measure* and *Troilus*), the sun comes out again, and sets at last, though still amid clouds, in the three romances of the final period.

Besides those early experimental comedies, the three *Henry VI* plays, *Titus Andronicus*, *Love's Labour's Lost*, the *Comedy of Errors*, *The Two Gentlemen of Verona*, three other plays, *The Taming of the Shrew*, *The Merry Wives of Windsor*, and *All's Well*, read like hack-work; and the historical plays *Richard III*, *King John*, and *Henry V* may also be placed perhaps in this category. *Timon of Athens* seems to be only partly of Shakespeare's composition, and *Pericles* and *Henry VIII* were plainly written in collaboration. I have sifted gold from these, though in smaller quantities of course than from the twenty masterpieces,—a few of which indeed, so all-golden are they, I have been forced to include with only minor eliminations. Curiously enough in that unpleasant and enigmatic play, *Troilus and Cressida*, which is generally regarded as one of Shakespeare's failures, I have found richer veins of gold than in some of the most famous masterpieces.

VII

Shakespeare's achievement has so many aspects, that the anthologist, from whatever angle he approaches it, will find abundant reward. Of these Shakespearean anthologists Pope may be regarded as the earliest, since, in his edition of 1725, he marked by commas in the margin what he regarded as ' the most shining passages '; and where the beauty of certain scenes lay, as he put it, ' not in particulars but in the whole ', he prefixed (thus anticipating Baedeker) a star to those which aroused his admiration.

Pope possessed, I suppose, the most exquisite taste of any of the exquisites of his time; and a study of his siftings and discriminations of Shakespeare's beauties would form one of the strangest chapters in that history of Taste which will, I hope, be one day written, since no more fascinating or disconcerting work lies still buried in the womb of time. And what a terrible warning (were we capable of listening to warnings) would be such a study to infatuated anthologists like myself. In performing what he rightly called ' the better half of criticism, namely, the pointing out of an author's excellencies ', Pope does mark a few shining passages which still shine for us; but his commendations of special scenes appear wildly capricious in their choice. No scenes in *Hamlet*, none in the *Henry IV* plays, none in *Romeo and Juliet* are starred by him; and, although he cannot refuse marginal commas of admiration to Launce and his dog, and to Juliet's Nurse, what he calls ' low scenes of mobs, plebeians and clowns ' find no favour in his sight. About some of these he feels indeed so strongly that he stabs them with daggers of disapproval; a few of them may, he says, have been of Shakespeare's composition, others he regarded as interpolations of the actors, but all of them could only be accounted for by the gross taste of Shakespeare's age. He wished, he said, that he had authority to leave them out, but he had done all he could by setting 'marks of reprobation' on them.

Of these reprobated scenes many, being composed as Pope describes them, of 'the lowest and most trifling conceits', deserve the marks they got; but we are astonished to find transfixed by these steely daggers the meeting of Viola and Feste at the beginning of the third act of *Twelfth Night*, or the enchanting talk of Rosalind and Celia about Orlando in the second scene of the third Act of *As You Like It*.

But most unbelievable to our comprehension are the lines which Pope says are so excessively bad that (thus proving himself the first of the 'disintegrators') he thinks they must be interpolations, and which he therefore omits from the text, degrading them (to use his own term) to notes in smaller type at the bottom of the page. This 'trash', these 'low and vicious passages' are sometimes what we consider the most magnificent things in Shakespeare; to enumerate them all (and they are numerous) would be too silly and too sad a task; I will only briefly describe his treatment of the text of three of the great tragedies, *Othello*, *Macbeth*, and *Lear*.

In the great scene of Othello before the Doge (I, iii) (which he does not star) Pope degrades the lines (143-144),

> The Anthropophagi, and the men whose heads
> Do grow beneath their shoulders.

And on Othello's simile of the Pontic Sea

> Whose icy current and compulsive course
> Ne'er feels retiring ebb, but keeps due on
> To the Propontic and the Hellespont,

he remarks, 'This simile is omitted in the first editions: I think it should be so, as an unnatural excursion in this place'.

In Act IV, Scene i, of *Othello*, he omits from the text some of Othello's mad outbursts, remarking, ' no hint of this trash in the 1st edition '.

Some of Pope's emendations are exquisite, as for instance *south* for *sound* in the opening speech of *Twelfth Night*,

> O, it came o'er my ear like the sweet south
> That breathes upon a bank of violets,

but when he emends the word *north* in Emilia's speech,

> No, I will speak as liberal as the north,

to *air*, we are astonished, and still more when in that most magical of lines,

> It is a sword of Spain, the ice-brook's temper
>
> (V, ii, 252),

he changes *ice-brook's* to *Ebro's* on the prosaic ground that ' the waters of that river in Spain are particularly famous for tempering of steel '.

Pope stars in *Macbeth* the scenes before and after Duncan's murder, and the banquet scene (the great sleep-walking scene he does not star) ; but even in these he degrades, as though they were interpolations foisted into the play by the actors, lines like that in Macbeth's invocation to sleep,

> Sleep that knits up the ravell'd sleave of care ;

and, in that stupendous expression of Macbeth's despair of cleansing his hand from blood,

> This my hand will rather
> The multitudinous seas incarnadine,
> Making the green one red,

Pope not only degrades the magnificent second line, but destroys as far as he can its beauty by printing the four words without authority as

> Thy multitudinous sea incarnadine.

' What are we to think ', as Professor Lounsbury justly exclaims, ' of an editor who coolly relegates to the obscurity of the margin a line which Homer might justly have felicitated himself upon writing, but which Homer's translator found himself incapable of appreciating ? ' [1]

And when, in Macbeth's great phrase,

> And all our yesterdays have lighted fools
> The way to dusty death,

Pope emends the text *dusty* to *study*, he reaches a height of ineptitude which might have made even the great Bentley envious.

In *Lear*, Pope degrades from the text some of Lear's talk with the Fool ; and in the sixth scene of the third act he takes from the Quarto of 1608 thirty-eight lines not printed in the Folio,—lines containing the great trial by stools,—all of which he describes as ' several speeches in the mad way, which probably were left out by the players, or by Shakespeare himself. I shall, however, insert them here,' he adds, ' and leave 'em to the reader's mercy.'

What can the reader say,—not in any endeavour to show mercy to Pope (who deserves no mercy, having so outrageously treated his text),—what can he say in the much more interesting attempt to understand his discriminations ? To Shakespeare Pope gives noble praise ; he was, he says, more of an ' original ' even than Homer ; for his characters were not copies, but Nature herself ; no author equalled him in pathetic, or in comic power, and ' in the coolness of Reflection and Reasoning ' Shakespeare was, Pope adds, ' full as admirable '.

Each generation lives in the glass palace of its own taste ; and rather than throwing stones at the windows of other periods (an outrage which Posterity shall certainly with its shattering blows avenge), it will do well to try to peer through these casements, dim and narrow and almost opaque to our eyes as they often seem. There can be no doubt that Shakespeare's greatness was visible from Pope's Twickenham villa : loomed before its windows indeed as something portentous,

---

[1] *The First Editors of Shakespeare*, T. R. Lounsbury, p. 97.

immense, and almost overwhelming,—like, as he says himself, some ancient and majestic piece of Gothic architecture, strong and solemn, with many noble apartments, and built of material enough to make more than one neat modern building. Many of its parts were, indeed, awkward, he felt, ill-placed and unequal to the grandeur of the whole ; yet that grandeur inspired in him a genuine reverence ; he found the vastness of Shakespeare's genius, the force and variety of his eloquent and moving scenes, and the deep knowledge he displayed of human nature, alike impressive. But the focus of appreciation changes from age to age, and many of the features of Shakespeare's achievement upon which we now fix our most rapt attention, were either unnoticed by Pope, or seemed childish and repulsive to him. Although he makes a general statement that Shakespeare's poetry was ' Inspiration indeed ', and marks with the approbation of his commas a few passages of Shakespeare's golden poetry, yet it would seem that the incomparable beauty of his lyric verse, which was as enchanting to Shakespeare's age as it is to ours, had little or no charm for Pope's fastidious ears. To none of Shakespeare's songs does he give marks of his approbation, and only partial ones to the spoken threnody, ' Fear no more the heat o' the sun ', of which, however, the refrain about ' golden lads and girls ', and the final stanza, failed to meet with his approval. Often, too, he will degrade as interpolations some of what seem to us the loveliest lines in the great lyric speeches in the plays ; as for instance in *Richard II*, when Gaunt speaks on his death-bed of

> The setting sun, and music at the close,

or when in the dethronement scene Richard gazes at his face in the mirror and says,

> A brittle glory shineth in this face :
> As brittle as the glory is the face.

The Aeschylean sublimity, the stupendous images and phrases of Shakespeare's later poetry, were plainly regarded by Pope as bombast ; while that sublime and unique effect of

Shakespearean tragedy,—the mention of trivial and mean things in moments of tensest passion,—evidently shocked him as gross offences against elegance, decorum, and good taste. Lear's talk with the Fool seemed to him stupid and vulgar trash ; he degrades as interpolations from the text the Porter's speeches in *Macbeth*, and Macduff's tragic cry on hearing of the murder of his wife and children,

> What ! all my pretty chickens and their dam
> At one fell swoop ?

VIII

If to read the first critical edition, and, as it were, the first anthology of Shakespeare,—the deliberate act of a man of exquisite taste in a time when taste was exquisite,—is a shattering experience, we find, twenty-seven years later, in the work of an inferior age and a much inferior writer, evidence of an immense advance in the aesthetic appreciation of Shakespeare's plays. Poor Dr. Dodd deserved a happier end than the hanging which fate allotted him ; his volume of ' Beauties ' has surprising merits, and has for a long period remained our best anthology of Shakespeare, and has been constantly reprinted. Although Dodd includes too many sententious passages for our modern taste, whose appreciation of what he called ' refined morality ' is on the wane, he includes also not a few single lines and subtle beauties which might easily escape the attention even of a modern anthologist, and my own debt to Dodd is one which I feel ought not to go without acknowledgement. The greater number of Shakespeare's lovely lyrics he includes also, omitting, however, as we might expect, the songs of exquisite nonsense, with their divine inconsequence and vulgar touches, which Autolycus and Feste sing. Although the appreciation of Shakespeare's art had been immensely deepened and enlarged between the time of Pope and Dodd, it was nearly a century before delicate good taste had learned to savour indelicacies of this and other kinds.

The 'sublimities' of Shakespeare, Dodd did, however, appreciate, and he includes many of what he calls Shakespeare's 'eagle-flights', although they had been condemned, he said (with obvious reference to Pope), by frigid critics as 'Rant and fustian and intolerable Bombast'. The low scenes of 'mobs, plebeians and clowns', which Pope also reprobated, are almost all omitted too; not that Dodd disliked them, but because his book was after all a book of 'Beauties', and the talk, for instance, of the 'inimitable Falstaff' could hardly find a place within his (to our minds) too narrow a conception of what may be regarded as 'Beauty' in art.

In 1784 the publisher Kearsley brought out another volume of the *Beauties of Shakespeare*,[1] which immediately ran through several editions. The name of the anthologist is not given, but he was probably the same writer in Kearsley's employment who compiled for him also the 'Beauties' of Milton and several other poets. Although the title of this Shakespearean anthology agrees, its anonymous compiler states, with that of a 'late unfortunate author', its object was not the same. Dodd's aim was, he somewhat unkindly remarks, chiefly to display his reading and critical attainments; his own purpose was rather to place in a clear light the noble moral system of a poet who, in the words of the great Mrs. Montagu, was 'one of the greatest Moral Philosophers who ever lived', and to assist the instructors of both sexes to impress on the memory of youth 'some of the sublimest lessons of Morality and Religion'. To fulfil this laudable purpose, he digests under headings, arranged in alphabetical order, a large number of edifying sentiments and reflections extracted from Shakespeare's plays, adding, however, a supplement of thirty-eight scenes which, though chosen with remarkable discrimination from a literary point of view, must, one thinks, have somewhat bewildered the youth of both sexes in their attempt to extract

[1] *The Beauties of Shakespeare; selected from his Works, to which are added, the principal Scenes in the same Author.* London, printed for C. & G. Kearsley, at No. 46 in Fleet Street.

any moral or religious lessons of a sublime,—or even a service-able,—nature from the talk (included in this edifying volume) of Juliet's Nurse, of Falstaff and Mistress Quickly, or from the obscenities of the Fool in *Lear*, or from Timon's terrible vituperation of the Athenian whores.

IX

The distinguished Shakespearean scholar, Dr. Caroline Spurgeon, when she was in America not long ago, had the good luck to make a wonderful discovery. For forty-seven years there had lain, in a private library at Princeton, Keats's pocket edition of Shakespeare, which no student had taken the trouble to look at during all this time. When she heard of this edition, Dr. Spurgeon went to Princeton, and found herself, as she tells us, one morning in Mr. Armour's fine library, with these seven stocky, rather shabby little volumes in her hands. This was the 1814 edition of Shakespeare's plays, which Keats had carried about with him during the last three and a half years of his life ; which he had taken with him on his voyage to Rome ; which he had given to Severn ; and which, at Severn's death in 1879, had passed into the possession of his doctor, and then been sold to America. In these volumes Dr. Spurgeon found not only notes and scribblings in Keats's hand, but thousands of marks of appreciation for the passages he chose out for admiration : words and phrases and long extracts, often underlined in ink, and marked as well in the margin with two or three lines of delight in their beauty. The book had evidently been read by Keats with special enthusiasm in his great year of Shakespeare study, the year 1817, during the period when he was rallying his forces between the *Poems* published in that year, and the composition of *Endymion*,—the period, as Dr. Spurgeon describes it, of ' miraculous re-birth, when Keats gradually found his way to his own deepest and most original convictions about life and poetry '. The four plays which Keats read at that time with special attention were *The Tempest*, the *Midsummer-Night's Dream*, *Measure for Measure*, and *Antony and Cleopatra*, and Dr. Spurgeon has beautifully edited, and the Oxford Press has beautifully printed (with many facsimile pages), Keats's markings of these plays and the notes written in them: adding from his folio reprint (now in the Dilke collection at Keats's house) his markings of *Troilus and Cressida*, and also a note of his markings in his edition of the *Poems and Sonnets*, which the Hampstead Public Library now possesses.

This volume of Dr. Spurgeon's editing, though it unluckily includes only a few of Shakespeare's plays, is to my mind the most exquisite and illuminating Shakespeare anthology that I know of. An unmeasurable distance in the growth of appreciation lies between the record left by the purblind Pope, the eighteenth-century ' Beauty '-compilers, and this memorial, as Dr. Spurgeon well describes it, of the passionate ardour and acute critical judgement with which Keats read Shakespeare. Like the roll that Ezekiel ate, these pages were, it is plain, like honey in his mouth for sweetness ; he pored and ruminated and mused and dreamt over them, with an exquisite and studious epicurism, filling his eyes and ears with their imagery and music, enriching his vocabulary with their diction, and deeply dyeing his imagination in their beauty. He notes the least suggestion of poetical effect: feels keenly the slightest touch ; hardly an exquisite word or epithet escapes him, hardly a suggestion of imaginative value. ' One's very breath while leaning over these pages ', he writes on one of them with reference to a special phrase, ' is held for fear of blowing the line away—as easily ', he beautifully adds, ' as the gentlest breath robs dandelion flowers of their fleecy crowns.'

When I have found that I have already noted, in my old perusals, passages which Keats marks, I have been delighted, and still more delighted when his underlinings have called my attention to phrases to which I have given no special notice,— Caliban's whisper to Stephano and Trinculo, for instance, when they are creeping up to kill Prospero in his cave,

Pray you tread softly, that the blind mole may not
Hear a foot fall.

Although, like Dodd, Keats omits many scenes of vulgar
life, he shows a real appreciation of the vigorous and even
vulgar touches which Pope regarded as such trash. Thus,
when Cleopatra crowns herself for death,

Give me my robe, put on my crown ; I have
Immortal longings in me,

and Charmian says to her, ' Your crown's awry ; I'll mend it ',
Keats underlines that homely poignant phrase with special
admiration.

Another phrase is worth noting as the indication of a
curious and profound change in taste. When in *The Tempest*
Ferdinand is led by the songs of Ariel before the sleeping
Miranda, Prospero wakes her up to see who is coming with
these words,

The fringed curtains of thine eye advance.

(I, ii, 405)

Pope degrades from the text this line, which he evidently
regarded as the grossest bombast, and which is quoted, or
rather misquoted, in *The Art of Sinking in Poetry* (printed with
Pope's works), as an instance of the exaltation of the ' most low
and vulgar actions of life ' to a ' ridiculous visibility '. Leigh
Hunt is equally severe in his condemnation of what he calls
the ' elaborate nothingness, not to say nonsense of this metaphor '. ' Why Shakespeare should have condescended to the
meaninglessness of " advancing curtains ", I cannot ', he writes,
' conceive, that is to say, if he did condescend ; for it looks
very like the interpolation of some pompous, declamatory
player.' [1]

This metaphor, which even to Coleridge, who admired
the line, seemed to need two pages of elaborate apology,[2]

[1] *Imagination and Fancy : Selections from English Poets, with an
Essay on Poetry*, Leigh Hunt, 1844, p. 162.
[2] *Coleridge's Shakespearean Criticism*, T. M. Raysor, 1930, vol. ii,
pp. 179-180.

Keats underlined with enthusiastic and unqualified delight; and he borrowed it as a gilt-edged phrase with which to load with golden ore more than one line of his *Endymion*.[1]

Keats will often mark (and sometimes borrow) a few simple words whose haunting quality is quite beyond analysis, like, for instance, Isabella's phrase in *Measure for Measure*, ' is it not strange, and strange ', which he also stole for his *Endymion*.

This simplicity of phrasing in Shakespeare's plays produces now and then an effect of exquisite pathos, which raises our admiration of his ' might and majesty of genius ' to what I can only call (if I may unabashedly describe my own feelings) a kind of idolatry for him. Now and then one of his shining souls will express themselves in a few words which are more moving and lovely in their unadorned plainness than any richness and splendour of metaphor or diction. Tennyson, a poet, like Keats, of exquisite appreciation, has noticed three of these phrases, which never failed, he confessed, to bring tears to his eyes : Cordelia's answer, ' So young, my lord, and true ', to Lear's reproach, ' So young and so untender ': the words of Posthumus to Imogen, ' Hang there like fruit, my soul ': and, in *The Winter's Tale*, ' When Florizel [I quote from Tennyson] takes Perdita's hand to lead her to the dance, and says " So turtles pair that never mean to part ", and little Perdita answers, giving her hand to Florizel, " I'll swear for 'em " '.[2]

To the unadorned beauty and tenderness of such phrases Keats was equally sensitive, noting for instance and underlining the request of Ferdinand to Miranda, soon after their meeting on the enchanted island,

> I do beseech you—
> Chiefly that I might set it in my prayers—
> What is your name ?

Keats's prompt and felicitous response to the fine phrases

[1] See Keats's Shakespeare, pp. 17-18.

[2] Quoted from Tennyson's *Life*, in *The Praise of Shakespeare*, compiled by C. E. Hughes, 1904.

upon which he looked, he said, like a lover: his 'trembling, delicate and snail-horn perception' (to borrow his own words) of their beauty, has led him to isolate and underline many single lines and phrases,—like, for instance,

Look, the unfolding star calls up the shepherd,—

lines and phrases which are often all the lovelier when we see them apart from their context. He would, I am sure, have approved of the choice of Robert Bridges, who, in his *Spirit of Man*, quoted by itself the line about

The setting sun, and music at the close,

which was degraded by Pope, as we have seen, from the dying speech of Gaunt. Emboldened by the example of these poets, I have in this selection allowed myself the liberty of sifting (no doubt to the exasperation of many readers) the minutest grains of gold from the rubble in which I have found them here and there embedded.

Dr. Mackail notes, in his fine essay on the Sonnets, the extraordinary effect which lines of Shakespeare produce in quotation. The concentration of poetry in them is so great, their sweetness so condensed,

that it must be disengaged to give out its full effect. 'Roses, damask and red,' says Bacon in his Essay of Gardens, 'are fast flowers of their smells, so that you may walk by a whole row of them and find nothing of their sweetness.' They must be approached closely if their 'royal scent' is to produce its full effect. The effect of Shakespeare's poetry is indeed universal and immediate. Yet a line or a phrase thus disengaged from it always thrills one with unexpected depths of beauty. It expands, takes colour, becomes as it were a live thing.[1]

If, then, a phrase or a lovely line is to produce on us the full effect,—' to expand ' (I again quote Dr. Mackail) ' as memory recalls it, association touches it, imagination kindles it ', such a phrase or line will sometimes flash upon us with a more vivid and essential beauty when we read it by itself, disengaged from its often less poetical surroundings.

[1] *Lectures on Poetry*, p. 207.

' Things real, such as existences of Sun, Moon and Stars—
and passages of Shakespeare '—in this phrase Keats gives
hyperbolical expression to his admiration for Shakespeare's
gold : a gold which I am not altogether sorry (such is our
fallen nature, and my sense of what must be my own short-
comings)—I am not altogether sorry to suspect so blinded
now and then his eyes—even the eyes of Keats—that he did
not notice certain lovely things : that, for instance, he omits
all marks of admiration for the magical, moonlit scene of
Enobarbus' remorseful suicide, and his address, so Keatsian
in its beauty, to the moon,

> O sovereign mistress of true melancholy.
> (*Antony and Cleopatra*, IV, ix, 12)

But for me to throw stones from my small house of glass at
the great shining windows of Keats's outlook would be not
only absurd presumption, but the grossest ingratitude as well,
since, like poor Haydon, I can say that I also have ' enjoyed
Shakespeare more with Keats than with any other human
creature '.

If to sift and select, to underline and mark and choose out
of literature what is delicate and rare and perfect : to pick
with fastidious fingers the goldenest fruit in the Hesperian
garden, and sip the dew on its most damasked roses,—if this
be a reprehensible indulgence (as many believe, who maintain
that we should swallow whole all that great men give us, or
nothing at all), it is pleasant at least for flower-gatherers like
myself to find a poet of Keats's quality addicted to this most
exquisite, most bird- or bee-like of literary vices. There are
other illustrious marauders too ; and if most anthologists
deserve the contumely heaped upon them, yet, when Charles
Lamb makes selections from Elizabethan plays, or Tennyson
guides Palgrave in his *Golden Treasury*, or Dr. Mackail sifts
out for us the gold from the Greek Anthology, or Robert
Bridges makes choice selections of verse or prose,—surely
chrystomathies, florileges such as these are among the most

delightful volumes which deserve a place of special honour by our bedsides or on our shelves. And our great Book of Common Prayer,—is not this holy volume in great part an anthology of exquisite extracts from the Bible, and from the prayers and liturgies of other ages ?

Although Keats's Shakespeare has been of greater value to me, as I have said, than any other Shakespearean anthology, it by no means follows that I have included in this volume all the passages which he marked and underlined. Keats was, as Dryden called Milton, a ' celestial thief ' ; he pillaged, like a robber-bee, honey from Shakespeare's hive to store up in his own ; he often underlines epithets and phrases for his private use rather than for their intrinsic beauty ; and the uses to which he puts these borrowings is beautifully shown in a section of Miss Spurgeon's invaluable book. He often, moreover, like the rest of us who mark our books, underlines passages because they chime in with his thoughts of the moment, or the feelings which haunt him as he reads.

X

Of the other Shakespearean anthologies which I have read (I cannot pretend to have read them all), there is little of interest for me to say. Charles Kemble, after his retirement from the stage, began to give readings of Shakespeare, first to Queens Adelaide and Victoria, then to the general public, which, at the request, as he writes, ' of numerous friends, who think they would be acceptable to families ', he published in two volumes under the title *Shakespeare Readings*. These volumes, though printed with the ' refinement of diction and feeling ' that marked Kemble's delivery, are of no help to the anthologist, being merely sixteen potted plays, each compressed into the compass of a single reading.

During the course of the nineteenth century, many selections were made from Shakespeare's voluminous volumes, *Temperance Calendars*, *Radical Thoughts from Shakespeare*,

Catholic Jewels, *Birthday Books* of ethical and uplifting sentiments, or books containing what he wrote about animals,
birds, and flowers. A sifting, however, as copious as this one
(and I hope as careful) of Shakespeare's authentic gold from
the baser metals which surround it has not, I think, been
made before. In spite of its abundant pages, it will be found
no doubt stinted and incomplete by many readers, and it will
incur the merited opprobium inseparable from all such undertakings. But I can plead for myself at least that I have not
performed this all-enchanting task in a hasty or perfunctory
manner; for many years I have been a re-reader of Shakespeare's plays; my favourite edition of them is enriched with
the deposit of many old and many recent appreciations, and
thousands of marks and underlinings; I have profited by the
study and collation of other anthologies, and have made my
selection with that care, difficulty, and moroseness with which
Landor said that he sought for words. I have availed myself,
moreover, of the advice and criticism of others who love
Shakespeare and are acquainted (as so few are) with the whole
body of his work. Among these I must mention with special
gratitude Robert Gathorne-Hardy, who has helped me in all
my considerations and reconsiderations, and has prepared
this book for the press, and my friend and neighbour, Sir
Trevor Bigham, who knows Shakespeare as few know him,
and has revised my selections with much concurrence, mingled
with much grieved or indignant expostulation. But the main
opprobrium for any exclusions or inclusions must rest upon
my own shoulders, and I must bear it as best I may. Quality
has been my one criterion; if I find the gold I seek for in the
tiniest phrase, I sift it out; but if, even in the most familiar
passages of Shakespearean declamation, I see no gleam of the
gold I seek, such passages have been omitted. Shakespeare
reciters, therefore (this book is no book for them), will not
find, for instance, in these pages the famous bombast of the
Bastard at the end of *King John*, while from the equally famous
rodomontade of Henry V before the walls of Harfleur—

Once more into the breach, dear friends, once more—

I include only the image of the wave-beaten rock,

    Swill'd with the wild and wasteful ocean.[1]

My tests of quality, my crucibles for extracting the gold I seek, and the scales in which I weigh it, are of course those of my own taste, and the taste of my own period, since we are all—willing or reluctant—children of the age we live in.

Other ages will bring, no doubt, other scales and standards to the valuing or disvaluing of Shakespeare's achievement; but Posterity, if it deigns to look at this compilation, will find in it an historical interest at least. Having made it for my own pleasure, I find, naturally enough, that I like it myself, and I hope that those persons,—whom Emerson said he was always glad to meet,—those persons who perceive the transcendental superiority of Shakespeare over all other writers, will like it too. Perhaps they will keep it, as I mean to keep it, by the bedside of their declining years, to look at now and then. Our appreciation of Shakespeare's achievement needs to be constantly renewed. His tragic vision of the world and our human fate is so darkly solemn that we cannot bear to think of it for long. His poetry is so sublime, and he pours his wealth before us in such extravagant profusion, that our purblind eyes can gaze in glimpses only on the dazzling hoard.

[1] I have left this passage as it stands, although, as will be seen, the mutilation, however poetically justifiable, of so famous an English monument, was afterwards somewhat mitigated. The mitigation was due to no pressure on my part (though I remember expressing some apprehension at the comments likely to follow on so drastic a carving up), but to the ' grieved and indignant expostulations ' of Sir Trevor Bigham.—R. G.-H.

DAWN

VENUS AND ADONIS
THE RAPE OF LUCRECE
2 HENRY VI
3 HENRY VI
RICHARD III
COMEDY OF ERRORS
TITUS ANDRONICUS
THE TAMING OF THE SHREW
THE TWO GENTLEMEN OF VERONA
LOVE'S LABOUR'S LOST

Venus and Adonis

More white and red than doves or roses are.

l. 10

Leading him prisoner in a red-rose chain.

l. 110

' Bid me discourse, I will enchant thine ear,
Or, like a fairy, trip upon the green,
Or, like a nymph, with long dishevell'd hair,
Dance on the sands, and yet no footing seen :
    Love is a spirit all compact of fire.'

ll. 145-149

O, learn to love ; the lesson is but plain,
And once made perfect, never lost again.

ll. 407-408

Shone like the moon in water seen by night.

l. 492

Echo replies
As if another chase were in the skies.

ll. 695-696

Lo, here the gentle lark, weary of rest,
From his moist cabinet mounts up on high,
And wakes the morning, from whose silver breast
The sun ariseth in his majesty ;
    Who doth the world so gloriously behold
    That cedar-tops and hills seem burnish'd gold.

ll. 853-858

Her eyes . . .
Like stars ashamed of day, themselves withdrew ;
Or, as the snail, whose tender horns being hit,
Shrinks backward in his shelly cave with pain,
And there, all smother'd up, in shade doth sit,
Long after fearing to creep forth again.

ll. 1031-1036

The Rape of Lucrece

As is the morning's silver-melting dew
Against the golden splendour of the sun !

ll. 24-25

Their silent war of lilies and of roses.

l. 71

O shame to knighthood and to shining arms !

l. 197

Without the bed her other fair hand was,
On the green coverlet ; whose perfect white
Show'd like an April daisy on the grass.

ll. 393-395

Time's glory is . . .
To feed oblivion with decay of things.

ll. 939, 947

Thou ceaseless lackey to eternity.

l. 967

Here feelingly she weeps Troy's painted woes :
For sorrow, like a heavy-hanging bell,
Once set on ringing, with his own weight goes.

ll. 1492-1494

And now this pale swan in her watery nest
Begins the sad dirge of her certain ending.

ll. 1611-1612

The Second Part of
King Henry VI

Wizards know their times :
Deep night, dark night, the silent of the night,
The time of night when Troy was set on fire.

ACT I, Scene iv, ll. 18-20

4

As the mournful crocodile
With sorrow snares relenting passengers.

ACT III, Scene i, ll. 226-227

The gaudy, blabbing and remorseful day
Is crept into the bosom of the sea.

ACT IV, Scene i, ll. 1-2

Cade. Be brave, then ; for your captain is brave, and vows
reformation.   There shall be in England seven halfpenny
loaves sold for a penny : the three-hooped pot shall have ten
hoops ; and I will make it felony to drink small beer.

ACT IV, Scene ii, ll. 70-74

Smith the Weaver. Sir, he made a chimney in my father's
house, and the bricks are alive at this day to testify it ; therefore deny it not.

ACT IV, Scene ii, ll. 156-158

Cade. I am the besom that must sweep the court clean of
such filth as thou art.   Thou hast most traitorously corrupted
the youth of the realm in erecting a grammar school : and
whereas, before, our forefathers had no other books but the
score and the tally, thou hast caused printing to be used, and,
contrary to the king, his crown and dignity, thou hast built a
paper-mill.

ACT IV, Scene vii, ll. 34-42

Tears virginal
Shall be to me even as the dew to fire.

ACT V, Scene ii, ll. 52-53

The Third Part of

King Henry VI

King. This battle fares like to the morning's war,
When dying clouds contend with growing light,
What time the shepherd, blowing of his nails,
Can neither call it perfect day nor night. . . .

5

O God ! methinks it were a happy life,
To be no better than a homely swain ;
To sit upon a hill, as I do now,
To carve out dials quaintly, point by point,
Thereby to see the minutes how they run,
How many make the hour full complete ;
How many hours bring about the day ;
How many days will finish up the year ;
How many years a mortal man may live.
When this is known, then to divide the times :
So many hours must I tend my flock ;
So many hours must I take my rest ;
So many hours must I contemplate ;
So many hours must I sport myself :
So many days my ewes have been with young ;
So many weeks ere the poor fools will ean ;
So many years ere I shall shear the fleece :
So minutes, hours, days, months, and years,
Pass'd over to the end they were created,
Would bring white hairs unto a quiet grave.
Ah, what a life were this ! how sweet ! how lovely !
Gives not the hawthorn-bush a sweeter shade
To shepherds looking on their silly sheep,
Than doth a rich embroider'd canopy
To kings that fear their subjects' treachery ?
O, yes, it doth ; a thousand-fold it doth.
And to conclude, the shepherd's homely curds,
His cold thin drink out of his leather bottle,
His wonted sleep under a fresh tree's shade,
All which secure and sweetly he enjoys,
Is far beyond a prince's delicates,
His viands sparkling in a golden cup,
His body couched in a curious bed,
When care, mistrust, and treason waits on him.

ACT II, Scene v, ll. 1-4, 21-54

Look, as I blow this feather from my face,
And as the air blows it to me again, . . .
Commanded always by the greater gust;
Such is the lightness of you common men.

ACT III, Scene i, ll. 84-85, 88-89

Wind-changing Warwick now can change no more.

ACT V, Scene i, l. 57

King Richard III

Now is the winter of our discontent
Made glorious summer by this sun of York.

ACT I, Scene i, l. 1

In a lady's chamber
To the lascivious pleasing of a lute.

ACT I, Scene i, ll. 12-13

To hear the piteous moan that Rutland made.

ACT I, Scene ii, l. 158

A sweeter and a lovelier gentleman . . .
The spacious world cannot again afford.

ACT I, Scene ii, ll. 243, 246

Our aery buildeth in the cedar's top,
And dallies with the wind and scorns the sun.

ACT I, Scene iii, ll. 264-265

Brakenbury. What was your dream? I long to hear you
tell it.

Clarence. Methoughts that I had broken from the
Tower,
And was embark'd to cross to Burgundy;
And, in my company, my brother Gloucester;
Who from my cabin tempted me to walk
Upon the hatches: thence we look'd toward England,
And cited up a thousand fearful times,
During the wars of York and Lancaster

7

That had befall'n us. As we paced along
Upon the giddy footing of the hatches,
Methought that Gloucester stumbled ; and, in falling,
Struck me, that thought to stay him, overboard,
Into the tumbling billows of the main.
Lord, Lord ! methought, what pain it was to drown !
What dreadful noise of waters in mine ears !
What ugly sights of death within mine eyes !
Methought I saw a thousand fearful wrecks ;
Ten thousand men that fishes gnaw'd upon ;
Wedges of gold, great anchors, heaps of pearl,
Inestimable stones, unvalued jewels,
All scatter'd in the bottom of the sea :
Some lay in dead men's skulls ; and, in those holes
Where eyes did once inhabit, there were crept,
As 'twere in scorn of eyes, reflecting gems,
Which woo'd the slimy bottom of the deep,
And mock'd the dead bones that lay scatter'd by.

    Brak. Had you such leisure in the time of death
To gaze upon the secrets of the deep ?

    Clar. Methought I had ; and often did I strive
To yield the ghost : but still the envious flood
Kept in my soul, and would not let it forth
To seek the empty, vast and wandering air ;
But smother'd it within my panting bulk,
Which almost burst to belch it in the sea.

    Brak. Awaked you not with this sore agony ?

    Clar. O, no, my dream was lengthen'd after life ;
O, then began the tempest to my soul,
Who pass'd, methought, the melancholy flood,
With that grim ferryman which poets write of,
Unto the kingdom of perpetual night.
The first that there did greet my stranger soul,
Was my great father-in-law, renowned Warwick ;
Who cried aloud, ' What scourge for perjury
Can this dark monarchy afford false Clarence ? '

And so he vanish'd : then came wandering by
A shadow like an angel, with bright hair
Dabbled in blood ; and he squeak'd out aloud,
' Clarence is come ; false, fleeting, perjured Clarence,
That stabb'd me in the field by Tewksbury.'

ACT I, Scene iv, ll. 8-56

Second Murderer. What, shall we stab him as he sleeps ?

First Murderer. No ; then he will say 'twas done cowardly, when he wakes.

Sec. Murd. When he wakes ! why, fool, he shall never wake till the judgement-day.

First Murd. Why, then he will say we stabbed him sleeping.

Sec. Murd. The urging of that word ' judgement ' hath bred a kind of remorse in me.

First Murd. What, art thou afraid ?

Sec. Murd. Not to kill him, having a warrant for it ; but to be damned for killing him, from which no warrant can defend us.

First Murd. I thought thou hadst been resolute.

Sec. Murd. So I am, to let him live.

First Murd. Back to the Duke of Gloucester, tell him so.

Sec. Murd. I pray thee, stay a while : I hope my holy humour will change ; 'twas wont to hold me but while one would tell twenty.

First Murd. How dost thou feel thyself now ?

Sec. Murd. 'Faith, some certain dregs of conscience are yet within me.

First Murd. Remember our reward, when the deed is done.

Sec. Murd. 'Zounds, he dies : I had forgot the reward.

First Murd. Where is thy conscience now ?

Sec. Murd. In the Duke of Gloucester's purse.

First Murd. So when he opens his purse to give us our reward, thy conscience flies out.

Sec. Murd. Let it go ; there's few or none will entertain it.

First Murd. How if it come to thee again ?

Sec. Murd. I'll not meddle with it : it is a dangerous thing : it makes a man a coward : a man cannot steal, but it accuseth him ; he cannot swear, but it checks him ; he cannot lie with his neighbour's wife, but it detects him : 'tis a blushing shamefast spirit that mutinies in a man's bosom ; it fills one full of obstacles : it made me once restore a purse of gold that I found ; it beggars any man that keeps it : it is turned out of all towns and cities for a dangerous thing ; and every man that means to live well endeavours to trust to himself and to live without it.

First Murd. 'Zounds, it is even now at my elbow, persuading me not to kill the duke.

Sec. Murd. Take the devil in thy mind, and believe him not : he would insinuate with thee but to make thee sigh.

First Murd. Tut, I am strong-framed, he cannot prevail with me, I warrant thee.

Sec. Murd. Spoke like a tall fellow that respects his reputation. Come, shall we to this gear ?

First Murd. Take him over the costard with the hilts of thy sword, and then we will chop him in the malmsey-butt in the next room.

Sec. Murd. O excellent device ! make a sop of him.

First Murd. Hark ! he stirs : shall I strike ?

Sec. Murd. No, first let's reason with him.

Clar. Where art thou, keeper ? give me a cup of wine.

Sec. Murd. You shall have wine enough, my lord, anon.

ACT I, Scene iv, ll. 101-168

O momentary grace of mortal men,
Which we more hunt for than the grace of God !
Who builds his hopes in air of your good looks,
Lives like a drunken sailor on a mast,
Ready, with every nod, to tumble down
Into the fatal bowels of the deep.

ACT III, Scene iv, ll. 98-103

' Lo, thus,' quoth Dighton, ' lay those tender babes : '
' Thus, thus,' quoth Forrest, ' girdling one another
Within their innocent alabaster arms :
Their lips were four red roses on a stalk,
Which in their summer beauty kiss'd each other.'

ACT IV, Scene iii, ll. 9-13

The silent hours steal on,
And flaky darkness breaks within the east.

ACT V, Scene iii, ll. 85-86

Thou quiet soul, sleep thou a quiet sleep.

ACT V, Scene iii, l. 164

' Jockey of Norfolk, be not too bold,
For Dickon thy master is bought and sold.'

ACT V, Scene iii, ll. 304-305

Titus Andronicus

The hunt is up, the morn is bright and grey,
The fields are fragrant and the woods are green.

ACT II, Scene ii, ll. 1-2

The birds chant melody on every bush,
The snake lies rolled in the cheerful sun,
The green leaves quiver with the cooling wind
And make a chequer'd shadow on the ground.

ACT II, Scene iii, ll. 12-15

Like to a bubbling fountain stirr'd with wind.

ACT II, Scene iv, l. 23

Fair Philomela, she but lost her tongue,
And in a tedious sampler sew'd her mind.

ACT II, Scene iv, ll. 38-39

O, had the monster seen those lily hands
Tremble, like aspen-leaves, upon a lute.

ACT II, Scene iv, ll. 44-45

O, that delightful engine of her thoughts,
That blabb'd them with such pleasing eloquence,
Is torn from forth that pretty hollow cage,
Where, like a sweet melodious bird, it sung
Sweet varied notes.　　　　　ACT III, Scene i, ll. 82-86

For now I stand as one upon a rock
Environ'd with a wilderness of sea,
Who marks the waxing tide grow wave by wave,
Expecting ever when some envious surge
Will in his brinish bowels swallow him.
　　　　　　　　　　　　ACT III, Scene i, ll. 93-97

　　Marcus. Alas, my lord, I have but kill'd a fly.
　　Titus. But how, if that fly had a father and mother ?
How would he hang his slender gilded wings,
And buzz lamenting doings in the air !
Poor harmless fly,
That, with his pretty buzzing melody,
Came here to make us merry ! and thou has kill'd him.
　　　　　　　　　　　　ACT III, Scene ii, ll. 59-65

Ravish'd and wrong'd, as Philomela was,
Forced in the ruthless, vast, and gloomy woods.
　　　　　　　　　　　　ACT IV, Scene i, ll. 52-53

　　Tit. We will solicit heaven and move the gods
To send down Justice for to wreak our wrongs.
Come, to this gear.　You are a good archer, Marcus.
　　　　　　　[*He gives them the arrows.* . . . .
　　Marc. My lord, I aim a mile beyond the moon ;
Your letter is with Jupiter by this.
　　　　　　　ACT IV, Scene iii, ll. 50-52, 65-66

King, be thy thoughts imperious, like thy name.
Is the sun dimm'd, that gnats do fly in it ?
The eagle suffers little birds to sing,
And is not careful what they mean thereby,
Knowing that with the shadow of his wings
He can at pleasure stint their melody.
　　　　　　　　　　　　ACT IV, Scene iv, ll. 81-86

Comedy of Errors

Sure, these are but imaginary wiles
And Lapland sorcerers inhabit here.

ACT IV, Scene iii, ll. 10-11

The Taming of the Shrew

A bedchamber in the Lord's *house.*

Enter aloft SLY, *with* Attendants ; *some with apparel, others
with basin and ewer and other appurtenances ; and* Lord.

Sly. For God's sake, a pot of small ale.

First Servant. Will't please your lordship drink a cup of
sack ?

Second Servant. Will't please your honour taste of these
conserves ?

Third Servant. What raiment will your honour wear to day ?

Sly. I am Christophero Sly ; call not me ' honour ' nor
' lordship : ' I ne'er drank sack in my life ; and if you give me
any conserves, give me conserves of beef : ne'er ask me what
raiment I'll wear ; for I have no more doublets than backs, no
more stockings than legs, nor no more shoes than feet ; nay,
sometime more feet than shoes, or such shoes as my toes look
through the over-leather.

Lord. Heaven cease this idle humour in your honour !
O, that a mighty man of such descent,
Of such possessions and so high esteem,
Should be infused with so foul a spirit !

Sly. What, would you make me mad ? Am not I Christopher Sly, old Sly's son of Burtonheath, by birth a pedlar, by
education a card-maker, by transmutation a bear-herd, and
now by present profession a tinker ? Ask Marian Hacket, the
fat ale-wife of Wincot, if she know me not : if she say I am
not fourteen pence on the score for sheer ale, score me up for
the lyingest knave in Christendom. . . .

13

Lord. . . . O noble lord, bethink thee of thy birth,
Call home thy ancient thoughts from banishment
And banish hence these abject lowly dreams.
Look how thy servants do attend on thee,
Each in his office ready at thy beck.
Wilt thou have music? hark! Apollo plays

[*Music.*

And twenty caged nightingales do sing:
Or wilt thou sleep? we'll have thee to a couch
Softer and sweeter than the lustful bed
On purpose trimm'd up for Semiramis.
Say thou wilt walk; we will bestrew the ground:
Or wilt thou ride? thy horses shall be trapp'd,
Their harness studded all with gold and pearl.
Dost thou love hawking? thou hast hawks will soar
Above the morning lark: or wilt thou hunt?
Thy hounds shall make the welkin answer them
And fetch shrill echoes from the hollow earth. . . .

    Sec. Serv. Dost thou love pictures? we will fetch
      thee straight
Adonis painted by a running brook,
And Cytherea all in sedges hid,
Which seem to move and wanton with her breath,
Even as the waving sedges play with wind. . . .

    Sly. Am I a lord? and have I such a lady?
Or do I dream? or have I dream'd till now?
I do not sleep: I see, I hear, I speak:
I smell sweet savours and I feel soft things:
Upon my life, I am a lord indeed
And not a tinker nor Christophero Sly.
Well, bring our lady hither to our sight;
And once again, a pot o' the smallest ale. . . .

           Come, madam wife, sit by my side and
let the world slip: we shall ne'er be younger.

INDUCTION, Scene ii, ll. 1-26, 32-48, 51-55, 70-77, 145-147

14

First Servant. My lord, you nod; you do not mind the play.

Sly. Yes, by Saint Anne, do I. A good matter, surely: comes there any more of it?

Page. My lord, 'tis but begun.

Sly. 'Tis a very excellent piece of work, madam lady: would 'twere done!   ACT I, Scene i, ll. 254-259

Kate like the hazel-twig
Is straight and slender and as brown in hue
As hazel nuts and sweeter than the kernels.

ACT II, Scene ii, 255-257

The Two Gentlemen of Verona

Proteus. If ever danger do environ thee,
Commend thy grievance to my holy prayers,
For I will be thy beadsman, Valentine.

Valentine. And on a love-book pray for my success?

Pro. Upon some book I love I'll pray for thee.

Val. That's on some shallow story of deep love:
How young Leander cross'd the Hellespont.

ACT I, Scene i, ll. 16-22

Other men, of slender reputation,
Put forth their sons to seek preferment out:
Some to the wars, to try their fortune there;
Some to discover islands far away;
Some to the studious universities.

ACT I, Scene iii, ll. 6-10

O, how this spring of love resembleth
The uncertain glory of an April day!

ACT I, Scene iii, ll. 84-85

Launce. Nay, 'twill be this hour ere I have done weeping; all the kind of the Launces have this very fault. I have received my proportion, like the prodigious son, and am going with Sir Proteus to the Imperial's court. I think Crab my dog be the sourest-natured dog that lives : my mother weeping, my father wailing, my sister crying, our maid howling, our cat wringing her hands, and all our house in a great perplexity, yet did not this cruel-hearted cur shed one tear : he is a stone, a very pebble stone, and has no more pity in him than a dog : a Jew would have wept to have seen our parting ; why, my grandam, having no eyes, look you, wept herself blind at my parting. Nay, I'll show you the manner of it. This shoe is my father : no, this left shoe is my father : no, no, this left shoe is my mother : nay, that cannot be so neither : yes, it is so, it is so, it hath the worser sole. This shoe, with the hole in it, is my mother, and this my father ; a vengeance on't ! there 'tis : now, sir, this staff is my sister, for, look you, she is as white as a lily and as small as a wand : this hat is Nan, our maid : I am the dog : no, the dog is himself, and I am the dog —Oh ! the dog is me, and I am myself ; ay, so, so. Now come I to my father ; Father, your blessing : now should not the shoe speak a word for weeping : now should I kiss my father ; well, he weeps on. Now come I to my mother : O, that she could speak now like a wood-woman ! Well, I kiss her ; why, there 'tis ; here's my mother's breath up and down. Now come I to my sister ; mark the moan she makes. Now the dog all this while sheds not a tear nor speaks a word ; but see how I lay the dust with my tears.   ACT II, Scene iii, ll. 1-35

Speed. But tell me true, will't be a match ?

Launce. Ask my dog : if he say ay, it will ; if he say no, it will ; if he shake his tail and say nothing, it will.

Speed. The conclusion is then that it will.

Launce. Thou shalt never get such a secret from me but by a parable.   ACT II, Scene v, ll. 35-41

Julia. The current that with gentle murmur glides,
Thou know'st, being stopp'd, impatiently doth rage ;

16

But when his fair course is not hindered,
He makes sweet music with the enamell'd stones,
Giving a gentle kiss to every sedge
He overtaketh in his pilgrimage,
And so by many winding nooks he strays
With willing sport to the wild ocean.
Then let me go and hinder not my course:
I'll be as patient as a gentle stream
And make a pastime of each weary step,
Till the last step have brought me to my love;
And there I'll rest, as after much turmoil
A blessed soul doth in Elysium.

Act II, Scene vii, ll. 25-38

What light is light, if Silvia be not seen?
What joy is joy, if Silvia be not by?
Unless it be to think that she is by
And feed upon the shadow of perfection.
Except I be by Silvia in the night,
There is no music in the nightingale;
Unless I look on Silvia in the day,
There is no day for me to look upon;
She is my essence. Act III, Scene i, ll. 174-182

But neither bended knees, pure hands held up,
Sad sighs, deep groans, nor silver-shedding tears.

Act III, Scene i, ll. 229-230

Say that upon the altar of her beauty
You sacrifice your tears, your sighs, your heart:
Write till your ink be dry, and with your tears
Moist it again, and frame some feeling line
That may discover such integrity:
For Orpheus' lute was strung with poets' sinews,
Whose golden touch could soften steel and stones,
Make tigers tame and huge leviathans
Forsake unsounded deeps to dance on sands.

Act III, Scene ii, ll. 73-81

17

Who is Silvia ? what is she,
    That all our swains commend her ?
Holy, fair and wise is she ;
    That heaven such grace did lend her,
That she might admired be.

Is she kind as she is fair ?
    For beauty lives with kindness.
Love doth to her eyes repair,
    To help him of his blindness,
And, being help'd, inhabits there.

Then to Silvia let us sing,
    That Silvia is excelling ;
She excels each mortal thing
    Upon the dull earth dwelling :
To her let us garlands bring.

ACT IV, Scene ii, ll. 39-53

Enter LAUNCE, *with his Dog*.

Launce. When a man's servant shall play the cur with him,
look you, it goes hard : one that I brought up of a puppy ; one
that I saved from drowning, when three or four of his blind
brothers and sisters went to it. I have taught him, even as one
would say precisely, ' thus I would teach a dog.' I was sent to
deliver him as a present to Mistress Silvia from my master ;
and I came no sooner into the dining-chamber but he steps me
to her trencher and steals her capon's leg : O, 'tis a foul thing
when a cur cannot keep himself in all companies ! I would
have, as one should say, one that takes upon him to be a dog
indeed, to be, as it were, a dog at all things. If I had not had
more wit than he, to take a fault upon me that he did, I think
verily he had been hanged for't ; sure as I live, he had suffered
for't : you shall judge. He thrusts me himself into the company of three or four gentlemanlike dogs, under the duke's
table : he had not been there—bless the mark !—a pissing
while, but all the chamber smelt him. ' Out with the dog ! '

says one : ' What cur is that ? ' says another : ' Whip him out '
says the third : ' Hang him up ' says the duke.   I, having been
acquainted with the smell before, knew it was Crab, and goes
me to the fellow that whips the dogs : ' Friend,' quoth I,
' you mean to whip the dog ? ' ' Ay, marry, do I,' quoth he.
' You do him the more wrong,' quoth I ; ' 'twas I did the
thing you wot of.' He makes me no more ado, but whips me
out of the chamber. How many masters would do this for his
servant ? Nay, I'll be sworn, I have sat in the stocks for
puddings he had stolen, otherwise he had been executed ; I
have stood on the pillory for geese he hath killed, otherwise he
had suffered for't. Thou thinkest not of this now. Nay, I
remember the trick you served me when I took my leave of
Madam Silvia : did not I bid thee still mark me and do as I
do ? when didst thou see me heave up my leg and make water
against a gentlewoman's farthingale ? didst thou ever see me
do such a trick ? ACT IV, Scene iv, ll. 1-43

Love's Labour's Lost

The huge army of the world's desires.

 ACT I, Scene i, l. 10

These earthly godfathers of heaven's lights
 That give a name to every fixed star
Have no more profit of their shining nights
 Than those that walk and wot not what they are.

 ACT I, Scene i, ll. 88-91

 King. . . . Our court, you know, is haunted
 With a refined traveller of Spain ;
A man in all the world's new fashion planted,
 That hath a mint of phrases in his brain ;
One whom the music of his own vain tongue
 Doth ravish like enchanting harmony.

 ACT I, Scene i, ll. 163-168

Armado. Comfort me, boy : what great men have been in love ?

Moth. Hercules, master.

Arm. Most sweet Hercules ! More authority, dear boy, name more ; and, sweet my child, let them be men of good repute and carriage.

Moth. Samson, master : he was a man of good carriage, great carriage, for he carried the town-gates on his back like a porter : and he was in love.

Arm. O well-knit Samson ! strong-jointed Samson ! I do excel thee in my rapier as much as thou didst me in carrying gates. I am in love too.   ACT I, Scene ii, ll. 67-79

> If she be made of white and red,
>   Her faults will ne'er be known.
>
> ACT I, Scene ii, ll. 104-105

Holophernes, the schoolmaster. This is a gift that I have, simple, simple ; a foolish extravagant spirit, full of forms, figures, shapes, objects, ideas, apprehensions, motions, revolutions : these are begot in the ventricle of memory, nourished in the womb of pia mater, and delivered upon the mellowing of occasion. But the gift is good in those in whom it is acute, and I am thankful for it.

Sir Nathaniel, the curate. Sir, I praise the Lord for you : and so may my parishioners.   ACT IV, Scene ii, ll. 67-76

> So sweet a kiss the golden sun gives not
>   To those fresh morning drops upon the rose.
>
> ACT IV, Scene iii, ll. 26-27

> Did not the heavenly rhetoric of thine eye,
>   'Gainst whom the world cannot hold argument,
> Persuade my heart to this false perjury ?
>
> ACT IV, Scene iii, ll. 60-62

> On a day—alack the day !—
> Love, whose month is ever May,

Spied a blossom passing fair
Playing in the wanton air :
Through the velvet leaves the wind,
All unseen, can passage find ;
That the lover, sick to death,
Wish himself the heaven's breath.
Air, quoth he, thy cheeks may blow ;
Air, would I might triumph so !
But, alack, my hand is sworn
Ne'er to pluck thee from thy thorn ;
Vow, alack, for youth unmeet,
Youth so apt to pluck a sweet !
Do not call it sin in me,
That I am forsworn for thee ;
Thou for whom Jove would swear
Juno but an Ethiope were ;
And deny himself for Jove,
Turning mortal for thy love.

ACT IV, Scene iii, ll. 101-120

The sea will ebb and flow, heaven show his face ;
Young blood doth not obey an old decree :

ACT IV, Scene iii, ll. 216-217

From women's eyes this doctrine I derive ;
They are the ground, the books, the academes
From whence doth spring the true Promethean fire. . . .
O, we have made a vow to study, lords,
And in that vow we have forsworn our books.
For when would you, my liege, or you, or you,
In leaden contemplation have found out
Such fiery numbers as the prompting eyes
Of beauty's tutors have enrich'd you with ?
Other slow arts entirely keep the brain ;
And therefore, finding barren practisers,
Scarce show a harvest of their heavy toil :
But love, first learned in a lady's eyes,

Lives not alone immured in the brain ;
But, with the motion of all elements,
Courses as swift as thought in every power,
And gives to every power a double power,
Above their functions and their offices.
It adds a precious seeing to the eye ;
A lover's eyes will gaze an eagle blind ;
A lover's ear will hear the lowest sound,
When the suspicious head of theft is stopp'd :
Love's feeling is more soft and sensible
Than are the tender horns of cockled snails ;
Love's tongue proves dainty Bacchus gross in taste :
For valour, is not Love a Hercules,
Still climbing trees in the Hesperides ?
Subtle as Sphinx ; as sweet and musical
As bright Apollo's lute, strung with his hair :
And when Love speaks, the voice of all the gods
Make heaven drowsy with the harmony.
Never durst poet touch a pen to write
Until his ink were temper'd with Love's sighs ;
O, then his lines would ravish savage ears
And plant in tyrants mild humility.
From women's eyes this doctrine I derive :
They sparkle still the right Promethean fire ;
They are the books, the arts, the academes,
That show, contain and nourish all the world :
Else none at all in ought proves excellent.
Then fools you were these women to forswear,
Or keeping what is sworn, you will prove fools.
For wisdom's sake, a word that all men love,
Or for love's sake, a word that loves all men,
Or for men's sake, the authors of these women,
Or women's sake, by whom we men are men,
Let us once lose our oaths to find ourselves,
Or else we lose ourselves to keep our oaths.
It is religion to be thus forsworn,

For charity itself fulfils the law,
And who can sever love from charity ?

ACT IV, Scene iii, ll. 302-304, 318-365

Enter HOLOFERNES, SIR NATHANIEL, *and* DULL.

Hol. Satis quod sufficit.

Nath. I praise God for you, sir : your reasons at dinner have been sharp and sententious ; pleasant without scurrility, witty without affection, audacious without impudency, learned without opinion, and strange without heresy. I did converse this quondam day with a companion of the king's, who is intituled, nominated, or called, Don Adriano de Armado.

Hol. Novi hominem tanquam te : his humour is lofty, his discourse peremptory, his tongue filed, his eye ambitious, his gait majestical, and his general behaviour vain, ridiculous, and thrasonical. He is too picked, too spruce, too affected, too odd, as it were, too peregrinate, as I may call it.

Nath. A most singular and choice epithet.

[*Draws out his table-book.*

Hol. He draweth out the thread of his verbosity finer than the staple of his argument. I abhor such fanatical phantasimes, such insociable and point-devise companions ; such rackers of orthography, as to speak dout, fine, when he should say doubt ; det, when he should pronounce debt,—d, e, b, t, not d, e, t : he clepeth a calf, cauf ; half, hauf ; neighbour vocatur nebour ; neigh abbreviated ne. This is abhominable,—which he would call abbominable : it insinuateth me of insanie : anne intelligis, domine ? to make frantic, lunatic.

Nath. Laus Deo, bene intelligo.

Hol. Bon, bon, fort bon ! Priscian a little scratched, 'twill serve.

Nath. Videsne quis venit ?

Hol. Video, et gaudeo.

Enter ARMADO, MOTH, *and* COSTARD.

Arm. Chirrah ! [*To Moth.*

Hol. Quare chirrah, not sirrah ?

23
C

Arm. Men of peace, well encountered.

Hol. Most military sir, salutation.

Moth. [*Aside to Costard*] They have been at a great feast of languages, and stolen the scraps.

Cost. O, they have lived long on the almsbasket of words. I marvel thy master hath not eaten thee for a word ; for thou art not so long by the head as honorificabilitudinitatibus : thou art easier swallowed than a flap-dragon.

ACT V, Scene i, ll. 1-45

Armado. Sir, it is the king's most sweet pleasure and affection to congratulate the princess at her pavilion in the posteriors of this day, which the rude multitude call the afternoon.

Holophernes. The posterior of the day, most generous sir, is liable, congruent and measurable for the afternoon : the word is well culled, chose, sweet and apt, I do assure you, sir, I do assure.

ACT V, Scene i, ll. 92-99

Taffeta phrases, silken terms precise.

ACT V, Scene ii, l. 406

Enter SIR NATHANIEL, *for Alexander.*

Nath. When in the world I lived, I was the world's commander ;

By east, west, north, and south, I spread my conquering might :

My scutcheon plain declares that I am Alisander, . . .

Costard. There, an't shall please you ; a foolish mild man ; an honest man, look you, and soon dashed. He is a marvellous good neighbour, faith, and a very good bowler : but, for Alisander,—alas, you see how 'tis,—a little o'erparted.

ACT V, Scene ii, ll. 565-567, 584-588

Enter ARMADO, *for Hector.*

Dumain. Hector's a greyhound.

Arm. The sweet war-man is dead and rotten ; sweet

24

chucks, beat not the bones of the buried : when he breathed,
he was a man. ACT V, Scene ii, ll. 664-667

SPRING

When daisies pied and violets blue
   And lady-smocks all silver-white
And cuckoo-buds of yellow hue
   Do paint the meadows with delight,
The cuckoo then, on every tree,
Mocks married men ; for thus sings he,
      Cuckoo ;
Cuckoo, cuckoo : O word of fear,
Unpleasing to a married ear !

When shepherds pipe on oaten straws .
   And merry larks are ploughmen's clocks,
When turtles tread, and rooks, and daws,
   And maidens bleach their summer smocks,
The cuckoo then, on every tree,
Mocks married men ; for thus sings he,
      Cuckoo ;
Cuckoo, cuckoo : O word of fear,
Unpleasing to a married ear !

WINTER

When icicles hang by the wall
   And Dick the shepherd blows his nail
And Tom bears logs into the hall
   And milk comes frozen home in pail,
When blood is nipp'd and ways be foul,
Then nightly sings the staring owl,
      Tu-whit ;
Tu-who, a merry note,
While greasy Joan doth keel the pot.

When all aloud the wind doth blow
    And coughing drowns the parson's saw
And birds sit brooding in the snow
    And Marian's nose looks red and raw,
When roasted crabs hiss in the bowl,
Then nightly sings the staring owl,
      Tu-whit ;
Tu-who, a merry note,
While greasy Joan doth keel the pot.

ACT V, Scene ii, ll. 904-939

SUNRISE

KING JOHN

RICHARD II

ROMEO AND JULIET

A MIDSUMMER-NIGHT'S DREAM

THE MERCHANT OF VENICE

The Life and Death of

King John

   Bastard. Well, now can I make any Joan a lady.
' Good den, sir Richard ! '—' God-a-mercy, fellow ! '—
And if his name be George, I'll call him Peter ;
For new-made honour doth forget men's names ;
'Tis too respective and too sociable
For your conversion. Now your traveller,
He and his toothpick at my worship's mess,
And when my knightly stomach is sufficed,
Why then I suck my teeth and catechize
My picked man of countries : ' My dear sir,'
Thus, leaning on mine elbow, I begin,
' I shall beseech you '—that is question now ;
And then comes answer like an Absey book :
' O sir,' says answer, ' at your best command ;
At your employment ; at your service, sir : '
' No, sir,' says question, ' I, sweet sir, at yours : '
And so, ere answer knows what question would,
Saving in dialogue of compliment,
And talking of the Alps and Apennines,
The Pyrenean and the river Po,
It draws toward supper in conclusion so.
But this is worshipful society
And fits the mounting spirit like myself,

Act I, Scene i, ll. 183-206

       That pale, that white-faced shore,
Whose foot spurns back the ocean's roaring tides.

Act II, Scene i, ll. 23-24

   Elinor.   Come to thy grandam, child.
   Constance. Do, child, go to it grandam, child ;

Give grandam kingdom, and it grandam will
Give it a plum, a cherry, and a fig:
There's a good grandam.

   Arthur.   Good my mother, peace!
I would that I were low laid in my grave:
I am not worth this coil that's made for me.

ACT II, Scene i, ll. 159-165

Then God forgive the sin of all those souls
That to their everlasting residence,
Before the dew of evening fall, shall fleet,
In dreadful trial of our kingdom's king!

ACT II, Scene i, ll. 283-286

And victory, with little loss, doth play
Upon the dancing banners of the French.

ACT II, Scene i, ll. 307-308

Of nature's gifts thou mayst with lilies boast
And with the half-blown rose.

ACT III, Scene i, ll. 53-54

I will instruct my sorrows to be proud;
For grief is proud and makes his owner stoop.
To me and to the state of my great grief
Let kings assemble; for my grief's so great
That no supporter but the huge firm earth
Can hold it up: here I and sorrows sit;
Here is my throne, bid kings come bow to it.

ACT III, Scene i, ll. 68-74

               The glorious sun
Stays in his course and plays the alchemist,
Turning with splendour of his precious eye
The meagre cloddy earth to glittering gold.

ACT III, Scene i, ll. 77-80

King John. Good Hubert, Hubert, Hubert, throw
   thine eye
On yon young boy: I'll tell thee what, my friend,

30

He is a very serpent in my way;
And whereso'er this foot of mine doth tread,
He lies before me: dost thou understand me?
Thou art his keeper.

Hubert.   And I'll keep him so,
That he shall not offend your majesty.

K. John.   Death.

Hub. My lord?

K. John.   A grave.

Hub.   He shall not live.

K. John   Enough.
I could be merry now.

          Act III, Scene iii, ll. 59-67

Constance. Death, death; O amiable lovely death! . . .
Arise forth from the couch of lasting night,
Thou hate and terror to prosperity,
And I will kiss thy detestable bones. . . .
And stop this gap of breath with fulsome dust
And be a carrion monster like thyself:
Come, grin on me, and I will think thou smilest
And buss thee as thy wife. Misery's love,
O, come to me! . . .

Pandulph. You hold too heinous a respect of grief.

Const. He talks to me that never had a son.

King Philip. You are as fond of grief as of your child.

Const. Grief fills the room up of my absent child,
Lies in his bed, walks up and down with me,
Puts on his pretty looks, repeats his words,
Remembers me of all his gracious parts,
Stuffs out his vacant garments with his form;
Then, have I reason to be fond of grief? . . .
O Lord! my boy, my Arthur, my fair son!
My life, my joy, my food, my all the world!
My widow-comfort and my sorrows' cure!

    Act III, Scene iv, ll. 25, 27-29, 32-36, 90-98, 103-105

How green you are and fresh in this old world !

ACT III, Scene iv, l. 145

A room in a castle.

Enter HUBERT *and* Executioners.

Hub. Heat me these irons hot ; and look thou stand
Within the arras : when I strike my foot
Upon the bosom of the ground, rush forth
And bind the boy which you shall find with me
Fast to the chair : be heedful : hence, and watch.

First Exec. I hope your warrant will bear out the deed.

Hub. Uncleanly scruples ! fear not you : look to't.

[*Exeunt Executioners.*

Young lad, come forth ; I have to say with you.

Enter ARTHUR.

Arth. Good morrow, Hubert.

Hub. Good morrow, little prince.

Arth. As little prince, having so great a title
To be more prince, as may be. You are sad.

Hub. Indeed, I have been merrier.

Arth. Mercy on me !

Methinks no body should be sad but I :
Yet, I remember, when I was in France,
Young gentlemen would be as sad as night,
Only for wantonness. By my christendom,
So I were out of prison and kept sheep,
I should be as merry as the day is long ;
And so I would be here, but that I doubt
My uncle practises more harm to me :
He is afraid of me and I of him :
Is it my fault that I was Geffrey's son ?
No, indeed, is't not ; and I would to heaven
I were your son, so you would love me, Hubert.

Hub. [*Aside*] If I talk to him, with his innocent prate
He will awake my mercy which lies dead :
Therefore I will be sudden and dispatch.

Arth. Are you sick, Hubert ? you look pale to-day :
In sooth, I would you were a little sick,
That I might sit all night and watch with you :
I warrant I love you more than you do me.

Hub. [*Aside*] His words do take possession of my bosom.
Read here, young Arthur.   [*Showing a paper.*
                    [*Aside*] How now, foolish rheum !
Turning dispiteous torture out of door !
I must be brief, lest resolution drop
Out at mine eyes in tender womanish tears.
Can you not read it ? is it not fair writ ?

Arth. Too fairly, Hubert, for so foul effect :
Must you with hot irons burn out both mine eyes ?

Hub. Young boy, I must.

Arth.   And will you ?

Hub.   And I will.

Arth. Have you the heart ? When your head did but
    ache,
I knit my handkercher about your brows,
The best I had, a princess wrought it me,
And I did never ask it you again ;
And with my hand at midnight held your head,
And like the watchful minutes to the hour,
Still and anon cheer'd up the heavy time,
Saying, ' What lack you ? ' and ' Where lies your grief ? '
Or ' What good love may I perform for you ? '
Many a poor man's son would have lien still
And ne'er have spoke a loving word to you ;
But you at your sick service had a prince.
Nay, you may think my love was crafty love
And call it cunning : do, an if you will :
If heaven be pleased that you must use me ill,
Why then you must. Will you put out mine eyes ?
These eyes that never did nor never shall
So much as frown on you.

Hub.   I have sworn to do it ;

33

And with hot irons must I burn them out. . . .

Arth. An if an angel should have come to me
And told me Hubert should put out mine eyes,
I would not have believed him,—no tongue but Hubert's.

Hub. Come forth. [*Stamps.*

Re-enter Executioners, *with a cord, irons, &c.*

Do as I bid you do.

Arth. O, save me, Hubert, save me ! my eyes are out
Even with the fierce looks of these bloody men.

Hub. Give me the iron, I say, and bind him here.

Arth. Alas, what need you be so boisterous-rough ?
I will not struggle, I will stand stone-still.
For heaven sake, Hubert, let me not be bound !
Nay, hear me, Hubert, drive these men away,
And I will sit as quiet as a lamb ;
I will not stir, nor wince, nor speak a word,
Nor look upon the iron angerly :
Thrust but these men away, and I'll forgive you,
Whatever torment you do put me to.

Hub. Go, stand within ; let me alone with him.

First Exec. I am best pleased to be from such a deed.

[*Exeunt Executioners.*

Arth. Alas, I then have chid away my friend !
He hath a stern look, but a gentle heart :
Let him come back, that his compassion may
Give life to yours.

Hub. Come, boy, prepare yourself.

Arth. Is there no remedy ?

Hub. None, but to lose your eyes.

Arth. O heaven, that there were but a mote in yours,
A grain, a dust, a gnat, a wandering hair,
Any annoyance in that precious sense !
Then feeling what small things are boisterous there,
Your vile intent must needs seem horrible.

Hub. Is this your promise ? go to, hold your tongue

Arth. Hubert, the utterance of a brace of tongues

Must needs want pleading for a pair of eyes :
Let me not hold my tongue, let me not, Hubert ;
Or, Hubert, if you will, cut out my tongue,
So I may keep mine eyes : O, spare mine eyes,
Though to no use but still to look on you !
Lo, by my troth, the instrument is cold
And would not harm me.

Hub.   I can heat it, boy.

Arth. No, in good sooth ; the fire is dead with grief,
Being create for comfort, to be used
In undeserved extremes : see else yourself ;
There is no malice in this burning coal ;
The breath of heaven hath blown his spirit out
And strew'd repentant ashes on his head.

Hub. But with my breath I can revive it, boy.

Arth. An if you do, you will but make it blush
And glow with shame of your proceedings, Hubert :
Nay, it perchance will sparkle in your eyes ;
And like a dog that is compell'd to fight,
Snatch at his master that doth tarre him on.
All things that you should use to do me wrong
Deny their office : only you do lack
That mercy which fierce fire and iron extends,
Creatures of note for mercy-lacking uses.

Hub. Well, see to live ; I will not touch thine eye
For all the treasure that thine uncle owes :
Yet am I sworn and I did purpose, boy,
With this same very iron to burn them out.

Arth. O, now you look like Hubert ! all this while
You were disguised.

Hub.   Peace ; no more. Adieu.
Your uncle must not know but you are dead ;
I'll fill these dogged spies with false reports :
And, pretty child, sleep doubtless and secure,
That Hubert, for the wealth of all the world,
Will not offend thee.

Arth.   O heaven ! I thank you, Hubert.

Hub. Silence ; no more : go closely in with me :
Much danger do I undergo for thee.   [*Exeunt.*

ACT IV, Scene i, ll. 1-59, 68-134

To guard a title that was rich before,
To gild refined gold, to paint the lily,
To throw a perfume on the violet,
To smooth the ice, or add another hue
Unto the rainbow, or with taper-light
To seek the beauteous eye of heaven to garnish,
Is wasteful and ridiculous excess.

ACT IV, Scene ii, ll. 10-16

I'll go with thee,
And find the inheritance of this poor child,
His little kingdom of a forced grave.

ACT IV, Scene ii, ll. 96-98

We will not line his thin bestained cloak
With our pure honours, nor attend the foot
That leaves the print of blood where'er it walks.

ACT IV, Scene iii, ll. 24-26

O death, made proud with pure and princely beauty !

ACT IV, Scene iii, l. 35

The burning crest
Of the old, feeble and day-wearied sun.

ACT V, Scene iv, ll. 34-35

Prince Henry.   'Tis strange that death should sing.
I am the cygnet to this pale faint swan,
Who chants a doleful hymn to his own death . . .
How fares your majesty ?

K. John. Poison'd,—ill fare—dead, forsook, cast off :
And none of you will bid the winter come
To thrust his icy fingers in my maw,
Nor let my kingdom's rivers take their course
Through my burn'd bosom, nor entreat the north

To make his bleak winds kiss my parched lips
And comfort me with cold. I do not ask you much,
I beg cold comfort.

ACT V, Scene vii, ll. 20-22, 34-42

The Tragedy of
Richard II

Old John of Gaunt, time-honoured Lancaster—

ACT I, Scene i, l. 1

My loving lord, I take my leave of you . . .
Not sick, although I have to do with death,
But lusty, young, and cheerly drawing breath.

ACT I, Scene iii, ll. 63, 65-66

The sly slow hours shall not determinate
The dateless limit of thy dear exile ;
The hopeless word of ' never to return '
Breathe I against thee.

ACT I, Scene iii, ll. 150-154

How long a time lies in one little word !
Four lagging winters and four wanton springs
End in a word : such is the breath of kings.

ACT I, Scene iii, ll. 213-215

    Gaunt. All places that the eye of heaven visits
Are to a wise man ports and happy havens.
Teach thy necessity to reason thus ;
There is no virtue like necessity.
Think not the king did banish thee,
But thou the king. Woe doth the heavier sit,
Where it perceives it is but faintly borne.
Go, say I sent thee forth to purchase honour
And not the king exiled thee ; or suppose
Devouring pestilence hangs in our air

37

And thou art flying to a fresher clime :
Look, what thy soul holds dear, imagine it
To lie that way thou go'st, not whence thou comest :
Suppose the singing birds musicians,
The grass whereon thou tread'st the presence strew'd,
The flowers fair ladies, and thy steps no more
Than a delightful measure or a dance ;
For gnarling sorrow hath less power to bite
The man that mocks at it and sets it light.

    Bolingbroke. O, who can hold a fire in his hand
By thinking on the frosty Caucasus ?
Or cloy the hungry edge of appetite
By bare imagination of a feast ?
Or wallow naked in December snow
By thinking on fantastic summer's heat ?

ACT I, Scene iii, ll. 275-299

The tongues of dying men
Enforce attention like deep harmony.

ACT II, Scene i, ll. 5-6

The setting sun, and music at the close.

ACT II, Scene i, l. 12

    Gaunt. This royal throne of kings, this scepter'd isle,
This earth of majesty, this seat of Mars,
This other Eden, demi-paradise,
This fortress built by Nature for herself
Against infection and the hand of war,
This happy breed of men, this little world,
This precious stone set in the silver sea,
Which serves it in the office of a wall
Or as a moat defensive to a house,
Against the envy of less happier lands,
This blessed plot, this earth, this realm, this England,
This nurse, this teeming womb of royal kings,
Fear'd by their breed and famous by their birth,
Renowned for their deeds as far from home,

For Christian service and true chivalry,
As is the sepulchre in stubborn Jewry
Of the world's ransom, blessed Mary's Son,
This land of such dear souls, this dear dear land,
Dear for her reputation through the world,
Is now leased out, I die pronouncing it,
Like to a tenement or pelting farm :
England, bound in with the triumphant sea,
Whose rocky shore beats back the envious siege
Of watery Neptune, is now bound in with shame,
With inky blots and rotten parchment bonds :
That England, that was wont to conquer others,
Hath made a shameful conquest of itself.
Ah, would the scandal vanish with my life,
How happy then were my ensuing death !

Act II, Scene i, ll. 40-68

Gaunt am I for the grave, gaunt as a grave.

Act II, Scene i, l. 82

Even through the hollow eyes of death
I spy life peering.　　　Act II, Scene i, ll. 270-271

Comfort's in heaven ; and we are on the earth.

Act II, Scene ii, l. 78

　　Captain. 'Tis thought the king is dead ; we will not
　　stay.
The bay-trees in our country are all wither'd
And meteors fright the fixed stars of heaven ;
The pale-faced moon looks bloody on the earth
And lean-look'd prophets whisper fearful change ;
Rich men look sad and ruffians dance and leap,
The one in fear to lose what they enjoy,
The other to enjoy by rage and war :
These signs forerun the death or fall of kings.
Farewell : our countrymen are gone and fled,
As well assured Richard their king is dead.　　　[*Exit.*
　　Salisbury. Ah, Richard, with the eyes of heavy mind

I see thy glory like a shooting star
Fall to the base earth from the firmament.
Thy sun sets weeping in the lowly west,
Witnessing storms to come.

ACT II, Scene iv, ll. 7-22

King Richard. Dear earth, I do salute thee with my
    hand,
Though rebels wound thee with their horses' hoofs :
As a long-parted mother with her child
Plays fondly with her tears and smiles in meeting,
So, weeping, smiling, greet I thee, my earth,
And do thee favours with my royal hands.
Feed not thy sovereign's foe, my gentle earth,
Nor with thy sweets comfort his ravenous sense ;
But let thy spiders, that suck up thy venom,
And heavy-gaited toads lie in their way,
Doing annoyance to the treacherous feet
Which with usurping steps do trample thee :
Yield stinging nettles to mine enemies ;
And when they from thy bosom pluck a flower,
Guard it, I pray thee, with a lurking adder
Whose double tongue may with a mortal touch
Throw death upon thy sovereign's enemies.

ACT III, Scene ii, ll. 6-22

Not all the water in the rough rude sea
Can wash the balm off from an anointed king ;
The breath of worldly men cannot depose
The deputy elected by the Lord :
For every man that Bolingbroke hath press'd
To lift shrewd steel against our golden crown,
God for his Richard hath in heavenly pay
A glorious angel.

ACT III, Scene ii, ll. 54-61

Of comfort no man speak :
Let's talk of graves, of worms and epitaphs ;

Make dust our paper and with rainy eyes
Write sorrow on the bosom of the earth,
Let's choose executors and talk of wills :
And yet not so, for what can we bequeath
Save our deposed bodies to the ground ?
Our lands, our lives and all are Bolingbroke's,
And nothing can we call our own but death
And that small model of the barren earth
Which serves as paste and cover to our bones.
For God's sake, let us sit upon the ground
And tell sad stories of the death of kings :
How some have been deposed ; some slain in war ;
Some haunted by the ghosts they have deposed ;
Some poison'd by their wives ; some sleeping kill'd ;
All murder'd : for within the hollow crown
That rounds the mortal temples of a king
Keeps Death his court and there the antic sits,
Scoffing his state and grinning at his pomp,
Allowing him a breath, a little scene,
To monarchize, be fear'd and kill with looks,
Infusing him with self and vain conceit,
As if this flesh which walls about our life
Were brass impregnable, and humour'd thus
Comes at the last and with a little pin
Bores through his castle wall, and farewell king !
Cover your heads and mock not flesh and blood
With solemn reverence : throw away respect,
Tradition, form and ceremonious duty,
For you have but mistook me all this while :
I live with bread like you, feel want,
Taste grief, need friends : subjected thus,
How can you say to me, I am a king ?

ACT III, Scene ii, ll. 144-177

King Richard.   O that I were as great
As is my grief, or lesser than my name !

Or that I could forget what I have been
Or not remember what I must be now !
Swell'st thou, proud heart ? I'll give thee scope to beat,
Since foes have scope to beat both thee and me.

    Aumerle. Northumberland comes back from Boling-
      broke.

    K. Rich. What must the king do now ? must he
     submit ?

The king shall do it : must he be deposed ?
The king shall be contented : must he lose
The name of king ? o' God's name, let it go :
I'll give my jewels for a set of beads,
My gorgeous palace for a hermitage,
My gay apparel for an almsman's gown,
My figured goblets for a dish of wood,
My sceptre for a palmer's walking-staff,
My subjects for a pair of carved saints
And my large kingdom for a little grave,
A little little grave, an obscure grave ;
Or I'll be buried in the king's highway,
Some way of common trade, where subjects' feet
May hourly trample on their sovereign's head ;
For on my heart they tread now whilst I live ;
And buried once, why not upon my head ?
Aumerle, thou weep'st, my tender-hearted cousin !
We'll make foul weather with despised tears ;
Our sighs and they shall lodge the summer corn,
And make a dearth in this revolting land.
Or shall we play the wantons with our woes,
And make some pretty match with shedding tears ?
As thus, to drop them still upon one place,
Till they have fretted us a pair of graves
Within the earth ; and, therein laid,—there lies
Two kinsmen digg'd their graves with weeping eyes.
Would not this ill do well ? Well, well, I see
I talk but idly, and you laugh at me.

Most mighty prince, my Lord Northumberland,
What says King Bolingbroke ? will his majesty
Give Richard leave to live till Richard die ?
You make a leg, and Bolingbroke says ay.
   Northumberland. My lord, in the base court he doth
    attend
To speak with you ; may it please you to come down.
   K. Rich. Down, down I come ; like glistering
    Phaethon,
Wanting the manage of unruly jades.

Act III, Scene iii, ll. 136-179

Shall I so much dishonour my fair stars ?

Act IV, Scene i, l. 21

Many a time hath banish'd Norfolk fought
For Jesu Christ in glorious Christian field,
Streaming the ensign of the Christian cross
Against black pagans, Turks, and Saracens ;
And toil'd with works of war, retired himself
To Italy ; and there at Venice gave
His body to that pleasant country's earth,
And his pure soul unto his captain Christ,
Under whose colours he had fought so long.

Act IV, Scene i, ll. 92-100

Enter York, *with* Richard, *and* Officers *bearing the regalia.*

   K. Rich. Alack, why am I sent for to a king,
Before I have shook off the regal thoughts
Wherewith I reign'd ? I hardly yet have learn'd
To insinuate, flatter, bow, and bend my limbs :
Give sorrow leave awhile to tutor me
To this submission. Yet I well remember
The favours of these men : were they not mine ?
Did they not sometime cry, ' all hail ! ' to me ?
So Judas did to Christ : but he, in twelve,
Found truth in all but one ; I, in twelve thousand, none.
God save the king ! Will no man say amen ?

43

Am I both priest and clerk ? well then, amen.
God save the king ! although I be not he ;
And yet, amen, if heaven do think him me.
To do what service am I sent for hither ?

    York. To do that office of thine own good will
Which tired majesty did make thee offer,
The resignation of thy state and crown
To Henry Bolingbroke.

        K. Rich. Give me the crown. Here, cousin, seize
        the crown ;
Here, cousin ;
On this side my hand, and on that side yours.
Now is this golden crown like a deep well
That owes two buckets, filling one another,
The emptier ever dancing in the air,
The other down, unseen and full of water :
That bucket down and full of tears am I,
Drinking my griefs, whilst you mount up on high.

    Bolingbroke. I thought you had been willing to
    resign.

    K. Rich. My crown I am ; but still my griefs are
    mine :
You may my glories and my state depose,
But not my griefs ; still am I king of those.

    Boling. Part of your cares you give me with your
    crown.

    K. Rich. Your cares set up do not pluck my cares
    down.
My care is loss of care, by old care done ;
Your care is gain of care, by new care won :
The cares I give I have, though given away ;
They tend the crown, yet still with me they stay.

    Boling. Are you contented to resign the crown ?.

    K. Rich. Ay, no ; no, ay ; for I must nothing be ;
Therefore no no, for I resign to thee.
Now mark me, how I will undo myself :

I give this heavy weight from off my head
And this unwieldly sceptre from my hand,
The pride of kingly sway from out my heart;
With mine own tears I wash away my balm,
With mine own hands I give away my crown,
With mine own tongue deny my sacred state,
With mine own breath release all duty's rites:
All pomp and majesty I do forswear;
My manors, rents, revenues I forego;
My acts, decrees, and statutes I deny:
God pardon all oaths that are broke to me!
God keep all vows unbroke that swear to thee!
Make me, that nothing have, with nothing grieved,
And thou with all pleased, that hast all achieved!
Long mayst thou live in Richard's seat to sit,
And soon lie Richard in an earthy pit!
God save King Harry, unking'd Richard says,
And send him many years of sunshine days!
What more remains?

    Northumberland.   No more, but that you read
These accusations and these grievous crimes
Committed by your person and your followers
Against the state and profit of this land;
That, by confessing them, the souls of men
May deem that you are worthily deposed.

    K. Rich. Must I do so? and must I ravel out
My weaved-up folly? Gentle Northumberland,
If thy offences were upon record,
Would it not shame thee in so fair a troop
To read a lecture of them? If thou wouldst,
There shouldst thou find one heinous article,
Containing the deposing of a king
And cracking the strong warrant of an oath,
Mark'd with a blot, damn'd in the book of heaven:
Nay, all of you that stand and look upon,
Whilst that my wretchedness doth bait myself,

Though some of you with Pilate wash your hands
Showing an outward pity ; yet you Pilates
Have here deliver'd me to my sour cross,
And water cannot wash away your sin.

   North. My lord, dispatch ; read o'er these articles.

   K. Rich. Mine eyes are full of tears, I cannot see :
And yet salt water blinds them not so much
But they can see a sort of traitors here.
Nay, if I turn mine eyes upon myself,
I find myself a traitor with the rest ;
For I have given here my soul's consent
To undeck the pompous body of a king :
Made glory base and sovereignty a slave,
Proud majesty a subject, state a peasant.

   North. My lord,—

   K. Rich. No lord of thine, thou haught insulting
     man,
Nor no man's lord ; I have no name, no title,
No, not that name was given me at the font,
But 'tis usurp'd : alack the heavy day,
That I have worn so many winters out,
And know not now what name to call myself !
O that I were a mockery king of snow,
Standing before the sun of Bolingbroke,
To melt myself away in water-drops !
Good king, great king, and yet not greatly good,
An if my word be sterling yet in England,
Let it command a mirror hither straight,
That it may show me what a face I have,
Since it is bankrupt of his majesty.

   Boling. Go some of you and fetch a looking-glass.

                          [Exit an attendant.

   North. Read o'er this paper while the glass doth
     come.

   K. Rich. Fiend, thou torment'st me ere I come to hell !

   Boling. Urge it no more, my Lord Northumberland.

North. The commons will not then be satisfied.

K. Rich. They shall be satisfied : I'll read enough,
When I do see the very book indeed
Where all my sins are writ, and that's myself.

Re-enter Attendant, *with a glass.*

Give me the glass, and therein will I read.
No deeper wrinkles yet ? hath sorrow struck
So many blows upon this face of mine,
And made no deeper wounds ? O flattering glass,
Like to my followers in prosperity,
Thou dost beguile me ! Was this face the face
That every day under his household roof
Did keep ten thousand men ? was this the face
That, like the sun, did make beholders wink ?
Was this the face that faced so many follies,
And was at last out-faced by Bolingbroke ?
A brittle glory shineth in this face :
As brittle as the glory is the face ;

                [*Dashes the glass against the ground.*
For there it is, crack'd in a hundred shivers.
Mark, silent king, the moral of this sport,
How soon my sorrow hath destroy'd my face.

Boling. The shadow of your sorrow hath destroy'd
The shadow of your face.

K. Rich.   Say that again.
The shadow of my sorrow ! ha ! let's see :
'Tis very true, my grief lies all within ;
And these external manners of laments
Are merely shadows to the unseen grief
That swells with silence in the tortured soul ;
There lies the substance : and I thank thee, king,
For thy great bounty, that not only givest
Me cause to wail but teachest me the way
How to lament the cause. I'll beg one boon,
And then be gone and trouble you no more.

Shall I obtain it ?

Boling.   Name it, fair cousin.

K. Rich. ' Fair cousin ' ?   I am greater than a king :
For when I was a king, my flatterers
Were then but subjects ; being now a subject,
I have a king here to my flatterer.
Being so great, I have no need to beg.

Boling. Yet ask.

K. Rich. And shall I have ?

Boling. You shall.

K. Rich. Then give me leave to go.

Boling. Whither ?

K. Rich. Whither you will, so I were from your
sights.   Act IV, Scene i, ll. 162-315

London.   A street leading to the Tower.

Enter QUEEN *and* Ladies.

Queen. This way the king will come ; this is the way
To Julius Caesar's ill-erected tower,
To whose flint bosom my condemned lord
Is doom'd a prisoner by proud Bolingbroke :
Here let us rest, if this rebellious earth
Have any resting for her true king's queen.

Enter RICHARD *and* Guard.

But soft, but see, or rather do not see,
My fair rose wither : yet look up, behold,
That you in pity may dissolve to dew,
And wash him fresh again with true-love tears. . . .

K. Rich. Join not with grief, fair woman, do not so
To make my end too sudden : learn, good soul,
To think our former state a happy dream ;
From which awaked, the truth of what we are
Shows us but this : I am sworn brother, sweet,
To grim Necessity, and he and I
Will keep a league till death. . . . .

Good sometime queen, prepare thee hence for France :
Think I am dead and that even here thou takest,
As from my death-bed, thy last living leave.
In winter's tedious nights sit by the fire
With good old folks and let them tell thee tales
Of woeful ages long ago betid ;
And ere thou bid good night, to quit their griefs,
Tell thou the lamentable tale of me
And send the hearers weeping to their beds . . .
Part us, Northumberland ; I towards the north,
Where shivering cold and sickness pines the clime ;
My wife to France : from whence, set forth in pomp,
She came adorned hither like sweet May,
Sent back like Hallowmas.

ACT V, Scene i, ll. 1-10, 16-22, 37-45, 76-80

As in a theatre, the eyes of men,
After a well-graced actor leaves the stage,
Are idly bent on him that enters next,
Thinking his prattle to be tedious ;
Even so, or with much more contempt, men's eyes
Did scowl on gentle Richard ; no man cried ' God save
  him ! '
No joyful tongue gave him his welcome home :
But dust was thrown upon his sacred head ;
Which with such gentle sorrow he shook off,
His face still combating with tears and smiles,
The badges of his grief and patience,
That had not God, for some strong purpose, steel'd
The hearts of men, they must perforce have melted
And barbarism itself have pitied him.

ACT V, Scene ii, ll. 23-36

Pomfret Castle.

To KING RICHARD *enter a* Groom of the Stable.
Groom. Hail, royal prince !
K. Rich.   Thanks, noble peer ;

The cheapest of us is ten groats too dear.
What art thou ? and how comest thou hither,
Where no man never comes but that sad dog
That brings me food to make misfortune live ?

    Groom. I was a poor groom of thy stable, king,
When thou wert king ; who, travelling towards York,
With much ado at length have gotten leave
To look upon my sometimes royal master's face.
O, how it yearn'd my heart when I beheld
In London streets, that coronation-day,
When Bolingbroke rode on roan Barbary,
That horse that thou so often hast bestrid,
That horse that I so carefully have dress'd !

    K. Rich. Rode he on Barbary ? Tell me, gentle friend,
How went he under him ?

    Groom. So proudly as if he disdain'd the ground.

    K. Rich. So proud that Bolingbroke was on his back !
That jade hath eat bread from my royal hand ;
This hand hath made him proud with clapping him.
Would he not stumble ? would he not fall down,
Since pride must have a fall, and break the neck
Of that proud man that did usurp his back ?
Forgiveness, horse ! why do I rail on thee,
Since thou, created to be awed by man,
Wast born to bear ? I was not made a horse ;
And yet I bear a burthen like an ass,
Spurr'd, gall'd and tired by jauncing Bolingbroke.

                Act V, Scene v, ll. 67-94

Romeo and Juliet

A pair of star-crossed lovers—
                Act I, Prologue, l. 6

To Sampson *and* Gregory *enter* Abraham *and* Balthasar.
  Abr. Do you bite your thumb at us, sir ?

Sampson. I do bite my thumb, sir.

Abr. Do you bite your thumb at us, sir ?

Sam. [*Aside to Gregory.*] Is the law of our side, if I say ay ?

Gre. No.

Sam. No, sir, I do not bite my thumb at you, sir, but I bite my thumb, sir.

Gre. Do you quarrel, sir ?

Abr. Quarrel, sir ! no, sir.

Sam. If you do, sir, I am for you : I serve as good a man as you.

ACT I, Scene i, ll. 51-62

So far from sounding and discovery,
As is the bud bit with an envious worm,
Ere he can spread his sweet leaves to the air,
Or dedicate his beauty to the sun.

ACT I, Scene i, ll. 156-159

Such comfort as do lusty young men feel
When well-apparell'd April on the heel
Of limping winter treads.

ACT I, Scene ii, ll. 26-28

A room in Capulet's house.

Enter LADY CAPULET *and* Nurse.

La. Cap. Nurse, where's my daughter ? call her forth to me.

Nurse. Now, by my maidenhead, at twelve year old,
I bade her come. What, lamb ! what, lady-bird !
God forbid ! Where's this girl ? What, Juliet !

Enter JULIET.

Jul. How now ! who calls ?

Nurse.   Your mother.

Jul.   Madam, I am here.
What is your will ?

La. Cap. This is the matter :—Nurse, give leave awhile,
We must talk in secret :—nurse, come back again ;

51

I have remember'd me, thou's hear our counsel.
Thou know'st my daughter's of a pretty age.

Nurse. Faith, I can tell her age unto an hour.

La. Cap. She's not fourteen.

Nurse. I'll lay fourteen of my teeth,—
And yet, to my teen be it spoken, I have but four,—
She is not fourteen. How long is it now
To Lammas-tide ?

La. Cap. A fortnight and odd days.

Nurse. Even or odd, of all days in the year,
Come Lammas-eve at night shall she be fourteen.
Susan and she—God rest all Christian souls !—
Were of an age : well, Susan is with God ;
She was too good for me : but, as I said,
On Lammas-eve at night shall she be fourteen ;
That shall she, marry ; I remember it well.
'Tis since the earthquake now eleven years ;
And she was wean'd,—I never shall forget it,—
Of all the days of the year, upon that day :
For I had then laid wormwood to my dug,
Sitting in the sun under the dove-house wall ;
My lord and you were then at Mantua :—
Nay, I do bear a brain :—but, as I said,
When it did taste the wormwood on the nipple
Of my dug and felt it bitter, pretty fool,
To see it tetchy and fall out with the dug !
' Shake ' quoth the dove-house : 'twas no need, I trow,
To bid me trudge :
And since that time it is eleven years ;
For then she could stand alone ; nay, by the rood,
She could have run and waddled all about ;
For even the day before, she broke her brow :
And then my husband—God be with his soul !
A' was a merry man—took up the child :
' Yea,' quoth he, ' dost thou fall upon thy face ?
Thou wilt fall backward when thou hast more wit ;

Wilt thou not, Jule ? ' and, by my holidame,
The pretty wretch left crying and said ' Ay.'
To see, now, how a jest shall come about !
I warrant, an I should live a thousand years,
I never should forget it : ' Wilt thou not, Jule ? ' quoth he ;
And, pretty fool, it stinted and said ' Ay.'

    La. Cap. Enough of this ; I pray thee, hold thy peace.

    Nurse. Yes, madam : yet I cannot choose but laugh,
To think it should leave crying and say ' Ay.'
And yet, I warrant, it had upon its brow
A bump as big as a young cockerel's stone ;
A parlous knock ; and it cried bitterly :
' Yea,' quoth my husband, ' fall'st upon thy face ?
Thou wilt fall backward when thou comest to age ;
Wilt thou not, Jule ? ' it stinted and said ' Ay.'

                          ACT I, Scene iii, ll. 1-57

    Romeo. I dream'd a dream to-night.

    Mercutio.   And so did I.

    Rom. Well, what was yours ?

    Mer.   That dreamers often lie.

    Rom. In bed asleep, while they do dream things true.

    Mer. O, then, I see Queen Mab hath been with you.
She is the fairies' midwife, and she comes
In shape no bigger than an agate-stone
On the fore-finger of an alderman,
Drawn with a team of little atomies
Athwart men's noses as they lie asleep ;
Her waggon-spokes made of long spinners' legs,
The cover of the wings of grasshoppers,
The traces of the smallest spider's web,
The collars of the moonshine's watery beams,
Her whip of cricket's bone, the lash of film,
Her waggoner a small grey-coated gnat,
Not half so big as a round little worm
Prick'd from the lazy finger of a maid ;

Her chariot is an empty hazel-nut
Made by the joiner squirrel or old grub,
Time out o' mind the fairies' coachmakers.
And in this state she gallops night by night
Through lovers' brains, and then they dream of love ;
O'er courtiers' knees, that dream on court'sies straight,
O'er lawyers' fingers, who straight dream on fees,
O'er ladies' lips, who straight on kisses dream,
Which oft the angry Mab with blisters plagues,
Because their breaths with sweetmeats tainted are :
Sometimes she gallops o'er a courtier's nose,
And then dreams he of smelling out a suit ;
And sometime comes she with a tithe-pig's tail
Tickling a parson's nose as a' lies asleep,
Then dreams he of another benefice :
Sometime she driveth o'er a soldier's neck,
And then dreams he of cutting foreign throats,
Of breaches, ambuscadoes, Spanish blades,
Of healths five-fathom deep ; and then anon
Drums in his ear, at which he starts and wakes,
And being thus frighted swears a prayer or two
And sleeps again. This is that very Mab
That plats the manes of horses in the night,
And bakes the elf-locks in foul sluttish hairs,
Which once untangled much misfortune bodes :
This is the hag, when maids lie on their backs,
That presses them and learns them first to bear,
Making them women of good carriage :
This is she—

    Rom.   Peace, peace, Mercutio, peace !
Thou talk'st of nothing.

    Mer.   True, I talk of dreams,
Which are the children of an idle brain,
Begot of nothing but vain fantasy,
Which is as thin of substance as the air
And more inconstant than the wind, who wooes

Even now the frozen bosom of the north,
And, being anger'd, puffs away from thence,
Turning his face to the dew-dropping south.

Benvolio. This wind, you talk of, blows us from ourselves ;
Supper is done, and we shall come too late.

Rom. I fear, too early : for my mind misgives
Some consequence yet hanging in the stars
Shall bitterly begin his fearful date
With this night's revels and expire the term
Of a despised life closed in my breast
By some vile forfeit of untimely death.
But He, that hath the steerage of my course,
Direct my sail ! On, lusty gentlemen.

Ben. Strike, drum.   [*Exeunt.*
                              ACT I, Scene iv, ll. 49-114

Romeo. [*To a Servingman*] What lady is that, which
doth enrich the hand
Of yonder knight ?

Serv. I know not, sir.

Rom. O, she doth teach the torches to burn bright !
It seems she hangs upon the cheek of night
Like a rich jewel in an Ethiope's ear ;
Beauty too rich for use, for earth too dear ! . . .
The measure done, I'll watch her place of stand,
And, touching hers, make blessed my rude hand.
Did my heart love till now ? forswear it, sight !
For I ne'er saw true beauty till this night.
                              ACT I, Scene v, ll. 44-49, 52-55

Juliet. What's he that follows there, that would not
dance ?

Nurse. I know not.

Jul. Go, ask his name : if he be married,
My grave is like to be my wedding bed.
                              ACT I, Scene v, ll. 134-137

Now old desire doth in his death-bed lie,
And young affection gapes to be his heir.

ACT II, Prologue, ll. 1-2

Capulet's orchard.

Enter ROMEO.

Rom. He jests at scars that never felt a wound.

[*Juliet appears above at a window.*

But, soft ! what light through yonder window breaks ?
It is the east, and Juliet is the sun.
Arise, fair sun, and kill the envious moon,
Who is already sick and pale with grief,
That thou her maid art far more fair than she :
Be not her maid, since she is envious ;
Her vestal livery is but sick and green
And none but fools do wear it ; cast it off.
It is my lady, O, it is my love !
O, that she knew she were !
She speaks, yet she says nothing : what of that ?
Her eye discourses ; I will answer it.
I am too bold, 'tis not to me she speaks :
Two of the fairest stars in all the heaven,
Having some business, do entreat her eyes
To twinkle in their spheres till they return.
What if her eyes were there, they in her head ?
The brightness of her cheek would shame those stars,
As daylight doth a lamp ; her eyes in heaven
Would through the airy region stream so bright
That birds would sing and think it were not night.
See, how she leans her cheek upon her hand !
O, that I were a glove upon that hand,
That I might touch that cheek !

    Jul.   Ay me !

    Rom.   She speaks :
O, speak again, bright angel ! for thou art
As glorious to this night, being o'er my head,

As is a winged messenger of heaven
Unto the white-upturned wondering eyes
Of mortals that fall back to gaze on him
When he bestrides the lazy-pacing clouds
And sails upon the bosom of the air.

Jul. O Romeo, Romeo ! wherefore art thou Romeo ?
Deny thy father and refuse thy name ;
Or, if thou wilt not, be but sworn my love,
And I'll no longer be a Capulet.

Rom. [*Aside*] Shall I hear more, or shall I speak at this ?

Jul. 'Tis but thy name that is my enemy ;
Thou art thyself, though not a Montague.
What's Montague ? it is nor hand, nor foot,
Nor arm, nor face, nor any other part
Belonging to a man. O, be some other name !
What's in a name ! that which we call a rose
By any other name would smell as sweet ;
So Romeo would, were he not Romeo call'd,
Retain that dear perfection which he owes
Without that title. Romeo, doff thy name,
And for that name which is no part of thee
Take all myself.

Rom.   I take thee at thy word :
Call me but love, and I'll be new baptized ;
Henceforth I never will be Romeo.

Jul. What man art thou that thus bescreen'd in night
So stumblest on my counsel ?

Rom.   By a name
I know not how to tell thee who I am :
My name, dear saint, is hateful to myself,
Because it is an enemy to thee ;
Had I it written, I would tear the word.

Jul. My ears have not yet drunk a hundred words
Of that tongue's utterance, yet I know the sound :
Art thou not Romeo and a Montague ?

Rom. Neither, fair saint, if either thee dislike.

Jul. How camest thou hither, tell me, and wherefore ?
The orchard walls are high and hard to climb,
And the place death, considering who thou art,
If any of my kinsmen find thee here.

    Rom. With love's light wings did I o'er-perch these
       walls ;
For stony limits cannot hold love out,
And what love can do that dares love attempt ;
Therefore thy kinsmen are no let to me.

    Jul. If they do see thee, they will murder thee.

    Rom. Alack, there lies more peril in thine eye
Than twenty of their swords : look thou but sweet,
And I am proof against their enmity.

    Jul. I would not for the world they saw thee here.

    Rom. I have night's cloak to hide me from their sight ;
And but thou love me, let them find me here :
My life were better ended by their hate,
Than death prorogued, wanting of thy love.

    Jul. By whose direction found'st thou out this place ?

    Rom. By love, who first did prompt me to inquire ;
He lent me counsel and I lent him eyes.
I am no pilot ; yet, wert thou as far
As that vast shore wash'd with the farthest sea,
I would adventure for such merchandise.

    Jul. Thou know'st the mask of night is on my face,
Else would a maiden blush bepaint my cheek
For that which thou hast heard me speak to-night.
Fain would I dwell on form, fain, fain deny
What I have spoke : but farewell compliment !
Dost thou love me ? I know thou wilt say 'Ay,'
And I will take thy word : yet, if thou swear'st,
Thou mayst prove false ; at lovers' perjuries,
They say, Jove laughs. O gentle Romeo,
If thou dost love, pronounce it faithfully :
Or if thou think'st I am too quickly won,
I'll frown and be perverse and say thee nay,

So thou wilt woo ; but else, not for the world.
In truth, fair Montague, I am too fond,
And therefore thou mayst think my 'haviour light :
But trust me, gentleman, I'll prove more true
Than those that have more cunning to be strange.
I should have been more strange, I must confess,
But that thou overheard'st, ere I was ware,
My true love's passion : therefore pardon me,
And not impute this yielding to light love,
Which the dark night hath so discovered.

Rom. Lady, by yonder blessed moon I swear
That tips with silver all these fruit-tree tops—

Jul. O, swear not by the moon, the inconstant moon,
That monthly changes in her circled orb,
Lest that thy love prove likewise variable.

Rom. What shall I swear by ?

Jul.   Do not swear at all ;
Or, if thou wilt, swear by thy gracious self,
Which is the god of my idolatry,
And I'll believe thee.

Rom.   If my heart's dear love—

Jul. Well, do not swear : although I joy in thee,
I have no joy of this contract to-night :
It is too rash, too unadvised, too sudden ;
Too like the lightning, which doth cease to be
Ere one can say ' It lightens.' Sweet, good night !
This bud of love, by summer's ripening breath,
May prove a beauteous flower when next we meet.
Good night, good night ! as sweet repose and rest
Come to thy heart as that within my breast !

Rom. O, wilt thou leave me so unsatisfied ?

Jul. What satisfaction canst thou have to-night ?

Rom. The exchange of thy love's faithful vow for mine.

Jul. I gave thee mine before thou didst request it :
And yet I would it were to give again.

Rom. Wouldst thou withdraw it ? for what purpose, love ?

59

Jul. But to be frank, and give it thee again.
And yet I wish but for the thing I have :
My bounty is as boundless as the sea,
My love as deep ; the more I give to thee,
The more I have, for both are infinite. [*Nurse calls within.*
I hear some noise within ; dear love, adieu !
Anon, good nurse ! Sweet Montague, be true.
Stay but a little, I will come again. [*Exit, above.*

Rom. O blessed, blessed night ! I am afeard,
Being in night, all this is but a dream,
Too flattering-sweet to be substantial.

Re-enter JULIET, *above.*

Jul. Three words, dear Romeo, and good night in-
        deed.
If that thy bent of love be honourable,
Thy purpose marriage, send me word to-morrow,
By one that I'll procure to come to thee,
Where and what time thou wilt perform the rite ;
And all my fortunes at thy foot I'll lay
And follow thee my lord throughout the world.

Nurse. [*Within*] Madam !

Jul. I come, anon.—But if thou mean'st not well,
I do beseech thee—

Nurse. [*Within*] Madam !

Jul.   By and by, I come :—
To cease thy suit, and leave me to my grief :
To-morrow will I send.

Rom.   So thrive my soul—

Jul. A thousand times good night ! [*Exit, above.*

Rom. A thousand times the worse, to want thy light.
Love goes toward love, as schoolboys from their books,
But love from love, toward school with heavy looks.

                                        [*Retiring.*

Re-enter JULIET, *above.*

Jul. Hist ! Romeo, hist ! O, for a falconer's voice,

To lure this tassel-gentle back again!
Bondage is hoarse, and may not speak aloud;
Else would I tear the cave where Echo lies,
And make her airy tongue more hoarse than mine,
With repetition of my Romeo's name.

Rom. It is my soul that calls upon my name:
How silver-sweet sound lovers' tongues by night,
Like softest music to attending ears!

Jul. Romeo!

Rom. My dear?

Jul. At what o'clock to-morrow
Shall I send to thee?

Rom. At the hour of nine.

Jul. I will not fail: 'tis twenty years till then.
I have forgot why I did call thee back.

Rom. Let me stand here till thou remember it.

Jul. I shall forget, to have thee still stand there,
Remembering how I love thy company.

Rom. And I'll still stay, to have thee still forget,
Forgetting any other home but this.

Jul. 'Tis almost morning; I would have thee gone:
And yet no further than a wanton's bird;
Who lets it hop a little from her hand,
Like a poor prisoner in his twisted gyves,
And with a silk thread plucks it back again,
So loving-jealous of his liberty.

Rom. I would I were thy bird.

Jul. Sweet, so would I:
Yet I should kill thee with much cherishing.
Good night, good night! parting is such sweet sorrow,
That I shall say good night till it be morrow. [*Exit above.*

Rom. Sleep dwell upon thine eyes, peace in thy breast!
Would I were sleep and peace, so sweet to rest!
Hence will I to my ghostly father's cell,
His help to crave, and my dear hap to tell. [*Exit.*

ACT II, Scene ii, ll. 1-190

To Mercutio *and* Benvolio *enter* Nurse *and* Peter.

Mercutio. A sail, a sail!

Benvolio. Two, two; a shirt and a smock.

Nurse. Peter!

Peter. Anon!

Nurse. My fan, Peter.

Mer. Good Peter, to hide her face; for her fan's the fairer face.

Nurse. God ye good morrow, gentlemen.

Mer. God ye good den, fair gentlewoman.

Nurse. Is it good den?

Mer. 'Tis no less, I tell you, for the bawdy hand of the dial is now upon the prick of noon.

Nurse. Out upon you! what a man are you!

Romeo. One, gentlewoman, that God hath made for himself to mar.

Nurse. By my troth, it is well said; ' for himself to mar,' quoth a'? Gentlemen, can any of you tell me where I may find the young Romeo?

Rom. I can tell you; but young Romeo will be older when you have found him than he was when you sought him: I am the youngest of that name, for fault of a worse.

Nurse. You say well.

Mer. Yea, is the worst well? very well took, i' faith; wisely, wisely.

Nurse. If you be he, sir, I desire some confidence with you.

Ben. She will indite him to some supper.

Mer. A bawd, a bawd, a bawd! So ho!

Rom. What hast thou found?

Mer. No hare, sir; unless a hare, sir, in a lenten pie, that is something stale and hoar ere it be spent,   [*Sings*.

An old hare hoar,
And an old hare hoar,
Is very good meat in lent:
But a hare that is hoar
Is too much for a score,
When it hoars ere it be spent.

Romeo, will you come to your father's? we'll to dinner, thither.

Rom. I will follow you.

Mer. Farewell, ancient lady: farewell, [*singing*] ' lady, lady, lady.' [*Exeunt Mercutio and Benvolio.*

Nurse. Marry, farewell! I pray you, sir, what saucy merchant was this, that was so full of his ropery?

Rom. A gentleman, nurse, that loves to hear himself talk, and will speak more in a minute than he will stand to in a month.

Nurse. An a' speak any thing against me, I'll take him down, an a' were lustier than he is, and twenty such Jacks; and if I cannot, I'll find those that shall. Scurvy knave! I am none of his flirt-gills; I am none of his skains-mates. And thou must stand by too, and suffer every knave to use me at his pleasure?

Peter. I saw no man use you at his pleasure; if I had, my weapon should quickly have been out, I warrant you: I dare draw as soon as another man, if I see occasion in a good quarrel, and the law on my side.

Nurse. Now, afore God, I am so vexed, that every part about me quivers. Scurvy knave!

ACT II, Scene iv, ll. 108-171

Here comes the lady: O, so light a foot
Will ne'er wear out the everlasting flint:
A lover may bestride the gossamer
That idles in the wanton summer air,
And yet not fall; so light is vanity.

ACT II, Scene vi, ll. 16-20

A public place.

Mercutio. Thou! why, thou wilt quarrel with a man that hath a hair more, or a hair less, in his beard, than thou hast: thou wilt quarrel with a man for cracking nuts, having no other reason but because thou hast hazel eyes: what eye but such an eye would spy out such a quarrel? Thy head is as full

of quarrels as an egg is full of meat, and yet thy head hath
been beaten as addle as an egg for quarrelling : thou hast
quarrelled with a man for coughing in the street, because he
hath wakened thy dog that hath lain asleep in the sun : didst
thou not fall out with a tailor for wearing his new doublet
before Easter ? with another, for tying his new shoes with
old riband ? and yet thou wilt tutor me from quarrelling !

ACT III, Scene i, ll. 18-33

Mercutio.   I am hurt.
A plague o' both your houses ! I am sped.
Is he gone, and hath nothing ?

  Benvolio.   What, art thou hurt ?

  Mer. Ay, ay, a scratch, a scratch ; marry, 'tis enough.
Where is my page ? Go, villain, fetch a surgeon.

             [*Exit Page.*

  Romeo. Courage, man ; the hurt cannot be much.

  Mer. No, 'tis not so deep as a well, nor so wide as a church-
door ; but 'tis enough, 'twill serve : ask for me to-morrow,
and you shall find me a grave man. I am peppered, I warrant,
for this world. A plague o' both your houses ! 'Zounds, a
dog, a rat, a mouse, a cat, to scratch a man to death ! a braggart,
a rogue, a villian, that fights by the book of arithmetic ! Why
the devil came you between us ? I was hurt under your arm.

  Rom. I thought all for the best.

  Mer. Help me into some house, Benvolio,
Or I shall faint. A plague o' both your houses !
They have made worms' meat of me : I have it,
And soundly too : your houses ! ACT III, Scene i, ll. 94-113

Capulet's orchard.

Enter JULIET.

  Jul. Gallop apace, you fiery-footed steeds,
Towards Phœbus' lodging : such a waggoner
As Phaethon would whip you to the west,
And bring in cloudy night immediately.

Spread thy close curtain, love-performing night,
That runaway's eyes may wink, and Romeo
Leap to these arms, untalk'd of and unseen.
Lovers can see to do their amorous rites
By their own beauties ; or, if love be blind,
It best agrees with night.   Come, civil night,
Thou sober-suited matron, all in black,
And learn me how to lose a winning match,
Play'd for a pair of stainless maidenhoods :
Hood my unmann'd blood, bating in my cheeks,
With thy black mantle ; till strange love, grown bold,
Think true love acted simple modesty.
Come, night ; come, Romeo ; come, thou day in night ;
For thou wilt lie upon the wings of night
Whiter than new snow on a raven's back.
Come, gentle night, come, loving, black-brow'd night,
Give me my Romeo ; and, when he shall die,
Take him and cut him out in little stars,
And he will make the face of heaven so fine
That all the world will be in love with night
And pay no worship to the garish sun.
O, I have bought the mansion of a love,
But not possess'd it, and, though I am sold,
Not yet enjoy'd : so tedious is this day
As is the night before some festival
To an impatient child that hath new robes
And may not wear them.   ACT III, Scene ii, ll. 1-31

Friar Lawrence. Romeo, come forth ; come forth,
      thou fearful man :
Affliction is enamour'd of thy parts,
And thou art wedded to calamity. . . .
Hence from Verona art thou banished :
Be patient, for the world is broad and wide.
  Romeo. There is no world without Verona walls.
                    ACT III, Scene iii, ll. 1-3, 15-17

Romeo.   Heaven is here,
Where Juliet lives ; and every cat and dog
And little mouse, every unworthy thing,
Live here in heaven and may look on her ;
But Romeo may not : more validity,
More honourable state, more courtship lives
In carrion-flies than Romeo : they may seize
On the white wonder of dear Juliet's hand
And steal immortal blessing from her lips.

ACT III, Scene iii, ll. 29-37

Capulet's orchard.

Enter ROMEO *and* JULIET *above, at the window.*

Jul. Wilt thou be gone ? it is not yet near day :
It was the nightingale, and not the lark,
That pierced the fearful hollow of thine ear ;
Nightly she sings on yon pomegranate-tree :
Believe me, love, it was the nightingale.

Rom. It was the lark, the herald of the morn,
No nightingale : look, love, what envious streaks
Do lace the severing clouds in yonder east :
Night's candles are burnt out, and jocund day
Stands tiptoe on the misty mountain tops.
I must be gone and live, or stay and die.

Jul. Yon light is not day-light, I know it, I :
It is some meteor that the sun exhales,
To be to thee this night a torch-bearer,
And light thee on thy way to Mantua :
Therefore stay yet ; thou need'st not to be gone.

Rom. Let me be ta'en, let me be put to death ;
I am content, so thou wilt have it so.
I'll say yon grey is not the morning's eye,
'Tis but the pale reflex of Cynthia's brow ;
Nor that is not the lark, whose notes do beat
The vaulty heaven so high above our heads :
I have more care to stay than will to go :

Come, death, and welcome ! Juliet wills it so.
How is't, my soul ? let's talk ; it is not day.

Jul. It is, it is : hie hence, be gone, away !
It is the lark that sings so out of tune,
Straining harsh discords and unpleasing sharps.
Some say the lark makes sweet division ;
This doth not so, for she divideth us :
Some say the lark and loathed toad change eyes ;
O, now I would they had changed voices too !
Since arm from arm that voice doth us affray,
Hunting thee hence with hunt's-up to the day.
O, now be gone ; more light and light it grows. . . .

O God, I have an ill-divining soul !
Methinks I see thee, now thou art below,
As one dead in the bottom of a tomb :
Either my eyesight fails, or thou look'st pale.

ACT III, Scene v, ll. 1-35, 54-57

Romeo. How doth my lady ? Is my father well ?
How fares my Juliet ? that I ask again ;
For nothing can be ill, if she be well.

Balthasar. Then she is well, and nothing can be ill :
Her body sleeps in Capel's monument,
And her immortal part with angels lives.
I saw her laid low in her kindred's vault,
And presently took post to tell it you :
O, pardon me for bringing these ill news,
Since you did leave it for my office, sir.

Rom. Is it even so ? then I defy you, stars ! . . .
Well, Juliet, I will lie with thee to-night.
Let's see for means : O mischief, thou art swift
To enter in the thoughts of desperate men !
I do remember an apothecary,—
And hereabouts he dwells,—which late I noted
In tatter'd weeds, with overwhelming brows
Culling of simples ; meagre were his looks

Sharp misery had worn him to the bones :
And in his needy shop a tortoise hung,
An alligator stuff'd, and other skins
Of ill-shaped fishes ; and about his shelves
A beggarly account of empty boxes,
Green earthen pots, bladders and musty seeds,
Remnants of packthread and old cakes of roses,
Were thinly scatter'd, to make up a show.
Noting this penury, to myself I said
' An if a man did need a poison now,
Whose sale is present death in Mantua,
Here lives a caitiff wretch would sell it him.'
O, this same thought did but forerun my need ;
And this same needy man must sell it me.

ACT V, Scene i, ll. 14-24, 34-54

A churchyard ; in it a tomb belonging to the Capulets.

 Paris. O, I am slain ! [*Falls.*] If thou be merciful,
Open the tomb, lay me with Juliet.   [*Dies.*
 Romeo. In faith, I will. Let me peruse this face.
Mercutio's kinsman, noble County Paris !
What said my man, when my betossed soul
Did not attend him as we rode ? I think
He told me Paris should have married Juliet :
Said he not so ? or did I dream it so ?
Or am I mad, hearing him talk of Juliet,
To think it was so ? O, give me thy hand,
One writ with me in sour misfortune's book !
I'll bury thee in a triumphant grave ;
A grave ? O, no ! a lantern, slaughter'd youth,
For here lies Juliet, and her beauty makes
This vault a feasting presence full of light.
Death, lie thou there, by a dead man interr'd.

[*Laying Paris in the tomb.*

How oft when men are at the point of death
Have they been merry ! which their keepers call

A lightning before death : O, how may I
Call this a lightning ? O my love ! my wife !
Death, that hath suck'd the honey of thy breath,
Hath had no power yet upon thy beauty :
Thou art not conquer'd ; beauty's ensign yet
Is crimson in thy lips and in thy cheeks,
And death's pale flag is not advanced there.
Tybalt, liest thou there in thy bloody sheet ?
O, what more favour can I do to thee,
Than with that hand that cut thy youth in twain
To sunder his that was thine enemy ?
Forgive me, cousin ! Ah, dear Juliet,
Why art thou yet so fair ? shall I believe
That unsubstantial death is amorous,
And that the lean abhorred monster keeps
Thee here in dark to be his paramour ?
For fear of that, I still will stay with thee ;
And never from this palace of dim night
Depart again : here, here will I remain
With worms that are thy chamber-maids ; O, here
Will I set up my everlasting rest,
And shake the yoke of inauspicious stars
From this world-wearied flesh. Eyes, look your last !
Arms, take your last embrace ! and, lips, O you
The doors of breath, seal with a righteous kiss
A dateless bargain to engrossing death !
Come, bitter conduct, come, unsavoury guide !
Thou desperate pilot, now at once run on
The dashing rocks thy sea-sick weary bark !
Here's to my love ! [*Drinks.*] O true apothecary !
Thy drugs are quick. Thus with a kiss I die. [*Dies.*

ACT V, Scene iii, ll. 72-120

A Midsummer-Night's Dream

Athens. The palace of THESEUS.

Enter THESEUS, HIPPOLYTA, PHILOSTRATE, *and* Attendants.

The. Now, fair Hippolyta, our nuptial hour
Draws on apace ; four happy days bring in
Another moon : but, O, methinks, how slow
This old moon wanes ! she lingers my desires,
Like to a step-dame or a dowager
Long withering out a young man's revenue.

Hip. Four days will quickly steep themselves in night ;
Four nights will quickly dream away the time ;
And then the moon, like to a silver bow
New-bent in heaven, shall behold the night
Of our solemnities.

The.   Go, Philostrate,
Stir up the Athenian youth to merriments ;
Awake the pert and nimble spirit of mirth :
Turn melancholy forth to funerals ;
The pale companion is not for our pomp.

[*Exit Philostrate.*

Hippolyta, I woo'd thee with my sword,
And won thy love, doing thee injuries ;
But I will wed thee in another key,
With pomp, with triumph and with revelling.

ACT I, Scene i, ll. 1-19

This man hath bewitch'd the bosom of my child :
Thou, thou, Lysander, thou hast given her rhymes
And interchanged love-tokens with my child :
Thou hast by moonlight at her window sung
With feigning voice verses of feigning love,
And stolen the impression of her fantasy
With bracelets of thy hair, rings, gawds, conceits.

ACT I, Scene i, ll. 27-33

Therefore, fair Hermia, question your desires ;
Know of your youth, examine well your blood,
Whether, if you yield not to your father's choice,
You can endure the livery of a nun,
For aye to be in shady cloister mew'd,
To live a barren sister all your life,
Chanting faint hymns to the cold fruitless moon.
Thrice-blessed they that master so their blood,
To undergo such maiden pilgrimage ;
But earthlier happy is the rose distill'd,
Than that which withering on the virgin thorn
Grows, lives and dies in single blessedness.

ACT I, Scene i, ll. 67-78

Ay me ! for aught that I could ever read,
Could ever hear by tale or history,
The course of true love never did run smooth ;
But, either it was different in blood. . . .
Or, if there were a sympathy in choice,
War, death, or sickness did lay siege to it,
Making it momentany as a sound,
Swift as a shadow, short as any dream ;
Brief as the lightning in the collied night,
That, in a spleen, unfolds both heaven and earth,
And ere a man hath power to say ' Behold ! '
The jaws of darkness do devour it up :
So quick bright things come to confusion.

ACT I, Scene i, ll. 132-135, 141-149

It is a customary cross,
As due to love as thoughts and dreams and sighs,
Wishes and tears, poor fancy's followers.

ACT I, Scene i, ll. 153-155

My good Lysander !
I swear to thee, by Cupid's strongest bow,
By his best arrow with the golden head,
By the simplicity of Venus' doves,

By that which knitteth souls and prospers loves,
And by that fire which burn'd the Carthage queen,
When the false Troyan under sail was seen,
By all the vows that ever men have broke,
In number more than ever women spoke,
In that same place thou hast appointed me,
To-morrow truly will I meet with thee.

ACT I, Scene i, ll. 168-178

Your eyes are lode-stars; and your tongue's sweet air
More tuneable than lark to shepherd's ear,
When wheat is green, when hawthorn buds appear.

ACT I, Scene i, ll. 183-185

Lysander. To-morrow night, when Phœbe doth behold
Her silver visage in the watery glass,
Decking with liquid pearl the bladed grass,
A time that lovers' flights doth still conceal,
Through Athens' gates have we devised to steal.

Hermia. And in the wood, where often you and I
Upon faint primrose-beds were wont to lie,
Emptying our bosoms of their counsel sweet,
There my Lysander and myself shall meet.

ACT I, Scene i, ll. 209-217

Athens. QUINCE'S *house.*
Enter QUINCE, SNUG, BOTTOM, FLUTE, SNOUT, *and*
STARVELING.

Quin. Is all our company here?

Bot. You were best to call them generally, man by man,
according to the scrip.

Quin. Here is the scroll of every man's name, which is
thought fit, through all Athens, to play in our interlude before
the duke and the duchess, on his wedding-day at night.

Bot. First, good Peter Quince, say what the play treats on,
then read the names of the actors, and so grow to a point.

Quin. Marry, our play is, The most lamentable comedy,
and most cruel death of Pyramus and Thisby.

Bot. A very good piece of work, I assure you, and a merry.
Now, good Peter Quince, call forth your actors by the scroll.
Masters, spread yourselves.

Quin. Answer as I call you. Nick Bottom, the weaver.

Bot. Ready. Name what part I am for, and proceed.

Quin. You, Nick Bottom, are set down for Pyramus.

Bot. What is Pyramus ? a lover, or a tyrant ?

Quin. A lover, that kills himself most gallant for love.

Bot. That will ask some tears in the true performing of it :
if I do it, let the audience look to their eyes ; I will move storms,
I will condole in some measure. To the rest : yet my chief
humour is for a tyrant : I could play Ercles rarely, or a part
to tear a cat in, to make all split.

> The raging rocks
> And shivering shocks
> Shall break the locks
>   Of prison gates ;
> And Phibbus' car
> Shall shine from far
> And make and mar
>   The foolish Fates.

This was lofty ! Now name the rest of the players. This is
Ercles' vein, a tyrant's vein ; a lover is more condoling.

Quin. Francis Flute, the bellows-mender.

Flu. Here, Peter Quince.

Quin. Flute, you must take Thisby on you.

Flu. What is Thisby ? a wandering knight ?

Quin. It is the lady that Pyramus must love.

Flu. Nay, faith, let not me play a woman ; I have a beard
coming.

Quin. That's all one : you shall play it in a mask, and you
may speak as small as you will.

Bot. An I may hide my face, let me play Thisby too,
I'll speak in a monstrous little voice, ' Thisne, Thisne ; '
' Ah Pyramus, my lover dear ! thy Thisby dear, and lady
dear ! '

Quin. No, no ; you must play Pyramus : and, Flute, you Thisby.

Bot. Well, proceed.

Quin. Robin Starveling, the tailor.

Star. Here, Peter Quince.

Quin. Robin Starveling, you must play Thisby's mother. Tom Snout, the tinker.

Snout. Here, Peter Quince.

Quin. You, Pyramus' father : myself, Thisby's father. Snug, the joiner ; you, the lion's part : and, I hope, here is a play fitted.

Snug. Have you the lion's part written ? pray you, if it be, give it me, for I am slow of study.

Quin. You may do it extempore, for it is nothing but roaring.

Bot. Let me play the lion too : I will roar, that I will do any man's heart good to hear me ; I will roar, that I will make the duke say ' Let him roar again, let him roar again.'

Quin. An you should do it too terribly, you would fright the duchess and the ladies, that they would shriek ; and that were enough to hang us all.

All. That would hang us, every mother's son.

Bot. I grant you, friends, if that you should fright the ladies out of their wits, they would have no more discretion but to hang us : but I will aggravate my voice so that I will roar you as gently as any sucking dove ; I will roar you an 'twere any nightingale.

Quin. You can play no part but Pyramus ; for Pyramus is a sweet-faced man ; a proper man, as one shall see in a summer's day ; a most lovely gentleman-like man : therefore you must needs play Pyramus.

Bot. Well, I will undertake it. What beard were I best to play it in ?

Quin. Why, what you will.

Bot. I will discharge it in either your straw-colour beard, your orange-tawny beard, your purple-in-grain beard, or your French-crown-colour beard, your perfect yellow.

Quin. Some of your French crowns have no hair at all, and then you will play barefaced. But masters, here are your parts : and I am to entreat you, request you and desire you, to con them by to-morrow night ; and meet me in the palace wood, a mile without the town, by moonlight ; there will we rehearse, for if we meet in the city, we shall be dogged with company, and our devices known. In the meantime I will draw a bill of properties, such as our play wants. I pray you, fail me not.

Bot. We will meet ; and there we may rehearse most obscenely and courageously. Take pains ; be perfect : adieu.

Quin. At the duke's oak we meet.

Bot. Enough ; hold or cut bow-strings.

ACT I, Scene ii, ll. 1-114

A wood near Athens.

Enter, from opposite sides, a Fairy, *and* PUCK.

Puck. How now, spirit ! whither wander you ?

Fai.   Over hill, over dale,
         Thorough bush, thorough brier,
      Over park, over pale,
         Thorough flood, thorough fire,
      I do wander every where,
      Swifter than the moon's sphere ;
      And I serve the fairy queen,
      To dew her orbs upon the green.
      The cowslips tall her pensioners be :
      In their gold coats spots you see ;
      Those be rubies, fairy favours,
      In those freckles live their savours.

ACT II, Scene i, ll. 1-13

And now they never meet in grove or green,
By fountain clear, or spangled starlight sheen,
But they do square, that all their elves for fear
Creep into acorn-cups and hide them there.

ACT II, Scene i, ll. 28-31

Enter, from one side, OBERON, *with his train; from the other,* TITANIA, *with hers.*

Obe. Ill met by moonlight, proud Titania.

Tita. What, jealous Oberon ! Fairies, skip hence :
I have forsworn his bed and company.

Obe. Tarry, rash wanton : am not I thy lord ?

Tita. Then I must be thy lady : but I know
When thou hast stolen away from fairy land,
And in the shape of Corin sat all day,
Playing on pipes of corn and versing love
To amorous Phillida. Why art thou here,
Come from the farthest steppe of India ?
But that, forsooth, the bouncing Amazon,
Your buskin'd mistress and your warrior love,
To Theseus must be wedded, and you come
To give their bed joy and prosperity.

Obe. How canst thou thus for shame, Titania,
Glance at my credit with Hippolyta,
Knowing I know thy love to Theseus ?
Didst thou not lead him through the glimmering night
From Perigenia, whom he ravished ?
And make him with fair Ægle break his faith,
With Ariadne and Antiopa ?

Tita. These are the forgeries of jealousy :
And never, since the middle summer's spring,
Met we on hill, in dale, forest or mead,
By paved fountain or by rushy brook,
Or in the beached margent of the sea,
To dance our ringlets to the whistling wind,
But with thy brawls thou hast disturb'd our sport.
Therefore the winds, piping to us in vain,
As in revenge, have suck'd up from the sea
Contagious fogs ; which falling in the land
Have every pelting river made so proud
That they have overborne their continents :
The ox hath therefore stretch'd his yoke in vain

The ploughman lost his sweat, and the green corn
Hath rotted ere his youth attain'd a beard ;
The fold stands empty in the drowned field,
And crows are fatted with the murrion flock ;
The nine men's morris is fill'd up with mud,
And the quaint mazes in the wanton green
For lack of tread are undistinguishable :
The human mortals want their winter here ;
No night is now with hymn or carol blest :
Therefore the moon, the governess of floods,
Pale in her anger, washes all the air,
That rheumatic diseases do abound :
And thorough this distemperature we see
The seasons alter : hoary-headed frosts
Fall in the fresh lap of the crimson rose,
And on old Hiems' thin and icy crown
An odorous chaplet of sweet summer buds
Is, as in mockery, set : the spring, the summer,
The childing autumn, angry winter, change
Their wonted liveries, and the mazed world,
By their increase, now knows not which is which :
And this same progeny of evils comes
From our debate, from our dissension ;
We are their parents and original.

   Obe. Do you amend it then ; it lies in you :
Why should Titania cross her Oberon ?
I do but beg a little changeling boy,
To be my henchman.

   Tita.   Set your heart at rest :
The fairy land buys not the child of me.
His mother was a votaress of my order :
And, in the spiced Indian air, by night,
Full often hath she gossip'd by my side,
And sat with me on Neptune's yellow sands,
Marking the embarked traders on the flood,
When we have laugh'd to see the sails conceive

And grow big-bellied with the wanton wind ;
Which she, with pretty and with swimming gait
Following,—her womb then rich with my young
    squire,—
Would imitate, and sail upon the land,
To fetch me trifles, and return again,
As from a voyage, rich with merchandise.
But she, being mortal, of that boy did die ;
And for her sake do I rear up her boy,
And for her sake I will not part with him.

Act II, Scene i, ll. 60-137

   Oberon. My gentle Puck, come hither. Thou re-
     memberest
Since once I sat upon a promontory,
And heard a mermaid on a dolphin's back
Uttering such dulcet and harmonious breath
That the rude sea grew civil at her song
And certain stars shot madly from their spheres,
To hear the sea-maid's music.
   Puck.   I remember.
   Obe. That very time I saw, but thou couldst not,
Flying between the cold moon and the earth,
Cupid all arm'd : a certain aim he took
At a fair vestal throned by the west,
And loosed his love-shaft smartly from his bow,
As it should pierce a hundred thousand hearts ;
But I might see young Cupid's fiery shaft
Quench'd in the chaste beams of the watery moon,
And the imperial votaress passed on,
In maiden meditation, fancy-free.
Yet mark'd I where the bolt of Cupid fell :
It fell upon a little western flower,
Before milk-white, now purple with love's wound,
And maidens call it love-in-idleness. . . .
Fetch me this herb ; and be thou here again
Ere the leviathan can swim a league.

78

Puck. I'll put a girdle round about the earth
In forty minutes.   [*Exit.*
                              ACT II, Scene i, ll. 148-168, 173-176

I know a bank where the wild thyme blows,
Where oxlips and the nodding violet grows,
Quite over-canopied with luscious woodbine,
With sweet musk-roses and with eglantine :
There sleeps Titania sometime of the night,
Lull'd in these flowers with dances and delight ;
And there the snake throws her enamell'd skin,
Weed wide enough to wrap a fairy in :
                              ACT II, Scene i, ll. 249-256

Another part of the wood.

Enter TITANIA, *with her train.*

Tita. Come, now a roundel and a fairy song ;
Then, for the third part of a minute, hence ;
Some to kill cankers in the musk-rose buds,
Some war with rere-mice for their leathern wings,
To make my small elves coats, and some keep back
The clamorous owl that nightly hoots and wonders
At our quaint spirits.   Sing me now asleep ;
Then to your offices and let me rest.

The Fairies sing.

You spotted snakes with double tongue,
    Thorny hedgehogs, be not seen ;
Newts and blind-worms, do no wrong,
    Come not near our fairy queen.
        Philomel, with melody
        Sing in our sweet lullaby ;
Lulla, lulla, lullaby, lulla, lulla, lullaby :
        Never harm,
        Nor spell nor charm,
    Come our lovely lady nigh ;
So, good night, with lullaby.

> Weaving spiders, come not here ;
>   Hence, you long-legg'd spinners, hence !
> Beetles black, approach not near ;
>   Worm nor snail, do no offence.
>   Philomel, with melody, &c.

ACT II, Scene ii, ll. 1-24

The wood. Titania lying asleep.

Enter QUINCE, SNUG, BOTTOM, FLUTE, SNOUT, *and* STARVELING.

Bot. Are we all met ?

Quin. Pat, pat ; and here's a marvellous convenient place for our rehearsal. This green plot shall be our stage, this hawthorn-brake our tiring-house ; and we will do it in action as we will do it before the duke.

Bot. Peter Quince,—

Quin. What sayest thou, bully Bottom ?

Bot. There are things in this comedy of Pyramus and Thisby that will never please. First, Pyramus must draw a sword to kill himself ; which the ladies cannot abide. How answer you that ?

Snout. By'r lakin, a parlous fear.

Star. I believe we must leave the killing out, when all is done.

Bot. Not a whit : I have a device to make all well. Write me a prologue ; and let the prologue seem to say, we will do no harm with our swords and that Pyramus is not killed indeed ; and, for the more better assurance, tell them that I Pyramus am not Pyramus, but Bottom the weaver : this will put them out of fear.

Quin. Well, we will have such a prologue ; and it shall be written in eight and six.

Bot. No, make it two more ; let it be written in eight and eight.

Snout. Will not the ladies be afeard of the lion ?

Star. I fear it, I promise you.

Bot. Masters, you ought to consider with yourselves : to bring in—God shield us !—a lion among ladies, is a most dreadful thing ; for there is not a more fearful wild-fowl than your lion living ; and we ought to look to 't.

Snout. Therefore another prologue must tell he is not a lion.

Bot. Nay, you must name his name, and half his face must be seen through the lion's neck : and he himself must speak through, saying thus, or to the same defect,—' Ladies,'—or ' Fair ladies,—I would wish you,'—or ' I would request you,' —or ' I would entreat you,—not to fear, not to tremble : my life for yours. If you think I come hither as a lion, it were pity of my life : no, I am no such thing ; I am a man as other men are ; ' and there indeed let him name his name, and tell them plainly he is Snug the joiner.

Quin. Well, it shall be so. But there is two hard things ; that is, to bring the moonlight into a chamber ; for, you know, Pyramus and Thisby meet by moonlight.

Snout. Doth the moon shine that night we play our play ?

Bot. A calendar, a calendar ! look in the almanac ; find out moonshine, find out moonshine.

Quin. Yes, it doth shine that night.

Bot. Why, then may you leave a casement of the great chamber window, where we play, open, and the moon may shine in at the casement.

Quin. Ay ; or else one must come in with a bush of thorns and a lanthorn, and say he comes to disfigure, or to present, the person of Moonshine. Then, there is another thing : we must have a wall in the great chamber ; for Pyramus and Thisby, says the story, did talk through the chink of a wall.

Snout. You can never bring in a wall. What say you, Bottom ?

Bot. Some man or other must present Wall : and let him have some plaster, or some loam, or some rough-cast about him, to signify wall ; and let him hold his fingers thus, and through that cranny shall Pyramus and Thisby whisper.

Quin. If that may be, then all is well. Come, sit down,

every mother's son, and rehearse your parts. Pyramus, you begin : when you have spoken your speech, enter into that brake : and so every one according to his cue.

Enter PUCK *behind.*

Puck. What hempen home-spuns have we swaggering here, So near the cradle of the fairy queen ? What, a play toward ! I'll be an auditor ; An actor too perhaps, if I see cause.

Quin. Speak, Pyramus. Thisby, stand forth.

Bot. Thisby, the flowers of odious savours sweet,——

Quin. Odours, odours.

Bot. —— odours savours sweet :

So hath thy breath, my dearest Thisby dear.
But hark, a voice ! stay thou but here awhile,
And by and by I will to thee appear. [*Exit.*

Puck. A stranger Pyramus than e'er played here. [*Exit.*

Flu. Must I speak now ?

Quin. Ay, marry, must you ; for you must understand he goes but to see a noise that he heard, and is to come again.

Flu. Most radiant Pyramus, most lily-white of hue,
Of colour like the red rose on triumphant brier,
Most brisky juvenal and eke most lovely Jew,
As true as truest horse that yet would never tire,
I'll meet thee, Pyramus, at Ninny's tomb.

Quin. ' Ninus' tomb,' man : why, you must not speak that yet ; that you answer to Pyramus : you speak all your part at once, cues and all. Pyramus enter : your cue is past ; it is, ' never tire.'

Flu. O,—As true as truest horse, that yet would never tire.

Re-enter PUCK, *and* BOTTOM *with an ass's head.*

Bot. If I were fair, Thisby, I were only thine.

Quin. O monstrous ! O strange ! we are haunted. Pray, masters ! fly, masters ! Help !

[*Exeunt Quince, Snug, Flute, Snout, and Starveling.*

Puck. I'll follow you, I'll lead you about a round,
    Through bog, through bush, through brake, through brier
Sometime a horse I'll be, sometime a hound,
    A hog, a headless bear, sometime a fire ;
And neigh, and bark, and grunt, and roar, and burn,
    Like horse, hound, hog, bear, fire, at every turn.   *[Exit.*

Bot. Why do they run away ? this is a knavery of them to
make me afeard.

Re-enter SNOUT.

Snout. O Bottom, thou art changed ! what do I see on thee ?

Bot. What do you see ? you see an ass-head of your own,
do you ?   *[Exit Snout.*

Re-enter QUINCE.

Quin. Bless thee, Bottom ! bless thee ! thou art translated.
                                                [Exit.

Bot. I see their knavery : this is to make an ass of me ; to
fright me, if they could. But I will not stir from this place,
do what they can : I will walk up and down here, and I will
sing, that they shall hear I am not afraid.   *[Sings.*

          The ousel cock so black of hue,
             With orange-tawny bill,
          The throstle with his note so true,
             The wren with little quill,—

Tita. [*Awaking*] What angel wakes me from my flowery
bed ?

Bot. [*Sings*]
            The finch, the sparrow and the lark,
              The plain-song cuckoo gray,
          Whose note full many a man doth mark,
             And dares not answer nay ;—
for, indeed, who would set his wit to so foolish a bird ? who
would give a bird the lie, though he cry ' cuckoo ' never so ?

Tita. I pray thee, gentle mortal, sing again :
Mine ear is much enamour'd of thy note ;
So is mine eye enthralled to thy shape ;

And thy fair virtue's force perforce doth move me
On the first view to say, to swear, I love thee.

Bot. Methinks, mistress, you should have little reason for that : and yet, to say the truth, reason and love keep little company together now-a-days ; the more the pity that some honest neighbours will not make them friends. Nay, I can gleek upon occasion.

Tita. Thou art as wise as thou art beautiful.

Bot. Not so, neither : but if I had wit enough to get out of this wood, I have enough to serve mine own turn

Tita. Out of this wood do not desire to go :
Thou shalt remain here, whether thou wilt or no
I am a spirit of no common rate :
The summer still doth tend upon my state ;
And I do love thee : therefore, go with me ;
I'll give thee fairies to attend on thee,
And they shall fetch thee jewels from the deep,
And sing while thou on pressed flowers dost sleep :
And I will purge thy mortal grossness so
That thou shalt like an airy spirit go.
Peaseblossom ! Cobweb ! Moth ! and Mustard-seed !

Enter PEASEBLOSSOM, COBWEB, MOTH, *and* MUSTARDSEED.

Peas. Ready.
Cob.　　　And I.
Moth.　　　　　And I.
Mus.　　　　　　　And I.
All.　　　　　　　　　Where shall we go ?

Tita. Be kind and courteous to this gentleman ;
Hop in his walks and gambol in his eyes ;
Feed him with apricocks and dewberries,
With purple grapes, green figs, and mulberries ;
The honey-bags steal from the humble-bees,
And for night-tapers crop their waxen thighs
And light them at the fiery glow-worm's eyes
To have my love to bed and to arise ;

84

And pluck the wings from painted butterflies
To fan the moonbeams from his sleeping eyes :
Nod to him, elves, and do him courtesies.

Peas. Hail, mortal !

Cob. Hail !

Moth. Hail !

Mus. Hail !

Bot. I cry your worships mercy, heartily : I beseech your
worship's name.

Cob. Cobweb.

Bot. I shall desire you of more acquaintance, good Master
Cobweb : if I cut my finger, I shall make bold with you.
Your name, honest gentleman ?

Peas. Peaseblossom.

Bot. I pray you, commend me to Mistress Squash, your
mother, and to Master Peascod, your father. Good Master
Peaseblossom, I shall desire you of more acquaintance too.
Your name, I beseech you, sir ?

Mus. Mustardseed.

Bot. Good Master Mustardseed, I know your patience
well : that same cowardly, giant-like ox-beef hath devoured
many a gentleman of your house : I promise you your kindred
hath made my eyes water ere now. I desire your more
acquaintance, good Master Mustardseed.

Tita. Come, wait upon him ; lead him to my bower.
  The moon methinks looks with a watery eye ;
And when she weeps, weeps every little flower,
  Lamenting some enforced chastity.
  Tie up my love's tongue, bring him silently.   [*Exeunt.*
                                    ACT III, Scene i, ll. 1-206

As wild geese that the creeping fowler eye,
Or russet-pated choughs, many in sort,
Rising and cawing at the gun's report,
Sever themselves and madly sweep the sky,

                                    ACT III, Scene ii, ll. 20-24

Puck. Shall we their fond pageant see ?
Lord, what fools these mortals be !

ACT III, Scene ii, ll. 114-115

Helena. Injurious Hermia ! most ungrateful maid !
Have you conspired, have you with these contrived
To bait me with this foul derision ?
Is all the counsel that we two have shared,
The sisters' vows, the hours that we have spent,
When we have chid the hasty-footed time
For parting us,—O, is it all forgot ?
All school-days' friendship, childhood innocence ?
We, Hermia, like two artificial gods,
Have with our needles created both one flower,
Both on one sampler, sitting on one cushion,
Both warbling of one song, both in one key,
As if our hands, our sides, voices and minds,
Had been incorporate. So we grew together,
Like to a double cherry, seeming parted,
But yet an union in partition ;
Two lovely berries moulded on one stem ;
So, with two seeming bodies, but one heart ;
Two of the first, like coats in heraldry,
Due but to one and crowned with one crest.
And will you rent our ancient love asunder,
To join with men in scorning your poor friend ?
It is not friendly, 'tis not maidenly :
Our sex, as well as I, may chide you for it,
Though I alone do feel the injury.

ACT III, Scene ii, ll. 195-219

Puck. My fairy lord, this must be done with haste,
For night's swift dragons cut the clouds full fast,
And yonder shines Aurora's harbinger ;
At whose approach, ghosts, wandering here and there,
Troop home to churchyards. . . .
Obe. But we are spirits of another sort :

86

I with the morning's love have oft made sport,
And, like a forester, the groves may tread,
Even till the eastern gate, all fiery-red,
Opening on Neptune with fair blessed beams,
Turns into yellow gold his salt green streams.
But, notwithstanding, haste; make no delay:
We may effect this business yet ere day.   [*Exit.*

Puck.   Up and down, up and down,
          I will lead them up and down:
          I am fear'd in field and town:
          Goblin, lead them up and down.
Here comes one.

ACT III, Scene ii, ll. 378-382, 388-400

The wood. LYSANDER, DEMETRIUS, HELENA, *and* HERMIA
          lying asleep.

Enter TITANIA *and* BOTTOM; PEASEBLOSSOM, COBWEB, MOTH,
    MUSTARDSEED, *and other* Fairies *attending;* OBERON
    behind unseen.

Tita. Come, sit thee down upon this flowery bed,
          While I thy amiable cheeks do coy,
          And stick musk-roses in thy sleek smooth head,
          And kiss thy fair large ears, my gentle joy.
Bot. Where's Peaseblossom?
Peas. Ready.
Bot. Scratch my head, Peaseblossom. Where's Mounsieur
Cobweb?
Cob. Ready.
Bot. Mounsieur Cobweb, good mounsieur, get you your
weapons in your hand, and kill me a red-hipped humble-bee
on the top of a thistle; and, good mounsieur, bring me the
honey-bag. Do not fret yourself too much in the action,
mounsieur; and, good mounsieur, have a care the honey-bag
break not; I would be loath to have you overflown with a
honey-bag, signior. Where's Mounsieur Mustardseed?
Mus. Ready.

Bot. Give me your neaf, Mounsieur Mustardseed. Pray you, leave your courtesy, good mounsieur.

Mus. What's your will?

Bot. Nothing, good mounsieur, but to help Cavalery Cobweb to scratch. I must to the barber's, mounsieur; for methinks I am marvellous hairy about the face; and I am such a tender ass, if my hair do but tickle me, I must scratch.

Tita. What, wilt thou hear some music, my sweet love?

Bot. I have a reasonable good ear in music. Let's have the tongs and the bones.

Tita. Or say, sweet love, what thou desirest to eat.

Bot. Truly, a peck of provender: I could munch your good dry oats. Methinks I have a great desire to a bottle of hay: good hay, sweet hay, hath no fellow.

Tita. I have a venturous fairy that shall seek
The squirrel's hoard, and fetch thee new nuts.

Bot. I had rather have a handful or two of dried peas. But, I pray you, let none of your people stir me: I have an exposition of sleep come upon me.

Tita. Sleep thou, and I will wind thee in my arms.
Fairies, be gone, and be all ways away.   [*Exeunt fairies.*
So doth the woodbine the sweet honeysuckle
Gently entwist; the female ivy so
Enrings the barky fingers of the elm.
O, how I love thee! how I dote on thee!   [*They sleep.*

Enter PUCK.

Obe. [*Advancing*] Welcome, good Robin. See'st thou this sweet sight?
Her dotage now I do begin to pity:
For, meeting her of late behind the wood,
Seeking sweet favours for this hateful fool,
I did upbraid her and fall out with her;
For she his hairy temples then had rounded
With coronet of fresh and fragrant flowers;
And that same dew, which sometime on the buds

Was wont to swell like round and orient pearls,
Stood now within the pretty flowerets' eyes
Like tears that did their own disgrace bewail.
When I had at my pleasure taunted her
And she in mild terms begg'd my patience,
I then did ask of her her changeling child ;
Which straight she gave me, and her fairy sent
To bear him to my bower in fairy land.
And now I have the boy, I will undo
This hateful imperfection of her eyes :
And, gentle Puck, take this transformed scalp
From off the head of this Athenian swain ;
That, he awaking when the other do,
May all to Athens back again repair
And think no more of this night's accidents ·
But as the fierce vexation of a dream.
But first I will release the fairy queen.

     Be as thou wast wont to be ;
     See as thou wast wont to see :
     Dian's bud o'er Cupid's flower
     Hath such force and blessed power.

Now, my Titania ; wake you, my sweet queen.

 Tita. My Oberon ! what visions have I seen !
Methought I was enamour'd of an ass.

 Obe. There lies your love.

 Tita.   How came these things to pass ?
O, how mine eyes do loathe his visage now !

 Obe. Silence awhile. Robin, take off this head.
Titania, music call ; and strike more dead
Than common sleep of all these five the sense.

 Tita. Music, ho ! music, such as charmeth sleep !

            [*Music, still.*

 Puck. Now, when thou wakest, with thine own fool's eyes
  peep.

 Obe. Sound, music ! Come, my queen, take hands with me,
And rock the ground whereon these sleepers be.

Now thou and I are new in amity
And will to-morrow midnight solemnly
Dance in Duke Theseus' house triumphantly
And bless it to all fair prosperity :
There shall the pairs of faithful lovers be
Wedded, with Theseus, all in jollity.

    Puck.   Fairy king, attend, and mark :
              I do hear the morning lark.

    Obe.   Then, my queen, in silence sad,
              Trip we after night's shade :
              We the globe can compass soon,
              Swifter than the wandering moon.

    Tita.   Come, my lord, and in our flight
              Tell me how it came this night
              That I sleeping here was found
              With these mortals on the ground.   [*Exeunt.*
                                [*Horns winded within.*

    Enter THESEUS, HIPPOLYTA, EGEUS, *and train.*

    The. Go, one of you, find out the forester ;
For now our observation is perform'd ;
And since we have the vaward of the day,
My love shall hear the music of my hounds.
Uncouple in the western valley ; let them go :
Dispatch, I say, and find the forester.
                            [*Exit an attendant.*
We will, fair queen, up to the mountain's top
And mark the musical confusion
Of hounds and echo in conjunction.

    Hip. I was with Hercules and Cadmus once,
When in a wood of Crete they bay'd the bear
With hounds of Sparta : never did I hear
Such gallant chiding ; for, besides the groves,
The skies, the fountains, every region near
Seem'd all one mutual cry : I never heard
So musical a discord, such sweet thunder.

The. My hounds are bred out of the Spartan kind,
So flew'd, so sanded, and their heads are hung
With ears that sweep away the morning dew ;
Crook-knee'd, and dew-lapp'd like Thessalian bulls ;
Slow in pursuit, but match'd in mouth like bells,
Each under each. A cry more tuneable
Was never holla'd to, nor cheer'd with horn,
In Crete, in Sparta, nor in Thessaly.

ACT IV, Scene i, ll. 1-130.

Bottom. [*Awaking*] When my cue comes, call me, and I
will answer : my next is, ' Most fair Pyramus.' Heigh-ho !
Peter Quince ! Flute, the bellows-mender ! Snout, the tinker !
Starveling ! God's my life, stolen hence, and left me asleep !
I have had a most rare vision. I have had a dream, past the
wit of man to say what dream it was : man is but an ass, if he
go about to expound this dream. Methought I was—there is
no man can tell what. Methought I was,—and methought I
had,—but man is but a patched fool, if he will offer to say
what methought I had. The eye of man hath not heard, the
ear of man hath not seen, man's hand is not able to taste, his
tongue to conceive, nor his heart to report, what my dream
was. I will get Peter Quince to write a ballad of this dream :
it shall be called Bottom's Dream, because it hath no bottom ;
and I will sing it in the latter end of a play, before the duke :
peradventure, to make it the more gracious, I shall sing it at
her death.

ACT IV, Scene i, ll. 204-225

Athens. QUINCE'S *house.*

Enter QUINCE, FLUTE, SNOUT, *and* STARVELING.

Quin. Have you sent to Bottom's house ? is he come home
yet ?

Star. He cannot be heard of. Out of doubt he is transported.

Flu. If he come not, then the play is marred : it goes not
forward, doth it ?

Quin. It is not possible : you have not a man in all Athens able to discharge Pyramus but he.

Flu. No, he hath simply the best wit of any handicraft man in Athens.

Quin. Yea, and the best person too ; and he is a very paramour for a sweet voice.

Flu. You must say ' paragon : ' a paramour is, God bless us, a thing of naught.   ACT IV, Scene ii, ll. 1-14

Athens. The palace of THESEUS.

Enter THESEUS, HIPPOLYTA, PHILOSTRATE, Lords, *and* Attendants.

Hip. 'Tis strange, my Theseus, that these lovers speak of.

The. More strange than true : I never may believe
These antique fables, nor these fairy toys.
Lovers and madmen have such seething brains,
Such shaping fantasies, that apprehend
More than cool reason ever comprehends.
The lunatic, the lover and the poet
Are of imagination all compact :
One sees more devils than vast hell can hold,
That is, the madman : the lover, all as frantic,
Sees Helen's beauty in a brow of Egypt :
The poet's eye, in a fine frenzy rolling,
Doth glance from heaven to earth, from earth to heaven ;
And as imagination bodies forth
The forms of things unknown, the poet's pen
Turns them to shapes and gives to airy nothing
A local habitation and a name.
                                        ACT V, Scene i, ll. 1-17

Enter QUINCE *for the* Prologue.

Pro. If we offend, it is with our good will.
        That you should think, we come not to offend,
    But with good will. To show our simple skill,
        That is the true beginning of our end.

Consider then we come but in despite.
   We do not come as minding to content you,
Our true intent is. All for your delight
   We are not here. That you should here repent you,
The actors are at hand and by their show
You shall know all that you are like to know.

Theseus. This fellow doth not stand upon points.

Lysander. He hath rid his prologue like a rough colt ; he knows not the stop. A good moral, my lord : it is not enough to speak, but to speak true.

Hippolyta. Indeed he hath played on his prologue like a child on a recorder ; a sound, but not in government.

The. His speech was like a tangled chain ; nothing impaired, but all disordered. Who is next ?

Enter PYRAMUS *and* THISBE, WALL, MOONSHINE,
and LION.

Pro. Gentles, perchance you wonder at this show ;
   But wonder on, till truth make all things plain.
This man is Pyramus, if you would know ;
   This beauteous lady Thisby is certain.
This man, with lime and rough-cast, doth present
   Wall, that vile Wall which did these lovers sunder ;
And through Wall's chink, poor souls, they are content
   To whisper. At the which let no man wonder.
This man, with lanthorn, dog, and brush of thorn,
   Presenteth Moonshine ; for, if you will know,
By moonshine did these lovers think no scorn
   To meet at Ninus' tomb, there, there to woo.
This grisly beast, which Lion hight by name,
The trusty Thisby, coming first by night,
Did scare away, or rather did affright ;
And, as she fled, her mantle she did fall,
   Which Lion vile with bloody mouth did stain.
Anon comes Pyramus, sweet youth and tall,
   And finds his trusty Thisby's mantle slain :

Whereat, with blade, with bloody blameful blade,
　　He bravely broach'd his boiling bloody breast ;
And Thisby, tarrying in mulberry shade,
　　His dagger drew, and died.　For all the rest,
Let Lion, Moonshine, Wall, and lovers twain
At large discourse, while here they do remain.

　　[*Exeunt Prologue, Pyramus, Thisbe, Lion, and Moonshine.*
　The. I wonder if the lion be to speak.

　Demetrius. No wonder, my lord : one lion may, when many asses do.

　Wall. In this same interlude it doth befall
That I, one Snout by name, present a wall ;
And such a wall, as I would have you think,
That had in it a crannied hole or chink,
Through which the lovers, Pyramus and Thisby,
Did whisper often very secretly.
This loam, this rough-cast and this stone doth show
That I am that same wall ; the truth is so :
And this the cranny is, right and sinister,
Through which the fearful lovers are to whisper.

　The. Would you desire lime and hair to speak better ?

　Dem. It is the wittiest partition that ever I heard discourse, my lord.

　　　　　　　　Re-enter PYRAMUS.

　The. Pyramus draws near the wall : silence !

　Pyr. O grim-look'd night ! O night with hue so black !
O night, which ever art when day is not !
O night, O night ! alack, alack, alack,
　I fear my Thisby's promise is forgot !
And thou, O wall, O sweet, O lovely wall,
　That stand'st between her father's ground and mine !
Thou wall, O wall, O sweet and lovely wall,
　Show me thy chink, to blink through with mine eyne !

　　　　　　　　　　　　[*Wall holds up his fingers.*
Thanks, courteous wall : Jove shield thee well for this
　But what see I ? No Thisby do I see.

94

O wicked wall, through whom I see no bliss!
 Cursed be thy stones for thus deceiving me!

The. The wall, methinks, being sensible, should curse again.

Pyr. No, in truth, sir, he should not. ' Deceiving me ' is Thisby's cue : she is to enter now, and I am to spy her through the wall. You shall see, it will fall pat as I told you. Yonder she comes.

Re-enter THISBE.

This. O wall, full often hast thou heard my moans,
 For parting my fair Pyramus and me!
 My cherry lips have often kiss'd thy stones,
 Thy stones with lime and hair knit up in thee.

Pyr. I see a voice : now will I to the chink,
To spy an I can hear my Thisby's face.
Thisby!

This. My love thou art, my love I think.

Pyr. Think what thou wilt, I am thy lover's grace ;
And, like Limander, am I trusty still.

This. And I like Helen, till the Fates me kill.

Pyr. Not Shafalus to Procrus was so true.

This. As Shafalus to Procrus, I to you.

Pyr. O, kiss me through the hole of this vile wall !

This. I kiss the wall's hole, not your lips at all.

Pyr. Wilt thou at Ninny's tomb meet me straightway ?

This. 'Tide life, 'tide death, I come without delay.

         [*Exeunt Pyramus and Thisbe.*

Wall. Thus have I, Wall, my part discharged so ;
And, being done, thus Wall away doth go.   [*Exit.*

The. Now is the mural down between the two neighbours.

Dem. No remedy, my lord, when walls are so wilful to hear without warning.

Hip. This is the silliest stuff that ever I heard.

The. The best in this kind are but shadows : and the worst are no worse, if imagination amend them.

Hip. It must be your imagination then, and not theirs.

The. If we imagine no worse of them than they of themselves, they may pass for excellent men. Here come two noble beasts in, a man and a lion.

Re-enter LION *and* MOONSHINE.

Lion. You, ladies, you, whose gentle hearts do fear
 The smallest monstrous mouse that creeps on floor,
May now perchance both quake and tremble here,
 When lion rough in wildest rage doth roar.
Then know that I, one Snug the joiner, am
A lion-fell, nor else no lion's dam;
For, if I should as lion come in strife
Into this place, 'twere pity on my life.

The. A very gentle beast, and of a good conscience.

Dem. The very best at a beast, my lord, that e'er I saw.

Lys. This lion is a very fox for his valour.

The. True; and a goose for his discretion.

Dem. Not so, my lord; for his valour cannot carry his discretion; and the fox carries the goose.

The. His discretion, I am sure, cannot carry his valour; for the goose carries not the fox. It is well: leave it to his discretion, and let us listen to the moon.

Moon. This lanthorn doth the horned moon present;—

Dem. He should have worn the horns on his head.

The. He is no crescent, and his horns are invisible within the circumference.

Moon. This lanthorn doth the horned moon present;
Myself the man i' the moon do seem to be.

The. This is the greatest error of all the rest: the man should be put into the lanthorn. How is it else the man i' the moon?

Dem. He dares not come there for the candle; for, you see, it is already in snuff.

Hip. I am aweary of this moon: would he would change!

The. It appears, by his small light of discretion, that he is in the wane; but yet, in courtesy, in all reason, we must stay the time.

Lys. Proceed, Moon.

Moon. All that I have to say, is, to tell you that the lanthorn is the moon; I, the man in the moon; this thorn-bush, my thorn-bush; and this dog, my dog.

Dem. Why, all these should be in the lanthorn; for all these are in the moon. But, silence! here comes Thisbe.

Re-enter THISBE.

This. This is old Ninny's tomb. Where is my love?

Lion. [*Roaring*] Oh——   [*Thisbe runs off.*

Dem. Well roared, Lion.

The. Well run, Thisbe.

Hip. Well shone, Moon. Truly, the moon shines with a good grace.   [*The Lion shakes Thisbe's mantle, and exit.*

The. Well moused, Lion.

Lys. And so the lion vanished.

Dem. And then came Pyramus.

Re-enter PYRAMUS.

Pyr. Sweet Moon, I thank thee for thy sunny beams;
    I thank thee, Moon, for shining now so bright;
For, by thy gracious, golden, glittering gleams,
    I trust to take of truest Thisby sight.
              But stay, O spite!
              But mark, poor knight,
      What dreadful dole is here!
              Eyes, do you see?
              How can it be?
      O dainty duck! O dear!
              Thy mantle good,
      What, stain'd with blood!
    Approach, ye Furies fell!
            O Fates, come, come,
            Cut thread and thrum;
    Quail, crush, conclude, and quell!

The. This passion, and the death of a dear friend, would go near to make a man look sad.

Hip. Beshrew my heart, but I pity the man.

Pyr. O wherefore, Nature, didst thou lions frame?
Since lion vile hath here deflower'd my dear:
Which is—no, no—which was the fairest dame
That lived, that loved, that liked, that look'd with cheer.
　　　　　　Come, tears, confound;
　　　　　　Out, sword, and wound
　　　　　The pap of Pyramus;
　　　　　　Ay, that left pap,
　　　　　　Where heart doth hop:　[*Stabs himself*.
　　　　Thus die I, thus, thus, thus.
　　　　　　Now am I dead,
　　　　　　Now am I fled;
　　　　My soul is in the sky:
　　　　　　Tongue, lose thy light;
　　　　　　Moon, take thy flight:　[*Exit Moonshine*.
　　　　Now die, die, die, die, die.　　　　[*Dies*.

Dem. No die, but an ace, for him; for he is but one.

Lys. Less than an ace, man; for he is dead; he is nothing.

The. With the help of a surgeon he might yet recover, and prove an ass.

Hip. How chance Moonshine is gone before Thisbe comes back and finds her lover?

The. She will find him by starlight. Here she comes; and her passion ends the play.

Re-enter THISBE.

Hip. Methinks she should not use a long one for such a Pyramus: I hope she will be brief.

Dem. A mote will turn the balance, which Pyramus, which Thisbe, is the better; he for a man, God warrant us; she for a woman, God bless us.

Lys. She hath spied him already with those sweet eyes.

Dem. And thus she means, videlicet:—

This. Asleep, my love?
    What, dead, my dove?
  O Pyramus, arise!
    Speak, speak. Quite dumb?
    Dead, dead? A tomb
  Must cover thy sweet eyes.
    These lily lips,
    This cherry nose,
  These yellow cowslip cheeks
    Are gone, are gone:
    Lovers, make moan:
  His eyes were green as leeks.
    O Sisters Three,
    Come, come to me,
  With hands as pale as milk;
    Lay them in gore,
    Since you have shore
  With shears his thread of silk.
    Tongue, not a word:
    Come, trusty sword;
  Come, blade, my breast imbrue:
          [*Stabs herself.*
    And, farewell, friends;
    Thus Thisby ends:
  Adieu, adieu, adieu.   [*Dies.*

The. Moonshine and Lion are left to bury the dead.

Dem. Ay, and Wall too.

Bot. [*Starting up*] No, I assure you; the wall is down that parted their fathers. Will it please you to see the epilogue, or to hear a Bergomask dance between two of our company?

The. No epilogue, I pray you; for your play needs no excuse. Never excuse; for when the players are all dead, there need none to be blamed. Marry, if he that writ it had played Pyramus and hanged himself in Thisbe's garter, it would have been a fine tragedy: and so it is, truly: and very notably discharged. But, come, your Bergomask: let your epilogue alone.   [*A dance.*

The iron tongue of midnight hath told twelve :
Lovers, to bed ; 'tis almost fairy time.
I fear we shall out-sleep the coming morn
As much as we this night have overwatch'd.
This palpable-gross play hath well beguiled
The heavy gait of night. Sweet friends, to bed.
A fortnight hold we this solemnity,
In nightly revels and new jollity.   [*Exeunt.*

Enter PUCK.

Puck. Now the hungry lion roars,
            And the wolf behowls the moon ;
        Whilst the heavy ploughman snores,
            All with weary task fordone.
        Now the wasted brands do glow,
            Whilst the screech-owl, screeching loud,
        Puts the wretch that lies in woe
            In remembrance of a shroud.
        Now it is the time of night
            That the graves all gaping wide,
        Every one lets forth his sprite,
            In the church-way paths to glide :
        And we fairies, that do run
            By the triple Hecate's team,
        From the presence of the sun,
            Following darkness like a dream,
        Now are frolic : not a mouse
        Shall disturb this hallow'd house :
        I am sent with broom before,
        To sweep the dust behind the door.

Enter OBERON *and* TITANIA *with their train.*

Obe.   Through the house give glimmering light,
            By the dead and drowsy fire :
        Every elf and fairy sprite
            Hop as light as bird from brier. . . .

Tita.   First, rehearse your song by rote,
    To each word a warbling note :
    Hand in hand, with fairy grace,
    Will we sing, and bless this place. [*Song and dance.*
                        ACT V, Scene i, ll. 108-401, 404-407

The Merchant of Venice

Antonio. In sooth, I know not why I am so sad :
It wearies me ; you say it wearies you ;
But how I caught it, found it, or came by it,
What stuff 'tis made of, whereof it is born,
I am to learn ;
And such a want-wit sadness makes of me,
That I have much ado to know myself.
    Salarino. Your mind is tossing on the ocean ;
There, where your argosies with portly sail,
Like signiors and rich burghers on the flood,
Or, as it were, the pageants of the sea,
Do overpeer the petty traffickers,
That curtsy to them, do them reverence,
As they fly by them with their woven wings.
                        ACT I, Scene i, ll. 1-14

Antonio. I hold the world but as the world, Gratiano ;
A stage where every man must play a part,
And mine a sad one.
    Gratiano.   Let me play the fool :
With mirth and laughter let old wrinkles come,
And let my liver rather heat with wine
Than my heart cool with mortifying groans.
Why should a man, whose blood is warm within,
Sit like his grandsire cut in alabaster ?
                        ACT I, Scene i, ll. 77-84

101

Portia. By my troth, Nerissa, my little body is aweary of this great world.   ACT I, Scene ii, ll. 1-2

Enter BASSANIO *and* SHYLOCK.

Shy. Three thousand ducats ; well.

Bass. Ay, sir, for three months.

Shy. For three months ; well.

Bass. For the which, as I told you, Antonio shall be bound.

Shy. Antonio shall become bound ; well.

Bass. May you stead me ? will you pleasure me ? shall I know your answer ?

Shy. Three thousand ducats for three months and Antonio bound.

Bass. Your answer to that.

Shy. Antonio is a good man.

Bass. Have you heard any imputation to the contrary ?

Shy. Oh, no, no, no, no : my meaning in saying he is a good man is to have you understand me that he is sufficient. Yet his means are in supposition : he hath an argosy bound to Tripolis, another to the Indies ; I understand, moreover, upon the Rialto, he hath a third at Mexico, a fourth for England, and other ventures he hath, squandered abroad. But ships are but boards, sailors but men : there be land-rats and water-rats, water-thieves and land-thieves, I mean pirates, and then there is the peril of waters, winds and rocks. The man is, notwithstanding, sufficient. Three thousand ducats ; I think I may take his bond.

Bass. Be assured you may.

Shy. I will be assured I may ; and, that I may be assured, I will bethink me. May I speak with Antonio ?

Bass. If it please you to dine with us.

Shy. Yes, to smell pork ; to eat of the habitation which your prophet the Nazarite conjured the devil into. I will buy with you, sell with you, talk with you, walk with you, and so following, but I will not eat with you, drink with you, nor pray with you. What news on the Rialto ? Who is he comes here ?

Enter ANTONIO.

Bass. This is Signior Antonio.

Shy. [*Aside*] How like a fawning publican he looks !
I hate him for he is a Christian,
But more for that in low simplicity
He lends out money gratis and brings down
The rate of usance here with us in Venice.
If I can catch him once upon the hip,
I will feed fat the ancient grudge I bear him.
He hates our sacred nation, and he rails,
Even there where merchants most do congregate,
On me, my bargains and my well-won thrift,
Which he calls interest. Cursed be my tribe,
If I forgive him !

    Bass.   Shylock, do you hear ?

    Shy. I am debating of my present store,
And, by the near guess of my memory,
I cannot instantly raise up the gross
Of full three thousand ducats. What of that ?
Tubal, a wealthy Hebrew of my tribe,
Will furnish me. But soft ! how many months
Do you desire ? [*To Ant.*] Rest you fair, good signior ;
Your worship was the last man in our mouths.

    Ant. Shylock, although I neither lend nor borrow
By taking nor by giving of excess,
Yet, to supply the ripe wants of my friend,
I'll break a custom. Is he yet possess'd
How much ye would ?

    Shy.   Ay, ay, three thousand ducats.

    Ant. And for three months.

    Shy. I had forgot ; three months ; you told me so.
Well then, your bond ; and let me see ; but hear you ;
Methought you said you neither lend nor borrow
Upon advantage.

    Ant.   I do never use it.

    Shy. When Jacob grazed his uncle Laban's sheep—

This Jacob from our holy Abram was,
As his wise mother wrought in his behalf,
The third possessor ; ay, he was the third—

    Ant. And what of him ? did he take interest ?

    Shy. No, not take interest, not, as you would say,
Directly interest : mark what Jacob did.
When Laban and himself were compromised
That all the eanlings which were streak'd and pied
Should fall as Jacob's hire, the ewes, being rank,
In the end of autumn turned to the rams,
And, when the work of generation was
Between these woolly breeders in the act,
The skilful shepherd peel'd me certain wands
And, in the doing of the deed of kind,
He stuck them up before the fulsome ewes,
Who then conceiving did in eaning time
Fall parti-colour'd lambs, and those were Jacob's.
This was a way to thrive, and he was blest :
And thrift is blessing, if men steal it not.

    Ant. This was a venture, sir, that Jacob served for ;
A thing not in his power to bring to pass,
But sway'd and fashion'd by the hand of heaven.
Was this inserted to make interest good ?
Or is your gold and silver ewes and rams ?

    Shy. I cannot tell ; I make it breed as fast :
But note me, signior.

    Ant.   Mark you this, Bassanio,
The devil can cite Scripture for his purpose.
An evil soul producing holy witness
Is like a villain with a smiling cheek,
A goodly apple rotten at the heart :
O, what a goodly outside falsehood hath ?

    Shy. Three thousand ducats ; 'tis a good round sum.
Three months from twelve ; then, let me see ; the
       rate—

    Ant. Well, Shylock, shall we be beholding to you ?

Shy. Signior Antonio, many a time and oft
In the Rialto you have rated me
About my moneys and my usances :
Still have I borne it with a patient shrug,
For sufferance is the badge of all our tribe.
You call me misbeliever, cut-throat dog,
And spit upon my Jewish gaberdine,
And all for use of that which is mine own.
Well then, it now appears you need my help :
Go to, then ; you come to me, and you say
' Shylock, we would have moneys : ' you say so ;
You, that did void your rheum upon my beard
And foot me as you spurn a stranger cur
Over your threshold : moneys is your suit.
What should I say to you ? Should I not say
' Hath a dog money ? is it possible
A cur can lend three thousand ducats ? ' Or
Shall I bend low and in a bondman's key,
With bated breath and whispering humbleness,
Say this ;
' Fair sir, you spit on me on Wednesday last ;
You spurn'd me such a day ; another time
You call'd me dog ; and for these courtesies
I'll lend you thus much moneys ' ?

Ant. I am as like to call thee so again,
To spit on thee again, to spurn thee too.
If thou wilt lend this money, lend it not
As to thy friends ; for when did friendship take
A breed for barren metal of his friend ?
But lend it rather to thine enemy,
Who, if he break, thou mayst with better face
Exact the penalty.

Shy. Why, look you, how you storm !
I would be friends with you and have your love,
Forget the shames that you have stain'd me with,
Supply your present wants and take no doit

Of usance for my moneys, and you'll not hear me :
This is kind I offer.

    Bass. This were kindness.

    Shy.   This kindness will I show.
Go with me to a notary, seal me there
Your single bond ; and, in a merry sport,
If you repay me not on such a day,
In such a place, such sum or sums as are
Express'd in the condition, let the forfeit
Be nominated for an equal pound
Of your fair flesh, to be cut off and taken
In what part of your body pleaseth me.

    Ant. Content, i' faith : I'll seal to such a bond
And say there is much kindness in the Jew.

    Bass. You shall not seal to such a bond for me :
I'll rather dwell in my necessity.

    Ant. Why, fear not, man ; I will not forfeit it :
Within these two months, that's a month before
This bond expires, I do expect return
Of thrice three times the value of this bond.

    Shy. O father Abram, what these Christians are,
Whose own hard dealings teaches them suspect
The thoughts of others ! Pray you, tell me this ;
If he should break his day, what should I gain
By the exaction of the forfeiture ?
A pound of man's flesh taken from a man
Is not so estimable, profitable neither,
As flesh of muttons, beefs, or goats. I say,
To buy his favour, I extend this friendship :
If he will take it, so ; if not, adieu ;
And, for my love, I pray you wrong me not.

    Ant. Yes, Shylock, I will seal unto this bond.

    Shy. Then meet me forthwith at the notary's ;
Give him direction for this merry bond,
And I will go and purse the ducats straight,
See to my house, left in the fearful guard

Of an unthrifty knave, and presently
I will be with you.

    Ant. Hie thee, gentle Jew.   *[Exit Shylock.*
The Hebrew will turn Christian : he grows kind.

    Bass. I like not fair terms and a villain's mind.

    Ant. Come on : in this there can be no dismay ;
My ships come home a month before the day.   *[Exeunt.*

                         Act I, Scene iii, ll. 1-182

    Prince of Morocco. Mislike me not for my complexion,
The shadow'd livery of the burnish'd sun,
To whom I am a neighbour and near bred.
Bring me the fairest creature northward born,
Where Phœbus' fire scarce thaws the icicles,
And let us make incision for your love,
To prove whose blood is reddest, his or mine.

                         Act II, Scene i, ll. 1-7

    Launcelot. Certainly my conscience will serve me to run from this Jew my master. The fiend is at mine elbow and tempts me saying to me ' Gobbo, Launcelot Gobbo, good Launcelot,' or ' good Gobbo,' or ' good Launcelot Gobbo, use your legs, take the start, run away.' My conscience says ' No ; take heed, honest Launcelot ; take heed, honest Gobbo,' or, as aforesaid, ' honest Launcelot Gobbo ; do not run ; scorn running with thy heels.' Well, the most courageous fiend bids me pack : ' Via ! ' says the fiend ; ' away ! ' says the fiend ; ' for the heavens, rouse up a brave mind,' says the fiend, ' and run.' Well, my conscience, hanging about the neck of my heart, says very wisely to me ' My honest friend Launcelot, being an honest man's son,' or rather an honest woman's son ; for, indeed, my father did something smack, something grow to, he had a kind of taste ; well, my conscience says ' Launcelot, budge not.' ' Budge,' says the fiend. ' Budge not,' says my conscience. ' Conscience,' say I, ' you counsel well ; ' ' Fiend,' say I, ' you counsel well : ' to be ruled by my conscience, I should stay with the Jew my master, who, God bless

the mark, is a kind of devil; and, to run away from the Jew,
I should be ruled by the fiend, who, saving your reverence, is
the devil himself. Certainly the Jew is the very devil incarnal;
and, in my conscience, my conscience is but a kind of hard
conscience, to offer to counsel me to stay with the Jew. The
fiend gives the more friendly counsel: I will run, fiend; my
heels are at your command; I will run.

Enter Old GOBBO, *with a basket.*

Gob. Master young man, you, I pray you, which is the
way to master Jew's?

Laun. [*Aside*] O heavens, this is my true-begotten father!
who, being more than sand-blind, high-gravel blind, knows
me not: I will try confusions with him.

Gob. Master young gentleman, I pray you, which is the
way to master Jew's?

Laun. Turn up on your right hand at the next turning,
but, at the next turning of all, on your left; marry, at the very
next turning, turn of no hand, but turn down indirectly to
the Jew's house.

Gob. By God's sonties, 'twill be a hard way to hit. Can
you tell me whether one Launcelot, that dwells with him,
dwell with him or no?

Laun. Talk you of young Master Launcelot? [*Aside*]
Mark me now; now will I raise the waters. Talk you of
young Master Launcelot?

Gob. No master, sir, but a poor man's son: his father,
though I say it, is an honest exceeding poor man and, God be
thanked, well to live.

Laun. Well, let his father be what a' will, we talk of young
Master Launcelot.

Gob. Your worship's friend and Launcelot, sir.

Laun. But I pray you, ergo, old man, ergo, I beseech you,
talk you of young Master Launcelot?

Gob. Of Launcelot, an't please your mastership.

Laun. Ergo, Master Launcelot. Talk not of Master

Launcelot, father; for the young gentleman, according to Fates and Destinies and such odd sayings, the Sisters Three and such branches of learning, is indeed deceased, or, as you would say in plain terms, gone to heaven.

Gob. Marry, God forbid! the boy was the very staff of my age, my very prop.

Laun. Do I look like a cudgel or a hovel-post, a staff or a prop? Do you know me, father?

Gob. Alack the day, I know you not, young gentleman: but, I pray you, tell me, is my boy, God rest his soul, alive or dead?

Laun. Do you not know me, father?

Gob. Alack, sir, I am sand-blind; I know you not.

Laun. Nay, indeed, if you had your eyes, you might fail of the knowing me: it is a wise father that knows his own child. Well, old man, I will tell you news of your son: give me your blessing: truth will come to light; murder cannot be hid long; a man's son may, but at the length truth will out.

Gob. Pray you, sir, stand up: I am sure you are not Launcelot, my boy.

Laun. Pray you, let's have no more fooling about it, but give me your blessing: I am Launcelot, your boy that was, your son that is, your child that shall be.

Gob. I cannot think you are my son.

Laun. I know not what I shall think of that: but I am Launcelot, the Jew's man, and I am sure Margery your wife is my mother.

Gob. Her name is Margery, indeed: I'll be sworn, if thou be Launcelot, thou art mine own flesh and blood. Lord worshipped might he be! what a beard hast thou got! thou hast got more hair on thy chin than Dobbin my fill-horse has on his tail.

Laun. It should seem, then, that Dobbin's tail grows backward: I am sure he had more hair of his tail than I have of my face when I last saw him.

Gob. Lord, how art thou changed! How dost thou and

thy master agree ? I have brought him a present. How 'gree
you now ?

Laun. Well, well : but, for mine own part, as I have set
up my rest to run away, so I will not rest till I have run some
ground. My master's a very Jew : give him a present ! give
him a halter : I am famished in his service ; you may tell
every finger I have with my ribs. Father, I am glad you are
come : give me your present to one Master Bassanio, who,
indeed, gives rare new liveries : if I serve not him, I will run
as far as God has any ground. O rare fortune ! here comes
the man : to him, father ; for I am a Jew, if I serve the Jew
any longer.   Act II, Scene ii, ll. 1-120

Fair Jessica shall be my torch-bearer.

Act II, Scene iv, l. 40

How like a younker or a prodigal
The scarfed bark puts from her native bay,
Hugg'd and embraced by the strumpet wind !
How like the prodigal doth she return,
With over-weather'd ribs and ragged sails,
Lean, rent and beggar'd by the strumpet wind !

Act II, Scene vi, ll. 14-19

From the four corners of the earth they come,
To kiss this shrine, this mortal-breathing saint :
The Hyrcanian deserts and the vasty wilds
Of wide Arabia are as throughfares now
For princes to come view fair Portia :
The watery kingdom, whose ambitious head
Spits in the face of heaven, is no bar
To stop the foreign spirits, but they come,
As o'er a brook, to see fair Portia.

Act II, Scene vii, ll. 39-47

Salanio. I never heard a passion so confused,
So strange, outrageous, and so variable,
As the dog Jew did utter in the streets :

' My daughter ! O my ducats ! O my daughter !
Fled with a Christian ! O my Christian ducats !
Justice ! the law ! my ducats, and my daughter !
A sealed bag, two sealed bags of ducats,
Of double ducats, stolen from me by my daughter !
And jewels, two stones, two rich and precious stones,
Stolen by my daughter ! Justice ! find the girl ;
She hath the stones upon her, and the ducats.'
   Salarino. Why, all the boys in Venice follow him,
Crying, his stones, his daughter, and his ducats.

ACT II, Scene viii, ll. 12-24

    Some there be that shadows kiss ;
    Some have but a shadow's bliss.

ACT II, Scene ix, ll. 66-67

I have not seen

So likely an ambassador of love :
A day in April never came so sweet,
To show how costly summer was at hand.

ACT II, Scene ix, ll. 91-94

   Salarino. Why, I am sure, if he forfeit, thou wilt not take
his flesh : what's that good for ?

   Shylock. To bait fish withal : if it will feed nothing else,
it will feed my revenge. He hath disgraced me, and hindered
me half a million ; laughed at my losses, mocked at my gains,
scorned my nation, thwarted my bargains, cooled my friends,
heated mine enemies ; and what's his reason ? I am a Jew.
Hath not a Jew eyes ? hath not a Jew hands, organs, dimensions, senses, affections, passions ? fed with the same food,
hurt with the same weapons, subject to the same diseases,
healed by the same means, warmed and cooled by the same
winter and summer, as a Christian is ? If you prick us, do we
not bleed ? if you tickle us, do we not laugh ? if you poison
us, do we not die ? and if you wrong us, shall we not revenge ?
If we are like you in the rest, we will resemble you in that. If
a Jew wrong a Christian, what is his humility ? Revenge. If a

Christian wrong a Jew, what should his sufferance be by
Christian example? Why, revenge. The villany you teach
me, I will execute, and it shall go hard but I will better the
instruction.   Act III, Scene i, ll. 53-76

Belmont. A room in PORTIA'S *house.*

Enter BASSANIO, PORTIA, GRATIANO, NERISSA,
and Attendants.

   Por. I pray you, tarry: pause a day or two
Before you hazard; for, in choosing wrong,
I lose your company: therefore forbear awhile.
There's something tells me, but it is not love,
I would not lose you; and you know yourself,
Hate counsels not in such a quality.
But lest you should not understand me well,—
And yet a maiden hath no tongue but thought,—
I would detain you here some month or two
Before you venture for me. I could teach you
How to choose right, but I am then forsworn;
So will I never be: so may you miss me;
But if you do, you'll make me wish a sin,
That I had been forsworn. Beshrew your eyes,
They have o'erlook'd me and divided me;
One half of me is yours, the other half yours,
Mine own, I would say; but if mine, then yours,
And so all yours. O, these naughty times
Put bars between the owners and their rights!
And so, though yours, not yours. Prove it so,
Let fortune go to hell for it, not I.
I speak too long; but 'tis to peize the time,
To eke it and to draw it out in length,
To stay you from election.
    Bass.   Let me choose;
For as I am, I live upon the rack.
   Por. Upon the rack, Bassanio! then confess
What treason there is mingled with your love.

Bass. None but that ugly treason of mistrust,
Which makes me fear the enjoying of my love :
There may as well be amity and life
'Tween snow and fire, as treason and my love.

Por. Ay, but I fear you speak upon the rack,
Where men enforced do speak anything.

Bass. Promise me life, and I'll confess the truth.

Por. Well then, confess and live.

Bass. 'Confess' and 'love'
Had been the very sum of my confession :
O happy torment, when my torturer
Doth teach me answers for deliverance !
But let me to my fortune and the caskets.

Por. Away, then ! I am lock'd in one of them :
If you do love me, you will find me out.
Nerissa and the rest, stand all aloof.
Let music sound while he doth make his choice ;
Then, if he lose, he makes a swan-like end,
Fading in music : that the comparison
May stand more proper, my eye shall be the stream
And watery death-bed for him. He may win ;
And what is music then ? Then music is
Even as the flourish when true subjects bow
To a new-crowned monarch : such it is
As are those dulcet sounds in break of day
That creep into the dreaming bridegroom's ear
And summon him to marriage. Now he goes,
With no less presence, but with much more love,
Than young Alcides, when he did redeem
The virgin tribute paid by howling Troy
To the sea-monster : I stand for sacrifice ;
The rest aloof are the Dardanian wives,
With bleared visages, come forth to view
The issue of the exploit. Go, Hercules !
Live thou, I live : with much much more dismay
I view the fight than thou that makest the fray.

Music, whilst BASSANIO *comments on the caskets
to himself.*

SONG.

Tell me where is fancy bred,
   Or in the heart or in the head ?
   How begot, how nourished ?
      Reply, reply.
   It is engender'd in the eyes,
   ' With gazing fed ; and fancy dies
   In the cradle where it lies.
      Let us all ring fancy's knell :
      I'll begin it,—Ding, dong, bell.
All. Ding, dong, bell. . . .

  Bass.   Thou gaudy gold,
Hard food for Midas, I will none of thee ;
Nor none of thee, thou pale and common drudge
'Tween man and man : but thou, thou meagre lead,
Which rather threatenest than dost promise aught,
Thy paleness moves me more than eloquence ;
And here choose I : joy be the consequence !
  Por. [*Aside*] How all the other passions fleet to air,
As doubtful thoughts, and rash-embraced despair,
And shuddering fear, and green-eyed jealousy !
O love,
Be moderate ; allay thy ecstasy ;
In measure rein thy joy ; scant this excess.
I feel too much thy blessing : make it less,
For fear I surfeit.

  Bass.   What find I here ?
                [*Opening the leaden casket.*
Fair Portia's counterfeit ! . . . .
Madam, you have bereft me of all words,
Only my blood speaks to you in my veins ;
And there is such confusion in my powers
As, after some oration fairly spoke

By a beloved prince, there doth appear
Among the buzzing pleased multitude;
Where every something, being blent together,
Turns to a wild of nothing, save of joy,
Express'd and not express'd.

ACT III, Scene ii, ll. 1-72, 100-116, 177-185

We are the Jasons, we have won the fleece.

ACT III, Scene ii, l. 244

Venice. A court of justice.

Enter the DUKE, *the* MAGNIFICOES, ANTONIO, BASSANIO,
GRATIANO, SALERIO, *and others.*

Duke. What, is Antonio here?
Ant. Ready, so please your grace.
Duke. I am sorry for thee: thou art come to answer
A stony adversary, an inhuman wretch
Uncapable of pity, void and empty
From any dram of mercy.
Ant.   I have heard
Your grace hath ta'en great pains to qualify
His rigorous course; but since he stands obdurate
And that no lawful means can carry me
Out of his envy's reach, I do oppose
My patience to his fury, and am arm'd
To suffer, with a quietness of spirit,
The very tyranny and rage of his.
Duke. Go one, and call the Jew into the court.
Saler. He is ready at the door: he comes, my lord.

Enter SHYLOCK.

Duke. Make room, and let him stand before our face.
Shylock, the world thinks, and I think so too,
That thou but lead'st this fashion of thy malice
To the last hour of act; and then 'tis thought
Thou'lt show thy mercy and remorse more strange
Than is thy strange apparent cruelty;

115

And where thou now exact'st the penalty,
Which is a pound of this poor merchant's flesh,
Thou wilt not only loose the forfeiture,
But, touch'd with human gentleness and love,
Forgive a moiety of the principal;
Glancing an eye of pity on his losses,
That have of late so huddled on his back,
Enow to press a royal merchant down
And pluck commiseration of his state
From brassy bosoms and rough hearts of flint,
From stubborn Turks and Tartars, never train'd
To offices of tender courtesy.
We all expect a gentle answer, Jew.

   Shy. I have possess'd your grace of what I purpose;
And by our holy Sabbath have I sworn
To have the due and forfeit of my bond:
If you deny it, let the danger light
Upon your charter and your city's freedom.
You'll ask me, why I rather choose to have
A weight of carrion flesh than to receive
Three thousand ducats: I'll not answer that:
But, say, it is my humour: is it answer'd?
What if my house be troubled with a rat
And I be pleased to give ten thousand ducats
To have it baned? What, are you answer'd yet?
Some men there are love not a gaping pig;
Some, that are mad if they behold a cat;
And others, when the bagpipe sings i' the nose,
Cannot contain their urine: for affection,
Mistress of passion, sways it to the mood
Of what it likes or loathes. Now, for your answer:
As there is no firm reason to be render'd,
Why he cannot abide a gaping pig;
Why he, a harmless necessary cat;
Why he, a woollen bag-pipe; but of force
Must yield to such inevitable shame

As to offend, himself being offended ;
So can I give no reason, nor I will not,
More than a lodged hate and a certain loathing
I bear Antonio, that I follow thus
A losing suit against him. Are you answer'd ?

Bass. This is no answer, thou unfeeling man,
To excuse the current of thy cruelty.

Shy. I am not bound to please thee with my answers.

Bass. Do all men kill the things they do not love ?

Shy. Hates any man the thing he would not kill ?

Bass. Every offence is not a hate at first.

Shy. What, wouldst thou have a serpent sting thee twice ?

Ant. I pray you, think you question with the Jew :
You may as well go stand upon the beach
And bid the main flood bate his usual height ;
You may as well use question with the wolf
Why he hath made the ewe bleat for the lamb ;
You may as well forbid the mountain pines
To wag their high tops and to make no noise,
When they are fretten with the gusts of heaven ;
You may as well do any thing most hard,
As seek to soften that—than which what's harder ?—
His Jewish heart : therefore, I do beseech you,
Make no more offers, use no farther means,
But with all brief and plain conveniency
Let me have judgement and the Jew his will.

Bass. For thy three thousand ducats here is six.

Shy. If every ducat in six thousand ducats
Were in six parts and every part a ducat,
I would not draw them ; I would have my bond.

Duke. How shalt thou hope for mercy, rendering none ?

Shy. What judgement shall I dread, doing no wrong ?
You have among you many a purchased slave,
Which, like your asses and your dogs and mules,

You use in abject and in slavish parts,
Because you bought them : shall I say to you,
Let them be free, marry them to your heirs ?
Why sweat they under burthens ? let their beds
Be made as soft as yours and let their palates
Be season'd with such viands ? You will answer
'The slaves are ours :' so do I answer you :
The pound of flesh, which I demand of him,
Is dearly bought ; 'tis mine and I will have it.
If you deny me, fie upon your law !
There is no force in the decrees of Venice.
I stand for judgement : answer ; shall I have it ?

   Duke. Upon my power I may dismiss this court,
Unless Bellario, a learned doctor,
Whom I have sent for to determine this,
Come here to-day.

   Saler.   My lord, here stays without
A messenger with letters from the doctor,
New come from Padua.

   Duke. Bring us the letters ; call the messenger.

   Bass. Good cheer, Antonio ! What, man, courage yet !
The Jew shall have my flesh, blood, bones and all,
Ere thou shalt lose for me one drop of blood.

   Ant. I am a tainted wether of the flock,
Meetest for death : the weakest kind of fruit
Drops earliest to the ground ; and so let me :
You cannot better be employ'd, Bassanio,
Than to live still and write mine epitaph.

     Enter NERISSA, *dressed like a lawyer's clerk.*

   Duke. Came you from Padua, from Bellario ?
   Ner. From both, my lord. Bellario greets your grace.
                          [*Presenting a letter.*
   Bass. Why dost thou whet thy knife so earnestly ?
   Shy. To cut the forfeiture from that bankrupt there.
   Gra. Not on thy sole, but on thy soul, harsh Jew,

Thou makest thy knife keen ; but no metal can,
No, not the hangman's axe, bear half the keenness
Of thy sharp envy. Can no prayers pierce thee ?

Shy. No, none that thou hast wit enough to make.

Gra. O, be thou damn'd, inexecrable dog !
And for thy life let justice be accused.
Thou almost makest me waver in my faith
To hold opinion with Pythagoras,
That souls of animals infuse themselves
Into the trunks of men : thy currish spirit
Govern'd a wolf, who, hang'd for human slaughter,
Even from the gallows did his fell soul fleet,
And, whilst thou lay'st in thy unhallow'd dam,
Infused itself in thee ; for thy desires
Are wolvish, bloody, starved and ravenous.

Shy. Till thou canst rail the seal from off my bond,
Thou but offend'st thy lungs to speak so loud :
Repair thy wit, good youth, or it will fall
To cureless ruin. I stand here for law.

Duke. This letter from Bellario doth commend
A young and learned doctor to our court.
Where is he ?

Ner.   He attendeth here hard by,
To know your answer, whether you'll admit him.

Duke. With all my heart. Some three or four of you
Go give him courteous conduct to this place.
Meantime the court shall hear Bellario's letter.

Clerk. [*Reads*] Your grace shall understand that at the
receipt of your letter I am very sick : but in the instant that
your messenger came, in loving visitation was with me a
young doctor of Rome ; his name is Balthasar. I acquainted
him with the cause in controversy between the Jew and
Antonio the merchant : we turned o'er many books together :
he is furnished with my opinion ; which, bettered with his
own learning, the greatness whereof I cannot enough commend, comes with him, at my importunity, to fill up your

grace's request in my stead. I beseech you, let his lack of
years be no impediment to let him lack a reverend estimation ;
for I never knew so young a body with so old a head. I leave
him to your gracious acceptance, whose trial shall better
publish his commendation.

Duke. You hear the learn'd Bellario, what he writes :
And here, I take it, is the doctor come.

Enter PORTIA, *dressed like a doctor of laws.*

Give me your hand. Come you from old Bellario ?

Por. I did, my lord.

Duke.　　　　　　　　You are welcome : take your place.
Are you acquainted with the difference
That holds this present question in the court ?

Por. I am informed throughly of the cause.
Which is the merchant here, and which the Jew ?

Duke. Antonio and old Shylock, both stand forth.

Por. Is your name Shylock ?

Shy.　　　　　　　　Shylock is my name.

Por. Of a strange nature is the suit you follow ;
Yet in such rule that the Venetian law
Cannot impugn you as you do proceed.　　　　[*To Antonio.*
You stand within his danger, do you not ?

Ant. Ay, so he says.

Por.　　　　　　　Do you confess the bond ?

Ant. I do.

Por.　　　　Then must the Jew be merciful.

Shy. On what compulsion must I ? tell me that.

Por. The quality of mercy is not strain'd,
It droppeth as the gentle rain from heaven
Upon the place beneath : it is twice blest ;
It blesseth him that gives and him that takes :
'Tis mightiest in the mightiest : it becomes
The throned monarch better than his crown ;
His sceptre shows the force of temporal power,
The attribute to awe and majesty,

Wherein doth sit the dread and fear of kings;
But mercy is above this sceptred sway;
It is enthroned in the hearts of kings,
It is an attribute of God himself;
And earthly power doth then show likest God's
When mercy seasons justice. Therefore, Jew,
Though justice be thy plea, consider this,
That, in the course of justice, none of us
Should see salvation: we do pray for mercy;
And that same prayer doth teach us all to render
The deeds of mercy. I have spoke thus much
To mitigate the justice of thy plea;
Which if thou follow, this strict court of Venice
Must needs give sentence 'gainst the merchant there.

Shy. My deeds upon my head! I crave the law,
The penalty and forfeit of my bond.

Por. Is he not able to discharge the money?

Bass. Yes, here I tender it for him in the court;
Yea, twice the sum: if that will not suffice,
I will be bound to pay it ten times o'er,
On forfeit of my hands, my head, my heart:
If this will not suffice, it must appear
That malice bears down truth. And I beseech you,
Wrest once the law to your authority:
To do a great right, do a little wrong,
And curb this cruel devil of his will.

Por. It must not be; there is no power in Venice
Can alter a decree established:
'Twill be recorded for a precedent,
And many an error by the same example
Will rush into the state: it cannot be.

Shy. A Daniel come to judgement! yea, a Daniel!
O wise young judge, how I do honour thee!

Por. I pray you, let me look upon the bond.

Shy. Here 'tis, most reverend doctor, here it is.

Por. Shylock, there's thrice thy money offer'd thee.

Shy. An oath, an oath, I have an oath in heaven :
Shall I lay perjury upon my soul ?
No, not for Venice.

Por.   Why, this bond is forfeit ;
And lawfully by this the Jew may claim
A pound of flesh, to be by him cut off
Nearest the merchant's heart. Be merciful :
Take thrice thy money ; bid me tear the bond.

Shy. When it is paid according to the tenour.
It doth appear you are a worthy judge ;
You know the law, your exposition
Hath been most sound : I charge you by the law,
Whereof you are a well-deserving pillar,
Proceed to judgement : by my soul I swear
There is no power in the tongue of man
To alter me : I stay here on my bond.

Ant. Most heartily I do beseech the court
To give the judgement.

Por.   Why then, thus it is :
You must prepare your bosom for his knife.

Shy. O noble judge ! O excellent young man !

Por. For the intent and purpose of the law
Hath full relation to the penalty,
Which here appeareth due upon the bond.

Shy. 'Tis very true : O wise and upright judge !
How much more elder art thou than thy looks !

Por. Therefore lay bare your bosom.

Shy.   Ay, his breast :
So says the bond : doth it not, noble judge ?
' Nearest his heart : ' those are the very words.

Por. It is so. Are there balance here to weigh
The flesh ?

Shy.   I have them ready.

Por. Have by some surgeon, Shylock, on your charge,
To stop his wounds, lest he do bleed to death.

Shy. Is it so nominated in the bond ?

Por. It is not so express'd : but what of that ?
'Twere good you do so much for charity.

Shy. I cannot find it ; 'tis not in the bond.

Por. You, merchant, have you any thing to say ?

Ant. But little : I am arm'd and well prepared.
Give me your hand, Bassanio : fare you well !
Grieve not that I am fallen to this for you ;
For herein Fortune shows herself more kind
Than is her custom : it is still her use
To let the wretched man outlive his wealth,
To view with hollow eye and wrinkled brow
An age of poverty ; from which lingering penance
Of such misery doth she cut me off.
Commend me to your honourable wife :
Tell her the process of Antonio's end ;
Say how I loved you, speak me fair in death ;
And, when the tale is told, bid her be judge
Whether Bassanio had not once a love.
Repent but you that you shall lose your friend,
And he repents not that he pays your debt ;
For if the Jew do cut but deep enough,
I'll pay it presently with all my heart.

Bass. Antonio, I am married to a wife
Which is as dear to me as life itself ;
But life itself, my wife, and all the world,
Are not with me esteem'd above thy life :
I would lose all, ay, sacrifice them all
Here to this devil, to deliver you.

Por. Your wife would give you little thanks for
        that,
If she were by, to hear you make the offer.

Gra. I have a wife, whom, I protest, I love :
I would she were in heaven, so she could
Entreat some power to change this currish Jew.

Ner. 'Tis well you offer it behind her back ;
The wish would make else an unquiet house.

Shy. These be the Christian husbands. I have a
    daughter ;
Would any of the stock of Barrabas
Had been her husband rather than a Christian ! [*Aside.*
We trifle time : I pray thee, pursue sentence.

Por. A pound of that same merchant's flesh is thine :
The court awards it, and the law doth give it.

Shy. Most rightful judge !

Por. And you must cut this flesh from off his breast :
The law allows it, and the court awards it.

Shy. Most learned judge ! A sentence ! Come, pre-
    pare !

Por. Tarry a little ; there is something else.
This bond doth give thee here no jot of blood ;
The words expressly are ' a pound of flesh : '
Take then thy bond, take thou thy pound of flesh ;
But, in the cutting it, if thou dost shed
One drop of Christian blood, thy lands and goods
Are, by the laws of Venice, confiscate
Unto the state of Venice.

Gra. O upright judge ! Mark, Jew : O learned judge !

Shy. Is that the law ?

Por.   Thyself shalt see the act :
For, as thou urgest justice, be assured
Thou shalt have justice, more than thou desirest.

Gra. O learned judge ! Mark, Jew : a learned judge !

Shy. I take this offer, then ; pay the bond thrice
And let the Christian go.

Bass.   Here is the money.

Por. Soft !
The Jew shall have all justice ; soft ! no haste :
He shall have nothing but the penalty.

Gra. O Jew ! an upright judge, a learned judge !

Por. Therefore prepare thee to cut off the flesh.
Shed thou no blood, nor cut thou less nor more
But just a pound of flesh : if thou cut'st more

Or less than a just pound, be it but so much
As makes it light or heavy in the substance,
Or the division of the twentieth part
Of one poor scruple, nay, if the scale do turn
But in the estimation of a hair,
Thou diest and all thy goods are confiscate.

Gra. A second Daniel, a Daniel, Jew !
Now, infidel, I have you on the hip.

Por. Why doth the Jew pause ? take thy forfeiture.

Shy. Give me my principal, and let me go.

Bass. I have it ready for thee ; here it is.

Por. He hath refused it in the open court :
He shall have merely justice and his bond.

Gra. A Daniel, still say I, a second Daniel !
I thank thee, Jew, for teaching me that word.

Shy. Shall I not have barely my principal ?

Por. Thou shalt have nothing but the forfeiture,
To be so taken at thy peril, Jew.

Shy. Why, then the devil give him good of it !
I'll stay no longer question.

Por.   Tarry, Jew :
The law hath yet another hold on you.
It is enacted in the laws of Venice,
If it be proved against an alien
That by direct or indirect attempts
He seek the life of any citizen,
The party 'gainst the which he doth contrive
Shall seize one half his goods ; the other half
Comes to the privy coffer of the state ;
And the offender's life lies in the mercy
Of the duke only, 'gainst all other voice.
In which predicament, I say, thou stand'st !
For it appears, by manifest proceeding,
That indirectly and directly too
Thou hast contrived against the very life
Of the defendant ; and thou hast incurr'd

The danger formerly by me rehearsed.
Down therefore and beg mercy of the duke.

Gra. Beg that thou mayst have leave to hang thyself :
And yet, thy wealth being forfeit to the state,
Thou hast not left the value of a cord ;
Therefore thou must be hang'd at the state's charge.

Duke. That thou shalt see the difference of our spirits,
I pardon thee thy life before thou ask it :
For half thy wealth, it is Antonio's ;
The other half comes to the general state,
Which humbleness may drive unto a fine.

Por. Ay, for the state, not for Antonio.

Shy. Nay, take my life and all ; pardon not that :
You take my house when you do take the prop
That doth sustain my house ; you take my life
When you do take the means whereby I live.

Por. What mercy can you render him, Antonio ?

Gra. A halter gratis ; nothing else, for God's sake.

Ant. So please my lord the duke and all the court
To quit the fine for one half of his goods,
I am content ; so he will let me have
The other half in use, to render it,
Upon his death, unto the gentleman
That lately stole his daughter :
Two things provided more, that, for this favour,
He presently become a Christian ;
The other, that he do record a gift,
Here in the court, of all he dies possess'd,
Unto his son Lorenzo and his daughter.

Duke. He shall do this, or else I do recant
The pardon that I late pronounced here.

Por. Art thou contented, Jew ? what dost thou say ?

Shy. I am content.

Por.   Clerk, draw a deed of gift.

Shy. I pray you, give me leave to go from hence ;
I am not well : send the deed after me,

And I will sign it.

Duke.   Get thee gone, but do it.

Gra. In christening shalt thou have two godfathers :
Had I been judge, thou shouldst have had ten more,
To bring thee to the gallows, not the font. [*Exit Shylock.*

ACT IV, Scene i, ll. 1-400.

Belmont. Avenue to PORTIA'S *house.*

Enter LORENZO *and* JESSICA.

Lor. The moon shines bright : in such a night as this,
When the sweet wind did gently kiss the trees
And they did make no noise, in such a night
Troilus methinks mounted the Troyan walls
And sigh'd his soul toward the Grecian tents,
Where Cressid lay that night.

Jes.   In such a night
Did Thisbe fearfully o'ertrip the dew
And saw the lion's shadow ere himself
And ran dismay'd away.

Lor.   In such a night
Stood Dido with a willow in her hand
Upon the wild sea banks and waft her love
To come again to Carthage.

Jes.   In such a night
Medea gather'd the enchanted herbs
That did renew old Æson.

Lor.   In such a night
Did Jessica steal from the wealthy Jew
And with an unthrift love did run from Venice
As far as Belmont.

Jes.   In such a night
Did young Lorenzo swear he loved her well,
Stealing her soul with many vows of faith
And ne'er a true one.

Lor.   In such a night
Did pretty Jessica, like a little shrew,

Slander her love, and he forgave it her.

Jes. I would out-night you, did no body come ;
But, hark, I hear the footing of a man.

Enter STEPHANO.

Lor. Who comes so fast in silence of the night ?
Steph. A friend.
Lor. A friend ! what friend ? your name, I pray you,
  friend ?
Steph. Stephano is my name ; and I bring word
My mistress will before the break of day
Be here at Belmont : she doth stray about
By holy crosses, where she kneels and prays
For happy wedlock hours.

  Lor.   Who comes with her ?

  Steph. None but a holy hermit and her maid. . . .

  Lor. Sweet soul, let's in, and there expect their
    coming.

And yet no matter : why should we go in ?
My friend Stephano, signify, I pray you,
Within the house, your mistress is at hand ;
And bring your music forth into the air. [*Exit Stephano.*
How sweet the moonlight sleeps upon this bank !
Here will we sit and let the sounds of music
Creep in our ears : soft stillness and the night
Become the touches of sweet harmony.
Sit, Jessica. Look how the floor of heaven
Is thick inlaid with patines of bright gold :
There's not the smallest orb which thou behold'st
But in his motion like an angel sings,
Still quiring to the young-eyed cherubins ;
Such harmony is in immortal souls ;
But whilst this muddy vesture of decay
Doth grossly close it in, we cannot hear it.

Enter Musicians.

Come, ho ! and wake Diana with a hymn :

With sweetest touches pierce your mistress' ear
And draw her home with music.   [*Music*.

  Jes. I am never merry when I hear sweet music.

  Lor. The reason is, your spirits are attentive :
For do but note a wild and wanton herd,
Or race of youthful and unhandled colts,
Fetching mad bounds, bellowing and neighing loud,
Which is the hot condition of their blood ;
If they but hear perchance a trumpet sound,
Or any air of music touch their ears,
You shall perceive them make a mutual stand,
Their savage eyes turn'd to a modest gaze
By the sweet power of music : therefore the poet
Did feign that Orpheus drew trees, stones and floods ;
Since nought so stockish, hard and full of rage,
But music for the time doth change his nature.
The man that hath no music in himself,
Nor is not moved with concord of sweet sounds,
Is fit for treasons, stratagems and spoils ;
The motions of his spirit are dull as night
And his affections dark as Erebus :
Let no such man be trusted.   Mark the music.

        Enter PORTIA *and* NERISSA.

  Por. That light we see is burning in my hall.
How far that little candle throws his beams !
So shines a good deed in a naughty world.

  Ner. When the moon shone, we did not see the candle.

  Por. So doth the greater glory dim the less :
A substitute shines brightly as a king
Until a king be by, and then his state
Empties itself, as doth an inland brook
Into the main of waters.   Music ! hark !

  Ner. It is your music, madam, of the house.

  Por. Nothing is good, I see, without respect :
Methinks it sounds much sweeter than by day.

Ner. Silence bestows that virtue on it, madam.

Por. The crow doth sing as sweetly as the lark
When neither is attended, and I think
The nightingale, if she should sing by day,
When every goose is cackling, would be thought
No better a musician than the wren.
How many things by season season'd are
To their right praise and true perfection !
Peace, ho ! the moon sleeps with Endymion
And would not be awaked.   [*Music ceases.*

Lor.   That is the voice,
Or I am much deceived, of Portia.

Por. He knows me as the blind man knows the cuckoo,
By the bad voice.

Lor.   Dear lady, welcome home.

Por. We have been praying for our husbands' healths,
Which speed, we hope, the better for our words.
Are they return'd ?

Lor.   Madam, they are not yet ;
But there is come a messenger before,
To signify their coming.

Por.   Go in, Nerissa ;
Give order to my servants that they take
No note at all of our being absent hence ;
Nor you, Lorenzo ; Jessica, nor you.   [*A tucket sounds.*

Lor. Your husband is at hand ; I hear his trumpet :
We are no tell-tales, madam ! fear you not.

Por. This night methinks is but the daylight sick ;
It looks a little paler : 'tis a day,
Such as the day is when the sun is hid.

ACT V, Scene i, ll. 1-33, 49-126

NOON

1 HENRY IV
2 HENRY IV
HENRY V
THE MERRY WIVES OF WINDSOR
MUCH ADO ABOUT NOTHING
AS YOU LIKE IT
TWELFTH NIGHT

The First Part of

King Henry the Fourth

King Henry. Therefore, friends,
As far as to the sepulchre of Christ,
Whose soldier now, under whose blessed cross
We are impressed and engaged to fight,
Forthwith a power of English shall we levy ;
Whose arms were moulded in their mothers' womb
To chase these pagans in those holy fields
Over whose acres walk'd those blessed feet
Which fourteen hundred years ago were nail'd
For our advantage on the bitter cross.

ACT I, Scene i, ll. 18-27

London. An apartment of the Prince's.

Enter the PRINCE OF WALES *and* FALSTAFF.

Fal. Now, Hal, what time of day is it, lad ?

Prince. Thou art so fat-witted, with drinking of old sack
and unbuttoning thee after supper and sleeping upon benches
after noon, that thou hast forgotten to demand that truly which
thou wouldst truly know. What a devil hast thou to do with
the time of the day ? Unless hours were cups of sack and
minutes capons and clocks the tongues of bawds and dials the
signs of leaping-houses and the blessed sun himself a fair hot
wench in flame-coloured taffeta, I see not reason why thou
shouldst be so superfluous to demand the time of the day.

Fal. Indeed, you come near me now, Hal ; for we that
take purses go by the moon and the seven stars, and not by
Phœbus, he, ' that wandering knight so fair.' And, I prithee,
sweet wag, when thou art king, as, God save thy grace,—
majesty I should say, for grace thou wilt have none,—

Prince. What, none ?

Fal. No, by my troth, not so much as will serve to be prologue to an egg and butter.

Prince. Well, how then ? come, roundly, roundly.

Fal. Marry, then, sweet wag, when thou art king, let not us
that are squires of the night's body be called thieves of the
day's beauty : let us be Diana's foresters, gentlemen of the
shade, minions of the moon ; and let men say we be men of
good government, being governed, as the sea is, by our noble
and chaste mistress the moon, under whose countenance we
steal.

Prince. Thou sayest well, and it holds well too ; for the
fortune of us that are the moon's men doth ebb and flow like
the sea, being governed, as the sea is, by the moon. As, for
proof, now : a purse of gold most resolutely snatched on
Monday night and most dissolutely spent on Tuesday morning ;
got with swearing ' Lay by ' and spent with crying ' Bring in ; '
now in as low an ebb as the foot of the ladder and by and by
in as high a flow as the ridge of the gallows.

Fal. By the Lord, thou sayest true, lad. And is not my
hostess of the tavern a most sweet wench ?

Prince. As the honey of Hybla, my old lad of the castle.
And is not a buff jerkin a most sweet robe of durance ?

Fal. How now, how now, mad wag ! what, in thy quips and
thy quiddities ? what a plague have I to do with a buff jerkin ?

Prince. Why, what a pox have I to do with my hostess of
the tavern ?

Fal. Well, thou hast called her to a reckoning many a time
and oft.

Prince. Did I ever call for thee to pay thy part ?

Fal. No ; I'll give thee thy due, thou hast paid all there.

Prince. Yea, and elsewhere, so far as my coin would
stretch ; and where it would not, I have used my credit.

Fal. Yea, and so used it that, were it not here apparent
that thou art heir apparent—But, I prithee, sweet wag, shall
there be gallows standing in England when thou art king ?

and resolution thus fobbed as it is with the rusty curb of old father antic the law ? Do not thou, when thou art king, hang a thief.

Prince. No ; thou shalt.

Fal. Shall I ? O rare ! By the Lord, I'll be a brave judge.

Prince. Thou judgest false already : I mean, thou shalt have the hanging of the thieves and so become a rare hang-man.

Fal. Well, Hal, well ; and in some sort it jumps with my humour as well as waiting in the court, I can tell you.

Prince. For obtaining of suits ?

Fal. Yea, for obtaining of suits, whereof the hangman hath no lean wardrobe. 'Sblood, I am as melancholy as a gib cat or a lugged bear.

Prince. Or an old lion, or a lover's lute.

Fal. Yea, or the drone of a Lincolnshire bagpipe.

Prince. What sayest thou to a hare, or the melancholy of Moor-ditch ?

Fal. Thou hast the most unsavoury similes and art indeed the most comparative, rascalliest, sweet young prince. But, Hal, I prithee, trouble me no more with vanity. I would to God thou and I knew where a commodity of good names were to be bought. An old lord of the council rated me the other day in the street about you, sir, but I marked him not ; and yet he talked very wisely, but I regarded him not ; and yet he talked wisely, and in the street too.

Prince. Thou didst well ; for wisdom cries out in the streets, and no man regards it.

Fal. O, thou hast damnable iteration and art indeed able to corrupt a saint. Thou hast done much harm upon me, Hal ; God forgive thee for it ! Before I knew thee, Hal, I knew nothing ; and now am I, if a man should speak truly, little better than one of the wicked. I must give over this life, and I will give it over : by the Lord, an I do not, I am a villain : I'll be damned for never a king's son in Christendom.

Prince. Where shall we take a purse to-morrow, Jack ?

Fal. 'Zounds, where thou wilt, lad; I'll make one; an I do not, call me villain and baffle me.

Prince. I see a good amendment of life in thee; from praying to purse-taking.

Fal. Why, Hal, 'tis my vocation, Hal; 'tis no sin for a man to labour in his vocation.

Enter POINS.

Poins! Now shall we know if Gadshill have set a match. O, if men were to be saved by merit, what hole in hell were hot enough for him? This is the most omnipotent villain that ever cried ' Stand ' to a true man.

Prince. Good morrow, Ned.

Poins. Good morrow, sweet Hal. What says Monsieur Remorse? what says Sir John Sack and Sugar? Jack! how agrees the devil and thee about thy soul, that thou soldest him on Good-Friday last for a cup of Madeira and a cold capon's leg?

Prince. Sir John stands to his word, the devil shall have his bargain; for he was never yet a breaker of proverbs: he will give the devil his due.

Poins. Then art thou damned for keeping thy word with the devil.

Prince. Else he had been damned for cozening the devil.

Poins. But, my lads, my lads, to-morrow morning, by four o'clock, early at Gadshill! there are pilgrims going to Canterbury with rich offerings, and traders riding to London with fat purses: I have vizards for you all; you have horses for yourselves: Gadshill lies to-night in Rochester: I have bespoke supper to-morrow night in Eastcheap: we may do it as secure as sleep. If you will go, I will stuff your purses full of crowns; if you will not, tarry at home and be hanged.

Fal. Hear ye, Yedward; if I tarry at home and go not, I'll hang you for going.

Poins. You will, chops?

Fal. Hal, wilt thou make one?

Prince. Who, I rob? I a thief? not I, by my faith.

Fal. There's neither honesty, manhood, nor good fellow-ship in thee, nor thou camest not of the blood royal, if thou darest not stand for ten shillings.

Prince. Well then, once in my days I'll be a madcap.

Fal. Why, that's well said.

Prince. Well, come what will, I'll tarry at home.

Fal. By the Lord, I'll be a traitor then, when thou art king.

Prince. I care not.

Poins. Sir John, I prithee, leave the prince and me alone: I will lay him down such reasons for this adventure that he shall go.

Fal. Well, God give thee the spirit of persuasion and him the ears of profiting, that what thou speakest may move and what he hears may be believed, that the true prince may, for recreation sake, prove a false thief; for the poor abuses of the time want countenance. Farewell: you shall find me in Eastcheap.

Prince. Farewell, thou latter spring! farewell, All-hallown summer!   *[Exit Falstaff.*

Poins. Now, my good sweet honey lord, ride with us to-morrow: I have a jest to execute that I cannot manage alone. Falstaff, Bardolph, Peto and Gadshill shall rob those men that we have already waylaid; yourself and I will not be there; and when they have the booty, if you and I do not rob them, cut this head off from my shoulders.

Prince. How shall we part with them in setting forth?

Poins. Why, we will set forth before or after them, and appoint them a place of meeting, wherein it is at our pleasure to fail, and then will they adventure upon the exploit themselves; which they shall have no sooner achieved, but we'll set upon them.

Prince. Yea, but 'tis like that they will know us by our horses, by our habits and by every other appointment, to be ourselves.

Poins. Tut! our horses they shall not see; I'll tie them in the wood ; our vizards we will change after we leave them : and, sirrah, I have cases of buckram for the nonce, to immask our noted outward garments.

Prince. Yea, but I doubt they will be too hard for us.

Poins. Well, for two of them, I know them to be as true-bred cowards as ever turned back ; and for the third, if he fight longer than he sees reason, I'll forswear arms. The virtue of this jest will be, the incomprehensible lies that this same fat rogue will tell us when we meet at supper : how thirty, at least, he fought with ; what wards, what blows, what extremities he endured ; and in the reproof of this lies the jest.

Prince. Well, I'll go with thee : provide us all things necessary and meet me to-morrow night in Eastcheap ; there I'll sup. Farewell.

Poins. Farewell, my lord. [*Exit.*

ACT I, Scene ii, ll. 1-217

Hotspur. My liege, I did deny no prisoners.
But I remember, when the fight was done,
When I was dry with rage and extreme toil,
Breathless and faint, leaning upon my sword,
Came there a certain lord, neat, and trimly dress'd,
Fresh as a bridegroom ; and his chin new reap'd
Show'd like a stubble-land at harvest-home ;
He was perfumed like a milliner ;
And 'twixt his finger and his thumb he held
A pouncet-box, which ever and anon
He gave his nose and took't away again ;
Who therewith angry, when it next came there,
Took it in snuff ; and still he smiled and talk'd,
And as the soldiers bore dead bodies by,
He call'd them untaught knaves, unmannerly,
To bring a slovenly unhandsome corse
Betwixt the wind and his nobility.
With many holiday and lady terms
He question'd me ; amongst the rest, demanded

My prisoners in your majesty's behalf.
I then, all smarting with my wounds being cold,
To be so pester'd with a popinjay,
Out of my grief and my impatience,
Answer'd neglectingly I know not what,
He should, or he should not ; for he made me mad
To see him shine so brisk and smell so sweet
And talk so like a waiting-gentlewoman
Of guns and drums and wounds,—God save the mark !—
And telling me the sovereign'st thing on earth
Was parmaceti for an inward bruise ;
And that it was great pity, so it was,
This villanous salt-petre should be digg'd
Out of the bowels of the harmless earth,
Which many a good tall fellow had destroy'd
So cowardly ; and but for these vile guns,
He would himself have been a soldier.
This bald unjointed chat of his, my lord,
I answer'd indirectly, as I said ;
And I beseech you, let not his report
Come current for an accusation
Betwixt my love and your high majesty. . . .
    King. Send us your prisoners, or you will hear of it.
                   [Exeunt King Henry and train.
    Hot. An if the devil come and roar for them,
I will not send them.   ACT I, Scene iii, ll. 29-69, 124-126

    Worcester. I'll read you matter deep and dangerous,
As full of peril and adventurous spirit
As to o'er-walk a current roaring loud
On the unsteadfast footing of a spear.
    Hotspur. If he fall in, good night ! or sink or swim :
Send danger from the east unto the west,
So honour cross it from the north to south,
And let them grapple : O, the blood more stirs
To rouse a lion than to start a hare ! . . .

139

By heaven, methinks it were an easy leap,
To pluck bright honour from the pale-faced moon,
Or dive into the bottom of the deep,
Where fathom-line could never touch the ground,
And pluck up drowned honour by the locks ;
So he that doth redeem her thence might wear
Without corrival all her dignities.

ACT I, Scene iii, ll. 190-198, 201-207

Rochester. An inn yard.

Enter a Carrier *with a lantern in his hand.*

First Car. Heigh-ho ! an it be not four by the day, I'll be hanged : Charles' wain is over the new chimney, and yet our horse not packed. What, ostler !

Ost. [*Within*] Anon, anon.

First Car. I prithee, Tom, beat Cut's saddle, put a few flocks in the point ; poor jade, is wrung in the withers out of all cess.

Enter another Carrier.

Sec. Car. Peas and beans are as dank here as a dog, and that is the next way to give poor jades the bots : this house is turned upside down since Robin Ostler died.

First Car. Poor fellow, never joyed since the price of oats rose ; it was the death of him.

Sec. Car. I think this be the most villanous house in all London road for fleas : I am stung like a tench.

First Car. Like a tench ! by the mass, there is ne'er a king christen could be better bit than I have been since the first cock.

Sec. Car. Why, they will allow us ne'er a jordan, and then we leak in your chimney ; and your chamber-lie breeds fleas like a loach.

First Car. What, ostler ! come away and be hanged ! come away.

Sec. Car. I have a gammon of bacon and two razes of ginger, to be delivered as far as Charing-cross.

First Car. God's body! the turkeys in my pannier are quite starved. What, ostler! A plague on thee! hast thou never an eye in thy head? canst not hear? An 'twere not as good deed as drink, to break the pate on thee, I am a very villain. Come, and be hanged! hast no faith in thee?

ACT II, Scene i, ll. 1-35

The highway, near Gadshill.

Enter PRINCE HENRY *and* POINS.

Poins. Come, shelter, shelter: I have removed Falstaff's horse, and he frets like a gummed velvet.

Prince. Stand close.

Enter FALSTAFF.

Fal. Poins! Poins, and be hanged! Poins!

Prince. Peace, ye fat-kidneyed rascal! what a brawling dost thou keep!

Fal. Where's Poins, Hal?

Prince. He is walked up to the top of the hill: I'll go seek him.

Fal. I am accursed to rob in that thief's company: the rascal hath removed my horse, and tied him I know not where. If I travel but four foot by the squier further afoot, I shall break my wind. Well, I doubt not but to die a fair death for all this, if I 'scape hanging for killing that rogue. I have forsworn his company hourly any time this two and twenty years, and yet I am bewitched with the rogue's company. If the rascal have not given me medicines to make me love him, I'll be hanged: it could not be else; I have drunk medicines. Poins! Hal! a plague upon you both! Bardolph! Peto! I'll starve ere I'll rob a foot further. An 'twere not as good a deed as drink, to turn true man and to leave these rogues, I am the veriest varlet that ever chewed with a tooth. Eight yards of uneven ground is threescore and ten miles afoot with me; and the stony-hearted villains know it well enough: a plague upon it when thieves cannot be true one to another! [*They*

141

whistle.] Whew! A plague upon you all! Give me my horse, you rogues; give me my horse, and be hanged!

Prince. Peace, ye fat-guts! lie down; lay thine ear close to the ground and list if thou canst hear the tread of travellers.

Fal. Have you any levers to lift me up again, being down? 'Sblood, I'll not bear mine own flesh so far afoot again for all the coin in thy father's exchequer. What a plague mean ye to colt me thus?

Prince. Thou liest; thou art not colted, thou art un-colted.

Fal. I prithee, good Prince Hal, help me to my horse, good king's son.

Prince. Out, ye rogue! shall I be your ostler?

Fal. Go hang thyself in thine own heir-apparent garters! If I be ta'en, I'll peach for this. An I have not ballads made on you all and sung to filthy tunes, let a cup of sack be my poison: when a jest is so forward, and afoot too! I hate it.

Enter GADSHILL, BARDOLPH *and* PETO *with him.*

Gads. Stand.

Fal. So I do, against my will.

Poins. O, 'tis our setter: I know his voice. Bardolph, what news?

Bard. Case ye, case ye; on with your vizards: there's money of the king's coming down the hill; 'tis going to the king's exchequer.

Fal. You lie, ye rogue; 'tis going to the king's tavern.

Gads. There's enough to make us all.

Fal. To be hanged.

Prince. Sirs, you four shall front them in the narrow lane; Ned Poins and I will walk lower: if they 'scape from your encounter, then they light on us.

Peto. How many be there of them?

Gads. Some eight or ten.

Fal. 'Zounds, will they not rob us?

Prince. What, a coward, Sir John Paunch?

Fal. Indeed, I am not John of Gaunt, your grandfather; but yet no coward, Hal.

Prince. Well, we leave that to the proof.

Poins. Sirrah Jack, thy horse stands behind the hedge: when thou needest him, there thou shalt find him. Farewell, and stand fast.

Fal. Now cannot I strike him, if I should be hanged.

Prince. Ned, where are our disguises?

Poins. Here, hard by: stand close.

[*Exeunt Prince and Poins.*

Fal. Now, my masters, happy man be his dole, say I: every man to his business.

Enter the Travellers.

First Trav. Come, neighbour: the boy shall lead our horses down the hill; we'll walk afoot awhile, and ease our legs.

Thieves. Stand!

Travellers. Jesus bless us!

Fal. Strike; down with them; cut the villains' throats: ah! whoreson caterpillars! bacon-fed knaves! they hate us youth: down with them: fleece them.

Travellers. O, we are undone, both we and ours for ever!

Fal. Hang ye, gorbellied knaves, are ye undone? No, ye fat chuffs; I would your store were here! On, bacons, on! What, ye knaves! young men must live. You are grandjurors, are ye? we'll jure ye, 'faith.

[*Here they rob them and bind them. Exeunt.*

Re-enter PRINCE HENRY *and* POINS.

Prince. The thieves have bound the true men. Now could thou and I rob the thieves and go merrily to London, it would be argument for a week, laughter for a month and a good jest for ever.

Poins. Stand close; I hear them coming.

Enter the Thieves again.

Fal. Come, my masters, let us share, and then to horse

before day. An the Prince and Poins be not two arrant cowards, there's no equity stirring : there's no more valour in that Poins than in a wild-duck.

Prince. Your money !

Poins. Villains !

[*As they are sharing, the Prince and Poins set upon them ; they all run away ; and Falstaff, after a blow or two, runs away too, leaving the booty behind them.*]

Prince. Got with much ease. Now merrily to horse :
The thieves are all scatter'd and possess'd with fear
So strongly that they dare not meet each other ;
Each takes his fellow for an officer.
Away, good Ned. Falstaff sweats to death,
And lards the lean earth as he walks along :
Were 't not for laughing, I should pity him.

Poins. How the rogue roar'd !

ACT II, Scene ii, ll. 1-118

The Boar's-Head Tavern, Eastcheap.

Prince. Sirrah, Falstaff and the rest of the thieves are at the door : shall we be merry ?

Poins. As merry as crickets, my lad. But hark ye ; what cunning match have you made with this jest of the drawer ? come, what's the issue ?

Prince. I am now of all humours that have showed themselves humours since the old days of goodman Adam to the pupil age of this present twelve o'clock at midnight.

Enter FRANCIS.

What's o'clock, Francis ?

Fran. Anon, anon, sir. [*Exit*.

Prince. That ever this fellow should have fewer words than a parrot, and yet the son of a woman ! His industry is up-stairs and down-stairs ; his eloquence the parcel of a reckoning. I am not yet of Percy's mind, the Hotspur of the north ; he that kills me some six or seven dozen of Scots at a breakfast, washes his hands, and says to his wife ' Fie upon this quiet life ! I want work.' ' O my sweet Harry,' says she, ' how many hast thou killed to-day ? ' ' Give my roan horse a drench,' says he ; and answers ' Some fourteen,' an hour after ; ' a trifle, a trifle.' I prithee, call in Falstaff : I'll play Percy, and that damned brawn shall play Dame Mortimer his wife. ' Rivo ! ' says the drunkard. Call in ribs, call in tallow.

Enter FALSTAFF, GADSHILL, BARDOLPH, *and* PETO ;
FRANCIS *following with wine.*

Poins. Welcome, Jack : where hast thou been ?

Fal. A plague of all cowards, I say, and a vengeance too ! marry, and amen ! Give me a cup of sack, boy. Ere I lead this life long, I'll sew nether stocks and mend them and foot them too. A plague of all cowards ! Give me a cup of sack, rogue. Is there no virtue extant ?   [*He drinks.*

Prince. Didst thou never see Titan kiss a dish of butter ? pitiful-hearted Titan, that melted at the sweet tale of the sun's ! if thou didst, then behold that compound.

Fal. You rogue, here's lime in this sack too : there is nothing but roguery to be found in villanous man : yet a coward is worse than a cup of sack with lime in it. A villanous coward ! Go thy ways, old Jack ; die when thou wilt, if manhood, good manhood, be not forgot upon the face of the earth, then am I a shotten herring. There live not three good men unhanged in England ; and one of them is fat and grows old : God help the while ! a bad world, I say. I would I were a weaver ; I could sing psalms or any thing. A plague of all cowards, I say still.

Prince. How now, wool-sack ! what mutter you ?

Fal. A king's son ! If I do not beat thee out of thy kingdom with a dagger of lath, and drive all thy subjects afore thee like a flock of wild-geese, I'll never wear hair on my face more. You Prince of Wales !

Prince. Why, you whoreson round man, what's the matter ?

Fal. Are not you a coward ? answer me to that : and Poins there ?

Poins. 'Zounds, ye fat paunch, an ye call me coward, by the Lord, I'll stab thee.

Fal. I call thee coward! I'll see thee damned ere I call thee coward: but I would give a thousand pound I could run as fast as thou canst. You are straight enough in the shoulders, you care not who sees your back: call you that backing of your friends? A plague upon such backing! give me them that will face me. Give me a cup of sack: I am a rogue, if I drunk to-day.

Prince. O villain! thy lips are scarce wiped since thou drunkest last.

Fal. All's one for that. [*He drinks.*] A plague of all cowards, still say I.

Prince. What's the matter?

Fal. What's the matter! there be four of us here have ta'en a thousand pound this day morning.

Prince. Where is it, Jack? where is it?

Fal. Where is it! taken from us it is: a hundred upon poor four of us.

Prince. What, a hundred, man?

Fal. I am a rogue, if I were not at half-sword with a dozen of them two hours together. I have 'scaped by miracle. I am eight times thrust through the doublet, four through the hose; my buckler cut through and through; my sword hacked like a hand-saw—ecce signum! I never dealt better since I was a man: all would not do. A plague of all cowards! Let them speak: if they speak more or less than truth, they are villains and the sons of darkness.

Prince. Speak, sirs; how was it?

Gads. We four set upon some dozen—

Fal. Sixteen at least, my lord.

Gads. And bound them.

Peto. No, no, they were not bound.

Fal. You rogue, they were bound, every man of them; or I am a Jew else, an Ebrew Jew.

Gads. As we were sharing, some six or seven fresh men set upon us—

Fal. And unbound the rest, and then come in the other.

Prince. What, fought you with them all?

Fal. All! I know not what you call all; but if I fought not with fifty of them, I am a bunch of radish: if there were not two or three and fifty upon poor old Jack, then am I no two-legged creature.

Prince. Pray God you have not murdered some of them.

Fal. Nay, that's past praying for: I have peppered two of them; two I am sure I have paid, two rogues in buckram suits. I tell thee what, Hal, if I tell thee a lie, spit in my face, call me horse. Thou knowest my old ward; here I lay, and thus I bore my point. Four rogues in buckram let drive at me—

Prince. What, four? thou saidst but two even now.

Fal. Four, Hal; I told thee four.

Poins. Ay, ay, he said four.

Fal. These four came all a-front, and mainly thrust at me. I made me no more ado but took all their seven points in my target, thus.

Prince. Seven? why, there were but four even now.

Fal. In buckram?

Poins. Ay, four, in buckram suits.

Fal. Seven, by these hilts, or I am a villain else.

Prince. Prithee, let him alone; we shall have more anon.

Fal. Dost thou hear me, Hal?

Prince. Ay, and mark thee too, Jack.

Fal. Do so, for it is worth the listening to. These nine in buckram that I told thee of—

Prince. So, two more already.

Fal. Their points being broken,—

Poins. Down fell their hose.

Fal. Began to give me ground: but I followed me close, came in foot and hand; and with a thought seven of the eleven I paid.

Prince. O monstrous! eleven buckram men grown out of two!

Fal. But, as the devil would have it, three misbegotten knaves in Kendal green came at my back, and let drive at me; for it was so dark, Hal, that thou couldst not see thy hand.

Prince. These lies are like their father that begets them; gross as a mountain, open, palpable. Why, thou clay-brained guts, thou knotty-pated fool, thou whoreson, obscene, greasy tallow-catch,—

Fal. What, art thou mad? art thou mad? is not the truth the truth?

Prince. Why, how couldst thou know these men in Kendal green, when it was so dark thou couldst not see thy hand? come, tell us your reason: what sayest thou to this?

Poins. Come, your reason, Jack, your reason.

Fal. What, upon compulsion? 'Zounds, an I were at the strappado, or all the racks in the world, I would not tell you on compulsion. Give you a reason on compulsion! if reasons were as plentiful as blackberries, I would give no man a reason upon compulsion, I.

Prince. I'll be no longer guilty of this sin; this sanguine coward, this bed-presser, this horse-back-breaker, this huge hill of flesh,—

Fal. 'Sblood, you starveling, you elf-skin, you dried neat's tongue, you bull's pizzle, you stock-fish! O for breath to utter what is like thee! you tailor's-yard, you sheath, you bow-case, you vile standing-tuck,—

Prince. Well, breathe awhile, and then to it again: and when thou hast tired thyself in base comparisons, hear me speak but this.

Poins. Mark, Jack.

Prince. We two saw you four set on four and bound them, and were masters of their wealth. Mark now, how a plain tale shall put you down. Then did we two set on you four; and, with a word, out-faced you from your prize, and have it; yea, and can show it you here in the house: and, Falstaff, you carried your guts away as nimbly, with as quick dexterity, and roared for mercy and still run and roared, as ever I heard bull-calf. What a slave art thou, to hack thy sword as thou hast done, and then say it was in fight! What trick, what device, what starting-hole, canst thou now find out to hide thee from this open and apparent shame?

Poins. Come, let's hear, Jack; what trick hast thou now?

Fal. By the Lord, I knew ye as well as he that made ye. Why, hear you, my masters: was it for me to kill the heir-apparent? should I turn upon the true prince? why, thou knowest I am as valiant as Hercules: but beware instinct; the lion will not touch the true prince. Instinct is a great matter; I was now a coward on instinct. I shall think the better of myself and thee during my life; I for a valiant lion, and thou for a true prince. But, by the Lord, lads, I am glad you have the money. Hostess, clap to the doors: watch to-night, pray to-morrow. Gallants, lads, boys, hearts of gold, all the titles of good fellowship come to you! What, shall we be merry? shall we have a play extempore?

Prince. Content; and the argument shall be thy running away.

Fal. Ah, no more of that, Hal, an thou lovest me!

Enter Hostess.

Host. O Jesu, my lord the prince!

Prince. How now, my lady the hostess! what sayest thou to me?

Host. Marry, my lord, there is a nobleman of the court at door would speak with you: he says he comes from your father.

Prince. Give him as much as will make him a royal man, and send him back again to my mother.

Fal. What manner of man is he?

Host. An old man.

Fal. What doth gravity out of his bed at midnight? Shall I give him his answer?

Prince. Prithee, do, Jack.

Fal. 'Faith, and I'll send him packing. [*Exit.*

Prince. Now, sirs : by'r lady, you fought fair ; so did you, Peto ; so did you, Bardolph : you are lions too, you ran away upon instinct, you will not touch the true prince ; no, fie !

Bard. 'Faith, I ran when I saw others run.

Prince. 'Faith, tell me now in earnest, how came Falstaff's sword so hacked ?

Peto. Why, he hacked it with his dagger, and said he would swear truth out of England but he would make you believe it was done in fight, and persuaded us to do the like.

Bard. Yea, and to tickle our noses with speargrass to make them bleed, and then to beslubber our garments with it and swear it was the blood of true men. I did that I did not this seven year before, I blushed to hear his monstrous devices.

Prince. O villain, thou stolest a cup of sack eighteen years ago, and wert taken with the manner, and ever since thou hast blushed extempore. Thou hadst fire and sword on thy side, and yet thou rannest away : what instinct hadst thou for it ?

Bard. My lord, do you see these meteors ? do you behold these exhalations ?

Prince. I do.

Bard. What think you they portend ?

Prince. Hot livers and cold purses.

Bard. Choler, my lord, if rightly taken.

Prince. No, if rightly taken, halter.

Re-enter FALSTAFF.

Here comes lean Jack, here comes bare-bone. How now, my sweet creature of bombast ! How long is't ago, Jack, since thou sawest thine own knee ?

Fal. My own knee ! when I was about thy years, Hal, I was not an eagle's talon in the waist ; I could have crept into any alderman's thumb-ring : a plague of sighing and grief ! it blows a man up like a bladder. There's villanous news abroad : here was Sir John Bracy from your father ; you must to the court in the morning. That same mad fellow of the north, Percy, and he of Wales, that gave Amamon the bastinado and made Lucifer cuckold and swore the devil his true liegeman upon the cross of a Welsh hook—what a plague call you him ?

Poins. O, Glendower.

Fal. Owen, Owen, the same ; and his son-in-law Mortimer, and old Northumberland, and that sprightly Scot of Scots, Douglas, that runs o' horseback up a hill perpendicular,—

Prince. He that rides at high speed and with his pistol kills a sparrow flying.

Fal. You have hit it.

Prince. So did he never the sparrow.

Fal. Well, that rascal hath good mettle in him ; he will not run.

Prince. Why, what a rascal art thou then, to praise him so for running !

Fal. O' horseback, ye cuckoo ; but afoot he will not budge a foot.

Prince. Yes, Jack, upon instinct.

Fal. I grant ye, upon instinct. Well, he is there too, and one Mordake, and a thousand blue-caps more : Worcester is stolen away to-night ; thy father's beard is turned white with the news : you may buy land now as cheap as stinking mackerel.

Prince. Why, then, it is like, if there come a hot June and this civil buffeting hold, we shall buy maidenheads as they buy hob-nails, by the hundreds.

Fal. By the mass, lad, thou sayest true ; it is like we shall have good trading that way. But tell me, Hal, art not thou horrible afeard ? thou being heir-apparent, could the world pick thee out three such enemies again as that fiend Douglas, that spirit Percy, and that devil Glendower ? Art thou not horribly afraid ? doth not thy blood thrill at it ?

Prince. Not a whit, i' faith ; I lack some of thy instinct.

Fal. Well, thou wilt be horribly chid to-morrow when thou comest to thy father : if thou love me, practise an answer.

Prince. Do thou stand for my father, and examine me upon the particulars of my life.

G

Fal. Shall I ? content : this chair shall be my state, this dagger my sceptre, and this cushion my crown.

Prince. Thy state is taken for a joined-stool, thy golden sceptre for a leaden dagger, and thy precious rich crown for a pitiful bald crown !

Fal. Well, an the fire of grace be not quite out of thee, now shalt thou be moved. Give me a cup of sack to make my eyes look red, that it may be thought I have wept ; for I must speak in passion, and I will do it in King Cambyses' vein.

Prince. Well, here is my leg.

Fal. And here is my speech. Stand aside, nobility.

Host. O Jesu, this is excellent sport, i' faith !

Fal. Weep not, sweet queen ; for trickling tears are vain.

Host. O, the father, how he holds his countenance !

Fal. For God's sake, lords, convey my tristful queen ;
For tears do stop the flood-gates of her eyes.

Host. O Jesu, he doth it as like one of these harlotry players as ever I see !

Fal. Peace, good pint-pot ; peace, good tickle-brain. Harry, I do not only marvel where thou spendest thy time, but also how thou art accompanied : for though the camomile, the more it is trodden on the faster it grows, yet youth, the more it is wasted the sooner it wears. That thou art my son, I have partly thy mother's word, partly my own opinion, but chiefly a villanous trick of thine eye and a foolish hanging of thy nether lip, that doth warrant me. If then thou be son to me, here lies the point ; why, being son to me, art thou so pointed at ? Shall the blessed sun of heaven prove a micher and eat blackberries ? a question not to be asked. Shall the son of England prove a thief and take purses ? a question to be asked. There is a thing, Harry, which thou hast often heard of and it is known to many in our land by the name of pitch : this pitch, as ancient writers do report, doth defile ; so doth the company thou keepest : for, Harry, now I do not speak to thee in drink but in tears, not in pleasure but in passion, not in words only, but in woes also : and yet there is a virtuous man whom I have often noted in thy company, but I know not his name.

Prince. What manner of man, an it like your majesty?

Fal. A goodly portly man, i' faith, and a corpulent; of a cheerful look, a pleasing eye and a most noble carriage; and, as I think, his age some fifty, or, by'r lady, inclining to three score; and now I remember me, his name is Falstaff: if that man should be lewdly given, he deceiveth me; for, Harry, I see virtue in his looks. If then the tree may be known by the fruit, as the fruit by the tree, then, peremptorily I speak it, there is virtue in that Falstaff: him keep with, the rest banish. And tell me now, thou naughty varlet, tell me, where hast thou been this month?

Prince. Dost thou speak like a king? Do thou stand for me, and I'll play my father.

Fal. Depose me? if thou dost it half so gravely, so majestically, both in word and matter, hang me up by the heels for a rabbit-sucker or a poulter's hare.

Prince. Well, here I am set.

Fal. And here I stand: judge, my masters.

Prince. Now, Harry, whence come you?

Fal. My noble lord, from Eastcheap.

Prince. The complaints I hear of thee are grievous.

Fal. 'Sblood, my lord, they are false: nay, I'll tickle ye for a young prince, i' faith.

Prince. Swearest thou, ungracious boy? henceforth ne'er look on me. Thou art violently carried away from grace: there is a devil haunts thee in the likeness of an old fat man; a tun of man is thy companion. Why dost thou converse with that trunk of humours, that bolting-hutch of beastliness, that swollen parcel of dropsies, that huge bombard of sack, that stuffed cloak-bag of guts, that roasted Manningtree ox with the pudding in his belly, that reverend vice, that grey iniquity, that father ruffian, that vanity in years? Wherein is he good, but to taste sack and drink it? wherein neat and cleanly, but to carve a capon and eat it? wherein cunning, but in craft?

wherein crafty, but in villany? wherein villanous, but in all things? wherein worthy, but in nothing?

Fal. I would your grace would take me with you: whom means your grace?

Prince. That villanous abominable misleader of youth, Falstaff, that old white-bearded Satan.

Fal. My lord, the man I know.

Prince. I know thou dost.

Fal. But to say I know more harm in him than in myself, were to say more than I know. That he is old, the more the pity, his white hairs do witness it; but that he is, saving your reverence, a whoremaster, that I utterly deny. If sack and sugar be a fault, God help the wicked! if to be old and merry be a sin, then many an old host that I know is damned: if to be fat be to be hated, then Pharaoh's lean kine are to be loved. No, my good lord; banish Peto, banish Bardolph, banish Poins: but for sweet Jack Falstaff, kind Jack Falstaff, true Jack Falstaff, valiant Jack Falstaff, and therefore more valiant, being, as he is, old Jack Falstaff, banish not him thy Harry's company, banish not him thy Harry's company: banish plump Jack, and banish all the world.

Prince. I do, I will.   *[A knocking heard.*

    [Exeunt Hostess, Francis, and Bardolph.

Re-enter BARDOLPH, *running.*

Bard. O, my lord, my lord! the sheriff with a most monstrous watch is at the door.

Fal. Out, ye rogue! Play out the play: I have much to say in the behalf of that Falstaff.

Re-enter the Hostess.

Host. O Jesu, my lord, my lord!

Prince. Heigh, heigh! the devil rides upon a fiddlestick: what's the matter?

Host. The sheriff and all the watch are at the door: they are come to search the house. Shall I let them in?

Fal. Dost thou hear, Hal ? never call a true piece of gold a counterfeit : thou art essentially mad, without seeming so.

Prince. And thou a natural coward, without instinct.

Fal. I deny your major : if you will deny the sheriff, so ; if not, let him enter : if I become not a cart as well as another man, a plague on my bringing up ! I hope I shall as soon be strangled with a halter as another.

Prince. Go, hide thee behind the arras : the rest walk up above. Now, my masters, for a true face and good conscience.

Fal. Both which I have had : but their date is out, and therefore I'll hide me.

Prince. Call in the sheriff.

[*Exeunt all except the Prince and Peto.*

Enter Sheriff *and the* Carrier.

Now, master sheriff, what is your will with me ?

Sher. First, pardon me, my lord. A hue and cry
Hath follow'd certain men unto this house.

Prince. What men ?

Sher. One of them is well known, my gracious lord,
A gross fat man.

Car.　　　　As fat as butter.

Prince. The man, I do assure you, is not here ;
For I myself at this time have employ'd him.
And, sheriff, I will engage my word to thee
That I will, by to-morrow dinner-time,
Send him to answer thee, or any man,
For any thing he shall be charged withal :
And so let me entreat you leave the house.

Sher. I will, my lord. There are two gentlemen
Have in this robbery lost three hundred marks.

Prince. It may be so : if he have robb'd these men,
He shall be answerable ; and so farewell.

Sher. Good night, my noble lord.

Prince. I think it is good morrow, is it not ?

Sher. Indeed, my lord, I think it be two o'clock.

[*Exeunt Sheriff and Carrier.*

Prince. This oily rascal is known as well as Paul's. Go, call him forth.

Peto. Falstaff !—Fast asleep behind the arras, and snorting like a horse.

Prince. Hark, how hard he fetches breath. Search his pockets. [*He searcheth his pockets, and findeth certain papers.*] What hast thou found ?

Peto. Nothing but papers, my lord.

Prince. Let's see what they be : read them.

Peto. [*reads*]

Item, A capon, ...	2s.	2d.
Item, Sauce, ...		4d.
Item, Sack, two gallons, . .	5s.	8d.
Item, Anchovies and sack after supper, ...	2s.	6d.
Item, Bread, ...		ob.

Prince. O monstrous ! but one half-pennyworth of bread to this intolerable deal of sack ! What there is else, keep close ; we'll read it at more advantage : there let him sleep till day. I'll to the court in the morning. We must all to the wars, and thy place shall be honourable. I'll procure this fat rogue a charge of foot ; and I know his death will be a march of twelve-score. The money shall be paid back again with advantage. Be with me betimes in the morning ; and so, good morrow, Peto.

Peto. Good morrow, good my lord.

Act II, Scene iv, ll. 98-602

Bangor. The Archdeacon's house.

Enter Hotspur, Worcester, Mortimer, *and* Glendower.

Mort. These promises are fair, the parties sure,
And our induction full of prosperous hope.

Hot. Lord Mortimer, and cousin Glendower,
Will you sit down ?
And uncle Worcester : a plague upon it !
I have forgot the map.

Glend.   No, here it is.

Sit, cousin Percy ; sit, good cousin Hotspur,
For by that name as oft as Lancaster
Doth speak of you, his cheek looks pale and with
A rising sigh he wisheth you in heaven.

    Hot. And you in hell, as oft as he hears Owen Glendower
spoke of.

    Glend. I cannot blame him : at my nativity
The front of heaven was full of fiery shapes,
Of burning cressets ; and at my birth
The frame and huge foundation of the earth
Shaked like a coward.

    Hot. Why, so it would have done at the same season, if
your mother's cat had but kittened, though yourself had never
been born.

    Glend. I say the earth did shake when I was born.

    Hot. And I say the earth was not of my mind,
If you suppose as fearing you it shook.

    Glend. The heavens were all on fire, the earth did tremble.

    Hot. O, then the earth shook to see the heavens on fire,
And not in fear of your nativity.
Diseased nature oftentimes breaks forth
In strange eruptions ; oft the teeming earth
Is with a kind of colic pinch'd and vex'd
By the imprisoning of unruly wind
Within her womb ; which, for enlargement striving,
Shakes the old beldam earth and topples down
Steeples and moss-grown towers. At your birth
Our grandam earth, having this distemperature,
In passion shook.

    Glend.   Cousin, of many men
I do not bear these crossings. Give me leave
To tell you once again that at my birth
The front of heaven was full of fiery shapes,
The goats ran from the mountains, and the herds
Were strangely clamorous to the frighted fields.
These signs have mark'd me extraordinary ;

And all the courses of my life do show
I am not in the roll of common men.
Where is he living, clipp'd in with the sea
That chides the banks of England, Scotland, Wales,
Which calls me pupil, or hath read to me?
And bring him out that is but woman's son
Can trace me in the tedious ways of art
And hold me pace in deep experiments.

Hot. I think there's no man speaks better Welsh. I'll to
dinner.

Mort. Peace, cousin Percy; you will make him mad.

Glend. I can call spirits from the vasty deep.

Hot. Why, so can I, or so can any man;
But will they come when you do call for them?

Glend. Why, I can teach you, cousin, to command
The devil.

Hot. And I can teach thee, coz, to shame the devil
By telling truth: tell truth and shame the devil.
If thou have power to raise him, bring him hither,
And I'll be sworn I have power to shame him hence.
O, while you live, tell truth and shame the devil!

Mort. Come, come, no more of this unprofitable chat.

Glend. Three times hath Henry Bolingbroke made head
Against my power; thrice from the banks of Wye
And sandy-bottom'd Severn have I sent him
Bootless home and weather-beaten back.

Hot. Home without boots, and in foul weather too!
How 'scapes he agues, in the devil's name? . . .

Mort. Fie, cousin Percy! how you cross my father!

Hot. I cannot choose: sometimes he angers me
With telling me of the moldwarp and the ant,
Of the dreamer Merlin and his prophecies,
And of a dragon and a finless fish,
A clip-wing'd griffin and a moulten raven,
A couching lion and a ramping cat,
And such a deal of skimble-skamble stuff

As puts me from my faith. I tell you what;
He held me last night at least nine hours
In reckoning up the several devils' names
That were his lackeys: I cried ' hum,' and ' well, go to,'
But mark'd him not a word. O, he is as tedious
As a tired horse, a railing wife;
Worse than a smoky house: I had rather live
With cheese and garlic in a windmill, far,
Than feed on cates and have him talk to me
In any summer-house in Christendom.
   Mort. In faith, he is a worthy gentleman,
Exceedingly well read, and profited
In strange concealments, valiant as a lion
And wondrous affable and as bountiful
As mines of India. Shall I tell you, cousin?
He holds your temper in a high respect
And curbs himself even of his natural scope
When you come 'cross his humour; faith, he does:
I warrant you, that man is not alive
Might so have tempted him as you have done,
Without the taste of danger and reproof:
But do not use it oft, let me entreat you.

                          ACT III, Scene i, ll. 1-69, 147-176

                    [The lady speaks in Welsh.
  Mortimer.   Thy tongue
Makes Welsh as sweet as ditties highly penn'd,
Sung by a fair queen in a summer's bower,
With ravishing division, to her lute.

                          ACT III, Scene i, ll. 208-211

Eastcheap. The Boar's-Head Tavern.

Enter FALSTAFF *and* BARDOLPH.

  Fal. Bardolph, am I not fallen away vilely since this last
action? do I not bate? do I not dwindle? Why, my skin
hangs about me like an old lady's loose gown; I am withered
like an old apple-john. Well, I'll repent, and that suddenly,

while I am in some liking ; I shall be out of heart shortly, and then I shall have no strength to repent. An I have not forgotten what the inside of a church is made of, I am a peppercorn, a brewer's horse : the inside of a church ! Company, villanous company, hath been the spoil of me.

Bard. Sir John, you are so fretful, you cannot live long.

Fal. Why, there is it : come sing me a bawdy song ; make me merry. I was as virtuously given as a gentleman need to be ; virtuous enough ; swore little ; diced not above seven times a week ; went to a bawdy-house not above once in a quarter—of an hour ; paid money that I borrowed, three or four times ; lived well and in good compass : and now I live out of all order, out of all compass.

Bard. Why, you are so fat, Sir John, that you must needs be out of all compass, out of all reasonable compass, Sir John.

Fal. Do thou amend thy face, and I'll amend my life : thou art our admiral, thou bearest the lantern in the poop, but 'tis in the nose of thee ; thou art the Knight of the Burning Lamp.

Bard. Why, Sir John, my face does you no harm.

Fal. No, I'll be sworn ; I make as good use of it as many a man doth of a Death's-head or a memento mori : I never see thy face but I think upon hell-fire and Dives that lived in purple ; for there he is in his robes, burning, burning. If thou wert any way given to virtue, I would swear by thy face ; my oath should be ' By this fire, that's God's angel : ' but thou art altogether given over ; and wert indeed, but for the light in thy face, the son of utter darkness. When thou rannest up Gadshill in the night to catch my horse, if I did not think thou hadst been an ignis fatuus or a ball of wildfire, there's no purchase in money. O, thou art a perpetual triumph, an everlasting bonfire-light ! Thou hast saved me a thousand marks in links and torches, walking with thee in the night betwixt tavern and tavern : but the sack that thou hast drunk me would have bought me lights as good cheap at the dearest chandler's in Europe. I have maintained that salamander of yours with fire any time this two and thirty years ; God reward me for it !

Bard. 'Sblood, I would my face were in your belly !

Fal. God-a-mercy ! so should I be sure to be heart-burned.

Enter Hostess.

How now, Dame Partlet the hen ! have you inquired yet who picked my pocket ?

Host. Why, Sir John, what do you think, Sir John ? do you think I keep thieves in my house ? I have searched, I have inquired, so has my husband, man by man, boy by boy, servant by servant : the tithe of a hair was never lost in my house before.

Fal. Ye lie, hostess : Bardolph was shaved and lost many a hair ; and I'll be sworn my pocket was picked. Go to, you are a woman, go.

Host. Who, I ? no ; I defy thee : God's light, I was never called so in mine own house before.

Fal. Go to, I know you well enough.

Host. No, Sir John ; you do not know me, Sir John. I know you, Sir John : you owe me money, Sir John ; and now you pick a quarrel to beguile me of it : I bought you a dozen of shirts to your back.

Fal. Dowlas, filthy dowlas : I have given them away to bakers' wives, and they have made bolters of them.

Host. Now, as I am a true woman, holland of eight shillings an ell. You owe money here besides, Sir John, for your diet and by-drinkings, and money lent you, four and twenty pound.

Fal. He had his part of it ; let him pay.

Host. He ? alas, he is poor ; he hath nothing.

Fal. How ! poor ? look upon his face ; what call you rich ? let them coin his nose, let them coin his cheeks : I'll not pay a denier. What, will you make a younker of me ? shall I not take mine ease in mine inn but I shall have my pocket picked ? I have lost a seal-ring of my grandfather's worth forty mark.

Host. O Jesu, I have heard the prince tell him, I know not how oft, that that ring was copper !

Fal. How ! the prince is a Jack, a sneak-cup : 'sblood, an he were here, I would cudgel him like a dog, if he would say so.

ACT III, Scene iii, ll. 1-101

Hotspur.   Where is his son,
The nimble-footed madcap Prince of Wales,
And his comrades, that daff'd the world aside,
And bid it pass ?
Vernon.   All furnish'd, all in arms ;
All plumed like estridges that with the wind
Baited like eagles having lately bathed ;
Glittering in golden coats, like images ;
As full of spirit as the month of May,
And gorgeous as the sun at midsummer ;
Wanton as youthful goats, wild as young bulls.
I saw young Harry, with his beaver on,
His cuisses on his thighs, gallantly arm'd,
Rise from the ground like feather'd Mercury,
And vaulted with such ease into his seat,
As if an angel dropp'd down from the clouds,
To turn and wind a fiery Pegasus
And witch the world with noble horsemanship.

ACT IV, Scene i, ll. 94-110

A public road near Coventry.

Falstaff. If I be not ashamed of my soldiers, I am a soused gurnet. I have misused the king's press damnably. I have got, in exchange of a hundred and fifty soldiers, three hundred and odd pounds. I press me none but good householders, yeomen's sons ; inquire me out contracted bachelors, such as had been asked twice on the banns ; such a commodity of warm slaves, as had as lieve hear the devil as a drum ; such as fear the report of a caliver worse than a struck fowl or a hurt wild-duck. I pressed me none but such toasts-and-butter, with hearts in their bellies no bigger than pins' heads, and they have bought out their services ; and now my whole charge consists of ancients, corporals, lieutenants, gentlemen of companies, slaves as ragged as Lazarus in the painted cloth, where the glutton's dogs licked his sores ; and such as indeed were never soldiers, but discarded unjust serving-men, younger sons to younger brothers, revolted tapsters and ostlers trade-fallen, the cankers of a calm world and a long peace, ten times more dishonourable ragged than an old faced ancient : and such have I, to fill up the rooms of them that have bought out their services, that you would think that I had a hundred and fifty tattered prodigals lately come from swine-keeping, from eating draff and husks. A mad fellow met me on the way and told me I had unloaded all the gibbets and pressed the dead bodies. No eye hath seen such scarecrows. I'll not march through Coventry with them, that's flat : nay, and the villains march wide betwixt the legs, as if they had gyves on ; for indeed I had the most of them out of prison. There's but a shirt and a half in all my company ; and the half shirt is two napkins tacked together and thrown over the shoulders like a herald's coat without sleeves ; and the shirt, to say the truth, stolen from my host at Saint Alban's, or the red-nose innkeeper of Daventry. But that's all one ; they'll find linen enough on every hedge.

Enter the PRINCE *and* WESTMORELAND.

Prince. How now, blown Jack ! how now, quilt !

Fal. What, Hal ! how now, mad wag ! what a devil dost thou in Warwickshire ? My good Lord of Westmoreland, I cry you mercy : I thought your honour had already been at Shrewsbury.

West. Faith, Sir John, 'tis more than time that I were there, and you too ; but my powers are there already. The king, I can tell you, looks for us all : we must away all night.

Fal. Tut, never fear me : I am as vigilant as a cat to steal cream.

Prince. I think, to steal cream indeed, for thy theft hath

already made thee butter. But tell me, Jack, whose fellows
are these that come after ?

Fal. Mine, Hal, mine.

Prince. I did never see such pitiful rascals.

Fal. Tut, tut ; good enough to toss ; food for powder,
food for powder ; they'll fill a pit as well as better : tush, man,
mortal men, mortal men.   ACT IV, Scene ii, ll. 12-73

King. How bloodily the sun begins to peer
Above yon busky hill ! the day looks pale
At his distemperature.

Prince.   The southern wind
Doth play the trumpet to his purposes,
And by his hollow whistling in the leaves
Foretells a tempest and a blustering day.

                              ACT V, Scene i, ll. 1-6

Falstaff. Hal, if thou see me down in the battle and bestride me, so ; 'tis a point of friendship.

Prince. Nothing but a colossus can do thee that friendship.
Say thy prayers, and farewell.

Fal. I would 'twere bed-time, Hal, and all well.

Prince. Why, thou owest God a death.   [*Exit.*

Fal. 'Tis not due yet ; I would be loath to pay him before
his day. What need I be so forward with him that calls not
on me ? Well, 'tis no matter ; honour pricks me on. Yea, but
how if honour prick me off when I come on ? how then ? Can
honour set to a leg ? no : or an arm ? no : or take away the
grief of a wound ? no. Honour hath no skill in surgery, then ?
no. What is honour ? a word. What is in that word honour ?
what is that honour ? air. A trim reckoning ! Who hath it ?
he that died o' Wednesday. Doth he feel it ? no. Doth he
hear it ? no. 'Tis insensible, then. Yea, to the dead. But
will it not live with the living ? no. Why ? detraction will not
suffer it. Therefore I'll none of it. Honour is a mere
scutcheon : and so ends my catechism.   [*Exit.*

                              ACT V, Scene i, ll. 121-144

Hotspur. My name is Harry Percy.

Prince.   Why, then I see
A very valiant rebel of the name.
I am the Prince of Wales; and think not, Percy,
To share with me in glory any more:
Two stars keep not their motion in one sphere;
Nor can one England brook a double reign,
Of Harry Percy and the Prince of Wales.

Hot. Nor shall it, Harry; for the hour is come
To end the one of us; and would to God
Thy name in arms were now as great as mine!

Prince. I'll make it greater ere I part from thee
And all the budding honours on thy crest
I'll crop, to make a garland for my head.

Hot. I can no longer brook thy vanities.   [*They fight.*

Enter FALSTAFF.

Fal. Well said, Hal! to it, Hal! Nay, you shall find no
boy's play here, I can tell you.

Enter DOUGLAS; *he fights with* FALSTAFF, *who falls down as
if he were dead, and exit* DOUGLAS. HOTSPUR *is wounded,
and falls.*

Hot. O, Harry, thou hast robb'd me of my youth!
I better brook the loss of brittle life
Than those proud titles thou hast won of me;
They wound my thoughts worse than thy sword my
        flesh:
But thought's the slave of life, and life time's fool;
And time, that takes survey of all the world,
Must have a stop. O, I could prophesy,
But that the earthy and cold hand of death
Lies on my tongue: no, Percy, thou art dust,
And food for—   [*Dies.*

Prince. For worms, brave Percy: fare thee well, great
        heart! . . .   [*He spieth Falstaff on the ground.*
What, old acquaintance! could not all this flesh

Keep in a little life? Poor Jack, farewell!
I could have better spared a better man:
O, I should have a heavy miss of thee,
If I were much in love with vanity!
Death hath not struck so fat a deer to-day,
Though many dearer, in this bloody fray.
Embowell'd will I see thee by and by:
Till then in blood by noble Percy lie. [*Exit.*

Fal. [*Rising up*] Embowelled! if thou embowel me to-day,
I'll give you leave to powder me and eat me too to-morrow.
'Sblood, 'twas time to counterfeit, or that hot termagant Scot
had paid me scot and lot too. Counterfeit? I lie, I am no
counterfeit: to die, is to be a counterfeit; for he is but
the counterfeit of a man who hath not the life of a man: but
to counterfeit dying, when a man thereby liveth, is to be no
counterfeit, but the true and perfect image of life indeed.
The better part of valour is discretion; in the which better
part I have saved my life. 'Zounds, I am afraid of this gun-
powder Percy, though he be dead: how, if he should counterfeit too and rise? by my faith, I am afraid he would prove the
better counterfeit. Therefore I'll make him sure; yea, and I'll
swear I killed him. Why may not he rise as well as I? Nothing
confutes me but eyes, and nobody sees me. Therefore, sirrah
[*stabbing him*], with a new wound in your thigh, come you
along with me. [*Takes up Hotspur on his back.* . . .

There is Percy [*throwing the body down*]: if your father
will do me any honour, so; if not, let him kill the next
Percy himself. I look to be either earl or duke, I can assure
you.

Prince. Why, Percy I killed myself and saw thee dead.

Fal. Didst thou? Lord, Lord, how this world is given to
lying! I grant you I was down and out of breath; and so was
he: but we rose both at an instant and fought a long hour by
Shrewsbury clock. If I may be believed, so; if not, let them
that should reward valour bear the sin upon their own heads.
I'll take it upon my death, I gave him this wound in the thigh:

if the man were alive and would deny it, 'zounds, I would
make him eat a piece of my sword. . . .

[*Exeunt Prince of Wales and Lancaster.*

I'll follow, as they say, for reward. He that rewards me,
God reward him! If I do grow great, I'll grow less; for
I'll purge, and leave sack, and live cleanly as a nobleman
should do. [*Exit.*

ACT V, Scene iv, ll. 61-87, 102-132, 143-157, 166-169

The Second Part of

King Henry IV

Even such a man, so faint, so spiritless,
So dull, so dead in look, so woe-begone,
Drew Priam's curtain in the dead of night,
And would have told him half his Troy was burnt.

ACT I, Scene i, ll. 70-74

London. A street.

Enter FALSTAFF, *with his* Page *bearing his
sword and buckler*.

Fal. Men of all sorts take a pride to gird at me: the brain
of this foolish-compounded clay, man, is not able to invent
any thing that tends to laughter, more than I invent or is
invented on me: I am not only witty in myself, but the cause
that wit is in other men. I do here walk before thee like a
sow that hath overwhelmed all her litter but one. . . .

Enter the Lord Chief-Justice *and* Servant.

Page. Sir, here comes the nobleman that committed the
prince for striking him about Bardolph.

Fal. Wait close; I will not see him.

Ch. Just. What's he that goes there?

Serv. Falstaff, an't please your lordship.

167

Ch. Just. He that was in question for the robbery?

Serv. He, my lord : but he hath since done good service at Shrewsbury ; and, as I hear, is now going with some charge to the Lord John of Lancaster.

Ch. Just. What, to York ? Call him back again.

Serv. Sir John Falstaff !

Fal. Boy, tell him I am deaf.

Page. You must speak louder ; my master is deaf.

Ch. Just. I am sure he is, to the hearing of any thing good. Go, pluck him by the elbow ; I must speak with him.

Serv. Sir John !

Fal. What ! a young knave, and begging ! Is there not wars ? is there not employment ? doth not the king lack subjects ? do not the rebels need soldiers ? . . .

Serv. Sir, my lord would speak with you.

Ch. Just. Sir John Falstaff, a word with you.

Fal. My good lord ! God give your lordship good time of day. I am glad to see your lordship abroad : I heard say your lordship was sick : I hope your lordship goes abroad by advice. Your lordship, though not clean past your youth, hath yet some smack of age in you, some relish of the saltness of time ; and I most humbly beseech your lordship to have a reverent care of your health.

Ch. Just. Sir John, I sent for you before your expedition to Shrewsbury.

Fal. An't please your lordship, I hear his majesty is returned with some discomfort from Wales.

Ch. Just. I talk not of his majesty : you would not come when I sent for you.

Fal. And I hear, moreover, his highness is fallen into this same whoreson apoplexy.

Ch. Just. Well, God mend him ! I pray you, let me speak with you.

Fal. This apoplexy is, as I take it, a kind of lethargy, an't please your lordship ; a kind of sleeping in the blood, a whoreson tingling.

Ch. Just. What tell you me of it ? be it as it is.

Fal. It hath it original from much grief, from study and perturbation of the brain : I have read the cause of his effects in Galen : it is a kind of deafness.

Ch. Just. I think you are fallen into the disease ; for you hear not what I say to you.

Fal. Very well, my lord, very well : rather, an't please you, it is the disease of not listening, the malady of not marking, that I am troubled withal.

Ch. Just. To punish you by the heels would amend the attention of your ears ; and I care not if I do become your physician.

Fal. I am as poor as Job, my lord, but not so patient : your lordship may minister the potion of imprisonment to me in respect of poverty ; but how I should be your patient to follow your prescriptions, the wise may make some dram of a scruple, or indeed a scruple itself.

Ch. Just. I sent for you, when there were matters against you for your life, to come speak with me.

Fal. As I was then advised by my learned counsel in the laws of this land-service, I did not come.

Ch. Just. Well, the truth is, Sir John, you live in great infamy.

Fal. He that buckles him in my belt cannot live in less.

Ch. Just. Your means are very slender, and your waste is great.

Fal. I would it were otherwise ; I would my means were greater, and my waist slenderer.

Ch. Just. You have misled the youthful prince.

Fal. The young prince hath misled me : I am the fellow with the great belly, and he my dog.

Ch. Just. Well, I am loath to gall a new-healed wound : your day's service at Shrewsbury hath a little gilded over your night's exploit on Gad's-hill : you may thank the unquiet time for your quiet o'er-posting that action.

Fal. My lord ?

Ch. Just. But since all is well, keep it so : wake not a sleeping wolf.

Fal. To wake a wolf is as bad as to smell a fox.

Ch. Just. What ! you are as a candle, the better part burnt out.

Fal. A wassail candle, my lord, all tallow : if I did say of wax, my growth would approve the truth.

Ch. Just. There is not a white hair on your face but should have his effect of gravity.

Fal. His effect of gravy, gravy, gravy.

Ch. Just. You follow the young prince up and down, like his ill angel.

Fal. Not so, my lord ; your ill angel is light ; but I hope he that looks upon me will take me without weighing : and yet, in some respects, I grant, I cannot go : I cannot tell. Virtue is of so little regard in these costermonger times that true valour is turned bear-herd : pregnancy is made a tapster, and hath his quick wit wasted in giving reckonings : all the other gifts appertinent to man, as the malice of this age shapes them, are not worth a gooseberry. You that are old consider not the capacities of us that are young ; you do measure the heat of our livers with the bitterness of your galls : and we that are in the vaward of our youth, I must confess, are wags too.

Ch. Just. Do you set down your name in the scroll of youth, that are written down old with all the characters of age ? Have you not a moist eye ? a dry hand ? a yellow cheek ? a white beard ? a decreasing leg ? an increasing belly ? is not your voice broken ? your wind short ? your chin double ? your wit single ? and every part about you blasted with antiquity ? and will you yet call yourself young ? Fie, fie, fie, Sir John !

Fal. My lord, I was born about three of the clock in the afternoon, with a white head and something a round belly. For my voice, I have lost it with halloing and singing of anthems. To approve my youth further, I will not : the truth is, I am only old in judgement and understanding ; and he that will caper with me for a thousand marks, let him lend me the money, and have at him ! For the box of the ear that the prince gave you, he gave it like a rude prince, and you took it like a sensible lord. I have checked him for it, and the young lion repents ; marry, not in ashes and sackcloth, but in new silk and old sack.

Ch. Just. Well, God send the prince a better companion !

Fal. God send the companion a better prince ! I cannot rid my hands of him.

Ch. Just. Well, the king hath severed you and Prince Harry : I hear you are going with Lord John of Lancaster against the Archbishop and the Earl of Northumberland.

Fal. Yea ; I thank your pretty sweet wit for it. But look you pray, all you that kiss my lady Peace at home, that our armies join not in a hot day ; for, by the Lord, I take but two shirts out with me, and I mean not to sweat extraordinarily : if it be a hot day, and I brandish any thing but a bottle, I would I might never spit white again. There is not a dangerous action can peep out his head but I am thrust upon it : well, I cannot last ever : but it was alway yet the trick of our English nation, if they have a good thing, to make it too common. If ye will needs say I am an old man, you should give me rest. I would to God my name were not so terrible to the enemy as it is : I were better to be eaten to death with a rust than to be scoured to nothing with perpetual motion.

Ch. Just. Well, be honest, be honest ; and God bless your expedition !

Fal. Will your lordship lend me a thousand pound to furnish me forth ?

Ch. Just. Not a penny, not a penny ; you are too impatient to bear crosses. Fare you well : commend me to my cousin Westmoreland. [*Exeunt Chief-Justice and Servant.*

Fal. If I do, fillip me with a three-man beetle. A man can no more separate age and covetousness than a' can part young limbs and lechery : but the gout galls the one, and the pox pinches the other ; and so both the degrees prevent my curses. Boy !

Page. Sir ?

Fal. What money is in my purse ?

Page. Seven groats and two pence.

Fal. I can get no remedy against this consumption of the purse : borrowing only lingers and lingers it out, but the disease is incurable. Go bear this letter to my Lord of Lancaster ; this to the prince ; this to the Earl of Westmoreland ; and this to old Mistress Ursula, whom I have weekly sworn to marry since I perceived the first white hair on my chin. About it : you know where to find me. [*Exit Page.*] A pox of this gout ! or, a gout of this pox ! for the one or the other plays the rogue with my great toe. 'Tis no matter if I do halt ; I have the wars for my colour, and my pension shall seem the more reasonable. A good wit will make use of any thing : I will turn diseases to commodity. [*Exit.*

ACT I, Scene ii, ll. 7-14, 62-86, 104-278

An habitation giddy and unsure
Hath he that buildeth on the vulgar heart.

ACT I, Scene iii, ll. 89-90

London. A street.

Enter Hostess, FANG *and his* Boy *with her, and*
SNARE *following.*

Fang. Snare, we must arrest Sir John Falstaff.

Host. Yea, good Master Snare ; I have entered him and all.

Snare. It may chance cost some of us our lives, for he will stab.

Host. Alas the day ! take heed of him ; he stabbed me in mine own house, and that most beastly : in good faith, he cares not what mischief he does, if his weapon be out : he will foin like any devil ; he will spare neither man, woman, nor child.

Fang. If I can close with him, I care not for his thrust.

Host. No, nor I neither : I'll be at your elbow.

Fang. An I but fist him once ; an a' come but within my vice,—

Host. I am undone by his going ; I warrant you, he's an infinitive thing upon my score. Good Master Fang, hold him sure : good Master Snare, let him not 'scape. A' comes continuantly to Pie-corner—saving your manhoods—to buy a saddle ; and he is indited to dinner to the Lubber's-head in Lumbert street, to Master Smooth's the silk-man : I pray ye, since my exion is entered and my case so openly known to the world, let him be brought in to his answer. A hundred mark is a long one for a poor lone woman to bear : and I have borne, and borne, and borne, and have been fubbed off, and fubbed off, and fubbed off, from this day to that day, that it is a shame to be thought on. There is no honesty in such dealing ; unless a woman should be made an ass and a beast, to bear every knave's wrong. Yonder he comes ; and that arrant malmsey-nose knave, Bardolph, with him. Do your offices, do your offices : Master Fang and Master Snare, do me, do me, do me your offices.

Enter FALSTAFF, Page, *and* BARDOLPH.

Fal. How now ! whose mare's dead ? what's the matter ?

Fang. Sir John, I arrest you at the suit of Mistress Quickly.

Fal. Away, varlets ! Draw, Bardolph : cut me off the villain's head : throw the quean in the channel.

Host. Throw me in the channel ! I'll throw thee in the channel. Wilt thou ? wilt thou ? thou bastardly rogue ! Murder, murder ! Ah, thou honey-suckle villain ! wilt thou kill God's officers and the king's ? Ah, thou honey-seed rogue ! thou art a honey-seed, a man-queller, and a woman-queller.

Fal. Keep them off, Bardolph.

Fang. A rescue ! a rescue !

Host. Good people, bring a rescue or two. Thou wo't, wo't thou ? thou wo't, wo't ta ? do, do, thou rogue ! do, thou hemp-seed !

Fal. Away, you scullion ! you rampallian ! you fustilarian ! I'll tickle your catastrophe.

Enter the LORD CHIEF-JUSTICE *and his men.*

Ch. Just. What is the matter ? keep the peace here, ho !

Host. Good my lord, be good to me. I beseech you, stand to me.

Ch. Just. How now, Sir John ! what are you brawling here ?
Doth this become your place, your time and business ?
You should have been well on your way to York.
Stand from him, fellow : wherefore hang'st upon him ?

Host. O my most worshipful lord, an't please your grace,
I am a poor widow of Eastcheap, and he is arrested at my suit.

Ch. Just. For what sum ?

Host. It is more than for some, my lord ; it is for all, all I have. He hath eaten me out of house and home ; he hath put all my substance into that fat belly of his : but I will have some of it out again, or I will ride thee o' nights like the mare.

Fal. I think I am as like to ride the mare, if I have any vantage of ground to get up.

Ch. Just. How comes this, Sir John ? Fie ! what man of good temper would endure this tempest of exclamation ? Are you not ashamed to enforce a poor widow to so rough a course to come by her own ?

Fal. What is the gross sum that I owe thee ?

Host. Marry, if thou wert an honest man, thyself and the money too. Thou didst swear to me upon a parcel-gilt goblet, sitting in my Dolphin-chamber, at the round table, by a sea-coal fire, upon Wednesday in Wheeson week, when the prince broke thy head for liking his father to a singing-man of Windsor, thou didst swear to me then, as I was washing thy wound, to marry me and make me my lady thy wife. Canst thou deny it ? Did not goodwife Keech, the butcher's wife, come in then and call me gossip Quickly ? coming in to borrow a mess of vinegar ; telling us she had a good dish of prawns ; whereby thou didst desire to eat some ; whereby I told thee they were ill for a green wound ? And didst thou not, when she was gone down stairs, desire me to be no more so familiarity with such poor people ; saying that ere long they should call me madam ? And didst thou not kiss me and bid me fetch thee thirty shillings ? I put thee now to thy book-oath : deny it, if thou canst.

Fal. My lord, this is a poor mad soul ; and she says up and down the town that her eldest son is like you : she hath been in good case, and the truth is, poverty hath distracted her. . . .

Host. By this heavenly ground I tread on, I must be fain to pawn both my plate and the tapestry of my dining-chambers.

Fal. Glasses, glasses, is the only drinking : and for thy walls, a pretty slight drollery, or the story of the Prodigal, or the German hunting in water-work, is worth a thousand of these bed-hangings and these fly-bitten tapestries. Let it be ten pound, if thou canst. Come, an 'twere not for thy humours, there's not a better wench in England. Go, wash thy face, and draw the action. Come, thou must not be in this humour with me ; dost not know me ? come, come, I know thou wast set on to this.

Host. Pray thee, Sir John, let it be but twenty nobles : i' faith, I am loath to pawn my plate, so God save me, la !

Fal. Let it alone ; I'll make other shift : you'll be a fool still.

Host. Well, you shall have it, though I pawn my gown. I hope you'll come to supper. You'll pay me all together ?

Fal. Will I live ? [*To Bardolph*] Go, with her, with her ; hook on, hook on. Act II, Scene i, ll. 28-127, 152-175

London. Another street.

Enter Prince Henry *and* Poins.

Prince. Before God, I am exceeding weary.

Poins. Is't come to that ? I had thought weariness durst not have attached one of so high blood.

Prince. Faith, it does me ; though it discolours the complexion of my greatness to acknowledge it. Doth it not show vilely in me to desire small beer?

Poins. Why, a prince should not be so loosely studied as to remember so weak a composition.

Prince. Belike then my appetite was not princely got; for, by my troth, I do now remember the poor creature, small beer. But, indeed, these humble considerations make me out of love with my greatness.

Act II, Scene ii, ll. 1-15

London. The Boar's-Head Tavern in Eastcheap.

Enter Hostess, DOLL TEARSHEET *and* FALSTAFF.

Doll Tearsheet. I'll be friends with thee, Jack: thou art going to the wars; and whether I shall ever see thee again or no, there is nobody cares.

Re-enter First Drawer.

First Draw. Sir, Ancient Pistol's below, and would speak with you.

Dol. Hang him, swaggering rascal! let him not come hither: it is the foul-mouthed'st rogue in England.

Host. If he swagger, let him not come here: no, by my faith; I must live among my neighbours; I'll no swaggerers: I am in good name and fame with the very best: shut the door; there comes no swaggerers here: I have not lived all this while, to have swaggering now: shut the door, I pray you.

Fal. Dost thou hear, hostess?

Host. Pray ye, pacify yourself, Sir John: there comes no swaggerers here.

Fal. Dost thou hear? it is mine ancient.

Host. Tilly-fally, Sir John, ne'er tell me: your ancient swaggerer comes not in my doors. I was before Master Tisick, the debuty, t'other day; and, as he said to me, 'twas no longer ago than Wednesday last, 'I' good faith, neighbour Quickly,' says he; Master Dumbe, our minister, was by then; 'neighbour Quickly,' says he, 'receive those that are civil; for,' said he, 'you are in an ill name:' now a' said so, I can

176

tell whereupon ; ' for,' says he, ' you are an honest woman, and well thought on ; therefore take heed what guests you receive : receive,' says he, ' no swaggering companions.' There comes none here : you would bless you to hear what he said : no, I'll no swaggerers.

Fal. He's no swaggerer, hostess ; a tame cheater, i' faith ; you may stroke him as gently as a puppy greyhound : he'll not swagger with a Barbary hen, if her feathers turn back in any show of resistance. Call him up, drawer. [*Exit First Drawer.*

Host. Cheater, call you him ? I will bar no honest man my house, nor no cheater : but I do not love swaggering, by my troth ; I am the worse, when one says swagger : feel, masters, how I shake ; look you, I warrant you.

Dol. So you do, hostess.

Host. Do I ? yea, in very truth, do I, an 'twere an aspen leaf : I cannot abide swaggerers. . . .

Dol. Thou whoreson little tidy Bartholomew boar-pig, when wilt thou leave fighting o' days and foining o' nights, and begin to patch up thine old body for heaven ?

Fal. Peace, good Doll ! do not speak like a death's-head ; do not bid me remember mine end.

ACT II, Scene iv, ll. 71-118, 250-254

Westminster. The palace.

Enter the KING *in his nightgown, with a* Page.

King. Go call the Earls of Surrey and of Warwick ;
But, ere they come, bid them o'er-read these letters,
And well consider of them : make good speed.

[*Exit Page.*

How many thousand of my poorest subjects
Are at this hour asleep ! O sleep, O gentle sleep,
Nature's soft nurse, how have I frighted thee,
That thou no more wilt weigh my eyelids down
And steep my senses in forgetfulness ?
Why rather, sleep, liest thou in smoky cribs,
Upon uneasy pallets stretching thee

And hush'd with buzzing night-flies to thy slumber,
Than in the perfumed chambers of the great,
Under the canopies of costly state,
And lull'd with sound of sweetest melody?
O thou dull god, why liest thou with the vile
In loathsome beds, and leavest the kingly couch
A watch-case or a common 'larum-bell?
Wilt thou upon the high and giddy mast
Seal up the ship-boy's eyes, and rock his brains
In cradle of the rude imperious surge
And in the visitation of the winds,
Who take the ruffian billows by the top,
Curling their monstrous heads and hanging them
With deafening clamour in the slippery clouds,
That, with the hurly, death itself awakes?
Canst thou, O partial sleep, give thy repose
To the wet sea-boy in an hour so rude,
And in the calmest and most stillest night,
With all appliances and means to boot,
Deny it to a king? Then happy low, lie down!
Uneasy lies the head that wears a crown. . . . .
O God! that one might read the book of fate,
And see the revolution of the times
Make mountains level, and the continent,
Weary of solid firmness, melt itself
Into the sea! and, other times, to see
The beachy girdle of the ocean
Too wide for Neptune's hips; how chances mock,
And changes fill the cup of alteration
With divers liquors! O, if this were seen,
The happiest youth, viewing his progress through,
What perils past, what crosses to ensue,
Would shut the book, and sit him down and die.

ACT III, Scene i, ll. 1-31, 45-56

Gloucestershire.   Before JUSTICE SHALLOW'S *house.*

Enter SHALLOW *and* SILENCE, *meeting;* MOULDY, SHADOW, WART, FEEBLE, BULLCALF, *a Servant or two with them.*

Shal. Come on, come on, come on, sir; give me your hand, sir, give me your hand, sir : an early stirrer, by the rood ! And how doth my good cousin Silence ?

Sil. Good morrow, good cousin Shallow.

Shal. And how doth my cousin, your bedfellow ? and your fairest daughter and mine, my god-daughter Ellen ?

Sil. Alas, a black ousel, cousin Shallow !

Shal. By yea and nay, sir, I dare say my cousin William is become a good scholar : he is at Oxford still, is he not ?

Sil. Indeed, sir, to my cost.

Shal. A' must, then, to the inns o' court shortly. I was once of Clement's Inn, where I think they will talk of mad Shallow yet.

Sil. You were called ' lusty Shallow ' then, cousin.

Shal. By the mass, I was called any thing; and I would have done any thing indeed too, and roundly too. There was I, and little John Doit of Staffordshire, and black George Barnes, and Francis Pickbone, and Will Squele, a Cotswold man ; you had not four such swinge-bucklers in all the inns o' court again : and I may say to you, we knew where the bona-robas were and had the best of them all at commandment. Then was Jack Falstaff, now Sir John, a boy, and page to Thomas Mowbray, Duke of Norfolk.

Sil. This Sir John, cousin, that comes hither anon about soldiers ?

Shal. The same Sir John, the very same. I see him break Skogan's head at the court-gate, when a' was a crack not thus high : and the very same day did I fight with one Sampson Stockfish, a fruiterer, behind Gray's Inn. Jesu, Jesu, the mad days that I have spent ! and to see how many of my old acquaintance are dead !

Sil. We shall all follow, cousin.

Shal. Certain, 'tis certain; very sure, very sure: death, as the Psalmist saith, is certain to all; all shall die. How a good yoke of bullocks at Stamford fair?

Sil. By my troth, I was not there.

Shal. Death is certain. Is old Double of your town living yet?

Sil. Dead, sir.

Shal. Jesu, Jesu, dead! a' drew a good bow; and dead! a' shot a fine shoot: John a Gaunt loved him well, and betted much money on his head. Dead! a' would have clapped i' the clout at twelve score; and carried you a forehand shaft a fourteen and fourteen and a half, that it would have done a man's heart good to see. How a score of ewes now?

Sil. Thereafter as they be: a score of good ewes may be worth ten pounds.

Shal. And is old Double dead?

Sil. Here come two of Sir John Falstaff's men, as I think.

Enter BARDOLPH *and one with him.*

Bard. Good morrow, honest gentlemen: I beseech you, which is Justice Shallow?

Shal. I am Robert Shallow, sir; a poor esquire of this county, and one of the king's justices of the peace: what is your good pleasure with me?

Bard. My captain, sir, commends him to you; my captain, Sir John Falstaff, a tall gentleman, by heaven, and a most gallant leader.

Shal. He greets me well, sir. I knew him a good back-sword man. How doth the good knight? may I ask how my lady his wife doth?

Bard. Sir, pardon; a soldier is better accommodated than with a wife.

Shal. It is well said, in faith, sir; and it is well said indeed too. Better accommodated! it is good; yea, indeed, is it: good phrases are surely, and ever were, very commendable. Accommodated! it comes of ' accommodo: ' very good; a good phrase.

Bard. Pardon me, sir; I have heard the word. Phrase call you it? by this good day, I know not the phrase; but I will maintain the word with my sword to be a soldier-like word, and a word of exceeding good command, by heaven. Accommodated; that is, when a man is, as they say, accommodated; or when a man is, being, whereby a' may be thought to be accommodated; which is an excellent thing.

Shal. It is very just.

Enter FALSTAFF.

Look, here comes good Sir John. Give me your good hand, give me your worship's good hand: by my troth, you like well and bear your years very well: welcome, good Sir John.

Fal. I am glad to see you well, good Master Robert Shallow: Master Surecard, as I think?

Shal. No, Sir John; it is my cousin Silence, in commission with me.

Fal. Good Master Silence, it well befits you should be of the peace.

Sil. Your good worship is welcome.

Fal. Fie! this is hot weather, gentlemen. Have you provided me here half a dozen sufficient men?

Shal. Marry, have we, sir. Will you sit?

Fal. Let me see them, I beseech you.

Shal. Where's the roll? where's the roll? where's the roll? Let me see, let me see, let me see. So, so, so, so, so, so, so: yea, marry, sir: Ralph Mouldy! Let them appear as I call; let them do so, let them do so. Let me see; where is Mouldy?

Moul. Here, an't please you.

Shal. What think you, Sir John? a good-limbed fellow; young, strong, and of good friends.

Fal. Is thy name Mouldy?

Moul. Yea, an't please you.

Fal. 'Tis the more time thou wert used.

Shal. Ha, ha, ha! most excellent, i' faith! things that are

mouldy lack use : very singular good ! in faith, well said, Sir
John, very well said.

Fal. Prick him.

Moul. I was pricked well enough before, an you could have
let me alone : my old dame will be undone now for one to do
her husbandry and her drudgery : you need not to have
pricked me ; there are other men fitter to go out than I.

Fal. Go to : peace, Mouldy ; you shall go. Mouldy, it is
time you were spent.

Moul. Spent !

Shal. Peace, fellow, peace ; stand aside : know you where
you are ? For the other, Sir John : let me see : Simon Shadow !

Fal. Yea, marry, let me have him to sit under : he's like to
be a cold soldier.

Shal. Where's Shadow ?

Shad. Here, sir.

Fal. Shadow, whose son art thou ?

Shad. My mother's son, sir.

Fal. Thy mother's son ! like enough, and thy father's
shadow : so the son of the female is the shadow of the male :
it is often so, indeed ; but much of the father's substance !

Shal. Do you like him, Sir John ?

Fal. Shadow will serve for summer ; prick him, for we
have a number of shadows to fill up the muster-book.

Shal. Thomas Wart !

Fal. Where's he ?

Wart. Here, sir.

Fal. Is thy name Wart ?

Wart. Yea, sir.

Fal. Thou art a very ragged wart.

Shal. Shall I prick him down, Sir John ?

Fal. It were superfluous ; for his apparel is built upon his
back and the whole frame stands upon pins : prick him no
more.

Shal. Ha, ha, ha ! you can do it, sir ; you can do it : I
commend you well. Francis Feeble !

Fee. Here, sir.

Fal. What trade art thou, Feeble?

Fee. A woman's tailor, sir.

Shal. Shall I prick him, sir?

Fal. You may: but if he had been a man's tailor, he'ld ha' pricked you. Wilt thou make as many holes in an enemy's battle as thou hast done in a woman's petticoat?

Fee. I will do my good will, sir: you can have no more.

Fal. Well said, good woman's tailor! well said, courageous Feeble! thou wilt be as valiant as the wrathful dove or most magnanimous mouse. Prick the woman's tailor: well, Master Shallow; deep, Master Shallow.

Fee. I would Wart might have gone, sir.

Fal. I would thou wert a man's tailor, that thou mightst mend him and make him fit to go. I cannot put him to a private soldier that is the leader of so many thousands: let that suffice, most forcible Feeble.

Fee. It shall suffice, sir.

Fal. I am bound to thee, reverend Feeble. Who is next?

Shal. Peter Bullcalf o' the green!

Fal. Yea, marry, let's see Bullcalf.

Bull. Here, sir.

Fal. 'Fore God, a likely fellow! Come, prick me Bullcalf till he roar again.

Bull. O Lord! good my lord captain,—

Fal. What, dost thou roar before thou art pricked?

Bull. O Lord, sir! I am a diseased man.

Fal. What disease hast thou?

Bull. A whoreson cold, sir, a cough, sir, which I caught with ringing in the king's affairs upon his coronation-day, sir.

Fal. Come, thou shalt go to the wars in a gown; we will have away thy cold; and I will take such order that thy friends shall ring for thee. Is here all?

Shal. Here is two more called than your number; you must have but four here, sir: and so, I pray you, go in with me to dinner.

Fal. Come, I will go drink with you, but I cannot tarry dinner. I am glad to see you, by my troth, Master Shallow.

Shal. O, Sir John, do you remember since we lay all night in the windmill in Saint George's field?

Fal. No more of that, good Master Shallow, no more of that.

Shal. Ha! 'twas a merry night. And is Jane Nightwork alive?

Fal. She lives, Master Shallow.

Shal. She never could away with me.

Fal. Never, never; she would always say she could not abide Master Shallow.

Shal. By the mass, I could anger her to the heart. She was then a bona-roba. Doth she hold her own well?

Fal. Old, old, Master Shallow.

Shal. Nay, she must be old; she cannot choose but be old; certain she's old; and had Robin Nightwork by old Nightwork before I came to Clement's Inn.

Sil. That's fifty five year ago.

Shal. Ha, cousin Silence, that thou hadst seen that that this knight and I have seen! Ha, Sir John, said I well?

Fal. We have heard the chimes at midnight, Master Shallow.

Shal. That we have, that we have, that we have; in faith, Sir John, we have: our watchword was 'Hem boys!' Come, let's to dinner; come, let's to dinner: Jesus, the days that we have seen! Come, come. . . .

[*Exeunt Justices, Bardolph, Recruits, etc.*

Fal. Lord, Lord, how subject we old men are to this vice of lying! This same starved justice hath done nothing but prate to me of the wildness of his youth, and the feats he hath done about Turnbull Street; and every third word a lie, duer paid to the hearer than the Turk's tribute. I do remember him at Clement's Inn like a man made after supper of a cheese-paring: when a' was naked, he was, for all the world, like a forked radish, with a head fantastically carved upon it with a knife : a' was so forlorn, that his dimensions to any thick sight were invincible : a' was the very genius of famine ; yet lecherous as a monkey, and the whores called him mandrake : a' came ever in the rearward of the fashion, and sung those tunes to the over-scutched huswives that he heard the carmen whistle, and sware they were his fancies or his good-nights. And now is this Vice's dagger become a squire, and talks as familiarly of John a Gaunt as if he had been sworn brother to him ; and I'll be sworn a' ne'er saw him but once in the Tilt-yard ; and then he burst his head for crowding among the marshal's men. I saw it, and told John a Gaunt he beat his own name ; for you might have thrust him and all his apparel into an eel-skin ; the case of a treble hautboy was a mansion for him, a court : and now has he land and beefs. Well, I'll be acquainted with him, if I return ; and it shall go hard but I will make him a philosopher's two stones to me : if the young dace be a bait for the old pike, I see no reason in the law of nature but I may snap at him. Let time shape, and there an end.

ACT III, Scene ii, ll. 1-234, 325-358

Falstaff. I have a whole school of tongues in this belly of mine, and not a tongue of them all speaks any other word but my name. An I had but a belly of any indifferency, I were simply the most active fellow in Europe : my womb, my womb, my womb, undoes me.

ACT IV, Scene iii, ll. 20-25

Prince. I will sit and watch here by the king.
Why doth the crown lie there upon his pillow,
Being so troublesome a bedfellow ?
O polish'd perturbation ! golden care !
That keep'st the ports of slumber open wide
To many a watchful night ! sleep with it now !
Yet not so sound and half so deeply sweet
As he whose brow with homely biggen bound
Snores out the watch of night. O majesty !

When thou dost pinch thy bearer, thou dost sit
Like a rich armour worn in heat of day,
That scalds with safety. By his gates of breath
There lies a downy feather which stirs not:
Did he suspire, that light and weightless down
Perforce must move. My gracious lord! my father!
This sleep is sound indeed; this is a sleep
That from this golden rigol hath divorced
So many English kings. Thy due from me
Is tears and heavy sorrows of the blood,
Which nature, love, and filial tenderness
Shall, O dear father, pay thee plenteously:
My due from thee is this imperial crown,
Which, as immediate from thy place and blood,
Derives itself to me. Lo, here it sits,
Which God shall guard: and put the world's whole strength
Into one giant arm, it shall not force
This lineal honour from me: this from thee
Will I to mine leave, as 'tis left to me.

ACT IV, Scene v, ll. 20-47

Not Amurath an Amurath succeeds,
But Harry Harry.

ACT V, Scene ii, ll. 48-49

Gloucestershire. SHALLOW's *orchard.*

Enter FALSTAFF, SHALLOW, SILENCE, DAVY,
BARDOLPH, *and the* Page.

Shal. Nay, you shall see my orchard, where, in an arbour,
we will eat a last year's pippin of my own graffing, with a dish
of caraways, and so forth: come, cousin Silence: and then to
bed.

Fal. 'Fore God, you have here a goodly dwelling and a
rich.

Shal. Barren, barren, barren; beggars all, beggars all,
Sir John: marry, good air. Spread, Davy; spread, Davy:
well said, Davy.

Fal. This Davy serves you for good uses ; he is your serving-man and your husband.

Shal. A good varlet, a good varlet, a very good varlet, Sir John : by the mass, I have drunk too much sack at supper : a good varlet. Now sit down, now sit down : come, cousin.

Sil. Ah, sirrah ! quoth-a, we shall
    Do nothing but eat, and make good cheer,   [*Singing*.
    And praise God for the merry year ;
    When flesh is cheap and females dear,
    And lusty lads roam here and there
        So merrily,
    And ever among so merrily.

Fal. There's a merry heart ! Good Master Silence, I'll give you a health for that anon.

Shal. Give Master Bardolph some wine, Davy.

Davy. Sweet sir, sit ; I'll be with you anon ; most sweet sir, sit. Master page, good master page, sit. Proface ! What you want in meat, we'll have in drink : but you must bear ; the heart's all.   [*Exit.*

Shal. Be merry, Master Bardolph ; and, my little soldier there, be merry.

Sil. Be merry, be merry, my wife has all ;   [*Singing*.
    For women are shrews, both short and tall :
    'Tis merry in hall when beards wag all,
        And welcome merry Shrove-tide.
    Be merry, be merry.

Fal. I did not think Master Silence had been a man of this mettle.

Sil. Who, I ? I have been merry twice and once ere now.

Re-enter DAVY.

Davy. There's a dish of leather-coats for you.

                  [*To Bardolph.*

Shal. Davy !

Davy. Your worship ! I'll be with you straight [*to Bar-dolph*]. A cup of wine, sir ?

Sil. A cup of wine that's brisk and fine,　　　[*Singing.*
　　　And drink unto the leman mine ;
　　　And a merry heart lives long-a.

Fal. Well said, Master Silence.

Sil. An we shall be merry, now comes in the sweet o' the night.

Fal. Health and long life to you, Master Silence.

Sil. Fill the cup, and let it come ;　　　[*Singing.*
　　　I'll pledge you a mile to the bottom.

Shal. Honest Bardolph, welcome : if thou wantest any thing, and wilt not call, beshrew thy heart. Welcome, my little tiny thief [*to the Page*], and welcome indeed too. I'll drink to Master Bardolph, and to all the cavaleros about London.

Davy. I hope to see London once ere I die.

Bard. An I might see you there, Davy,—

Shall. By the mass, you'll crack a quart together, ha ! will you not, Master Bardolph ?

Bard. Yea, sir, in a pottle-pot.

Shal. By God's liggens, I thank thee : the knave will stick by thee, I can assure thee that. A' will not out ; he is true bred.

Bard. And I'll stick by him, sir.

Shal. Why, there spoke a king. Lack nothing : be merry. [*Knocking within.*] Look who's at door there, ho ! who knocks ?　　　[*Exit Davy.*

Fal. Why, now you have done me right.

　　　　　[*To Silence, seeing him take off a bumper.*

Sil.　　　Do me right,　　　[*Singing.*
　　　And dub me knight :
　　　　　Samingo.
Is't not so ?

Fal. 'Tis so.

Sil. Is't so ? Why then, say an old man can do somewhat.

Re-enter DAVY.

188

Davy. An't please your worship, there's one Pistol come from the court with news.

Fal. From the court! let him come in.

Enter PISTOL.

How now, Pistol!

Pist. Sir John, God save you!

Fal. What wind blew you hither, Pistol?

Pist. Not the ill wind which blows no man to good. Sweet knight, thou art now one of the greatest men in this realm.

Sil. By'r lady, I think a' be, but goodman Puff of Barson.

Pist. Puff!

Puff in thy teeth, most recreant coward base!

Sir John, I am thy Pistol and thy friend,

And helter-skelter have I rode to thee,

And tidings do I bring and lucky joys

And golden times and happy news of price.

Fal. I pray thee now, deliver them like a man of this world.

Pist. A foutre for the world and worldlings base!

I speak of Africa and golden joys.

Fal. O base Assyrian knight, what is thy news?

Let King Cophetua know the truth thereof.

Sil. And Robin Hood, Scarlet, and John. [*Singing.*

Pist. Shall dunghill curs confront the Helicons?

And shall good news be baffled?

Then, Pistol, lay thy head in Furies' lap.

Shal. Honest gentleman, I know not your breeding.

Pist. Why then, lament therefore.

Shal. Give me pardon, sir: if, sir, you come with news from the court, I take it there's but two ways, either to utter them, or to conceal them. I am, sir, under the king, in some authority.

Pist. Under which king, Besonian? speak, or die.

Shal. Under King Harry.

Pist.   Harry the Fourth? or Fifth?

189

Shal. Harry the Fourth.

Pist.   A foutre for thine office!
Sir John, thy tender lambkin now is king;
Harry the Fifth's the man. I speak the truth:
When Pistol lies, do this; and fig me, like
The bragging Spaniard.

Fal. What, is the old king dead?

Pist. As nail in door: the things I speak are just.

Fal. Away, Bardolph! saddle my horse. Master Robert
Shallow, choose what office thou wilt in the land, 'tis thine.
Pistol, I will double-charge thee with dignities.

Bard. O joyful day!
I would not take a knighthood for my fortune.

Pist. What! I do bring good news.

Fal. Carry Master Silence to bed. Master Shallow, my
Lord Shallow,—be what thou wilt; I am fortune's steward—
get on thy boots: we'll ride all night. O sweet Pistol! Away,
Bardolph! [*Exit Bard.*] Come, Pistol, utter more to me;
and withal devise something to do thyself good. Boot, boot,
Master Shallow: I know the young king is sick for me. Let
us take any man's horses; the laws of England are at my commandment. Blessed are they that have been my friends; and
woe to my lord chief-justice!

Pist. Let vultures vile seize on his lungs also!
' Where is the life that late I led?' say they:
Why, here it is; welcome these pleasant days!
                                                              [*Exeunt.*

ACT V, Scene iii, ll. 1-148

A public place near Westminster Abbey.

Enter FALSTAFF, SHALLOW, PISTOL, BARDOLPH, *and* Page.

Fal. Stand here by me, Master Robert Shallow; I will
make the king do you grace: I will leer upon him as a' comes
by; and do but mark the countenance that he will give me.

Pist. God bless thy lungs, good knight.

Fal. Come here, Pistol; stand behind me. O, if I had had

time to have made new liveries, I would have bestowed the thousand pound I borrowed of you. But 'tis no matter; this poor show doth better: this doth infer the zeal I had to see him.

Shal. It doth so.

Fal. It shows my earnestness of affection,—

Shal. It doth so.

Fal. My devotion,—

Shal. It doth, it doth, it doth.

Fal. As it were, to ride day and night; and not to deliberate, not to remember, not to have patience to shift me,—

Shal. It is best, certain.

Fal. But to stand stained with travel, and sweating with desire to see him; thinking of nothing else, putting all affairs else in oblivion, as if there were nothing else to be done but to see him.

Pist. 'Tis ' semper idem,' for ' obsque hoc nihil est : ' 'tis all in every part.

Shal. 'Tis so, indeed.

Pist. My knight, I will inflame thy noble liver,
And make thee rage.
Thy Doll, and Helen of thy noble thoughts,
Is in base durance and contagious prison;
Haled thither
By most mechanical and dirty hand :
Rouse up revenge from ebon den with fell Alecto's snake,
For Doll is in. Pistol speaks nought but truth.

Fal. I will deliver her.

[*Shouts within, and the trumpets sound.*

Pist. There roar'd the sea, and trumpet-clangor sounds.

Enter the KING *and his train, the* Lord Chief-Justice
among them.

Fal. God save thy grace, King Hal! my royal Hal!

Pist. The heavens thee guard and keep, most royal imp of fame!

Fal. God save thee, my sweet boy !

King. My lord chief-justice, speak to that vain man.

Ch. Just. Have you your wits ? know you what 'tis you
    speak ?

Fal. My king ! my Jove ! I speak to thee, my heart !

King. I know thee not, old man : fall to thy prayers ;
How ill white hairs become a fool and jester !
I have long dream'd of such a kind of man,
So surfeit-swell'd, so old and so profane ;
But, being awaked, I do despise my dream.
Make less thy body hence, and more thy grace ;
Leave gormandizing ; know the grave doth gape
For thee thrice wider than for other men.
Reply not to me with a fool-born jest :
Presume not that I am the thing I was ;
For God doth know, so shall the world perceive,
That I have turn'd away my former self ;
So will I those that kept me company.
When thou dost hear I am as I have been,
Approach me, and thou shalt be as thou wast,
The tutor and the feeder of my riots :
Till then, I banish thee, on pain of death,
As I have done the rest of my misleaders,
Not to come near our person by ten mile.
For competence of life I will allow you,
That lack of means enforce you not to evil :
And, as we hear you do reform yourselves,
We will, according to your strengths and qualities,
Give you advancement. Be it your charge, my lord,
To see perform'd the tenour of our word.
Set on.   [*Exeunt King, &c.*

Fal. Master Shallow, I owe you a thousand pound.

ACT V, Scene v, ll. 5-78

192

The Life of

King Henry the Fifth

O for a Muse of fire, that would ascend
The brightest heaven of invention,
A kingdom for a stage, princes to act
And monarchs to behold the swelling scene !
Then should the warlike Harry, like himself,
Assume the port of Mars ; and at his heels,
Leash'd in like hounds, should famine, sword and fire
Crouch for employment. But pardon, gentles all,
The flat unraised spirits that have dared
On this unworthy scaffold to bring forth
So great an object : can this cockpit hold
The vasty fields of France ? or may we cram
Within this wooden O the very casques
That did affright the air at Agincourt ?
O, pardon ! since a crooked figure may
Attest in little place a million ;
And let us, ciphers to this great accompt,
On your imaginary forces work.
Suppose within the girdle of these walls
Are now confined two mighty monarchies,
Whose high upreared and abutting fronts
The perilous narrow ocean parts asunder :
Piece out our imperfections with your thoughts ;
Into a thousand parts divide one man,
And make imaginary puissance ;
Think, when we talk of horses, that you see them
Printing their proud hoofs i' the receiving earth ;
For 'tis your thoughts that now must deck our kings
Carry them here and there ; jumping o'er times,
Turning the accomplishment of many years
Into an hour-glass.

Prologue, ll. 1-31

List his discourse of war, and you shall hear
A fearful battle render'd you in music :
Turn him to any cause of policy,
The Gordian knot of it he will unloose,
Familiar as his garter : that, when he speaks,
The air, a charter'd libertine, is still,
And the mute wonder lurketh in men's ears,
To steal his sweet and honey'd sentences.

ACT I, Scene i, ll. 43-50

So work the honey-bees,
Creatures that by a rule in nature teach
The act of order to a peopled kingdom
They have a king and officers of sorts ;
Where some, like magistrates, correct at home,
Others, like merchants, venture trade abroad,
Others, like soldiers, armed in their stings,
Make boot upon the summer's velvet buds,
Which pillage they with merry march bring home
To the tent-royal of their emperor ;
Who, busied in his majesty, surveys
The singing masons building roofs of gold,
The civil citizens kneading up the honey,
The poor mechanic porters crowding in
Their heavy burdens at his narrow gate,
The sad-eyed justice, with his surly hum,
Delivering o'er to executors pale
The lazy yawning drone

ACT I, Scene ii, ll. 187-204

Now all the youth of England are on fire,
And silken dalliance in the wardrobe lies :
Now thrive the armourers, and honour's thought
Reigns solely in the breast of every man :
They sell the pasture now to buy the horse,
Following the mirror of all Christian kings,
With winged heels, as English Mercuries.

194

For now sits Expectation in the air,
And hides a sword from hilts unto the point
With crowns imperial, crowns and coronets,
Promised to Harry and his followers.

ACT II, Prologue, ll. 1-11

London. A street.

Enter Corporal NYM *and* Lieutenant BARDOLPH.

Bard. Well met, Corporal Nym.

Nym. Good morrow, Lieutenant Bardolph.

Bard. What, are Ancient Pistol and you friends yet?

Nym. For my part, I care not: I say little; but when time shall serve, there shall be smiles; but that shall be as it may. I dare not fight; but I will wink and hold out mine iron: it is a simple one; but what though? it will toast cheese, and it will endure cold as another man's sword will: and there's an end. . . .

Enter PISTOL *and* Hostess. . . .

Enter the Boy.

Boy. Mine host Pistol, you must come to my master, and you, hostess: he is very sick, and would to bed. Good Bardolph, put thy face between his sheets, and do the office of a warming-pan. Faith, he's very ill.

Bard. Away, you rogue!

Hostess. By my troth, he'll yield the crow a pudding one of these days. The king has killed his heart. Good husband, come home presently. [*Exeunt Hostess and Boy.* . . .

Re-enter Hostess.

Host. As ever you came of women, come in quickly to Sir John. Ah, poor heart! he is so shaked of a burning quotidian tertian, that it is most lamentable to behold. Sweet men, come to him.

Nym. The king hath run bad humours on the knight; that's the even of it.

Pistol. Nym, thou hast spoke the right ;
His heart is fracted and corroborate.

ACT II, Scene i, ll. 1-11, 85-93, 122-130

Pist. Falstaff he is dead,
And we must yearn therefore.

Bardolph. Would I were with him, wheresome'er he is,
either in heaven or in hell !

Host. Nay, sure, he's not in hell : he's in Arthur's bosom,
if ever man went to Arthur's bosom. A' made a finer end and
went away an it had been any christom child ; a' parted even
just between twelve and one, even at the turning o' the tide :
for after I saw him fumble with the sheets and play with
flowers and smile upon his fingers' ends, I knew there was but
one way ; for his nose was as sharp as a pen, and a' babbled of
green fields. 'How now, Sir John !' quoth I : 'what, man !
be o' good cheer.' So a' cried out 'God, God, God !' three
or four times. Now I, to comfort him, bid him a' should not
think of God ; I hoped there was no need to trouble himself
with any such thoughts yet. So a' bade me lay more clothes
on his feet : I put my hand into the bed and felt them, and
they were as cold as any stone ; then I felt to his knees, and
they were as cold as any stone, and so upward and upward,
and all was as cold as any stone.

Nym. They say he cried out of sack.

Host. Ay, that a' did.

Bard. And of women.

Host. Nay, that a' did not.

Boy. Yes, that a' did ; and said they were devils incarnate.

Host. A' could never abide carnation ; 'twas a colour he
never liked.

Boy. A' said once, the devil would have him about women.

Host. A' did in some sort, indeed, handle women ; but
then he was rheumatic, and talked of the whore of Babylon.

Boy. Do you not remember, a' saw a flea stick upon
Bardolph's nose, and a' said it was a black soul burning in
hell-fire ?

Bard. Well, the fuel is gone that maintained that fire: that's all the riches I got in his service.

Nym. Shall we shog? the king will be gone from Southampton.

ACT II, Scene iii, ll. 4-48

In fierce tempest is he coming,
In thunder and in earthquake, like a Jove,

ACT II, Scene iv, ll. 99-100

Thus with imagined wing our swift scene flies
In motion of no less celerity
Than that of thought. Suppose that you have seen
The well-appointed king at Hampton pier
Embark his royalty; and his brave fleet
With silken streamers the young Phœbus fanning:
Play with your fancies, and in them behold
Upon the hempen tackle ship-boys climbing;
Hear the shrill whistle which doth order give
To sounds confused; behold the threaden sails,
Borne with the invisible and creeping wind,
Draw the huge bottoms through the furrow'd sea,
Breasting the lofty surge: O, do but think
You stand upon the rivage and behold
A city on the inconstant billows dancing;
For so appears this fleet majestical,
Holding due course to Harfleur. Follow, follow.

ACT III, Prologue, ll. 1-17

France. Before Harfleur.

King Henry. Once more unto the breach, dear friends,
    once more;
Or close the wall up with our English dead.
In peace there's nothing so becomes a man
As modest stillness and humility:
But when the blast of war blows in our ears,
Then imitate the action of the tiger;
Stiffen the sinews, summon up the blood,
Disguise fair nature with hard-favour'd rage;

197

Then lend the eye a terrible aspect ;
Let it pry through the portage of the head
Like the brass cannon ; let the brow o'erwhelm it
As fearfully as doth a galled rock
O'erhang and jutty his confounded base,
Swill'd with the wild and wasteful ocean. . . .
I see you stand like greyhounds in the slips,
Straining upon the start.   The game's afoot :
Follow your spirit.

ACT III, Scene i, ll. 1-14, 31-33

Pistol. Fortune is Bardolph's foe, and frowns on him ;
For he hath stolen a pax, and hanged must a' be :
A damned death !
Let gallows gape for dog ; let man go free
And let not hemp his wind-pipe suffocate :
But Exeter hath given the doom of death
For pax of little price.
Therefore, go speak : the duke will hear thy voice ;
And let not Bardolph's vital thread be cut
With edge of penny cord and vile reproach :
Speak, captain, for his life, and I will thee requite.

Fluellen. Aunchient Pistol, I do partly understand your
meaning.

ACT III, Scene vi, ll. 41-53

The French camp, near Agincourt.

Dauphin. What a long night is this ! I will not change my
horse with any that treads but on four pasterns. Ça, ha ! he
bounds from the earth, as if his entrails were hairs ; le cheval
volant, the Pegasus, chez les narines de feu ! When I bestride
him, I soar, I am a hawk : he trots the air ; the earth sings
when he touches it ; the basest horn of his hoof is more
musical than the pipe of Hermes.

Orleans. He's of the colour of the nutmeg.

Dau. And of the heat of the ginger   It is a beast for
Perseus : he is pure air and fire ; and the dull elements of

earth and water never appear in him, but only in patient stillness while his rider mounts him : he is indeed a horse ; and
all other jades you may call beasts.

ACT III, Scene vii, ll. 11-26

Now entertain conjecture of a time
When creeping murmur and the poring dark
Fills the wide vessel of the universe.
From camp to camp through the foul womb of night
The hum of either army stilly sounds,
That the fix'd sentinels almost receive
The secret whispers of each other's watch :
Fire answers fire, and through their paly flames
Each battle sees the other's umber'd face ;
Steed threatens steed, in high and boastful neighs
Piercing the night's dull ear ; and from the tents
The armourers, accomplishing the knights,
With busy hammers closing rivets up,
Give dreadful note of preparation :
The country cocks do crow, the clocks do toll,
And the third hour of drowsy morning name.
Proud of their numbers and secure in soul,
The confident and over-lusty French
Do the low-rated English play at dice ;
And chide the cripple tardy-gaited night
Who, like a foul and ugly witch, doth limp
So tediously away. The poor condemned English,
Like sacrifices, by their watchful fires
Sit patiently and inly ruminate
The morning's danger, and their gesture sad
Investing lank-lean cheeks and war-worn coats
Presenteth them unto the gazing moon
So many horrid ghosts. O now, who will behold
The royal captain of this ruin'd band
Walking from watch to watch, from tent to tent,
Let him cry ' Praise and glory on his head ! '
For forth he goes and visits all his host,

Bids them good morrow with a modest smile
And calls them brothers, friends and countrymen.
Upon his royal face there is no note
How dread an army hath enrounded him;
Nor doth he dedicate one jot of colour
Unto the weary and all-watched night,
But freshly looks and over-bears attaint
With cheerful semblance and sweet majesty;
That every wretch, pining and pale before,
Beholding him, plucks comfort from his looks:
A largess universal like the sun
His liberal eye doth give to every one,
Thawing cold fear, that mean and gentle all
Behold, as may unworthiness define,
A little touch of Harry in the night.

ACT IV, Prologue, ll. 1-47

God Almighty!
There is some soul of goodness in things evil,
Would men observingly distil it out.
For our bad neighbour makes us early stirrers,
Which is both healthful and good husbandry:
Besides, they are our outward consciences,
And preachers to us all, admonishing
That we should dress us fairly for our end.
Thus may we gather honey from the weed,
And make a moral of the devil himself.

ACT IV, Scene i, ll. 3-12

'Tis not the balm, the sceptre and the ball,
The sword, the mace, the crown imperial,
The intertissued robe of gold and pearl,
The farced title running 'fore the king,
The throne he sits on, nor the tide of pomp
That beats upon the high shore of this world,
No, not all these, thrice-gorgeous ceremony,
Not all these, laid in bed majestical,

Can sleep so soundly as the wretched slave,
Who with a body fill'd and vacant mind
Gets him to rest, cramm'd with distressful bread ;
Never sees horrid night, the child of hell,
But, like a lackey, from the rise to set
Sweats in the eye of Phœbus and all night
Sleeps in Elysium ; next day after dawn,
Doth rise and help Hyperion to his horse,
And follows so the ever-running year,
With profitable labour, to his grave.

ACT IV, Scene i, ll. 277-294

King Henry. O God of battles ! steel my soldiers'
  hearts ;
Possess them not with fear ; take from them now
The sense of reckoning, if the opposed numbers
Pluck their hearts from them. Not to-day, O Lord,
O, not to-day, think not upon the fault
My father made in compassing the crown !
I Richard's body have interred new ;
And on it have bestow'd more contrite tears
Than from it issued forced drops of blood :
Five hundred poor I have in yearly pay,
Who twice a-day their wither'd hands hold up
Toward heaven, to pardon blood ; and I have built
Two chantries, where the sad and solemn priests
Sing still for Richard's soul. More will I do ;
Though all that I can do is nothing worth,
Since that my penitence comes after all,
Imploring pardon.   ACT IV, Scene i, ll. 306-322

Westmorland.   O that we now had here
But one ten thousand of those men in England
That do no work to-day !
  King Henry.   What's he that wishes so ?
My cousin Westmoreland ? No, my fair cousin :
If we are mark'd to die, we are enow

To do our country loss; and if to live,
The fewer men, the greater share of honour.
God's will! I pray thee, wish not one man more.
By Jove, I am not covetous for gold,
Nor care I who doth feed upon my cost;
It yearns me not if men my garments wear;
Such outward things dwell not in my desires:
But if it be a sin to covet honour,
I am the most offending soul alive.
No, faith, my coz, wish not a man from England:
God's peace! I would not lose so great an honour
As one man more, methinks, would share from me
For the best hope I have. O, do not wish one more
Rather proclaim it, Westmoreland, through my host,
That he which hath no stomach to this fight,
Let him depart; his passport shall be made
And crowns for convoy put into his purse:
We would not die in that man's company
That fears his fellowship to die with us.
This day is call'd the feast of Crispian:
He that outlives this day, and comes safe home,
Will stand a tip-toe when this day is named,
And rouse him at the name of Crispian.
He that shall live this day, and see old age,
Will yearly on the vigil feast his neighbours,
And say ' To-morrow is Saint Crispian:'
Then will he strip his sleeve and show his scars,
And say ' These wounds I had on Crispin's day.'
Old men forget; yet all shall be forgot,
But he'll remember with advantages
What feats he did that day: then shall our names,
Familiar in his mouth as household words,
Harry the King, Bedford and Exeter,
Warwick and Talbot, Salisbury and Gloucester,
Be in their flowing cups freshly remember'd.
This story shall the good man teach his son;

And Crispin Crispian shall ne'er go by,
From this day to the ending of the world,
But we in it shall be remembered ;
We few, we happy few, we band of brothers ;
For he to-day that sheds his blood with me
Shall be my brother ; be he ne'er so vile,
This day shall gentle his condition :
And gentlemen in England now a-bed
Shall think themselves accursed they were not here,
And hold their manhoods cheap whiles any speaks
That fought with us upon Saint Crispin's day.

ACT IV, Scene iii, ll. 16-67

The field of battle.

Enter FLUELLEN *and* GOWER.

Gow. O, 'tis a gallant king !

Flu. Ay, he was porn at Monmouth, Captain Gower. What call you the town's name where Alexander the Pig was born ?

Gow. Alexander the Great.

Flu. Why, I pray you, is not pig great ? the pig, or the great, or the mighty, or the huge, or the magnanimous, are all one reckonings, save the phrase is a little variations.

Gow. I think Alexander the Great was born in Macedon : his father was called Philip of Macedon, as I take it.

Flu. I think it is in Macedon where Alexander is porn. I tell you, captain, if you look in the maps of the 'orld, I warrant you sall find, in the comparisons between Macedon and Monmouth, that the situations, look you, is both alike. There is a river in Macedon ; and there is also moreover a river at Monmouth : it is called Wye at Monmouth ; but it is out of my prains what is the name of the other river ; but 'tis all one, 'tis alike as my fingers is to my fingers, and there is salmons in both. If you mark Alexander's life well, Harry of Monmouth's life is come after it indifferent well ; for there is figures in all things. Alexander, God knows, and you know, in his rages, and his furies, and his wraths, and his cholers, and his moods, and his displeasures, and his indignations, and also being a little intoxicates in his prains, did, in his ales and his angers, look you, kill his best friend, Cleitus.

Gow. Our king is not like him in that: he never killed any of his friends.

Flu. It is not well done, mark you now, to take the tales out of my mouth, ere it is made and finished. I speak but in the figures and comparisons of it: As Alexander killed his friend Cleitus, being in his ales and his cups; so also Harry Monmouth, being in his right wits and his good judgements, turned away the fat knight with the great belly-doublet: he was full of jests, and gipes, and knaveries, and mocks; I have forgot his name.

Gow. Sir John Falstaff.

Flu. That is he: I'll tell you there is good men porn at Monmouth. Act IV, Scene vii, ll. 10-56

Before God, Kate, I cannot look greenly nor gasp out my eloquence, nor I have no cunning in protestation; only downright oaths, which I never use till urged, nor never break for urging. If thou canst love a fellow of this temper, Kate, whose face is not worth sun-burning, that never looks in his glass for love of any thing he sees there, let thine eye be thy cook. I speak to thee plain soldier: if thou canst love me for this, take me; if not, to say to thee that I shall die, is true; but for thy love, by the Lord, no; yet I love thee too. And while thou livest, dear Kate, take a fellow of plain and uncoined constancy; for he perforce must do thee right, because he hath not the gift to woo in other places: for these fellows of infinite tongue, that can rhyme themselves into ladies' favours, they do always reason themselves out again. What! a speaker is but a prater; a rhyme is but a ballad. A good leg will fall; a straight back will stoop; a black beard will turn white; a curled pate will grow bald; a fair face will wither; a full eye will wax hollow: but a good heart, Kate, is the sun and the moon; or rather the sun and not the moon; for it shines bright and never changes, but keeps his course truly. If thou would have such a one, take me ; and take me, take a soldier ; take a soldier, take a king. . . . Shall not thou and I, between Saint Denis and Saint George, compound a boy, half French, half English, that shall go to Constantinople and take the Turk by the beard ? shall we not ? what sayest thou, my fair flower-de-luce ?

ACT V, Scene ii, ll. 148-176, 219-224

Small time, but in that small most greatly lived
This star of England.

Epilogue, ll. 5-6

The Merry Wives of Windsor

Windsor. Before PAGE'S *house.*

Enter JUSTICE SHALLOW, SLENDER, *and* SIR HUGH EVANS.

Shal. Sir Hugh, persuade me not ; I will make a Star-chamber matter of it : if he were twenty Sir John Falstaffs, he shall not abuse Robert Shallow, esquire.

Slen. In the county of Gloucester, justice of peace and ' Coram.'

Shal. Ay, cousin Slender, and ' Custalorum.'

Slen. Ay, and ' Rato-lorum ' too ; and a gentleman born, master parson ; who writes himself ' Armigero,' in any bill, warrant, quittance, or obligation, ' Armigero.'

Shal. Ay, that I do ; and have done any time these three hundred years.

Slen. All his successors gone before him hath done't ; and all his ancestors that come after him may : they may give the dozen white luces in their coat.

Shal. It is an old coat.

Evans. The dozen white louses do become an old coat well ; it agrees well, passant ; it is a familiar beast to man, and signifies love.

ACT I, Scene i, ll. 1-21

A room in DOCTOR CAIUS's *house*.

Enter MISTRESS QUICKLY, SIMPLE, *and* RUGBY.

Quick. What, John Rugby ! I pray thee, go to the casement, and see if you can see my master, Master Doctor Caius, coming. If he do, i' faith, and find any body in the house, here will be an old abusing of God's patience and the king's English.

Rug. I'll go watch.

Quick. Go ; and we'll have a posset for't soon at night, in faith, at the latter end of a sea-coal fire. [*Exit Rugby.*] An honest, willing, kind fellow, as ever servant shall come in house withal, and, I warrant you, no tell-tale nor no breed-bate : his worst fault is, that he is given to prayer ; he is something peevish that way : but nobody but has his fault ; but let that pass. Peter Simple, you say your name is ?

Sim. Ay, for fault of a better.   ACT I, Scene iv, ll. 1-17

What, have I scaped love-letters in the holiday-time of my beauty, and am I now a subject for them ?

ACT II, Scene i, ll. 1-3

You'll not bear a letter. . . . Why, thou unconfinable baseness, it is as much as I can do to keep the terms of my honour precise : I, I, I myself sometimes, leaving the fear of God on the left hand and hiding mine honour in my necessity, am fain to shuffle, to hedge and to lurch ; and yet you, rogue, will ensconce your rags, your cat-a-mountain looks, your red-lattice phrases, and your bold-beating oaths, under the shelter of your honour !   ACT II, Scene ii, ll. 19, 21-29

Evans. 'Pless my soul, how full of chollors I am, and trempling of mind ! I shall be glad if he have deceived me. How melancholies I am ! I will knog his urinals about his knave's costard when I have good opportunities for the ork. 'Pless my soul !   [*Sings.*

To shallow rivers, to whose falls
Melodious birds sing madrigals ;

There will we make our peds of roses,
And a thousand fragrant posies.
To shallow—
Mercy on me! I have a great dispositions to cry.   [*Sings.*
Melodious birds sing madrigals—
When as I sat in Pabylon—
And a thousand vagram posies.
To shallow, &c.

Enter SIMPLE.

Sim. Yonder he is coming, this way, Sir Hugh.
Evans. He's welcome.   [*Sings.*
To shallow rivers, to whose falls—
Heaven prosper the right!

ACT III, Scene i, ll. 11-30

What say you to young Master Fenton? he capers, he
dances, he has eyes of youth, he writes verses, he speaks holiday, he smells April and May: he will carry't, he will carry't;
'tis in his buttons; he will carry't.

ACT III, Scene ii, ll. 67-71

Falstaff. Go fetch me a quart of sack; put a toast in't.
Have I lived to be carried in a basket, like a barrow of butcher's
offal, and to be thrown in the Thames? Well, if I be served
such another trick, I'll have my brains ta'en out and buttered,
and give them to a dog for a new-year's gift. The rogues
slighted me into the river with as little remorse as they would
have drowned a blind bitch's puppies, fifteen i' the litter: and
you may know by my size that I have a kind of alacrity in
sinking; if the bottom were as deep as hell, I should down.
I had been drowned, but that the shore was shelvy and
shallow,—a death that I abhor; for the water swells a man;
and what a thing should I have been when I had been swelled!
I should have been a mountain of mummy.

ACT III, Scene v, ll. 3-19

Much Ado about Nothing

Messina. Before LEONATO'S *house.*

Beatrice. I wonder that you will still be talking, Signior Benedick : nobody marks you.

Benedick. What, my dear Lady Disdain ! are you yet living ?

Beat. Is it possible disdain should die while she hath such meet food to feed it as Signior Benedick ? Courtesy itself must convert to disdain, if you come in her presence.

Bene. Then is courtesy a turncoat. But it is certain I am loved of all ladies, only you excepted : and I would I could find in my heart that I had not a hard heart ; for, truly, I love none.

Beat. A dear happiness to women : they would else have been troubled with a pernicious suitor. I thank God and my cold blood, I am of your humour for that : I had rather hear my dog bark at a crow than a man swear he loves me.

Bene. God keep your ladyship still in that mind ! so some gentleman or other shall 'scape a predestinate scratched face.

Beat. Scratching could not make it worse, an 'twere such a face as yours were.

Bene. Well, you are a rare parrot-teacher.

Beat. A bird of my tongue is better than a beast of yours.

Bene. I would my horse had the speed of your tongue, and so good a continuer. But keep your way, i' God's name ; I have done.

Beat. You always end with a jade's trick : I know you of old.

ACT I, Scene i, ll. 117-146

Don Pedro. I shall see thee, ere I die, look pale with love.

Benedick. With anger, with sickness, or with hunger, my lord, not with love : prove that ever I lose more blood with love than I will get again with drinking, pick out mine eyes with a ballad-maker's pen and hang me up at the door of a brothel-house for the sign of blind Cupid.

D. Pedro. Well, if ever thou dost fall from this faith, thou wilt prove a notable argument.

Bene. If I do, hang me in a bottle like a cat and shoot at me ; and he that hits me, let him be clapped on the shoulder, and called Adam.

D. Pedro. Well, as time shall try :
' In time the savage bull doth bear the yoke.'

Bene. The savage bull may ; but if ever the sensible Benedick bear it, pluck off the bull's horns and set them in my forehead : and let me be vilely painted, and in such great letters as they write ' Here is good horse to hire,' let them signify under my sign ' Here you may see Benedick the married man.'   ACT I, Scene i, ll. 249-270

Leonato. Well, then, go you into hell ?
Beatrice. No, but to the gate ; and there will the devil meet me, like an old cuckold, with horns on his head, and say ' Get you to heaven, Beatrice, get you to heaven ; here's no place for you maids : ' so deliver I up my apes, and away to Saint Peter for the heavens ; he shows me where the bachelors sit, and there live we as merry as the day is long.
                                              ACT II, Scene i, ll. 44-52

Speak low, if you speak love.
                                              ACT II, Scene i, l. 103

Don Pedro. The Lady Beatrice hath a quarrel to you : the gentleman that danced with her told her she is much wronged by you.

Benedick. O, she misused me past the endurance of a block ! an oak but with one green leaf on it would have answered her ; my very visor began to assume life and scold with her. She told me, not thinking I had been myself, that I was the prince's jester, that I was duller than a great thaw ; huddling jest upon jest with such impossible conveyance upon me that I stood like a man at a mark, with a whole army shooting at me. She speaks poniards, and every word stabs: if her breath were as terrible as her terminations, there were no living near her; she would infect to the north star. I would not marry her, though she were endowed with all that Adam had left him before he transgressed: she would have made Hercules have turned spit, yea, and have cleft his club to make the fire too. Come, talk not of her: you shall find her the infernal Ate in good apparel. I would to God some scholar would conjure her; for certainly, while she is here, a man may live as quiet in hell as in a sanctuary; and people sin upon purpose, because they would go thither; so, indeed, all disquiet, horror and perturbation follows her.

D. Pedro. Look, here she comes.

Bene. Will your grace command me any service to the world's end? I will go on the slightest errand now to the Antipodes that you can devise to send me on; I will fetch you a tooth-picker now from the furthest inch of Asia, bring you the length of Prester John's foot, fetch you a hair off the great Cham's beard, do you any embassage to the Pigmies, rather than hold three words' conference with this harpy. You have no employment for me?   ACT II, Scene i, ll. 243-280

Don Pedro. In faith, lady, you have a merry heart.

Beatrice. Yea, my lord; I thank it, poor fool, it keeps on the windy side of care. My cousin tells him in his ear that he is in her heart.

Claudio. And so she doth, cousin.

Beat. Good Lord, for alliance! Thus goes every one to the world but I, and I am sunburnt; I may sit in a corner and cry heigh-ho for a husband!

D. Pedro. Lady Beatrice, I will get you one.

Beat. I would rather have one of your father's getting. Hath your grace ne'er a brother like you? Your father got excellent husbands, if a maid could come by them.

D. Pedro. Will you have me, lady?

Beat. No, my lord, unless I might have another for working-days : your grace is too costly to wear every day. But, I beseech your grace, pardon me : I was born to speak all mirth and no matter.

D. Pedro. Your silence most offends me, and to be merry best becomes you ; for, out of question, you were born in a merry hour.

Beat. No, sure, my lord, my mother cried ; but then there was a star danced, and under that was I born.

ACT II, Scene i, ll. 324-350

Sigh no more, ladies, sigh no more,
    Men were deceivers ever,
One foot in sea and one on shore,
    To one thing constant never :
Then sigh not so, but let them go,
    And be you blithe and bonny,
Converting all your sounds of woe
    Into Hey nonny, nonny.

Sing no more ditties, sing no moe,
    Of dumps so dull and heavy ;
The fraud of men was ever so,
    Since summer first was leavy :
Then sigh not so, but let them go,
    And be you blithe and bonny,
Converting all your sounds of woe
    Into Hey nonny, nonny.

ACT II, Scene iii, ll. 64-79

Bid her steal into the pleached bower,
Where honeysuckles, ripen'd by the sun
Forbid the sun to enter, like favourites,
Made proud by princes, that advance their pride
Against that power that bred it.

ACT III, Scene i, ll. 7-11

Benedick. Gallants, I am not as I have been.

Leonato. So say I : methinks you are sadder.

Claudio. I hope he be in love.

Don Pedro. Hang him, truant ! there's no true drop of blood in him, to be truly touched with love : if he be sad, he wants money.

Bene. I have the toothache. . . .

Claud. If he be not in love with some woman, there is no believing old signs : a' brushes his hat o' mornings ; what should that bode ?

D. Pedro. Hath any man seen him at the barber's ?

Claud. No, but the barber's man hath been seen with him, and the old ornament of his cheek hath already stuffed tennis-balls.

Leon. Indeed, he looks younger than he did, by the loss of a beard.

D. Pedro. Nay, a' rubs himself with civet : can you smell him out by that ?

Claud. That's as much as to say, the sweet youth's in love.

D. Pedro. The greatest note of it is his melancholy.

Claud. And when was he wont to wash his face ?

D. Pedro. Yea, or to paint himself ? for the which, I hear what they say of him.

Claud. Nay, but his jesting spirit ; which is now crept into a lute-string and now governed by stops.

D. Pedro. Indeed, that tells a heavy tale for him : conclude, conclude he is in love. ACT III, Scene ii, ll. 15-21, 40-64

A street.

Enter DOGBERRY and VERGES with the Watch.

Dog. Are you good men and true ?

Verg. Yea, or else it were pity but they should suffer salvation, body and soul.

Dog. Nay, that were a punishment too good for them, if they should have any allegiance in them, being chosen for the prince's watch.

Verg. Well, give them their charge, neighbour Dogberry.

Dog. First, who think you the most desartless man to be constable?

First Watch. Hugh Otecake, sir, or George Seacole; for they can write and read.

Dog. Come hither, neighbour Seacole. God hath blessed you with a good name: to be a well-favoured man is the gift of fortune; but to write and read comes by nature.

Second Watch. Both which, master constable,—

Dog. You have: I knew it would be your answer. Well, for your favour, sir, why, give God thanks, and make no boast of it; and for your writing and reading, let that appear when there is no need of such vanity. You are thought here to be the most senseless and fit man for the constable of the watch; therefore bear you the lantern. This is your charge: you shall comprehend all vagrom men; you are to bid any man stand, in the prince's name.

Sec. Watch. How if a' will not stand?

Dog. Why, then, take no note of him, but let him go; and presently call the rest of the watch together and thank God you are rid of a knave. . . .

Enter BORACHIO *and* CONRADE.

Bora. What, Conrade!

Watch. [*Aside*] Peace! stir not.

Bora. Conrade, I say!

Con. Here, man; I am at thy elbow.

Bora. Mass, and my elbow itched; I thought there would a scab follow.

Con. I will owe thee an answer for that: and now forward with thy tale.

Bora. Stand thee close, then, under this pent-house, for it drizzles rain; and I will, like a true drunkard, utter all to thee.

Watch. [*Aside*] Some treason, masters: yet stand close.

Bora. Therefore know I have earned of Don John a thousand ducats.

Con. Is it possible that any villany should be so dear ?

Bora. Thou shouldst rather ask if it were possible any villany should be so rich ; for when rich villains have need of poor ones, poor ones may make what price they will.

Con. I wonder at it.

Bora. That shows thou art unconfirmed. Thou knowest that the fashion of a doublet, or a hat, or a cloak, is nothing to a man.

Con. Yes, it is apparel.

Bora. I mean, the fashion.

Con. Yes, the fashion is the fashion.

· *Bora.* Tush ! I may as well say the fool's the fool. But seest thou not what a deformed thief this fashion is ?

Watch. [*Aside*] I know that Deformed ; a' has been a vile thief this seven year ; a' goes up and down like a gentleman : I remember his name.

Bora. Didst thou not hear somebody ?

Con. No ; 'twas the vane on the house.

Bora. Seest thou not, I say, what a deformed thief this fashion is ? how giddily a' turns about all the hot bloods between fourteen and five-and-thirty ? sometimes fashioning them like Pharaoh's soldiers in the reechy painting, sometime like god Bel's priests in the old church-window, sometime like the shaven Hercules in the smirched worm-eaten tapestry, where his codpiece seems as massy as his club ?

Con. All this I see ; and I see that the fashion wears out more apparel than the man. But art not thou thyself giddy with the fashion too, that thou hast shifted out of thy tale into telling me of the fashion ?

Bora. Not so, neither : but know that I have to-night wooed Margaret, the Lady Hero's gentlewoman, by the name of Hero : she leans me out at her mistress' chamber-window, bids me a thousand times good night,—I tell this tale vilely : —I should first tell thee how the prince, Claudio and my master, planted and placed and possessed by my master Don John, saw afar off in the orchard this amiable encounter. . . .

First Watch. We charge you, in the prince's name, stand !

Sec. Watch. Call up the right master constable. We have here recovered the most dangerous piece of lechery that ever was known in the commonwealth.

First Watch. And one Deformed is one of them : I know him ; a' wears a lock.

ACT III, Scene iii, ll. 1-31, 102-161, 176-183

Dogberry. A good old man, sir ; he will be talking : as they say, When the age is in, the wit is out : God help us ! it is a world to see. Well said, i' faith, neighbour Verges : well, God's a good man ; an two men ride of a horse, one must ride behind. An honest soul, i' faith, sir ; by my troth he is, as ever broke bread ; but God is to be worshipped ; all men are not alike ; alas, good neighbour !

ACT III, Scene v, ll. 36-44

You seem to me as Dian in her orb,
As chaste as is the bud ere it be blown.

ACT IV, Scene i, ll. 58-59

Benedick. Lady Beatrice, have you wept all this while ?

Beatrice. Yea, and I will weep a while longer.

Bene. I will not desire that.

Beat. You have no reason ; I do it freely.

Bene. Surely I do believe your fair cousin is wronged.

Beat. Ah, how much might the man deserve of me that would right her !

Bene. Is there any way to show such friendship ?

Beat. A very even way, but no such friend.

Bene. May a man do it ?

Beat. It is a man's office, but not yours.

Bene. I do love nothing in the world so well as you : is not that strange ?

Beat. As strange as the thing I know not. It were as possible for me to say I loved nothing so well as you : but believe me not ; and yet I lie not ; I confess nothing, nor I deny nothing. I am sorry for my cousin.

215

Bene. By my sword, Beatrice, thou lovest me.

Beat. Do not swear, and eat it.

Bene. I will swear by it that you love me; and I will make him eat it that says I love not you.

Beat. Will you not eat your word?

Bene. With no sauce that can be devised to it. I protest I love thee.

Beat. Why, then, God forgive me!

Bene. What offence, sweet Beatrice?

Beat. You have stayed me in a happy hour: I was about to protest I loved you.

Bene. And do it with all thy heart.

Beat. I love you with so much of my heart that none is left to protest.

Bene. Come, bid me do any thing for thee.

Beat. Kill Claudio.

Bene. Ha! not for the wide world.

Beat. You kill me to deny it. Farewell.

Bene. Tarry, sweet Beatrice.

Beat. I am gone, though I am here: there is no love in you: nay, I pray you, let me go.

Bene. Beatrice,—

Beat. In faith, I will go.

Bene. We'll be friends first.

Beat. You dare easier be friends with me than fight with mine enemy.

Bene. Is Claudio thine enemy?

Beat. Is he not approved in the height a villain, that hath slandered, scorned, dishonoured my kinswoman? O that I were a man! What, bear her in hand until they come to take hands; and then, with public accusation, uncovered slander, unmitigated rancour,—O God, that I were a man! I would eat his heart in the market-place.

Bene. Hear me, Beatrice,—

Beat. Talk with a man out at a window! A proper saying!

Bene. Nay, but, Beatrice,—

Beat. Sweet Hero! She is wronged, she is slandered, she is undone.

Bene. Beat—

Beat. Princes and counties! Surely, a princely testimony, a goodly count, Count Comfect; a sweet gallant, surely! O that I were a man for his sake! or that I had any friend would be a man for my sake! But manhood is melted into courtesies, valour into compliment, and men are only turned into tongue, and trim ones too: he is now as valiant as Hercules that only tells a lie and swears it. I cannot be a man with wishing, therefore I will die a woman with grieving.

Bene. Tarry, good Beatrice. By this hand, I love thee.

Beat. Use it for my love some other way than swearing by it.

Bene. Think you in your soul the Count Claudio hath wronged Hero?

Beat. Yea, as sure as I have a thought or a soul.

Bene. Enough, I am engaged; I will challenge him. I will kiss your hand, and so I leave you. By this hand, Claudio shall render me a dear account. As you hear of me, so think of me. Go, comfort your cousin: I must say she is dead: and so, farewell.

ACT IV, Scene i, ll. 257-339

A prison.

Enter DOGBERRY, VERGES, *and* Sexton, *in gowns; and the* Watch, *with* CONRADE *and* BORACHIO.

Dog. Is our whole dissembly appeared?

Verg. O, a stool and a cushion for the sexton.

Sex. Which be the malefactors?

Dog. Marry, that am I and my partner.

Verg. Nay, that's certain; we have the exhibition to examine.

Sex. But which are the offenders that are to be examined? let them come before master constable.

Dog. Yea, marry, let them come before me. What is your name, friend?

Bora. Borachio.

217

Dog. Pray, write down, Borachio. Yours, sirrah ?

Con. I am a gentleman, sir, and my name is Conrade.

Dog. Write down, master gentleman Conrade. Masters, do you serve God ?

Con. }
Bora. } Yea, sir, we hope.

Dog. Write down, that they hope they serve God : and write God first ; for God defend but God should go before such villains ! Masters, it is proved already that you are little better than false knaves ; and it will go near to be thought so shortly. How answer you for yourselves ?

Con. Marry, sir, we say we are none.

Dog. A marvellous witty fellow, I assure you ; but I will go about with him. Come you hither, sirrah ; a word in your ear : sir, I say to you, it is thought you are false knaves.

Bora. Sir, I say to you we are none.

Dog. Well, stand aside. 'Fore God, they are both in a tale. Have you writ down, that they are none ?

Sex. Master constable, you go not the way to examine : you must call forth the watch that are their accusers.

Dog. Yea, marry, that's the eftest way. Let the watch come forth. Masters, I charge you, in the prince's name, accuse these men.

First Watch. This man said, sir, that Don John, the prince's brother, was a villain.

Dog. Write down Prince John a villain. Why, this is flat perjury, to call a prince's brother villain.

Bora. Master constable,—

Dog. Pray thee, fellow, peace : I do not like thy look, I promise thee.

Sex. What heard you him say else ?

Sec. Watch. Marry, that he had received a thousand ducats of Don John for accusing the Lady Hero wrongfully.

Dog. Flat burglary as ever was committed.

Verg. Yea, by mass, that it is.

Sex. What else, fellow?

First Watch. And that Count Claudio did mean, upon his words, to disgrace Hero before the whole assembly, and not marry her.

Dog. O villain! thou wilt be condemned into everlasting redemption for this.

Sex. What else?

Watch. This is all.

Sex. And this is more, masters, than you can deny. Prince John is this morning secretly stolen away; Hero was in this manner accused, in this very manner refused, and upon the grief of this suddenly died. Master constable, let these men be bound, and brought to Leonato's: I will go before and show him their examination. [*Exit.*

Dog. Come, let them be opinioned.

Verg. Let them be in the hands—

Con. Off, coxcomb!

Dog. God's my life, where's the sexton? let him write down the prince's officer coxcomb. Come, bind them. Thou naughty varlet!

Con. Away! you are an ass, you are an ass.

Dog. Dost thou not suspect my place? dost thou not suspect my years? O that he were here to write me down an ass! But, masters, remember that I am an ass; though it be not written down, yet forget not that I am an ass. No, thou villain, thou art full of piety, as shall be proved upon thee by good witness. I am a wise fellow, and, which is more, an officer, and, which is more, a householder, and, which is more, as pretty a piece of flesh as any is in Messina, and one that knows the law, go to; and a rich fellow enough, go to; and a fellow that hath had losses, and one that hath two gowns and every thing handsome about him. Bring him away. O that I had been writ down an ass!

ACT IV, Scene ii, ll. 1-90

Benedick. Shall I speak a word in your ear?

Claudio. God bless me from a challenge!

Bene. [*Aside to Claudio*] You are a villain; I jest not: I will make it good how you dare, with what you dare, and when you dare. Do me right, or I will protest your cowardice. You have killed a sweet lady, and her death shall fall heavy on you. Let me hear from you. . . .

Fare you well, boy: you know my mind. I will leave you now to your gossip-like humour: you break jests as braggarts do their blades, which, God be thanked, hurt not. My lord, for your many courtesies I thank you: I must discontinue your company: your brother the bastard is fled from Messina: you have among you killed a sweet and innocent lady. For my Lord Lackbeard there, he and I shall meet: and, till then, peace be with him. [*Exit.*

Don Pedro. He is in earnest.

Claud. In most profound earnest; and, I'll warrant you, for the love of Beatrice.

D. Pedro. And hath challenged thee.

Claud. Most sincerely.

D. Pedro. What a pretty thing man is when he goes in his doublet and hose and leaves off his wit!

ACT V, Scene i, ll. 144-151, 187-204

Benedick. A miracle! here's our own hands against our hearts. Come, I will have thee; but, by this light, I take thee for pity.

ACT V, Scene iv, ll. 91-93

As You Like It

Charles. Good morrow to your worship.

Oliver. Good Monsieur Charles, what's the new news at the new court?

Cha. There's no news at the court, sir, but the old news: that is, the old duke is banished by his younger brother the new duke; and three or four loving lords have put themselves into voluntary exile with him, whose lands and revenues enrich the new duke; therefore he gives them good leave to wander.

Oli. Can you tell if Rosalind, the duke's daughter, be banished with her father?

Cha. O, no; for the duke's daughter, her cousin, so loves her, being ever from their cradles bred together, that she would have followed her exile, or have died to stay behind her. She is at the court, and no less beloved of her uncle than his own daughter; and never two ladies loved as they do.

Oli. Where will the old duke live?

Cha. They say he is already in the forest of Arden, and a many merry men with him; and there they live like the old Robin Hood of England: they say many young gentlemen flock to him every day, and fleet the time carelessly, as they did in the golden world.

ACT I, Scene i, ll. 100-125

Rosalind. Young man, have you challenged Charles the wrestler?

Orlando. No, fair princess; he is the general challenger: I come but in, as others do, to try with him the strength of my youth.

Celia. Young gentleman, your spirits are too bold for your years. You have seen cruel proof of this man's strength: if you saw yourself with your eyes or knew yourself with your judgement, the fear of your adventure would counsel you to a more equal enterprise. We pray you, for your own sake, to embrace your own safety and give over this attempt.

Ros. Do, young sir; your reputation shall not therefore be misprised: we will make it our suit to the duke that the wrestling might not go forward.

Orl. I beseech you, punish me not with your hard thoughts; wherein I confess me much guilty, to deny so fair and excellent ladies any thing. But let your fair eyes and gentle wishes go with me to my trial: wherein if I be foiled, there is but one shamed that was never gracious; if killed, but one dead that is willing to be so: I shall do my friends no wrong, for I have none to lament me, the world no injury, for in it I have nothing; only in the world I fill up a place, which may be better supplied when I have made it empty.

Act I, Scene ii, ll. 178-205

A room in the palace.

Enter CELIA *and* ROSALIND.

Cel. Why, cousin! why, Rosalind! Cupid have mercy! not a word?

Ros. Not one to throw at a dog.

Cel. No, thy words are too precious to be cast away upon curs; throw some of them at me; come, lame me with reasons.

Ros. Then there were two cousins laid up; when the one should be lamed with reasons and the other mad without any.

Cel. But is all this for your father?

Ros. No, some of it is for my child's father. O, how full of briers is this working-day world!

Cel. They are but burs, cousin, thrown upon thee in holiday foolery: if we walk not in the trodden paths, our very petticoats will catch them.

Ros. I could shake them off my coat: these burs are in my heart.

Act I, Scene iii, ll. 1-17

I was too young that time to value her;
But now I know her: if she be a traitor,
Why so am I; we still have slept together,
Rose at an instant, learn'd, play'd, eat together,
And whereso'er we went, like Juno's swans,
Still we went coupled and inseparable.

Act I, Scene iii, ll. 73-78

The Forest of Arden.

Enter DUKE senior, AMIENS, *and two or three* Lords
like foresters.

Duke S. Now, my co-mates and brothers in exile,
Hath not old custom made this life more sweet

222

Than that of painted pomp ? Are not these woods
More free from peril than the envious court ?
Here feel we but the penalty of Adam,
The seasons' difference, as the icy fang
And churlish chiding of the winter's wind,
Which, when it bites and blows upon my body,
Even till I shrink with cold, I smile and say
' This is no flattery : these are counsellors
That feelingly persuade me what I am.'
Sweet are the uses of adversity,
Which, like the toad, ugly and venomous,
Wears yet a precious jewel in his head ;
And this our life exempt from public haunt
Finds tongues in trees, books in the running brooks,
Sermons in stones and good in every thing.
I would not change it.

  Ami.   Happy is your grace,
That can translate the stubbornness of fortune
Into so quiet and so sweet a style.

  Duke S. Come, shall we go and kill us venison ?
And yet it irks me the poor dappled fools,
Being native burghers of this desert city,
Should in their own confines with forked heads
Have their round haunches gored.

  First Lord.   Indeed, my lord,
The melancholy Jaques grieves at that,
And, in that kind, swears you do more usurp
Than doth your brother that hath banish'd you.
To-day my Lord of Amiens and myself
Did steal behind him as he lay along
Under an oak whose antique root peeps out
Upon the brook that brawls along this wood :
To the which place a poor sequester'd stag,
That from the hunter's aim had ta'en a hurt,
Did come to languish, and indeed, my lord,
The wretched animal heaved forth such groans

That their discharge did stretch his leathern coat
Almost to bursting, and the big round tears
Coursed one another down his innocent nose
In piteous chase ; and thus the hairy fool,
Much marked of the melancholy Jaques,
Stood on the extremest verge of the swift brook,
Augmenting it with tears.

    Duke S.   But what said Jaques ?
Did he not moralize this spectacle ?

    First Lord. O, yes, into a thousand similes.
First, for his weeping into the needless stream ;
' Poor deer,' quoth he, ' thou makest a testament
As worldlings do, giving thy sum of more
To that which had too much : ' then, being there alone,
Left and abandon'd of his velvet friends,
' 'Tis right,' quoth he ; ' thus misery doth part
The flux of company : ' anon a careless herd,
Full of the pasture, jumps along by him
And never stays to greet him ; ' Ay,' quoth Jaques,
' Sweep on, you fat and greasy citizens ;
'Tis just the fashion : wherefore do you look
Upon that poor and broken bankrupt there ? '
Thus most invectively he pierceth through
The body of the country, city, court,
Yea, and of this our life, swearing that we
Are mere usurpers, tyrants and what's worse,
To fright the animals and to kill them up
In their assign'd and native dwelling-place.

    Duke S. And did you leave him in this contempla-
        tion ?

    Sec. Lord. We did, my lord, weeping and com-
        menting
Upon the sobbing deer.

    Duke S.   Show me the place :
I love to cope him in these sullen fits,
For then he's full of matter.

First Lord. I'll bring you to him straight.

ACT II, Scene i, ll. 1-69

O good old man, how well in thee appears
The constant service of the antique world,
When service sweat for duty, not for meed !

ACT II, Scene iii, ll. 56-58

The Forest of Arden.

Enter ROSALIND *for* GANYMEDE, CELIA *for* ALIENA, *and*
TOUCHSTONE.

Ros. O Jupiter, how weary are my spirits !

Touch. I care not for my spirits, if my legs were not weary.

Ros. I could find in my heart to disgrace my man's apparel
and to cry like a woman ; but I must comfort the weaker
vessel, as doublet and hose ought to show itself courageous to
petticoat : therefore courage, good Aliena !

Cel. I pray you, bear with me ; I cannot go no further.

Touch. For my part, I had rather bear with you than bear
you ; yet I should bear no cross if I did bear you, for I think
you have no money in your purse.

Ros. Well, this is the forest of Arden.

Touch. Ay, now am I in Arden ; the more fool I ; when I
was at home, I was in a better place : but travellers must be
content.

ACT II, Scene iv, ll. 1-18

The forest.

Enter AMIENS, JAQUES, *and others.*

SONG.

Ami.　　　Under the greenwood tree
　　　　　Who loves to lie with me,
　　　　　And turn his merry note
　　　　　Unto the sweet bird's throat,
　　　Come hither, come hither, come hither :
　　　　　Here shall he see
　　　　　No enemy
　　　But winter and rough weather.

225

Jaq. More, more, I prithee, more.

Ami It will make you melancholy, Monsieur Jaques.

Jaq. I thank it. More, I prithee, more. I can suck melancholy out of a song, as a weasel sucks eggs. More, I prithee, more.

Ami. My voice is ragged : I know I cannot please you.

Jaq. I do not desire you to please me ; I do desire you to sing. Come, more ; another stanzo : call you 'em stanzos ?

Ami. What you will, Monsieur Jaques.

Jaq. Nay, I care not for their names ; they owe me nothing. Will you sing ?

Ami. More at your request than to please myself.

Jaq. Well then, if ever I thank any man, I'll thank you ; but that they call compliment is like the encounter of two dog-apes, and when a man thanks me heartily, methinks I have given him a penny and he renders me the beggarly thanks. Come, sing ; and you that will not, hold your tongues.

Ami. Well, I'll end the song. Sirs, cover the while ; the duke will drink under this tree. He hath been all this day to look you.

Jaq. And I have been all this day to avoid him. He is too disputable for my company : I think of as many matters as he, but I give heaven thanks and make no boast of them. Come, warble, come.

SONG.

Who doth ambition shun   [*All together here.*
And loves to live i' the sun,
Seeking the food he eats
And pleased with what he gets,
Come hither, come hither, come hither :
Here shall he see
No enemy
But winter and rough weather.

Jaq. I'll give you a verse to this note that I made yesterday in despite of my invention.

Ami. And I'll sing it.

Jaq. Thus it goes :—

> If it do come to pass
> That any man turn ass,
> Leaving his wealth and ease,
> A stubborn will to please,
> Ducdame, ducdame, ducdame :
> Here shall he see
> Gross fools as he,
> An if he will come to me.

Ami. What's that ' ducdame ' ?

Jaq. 'Tis a Greek invocation, to call fools into a circle. I'll go sleep, if I can ; if I cannot, I'll rail against all the first-born of Egypt.

Ami. And I'll go seek the duke : his banquet is prepared.

ACT II, Scene v, ll. 1-65

A table set out. Enter DUKE *senior,* AMIENS, *and* Lords *like outlaws.*

Duke S. I think he be transform'd into a beast ;
For I can no where find him like a man.

First Lord. My lord, he is but even now gone hence :
Here was he merry, hearing of a song.

Duke S. If he, compact of jars, grow musical,
We shall have shortly discord in the spheres.
Go, seek him : tell him I would speak with him.

Enter JAQUES.

First Lord. He saves my labour by his own approach.

Duke S. Why, how now, monsieur ! what a life is this,
That your poor friends must woo your company ?
What, you look merrily !

Jaq. A fool, a fool ! I met a fool i' the forest,
A motley fool ; a miserable world !
As I do live by food, I met a fool ;
Who laid him down and bask'd him in the sun,
And rail'd on Lady Fortune in good terms,
In good set terms and yet a motley fool.

227

' Good morrow, fool,' quoth I. ' No, sir,' quoth he,
' Call me not fool till heaven hath sent me fortune : '
And then he drew a dial from his poke,
And, looking on it with lack-lustre eye,
Says very wisely, ' It is ten o'clock :
Thus we may see,' quoth he, ' how the world wags :
'Tis but an hour ago since it was nine,
And after one hour more 'twill be eleven ;
And so, from hour to hour, we ripe and ripe,
And then, from hour to hour, we rot and rot ;
And thereby hangs a tale.' When I did hear
The motley fool thus moral on the time,
My lungs began to crow like chanticleer,
That fools should be so deep-contemplative,
And I did laugh sans intermission
An hour by his dial. O noble fool !
A worthy fool ! Motley's the only wear.

Duke S. What fool is this ?

Jaq. O worthy fool ! One that hath been a courtier,
And says, if ladies be but young and fair,
They have the gift to know it : and in his brain,
Which is as dry as the remainder biscuit
After a voyage, he hath strange places cramm'd
With observation, the which he vents
In mangled forms. O that I were a fool !
I am ambitious for a motley coat.

Duke S. Thou shalt have one.

Jaq.   It is my only suit ;
Provided that you weed your better judgements
Of all opinion that grows rank in them
That I am wise. I must have liberty
Withal, as large a charter as the wind,
To blow on whom I please ; for so fools have ;
And they that are most galled with my folly,
They most must laugh. And why, sir, must they so ?
The ' why ' is plain as way to parish church :

He that a fool doth very wisely hit
Doth very foolishly, although he smart,
Not to seem senseless of the bob : if not,
The wise man's folly is anatomized
Even by the squandering glances of the fool.
Invest me in my motley ; give me leave
To speak my mind, and I will through and through
Cleanse the foul body of the infected world,
If they will patiently receive my medicine.

    Duke S. Fie on thee ! I can tell what thou wouldst do.

    Jaq. What, for a counter, would I do but good ?

    Duke S. Most mischievous foul sin, in chiding sin :
For thou thyself hast been a libertine,
As sensual as the brutish sting itself ;
And all the embossed sores and headed evils,
That thou with license of free foot hast caught,
Wouldst thou disgorge into the general world.

    Jaq. Why, who cries out on pride,
That can therein tax any private party ?
Doth it not flow as hugely as the sea,
Till that the weary very means do ebb ?
What woman in the city do I name,
When that I say the city-woman bears
The cost of princes on unworthy shoulders ?
Who can come in and say that I mean her,
When such a one as she such is her neighbour ?
Or what is he of basest function
That says his bravery is not on my cost,
Thinking that I mean him, but therein suits
His folly to the mettle of my speech ?
There then ; how then ? what then ? Let me see wherein
My tongue hath wrong'd him : if it do him right,
Then he hath wrong'd himself ; if he be free,
Why then my taxing like a wild-goose flies,
Unclaim'd of any man. But who comes here ?

    Enter ORLANDO, *with his sword drawn.*

Orl. Forbear, and eat no more.

Jaq.   Why, I have eat none yet.

Orl. Nor shalt not, till necessity be served.

Jaq. Of what kind should this cock come of?

Duke S. Art thou thus bolden'd, man, by thy distress,
Or else a rude despiser of good manners,
That in civility thou seem'st so empty?

Orl. You touch'd my vein at first: the thorny point
Of bare distress hath ta'en from me the show
Of smooth civility: yet am I inland bred
And know some nurture. But forbear, I say:
He dies that touches any of this fruit
Till I and my affairs are answered.

Jaq. An you will not be answered with reason, I must die.

Duke S. What would you have? Your gentleness shall force
More than your force move us to gentleness.

Orl. I almost die for food; and let me have it.

Duke S. Sit down and feed, and welcome to our table.

Orl. Speak you so gently? Pardon me, I pray you:
I thought that all things had been savage here;
And therefore put I on the countenance
Of stern commandment. But whate'er you are
That in this desert inaccessible,
Under the shade of melancholy boughs,
Lose and neglect the creeping hours of time;
If ever you have look'd on better days,
If ever been where bells have knoll'd to church,
If ever sat at any good man's feast,
If ever from your eyelids wiped a tear
And know what 'tis to pity and be pitied,
Let gentleness my strong enforcement be:
In the which hope I blush, and hide my sword.

Duke S. True is it that we have seen better days,
And have with holy bell been knoll'd to church
And sat at good men's feasts and wiped our eyes

Of drops that sacred pity hath engender'd :
And therefore sit you down in gentleness
And take upon command what help we have
That to your wanting may be minister'd.

Orl. Then but forbear your food a little while,
Whiles, like a doe, I go to find my fawn
And give it food. There is an old poor man,
Who after me hath many a weary step
Limp'd in pure love : till he be first sufficed,
Oppress'd with two weak evils, age and hunger,
I will not touch a bit.

Duke S.　　　　　Go find him out,
And we will nothing waste till you return.

Orl. I thank ye ; and be blest for your good comfort !
　　　　　　　　　　　　　　　　　　[*Exit.*

Duke S. Thou seest we are not all alone unhappy :
This wide and universal theatre
Presents more woeful pageants than the scene
Wherein we play in.

Jaq.　　　　　All the world's a stage,
And all the men and women merely players :
They have their exits and their entrances ;
And one man in his time plays many parts,
His acts being seven ages. At first the infant,
Mewling and puking in the nurse's arms.
And then the whining school-boy, with his satchel
And shining morning face, creeping like snail
Unwillingly to school. And then the lover,
Sighing like furnace, with a woeful ballad
Made to his mistress' eyebrow. Then a soldier,
Full of strange oaths and bearded like the pard,
Jealous in honour, sudden and quick in quarrel,
Seeking the bubble reputation
Even in the cannon's mouth. And then the justice
In fair round belly with good capon lined,
With eyes severe and beard of formal cut,

Full of wise saws and modern instances;
And so he plays his part. The sixth age shifts
Into the lean and slipper'd pantaloon,
With spectacles on nose and pouch on side,
His youthful hose, well saved, a world too wide
For his shrunk shank; and his big manly voice,
Turning again toward childish treble, pipes
And whistles in his sound. Last scene of all,
That ends this strange eventful history,
Is second childishness and mere oblivion,
Sans teeth, sans eyes, sans taste, sans every thing.

Re-enter ORLANDO, *with* ADAM.

Duke S. Welcome. Set down your venerable burden
And let him feed.

Orl. I thank you most for him.

Adam. So had you need:
I scarce can speak to thank you for myself.

Duke S. Welcome; fall to: I will not trouble you
As yet, to question you about your fortunes.
Give us some music; and, good cousin, sing.

SONG.

Ami. Blow, blow, thou winter wind,
     Thou art not so unkind
          As man's ingratitude;
     Thy tooth is not so keen,
     Because thou art not seen,
          Although thy breath be rude.
Heigh-ho! sing, heigh-ho! unto the green holly:
Most friendship is feigning, most loving mere folly:
     Then, heigh-ho, the holly!
          This life is most jolly.

     Freeze, freeze, thou bitter sky,
     That dost not bite so nigh
          As benefits forgot:

232

Though thou the waters warp,
Thy sting is not so sharp
As friend remember'd not.
Heigh-ho ! sing, &c.

Duke S. If that you were the good Sir Rowland's son,
As you have whisper'd faithfully you were,
And as mine eye doth his effigies witness
Most truly limn'd and living in your face,
Be truly welcome hither : I am the duke
That loved your father : the residue of your fortune,
Go to my cave and tell me. Good old man,
Thou art right welcome as thy master is.
Support him by the arm. Give me your hand,
And let me all your fortunes understand.

ACT II, Scene vii, ll. 1-200

Hang there, my verse, in witness of my love :
And thou, thrice-crowned queen of night, survey
With thy chaste eye, from thy pale sphere above,
Thy huntress' name that my full life doth sway.
O Rosalind ! these trees shall be my books
And in their barks my thoughts I'll character ;
That every eye which in this forest looks
Shall see thy virtue witness'd every where.
Run, run, Orlando ; carve on every tree
The fair, the chaste and unexpressive she.

ACT III, Scene ii, ll. 1-10

Why should this a desert be ?
For it is unpeopled ? No ;
Tongues I'll hang on every tree,
That shall civil sayings show :
Some, how brief the life of man
Runs his erring pilgrimage,
That the stretching of a span
Buckles in his sum of age ;
Some, of violated vows
'Twixt the souls of friend and friend :

233

But upon the fairest boughs,
  Or at every sentence end,
Will I Rosalinda write,
  Teaching all that read to know
The quintessence of every sprite
  Heaven would in little show.
Therefore Heaven Nature charged
  That one body should be fill'd
With all graces wide-enlarged :
  Nature presently distill'd
Helen's cheek, but not her heart,
  Cleopatra's majesty,
Atalanta's better part,
  Sad Lucretia's modesty.
Thus Rosalind of many parts
  By heavenly synod was devised,
Of many faces, eyes and hearts,
  To have the touches dearest prized.

                              ACT III, Scene ii, ll. 133-160

Rosalind. O, ominous ! he comes to kill my heart.

Celia. I would sing my song without a burden : thou bringest me out of tune.

Ros. Do you not know I am a woman ? when I think, I must speak. Sweet, say on.

Cel. You bring me out. Soft ! comes he not here ?

Enter ORLANDO *and* JAQUES.

Ros. 'Tis he : slink by, and note him.

Jaq. I thank you for your company ; but, good faith, I had as lief have been myself alone.

Orl. And so had I ; but yet, for fashion sake, I thank you too for your society.

Jaq. God be wi' you : let's meet as little as we can.

Orl. I do desire we may be better strangers.

Jaq. I pray you, mar no more trees with writing love-songs in their barks.

Orl. I pray you, mar no moe of my verses with reading them ill-favouredly.

Jaq. Rosalind is your love's name?

Orl. Yes, just.

Jaq. I do not like her name.

Orl. There was no thought of pleasing you when she was christened.

Jaq. What stature is she of?

Orl. Just as high as my heart.

Jaq. You are full of pretty answers. Have you not been acquainted with goldsmiths' wives, and conned them out of rings?

Orl. Not so; but I answer you right painted cloth, from whence you have studied your questions.

Jaq. You have a nimble wit: I think 'twas made of Atalanta's heels. Will you sit down with me? and we two will rail against our mistress the world and all our misery.

Orl. I will chide no breather in the world but myself, against whom I know most faults.

Jaq. The worst fault you have is to be in love.

Orl. 'Tis a fault I will not change for your best virtue. I am weary of you.

Jaq. By my troth, I was seeking for a fool when I found you.

Orl. He is drowned in the brook: look but in, and you shall see him.

Jaq. There I shall see mine own figure.

Orl. Which I take to be either a fool or a cipher.

Jaq. I'll tarry no longer with you: farewell, good Signior Love.

Orl. I am glad of your departure: adieu, good Monsieur Melancholy. [*Exit Jaques.*

Ros. [*Aside to Celia*] I will speak to him like a saucy lackey and under that habit play the knave with him. Do you hear, forester?

Orl. Very well: what would you?

Ros. I pray you, what is't o'clock?

Orl. You should ask me what time o' day : there's no clock in the forest.

Ros. Then there is no true lover in the forest ; else sighing every minute and groaning every hour would detect the lazy foot of Time as well as a clock.

Orl. And why not the swift foot of Time ? had not that been as proper ?

Ros. By no means, sir : Time travels in divers paces with divers persons. I'll tell you who Time ambles withal, who Time trots withal, who Time gallops withal and who he stands still withal.

Orl. I prithee, who doth he trot withal ?

Ros. Marry, he trots hard with a young maid between the contract of her marriage and the day it is solemnized : if the interim be but a se'nnight, Time's pace is so hard that it seems the length of seven year.

Orl. Who ambles Time withal ?

Ros. With a priest that lacks Latin and a rich man that hath not the gout, for the one sleeps easily because he cannot study and the other lives merrily because he feels no pain, the one lacking the burden of lean and wasteful learning, the other knowing no burden of heavy tedious penury ; these Time ambles withal.

Orl. Who doth he gallop withal ?

Ros. With a thief to the gallows, for though he go as softly as foot can fall, he thinks himself too soon there.

Orl. Who stays it still withal ?

Ros. With lawyers in the vacation ; for they sleep between term and term and then they perceive not how Time moves.

Orl. Where dwell you, pretty youth ?

Ros. With this shepherdess, my sister ; here in the skirts of the forest, like fringe upon a petticoat.

Orl. Are you native of this place ?

Ros. As the cony that you see dwell where she is kindled.

Orl. Your accent is something finer than you could purchase in so removed a dwelling.

Ros. I have been told so of many : but indeed an old religious uncle of mine taught me to speak, who was in his youth an inland man ; one that knew courtship too well, for there he fell in love. I have heard him read many lectures against it, and I thank God I am not a woman, to be touched with so many giddy offences as he hath generally taxed their whole sex withal.

Orl. Can you remember any of the principal evils that he laid to the charge of women ?

Ros. There were none principal ; they were all like one another as half-pence are, every one fault seeming monstrous till his fellow-fault came to match it.

Orl. I prithee, recount some of them.

Ros. No, I will not cast away my physic but on those that are sick. There is a man haunts the forest, that abuses our young plants with carving ' Rosalind ' on their barks ; hangs odes upon hawthorns and elegies on brambles, all, forsooth, deifying the name of Rosalind : if I could meet that fancy-monger, I would give him some good counsel, for he seems to have the quotidian of love upon him.

Orl. I am he that is so love-shaked : I pray you, tell me your remedy.

Ros. There is none of my uncle's marks upon you : he taught me how to know a man in love ; in which cage of rushes I am sure you are not prisoner.

Orl. What were his marks ?

Ros. A lean cheek, which you have not, a blue eye and sunken, which you have not, an unquestionable spirit, which you have not, a beard neglected, which you have not ; but I pardon you for that, for simply your having in beard is a younger brother's revenue : then your hose should be un-gartered, your bonnet unbanded, your sleeve unbuttoned, your shoe untied and every thing about you demonstrating a careless desolation ; but you are no such man ; you are rather point-device in your accoutrements as loving yourself than seeming the lover of any other.

Orl. Fair youth, I would I could make thee believe I love.

Ros. Me believe it! you may as soon make her that you love believe it; which, I warrant, she is apter to do than to confess she does: that is one of the points in the which women still give the lie to their consciences. But, in good sooth, are you he that hangs the verses on the trees, wherein Rosalind is so admired?

Orl. I swear to thee, youth, by the white hand of Rosalind, I am that he, that unfortunate he.

Ros. But are you so much in love as your rhymes speak?

Orl. Neither rhyme nor reason can express how much.

Ros. Love is merely a madness, and, I tell you, deserves as well a dark house and a whip as madmen do: and the reason why they are not so punished and cured is, that the lunacy is so ordinary that the whippers are in love too. Yet I profess curing it by counsel.

Orl. Did you ever cure any so?

Ros. Yes, one, and in this manner. He was to imagine me his love, his mistress; and I set him every day to woo me: at which time would I, being but a moonish youth, grieve, be effeminate, changeable, longing and liking, proud, fantastical, apish, shallow, inconstant, full of tears, full of smiles, for every passion something and for no passion truly any thing, as boys and women are for the most part cattle of this colour; would now like him, now loathe him; then entertain him, then forswear him; now weep for him, then spit at him; that I drave my suitor from his mad humour of love to a living humour of madness; which was, to forswear the full stream of the world and to live in a nook merely monastic. And thus I cured him; and this way will I take upon me to wash your liver as clean as a sound sheep's heart, that there shall not be one spot of love in't.

Orl. I would not be cured, youth.

Ros. I would cure you, if you would but call me Rosalind and come every day to my cote and woo me.

Orl. Now, by the faith of my love, I will : tell me where it is.

Ros. Go with me to it and I'll show it you : and by the way you shall tell me where in the forest you live. Will you go ?

Orl. With all my heart, good youth.

Ros. Nay, you must call me Rosalind. Come, sister, will you go ? *[Exeunt.*

Act III, Scene ii, ll. 260-456

Enter Touchstone *and* Audrey ; Jaques *behind.*

Touch. Come apace, good Audrey : I will fetch up your goats, Audrey. And how, Audrey ? am I the man yet ? doth my simple feature content you ?

Aud. Your features ! Lord warrant us ! what features ?

Touch. I am here with thee and thy goats, as the most capricious poet, honest Ovid, was among the Goths.

Jaq. [*Aside*] O knowledge ill-inhabited, worse than Jove in a thatched house !

Touch. When a man's verses cannot be understood, nor a man's good wit seconded with the forward child Understanding, it strikes a man more dead than a great reckoning in a little room. Truly, I would the gods had made thee poetical.

Aud. I do not know what ' poetical ' is : is it honest in deed and word ? is it a true thing ?

Touch. No, truly ; for the truest poetry is the most feigning ; and lovers are given to poetry, and what they swear in poetry may be said as lovers they do feign.

Aud. Do you wish then that the gods had made me poetical ?

Touch. I do, truly ; for thou swearest to me thou art honest : now, if thou wert a poet, I might have some hope thou didst feign.

Aud. Would you not have me honest ?

Touch. No, truly, unless thou wert hard-favoured ; for honesty coupled to beauty is to have honey a sauce to sugar.

Jaq. [*Aside*] A material fool !

Aud. Well, I am not fair; and therefore I pray the gods make me honest.

Touch. Truly, and to cast away honesty upon a foul slut were to put good meat into an unclean dish.

Aud. I am not a slut, though I thank the gods I am foul.

Touch. Well, praised be the gods for thy foulness! sluttishness may come hereafter. But be it as it may be, I will marry thee, and to that end I have been with Sir Oliver Martext, the vicar of the next village, who hath promised to meet me in this place of the forest and to couple us.

Jaq. [*Aside*] I would fain see this meeting.

Aud. Well, the gods give us joy!

Touch. Amen. A man may, if he were of a fearful heart, stagger in this attempt; for here we have no temple but the wood, no assembly but horn-beasts. But what though? Courage! . . . Here comes Sir Oliver. . . .

Come, sweet Audrey:
We must be married, or we must live in bawdry.

Farewell, good Master Oliver: not,—

O sweet Oliver,
O brave Oliver,
Leave me not behind thee:

but,—

Wind away,
Begone, I say,
I will not to wedding with thee.

[*Exeunt Jacques, Touchstone and Audrey.*

Sir Oliver Martext. 'Tis no matter: ne'er a fantastical knave of them all shall flout me out of my calling.

ACT III, Scene iii, ll. 1-51, 64, 98-119

Enter ROSALIND *and* CELIA.

Ros. Never talk to me; I will weep.

Cel. Do, I prithee; but yet have the grace to consider that tears do not become a man.

Ros. But have I not cause to weep?

Cel. As good cause as one would desire; therefore weep.

Ros. His very hair is of the dissembling colour.

Cel. Something browner than Judas's : marry, his kisses are Judas's own children.

Ros. I' faith, his hair is of a good colour.

Cel. An excellent colour : your chestnut was ever the only colour.

Ros. And his kissing is as full of sanctity as the touch of holy bread.

Cel. He hath bought a pair of cast lips of Diana : a nun of winter's sisterhood kisses not more religiously ; the very ice of chastity is in them.

Ros. But why did he swear he would come this morning, and comes not ?

Cel. Nay, certainly, there is no truth in him.

Ros. Do you think so ?

Cel. Yes ; I think he is not a pick-purse nor a horse-stealer, but for his verity in love, I do think him as concave as a covered goblet or a worm-eaten nut.

Ros. Not true in love ?

Cel. Yes, when he is in ; but I think he is not in.

Ros. You have heard him swear downright he was.

Cel. ' Was ' is not ' is : ' besides, the oath of a lover is no stronger than the word of a tapster ; they are both the confirmer of false reckonings. He attends here in the forest on the duke your father.

Ros. I met the duke yesterday and had much question with him : he asked me of what parentage I was ; I told him, of as good as he ; so he laughed and let me go. But what talk we of fathers, when there is such a man as Orlando ?

Cel. O, that's a brave man ! he writes brave verses, speaks brave words, swears brave oaths and breaks them bravely, quite traverse, athwart the heart of his lover ; as a puisny tilter, that spurs his horse but on one side, breaks his staff like a noble goose : but all's brave that youth mounts and folly guides.

ACT III, Scene iv, ll. 1-49

'Tis pretty, sure, and very probable,
That eyes, that are the frail'st and softest things,
Who shut their coward gates on atomies,
Should be call'd tyrants, butchers, murderers!

ACT III, Scene v, ll. 11-14

The forest.

Enter ROSALIND, CELIA, and JAQUES.

Jaq. I prithee, pretty youth, let me be better acquainted with thee.

Ros. They say you are a melancholy fellow.

Jaq. I am so; I do love it better than laughing.

Ros. Those that are in extremity of either are abominable fellows and betray themselves to every modern censure worse than drunkards.

Jaq. Why, 'tis good to be sad and say nothing.

Ros. Why then, 'tis good to be a post.

Jaq. I have neither the scholar's melancholy, which is emulation, nor the musician's, which is fantastical, nor the courtier's, which is proud, nor the soldier's, which is ambitious, nor the lawyer's, which is politic, nor the lady's, which is nice, nor the lover's, which is all these: but it is a melancholy of mine own, compounded of many simples, extracted from many objects, and indeed the sundry contemplation of my travels, in which my often rumination wraps me in a most humorous sadness.

Ros. A traveller! By my faith, you have great reason to be sad: I fear you have sold your own lands to see other men's; then, to have seen much and to have nothing, is to have rich eyes and poor hands.

Jaq. Yes, I have gained my experience.

Ros. And your experience makes you sad: I had rather have a fool to make me merry than experience to make me sad; and to travel for it too!

Enter ORLANDO.

Orl. Good day and happiness, dear Rosalind

242

Jaq. Nay, then, God be wi' you, an you talk in blank verse.   [*Exit.*

Ros. Farewell, Monsieur Traveller : look you lisp and wear strange suits, disable all the benefits of your own country, be out of love with your nativity and almost chide God for making you that countenance you are, or I will scarce think you have swam in a gondola. Why, how now, Orlando ! where have you been all this while ? You a lover ! An you serve me such another trick, never come in my sight more.

Orl. My fair Rosalind, I come within an hour of my promise.

Ros. Break an hour's promise in love ! He that will divide a minute into a thousand parts and break but a part of the thousandth part of a minute in the affairs of love, it may be said of him that Cupid hath clapped him o' the shoulder, but I'll warrant him heart-whole.

Orl. Pardon me, dear Rosalind.

Ros. Nay, an you be so tardy, come no more in my sight : I had as lief be wooed of a snail.

Orl. Of a snail ?

Ros. Ay, of a snail ; for though he comes slowly, he carries his house on his head ; a better jointure, I think, than you make a woman : besides, he brings his destiny with him.

Orl. What's that ?

Ros. Why, horns, which such as you are fain to be beholding to your wives for : but he comes armed in his fortune and prevents the slander of his wife.

Orl. Virtue is no horn-maker ; and my Rosalind is virtuous.

Ros. And I am your Rosalind.

Cel. It pleases him to call you so ; but he hath a Rosalind of a better leer than you.

Ros. Come, woo me, woo me, for now I am in a holiday humour and like enough to consent. What would you say to me now, an I were your very very Rosalind ?

Orl. I would kiss before I spoke.

Ros. Nay, you were better speak first, and when you were

243

gravelled for lack of matter, you might take occasion to kiss. Very good orators, when they are out, they will spit ; and for lovers lacking—God warn us !—matter, the cleanliest shift is to kiss.

Orl. How if the kiss be denied ?

Ros. Then she puts you to entreaty, and there begins new matter.

Orl. Who could be out, being before his beloved mistress ?

Ros. Marry, that should you, if I were your mistress, or I should think my honesty ranker than my wit.

Orl. What, of my suit ?

Ros. Not out of your apparel, and yet out of your suit. Am not I your Rosalind ?

Orl. I take some joy to say you are, because I would be talking of her.

Ros. Well in her person I say I will not have you.

Orl. Then in mine own person I die.

Ros. No, faith, die by attorney. The poor world is almost six thousand years old, and in all this time there was not any man died in his own person, videlicet, in a love-cause. Troilus had his brains dashed out with a Grecian club ; yet he did what he could to die before, and he is one of the patterns of love. Leander, he would have lived many a fair year, though Hero had turned nun, if it had not been for a hot midsummer night ; for, good youth, he went but forth to wash him in the Hellespont and being taken with the cramp was drowned : and the foolish chroniclers of that age found it was ' Hero of Sestos.' But these are all lies : men have died from time to time and worms have eaten them, but not for love.

Orl. I would not have my right Rosalind of this mind, for, I protest, her frown might kill me.

Ros. By this hand, it will not kill a fly. But come, now I will be your Rosalind in a more coming-on disposition, and ask me what you will, I will grant it.

Orl. Then love me, Rosalind.

Ros. Yes, faith, will I, Fridays and Saturdays and all. . . .

Cel. Go to. Will you, Orlando, have to wife this Rosalind ?

Orl. I will.

Ros. Ay, but when ?

Orl. Why now ; as fast as she can marry us.

Ros. Then you must say ' I take thee, Rosalind, for wife.'

Orl. I take thee, Rosalind, for wife.

Ros. I might ask you for your commission ; but I do take thee, Orlando, for my husband : there's a girl goes before the priest ; and certainly a woman's thought runs before her actions.

Orl. So do all thoughts ; they are winged.

Ros. Now tell me how long you would have her after you have possessed her.

Orl. For ever and a day.

Ros. Say ' a day,' without the ' ever.' No, no, Orlando ; men are April when they woo, December when they wed : maids are May when they are maids, but the sky changes when they are wives. I will be more jealous of thee than a Barbary cock-pigeon over his hen, more clamorous than a parrot against rain, more new-fangled than an ape, more giddy in my desires than a monkey : I will weep for nothing, like Diana in the fountain, and I will do that when you are disposed to be merry ; I will laugh like a hyen, and that when thou art inclined to sleep.

Orl. But will my Rosalind do so ?

Ros. By my life, she will do as I do.

Orl. O, but she is wise.

Ros. Or else she could not have the wit to do this : the wiser, the waywarder : make the doors upon a woman's wit and it will out at the casement ; shut that and 'twill out at the key-hole ; stop that, 'twill fly with the smoke out at the chimney. . . .

Orl. For these two hours, Rosalind, I will leave thee.

Ros. Alas ! dear love, I cannot lack thee two hours.

Orl. I must attend the duke at dinner : by two o'clock I will be with thee again.

Ros. Ay, go your ways, go your ways; I knew what you would prove: my friends told me as much, and I thought no less: that flattering tongue of yours won me: 'tis but one cast away, and so, come, death! Two o'clock is your hour?

Orl. Ay, sweet Rosalind.

Ros. By my troth, and in good earnest, and so God mend me, and by all pretty oaths that are not dangerous, if you break one jot of your promise or come one minute behind your hour, I will think you the most pathetical break-promise and the most hollow lover and the most unworthy of her you call Rosalind that may be chosen out of the gross band of the unfaithful: therefore beware my censure and keep your promise.

Orl. With no less religion than if thou wert indeed my Rosalind: so adieu.

Ros. Well, Time is the old justice that examines all such offenders, and let Time try: adieu.   [*Exit Orlando.*

Cel. You have simply misused our sex in your love-prate: we must have your doublet and hose plucked over your head, and show the world what the bird hath done to her own nest.

Ros. O coz, coz, coz, my pretty little coz, that thou didst know how many fathom deep I am in love! But it cannot be sounded: my affection hath an unknown bottom, like the bay of Portugal.

Cel. Or rather, bottomless, that as fast as you pour affection in, it runs out.

Ros. No, that same wicked bastard of Venus that was begot of thought, conceived of spleen and born of madness, that blind rascally boy that abuses every one's eyes because his own are out, let him be judge how deep I am in love. I'll tell thee, Aliena, I cannot be out of the sight of Orlando: I'll go find a shadow and sigh till he come.

Cel. And I'll sleep.

ACT IV, Scene i, ll. 1-117, 130-166, 180-224

What shall he have that kill'd the deer?

ACT IV, Scene ii, l. 11

> Pacing through the forest,
> Chewing the food of sweet and bitter fancy.

Act IV, Scene iii, ll. 101-102

Enter Touchstone *and* Audrey.

Touch. To-morrow is the joyful day, Audrey ; to-morrow will we be married.

Aud. I do desire it with all my heart ; and I hope it is no dishonest desire to desire to be a woman of the world. Here come two of the banished duke's pages.

Enter two Pages.

First Page. Well met, honest gentleman.

Touch. By my troth, well met. Come, sit, sit, and a song.

Sec. Page. We are for you : sit i' the middle.

First Page. Shall we clap into 't roundly, without hawking or spitting or saying we are hoarse, which are the only prologues to a bad voice ?

Sec. Page. I 'faith, i 'faith ; and both in a tune, like two gipsies on a horse.

Song.

> It was a lover and his lass,
>   With a hey, and a ho, and a hey nonino,
> That o'er the green corn-field did pass
>   In the spring time, the only pretty ring time,
> When birds do sing, hey ding a ding, ding :
>   Sweet lovers love the spring.
>
> Between the acres of the rye,
>   With a hey, and a ho, and a hey nonino,
> These pretty country folks would lie,
>   In spring time, &c.
>
> This carol they began that hour,
>   With a hey, and a ho, and a hey nonino,
> How that a life was but a flower
>   In spring time, &c.

247

K

And therefore take the present time,
  With a hey, and a ho, and a hey nonino ;
For love is crowned with the prime
  In spring time, &c.

Touch. Truly, young gentlemen, though there was no great matter in the ditty, yet the note was very untuneable.

First Page. You are deceived, sir : we kept time, we lost not our time.

Touch. By my troth, yes ; I count it but time lost to hear such a foolish song. God be wi' you ; and God mend your voices ! Come, Audrey.

ACT V, Scene iii, ll. 1-43

To DUKE *senior and* JAQUES *enter* TOUCHSTONE *and* AUDREY.

Jaq. There is, sure, another flood toward, and these couples are coming to the ark. Here comes a pair of very strange beasts, which in all tongues are called fools.

Touch. Salutation and greeting to you all !

Jaq. Good my lord, bid him welcome : this is the motley-minded gentleman that I have so often met in the forest : he hath been a courtier, he swears.

Touch. If any man doubt that, let him put me to my purgation. I have trod a measure ; I have flattered a lady ; I have been politic with my friend, smooth with mine enemy ; I have undone three tailors ; I have had four quarrels, and like to have fought one.

Jaq. And how was that ta'en up ?

Touch. Faith, we met, and found the quarrel was upon the seventh cause.

Jaq. How seventh cause ? Good my lord, like this fellow.

Duke S. I like him very well.

Touch. God 'ild you, sir ; I desire you of the like. I press in here, sir, amongst the rest of the country copulatives, to swear and to forswear ; according as marriage binds and blood breaks : a poor virgin, sir, an ill-favoured thing, sir, but mine own ; a poor humour of mine, sir, to take that that no man else will : rich honesty dwells like a miser, sir, in a poor house ; as your pearl in your foul oyster.

Duke S. By my faith, he is very swift and sententious.

Touch. According to the fool's bolt, sir, and such dulcet diseases.

Jaq. But, for the seventh cause ; how did you find the quarrel on the seventh cause ?

Touch. Upon a lie seven times removed :—bear your body more seeming, Audrey :—as thus, sir. I did dislike the cut of a certain courtier's beard : he sent me word, if I said his beard was not cut well, he was in the mind it was : this is called the Retort Courteous. If I sent him word again ' it was not well cut,' he would send me word, he cut it to please himself : this is called the Quip Modest. If again ' it was not well cut,' he disabled my judgement : this is called the Reply Churlish. If again ' it was not well cut,' he would answer, I spake not true : this is called the Reproof Valiant. If again ' it was not well cut,' he would say, I lied : this is called the Countercheck Quarrelsome : and so to the Lie Circumstantial and the Lie Direct.

Jaq. And how oft did you say his beard was not well cut ?

Touch. I durst go no further than the Lie Circumstantial, nor he durst not give me the Lie Direct ; and so we measured swords and parted.

Jaq. Can you nominate in order now the degrees of the lie ?

Touch. O sir, we quarrel in print, by the book ; as you have books for good manners : I will name you the degrees. The first, the Retort Courteous ; the second, the Quip Modest ; the third, the Reply Churlish ; the fourth, the Reproof Valiant ; the fifth, the Countercheck Quarrelsome ; the sixth, the Lie with Circumstance ; the seventh, the Lie Direct. All these you may avoid but the Lie Direct ; and you may avoid that too, with an If. I knew when seven justices could not take up a quarrel, but when the parties were met themselves, one of them thought but of an If, as, ' If you said so, then I

said so ; ' and they shook hands and swore brothers. Your
If is the only peace-maker ; much virtue in If.

Jaq. Is not this a rare fellow, my lord ? he's as good at any
thing and yet a fool.

Duke S. He uses his folly like a stalking-horse and under
the presentation of that he shoots his wit.

ACT V, Scene iv, ll. 35-113

Twelfth Night ;

or, What You Will

The DUKE'S *palace.*

Enter DUKE, CURIO, *and other* Lords *;* Musicians *attending.*

Duke. If music be the food of love, play on ;
Give me excess of it, that, surfeiting,
The appetite may sicken, and so die.
That strain again ! it had a dying fall :
O, it came o'er my ear like the sweet south,
That breathes upon a bank of violets,
Stealing and giving odour ! Enough ; no more :
'Tis not so sweet now as it was before.
O spirit of love ! how quick and fresh art thou,
That, notwithstanding thy capacity
Receiveth as the sea, nought enters there,
Of what validity and pitch soe'er,
But falls into abatement and low price,
Even in a minute : so full of shapes is fancy
That it alone is high fantastical.

Cur. Will you go hunt, my lord ?

Duke.   What, Curio ?

Cur. The hart.

Duke. Why, so I do, the noblest that I have :
O, when mine eyes did see Olivia first,
Methought she purged the air of pestilence !

That instant was I turn'd into a hart ;
And my desires, like fell and cruel hounds,
E'er since pursue me. . . .
How will she love, when the rich golden shaft
Hath kill'd the flock of all affections else
That live in her ; when liver, brain and heart,
These sovereign thrones, are all supplied, and fill'd
Her sweet perfections with one self king !
Away before me to sweet beds of flowers :
Love-thoughts lie rich when canopied with bowers.

ACT I, Scene i, ll. 1-23, 35-41

OLIVIA'S *house*.

Enter SIR TOBY BELCH *and* MARIA.

Sir Toby. What a plague means my niece, to take the death of her brother thus ? I am sure care's an enemy to life.

Maria. By my troth, Sir Toby, you must come in earlier o' nights : your cousin, my lady, takes great exceptions to your ill hours.

Sir To. Why, let her except, before excepted.

Mar. Ay, but you must confine yourself within the modest limits of order.

Sir To. Confine ! I'll confine myself no finer than I am : these clothes are good enough to drink in ; and so be these boots too : an they be not, let them hang themselves in their own straps.

Mar. That quaffing and drinking will undo you : I heard my lady talk of it yesterday ; and of a foolish knight that you brought in one night here to be her wooer.

Sir To. Who, Sir Andrew Aguecheek ?

Mar. Ay, he.

Sir To. He's as tall a man as any's in Illyria.

Mar. What's that to the purpose ?

Sir To. Why, he has three thousand ducats a year.

Mar. Ay, but he'll have but a year in all these ducats : he's a very fool and a prodigal.

Sir To. Fie, that you'll say so! he plays o' the viol-de-gamboys, and speaks three or four languages word for word without book, and hath all the good gifts of nature.

Mar. He hath indeed, almost natural: for besides that he's a fool, he's a great quarreller; and but that he hath the gift of a coward to allay the gust he hath in quarrelling, 'tis thought among the prudent he would quickly have the gift of a grave.

Sir To. By this hand, they are scoundrels and substractors that say so of him. Who are they?

Mar. They that add, moreover, he's drunk nightly in your company.

Sir To. With drinking healths to my niece: I'll drink to her as long as there is a passage in my throat and drink in Illyria: he's a coward and a coystrill that will not drink to my niece till his brains turn o' the toe like a parish-top. What, wench! Castiliano vulgo! for here comes Sir Andrew Agueface.

Enter Sir Andrew Aguecheek.

Sir And. Sir Toby Belch! how now, Sir Toby Belch!

Sir To. Sweet Sir Andrew!

Sir And. Bless you, fair shrew.

Mar. And you too, sir.

Sir To. Accost, Sir Andrew, accost.

Sir And. What's that?

Sir To. My niece's chambermaid.

Sir And. Good Mistress Accost, I desire better acquaintance.

Mar. My name is Mary, sir. . . .

Sir To. O knight, thou lackest a cup of canary: when did I see thee so put down?

Sir And. Never in your life, I think; unless you see canary put me down. Methinks sometimes I have no more wit than a Christian or an ordinary man has: but I am a great eater of beef and I believe that does harm to my wit.

Sir To. No question.

Sir And. An I thought that, I'ld forswear it. I'll ride home to-morrow, Sir Toby.

Sir To. Pourquoi, my dear knight ?

Sir And. What is ' pourquoi ' ? do or not do ? I would I had bestowed that time in the tongues that I have in fencing, dancing and bear-baiting : O, had I but followed the arts !

Sir To. Then hadst thou had an excellent head of hair.

Sir And. Why, would that have mended my hair ?

Sir To. Past question ; for thou seest it will not curl by nature.

Sir And. But it becomes me well enough, does't not ?

Sir To. Excellent ; it hangs like flax on a distaff ; and I hope to see a housewife take thee between her legs and spin it off.

Sir And. Faith, I'll home to-morrow, Sir Toby : your niece will not be seen ; or if she be, it's four to one she'll none of me : the count himself here hard by woos her.

Sir To. She'll none o' the count : she'll not match above her degree, neither in estate, years, nor wit ; I have heard her swear't. Tut, there's life in't, man.

Sir And. I'll stay a month longer. I am a fellow o' the strangest mind i' the world ; I delight in masques and revels sometimes altogether.

Sir To. Art thou good at these kickshawses, knight ?

Sir And. As any man in Illyria, whatsoever he be, under the degree of my betters ; and yet I will not compare with an old man.

Sir To. What is thy excellence in a galliard, knight ?

Sir And. Faith, I can cut a caper.

Sir To. And I can cut the mutton to't.

Sir And. And I think I have the back-trick simply as strong as any man in Illyria.

Sir To. Wherefore are these things hid ? wherefore have these gifts a curtain before 'em ? are they like to take dust, like Mistress Mall's picture ? why dost thou not go to church in a galliard and come home in a coranto ? My very walk should

be a jig ; I would not so much as make water but in a sink-a-
pace. What dost thou mean ? Is it a world to hide virtues
in ? I did think, by the excellent constitution of thy leg, it
was formed under the star of a galliard.

Sir And. Ay, 'tis strong, and it does indifferent well in a
flame-coloured stock. Shall we set about some revels ?

Sir To. What shall we do else ? were we not born under
Taurus ?

Sir And. Taurus ! That's sides and heart.

Sir To. No, sir ; it is legs and thighs. Let me see thee
caper : ha ! higher : ha, ha ! excellent !

ACT I, Scene iii, ll. 1-57, 85-151

Enter MARIA *and* CLOWN.

Mar. Nay, either tell me where thou hast been, or I will
not open my lips so wide as a bristle may enter in way of thy
excuse : my lady will hang thee for thy absence.

Clo. Let her hang me : he that is well hanged in this
world needs to fear no colours.

Mar. Make that good.

Clo. He shall see none to fear.

Mar. A good lenten answer : I can tell thee where that
saying was born, of ' I fear no colours.'

Clo. Where, good Mistress Mary ?

Mar. In the wars ; and that may you be bold to say in your
foolery.

Clo. Well, God give them wisdom that have it ; and those
that are fools, let them use their talents.

Mar. Yet you will be hanged for being so long absent ; or
to be turned away, is not that as good as a hanging to you ?

Clo. Many a good hanging prevents a bad marriage ; and,
for turning away, let summer bear it out.

Mar. You are resolute, then ?

Clo. Not so, neither ; but I am resolved on two points.

Mar. That if one break, the other will hold ; or, if both
break, your gaskins fall.

Clo. Apt, in good faith ; very apt. Well, go thy way ; if Sir Toby would leave drinking, thou wert as witty a piece of Eve's flesh as any in Illyria.

Mar. Peace, you rogue, no more o' that. Here comes my lady : make your excuse wisely, you were best.   [*Exit*.

Clo. Wit, an't be thy will, put me into good fooling ! Those wits, that think they have thee, do very oft prove fools ; and I, that am sure I lack thee, may pass for a wise man : for what says Quinapalus ? 'Better a witty fool than a foolish wit.'

Enter Lady OLIVIA *with* MALVOLIO.

God bless thee, lady !

Oli. Take the fool away.

Clo. Do you not hear, fellows ? Take away the lady.

Oli. Go to, you're a dry fool ; I'll no more of you : besides, you grow dishonest.

Clo. Two faults, madonna, that drink and good counsel will amend : for give the dry fool drink, then is the fool not dry : bid the dishonest man mend himself ; if he mend, he is no longer dishonest ; if he cannot, let the botcher mend him. Any thing that's mended is but patched : virtue that transgresses is but patched with sin ; and sin that amends is but patched with virtue. If that this simple syllogism will serve, so ; if it will not, what remedy ? As there is no true cuckold but calamity, so beauty's a flower. The lady bade take away the fool ; therefore, I say again, take her away.

Oli. Sir, I bade them take away you.

Clo. Misprision in the highest degree ! Lady, *cucullus non facit monachum* ; that's as much to say as I wear not motley in my brain. Good madonna, give me leave to prove you a fool.

Oli. Can you do it ?

Clo. Dexteriously, good madonna.

Oli. Make your proof.

Clo. I must catechize you for it, madonna : good my mouse of virtue, answer me.

Oli. Well, sir, for want of other idleness, I'll bide your proof.

Clo. Good madonna, why mournest thou ?

Oli. Good fool, for my brother's death.

Clo. I think his soul is in hell, madonna.

Oli. I know his soul is in heaven, fool.

Clo. The more fool, madonna, to mourn for your brother's soul being in heaven. Take away the fool, gentlemen.

Oli. What think you of this fool, Malvolio ? doth he not mend ?

Mal. Yes, and shall do till the pangs of death shake him : infirmity, that decays the wise, doth ever make the better fool.

Clo. God send you, sir, a speedy infirmity, for the better increasing your folly ! Sir Toby will be sworn that I am no fox ; but he will not pass his word for two pence that you are no fool.

Oli. How say you to that, Malvolio ?

Mal. I marvel your ladyship takes delight in such a barren rascal : I saw him put down the other day with an ordinary fool that has no more brain than a stone. Look you now, he's out of his guard already ; unless you laugh and minister occasion to him, he is gagged. I protest, I take these wise men, that crow so at these set kind of fools, no better than the fools' zanies.

Oli. O, you are sick of self-love, Malvolio, and taste with a distempered appetite. To be generous, guiltless and of free disposition, is to take those things for bird-bolts that you deem cannon-bullets. . . . [*Exit Malvolio.*] Now you see, sir how your fooling grows old, and people dislike it. . . .

Give me my veil : come, throw it o'er my face.
We'll once more hear Orsino's embassy.

Enter VIOLA *in man's attire, and* Attendants.

Vio. The honourable lady of the house, which is she ?

Oli. Speak to me ; I shall answer for her. Your will ?

Vio. Most radiant, exquisite and unmatchable beauty,—

I pray you, tell me if this be the lady of the house, for I never saw her : I would be loath to cast away my speech, for besides that it is excellently well penned, I have taken great pains to con it. Good beauties, let me sustain no scorn ; I am very comptible, even to the least sinister usage.

Oli. Whence came you, sir ?

Vio. I can say little more than I have studied, and that question's out of my part. Good gentle one, give me modest assurance if you be the lady of the house, that I may proceed in my speech.

Oli. Are you a comedian ?

Vio. No, my profound heart : and yet, by the very fangs of malice I swear, I am not that I play. Are you the lady of the house ?

Oli. If I do not usurp myself, I am.

Vio. Most certain, if you are she, you do usurp yourself ; for what is yours to bestow is not yours to reserve. But this is from my commission : I will on with my speech in your praise, and then show you the heart of my message.

Oli. Come to what is important in't : I forgive you the praise.

Vio. Alas, I took great pains to study it, and 'tis poetical.

Oli. It is the more like to be feigned : I pray you, keep it in. I heard you were saucy at my gates, and allowed your approach rather to wonder at you than to hear you. If you be not mad, be gone ; if you have reason, be brief : 'tis not that time of moon with me to make one in so skipping a dialogue. . . . Give us the place alone : we will hear this divinity. [*Exeunt Maria and Attendants.*] Now, sir, what is your text ?

Vio. Most sweet lady,—

Oli. A comfortable doctrine, and much may be said of it. Where lies your text ?

Vio. In Orsino's bosom.

Oli. In his bosom ! In what chapter of his bosom ?

Vio. To answer by the method, in the first of his heart.

Oli. O, I have read it : it is heresy. Have you no more to say ?

Vio. Good madam, let me see your face.

Oli. Have you any commission from your lord to negotiate
with my face ? You are now out of your text : but we will
draw the curtain and show you the picture. Look you, sir,
such a one I was this present : is't not well done ? [*Unveiling.*

Vio. Excellently done, if God did all.

Oli. 'Tis in grain, sir ; 'twill endure wind and weather.

Vio. 'Tis beauty truly blent, whose red and white
Nature's own sweet and cunning hand laid on :
Lady, you are the cruell'st she alive,
If you will lead these graces to the grave
And leave the world no copy.

Oli. O, sir, I will not be so hard-hearted ; I will give out
divers schedules of my beauty : it shall be inventoried, and
every particle and utensil labelled to my will : as, item, two
lips, indifferent red ; item, two grey eyes, with lids to them ;
item, one neck, one chin, and so forth. Were you sent hither
to praise me ?

Vio. I see you what you are, you are too proud ;
But, if you were the devil, you are fair.
My lord and master loves you : O, such love
Could be but recompensed, though you were crown'd
The nonpareil of beauty !

Oli.   How does he love me ?

Vio. With adorations, fertile tears,
With groans that thunder love, with sighs of fire.

Oli. Your lord does know my mind ; I cannot love him :
Yet I suppose him virtuous, know him noble,
Of great estate, of fresh and stainless youth ;
In voices well divulged, free, learn'd and valiant ;
And in dimension and the shape of nature
A gracious person : but yet I cannot love him ;
He might have took his answer long ago.

Vio. If I did love you in my master's flame,
With such a suffering, such a deadly life,
In your denial I would find no sense ;

258

I would not understand it.

Oli.   Why, what would you ?

Vio. Make me a willow cabin at your gate,
And call upon my soul within the house ;
Write loyal cantons of contemned love
And sing them loud even in the dead of night ;
Halloo your name to the reverberate hills
And make the babbling gossip of the air
Cry out ' Olivia ! ' O, you should not rest
Between the elements of air and earth,
But you should pity me !

Oli.   You might do much.
What is your parentage ?

Vio. Above my fortunes, yet my state is well :
I am a gentleman.

Oli.   Get you to your lord ;
I cannot love him : let him send no more ;
Unless, perchance, you come to me again,
To tell me how he takes it. Fare you well :
I thank you for your pains : spend this for me.

Vio. I am no fee'd post, lady ; keep your purse :
My master, not myself, lacks recompense.
Love make his heart of flint that you shall love ;
And let your fervour, like my master's, be
Placed in contempt ! Farewell, fair cruelty. [*Exit.*

Oli. ' What is your parentage ? '
' Above my fortunes, yet my state is well :
I am a gentleman.' I'll be sworn thou art ;
Thy tongue, thy face, thy limbs, actions and spirit,
Do give thee five-fold blazon : not too fast : soft, soft !
Unless the master were the man. How now !
Even so quickly may one catch the plague ?
Methinks I feel this youth's perfections
With an invisible and subtle stealth
To creep in at mine eyes.

ACT I, Scene v, ll. 1-101, 119-120, 175-214, 235-317

OLIVIA'S *house*.

Enter SIR TOBY *and* SIR ANDREW.

Sir To. Approach, Sir Andrew: not to be a-bed after midnight is to be up betimes; and ' diluculo surgere,' thou know'st,—

Sir And. Nay, by my troth, I know not: but I know, to be up late is to be up late.

Sir To. A false conclusion: I hate it as an unfilled can. To be up after midnight and to go to bed then, is early: so that to go to bed after midnight is to go to bed betimes. Does not our life consist of the four elements?

Sir And. Faith, so they say: but I think it rather consists of eating and drinking.

Sir To. Thou'rt a scholar; let us therefore eat and drink. Marian, I say! a stoup of wine!

Enter CLOWN.

Sir And. Here comes the fool, i' faith.

Clo. How now, my hearts! did you never see the picture of ' we three '?

Sir To. Welcome, ass. Now let's have a catch.

Sir And. By my troth, the fool has an excellent breast. I had rather than forty shillings I had such a leg, and so sweet a breath to sing, as the fool has. In sooth, thou wast in very gracious fooling last night, when thou spokest of Pigrogromitus, of the Vapians passing the equinoctial of Queubus: 'twas very good, i' faith. I sent thee sixpence for thy leman: hadst it?

Clo. I did impeticos thy gratillity; for Malvolio's nose is no whipstock: my lady has a white hand, and the Myrmidons are no bottle-ale houses.

Sir And. Excellent! why, this is the best fooling, when all is done. Now, a song.

Sir To. Come on; there is sixpence for you: let's have a song.

Sir And. There's a testril of me too: if one knight give a—

Clo. Would you have a love-song, or a song of good life?

Sir To. A love-song, a love-song.

Sir And. Ay, ay: I care not for good life.

Clo. [*Sings*]

> O mistress mine, where are you roaming?
> O, stay and hear; your true love's coming,
>   That can sing both high and low:
> Trip no further, pretty sweeting;
> Journeys end in lovers meeting,
>   Every wise man's son doth know.

Sir And. Excellent good, i' faith.

Sir To. Good, good.

Clo. [*Sings*]

> What is love? 'tis not hereafter;
> Present mirth hath present laughter;
>   What's to come is still unsure:
> In delay there lies no plenty;
> Then come kiss me, sweet and twenty,
>   Youth's a stuff will not endure. . . .

Enter MARIA.

Mar. What a caterwauling do you keep here! If my lady have not called up her steward Malvolio and bid him turn you out of doors, never trust me.

Sir To. My lady's a Cataian, we are politicians, Malvolio's a Peg-a-Ramsey, and 'Three merry men be we.' Am not I consanguineous? am I not of her blood? Tillyvally. Lady! [*Sings*] 'There dwelt a man in Babylon, lady, lady!'

Clo. Beshrew me, the knight's in admirable fooling.

Sir And. Ay, he does well enough if he be disposed, and so do I too: he does it with a better grace, but I do it more natural.

Sir To. [*Sings*] 'O, the twelfth day of December,'—

Mar. For the love o' God, peace!

Enter MALVOLIO.

Mal. My masters, are you mad ? or what are you ? Have you no wit, manners, nor honesty, but to gabble like tinkers at this time of night ? Do ye make an alehouse of my lady's house, that ye squeak out your coziers' catches without any mitigation or remorse of voice ? Is there no respect of place, persons, nor time in you ?

Sir To. We did keep time, sir, in our catches. Sneck up !

Mal. Sir Toby, I must be round with you. My lady bade me tell you, that, though she harbours you as her kinsman, she's nothing allied to your disorders. If you can separate yourself and your misdemeanours, you are welcome to the house ; if not, an it would please you to take leave of her, she is very willing to bid you farewell.

Sir To. ' Farewell, dear heart, since I must needs be gone.'

Mar. Nay, good Sir Toby.

Clo. ' His eyes do show his days are almost done.'

Mal. Is't even so ?

Sir To. ' But I will never die.'

Clo. Sir Toby, there you lie.

Mal. This is much credit to you.

Sir To. ' Shall I bid him go ? '

Clo. ' What an if you do ? '

Sir To. ' Shall I bid him go, and spare not ? '

Clo. ' O no, no, no, no, you dare not.'

Sir To. Out o' tune, sir : ye lie. Art any more than a steward ? Dost thou think, because thou art virtuous, there shall be no more cakes and ale ?

Clo. Yes, by Saint Anne, and ginger shall be hot i' the mouth too. . . .

Sir To. Good night, Penthesilea.

Sir And. Before me, she's a good wench.

Sir To. She's a beagle, true-bred, and one that adores me : what o' that ?

Sir And. I was adored once too.

Sir To. Let's to bed, knight. Thou hadst need send for more money.

Sir And. If I cannot recover your niece, I am a foul way out.

Sir To. Send for money, knight: if thou hast her not i' the end, call me cut.

Sir And. If I do not, never trust me, take it how you will.

Sir To. Come, come, I'll go burn some sack; 'tis too late to go to bed now: come, knight; come, knight.

ACT II, Scene iii, ll. 1-53, 76-127, 193-208

The DUKE'S *palace.*

Enter DUKE, VIOLA, CURIO, *and others.*

Duke. Give me some music. Now, good morrow, friends.
Now, good Cesario, but that piece of song,
That old and antique song we heard last night:
Methought it did relieve my passion much,
More than light airs and recollected terms
Of these most brisk and giddy-paced times:
Come, but one verse.

Cur. He is not here, so please your lordship, that should sing it.

Duke. Who was it?

Cur. Feste, the jester, my lord; a fool that the lady Olivia's father took much delight in. He is about the house.

Duke. Seek him out, and play the tune the while.

[Exit Curio. Music plays.

Come hither, boy: if ever thou shalt love,
In the sweet pangs of it remember me;
For such as I am all true lovers are,
Unstaid and skittish in all motions else,
Save in the constant image of the creature
That is beloved. How dost thou like this tune?

Vio. It gives a very echo to the seat
Where Love is throned. . . .

263

Re-enter CURIO *and* CLOWN.

Duke. O, fellow, come, the song we had last night.
Mark it, Cesario, it is old and plain ;
The spinsters and the knitters in the sun
And the free maids that weave their thread with bones
Do use to chant it : it is silly sooth,
And dallies with the innocence of love,
Like the old age.

    Clo. Are you ready, sir ?

    Duke. Ay ; prithee, sing.   [*Music.*

SONG.

Clo. Come away, come away, death,
    And in sad cypress let me be laid ;
Fly away, fly away, breath ;
    I am slain by a fair cruel maid.
My shroud of white, stuck all with yew,
        O, prepare it !
My part of death, no one so true
    Did share it.

Not a flower, not a flower sweet,
    On my black coffin let there be strown ;
Not a friend, not a friend greet
    My poor corpse, where my bones shall be thrown :
A thousand thousand sighs to save,
        Lay me, O, where
Sad true lover never find my grave,
        To weep there !

Duke. There's for thy pains.

Clo. No pains, sir ; I take pleasure in singing, sir. . . .

Duke. Let all the rest give place.
          [*Curio and Attendants retire.*
          Once more, Cesario,
Get thee to yond same sovereign cruelty :
Tell her, my love, more noble than the world,
Prizes not quantity of dirty lands ;

The parts that fortune hath bestow'd upon her,
Tell her, I hold as giddily as fortune;
But 'tis that miracle and queen of gems
That nature pranks her in attracts my soul.

Vio. But if she cannot love you, sir?

Duke. I cannot be so answer'd.

Vio.   Sooth, but you must.
Say that some lady, as perhaps there is,
Hath for your love as great a pang of heart
As you have for Olivia: you cannot love her;
You tell her so; must she not then be answer'd?

Duke. There is no woman's sides
Can bide the beating of so strong a passion
As love doth give my heart; no woman's heart
So big, to hold so much; they lack retention.
Alas, their love may be call'd appetite,
No motion of the liver, but the palate,
That suffer surfeit, cloyment and revolt;
But mine is all as hungry as the sea,
And can digest as much: make no compare
Between that love a woman can bear me
And that I owe Olivia.

Vio.   Ay, but I know—

Duke. What dost thou know?

Vio. Too well what love women to men may owe:
In faith, they are as true of heart as we.
My father had a daughter loved a man,
As it might be, perhaps, were I a woman,
I should your lordship.

Duke.   And what's her history?

Vio. A blank, my lord. She never told her love,
But let concealment, like a worm i' the bud,
Feed on her damask cheek: she pined in thought,
And with a green and yellow melancholy
She sat like patience on a monument,
Smiling at grief. Was not this love indeed?

We men may say more, swear more : but indeed
Our shows are more than will ; for still we prove
Much in our vows, but little in our love.

Duke. But died thy sister of her love, my boy ?

Vio. I am all the daughters of my father's house,
And all the brothers too : and yet I know not.

ACT II, Scene iv, ll. 1-22, 43-70, 82-124

OLIVIA'S garden.

Enter SIR TOBY, SIR ANDREW, and FABIAN.

Sir To. Here comes the little villain.

Enter MARIA.

How now, my metal of India !

Mar. Get ye all three into the box-tree : Malvolio's coming
down this walk : he has been yonder i' the sun practising
behaviour to his own shadow this half hour : observe him, for
the love of mockery ; for I know this letter will make a con-
templative idiot of him. Close, in the name of jesting ! Lie
thou there [*throws down a letter*] ; for here comes the trout
that must be caught with tickling. [*Exit.*

Enter MALVOLIO.

Mal. 'Tis but fortune ; all is fortune. Maria once told
me she did affect me : and I have heard herself come thus
near, that, should she fancy, it should be one of my complexion. Besides, she uses me with a more exalted respect
than any one else that follows her. What should I think on't ?

Sir To. Here's an overweening rogue !

Fab. O, peace ! Contemplation makes a rare turkey-cock
of him : how he jets under his advanced plumes !

Sir And. 'Slight, I could so beat the rogue !

Sir To. Peace, I say.

Mal. To be Count Malvolio !

Sir To. Ah, rogue !

Sir And. Pistol him, pistol him.

Sir To. Peace, peace !

266

Mal. There is example for't ; the lady of the Strachy married the yeoman of the wardrobe.

Sir And. Fie on him, Jezebel !

Fab. O, peace ! now he's deeply in : look how imagination blows him.

Mal. Having been three months married to her, sitting in my state,—

Sir To. O, for a stone-bow, to hit him in the eye !

Mal. Calling my officers about me, in my branched velvet gown ; having come from a daybed, where I have left Olivia sleeping,—

Sir To. Fire and brimstone !

Fab. O, peace, peace !

Mal. And then to have the humour of state ; and after a demure travel of regard, telling them I know my place as I would they should do theirs, to ask for my kinsman Toby,—

Sir To. Bolts and shackles !

Fab. O peace, peace, peace ! now, now.

Mal. Seven of my people, with an obedient start, make out for him : I frown the while ; and perchance wind up my watch, or play with my—some rich jewel. Toby approaches ; courtesies there to me,—

Sir To. Shall this fellow live ?

Fab. Though our silence be drawn from us with cars, yet peace.

Mal. I extend my hand to him thus, quenching my familiar smile with an austere regard of control,—

Sir To. And does not Toby take you a blow o' the lips then ?

Mal. Saying, ' Cousin Toby, my fortunes having cast me on your niece give me this prerogative of speech,'—

Sir To. What, what ?

Mal. ' You must amend your drunkenness.'

Sir To. Out, scab !

Fab. Nay, patience, or we break the sinews of our plot.

Mal. ' Besides, you waste the treasure of your time with a foolish knight,'—

Sir And. That's me, I warrant you.

Mal. ' One Sir Andrew,'——

Sir And. I knew 'twas I ; for many do call me fool.

Mal. What employment have we here ?

[*Taking up the letter.*

Fab. Now is the woodcock near the gin.

Sir To. O, peace ! and the spirit of humours intimate reading aloud to him !

Mal. By my life, this is my lady's hand : these be her very C's, her U's and her T's ; and thus makes she her great P's. It is, in contempt of question, her hand.

Sir And. Her C's, her U's and her T's : why that ?

Mal. [*Reads*] ' To the unknown beloved, this, and my good wishes : '——her very phrases ! By your leave, wax. Soft ! and the impressure her Lucrece, with which she uses to seal : 'tis my lady. . . .

[*Reads*] ' If this fall into thy hand, revolve. In my stars I am above thee ; but be not afraid of greatness : some are born great, some achieve greatness and some have greatness thrust upon 'em. Thy Fates open their hands ; let thy blood and spirit embrace them ; and, to inure thyself to what thou art like to be, cast thy humble slough and appear fresh. Be opposite with a kinsman, surly with servants ; let thy tongue tang arguments of state ; put thyself into the trick of singularity : she thus advises thee that sighs for thee. Remember who commended thy yellow stockings, and wished to see thee ever cross-gartered : I say, remember. Go to, thou art made, if thou desirest to be so ; if not, let me see thee a steward still, the fellow of servants, and not worthy to touch Fortune's fingers. Farewell. She that would alter services with thee,

THE FORTUNATE-UNHAPPY.'

Daylight and champain discovers not more : this is open. I will be proud, I will read politic authors, I will baffle Sir Toby, I will wash off gross acquaintance, I will be point-devise the very man. I do not now fool myself, to let imagination jade me ; for every reason excites to this, that my lady loves me. She did commend my yellow stockings of late, she did praise my leg being cross-gartered ; and in this she manifests herself to my love, and with a kind of injunction drives me to these habits of her liking. I thank my stars I am happy. I will be strange, stout, in yellow stockings, and cross-gartered, even with the swiftness of putting on. Jove and my stars be praised ! Here is yet a postscript.

[*Reads*] ' Thou canst not choose but know who I am. If thou entertainest my love, let it appear in thy smiling ; thy smiles become thee well ; therefore in my presence still smile, dear my sweet, I prithee.'

Jove, I thank thee : I will smile ; I will do everything that thou wilt have me.   [*Exit.*

Fab. I will not give my part of this sport for a pension of thousands to be paid from the Sophy.

Act II, Scene v, ll. 16-105, 155-197

O, what a deal of scorn looks beautiful
In the contempt and anger of his lip !
A murderous guilt shows not itself more soon
Than love that would seem hid : love's night is noon.
Cesario, by the roses of the spring,
By maidhood, honour, truth and every thing,
I love thee so, that, maugre all thy pride,
Nor wit nor reason can my passion hide.

Act III, Scene i, ll. 157-164

Olivia's garden.

Enter Olivia and Maria.

Oli. I have sent after him : he says he'll come ;
How shall I feast him ? what bestow of him ?
For youth is bought more oft than begg'd or borrow'd.
I speak too loud.
Where is Malvolio ? he is sad and civil,
And suits well for a servant with my fortunes :
Where is Malvolio ?

269

Mar. He's coming, madam ; but in very strange manner. He is, sure, possessed, madam.

Oli. Why, what's the matter ? does he rave ?

Mar. No, madam, he does nothing but smile : your ladyship were best to have some guard about you, if he come ; for, sure, the man is tainted in's wits.

Oli. Go call him hither. [*Exit Maria.*] I am as mad as he, If sad and merry madness equal be.

Re-enter MARIA, *with* MALVOLIO.

How now, Malvolio !

Mal. Sweet lady, ho, ho.

Oli. Smilest thou ?
I sent for thee upon a sad occasion.

Mal. Sad, lady ! I could be sad : this does make some obstruction in the blood, this cross-gartering ; but what of that ? if it please the eye of one, it is with me as the very true sonnet is, ' Please one, and please all.'

Oli. Why, how dost thou, man ? what is the matter with thee ?

Mal. Not black in my mind, though yellow in my legs. It did come to his hands, and commands shall be executed : I think we do know the sweet Roman hand.

Oli. Wilt thou go to bed, Malvolio ?

Mal. To bed ! ay, sweet-heart, and I'll come to thee.

Oli. God comfort thee ! Why dost thou smile so and kiss thy hand so oft ?

Mar. How do you, Malvolio ?

Mal. At your request ! yes ; nightingales answer daws.

Mar. Why appear you with this ridiculous boldness before my lady ?

Mal. ' Be not afraid of greatness : ' 'twas well writ.

Oli. What meanest thou by that, Malvolio ?

Mal. ' Some are born great,'—

Oli. Ha !

Mal. ' Some achieve greatness,'—

Oli. What sayest thou ?

Mal. ' And some have greatness thrust upon them.'

Oli. Heaven restore thee !

Mal. ' Remember who commended thy yellow stockings,'—

Oli. Thy yellow stockings !

Mal. ' And wished to see thee cross-gartered.'

Oli. Cross-gartered !

Mal. ' Go to, thou art made, if thou desirest to be so ; '—

Oli. Am I made ?

Mal. ' If not, let me see thee a servant still.'

Oli. Why, this is very midsummer madness.

Enter Servant.

Ser. Madam, the young gentleman of the Count Orsino's is returned : I could hardly entreat him back : he attends your ladyship's pleasure.

Oli. I'll come to him. [*Exit Servant.*] Good Maria, let this fellow be looked to. Where's my cousin Toby ? Let some of my people have a special care of him : I would not have him miscarry for the half of my dowry.

[*Exeunt Olivia and Maria.*

Mal. O, ho ! do you come near me now ? no worse man than Sir Toby to look to me ! This concurs directly with the letter : she sends him on purpose, that I may appear stubborn to him ; for she incites me to that in the letter. ' Cast thy humble slough,' says she ; ' be opposite with a kinsman, surly with servants ; let thy tongue tang with arguments of state ; put thyself into the trick of singularity ; ' and consequently sets down the manner how ; as, a sad face, a reverend carriage, a slow tongue, in the habit of some sir of note, and so forth. I have limed her ; but it is Jove's doing, and Jove make me thankful ! And when she went away now, ' Let this fellow be looked to : ' fellow ! not Malvolio, nor after my degree, but fellow. Why, every thing adheres together, that no dram of a scruple, no scruple of a scruple, no obstacle, no incredulous or unsafe circumstance—What can be said ?

Nothing that can be can come between me and the full prospect of my hopes. Well, Jove, not I, is the doer of this, and he is to be thanked.

Re-enter MARIA, *with* SIR TOBY *and* FABIAN.

Sir To. Which way is he, in the name of sanctity? If all the devils of hell be drawn in little, and Legion himself possessed him, yet I'll speak to him.

Fab. Here he is, here he is. How is't with you, sir? how is't with you, man?

Mal. Go off; I discard you: let me enjoy my private: go off.

Mar. Lo, how hollow the fiend speaks within him! did not I tell you? Sir Toby, my lady prays you to have a care of him.

Mal. Ah, ha! does she so?

Sir To. Go to, go to; peace, peace; we must deal gently with him: let me alone. How do you, Malvolio? how is't with you? What, man! defy the devil: consider, he's an enemy to mankind.

Mal. Do you know what you say?

Mar. La you, an you speak ill of the devil, how he takes it at heart! Pray God, he be not bewitched!

Fab. Carry his water to the wise woman.

Mar. Marry, and it shall be done to-morrow morning, if I live. My lady would not lose him for more than I'll say.

Mal. How now, mistress!

Mar. O Lord!

Sir To. Prithee, hold thy peace; this is not the way: do you not see you move him? let me alone with him.

Fab. No way but gentleness; gently, gently: the fiend is rough, and will not be roughly used.

Sir To. Why, how now, my bawcock! how dost thou, chuck?

Mal. Sir!

Sir To. Ay, Biddy, come with me. What, man! 'tis not

for gravity to play at cherry-pit with Satan : hang him, foul collier !

Mar. Get him to say his prayers, good Sir Toby, get him to pray.

Mal. My prayers, minx !

Mar. No, I warrant you, he will not hear of godliness.

Mal. Go, hang yourselves all ! you are idle shallow things : I am not of your element : you shall know more hereafter. . . .

[*Exit*.

Enter SIR ANDREW.

Fab. More matter for a May morning.

Sir And. Here's the challenge, read it : I warrant there's vinegar and pepper in't.

Fab. Is't so saucy ?

Sir And. Ay, is't, I warrant him : do but read.

Sir To. Give me. [*Reads*] ' Youth, whatsoever thou art, thou art but a scurvy fellow.'

Fab. Good, and valiant.

Sir To. [*Reads*] ' Wonder not, nor admire not in thy mind, why I do call thee so, for I will show thee no reason for't.'

Fab. A good note ; that keeps you from the blow of the law.

Sir To. [*Reads*] ' Thou comest to the lady Olivia, and in my sight she uses thee kindly : but thou liest in thy throat ; that is not the matter I challenge thee for.'

Fab. Very brief, and to exceeding good sense—less.

Sir To. [*Reads*] ' I will waylay thee going home ; where if it be thy chance to kill me,'—

Fab. Good.

Sir To. [*Reads*] ' Thou killest me like a rogue and a villain.'

Fab. Still you keep o' the windy side of the law : good.

Sir To. [*Reads*] ' Fare thee well ; and God have mercy upon one of our souls ! He may have mercy upon mine ; but my hope is better, and so look to thyself. Thy friend, as thou usest him, and thy sworn enemy,   ANDREW AGUECHEEK.'

If this letter move him not, his legs cannot : I'll give't him.

Mar. You may have very fit occasion for't : he is now in some commerce with my lady, and will by and by depart.

Sir To. Go, Sir Andrew ; scout me for him at the corner of the orchard like a bum-baily : so soon as ever thou seest him, draw ; and, as thou drawest, swear horrible ; for it comes to pass oft that a terrible oath, with a swaggering accent, sharply twanged off, gives manhood more approbation than ever proof itself would have earned him. Away !

Sir And. Nay, let me alone for swearing.   [*Exit*. . . .

Enter VIOLA.

Sir To. Gentleman, God save thee.

Vio. And you, sir.

Sir To. That defence thou hast, betake thee to't : of what nature the wrongs are thou hast done him, I know not ; but thy intercepter, full of despite, bloody as the hunter, attends thee at the orchard-end : dismount thy tuck, be yare in thy preparation, for thy assailant is quick, skilful and deadly.

Vio. You mistake, sir ; I am sure no man hath any quarrel to me : my remembrance is very free and clear from any image of offence done to any man.

Sir To. You'll find it otherwise, I assure you : therefore, if you hold your life at any price, betake you to your guard ; for your opposite hath in him what youth, strength, skill and wrath can furnish man withal.

Vio. I pray you, sir, what is he ?

Sir To. He is knight, dubbed with unhatched rapier and on carpet consideration ; but he is a devil in private brawl : souls and bodies hath he divorced three ; and his incensement at this moment is so implacable, that satisfaction can be none but by pangs of death and sepulchre. Hob, nob, is his word ; give't or take't.

Vio. I will return again into the house and desire some conduct of the lady. I am no fighter. I have heard of some kind of men that put quarrels purposely on others, to taste their valour : belike this is a man of that quirk.

Sir To. Sir, no; his indignation derives itself out of a very competent injury: therefore, get you on and give him his desire. Back you shall not to the house, unless you undertake that with me which with as much safety you might answer him: therefore, on, or strip your sword stark naked; for meddle you must, that's certain, or forswear to wear iron about you.

Vio. This is as uncivil as strange. I beseech you, do me this courteous office, as to know of the knight what my offence to him is: it is something of my negligence, nothing of my purpose.

Sir To. I will do so. Signior Fabian, stay you by this gentleman till my return. [*Exit.*

Vio. Pray you, sir, do you know of this matter?

Fab. I know the knight is incensed against you, even to a mortal arbitrement; but nothing of the circumstance more.

Vio. I beseech you, what manner of man is he?

Fab. Nothing of that wonderful promise, to read him by his form, as you are like to find him in the proof of his valour. He is, indeed, sir, the most skilful, bloody and fatal opposite that you could possibly have found in any part of Illyria. Will you walk towards him? I will make your peace with him if I can.

Vio. I shall be much bound to you for't: I am one that had rather go with sir priest than sir knight: I care not who knows so much of my mettle. [*Exeunt.*

Re-enter Sir Toby, *with* Sir Andrew.

Sir To. Why, man, he's a very devil; I have not seen such a firago. I had a pass with him, rapier, scabbard and all, and he gives me the stuck in with such a mortal motion, that it is inevitable; and on the answer, he pays you as surely as your feet hit the ground they step on. They say he has been fencer to the Sophy.

Sir And. Pox on't, I'll not meddle with him.

Sir To. Ay, but he will not now be pacified : Fabian can scarce hold him yonder.

Sir And. Plague on't, an I thought he had been valiant and so cunning in fence, I'ld have seen him damned ere I'ld have challenged him. Let him let the matter slip, and I'll give him my horse, grey Capilet.

Sir To. I'll make the motion : stand here, make a good show on't : this shall end without the perdition of souls. [*Aside*] Marry, I'll ride your horse as well as I ride you.

Re-enter FABIAN *and* VIOLA.

[*To Fab.*] I have his horse to take up the quarrel : I have persuaded him the youth's a devil.

Fab. He is as horribly conceited of him ; and pants and looks pale, as if a bear were at his heels.

Sir To. [*To Vio.*] There's no remedy, sir ; he will fight with you for's oath sake : marry, he hath better bethought him of his quarrel, and he finds that now scarce to be worth talking of : therefore draw, for the supportance of his vow ; he protests he will not hurt you.

Vio. [*Aside*] Pray God defend me ! A little thing would make me tell them how much I lack of a man.

Fab. Give ground, if you see him furious.

Sir To. Come, Sir Andrew, there's no remedy ; the gentleman will, for his honour's sake, have one bout with you ; he cannot by the duello avoid it : but he has promised me, as he is a gentleman and a soldier, he will not hurt you. Come on ; to't.

Sir And. Pray God, he keep his oath !

Vio. I do assure you, 'tis against my will.   [*They draw.*

ACT III, Scene iv, ll. 1-138, 156-201, 238-342

OLIVIA'S *house.*

Enter MARIA *and* CLOWN.

Mar. Nay, I prithee, put on this gown and this beard ; make him believe thou art Sir Topas the curate : do it quickly ; I'll call Sir Toby the whilst.   [*Exit.*

Clo. Well, I'll put it on, and I will dissemble myself in't ; and I would I were the first that ever dissembled in such a gown. I am not tall enough to become the function well, nor lean enough to be thought a good student ; but to be said an honest man and a good housekeeper goes as fairly as to say a careful man and a great scholar. The competitors enter.

Enter SIR TOBY *and* MARIA.

Sir To. Jove bless thee, master Parson.

Clo. Bonos dies, Sir Toby : for, as the old hermit of Prague, that never saw pen and ink, very wittily said to a niece of King Gorboduc, ' That that is is ; ' so I, being master Parson, am master Parson ; for, what is ' that ' but ' that,' and ' is ' but ' is ' ?

Sir To. To him, Sir Topas.

Clo. What, ho, I say ! peace in this prison !

Sir To. The knave counterfeits well ; a good knave.

Mal. [*Within*] Who calls there ?

Clo. Sir Topas the curate, who comes to visit Malvolio the lunatic.

Mal. Sir Topas, Sir Topas, good Sir Topas, go to my lady.

Clo. Out, hyperbolical fiend ! how vexest thou this man ! talkest thou nothing but of ladies ?

Sir To. Well said, master Parson.

Mal. Sir Topas, never was man thus wronged : good Sir Topas, do not think I am mad : they have laid me here in hideous darkness.

Clo. Fie, thou dishonest Satan ! I call thee by the most modest terms ; for I am one of those gentle ones that will use the devil himself with courtesy : sayest thou that house is dark ?

Mal. As hell, Sir Topas.

Clo. Why, it hath bay windows transparent as barricadoes, and the clearstores toward the south north are as lustrous as ebony ; and yet complainest thou of obstruction ?

Mal. I am not mad, Sir Topas : I say to you, this house is dark.

Clo. Madman, thou errest : I say, there is no darkness but ignorance ; in which thou art more puzzled than the Egyptians in their fog.

Mal. I say, this house is as dark as ignorance, though ignorance were as dark as hell ; and I say, there was never man thus abused. I am no more mad than you are : make the trial of it in any constant question.

Clo. What is the opinion of Pythagoras concerning wild fowl ?

Mal. That the soul of our grandam might haply inhabit a bird.

Clo. What thinkest thou of his opinion ?

Mal. I think nobly of the soul, and no way approve his opinion.

Clo. Fare thee well. Remain thou still in darkness : thou shalt hold the opinion of Pythagoras ere I will allow of thy wits, and fear to kill a woodcock, lest thou dispossess the soul of thy grandam. Fare thee well.

Mal. Sir Topas, Sir Topas !

Sir To. My most exquisite Sir Topas !

Clo. Nay, I am for all waters.

Mar. Thou mightst have done this without thy beard and gown : he sees thee not.

Sir To. To him in thine own voice, and bring me word how thou findest him : I would we were well rid of this knavery. If he may be conveniently delivered, I would he were, for I am now so far in offence with my niece that I cannot pursue with any safety this sport to the upshot. Come by and by to my chamber. *[Exeunt Sir Toby and Maria.*

Clo. [*Singing*] ' Hey, Robin, jolly Robin,
            Tell me how thy lady does.'

Mal. Fool !

Clo. ' My lady is unkind, perdy.'

Mal. Fool !

Clo. ' Alas, why is she so ? '

Mal. Fool, I say !

Clo. ' She loves another '—Who calls, ha ?

Mal. Good fool, as ever thou wilt deserve well at my hand, help me to a candle, and pen, ink and paper : as I am a gentleman, I will live to be thankful to thee for't.

Clo. Master Malvolio ?

Mal. Ay, good fool.

Clo. Alas, sir, how fell you besides your five wits ?

Mal. Fool, there was never man so notoriously abused : I am as well in my wits, fool, as thou art.

Clo. But as well ? then you are mad indeed, if you be no better in your wits than a fool.

Mal. They have here propertied me ; keep me in darkness, send ministers to me, asses, and do all they can to face me out of my wits.

Clo. Advise you what you say ; the minister is here. Malvolio, Malvolio, thy wits the heavens restore ! endeavour thyself to sleep, and leave thy vain bibble babble.

Mal. Sir Topas !

Clo. Maintain no words with him, good fellow. Who, I, sir ? not I, sir. God be wi' you, good Sir Topas. Marry, amen. I will, sir, I will.

Mal. Fool, fool, fool, I say !

Clo. Alas, sir, be patient. What say you, sir ? I am shent for speaking to you.

Mal. Good fool, help me to some light and some paper : I tell thee, I am as well in my wits as any man in Illyria.

Clo. Well-a-day that you were, sir !

Mal. By this hand, I am. Good fool, some ink, paper and light ; and convey what I will set down to my lady : it shall advantage thee more than ever the bearing of letter did.

Clo. I will help you to't. But tell me true, are you not mad indeed ? or do you but counterfeit ?

Mal. Believe me, I am not ; I tell thee true.

Clo. Nay, I'll ne'er believe a madman till I see his brains.

L

I will fetch you light and paper and ink.

Mal. Fool, I'll requite it in the highest degree: I prithee, be gone.   ACT IV, Scene ii, ll. 1-129

Oli. How now, Malvolio!

Mal.   Madam, you have done me wrong, Notorious wrong. . . .

Oli. Alas, poor fool, how have they baffled thee!

Clo. Why, ' some are born great, some achieve greatness, and some have greatness thrown upon them.' I was one, sir, in this interlude; one Sir Topas, sir; but that's all one. ' By the Lord, fool, I am not mad.' But do you remember? ' Madam, why laugh you at such a barren rascal? an you smile not, he's gagged:' and thus the whirligig of time brings in his revenges.

Mal. I'll be revenged on the whole pack of you.   [*Exit.*

Oli. He hath been most notoriously abused.

Duke. Pursue him, and entreat him to a peace:
He hath not told us of the captain yet:
When that is known and golden time convents,
A solemn combination shall be made
Of our dear souls. . . .   [*Exeunt all, except* CLOWN.

Clo. [*Sings*]

> When that I was and a little tiny boy,
> With hey, ho, the wind and the rain,
> A foolish thing was but a toy,
> For the rain it raineth every day.

> But when I came to man's estate,
> With hey, ho, &c.
> 'Gainst knaves and thieves men shut their gate,
> For the rain, &c.

> But when I came, alas! to wive,
> With hey, ho, &c.
> By swaggering could I never thrive,
> For the rain, &c.

But when I came unto my beds,
   With hey, ho, &c.
With toss-pots still had drunken heads,
   For the rain, &c.

A great while ago the world begun,
   With hey, ho, &c.
But that's all one, our play is done,
   And we'll strive to please you every day.
        Act V, Scene i, ll. 336-337, 377-393, 398-417

AFTERNOON

PART I

Julius Caesar

Second Commoner. We make holiday, to see Caesar and to
rejoice in his triumph.

    Marullus. Wherefore rejoice ? What conquest brings he
        home ?
What tributaries follow him to Rome,
To grace in captive bonds his chariot-wheels ?
You blocks, you stones, you worse than senseless things !
O you hard hearts, you cruel men of Rome,
Knew you not Pompey ? Many a time and oft
Have you climb'd up to walls and battlements,
To towers and windows, yea, to chimney-tops,
Your infants in your arms, and there have sat
The live-long day, with patient expectation,
To see great Pompey pass the streets of Rome :
And when you saw his chariot but appear,
Have you not made an universal shout,
That Tiber trembled underneath her banks,
To hear the replication of your sounds
Made in her concave shores ?
And do you now put on your best attire ?
And do you now cull out a holiday ?
And do you now strew flowers in his way
That comes in triumph over Pompey's blood ?
Be gone !
Run to your houses, fall upon your knees,
Pray to the gods to intermit the plague
That needs must light on this ingratitude.

Act I, Scene i, ll. 35-60

    Caesar. Who is it in the press that calls on me ?
I hear a tongue, shriller than all the music,

285

Cry ' Caesar ! ' Speak ; Caesar is turn'd to hear.

   Soothsayer. Beware the ides of March.

   Caes.   What man is that ?

   Brutus. A soothsayer bids you beware the ides of March.

   Caes. Set him before me ; let me see his face.

   Cassius. Fellow, come from the throng ; look upon Caesar.

   Caes. What say'st thou to me now ? speak once again.

   Sooth. Beware the ides of March.

   Caes. He is a dreamer ; let us leave him : pass.

ACT I, Scene ii, ll. 15-24

   Brutus. What means this shouting ? I do fear, the people
Choose Caesar for their king.

   Cassius.   Ay, do you fear it ?
Then must I think you would not have it so.

   Bru. I would not, Cassius ; yet I love him well.
But wherefore do you hold me here so long ?
What is it that you would impart to me ?
If it be aught toward the general good,
Set honour in one eye and death i' the other,
And I will look on both indifferently,
For let the gods so speed me as I love
The name of honour more than I fear death.

   Cas. I know that virtue to be in you, Brutus,
As well as I do know your outward favour.
Well, honour is the subject of my story.
I cannot tell what you and other men
Think of this life ; but, for my single self,
I had as lief not be as live to be
In awe of such a thing as I myself.
I was born free as Caesar ; so were you :
We both have fed as well, and we can both
Endure the winter's cold as well as he :
For once, upon a raw and gusty day,
The troubled Tiber chafing with her shores,
Caesar said to me ' Darest thou, Cassius, now

Leap in with me into this angry flood,
And swim to yonder point?' Upon the word,
Accoutred as I was, I plunged in
And bade him follow; so indeed he did.
The torrent roar'd, and we did buffet it
With lusty sinews, throwing it aside
And stemming it with hearts of controversy;
But ere we could arrive the point proposed,
Caesar cried 'Help me, Cassius, or I sink!'
I, as Æneas, our great ancestor,
Did from the flames of Troy upon his shoulder
The old Anchises bear, so from the waves of Tiber
Did I the tired Caesar. And this man
Is now become a god, and Cassius is
A wretched creature and must bend his body,
If Caesar carelessly but nod on him.
He had a fever when he was in Spain,
And when the fit was on him, I did mark
How he did shake: 'tis true, this god did shake:
His coward lips did from their colour fly,
And that same eye whose bend doth awe the world
Did lose his lustre: I did hear him groan:
Ay, and that tongue of his that bade the Romans
Mark him and write his speeches in their books,
Alas, it cried 'Give me some drink, Titinius,'
As a sick girl. Ye gods, it doth amaze me
A man of such a feeble temper should
So get the start of the majestic world
And bear the palm alone.   [*Shout. Flourish.*

 Bru. Another general shout!
I do believe that these applauses are
For some new honours that are heap'd on Caesar.

 Cas. Why, man, he doth bestride the narrow world
Like a Colossus, and we petty men
Walk under his huge legs and peep about
To find ourselves dishonourable graves.

Men at some time are masters of their fates :
The fault, dear Brutus, is not in our stars,
But in ourselves, that we are underlings.
Brutus and Caesar : what should be in that ' Caesar ' ?
Why should that name be sounded more than yours ?
Write them together, yours is as fair a name ;
Sound them, it doth become the mouth as well ;
Weigh them, it is as heavy ; conjure with 'em,
Brutus will start a spirit as soon as Caesar.
Now, in the names of all the gods at once,
Upon what meat doth this our Caesar feed,
That he is grown so great ? Age, thou art shamed !
Rome, thou hast lost the breed of noble bloods !
When went there by an age, since the great flood,
But it was famed with more than with one man ?
When could they say till now, that talk'd of Rome,
That her wide walls encompass'd but one man ?
Now is it Rome indeed and room enough,
When there is in it but one only man.
O, you and I have heard our fathers say,
There was a Brutus once that would have brook'd
The eternal devil to keep his state in Rome
As easily as a king. . . .

Enter CAESAR *and his Train.*

Bru. But, look you, Cassius,
The angry spot doth glow on Caesar's brow,
And all the rest look like a chidden train :
Calpurnia's cheek is pale ; and Cicero
Looks with such ferret and such fiery eyes
As we have seen him in the Capitol,
Being cross'd in conference by some senators.

Cas. Casca will tell us what the matter is.

Caes. Antonius !

Antony. Caesar ?

Caes. Let me have men about me that are fat :

Sleek-headed men and such as sleep o' nights :
Yond Cassius has a lean and hungry look ;
He thinks too much : such men are dangerous.

    Ant. Fear him not, Caesar ; he's not dangerous ;
He is a noble Roman and well given.

    Caes. Would he were fatter ! But I fear him not :
Yet if my name were liable to fear,
I do not know the man I should avoid
So soon as that spare Cassius. He reads much ;
He is a great observer and he looks
Quite through the deeds of men ; he loves no plays,
As thou dost, Antony ; he hears no music ;
Seldom he smiles, and smiles in such a sort
As if he mock'd himself and scorn'd his spirit
That could be moved to smile at any thing.
Such men as he be never at heart's ease
Whiles they behold a greater than themselves,
And therefore are they very dangerous.
I rather tell thee what is to be fear'd
Than what I fear ; for always I am Caesar.

                           Act I, Scene ii, ll. 79-161, 182-212

A street.

Thunder and lightning. Enter, from opposite sides, Casca, *with his sword drawn, and* Cicero.

    Cic. Good even, Casca : brought you Caesar home ?
Why are you breathless ? and why stare you so ?

    Casca. Are not you moved, when all the sway of earth
Shakes like a thing unfirm ? O Cicero,
I have seen tempests, when the scolding winds
Have rived the knotty oaks, and I have seen
The ambitious ocean swell and rage and foam,
To be exalted with the threatening clouds :
But never till to-night, never till now,
Did I go through a tempest dropping fire.
Either there is a civil strife in heaven,

Or else the world, too saucy with the gods,
Incenses them to send destruction.

   Cic. Why, saw you any thing more wonderful?

   Casca. A common slave—you know him well by sight—
Held up his left hand, which did flame and burn
Like twenty torches join'd, and yet his hand,
Not sensible of fire, remain'd unscorch'd.
Besides—I ha' not since put up my sword—
Against the Capitol I met a lion,
Who glared upon me, and went surly by,
Without annoying me: and there were drawn
Upon a heap a hundred ghastly women,
Transformed with their fear; who swore they saw
Men all in fire walk up and down the streets.
And yesterday the bird of night did sit
Even at noon-day upon the market-place,
Hooting and shrieking. When these prodigies
Do so conjointly meet, let not men say
' These are their reasons; they are natural; '
For, I believe, they are portentous things
Unto the climate that they point upon.

                         ACT I, Scene iii, ll. 1-32

Brutus's orchard.

   Brutus. It must be by his death: and for my part,
I know no personal cause to spurn at him,
But for the general. He would be crown'd:
How that might change his nature, there's the question.
It is the bright day that brings forth the adder; . . .
Since Cassius first did whet me against Caesar,
I have not slept.
Between the acting of a dreadful thing
And the first motion, all the interim is
Like a phantasma, or a hideous dream:
The Genius and the mortal instruments
Are then in council; and the state of man,

Like to a little kingdom, suffers then
The nature of an insurrection.

ACT II, Scene i, ll. 9-14, 61-69

   Brutus. Boy! Lucius! Fast asleep? It is no matter;
Enjoy the honey-heavy dew of slumber:
Thou hast no figures nor no fantasies,
Which busy care draws in the brains of men;
Therefore thou sleep'st so sound.

Enter PORTIA.

   Por.   Brutus, my lord!
   Bru. Portia, what mean you? wherefore rise you now?
It is not for your health thus to commit
Your weak condition to the raw cold morning.
   Por. Nor for yours neither. You've ungently, Brutus,
Stole from my bed: and yesternight, at supper,
You suddenly arose, and walk'd about,
Musing and sighing, with your arms across,
And when I ask'd you what the matter was,
You stared upon me with ungentle looks;
I urged you further; then you scratch'd your head,
And too impatiently stamp'd with your foot;
Yet I insisted, yet you answer'd not,
But, with an angry wafture of your hand,
Gave sign for me to leave you: so I did;
Fearing to strengthen that impatience
Which seem'd too much enkindled, and withal
Hoping it was but an effect of humour,
Which sometime hath his hour with every man.
It will not let you eat, nor talk, nor sleep,
And could it work so much upon your shape
As it hath much prevail'd on your condition,
I should not know you, Brutus. Dear my lord,
Make me acquainted with your cause of grief.
   Bru. I am not well in health, and that is all.
   Por. Brutus is wise, and, were he not in health,

291

He would embrace the means to come by it.

    Bru. Why, so I do. Good Portia, go to bed.

    Por. Is Brutus sick ? and is it physical
To walk unbraced and suck up the humours
Of the dank morning ? What, is Brutus sick,
And will he steal out of his wholesome bed,
To dare the vile contagion of the night
And tempt the rheumy and unpurged air
To add unto his sickness ? No, my Brutus ;
You have some sick offence within your mind,
Which, by the right and virtue of my place,
I ought to know of : and, upon my knees,
I charm you, by my once-commended beauty,
By all your vows of love and that great vow
Which did incorporate and make us one,
That you unfold to me, yourself, your half,
Why you are heavy, and what men to-night
Have had resort to you : for here have been
Some six or seven, who did hide their faces
Even from darkness.

    Bru.   Kneel not, gentle Portia.

    Por. I should not need, if you were gentle Brutus.
Within the bond of marriage, tell me, Brutus,
Is it excepted I should know no secrets
That appertain to you ? Am I yourself
But, as it were, in sort or limitation,
To keep with you at meals, comfort your bed,
And talk to you sometimes ? Dwell I but in the suburbs
Of your good pleasure ? If it be no more,
Portia is Brutus' harlot, not his wife.

    Bru. You are my true and honourable wife,
As dear to me as are the ruddy drops
That visit my sad heart.

    Por. If this were true, then should I know this secret.
I grant I am a woman ; but withal
A woman that Lord Brutus took to wife :

I grant I am a woman ; but withal
A woman well-reputed, Cato's daughter.
Think you I am no stronger than my sex,
Being so father'd and so husbanded ?
Tell me your counsels, I will not disclose 'em :
I have made strong proof of my constancy,
Giving myself a voluntary wound
Here, in the thigh : can I bear that with patience,
And not my husband's secrets ?

Bru.   O ye gods,
Render me worthy of this noble wife !

                                                    [*Knocking within.*

Hark, hark ! one knocks : Portia, go in awhile ;
And by and by thy bosom shall partake
The secrets of my heart.
All my engagements I will construe to thee,
All the charactery of my sad brows :
Leave me with haste.

                                        ACT II, Scene i, ll. 229-309

Caesar's house.

Thunder and lightning. Enter CAESAR, *in his night-gown.*

Caes. Nor heaven nor earth have been at peace to-night :
Thrice hath Calpurnia in her sleep cried out,
' Help, ho ! they murder Caesar ! ' Who's within ?

Enter a Servant.

Serv. My lord ?
Caes. Go bid the priests do present sacrifice
And bring me their opinions of success.
Serv. I will, my lord.   [*Exit*

Enter CALPURNIA.

Cal. What mean you, Caesar ? think you to walk forth ?
You shall not stir out of your house to-day.
Caes. Caesar shall forth : the things that threaten'd me

Ne'er look'd but on my back ; when they shall see
The face of Caesar, they are vanished.

Cal. Caesar, I never stood on ceremonies,
Yet now they fright me. There is one within,
Besides the things that we have heard and seen,
Recounts most horrid sights seen by the watch.
A lioness hath whelped in the streets ;
And graves have yawn'd, and yielded up their dead ;
Fierce fiery warriors fought upon the clouds,
In ranks and squadrons and right form of war,
Which drizzled blood upon the Capitol ;
The noise of battle hurtled in the air,
Horses did neigh, and dying men did groan,
And ghosts did shriek and squeal about the streets.
O Caesar ! these things are beyond all use,
And I do fear them.

Caes.   What can be avoided
Whose end is purposed by the mighty gods ?
Yet Caesar shall go forth ; for these predictions
Are to the world in general as to Caesar.

Cal. When beggars die, there are no comets seen ;
The heavens themselves blaze forth the death of princes.

Caes. Cowards die many times before their deaths ;
The valiant never taste of death but once.
Of all the wonders that I yet have heard,
It seems to me most strange that men should fear ;
Seeing that death, a necessary end,
Will come when it will come.

Re-enter Servant.

                              What say the augurers ?

Serv. They would not have you to stir forth to-day.
Plucking the entrails of an offering forth,
They could not find a heart within the beast.

Caes. The gods do this in shame of cowardice :
Caesar should be a beast without a heart,

If he should stay at home to-day for fear.
No, Caesar shall not : danger knows full well
That Caesar is more dangerous than he :
We are two lions litter'd in one day,
And I the elder and more terrible :
And Caesar shall go forth.

ACT II, Scene ii, ll. 1-48

The Senate-House.

Brutus. I kiss thy hand, but not in flattery, Caesar ;
Desiring thee that Publius Cimber may
Have an immediate freedom of repeal.

Caesar. What, Brutus !

Cassius.   Pardon, Caesar ; Caesar, pardon :
As low as to thy foot doth Cassius fall,
To beg enfranchisement for Publius Cimber.

Caes. I could be well moved, if I were as you ;
If I could pray to move, prayers would move me :
But I am constant as the northern star,
Of whose true-fix'd and resting quality
There is no fellow in the firmament.
The skies are painted with unnumber'd sparks,
They are all fire and every one doth shine,
But there's but one in all doth hold his place :
So in the world ; 'tis furnish'd well with men,
And men are flesh and blood, and apprehensive ;
Yet in the number I do know but one
That unassailable holds on his rank,
Unshaked of motion : and that I am he,
Let me a little show it, even in this ;
That I was constant Cimber should be banish'd,
And constant do remain to keep him so.

Cinna. O Caesar,—

Caes.   Hence ! wilt thou lift up Olympus ?

Decius. Great Caesar,—

Caes.   Doth not Brutus bootless kneel ?

Casca. Speak, hands, for me !

   [Casca first, then the other Conspirators and
                     Marcus Brutus stab Caesar.

Caes. Et tu, Brute ! Then fall, Caesar !   *[Dies.* . . .

   Bru.   Stoop, Romans, stoop,

And let us bathe our hands in Caesar's blood
Up to the elbows, and besmear our swords :
Then walk we forth, even to the market-place,
And, waving our red weapons o'er our heads,
Let's all cry ' Peace, freedom and liberty ! '

   Cas. Stoop, then, and wash. How many ages hence
Shall this our lofty scene be acted over
In states unborn and accents yet unknown !

   Bru. How many times shall Caesar bleed in sport
That now on Pompey's basis lies along
No worthier than the dust !

   Cas.   So oft as that shall be,
So often shall the knot of us be call'd
The men that gave their country liberty. . . .

   Bru. But here comes Antony.

Enter ANTONY.

                         Welcome, Mark Antony.

   Ant. O mighty Caesar ! dost thou lie so low ?
Are all thy conquests, glories, triumphs, spoils,
Shrunk to this little measure ? Fare thee well.
I know not, gentlemen, what you intend,
Who else must be let blood, who else is rank :
If I myself, there is no hour so fit
As Caesar's death hour, nor no instrument
Of half that worth as those your swords, made rich
With the most noble blood of all this world.
I do beseech ye, if you bear me hard,
Now, whilst your purpled hands do reek and smoke,
Fulfil your pleasure. Live a thousand years,
I shall not find myself so apt to die :

No place will please me so, no mean of death,
As here by Caesar, and by you cut off,
The choice and master spirits of this age. . . .
That I did love thee, Caesar, O, 'tis true :
If then thy spirit look upon us now,
Shall it not grieve thee dearer than thy death,
To see thy Antony making his peace,
Shaking the bloody fingers of thy foes,
Most noble ! in the presence of thy corse ?
Had I as many eyes as thou hast wounds,
Weeping as fast as they stream forth thy blood,
It would become me better than to close
In terms of friendship with thine enemies.
Pardon me, Julius ! Here wast thou bay'd, brave hart ;
Here didst thou fall ; and here thy hunters stand,
Sign'd in thy spoil, and crimson'd in thy lethe.
O world, thou wast the forest to this hart ;
And this, indeed, O world, the heart of thee.
How like a deer, strucken by many princes,
Dost thou here lie ! . . .

[Exeunt all but Antony.

   Ant. O, pardon me, thou bleeding piece of earth,
That I am meek and gentle with these butchers !
Thou art the ruins of the noblest man
That ever lived in the tide of times.
Woe to the hand that shed this costly blood !
Over thy wounds now do I prophesy,—
Which, like dumb mouths, do ope their ruby lips,
To beg the voice and utterance of my tongue—
A curse shall light upon the limbs of men ;
Domestic fury and fierce civil strife
Shall cumber all the parts of Italy ;
Blood and destruction shall be so in use
And dreadful objects so familiar
That mothers shall but smile when they behold
Their infants quarter'd with the hands of war ;

All pity choked with custom of fell deeds :
And Caesar's spirit, ranging for revenge,
With Ate by his side come hot from hell,
Shall in these confines with a monarch's voice
Cry ' Havoc,' and let slip the dogs of war ;
That this foul deed shall smell above the earth
With carrion men, groaning for burial.

ACT III, Scene i, ll. 52-77, 105-119, 147-163, 194-210, 254-275

The Forum.

Enter BRUTUS *and* CASSIUS, *and a throng of* Citizens.

First Cit. I will hear Brutus speak.

Sec. Cit. I will hear Cassius ; and compare their reasons,
When severally we hear them rendered.

[*Exit Cassius, with some of the Citizens.*
Brutus goes into the pulpit.

Third Cit. The noble Brutus is ascended : silence !

Bru. Be patient till the last.

Romans, countrymen, and lovers ! hear me for my cause, and
be silent, that you may hear : believe me for mine honour,
and have respect to mine honour, that you may believe : censure me in your wisdom, and awake your senses, that you may
the better judge. If there be any in this assembly, any dear
friend of Caesar's, to him I say, that Brutus' love to Caesar was
no less than his. If then that friend demand why Brutus rose
against Caesar, this is my answer :—Not that I loved Caesar
less, but that I loved Rome more. Had you rather Caesar
were living and die all slaves, than that Caesar were dead, to
live all free men ? As Caesar loved me, I weep for him ; as
he was fortunate, I rejoice at it ; as he was valiant, I honour
him : but, as he was ambitious, I slew him. There is tears for
his love ; joy for his fortune ; honour for his valour ; and
death for his ambition. Who is here so base that would be a
bondman ? If any, speak ; for him have I offended. Who is
here so rude that would not be a Roman ? If any, speak ; for
him have I offended. Who is here so vile that will not love

his country? If any, speak; for him have I offended. I
pause for a reply.

All. None, Brutus, none.

Bru. Then none have I offended. I have done no more to
Caesar than you shall do to Brutus. The question of his
death is enrolled in the Capitol; his glory not extenuated,
wherein he was worthy, nor his offences enforced, for which
he suffered death.

Enter ANTONY *and others, with* CAESAR'S *body.*

Here comes his body, mourned by Mark Antony: who,
though he had no hand in his death, shall receive the benefit of
his dying, a place in the commonwealth; as which of you shall
not? With this I depart,—that, as I slew my best lover for the
good of Rome, I have the same dagger for myself, when it
shall please my country to need my death.

Ant. You gentle Romans,—

Citizens. Peace, ho! let us hear him.

Ant. Friends, Romans, countrymen, lend me your ears;
I come to bury Caesar, not to praise him.
The evil that men do lives after them;
The good is oft interred with their bones;
So let it be with Caesar. The noble Brutus
Hath told you Caesar was ambitious:
If it were so, it was a grievous fault,
And grievously hath Caesar answer'd it.
Here, under leave of Brutus and the rest—
For Brutus is an honourable man;
So are they all, all honourable men—
Come I to speak in Caesar's funeral.
He was my friend, faithful and just to me:
But Brutus says he was ambitious;
And Brutus is an honourable man.
He hath brought many captives home to Rome,
Whose ransoms did the general coffers fill:
Did this in Caesar seem ambitious?

When that the poor have cried, Caesar hath wept:
Ambition should be made of sterner stuff:
Yet Brutus says he was ambitious;
And Brutus is an honourable man.
You all did see that on the Lupercal
I thrice presented him a kingly crown,
Which he did thrice refuse: was this ambition?
Yet Brutus says he was ambitious;
And, sure, he is an honourable man.
I speak not to disprove what Brutus spoke,
But here I am to speak what I do know.
You all did love him once, not without cause:
What cause withholds you then, to mourn for him?
O judgement! thou art fled to brutish beasts,
And men have lost their reason. Bear with me;
My heart is in the coffin there with Caesar,
And I must pause till it come back to me.

 First Cit. Methinks there is much reason in his sayings.

 Sec. Cit. If thou consider rightly of the matter,
Caesar has had great wrong.

 Third Cit.   Has he, masters?
I fear there will a worse come in his place.

 Fourth Cit. Mark'd ye his words? He would not take the
  crown;
Therefore 'tis certain he was not ambitious.

 First Cit. If it be found so, some will dear abide it.

 Sec. Cit. Poor soul! his eyes are red as fire with weeping.

 Third Cit. There's not a nobler man in Rome than Antony.

 Fourth Cit. Now mark him, he begins again to speak.

 Ant. But yesterday the word of Caesar might
Have stood against the world; now lies he there,
And none so poor to do him reverence.
O masters, if I were disposed to stir
Your hearts and minds to mutiny and rage,
I should do Brutus wrong, and Cassius wrong,
Who, you all know, are honourable men:

I will not do them wrong ; I rather choose
To wrong the dead, to wrong myself and you,
Than I will wrong such honourable men.
But here's a parchment with the seal of Caesar ;
I found it in his closet, 'tis his will :
Let but the commons hear this testament—
Which, pardon me, I do not mean to read—
And they would go and kiss dead Caesar's wounds
And dip their napkins in his sacred blood,
Yea, beg a hair of him for memory,
And, dying, mention it within their wills,
Bequeathing it as a rich legacy
Unto their issue.

 Fourth Cit. We'll hear the will : read it, Mark Antony.

 All. The will, the will ! we will hear Caesar's will.

 Ant. Have patience, gentle friends, I must not read it ;
It is not meet you know how Caesar loved you.
You are not wood, you are not stones, but men ;
And, being men, hearing the will of Caesar,
It will inflame you, it will make you mad :
'Tis good you know not that you are his heirs ;
For, if you should, O, what would come of it !

 Fourth Cit. Read the will ; we'll hear it, Antony ;
You shall read us the will, Caesar's will.

 Ant. Will you be patient ? will you stay awhile ?
I have o'ershot myself to tell you of it :
I fear I wrong the honourable men
Whose daggers have stabb'd Caesar ; I do fear it.

 Fourth Cit. They were traitors : honourable men !

 All. The will ! the testament !

 Sec. Cit. They were villains, murderers : the will ! read
the will.

 Ant. You will compel me, then, to read the will ?
Then make a ring about the corpse of Caesar,
And let me show you him that made the will.
Shall I descend ? and will you give me leave ?

Several Cit. Come down.

Sec. Cit. Descend.

Third Cit. You shall have leave.   [*Antony comes down.*

Fourth Cit. A ring ; stand round.

First Cit. Stand from the hearse, stand from the body.

Sec. Cit. Room for Antony, most noble Antony.

Ant. Nay, press not so upon me ; stand far off.

Several Cit. Stand back ; room ; bear back.

Ant. If you have tears, prepare to shed them now.
You all do know this mantle : I remember
The first time ever Caesar put it on ;
'Twas on a summer's evening, in his tent,
That day he overcame the Nervii :
Look, in this place ran Cassius' dagger through :
See what a rent the envious Casca made :
Through this the well-beloved Brutus stabb'd ;
And as he pluck'd his cursed steel away,
Mark how the blood of Caesar follow'd it,
As rushing out of doors, to be resolved
If Brutus so unkindly knock'd, or no ;
For Brutus, as you know, was Caesar's angel :
Judge, O you gods, how dearly Caesar loved him !
This was the most unkindest cut of all ;
For when the noble Caesar saw him stab,
Ingratitude, more strong than traitors' arms,
Quite vanquish'd him : then burst his mighty heart ;
And, in his mantle muffling up his face,
Even at the base of Pompey's statua,
Which all the while ran blood, great Caesar fell.
O, what a fall was there, my countrymen !
Then I, and you, and all of us fell down,
Whilst bloody treason flourish'd over us.
O, now you weep ; and, I perceive, you feel
The dint of pity : these are gracious drops.
Kind souls, what, weep you when you but behold
Our Caesar's vesture wounded ? Look you here

Here is himself, marr'd, as you see, with traitors.

First Cit. O piteous spectacle !

Sec. Cit. O noble Caesar !

Third Cit. O woful day !

Fourth Cit. O traitors, villains !

First Cit. O most bloody sight !

Sec. Cit. We will be revenged.

All. Revenge ! About ! Seek ! Burn ! Fire ! Kill !
Slay ! Let not a traitor live !

Ant. Stay, countrymen.

First Cit. Peace there ! hear the noble Antony.

Sec. Cit. We'll hear him, we'll follow him, we'll die with
him.

Ant. Good friends, sweet friends, let me not stir you up
To such a sudden flood of mutiny.
They that have done this deed are honourable :
What private griefs they have, alas, I know not,
That made them do it : they are wise and honourable,
And will, no doubt, with reasons answer you.
I come not, friends, to steal away your hearts :
I am no orator, as Brutus is ;
But, as you know me all, a plain blunt man,
That love my friend ; and that they know full well
That gave me public leave to speak of him :
For I have neither wit, nor words, nor worth,
Action, nor utterance, nor the power of speech,
To stir men's blood : I only speak right on ;
I tell you that which you yourselves do know ;
Show you sweet Caesar's wounds, poor poor dumb mouths,
And bid them speak for me : but were I Brutus,
And Brutus Antony, there were an Antony
Would ruffle up your spirits and put a tongue
In every wound of Caesar that should move
The stones of Rome to rise and mutiny.

ACT III, Scene ii, ll. 8-52, 77-234

303

Brutus's tent.

Enter BRUTUS *and* CASSIUS.

Cas. That you have wrong'd me doth appear in this :
You have condemn'd and noted Lucius Pella
For taking bribes here of the Sardians ;
Wherein my letters, praying on his side,
Because I knew the man, were slighted off.

Bru. You wrong'd yourself to write in such a case.

Cas. In such a time as this it is not meet
That every nice offence should bear his comment.

Bru. Let me tell you, Cassius, you yourself
Are much condemn'd to have an itching palm ;
To sell and mart your offices for gold
To undeservers.

Cas.   I an itching palm !
You know that you are Brutus that speak this,
Or, by the gods, this speech were else your last.

Bru. The name of Cassius honours this corruption,
And chastisement doth therefore hide his head.

Cas. Chastisement !

Bru. Remember March, the ides of March remember :
Did not great Julius bleed for justice' sake ?
What villain touch'd his body, that did stab,
And not for justice ? What, shall one of us,
That struck the foremost man of all this world
But for supporting robbers, shall we now
Contaminate our fingers with base bribes,
And sell the mighty space of our large honours
For so much trash as may be grasped thus ?—
I had rather be a dog, and bay the moon,
Than such a Roman.

Cas.   Brutus, bay not me ;
I'll not endure it : you forget yourself,
To hedge me in ; I am a soldier, I,
Older in practice, abler than yourself

304

To make conditions.

Bru.   Go to; you are not, Cassius.

Cas. I am.

Bru. I say you are not.

Cas. Urge me no more, I shall forget myself;
Have mind upon your health, tempt me no further.

Bru. Away, slight man!

Cas. Is't possible?

Bru.   Hear me, for I will speak.
Must I give way and room to your rash choler?
Shall I be frighted when a madman stares?

Cas. O ye gods, ye gods! must I endure all this?

Bru. All this! ay, more: fret till your proud heart
       break;
Go show your slaves how choleric you are,
And make your bondmen tremble. Must I budge?
Must I observe you? must I stand and crouch
Under your testy humour? By the gods,
You shall digest the venom of your spleen,
Though it do split you; for, from this day forth,
I'll use you for my mirth, yea, for my laughter,
When you are waspish.

Cas.   Is it come to this?

Bru. You say you are a better soldier:
Let it appear so; make your vaunting true,
And it shall please me well: for mine own part,
I shall be glad to learn of noble men.

Cas. You wrong me every way; you wrong me, Brutus;
I said, an elder soldier, not a better:
Did I say 'better'?

Bru.   If you did, I care not.

Cas. When Caesar lived, he durst not thus have moved
       me.

Bru. Peace, peace! you durst not so have tempted him.

Cas. I durst not!

Bru. No.

Cas. What, durst not tempt him !

Bru. For your life you durst not.

Cas. Do not presume too much upon my love ;
I may do that I shall be sorry for.

Bru. You have done that you should be sorry for.
There is no terror, Cassius, in your threats,
For I am arm'd so strong in honesty
That they pass by me as the idle wind,
Which I respect not. I did send to you
For certain sums of gold, which you denied me :
For I can raise no money by vile means :
By heaven, I had rather coin my heart,
And drop my blood for drachmas, than to wring
From the hard hands of peasants their vile trash
By any indirection : I did send
To you for gold to pay my legions,
Which you denied me : was that done like Cassius ?
Should I have answer'd Caius Cassius so ?
When Marcus Brutus grows so covetous,
To lock such rascal counters from his friends,
Be ready, gods, with all your thunderbolts ;
Dash him to pieces !

Cas. I denied you not.

Bru. You did.

Cas. I did not : he was but a fool that brought
My answer back. Brutus hath rived my heart :
A friend should bear his friend's infirmities,
But Brutus makes mine greater than they are.

Bru. I do not, till you practise them on me.

Cas. You love me not.

Bru. I do not like your faults.

Cas. A friendly eye could never see such faults.

Bru. A flatterer's would not, though they do appear
As huge as high Olympus.

Cas. Come, Antony, and young Octavius, come,
Revenge yourselves alone on Cassius,

For Cassius is aweary of the world ;
Hated by one he loves ; braved by his brother ;
Check'd like a bondman ; all his faults observed,
Set in a note-book, learn'd, and conn'd by rote,
To cast into my teeth. O, I could weep
My spirit from mine eyes ! There is my dagger,
And here my naked breast ; within, a heart
Dearer than Plutus' mine, richer than gold :
If that thou be'st a Roman, take it forth ;
I, that denied thee gold, will give my heart :
Strike, as thou didst at Caesar ; for, I know,
When thou didst hate him worst, thou lovedst him better
Than ever thou lovedst Cassius.

Bru.   Sheathe your dagger :
Be angry when you will, it shall have scope ;
Do what you will, dishonour shall be humour.
O Cassius, you are yoked with a lamb
That carries anger as the flint bears fire ;
Who, much enforced, shows a hasty spark,
And straight is cold again.

Cas.   Hath Cassius lived
To be but mirth and laughter to his Brutus,
When grief, and blood ill-temper'd, vexeth him ?

Bru. When I spoke that, I was ill-temper'd too.

Cas. Do you confess so much ? Give me your hand.

Bru. And my heart too.

Cas.   O Brutus !

Bru.   What's the matter ?

Cas. Have not you love enough to bear with me,
When that rash humour which my mother gave me
Makes me forgetful ?

Bru.   Yes, Cassius ; and, from henceforth,
When you are over-earnest with your Brutus,
He'll think your mother chides, and leave you so. . . .

      Enter LUCIUS.

Bru. Lucius, a bowl of wine !   [*Exit Lucius.*

Cas. I did not think you could have been so angry.

Bru. O Cassius, I am sick of many griefs.

Cas. Of your philosophy you make no use,
If you give place to accidental evils.

Bru. No man bears sorrow better. Portia is dead.

Cas. Ha! Portia!

Bru. She is dead.

Cas. How 'scaped I killing when I cross'd you so?
O insupportable and touching loss!
Upon what sickness?

Bru.   Impatient of my absence,
And grief that young Octavius with Mark Antony
Have made themselves so strong:—for with her death
That tidings came;—with this she fell distract,
And, her attendants absent, swallow'd fire.

Cas. And died so?

Bru.   Even so.

Cas.   O ye immortal gods!

Re-enter LUCIUS, *with wine and taper.*

Bru. Speak no more of her. Give me a bowl of wine.
In this I bury all unkindness, Cassius.

Cas. My heart is thirsty for that noble pledge.
Fill, Lucius, till the wine o'erswell the cup;
I cannot drink too much of Brutus' love. . . .

Bru. Our legions are brim-full, our cause is ripe:
The enemy increaseth every day;
We, at the height, are ready to decline.
There is a tide in the affairs of men,
Which, taken at the flood, leads on to fortune;
Omitted, all the voyage of their life
Is bound in shallows and in miseries.
On such a full sea are we now afloat;
And we must take the current when it serves,
Or lose our ventures.

Cas.   Then, with your will, go on:

308

We'll along ourselves, and meet them at Philippi.

Bru. The deep of night is crept upon our talk,
And nature must obey necessity;
Which we will niggard with a little rest.
There is no more to say?

Cas.   No more. Good night:
Early to-morrow will we rise, and hence.

Bru.   Lucius! [*Enter Lucius.*] My gown. . . .
                              [*Exit Lucius.*
Noble, noble Cassius,
Good night, and good repose.

Cas.   O my dear brother!
This was an ill beginning of the night:
Never come such division 'tween our souls!
Let it not, Brutus.

Bru.   Every thing is well.

Cas. Good night, my lord.

Bru.   Good night, good brother. . . .
                             [*Exit Cassius.*

Re-enter LUCIUS, *with the gown.*

Give me the gown. Where is thy instrument?

Luc. Here in the tent.

Bru.   What, thou speak'st drowsily?
Poor knave, I blame thee not; thou art o'er-watch'd.
Call Claudius and some other of my men;
I'll have them sleep on cushions in my tent.

Luc. Varro and Claudius!

Enter VARRO *and* CLAUDIUS.

Var. Calls my lord?

Bru. I pray you, sirs, lie in my tent and sleep;
It may be I shall raise you by and by
On business to my brother Cassius.

Var. So please you, we will stand and watch your
     pleasure.

Bru. I will not have it so : lie down, good sirs ;
It may be I shall otherwise bethink me.
Look, Lucius, here's the book I sought for so ;
I put it in the pocket of my gown.

                          [Var. and Clau. lie down.

    Luc. I was sure your lordship did not give it me.

    Bru. Bear with me, good boy, I am much forgetful.
Canst thou hold up thy heavy eyes awhile,
And touch thy instrument a strain or two ?

    Luc. Ay, my lord, an't please you.

    Bru.   It does, my boy :
I trouble thee too much, but thou art willing.

    Luc. It is my duty, sir.

    Bru. I should not urge thy duty past thy might ;
I know young bloods look for a time of rest.

    Luc. I have slept, my lord, already.

    Bru. It was well done ; and thou shalt sleep again ;
I will not hold thee long : if I do live,
I will be good to thee.   *[Music, and a song.*
This is a sleepy tune. O murderous slumber,
Lay'st thou thy leaden mace upon my boy,
That plays thee music ? Gentle knave, good night ;
I will not do thee so much wrong to wake thee :
If thou dost nod, thou break'st thy instrument ;
I'll take it from thee ; and, good boy, good night.
Let me see, let me see ; is not the leaf turn'd down
Where I left reading ? Here it is, I think.

            Enter the Ghost of CAESAR.

How ill this taper burns ! Ha ! who comes here ?
I think it is the weakness of mine eyes
That shapes this monstrous apparition.
It comes upon me. Art thou any thing ?
Art thou some god, some angel, or some devil,
That makest my blood cold and my hair to stare ?
Speak to me what thou art.

Ghost. Thy evil spirit, Brutus.
Bru. Why comest thou ?
Ghost. To tell thee thou shalt see me at Philippi.
Bru. Well ; then I shall see thee again ?
Ghost. Ay, at Philippi.
Bru. Why, I will see thee at Philippi, then.

[*Exit Ghost.*

Now I have taken heart thou vanishest :
Ill spirit, I would hold more talk with thee.
Boy, Lucius ! Varro ! Claudius ! Sirs, awake !
Claudius !

ACT IV, Scene iii, ll. 1-123, 142-162, 215-237, 239-291

The plains of Philippi.

Cassius. Messala !
Mes. [*Standing forth*] What says my general ?
Cas. Messala,
This is my birth-day ; as this very day
Was Cassius born. Give me thy hand, Messala :
Be thou my witness that against my will,
As Pompey was, am I compell'd to set
Upon one battle all our liberties.
You know that I held Epicurus strong
And his opinion : now I change my mind,
And partly credit things that do presage.
Coming from Sardis, on our former ensign
Two mighty eagles fell, and there they perch'd,
Gorging and feeding from our soldiers' hands ;
Who to Philippi here consorted us :
This morning are they fled away and gone ;
And in their steads do ravens, crows and kites,
Fly o'er our heads and downward look on us,
As we were sickly prey : their shadows seem
A canopy most fatal, under which
Our army lies, ready to give up the ghost.
Mes. Believe not so.

Cas.   I but believe it partly ;
For I am fresh of spirit and resolved
To meet all perils very constantly.

Brutus. Even so, Lucilius.

Cas.   Now, most noble Brutus,
The gods to-day stand friendly, that we may,
Lovers in peace, lead on our days to age !
But since the affairs of men rest still incertain,
Let's reason with the worst that may befall.
If we do lose this battle, then is this
The very last time we shall speak together :
What are you then determined to do ?

Bru. Even by the rule of that philosophy
By which I did blame Cato for the death
Which he did give himself, I know not how,
But I do find it cowardly and vile,
For fear of what might fall, so to prevent
The time of life : arming myself with patience
To stay the providence of some high powers
That govern us below.

Cas.   Then, if we lose this battle,
You are contented to be led in triumph
Thorough the streets of Rome ?

Bru. No, Cassius, no : think not, thou noble Roman,
That ever Brutus will go bound to Rome ;
He bears too great a mind. But this same day
Must end that work the ides of March begun ;
And whether we shall meet again I know not.
Therefore our everlasting farewell take :
For ever, and for ever, farewell, Cassius !
If we do meet again, why, we shall smile ;
If not, why then, this parting was well made.

Cas. For ever, and for ever, farewell, Brutus !
If we do meet again, we'll smile indeed ;
If not, 'tis true this parting was well made.

Bru. Why, then, lead on. O, that a man might know

The end of this day's business ere it come !
But it sufficeth that the day will end,
And then the end is known.   Come, ho ! away !

ACT V, Scene i, ll. 70-126

Alarum.   Enter MESSALA, *with* BRUTUS, *young* CATO,
STRATO, VOLUMNIUS, *and* LUCILIUS.

Bru. Where, where, Messala, doth his body lie ?
Mes. Lo, yonder, and Titinius mourning it.
Bru. Titinius' face is upward.
Cato. He is slain.
Bru. O Julius Caesar, thou art mighty yet !
Thy spirit walks abroad, and turns our swords
In our own proper entrails.   [*Low alarums.*
Cato.   Brave Titinius !
Look, whether he have not crown'd dead Cassius !
Bru. Are yet two Romans living such as these ?
The last of all the Romans, fare thee well !
It is impossible that ever Rome
Should breed thy fellow.   Friends, I owe more tears
To this dead man than you shall see me pay.
I shall find time, Cassius, I shall find time.

ACT V, Scene iii, ll. 90-103

Another part of the field.

Enter BRUTUS, DARDANIUS, CLITUS, STRATO, *and*
VOLUMNIUS.

Bru. Come, poor remains of friends, rest on this rock.
Cli. Statilius show'd the torch-light, but, my lord,
He came not back : he is or ta'en or slain.
Bru. Sit thee down, Clitus : slaying is the word ;
It is a deed in fashion.   Hark thee, Clitus.   [*Whispers.*
Cli. What, I, my lord ?   No, not for all the world.
Bru. Peace then ! no words.
Cli. I'll rather kill myself.
Bru. Hark thee, Dardanius.   [*Whispers.*
Dar.   Shall I do such a deed ?
Cli. O Dardanius !

313

Dar. O Clitus !

Cli. What ill request did Brutus make to thee ?

Dar. To kill him, Clitus. Look, he meditates.

Cli. Now is that noble vessel full of grief,
That it runs over even at his eyes.

Bru. Come hither, good Volumnius ; list a word.

Vol. What says my lord ?

Bru.   Why, this, Volumnius :
The ghost of Caesar hath appear'd to me
Two several times by night ; at Sardis once,
And, this last night, here in Philippi fields :
I know my hour is come.

Vol.   Not so, my lord.

Bru. Nay, I am sure it is, Volumnius.
Thou seest the world, Volumnius, how it goes ;
Our enemies have beat us to the pit :   [*Low alarums.*
It is more worthy to leap in ourselves,
Than tarry till they push us. Good Volumnius,
Thou know'st that we two went to school together :
Even for that our love of old, I prithee,
Hold thou my sword-hilts, whilst I run on it.

Vol. That's not an office for a friend, my lord.
                                            [*Alarum still.*

Cli. Fly, fly, my lord ; there is no tarrying here.

Bru. Farewell to you ; and you ; and you, Volumnius.
Strato, thou hast been all this while asleep ;
Farewell to thee too, Strato. Countrymen,
My heart doth joy that yet in all my life
I found no man but he was true to me.
I shall have glory by this losing day
More than Octavius and Mark Antony
By this vile conquest shall attain unto.
So fare you well at once ; for Brutus' tongue
Hath almost ended his life's history :
Night hangs upon mine eyes ; my bones would rest,
That have but labour'd to attain this hour.

[*Alarum. Cry within,* ' Fly, fly, fly ! '
Cli. Fly, my lord, fly.
Bru.   Hence ! I will follow.
                    [*Exeunt Clitus, Dardanius, and Volumnius.*
I prithee, Strato, stay thou by thy lord :
Thou art a fellow of a good respect ;
Thy life hath had some smatch of honour in it :
Hold then my sword, and turn away thy face,
While I do run upon it. Wilt thou, Strato ?
    Stra. Give me your hand first. Fare you well, my lord.
    Bru. Farewell, good Strato. [*Runs on his sword.*] Caesar,
        now be still :
I kill'd not thee with half so good a will.   [*Dies.*

Alarum. Retreat. Enter OCTAVIUS, ANTONY, MESSALA,
                LUCILIUS, *and the army.*

    Oct. What man is that ?
    Mes. My master's man. Strato, where is thy master ?
    Stra. Free from the bondage you are in, Messala :
The conquerors can but make a fire of him ;
For Brutus only overcame himself,
And no man else hath honour by his death.
    Lucil. So Brutus should be found. I thank thee, Brutus,
That thou hast proved Lucilius' saying true.
    Oct. All that served Brutus, I will entertain them.
Fellow, wilt thou bestow thy time with me ?
    Stra. Ay, if Messala will prefer me to you.
    Oct. Do so, good Messala.
    Mes. How died my master, Strato ?
    Stra. I held the sword, and he did run on it.
    Mes. Octavius, then take him to follow thee,
That did the latest service to my master.
    Ant. This was the noblest Roman of them all :
All the conspirators save only he
Did that they did in envy of great Caesar ;
He only, in a general honest thought

315

And common good to all, made one of them.
His life was gentle, and the elements
So mix'd in him that Nature might stand up
And say to all the world ' This was a man ! '
    Oct. According to his virtue let us use him,
With all respect and rites of burial.
Within my tent his bones to-night shall lie,
Most like a soldier, order'd honourably.
So call the field to rest ; and let's away,
To part the glories of this happy day.

ACT V, Scene v, ll. 1-81

Hamlet, Prince of Denmark

Elsinore. A platform before the castle.
FRANCISCO *at his post. Enter to him* BERNARDO.

    Ber. Who's there ?
    Fran. Nay, answer me : stand, and unfold yourself.
    Ber. Long live the king !
    Fran. Bernardo ?
    Ber. He.
    Fran. You come most carefully upon your hour.
    Ber. 'Tis now struck twelve ; get thee to bed, Francisco.
    Fran. For this relief much thanks : 'tis bitter cold,
And I am sick at heart.
    Ber. Have you had quiet guard ?
    Fran.   Not a mouse stirring.
    Ber. Well, good night.
If you do meet Horatio and Marcellus,
The rivals of my watch, bid them make haste.
    Fran. I think I hear them. Stand, ho ! Who's there ?

Enter HORATIO *and* MARCELLUS.

Hor. Friends to this ground.

Mar.   And liegemen to the Dane.

Fran. Give you good night.

Mar.   O, farewell, honest soldier :
Who hath relieved you ?

Fran.   Bernardo has my place.
Give you good night.   [*Exit.*

Mar.   Holla ! Bernardo !

Ber.   Say,
What, is Horatio there ?

Hor.   A piece of him.

Ber. Welcome, Horatio : welcome, good Marcellus.

Mar. What, has this thing appear'd again to-night ?

Ber. I have seen nothing.

Mar. Horatio says 'tis but our fantasy,
And will not let belief take hold of him
Touching this dreaded sight, twice seen of us :
Therefore I have entreated him along
With us to watch the minutes of this night ;
That if again this apparition come,
He may approve our eyes and speak to it.

Hor. Tush, tush, 'twill not appear.

Ber.   Sit down awhile ;
And let us once again assail your ears,
That are so fortified against our story
What we have two nights seen.

Hor.   Well, sit we down,
And let us hear Bernardo speak of this.

Ber. Last night of all,
When yond same star that's westward from the pole
Had made his course to illume that part of heaven
Where now it burns, Marcellus and myself,
The bell then beating one,—

Enter Ghost.

Mar. Peace, break thee off ; look, where it comes again !

Ber. In the same figure, like the king that's dead.

Mar. Thou art a scholar ; speak to it, Horatio.

Ber. Looks it not like the king ? mark it, Horatio.

Hor. Most like : it harrows me with fear and wonder.

Ber. It would be spoke to.

Mar.　　　　　　　　　Question it, Horatio.

Hor. What art thou that usurp'st this time of night,
Together with that fair and warlike form
In which the majesty of buried Denmark
Did sometimes march ? by heaven I charge thee, speak !

Mar. It is offended.

Ber.　　　　　　See, it stalks away !

Hor. Stay ! speak, speak ! I charge thee, speak !

　　　　　　　　　　　　　　　　[Exit Ghost.

Mar. 'Tis gone, and will not answer.

Ber. How now, Horatio ! you tremble and look pale :
Is not this something more than fantasy ?
What think you on't ?

Hor. Before my God, I might not this believe
Without the sensible and true avouch
Of mine own eyes.

Mar.　　　　　　Is it not like the king ?

Hor. As thou art to thyself :
Such was the very armour he had on
When he the ambitious Norway combated ;
So frown'd he once, when, in an angry parle,
He smote the sledded Polacks on the ice.
'Tis strange.

Mar. Thus twice before, and jump at this dead hour,
With martial stalk hath he gone by our watch.

Hor. In what particular thought to work I know not ;
But in the gross and scope of my opinion,
This bodes some strange eruption to our state. . . .
In the most high and palmy state of Rome,
A little ere the mightiest Julius fell,
The graves stood tenantless and the sheeted dead

Did squeak and gibber in the Roman streets:
As stars with trains of fire and dews of blood,
Disasters in the sun; and the moist star
Upon whose influence Neptune's empire stands
Was sick almost to doomsday with eclipse:
And even the like precurse of fierce events,
As harbingers preceding still the fates
And prologue to the omen coming on,
Have heaven and earth together demonstrated
Unto our climatures and countrymen.——
But soft, behold! lo, where it comes again!

Re-enter Ghost.

I'll cross it, though it blast me. Stay, illusion!
If thou hast any sound, or use of voice,
Speak to me:
If there be any good thing to be done,
That may to thee do ease and grace to me,
Speak to me: [*Cock crows.*
If thou art privy to thy country's fate,
Which, happily, foreknowing may avoid,
O, speak!
Or if thou hast uphoarded in thy life
Extorted treasure in the womb of earth,
For which, they say, you spirits oft walk in death,
Speak of it: stay, and speak! Stop it, Marcellus.

   Mar. Shall I strike at it with my partisan?
   Hor. Do, if it will not stand.
   Ber.   'Tis here!
   Hor.   'Tis here!
   Mar. 'Tis gone!   [*Exit Ghost.*
We do it wrong, being so majestical,
To offer it the show of violence;
For it is, as the air, invulnerable,
And our vain blows malicious mockery.

   Ber. It was about to speak, when the cock crew.

Hor. And then it started like a guilty thing
Upon a fearful summons. I have heard,
The cock, that is the trumpet to the morn,
Doth with his lofty and shrill-sounding throat
Awake the god of day ; and, at his warning,
Whether in sea or fire, in earth or air,
The extravagant and erring spirit hies
To his confine : and of the truth herein
This present object made probation.

    Mar. It faded on the crowing of the cock.
Some say that ever 'gainst that season comes
Wherein our Saviour's birth is celebrated,
The bird of dawning singeth all night long :
And then, they say, no spirit dare stir abroad ;
The nights are wholesome ; then no planets strike,
No fairy takes, nor witch hath power to charm,
So hallow'd and so gracious is the time.

    Hor. So have I heard and do in part believe it.
But, look, the morn, in russet mantle clad,
Walks o'er the dew of yon high eastward hill :
Break we our watch up ; and by my advice,
Let us impart what we have seen to-night
Unto young Hamlet ; for, upon my life,
This spirit, dumb to us, will speak to him.
Do you consent we shall acquaint him with it,
As needful in our loves, fitting our duty ?

    Mar. Let's do 't, I pray ; and I this morning know
Where we shall find him most conveniently.

                ACT I, Scene i, ll. 1-69, 113-175

A room of state in the castle.

Enter the KING, QUEEN, HAMLET, LAERTES, Lords,
and Attendants.

    King. Take thy fair hour, Laertes ; time be thine,
And thy best graces spend it at thy will !
But now, my cousin Hamlet, and my son,—

Ham. [*Aside*] A little more than kin, and less than kind.

King. How is it that the clouds still hang on you?

Ham. Not so, my lord; I am too much i' the sun.

Queen. Good Hamlet, cast thy nighted colour off,
And let thine eye look like a friend on Denmark.
Do not for ever with thy vailed lids
Seek for thy noble father in the dust :
Thou know'st 'tis common; all that lives must die,
Passing through nature to eternity.

Ham. Ay, madam, it is common.

Queen. If it be,
Why seems it so particular with thee?

Ham. Seems, madam! nay, it is; I know not ' seems.'
'Tis not alone my inky cloak, good mother,
Nor customary suits of solemn black,
Nor windy suspiration of forced breath,
No, nor the fruitful river in the eye,
Nor the dejected 'haviour of the visage,
Together with all forms, moods, shapes of grief,
That can denote me truly : these indeed seem,
For they are actions that a man might play :
But I have that within which passeth show;
These but the trappings and the suits of woe. . . .

Queen. Let not thy mother lose her prayers, Hamlet
I pray thee, stay with us; go not to Wittenberg.

Ham. I shall in all my best obey you, madam.

King. Why, 'tis a loving and a fair reply :
Be as ourself in Denmark. Madam, come;
This gentle and unforced accord of Hamlet
Sits smiling to my heart : in grace whereof,
No jocund health that Denmark drinks to-day,
But the great cannon to the clouds shall tell,
And the king's rouse the heavens shall bruit again,
Re-speaking earthly thunder. Come away.

[*Exeunt all but Hamlet.*

Ham. O, that this too too solid flesh would melt,

Thaw and resolve itself into a dew !
Or that the Everlasting had not fix'd
His canon 'gainst self-slaughter ! O God ! God !
How weary, stale, flat and unprofitable,
Seem to me all the uses of this world !
Fie on 't ! ah fie ! 'tis an unweeded garden,
That grows to seed ; things rank and gross in nature
Possess it merely. That it should come to this !
But two months dead : nay, not so much, not two :
So excellent a king ; that was, to this,
Hyperion to a satyr ; so loving to my mother
That he might not beteem the winds of heaven
Visit her face too roughly. Heaven and earth !
Must I remember ? why, she would hang on him,
As if increase of appetite had grown
By what it fed on : and yet, within a month—
Let me not think on't—Frailty, thy name is woman !—
A little month, or ere those shoes were old
With which she follow'd my poor father's body,
Like Niobe, all tears :—why she, even she—
O God ! a beast, that wants discourse of reason,
Would have mourn'd longer—married with my uncle,
My father's brother, but no more like my father
Than I to Hercules : within a month :
Ere yet the salt of most unrighteous tears
Had left the flushing in her galled eyes,
She married. O, most wicked speed, to post
With such dexterity to incestuous sheets !
It is not nor it cannot come to good :
But break, my heart ; for I must hold my tongue.

Enter HORATIO, MARCELLUS, *and* BERNARDO.

Hor. Hail to your lordship !

Ham. I am glad to see you well :
Horatio,—or I do forget myself.

Hor. The same, my lord, and your poor servant ever.

Ham. Sir, my good friend ; I'll change that name with
you :
And what make you from Wittenberg, Horatio ?
Marcellus ?

Mar. My good lord—

Ham. I am very glad to see you. Good even, sir.
But what, in faith, make you from Wittenberg ?

Hor. A truant disposition, good my lord.

Ham. I would not hear your enemy say so,
Nor shall you do mine ear that violence,
To make it truster of your own report
Against yourself : I know you are no truant.
But what is your affair in Elsinore ?
We'll teach you to drink deep ere you depart.

Hor. My lord, I came to see your father's funeral.

Ham. I pray thee, do not mock me, fellow-student ;
I think it was to see my mother's wedding.

Hor. Indeed, my lord, it follow'd hard upon.

Ham. Thrift, thrift, Horatio ! the funeral baked meats
Did coldly furnish forth the marriage tables.
Would I had met my dearest foe in heaven
Or ever I had seen that day, Horatio !
My father !—methinks I see my father.

Hor. Where, my lord ?

Ham.   In my mind's eye, Horatio.

Hor. I saw him once ; he was a goodly king.

Ham. He was a man, take him for all in all,
I shall not look upon his like again.

Hor. My lord, I think I saw him yesternight.

Ham. Saw ? who ?

Hor. My lord, the king your father.

Ham.   The king my father !

Hor. Season your admiration for a while
With an attent ear, till I may deliver,
Upon the witness of these gentlemen,
This marvel to you.

Ham.   For God's love, let me hear.

Hor. Two nights together had these gentlemen,
Marcellus and Bernardo, on their watch,
In the dead vast and middle of the night,
Been thus encounter'd. A figure like your father,
Armed at point exactly, cap-a-pe,
Appears before them, and with solemn march
Goes slowly and stately by them : thrice he walk'd
By their oppress'd and fear-surprised eyes,
Within his truncheon's length ; whilst they, distill'd
Almost to jelly with the act of fear,
Stand dumb and speak not to him. This to me
In dreadful secrecy impart they did ;
And I with them the third night kept the watch :
Where, as they had deliver'd, both in time,
Form of the thing, each word made true and good,
The apparition comes : I knew your father ;
These hands are not more like.

Ham.   But where was this ?

Mar. My lord, upon the platform where we watch'd.

Ham. Did you not speak to it ?

Hor.   My lord, I did ;
But answer made it none : yet once methought
It lifted up it head and did address
Itself to motion, like as it would speak ;
But even then the morning cock crew loud,
And at the sound it shrunk in haste away,
And vanish'd from our sight.

Ham.   'Tis very strange.

Hor. As I do live, my honour'd lord, 'tis true ;
And we did think it writ down in our duty
To let you know of it.

Ham. Indeed, indeed, sirs, but this troubles me.
Hold you the watch to-night ?

Mar.⎫
Ber. ⎭   We do, my lord.

324

Ham. Arm'd, say you ?

Mar.⎱
Ber.⎰ Arm'd, my lord.

Ham. From top to toe ?

Mar.⎱
Ber.⎰   My lord, from head to foot.

Ham. Then saw you not his face ?

Hor. O, yes, my lord ; he wore his beaver up.

Ham. What, look'd he frowningly ?

Hor. A countenance more in sorrow than in anger.

Ham. Pale or red ?

Hor. Nay, very pale.

Ham.   And fix'd his eyes upon you ?

Hor. Most constantly.

Ham.   I would I had been there.

Hor. It would have much amazed you.

Ham. Very like, very like. Stay'd it long ?

Hor. While one with moderate haste might tell a hun-
     dred.

Mar.⎱
Ber.⎰ Longer, longer.

Hor. Not when I saw 't.

Ham.   His beard was grizzled,—no ?

Hor. It was, as I have seen it in his life,
A sable silver'd.

Ham.   I will watch to-night ;
Perchance 'twill walk again.

Hor.   I warrant it will.

Ham If it assume my noble father's person,
I'll speak to it, though hell itself should gape
And bid me hold my peace I pray you all,
If you have hitherto conceal'd this sight,
Let it be tenable in your silence still ;
And whatsoever else shall hap to-night,
Give it an understanding, but no tongue :
I will requite your loves. So, fare you well :

Upon the platform, 'twixt eleven and twelve,
I'll visit you.

    All.   Our duty to your honour.

    Ham. Your loves, as mine to you : farewell.

                       [*Exeunt all but Hamlet.*

My father's spirit in arms ! all is not well ;
I doubt some foul play : would the night were come !

                 ACT I, Scene ii, ll. 62-86, 118-256

A room in Polonius' house.

Enter LAERTES *and* OPHELIA.

    Laer. My necessaries are embark'd : farewell :
And, sister, as the winds give benefit
And convoy is assistant, do not sleep,
But let me hear from you.

    Oph.   Do you doubt that ?

    Laer. For Hamlet and the trifling of his favour,
Hold it a fashion and a toy in blood,
A violet in the youth of primy nature,
Forward, not permanent, sweet, not lasting,
The perfume and suppliance of a minute ;
No more.

    Oph. No more but so ?

    Laer.   Think it no more :
For nature, crescent, does not grow alone
In thews and bulk, but, as this temple waxes,
The inward service of the mind and soul
Grows wide withal. Perhaps he loves you now,
And now no soil nor cautel doth besmirch
The virtue of his will : but you must fear,
His greatness weigh'd, his will is not his own ; . . .
Fear it, Ophelia, fear it, my dear sister,
And keep you in the rear of your affection,
Out of the shot and danger of desire.
The chariest maid is prodigal enough,
If she unmask her beauty to the moon :

Virtue itself 'scapes not calumnious strokes :
The canker galls the infants of the spring,
Too oft before their buttons be disclosed,
And in the morn and liquid dew of youth
Contagious blastments are most imminent.
Be wary then ; best safety lies in fear :
Youth to itself rebels, though none else near.

   Oph. I shall the effect of this good lesson keep,
As watchman to my heart. But, good my brother,
Do not, as some ungracious pastors do,
Show me the steep and thorny way to heaven ;
Whiles, like a puff'd and reckless libertine,
Himself the primrose path of dalliance treads,
And recks not his own rede.

     Laer.   O, fear me not.
I stay too long : but here my father comes.

           Enter POLONIUS.

A double blessing is a double grace ;
Occasion smiles upon a second leave.

   Pol. Yet here, Laertes ! aboard, aboard, for shame !
The wind sits in the shoulder of your sail,
And you are stay'd for. There ; my blessing with thee !
And these few precepts in thy memory
See thou character. Give thy thoughts no tongue,
Nor any unproportioned thought his act.
Be thou familiar, but by no means vulgar.
Those friends thou hast, and their adoption tried,
Grapple them to thy soul with hoops of steel ;
But do not dull thy palm with entertainment
Of each new-hatch'd, unfledged comrade. Beware
Of entrance to a quarrel, but being in,
Bear 't that the opposed may beware of thee.
Give every man thy ear, but few thy voice ;
Take each man's censure, but reserve thy judgement.
Costly thy habit as thy purse can buy,

But not express'd in fancy ; rich, not gaudy ;
For the apparel oft proclaims the man,
And they in France of the best rank and station
Are of a most select and generous chief in that.
Neither a borrower nor a lender be ;
For loan oft loses both itself and friend,
And borrowing dulls the edge of husbandry.
This above all : to thine own self be true,
And it must follow, as the night the day,
Thou canst not then be false to any man.
Farewell : my blessing season this in thee !

    Laer. Most humbly do I take my leave, my lord.

    Pol. The time invites you ; go ; your servants tend.

    Laer. Farewell, Ophelia ; and remember well
What I have said to you.

    Oph.   'Tis in my memory lock'd,
And you yourself shall keep the key of it.

    Laer. Farewell.   [*Exit.*

    Pol. What is't, Ophelia, he hath said to you ?

    Oph. So please you, something touching the Lord Hamlet.

    Pol. Marry, well bethought :
'Tis told me, he hath very oft of late
Given private time to you ; and you yourself
Have of your audience been most free and bounteous :
If it be so, as so 'tis put on me,
And that in way of caution, I must tell you,
You do not understand yourself so clearly
As it behoves my daughter and your honour.
What is between you ? give me up the truth.

    Oph. He hath, my lord, of late made many tenders
Of his affection to me.

    Pol. Affection ! pooh ! you speak like a green girl,
Unsifted in such perilous circumstance.
Do you believe his tenders, as you call them ?

    Oph. I do not know, my lord, what I should think.

    Pol. Marry, I'll teach you : think yourself a baby ;

That you have ta'en these tenders for true pay,
Which are not sterling.   Tender yourself more dearly ;
Or—not to crack the wind of the poor phrase,
Running it thus—you'll tender me a fool.

    Oph. My lord, he hath importuned me with love
In honourable fashion.

    Pol. Ay, fashion you may call it ; go to, go to.

    Oph. And hath given countenance to his speech, my lord,
With almost all the holy vows of heaven.

    Pol. Ay, springes to catch woodcocks

ACT I, Scene iii, ll. 1-17, 33-115

The platform.

Enter HAMLET, HORATIO, *and* MARCELLUS.

    Ham. The air bites shrewdly ; it is very cold.

    Hor. It is a nipping and an eager air.

    Ham. What hour now ?

    Hor.   I think it lacks of twelve.

    Mar. No, it is struck.

    Hor. Indeed ? I heard it not : then it draws near the season
Wherein the spirit held his wont to walk.

    [*A flourish of trumpets, and ordnance shot off, within.*
What does this mean, my lord ?

    Ham. The king doth wake to-night and takes his rouse,
Keeps wassail, and the swaggering up-spring reels ;
And, as he drains his draught of Rhenish down,
The kettle-drum and trumpet thus bray out
The triumph of his pledge.

    Hor.   Is it a custom ?

    Ham. Ay, marry, is 't :
But to my mind, though I am native here
And to the manner born, it is a custom
More honour'd in the breach than the observance. . . .

    Hor.   Look, my lord, it comes !

329

Enter Ghost.

Ham. Angels and ministers of grace defend us !
Be thou a spirit of health or goblin damn'd,
Bring with thee airs from heaven or blasts from hell,
Be thy intents wicked or charitable,
Thou comest in such a questionable shape
That I will speak to thee : I'll call thee Hamlet,
King, father, royal Dane : O, answer me !
Let me not burst in ignorance ; but tell
Why thy canonized bones, hearsed in death,
Have burst their cerements ; why the sepulchre,
Wherein we saw thee quietly inurn'd,
Hath oped his ponderous and marble jaws,
To cast thee up again. What may this mean,
That thou, dead corse, again in complete steel
Revisit'st thus the glimpses of the moon,
Making night hideous ; and we fools of nature
So horridly to shake our disposition
With thoughts beyond the reaches of our souls ?
Say, why is this ? wherefore ? what should we do ?

                                  [Ghost beckons Hamlet.

   Hor. It beckons you to go away with it,
As if it some impartment did desire
To you alone.

    Mar.   Look, with what courteous action
It waves you to a more removed ground :
But do not go with it.

    Hor.   No, by no means.

   Ham. It will not speak ; then I will follow it.

   Hor. Do not, my lord.

    Ham.   Why, what should be the fear ?
I do not set my life at a pin's fee ;
And for my soul, what can it do to that,
Being a thing immortal as itself ?
It waves me forth again : I'll follow it.

   Hor. What if it tempt you toward the flood, my lord,

Or to the dreadful summit of the cliff
That beetles o'er his base into the sea,
And there assume some other horrible form,
Which might deprive your sovereignty of reason
And draw you into madness ? think of it :
The very place puts toys of desperation,
Without more motive, into every brain
That looks so many fathoms to the sea
And hears it roar beneath.

 Ham.   It waves me still.
Go on ; I'll follow thee.

 Mar. You shall not go, my lord.

 Ham.   Hold off your hands.

 Hor. Be ruled ; you shall not go.

 Ham.   My fate cries out,
And makes each petty artery in this body
As hardy as the Nemean lion's nerve.
Still am I call'd. Unhand me, gentlemen.
By heaven, I'll make a ghost of him that lets me !
I say, away ! Go on ; I'll follow thee.

        Act I, Scene iv, ll. 1-16, 38-86

   Another part of the platform.

   Enter GHOST *and* HAMLET.

 Ham. Where wilt thou lead me? speak; I'll go no further.

 Ghost. Mark me.

 Ham.   I will.

 Ghost.   My hour is almost come,
When I to sulphurous and tormenting flames
Must render up myself.

 Ham.   Alas, poor ghost !

 Ghost. Pity me not, but lend thy serious hearing
To what I shall unfold.

 Ham.   Speak ; I am bound to hear.

 Ghost. So art thou to revenge, when thou shalt hear.

 Ham. What ?

        331

Ghost. I am thy father's spirit,
Doom'd for a certain term to walk the night,
And for the day confined to fast in fires,
Till the foul crimes done in my days of nature
Are burnt and purged away. But that I am forbid
To tell the secrets of my prison-house,
I could a tale unfold whose lightest word
Would harrow up thy soul, freeze thy young blood,
Make thy two eyes, like stars, start from their spheres,
Thy knotted and combined locks to part
And each particular hair to stand an end,
Like quills upon the fretful porpentine:
But this eternal blazon must not be
To ears of flesh and blood. List, list, O, list!
If thou didst ever thy dear father love—

Ham. O God!

Ghost. Revenge his foul and most unnatural murder.

Ham. Murder!

Ghost. Murder most foul, as in the best it is;
But this most foul, strange and unnatural.

Ham. Haste me to know't, that I, with wings as swift
As meditation or the thoughts of love,
May sweep to my revenge.

Ghost.   I find thee apt;
And duller shouldst thou be than the fat weed
That roots itself in ease on Lethe wharf,
Wouldst thou not stir in this. Now, Hamlet, hear:
'Tis given out that, sleeping in my orchard,
A serpent stung me; so the whole ear of Denmark
Is by a forged process of my death
Rankly abused: but know, thou noble youth,
The serpent that did sting thy father's life
Now wears his crown.

Ham.   O my prophetic soul!
My uncle! . . .

Ghost. But, soft! methinks I scent the morning air;

Brief let me be. . . .
Thus was I, sleeping, by a brother's hand
Of life, of crown, of queen, at once dispatch'd :
Cut off even in the blossoms of my sin,
Unhousel'd, disappointed, unaneled,
No reckoning made, but sent to my account
With all my imperfections on my head :
O, horrible ! O, horrible ! most horrible !
If thou hast nature in thee, bear it not ;
Let not the royal bed of Denmark be
A couch for luxury and damned incest.
But, howsoever thou pursuest this act,
Taint not thy mind, nor let thy soul contrive
Against thy mother aught : leave her to heaven
And to those thorns that in her bosom lodge,
To prick and sting her. Fare thee well at once !
The glow-worm shows the matin to be near,
And 'gins to pale his uneffectual fire :
Adieu, adieu ! Hamlet, remember me.   [*Exit.*

    Ham. O all you host of heaven ! O earth ! what else ?
And shall I couple hell ? O, fie ! Hold, hold, my heart ;
And you, my sinews, grow not instant old,
But bear me stiffly up. Remember thee !
Ay, thou poor ghost, while memory holds a seat
In this distracted globe. Remember thee !
Yea, from the table of my memory
I'll wipe away all trivial fond records,
All saws of books, all forms, all pressures past,
That youth and observation copied there ;
And thy commandment all alone shall live
Within the book and volume of my brain,
Unmix'd with baser matter : yes, by heaven !
O most pernicious woman !
O villain, villain, smiling, damned villain !
My tables,—meet it is I set it down,
That one may smile, and smile, and be a villain ;

At least I'm sure it may be so in Denmark :   [*Writing*.
So, uncle, there you are. Now to my word ;
It is ' Adieu, adieu ! remember me.'
I have sworn 't.

 Mar. ⎫
 Hor. ⎭ [*Within*] My lord, my lord,—

 Mar.   [*Within*] Lord Hamlet,—

 Hor.   [*Within*] Heaven secure him

 Ham. So be it !

 Hor. [*Within*] Hillo, ho, ho, my lord !

 Ham. Hillo, ho, ho, boy ! come, bird, come.

Enter HORATIO *and* MARCELLUS.

 Mar. How is 't, my noble lord ?

 Hor.   What news, my lord ?

 Ham. O, wonderful !

 Hor.   Good my lord, tell it.

 Ham. No ; you'll reveal it.

 Hor. Not I, my lord, by heaven.

 Mar.   Nor I, my lord.

 Ham. How say you, then ; would heart of man once
  think it ?
But you'll be secret ?

 Hor. ⎫
 Mar. ⎭   Ay, by heaven, my lord.

 Ham. There's ne'er a villain dwelling in all Denmark
But he's an arrant knave.

 Hor. There needs no ghost, my lord, come from the grave
To tell us this.

 Ham.   Why, right ; you are i' the right ;
And so, without more circumstance at all,
I hold it fit that we shake hands and part :
You, as your business and desire shall point you :
For every man has business and desire,
Such as it is ; and for mine own poor part,
Look you, I'll go pray.

Hor. These are but wild and whirling words, my lord.

Ham. I'm sorry they offend you, heartily ;
Yes, 'faith, heartily.

Hor.   There's no offence, my lord.

Ham. Yes, by Saint Patrick, but there is, Horatio,
And much offence too. Touching this vision here,
It is an honest ghost, that let me tell you :
For your desire to know what is between us,
O'ermaster 't as you may. And now, good friends,
As you are friends, scholars and soldiers,
Give me one poor request.

Hor. What is 't, my lord ? we will.

Ham. Never make known what you have seen to-night.

Hor. }
Mar. } My lord, we will not.

Ham.   Nay, but swear 't.

Hor.   In faith,
My lord, not I.

Mar.   Nor I, my lord, in faith.

Ham. Upon my sword.

Mar.   We have sworn, my lord, already.

Ham. Indeed, upon my sword, indeed.

Ghost. [*Beneath*] Swear.

Ham. Ah, ha, boy ! say'st thou so ? art thou there, true-
penny ?
Come on—you hear this fellow in the cellarage—
Consent to swear.

Hor.   Propose the oath, my lord.

Ham. Never to speak of this that you have seen,
Swear by my sword.

Ghost. [*Beneath*] Swear.

Ham. Hic et ubique ? then we'll shift our ground.
Come hither, gentlemen,
And lay your hands again upon my sword :
Never to speak of this that you have heard,
Swear by my sword.

Ghost. [*Beneath*] Swear.

Ham. Well said, old mole! canst work i' the earth so
    fast?

A worthy pioner! Once more remove, good friends.

Hor. O day and night, but this is wondrous strange!

Ham. And therefore as a stranger give it welcome.

There are more things in heaven and earth, Horatio,

Than are dreamt of in your philosophy.

But come;

Here, as before, never, so help you mercy,

How strange or odd soe'er I bear myself,

As I perchance hereafter shall think meet

To put an antic disposition on,

That you, at such times seeing me, never shall,

With arms encumber'd thus, or this head-shake,

Or by pronouncing of some doubtful phrase,

As ' Well, well, we know,' or ' We could, an if we would,'

Or ' If we list to speak,' or ' There be, an if they might,'

Or such ambiguous giving out, to note

That you know aught of me: this not to do,

So grace and mercy at your most need help you,

Swear.

Ghost. [*Beneath*] Swear.

Ham. Rest, rest, perturbed spirit! [*They swear.*] So,
    gentlemen,

With all my love I do commend me to you:

And what so poor a man as Hamlet is

May do, to express his love and friending to you,

God willing, shall not lack. Let us go in together;

And still your fingers on your lips, I pray.

The time is out of joint: O cursed spite,

That ever I was born to set it right!

Nay, come, let's go together.

                      ACT I, Scene v, ll. 1-41, 58-59, 74-191

A room in Polonius' house.

Enter OPHELIA.

Polonius. How now, Ophelia! what's the matter?

Oph. O, my lord, my lord, I have been so affrighted!

Pol. With what, i' the name of God?

Oph. My lord, as I was sewing in my closet,
Lord Hamlet, with his doublet all unbraced;
No hat upon his head; his stockings foul'd,
Ungarter'd, and down-gyved to his ancle;
Pale as his shirt; his knees knocking each other;
And with a look so piteous in purport
As if he had been loosed out of hell
To speak of horrors,—he comes before me.

Pol. Mad for thy love?

Oph.   My lord, I do not know;
But truly, I do fear it.

Pol.   What said he?

Oph. He took me by the wrist and held me hard;
Then goes he to the length of all his arm;
And, with his other hand thus o'er his brow,
He falls to such perusal of my face
As he would draw it. Long stay'd he so;
At last, a little shaking of mine arm
And thrice his head thus waving up and down,
He raised a sigh so piteous and profound
As it did seem to shatter all his bulk
And end his being: that done, he lets me go:
And, with his head over his shoulder turn'd,
He seem'd to find his way without his eyes;
For out o' doors he went without their helps,
And, to the last, bended their light on me.

Pol. Come, go with me: I will go seek the king.
This is the very ecstasy of love,
Whose violent property fordoes itself
And leads the will to desperate undertakings

As oft as any passion under heaven
That does afflict our natures.

ACT II, Scene i, ll. 74-106

A room in the castle.

Polonius. My liege, and madam, to expostulate
What majesty should be, what duty is,
Why day is day, night night, and time is time,
Were nothing but to waste night, day and time.
Therefore, since brevity is the soul of wit,
And tediousness the limbs and outward flourishes,
I will be brief : your noble son is mad :
Mad call I it ; for, to define true madness,
What is't but to be nothing else but mad ?
But let that go.

  Queen.   More matter, with less art.

  Pol. Madam, I swear I use no art at all.
That he is mad, 'tis true : 'tis true 'tis pity ;
And pity 'tis 'tis true : a foolish figure ;
But farewell it, for I will use no art.
Mad let us grant him, then : and now remains
That we find out the cause of this effect,
Or rather say, the cause of this defect,
For this effect defective comes by cause :
Thus it remains, and the remainder thus.
Perpend.
I have a daughter—have while she is mine—
Who, in her duty and obedience, mark,
Hath given me this : now gather, and surmise. [*Reads.*
' To the celestial and my soul's idol, the most beautified
  Ophelia,'—
That's an ill phrase, a vile phrase ; ' beautified ' is a vile
phrase : but you shall hear. Thus :   [*Reads.*
' In her excellent white bosom, these, &c.'

  Queen. Came this from Hamlet to her ?

  Pol. Good madam, stay awhile ; I will be faithful. [*Reads.*

' Doubt thou the stars are fire ;
    Doubt that the sun doth move ;
    Doubt truth to be a liar ;
    But never doubt I love.

' O dear Ophelia, I am ill at these numbers ; I have not art to reckon my groans : but that I love thee best, O most best, believe it.   Adieu.

' Thine evermore, most dear lady, whilst this machine is
                        to him, HAMLET.' . . .

Queen. But, look, where sadly the poor wretch comes reading.

Pol. Away, I do beseech you, both away :
I'll board him presently.

[*Exeunt King, Queen, and Attendants.*

Enter HAMLET, *reading.*

                        O, give me leave :
How does my good Lord Hamlet ?

Ham. Well, God-a-mercy.

Pol. Do you know me, my lord ?

Ham. Excellent well ; you are a fishmonger.

Pol. Not I, my lord.

Ham. Then I would you were so honest a man.

Pol. Honest, my lord !

Ham. Ay, sir ; to be honest, as this world goes, is to be one man picked out of ten thousand.

Pol. That's very true, my lord.

Ham. For if the sun breed maggots in a dead dog, being a god kissing carrion,—Have you a daughter ?

Pol. I have, my lord.

Ham. Let her not walk i' the sun : conception is a blessing : but not as your daughter may conceive.   Friend, look to 't.

Pol. [*Aside*] How say you by that ?   Still harping on my daughter : yet he knew me not at first ; he said I was a fishmonger : he is far gone, far gone : and truly in my youth I suffered much extremity for love ; very near this.   I'll speak to him again.   What do you read, my lord ?

Ham. Words, words, words.

Pol. What is the matter, my lord ?

Ham. Between who ?

Pol. I mean, the matter that you read, my lord.

Ham. Slanders, sir : for the satirical rogue says here that old men have grey beards, that their faces are wrinkled, their eyes purging thick amber and plum-tree gum and that they have a plentiful lack of wit, together with most weak hams : all which, sir, though I most powerfully and potently believe, yet I hold it not honesty to have it thus set down, for yourself, sir, should be old as I am, if like a crab you could go backward.

Pol. [*Aside*] Though this be madness, yet there is method in 't. Will you walk out of the air, my lord ?

Ham. Into my grave.

Pol. Indeed, that is out o' the air. [*Aside*] How pregnant sometimes his replies are ? a happiness that often madness hits on, which reason and sanity could not so prosperously be delivered of. I will leave him, and suddenly contrive the means of meeting between him and my daughter.—My honourable lord, I will most humbly take my leave of you.

Ham. You cannot, sir, take from me any thing that I will more willingly part withal : except my life, except my life, except my life.

Pol. Fare you well, my lord.

Ham. These tedious old fools !

Enter ROSENCRANTZ *and* GUILDENSTERN.

Pol. You go to seek the Lord Hamlet ; there he is.

Ros. [*To Polonius*] God save you, sir !   [*Exit Polonius.*

Guil. My honoured lord !

Ros. My most dear lord !

Ham. My excellent good friends ! How dost thou, Guildenstern ? Ah, Rosencrantz ? Good lads, how do ye both ?

Ros. As the indifferent children of the earth.

Guil. Happy, in that we are not over-happy ;
On fortune's cap we are not the very button.

340

Ham. Nor the soles of her shoe ?

Ros. Neither, my lord.

Ham. Then you live about her waist, or in the middle of her favours ?

Guil. 'Faith, her privates we.

Ham. In the secret parts of fortune ? O, most true ; she is a strumpet. What's the news ?

Ros. None, my lord, but that the world's grown honest.

Ham. Then is doomsday near : but your news is not true. Let me question more in particular : what have you, my good friends, deserved at the hands of fortune, that she sends you to prison hither ?

Guil. Prison, my lord !

Ham. Denmark's a prison.

Ros. Then is the world one.

Ham. A goodly one ; in which there are many confines, wards and dungeons, Denmark being one o' the worst.

Ros. We think not so, my lord.

Ham. Why, then, 'tis none to you ; for there is nothing either good or bad, but thinking makes it so : to me it is a prison.

Ros. Why then, your ambition makes it one ; 'tis too narrow for your mind.

Ham. O God, I could be bounded in a nutshell and count myself a king of infinite space, were it not that I have bad dreams.

Guil. Which dreams indeed are ambition, for the very substance of the ambitious is merely the shadow of a dream.

Ham. A dream itself is but a shadow.

Ros. Truly, and I hold ambition of so airy and light a quality that it is but a shadow's shadow.

Ham. Then are our beggars bodies, and our monarchs and outstretched heroes the beggars' shadows. Shall we to the court ? for, by my fay, I cannot reason.

Ros. }
Guil. } We'll wait upon you.

341

Ham. No such matter; I will not sort you with the rest of my servants, for, to speak to you like an honest man, I am most dreadfully attended. But, in the beaten way of friendship, what make you at Elsinore?

Ros. To visit you, my lord; no other occasion.

Ham. Beggar that I am, I am even poor in thanks; but I thank you: and sure, dear friends, my thanks are too dear a halfpenny. Were you not sent for? Is it your own inclining? Is it a free visitation? Come, deal justly with me: come, come; nay, speak.

Guil. What should we say, my lord?

Ham. Why, any thing, but to the purpose. You were sent for; and there is a kind of confession in your looks which your modesties have not craft enough to colour: I know the good king and queen have sent for you.

Ros. To what end, my lord?

Ham. That you must teach me. But let me conjure you, by the rights of our fellowship, by the consonancy of our youth, by the obligation of our ever-preserved love, and by what more dear a better proposer could charge you withal, be even and direct with me, whether you were sent for, or no?

Ros. [*Aside to Guil.*] What say you?

Ham. [*Aside*] Nay, then, I have an eye of you.—If you love me, hold not off.

Guil. My lord, we were sent for.

Ham. I will tell you why; so shall my anticipation prevent your discovery, and your secrecy to the king and queen moult no feather. I have of late—but wherefore I know not—lost all my mirth, forgone all custom of exercises; and indeed it goes so heavily with my disposition that this goodly frame, the earth, seems to me a sterile promontory, this most excellent canopy, the air, look you, this brave o'erhanging firmament, this majestical roof fretted with golden fire, why, it appears no other thing to me than a foul and pestilent congregation of vapours. What a piece of work is a man! how noble in reason! how infinite in faculty! in form and moving how express and admirable ! in action how like an angel ! in apprehension how like a god ! the beauty of the world ! the paragon of animals ! And yet, to me, what is this quintessence of dust ? man delights not me : no, nor woman neither, though by your smiling you seem to say so.

Ros. My lord, there was no such stuff in my thoughts.

Ham. Why did you laugh then, when I said ' man delights not me ' ?

Ros. To think, my lord, if you delight not in man, what lenten entertainment the players shall receive from you : we coted them on the way ; and hither are they coming, to offer you service.

Ham. He that plays the king shall be welcome ; his majesty shall have tribute of me ; the adventurous knight shall use his foil and target ; the lover shall not sigh gratis ; the humorous man shall end his part in peace ; the clown shall make those laugh whose lungs are tickled o' the sere ; and the lady shall say her mind freely, or the blank verse shall halt for 't. . . .

Enter POLONIUS.

Pol. Well be with you, gentlemen !

Ham. Hark you, Guildenstern ; and you too : at each ear a hearer : that great baby you see there is not yet out of his swaddling-clouts.

Ros. Happily he's the second time come to them ; for they say an old man is twice a child.

Ham. I will prophesy he comes to tell me of the players ; mark it. You say right, sir : o' Monday morning ; 'twas so indeed.

Pol. My lord, I have news to tell you.

Ham. My lord, I have news to tell you. When Roscius was an actor in Rome,—

Pol. The actors are come hither, my lord.

Ham. Buz, buz !

Pol. Upon mine honour,—

Ham. Then came each actor on his ass,—

Pol. The best actors in the world, either for tragedy, comedy, history, pastoral, pastoral-comical, historical-pastoral, tragical-historical, tragical-comical-historical-pastoral, scene individable, or poem unlimited : Seneca cannot be too heavy, nor Plautus too light. For the law of writ and the liberty, these are the only men.

Ham. O Jephthah, judge of Israel, what a treasure hadst thou !

Pol. What a treasure had he, my lord ?

Ham. Why,

> ' One fair daughter, and no more,
> The which he loved passing well.'

Pol. [*Aside*] Still on my daughter.

Ham. Am I not i' the right, old Jephthah ?

Pol. If you call me Jephthah, my lord, I have a daughter that I love passing well. . . .

Ham. Good my lord, will you see the players well bestowed ? Do you hear, let them be well used ; for they are the abstract and brief chronicles of the time : after your death you were better have a bad epitaph than their ill report while you live.

Pol. My lord, I will use them according to their desert.

Ham. God's bodykins, man, much better : use every man after his desert, and who should 'scape whipping ? Use them after your own honour and dignity : the less they deserve, the more merit is in your bounty. Take them in.

ACT II, Scene ii, ll. 86-124, 168-339, 398-431, 546-558

Hamlet. O, what a rogue and peasant slave am I !
Is it not monstrous that this player here,
But in a fiction, in a dream of passion,
Could force his soul so to his own conceit
That from her working all his visage wann'd,
Tears in his eyes, distraction in 's aspect,
A broken voice, and his whole function suiting
With forms to his conceit ? and all for nothing !
For Hecuba !

What's Hecuba to him, or he to Hecuba,
That he should weep for her ? What would he do,
Had he the motive and the cue for passion
That I have ? He would drown the stage with tears
And cleave the general ear with horrid speech,
Make mad the guilty and appal the free,
Confound the ignorant, and amaze indeed
The very faculties of eyes and ears.
Yet I,
A dull and muddy-mettled rascal, peak,
Like John-a-dreams, unpregnant of my cause,
And can say nothing ; no, not for a king,
Upon whose property and most dear life
A damn'd defeat was made. Am I a coward ?
Who calls me villain ? breaks my pate across ?
Plucks off my beard, and blows it in my face ?
Tweaks me by the nose ? gives me the lie i' the throat,
As deep as to the lungs ? who does me this ?
Ha !
'Swounds, I should take it : for it cannot be
But I am pigeon-liver'd and lack gall
To make oppression bitter, or ere this
I should have fatted all the region kites
With this slave's offal : bloody, bawdy villain !
Remorseless, treacherous, lecherous, kindless villain !
O, vengeance !
Why, what an ass am I ! This is most brave,
That I, the son of a dear father murder'd,
Prompted to my revenge by heaven and hell,
Must, like a whore, unpack my heart with words,
And fall a-cursing, like a very drab,
A scullion !
Fie upon 't ! foh ! . . .
I know my course. The spirit that I have seen
May be the devil : and the devil hath power
To assume a pleasing shape ; yea, and perhaps

Out of my weakness and my melancholy,
As he is very potent with such spirits,
Abuses me to damn me : I'll have grounds
More relative than this : the play's the thing
Wherein I'll catch the conscience of the king.

ACT II, Scene ii, ll. 576-617, 627-634

King.   Sweet Gertrude, leave us too ;
For we have closely sent for Hamlet hither,
That he, as 'twere by accident, may here
Affront Ophelia. . . .
    Queen.   I shall obey you.
And for your part, Ophelia, I do wish
That your good beauties be the happy cause
Of Hamlet's wildness : so shall I hope your virtues
Will bring him to his wonted way again,
To both your honours.
    Ophelia. Madam, I wish it may.   [*Exit Queen*.
    Polonius. Ophelia, walk you here.   Gracious, so please you,
We will bestow ourselves.   [*To Ophelia*]   Read on this book ;
That show of such an exercise may colour
Your loneliness. . . .   [*Exeunt King and Polonius*.

Enter HAMLET.

Ham. To be, or not to be : that is the question :
Whether 'tis nobler in the mind to suffer
The slings and arrows of outrageous fortune,
Or to take arms against a sea of troubles,
And by opposing end them ? To die : to sleep ;
No more ; and by a sleep to say we end
The heart-ache and the thousand natural shocks
That flesh is heir to, 'tis a consummation
Devoutly to be wish'd.   To die, to sleep ;
To sleep : perchance to dream : ay, there's the rub ;
For in that sleep of death what dreams may come
When we have shuffled off this mortal coil,
Must give us pause : there's the respect

346

That makes calamity of so long life ;
For who would bear the whips and scorns of time,
The oppressor's wrong, the proud man's contumely,
The pangs of despised love, the law's delay,
The insolence of office and the spurns
That patient merit of the unworthy takes,
When he himself might his quietus make
With a bare bodkin ? who would fardels bear,
To grunt and sweat under a weary life,
But that the dread of something after death,
The undiscover'd country from whose bourn
No traveller returns, puzzles the will
And makes us rather bear those ills we have
Than fly to others that we know not of ?
Thus conscience does make cowards of us all ;
And thus the native hue of resolution
Is sicklied o'er with the pale cast of thought,
And enterprises of great pith and moment
With this regard their currents turn awry,
And lose the name of action.—Soft you now !
The fair Ophelia ! Nymph, in thy orisons
Be all my sins remember'd.

Oph.   Good my lord,
How does your honour for this many a day ?

　Ham. I humbly thank you ; well, well, well.

　Oph. My lord, I have remembrances of yours,
That I have longed long to re-deliver ;
I pray you, now receive them.

　Ham.   No, not I ;
I never gave you aught.

　Oph. My honour'd lord, you know right well you did ;
And, with them, words of so sweet breath composed
As made the things more rich : their perfume lost,
Take these again ; for to the noble mind
Rich gifts wax poor when givers prove unkind.
There, my lord.

Ham. Ha, ha ! are you honest ?

Oph. My lord ?

Ham. Are you fair ?

Oph. What means your lordship ?

Ham. That if you be honest and fair, your honesty should admit no discourse to your beauty.

Oph. Could beauty, my lord, have better commerce than with honesty ?

Ham. Ay, truly ; for the power of beauty will sooner transform honesty from what it is to a bawd than the force of honesty can translate beauty into his likeness : this was sometime a paradox, but now the time gives it proof. I did love you once.

Oph. Indeed, my lord, you made me believe so.

Ham. You should not have believed me ; for virtue cannot so inoculate our old stock but we shall relish of it ; I loved you not.

Oph. I was the more deceived.

Ham. Get thee to a nunnery : why wouldst thou be a breeder of sinners ? I am myself indifferent honest ; but yet I could accuse me of such things that it were better my mother had not borne me : I am very proud, revengeful, ambitious, with more offences at my beck than I have thoughts to put them in, imagination to give them shape, or time to act them in. What should such fellows as I do crawling between earth and heaven ? We are arrant knaves, all ; believe none of us. Go thy ways to a nunnery. Where's your father ?

Oph. At home, my lord.

Ham. Let the doors be shut upon him, that he may play the fool no where but in 's own house. Farewell.

Oph. O, help him, you sweet heavens !

Ham. If thou dost marry, I'll give thee this plague for thy dowry : be thou as chaste as ice, as pure as snow, thou shalt not escape calumny. Get thee to a nunnery, go : farewell. Or, if thou wilt needs marry, marry a fool ; for wise men know well enough what monsters you make of them. To a nunnery, go, and quickly too. Farewell.

Oph. O heavenly powers, restore him !

Ham. I have heard of your paintings too, well enough ; God has given you one face, and you make yourselves another : you jig, you amble, and you lisp, and nick-name God's creatures, and make your wantonness your ignorance. Go to, I'll no more on 't ; it hath made me mad. I say, we will have no more marriages : those that are married already, all but one, shall live ; the rest shall keep as they are. To a nunnery, go.

[Exit.

Oph. O, what a noble mind is here o'erthrown !
The courtier's, soldier's, scholar's, eye, tongue, sword ;
The expectancy and rose of the fair state,
The glass of fashion and the mould of form,
The observed of all observers, quite, quite down !
And I, of ladies most deject and wretched,
That suck'd the honey of his music vows,
Now see that noble and most sovereign reason,
Like sweet bells jangled, out of tune and harsh ;
That unmatch'd form and feature of blown youth
Blasted with ecstasy.

ACT III, Scene i, ll. 28-31, 36-46, 56-168

Enter HAMLET *and* Players.

Ham. Speak the speech, I pray you, as I pronounced it to you, trippingly on the tongue : but if you mouth it, as many of your players do, I had as lief the town-crier spoke my lines. Nor do not saw the air too much with your hand, thus, but use all gently ; for in the very torrent, tempest, and, as I may say, the whirlwind of passion, you must acquire and beget a temperance that may give it smoothness. O, it offends me to the soul to hear a robustious periwig-pated fellow tear a passion to tatters, to very rags, to split the ears of the groundlings, who for the most part are capable of nothing but inexplicable dumb-shows and noise : I would have such a fellow whipped for o'erdoing Termagant ; it out-herods Herod : pray you, avoid it.

First Play. I warrant your honour.

349

Ham. Be not too tame neither, but let your own discretion be your tutor : suit the action to the word, the word to the action ; with this special observance, that you o'erstep not the modesty of nature : for any thing so overdone is from the purpose of playing, whose end, both at the first and now, was and is, to hold, as 'twere, the mirror up to nature ; to show virtue her own feature, scorn her own image, and the very age and body of the time his form and pressure. Now this overdone, or come tardy off, though it make the unskilful laugh, cannot but make the judicious grieve ; the censure of the which one must in your allowance o'erweigh a whole theatre of others. O, there be players that I have seen play, and heard others praise, and that highly, not to speak it profanely, that, neither having the accent of Christians nor the gait of Christian, pagan, nor man, have so strutted and bellowed that I have thought some of nature's journeymen had made men and not made them well, they imitated humanity so abominably.

First Play. I hope we have reformed that indifferently with us, sir.

Ham. O, reform it altogether. And let those that play your clowns speak no more than is set down for them ; for there be of them that will themselves laugh, to set on some quantity of barren spectators to laugh too ; though, in the mean time, some necessary question of the play be then to be considered : that's villanous, and shows a most pitiful ambition in the fool that uses it. Go, make you ready. . . .

What ho ! Horatio !

Enter HORATIO.

Hor. Here, sweet lord, at your service.

Ham. Horatio, thou art e'en as just a man
As e'er my conversation coped withal.

Hor. O, my dear lord,—

Ham. Nay, do not think I flatter ;
For what advancement may I hope from thee
That no revenue hast but thy good spirits,

To feed and clothe thee? Why should the poor be flatter'd?
No, let the candied tongue lick absurd pomp,
And crook the pregnant hinges of the knee
Where thrift may follow fawning. Dost thou hear?
Since my dear soul was mistress of her choice
And could of men distinguish, her election
Hath seal'd thee for herself; for thou hast been
As one, in suffering all, that suffers nothing,
A man that fortune's buffets and rewards
Hast ta'en with equal thanks: and blest are those
Whose blood and judgement are so well commingled,
That they are not a pipe for fortune's finger
To sound what stop she please. Give me that man
That is not passion's slave, and I will wear him
In my heart's core, ay, in my heart of heart,
As I do thee.—Something too much of this.—

ACT III, Scene ii, ll. 1-50, 57-79

Hamlet. Is this a prologue, or the posy of a ring?

Ophelia. 'Tis brief, my lord.

Ham. As woman's love. . . .

Madam, how like you this play?

Queen. The lady doth protest too much, methinks.

Ham. O, but she'll keep her word.

King. Have you heard the argument? Is there no offence in 't?

Ham. No, no, they do but jest, poison in jest; no offence i' the world.

King. What do you call the play? . . .

Ham. The Mouse-trap. Marry, how? Tropically. This play is the image of a murder done in Vienna: Gonzago is the duke's name; his wife, Baptista: you shall see anon; 'tis a knavish piece of work: but what o' that? your majesty and we that have free souls, it touches us not: let the galled jade wince, our withers are unwrung. . . .

Oph. The king rises.

Ham. What, frighted with false fire !

Queen. How fares my lord ?

Polonius. Give o'er the play.

King. Give me some light : away !

All. Lights, lights, lights !

[*Exeunt all but Hamlet and Horatio.*

Ham. Why, let the stricken deer go weep,
  The hart ungalled play ;
  For some must watch, while some must sleep :
  So runs the world away.

Would not this, sir, and a forest of feathers—if the rest of my
fortunes turn Turk with me—with two Provincial roses on
my razed shoes, get me a fellowship in a cry of players, sir ?

Hor. Half a share.

Ham. A whole one, I.
  For thou dost know, O Damon dear,
  This realm dismantled was
  Of Jove himself ; and now reigns here
  A very, very—pajock.

Hor. You might have rhymed.

Ham. O good Horatio, I'll take the ghost's word for a
thousand pound. Didst perceive ?

Hor. Very well, my lord.

Ham. Upon the talk of the poisoning ?

Hor. I did very well note him.

Ham. Ah, ha ! Come, some music ! come, the recorders !
  For if the king like not the comedy,
  Why then, belike, he likes it not, perdy.

Come, some music ! . . .

Re-enter Players *with recorders.*

O, the recorders ! let me see one. To withdraw with you :—
why do you go about to recover the wind of me, as if you would
drive me into a toil ?

Guildenstern. O, my lord, if my duty be too bold, my love
is too unmannerly.

Ham. I do not well understand that. Will you play upon this pipe ?

Guil. My lord, I cannot.

Ham. I pray you.

Guil. Believe me, I cannot.

Ham. I do beseech you.

Guil. I know no touch of it, my lord.

Ham. 'Tis as easy as lying : govern these ventages with your fingers and thumb, give it breath with your mouth, and it will discourse most eloquent music. Look you, these are the stops.

Guil. But these cannot I command to any utterance of harmony ; I have not the skill.

Ham. Why, look you now, how unworthy a thing you make of me ! You would play upon me ; you would seem to know my stops ; you would pluck out the heart of my mystery ; you would sound me from my lowest note to the top of my compass : and there is much music, excellent voice, in this little organ ; yet cannot you make it speak. 'Sblood, do you think I am easier to be played on than a pipe ? Call me what instrument you will, though you can fret me, yet you cannot play upon me.

Re-enter POLONIUS.

God bless you, sir !

Pol. My lord, the queen would speak with you, and presently.

Ham. Do you see yonder cloud that's almost in shape of a camel ?

Pol. By the mass, and 'tis like a camel, indeed.

Ham. Methinks it is like a weasel.

Pol. It is backed like a weasel.

Ham. Or like a whale ?

Pol. Very like a whale.

Ham. Then I will come to my mother by and by. They fool me to the top of my bent. I will come by and by.

Pol. I will say so.

Ham. By and by is easily said. [*Exit Polonius.*] Leave me,
    friends.   [*Exeunt all but Hamlet.*
'Tis now the very witching time of night,
When churchyards yawn and hell itself breathes out
Contagion to this world : now could I drink hot blood,
And do such bitter business as the day
Would quake to look on. Soft ! now to my mother.
O heart, lose not thy nature ; let not ever
The soul of Nero enter this firm bosom :
Let me be cruel, not unnatural :
I will speak daggers to her, but use none ;
My tongue and soul in this be hypocrites ;
How in my words soever she be shent,
To give them seals never, my soul, consent !
         Act III, Scene ii, ll. 162-164, 239-254, 276-306, 360-417

A room in the castle.
Enter King.

King. O, my offence is rank, it smells to heaven ;
It hath the primal eldest curse upon 't,
A brother's murder. Pray can I not,
Though inclination be as sharp as will :
My stronger guilt defeats my strong intent ;
And, like a man to double business bound,
I stand in pause where I shall first begin,
And both neglect. What if this cursed hand
Were thicker than itself with brother's blood,
Is there not rain enough in the sweet heavens
To wash it white as snow ? . . .

Enter Hamlet.

Ham. Now might I do it pat, now he is praying ;
And now I'll do't. And so he goes to heaven ;
And so am I revenged. That would be scann'd :
A villain kills my father ; and for that,
I, his sole son, do this same villain send
To heaven.

O, this is hire and salary, not revenge.
He took my father grossly, full of bread ;
With all his crimes broad blown, as flush as May ;
And how his audit stands who knows save heaven ?
But in our circumstance and course of thought,
'Tis heavy with him : and am I then revenged,
To take him in the purging of his soul,
When he is fit and season'd for his passage ?
No !
Up, sword ; and know thou a more horrid hent.

ACT III, Scene iii, ll. 36-46, 73-88

The Queen's closet.

Hamlet. Now, mother, what's the matter ?
Queen. Hamlet, thou hast thy father much offended.
Ham. Mother, you have my father much offended.
Queen. Come, come, you answer with an idle tongue.
Ham. Go, go, you question with a wicked tongue.
Queen. Why, how now, Hamlet !
Ham.   What's the matter now ?
Queen. Have you forgot me ?
Ham.   No, by the rood, not so :
You are the queen, your husband's brother's wife ;
And—would it were not so !—you are my mother.
Queen. Nay, then, I'll set those to you that can speak.
Ham. Come, come, and sit you down ; you shall not budge ;
You go not till I set you up a glass
Where you may see the inmost part of you.
Queen. What wilt thou do ? thou wilt not murder me ?
Help, help, ho !
Pol. [*Behind*] What, ho ! help, help, help !
Ham. [*Drawing*] How now ! a rat ? Dead, for a ducat,
  dead !   [*Makes a pass through the arras.*
Pol. [*Behind*] O, I am slain !   [*Falls and dies.*
Queen. O me, what hast thou done ?
Ham.   Nay, I know not :

355

Is it the king?

Queen. O, what a rash and bloody deed is this!

Ham. A bloody deed! almost as bad, good mother,
As kill a king, and marry with his brother.

Queen. As kill a king!

Ham.   Ay, lady, 'twas my word.

                    [Lifts up the arras and discovers Polonius.
Thou wretched, rash, intruding fool, farewell!
I took thee for thy better: take thy fortune;
Thou find'st to be too busy is some danger.
Leave wringing of your hands: peace! sit you down,
And let me wring your heart; for so I shall,
If it be made of penetrable stuff,
If damned custom have not brass'd it so
That it be proof and bulwark against sense.

Queen. What have I done, that thou darest wag thy tongue
In noise so rude against me?

Ham.   Such an act
That blurs the grace and blush of modesty,
Calls virtue hypocrite, takes off the rose
From the fair forehead of an innocent love
And sets a blister there, makes marriage-vows
As false as dicers' oaths: O, such a deed
As from the body of contraction plucks
The very soul, and sweet religion makes
A rhapsody of words: heaven's face doth glow;
Yea, this solidity and compound mass,
With tristful visage, as against the doom,
Is thought-sick at the act.

Queen.   Ay me, what act,
That roars so loud, and thunders in the index?

Ham. Look here, upon this picture, and on this,
The counterfeit presentment of two brothers.
See, what a grace was seated on this brow;
Hyperion's curls; the front of Jove himself;
An eye like Mars, to threaten and command;

A station like the herald Mercury
New-lighted on a heaven-kissing hill ;
A combination and a form indeed,
Where every god did seem to set his seal,
To give the world assurance of a man :
This was your husband. Look you now, what follows :
Here is your husband ; like a mildew'd ear,
Blasting his wholesome brother. Have you eyes ?
Could you on this fair mountain leave to feed,
And batten on this moor ? Ha ! have you eyes ?
You cannot call it love ; for at your age
The hey-day in the blood is tame, it's humble,
And waits upon the judgement : and what judgement
Would step from this to this ? Sense, sure, you have,
Else could you not have motion ; but sure, that sense
Is apoplex'd ; for madness would not err,
Nor sense to ecstasy was ne'er so thrall'd
But it reserved some quantity of choice,
To serve in such a difference. What devil was't
That thus hath cozen'd you at hoodman-blind ?
Eyes without feeling, feeling without sight,
Ears without hands or eyes, smelling sans all,
Or but a sickly part of one true sense
Could not so mope.
O shame ! where is thy blush ? Rebellious hell,
If thou canst mutine in a matron's bones,
To flaming youth let virtue be as wax,
And melt in her own fire : proclaim no shame
When the compulsive ardour gives the charge,
Since frost itself as actively doth burn
And reason pandars will.
    Queen.   O Hamlet, speak no more :
Thou turn'st mine eyes into my very soul ;
And there I see such black and grained spots
As will not leave their tinct.
    Ham.   Nay, but to live

In the rank sweat of an enseamed bed,
Stew'd in corruption, honeying and making love
Over the nasty sty,—

    Queen.   O, speak to me no more ;
These words, like daggers, enter in mine ears ;
No more, sweet Hamlet !

    Ham.   A murderer and a villain ;
A slave that is not twentieth part the tithe
Of your precedent lord ; a vice of kings ;
A cutpurse of the empire and the rule,
That from a shelf the precious diadem stole,
And put it in his pocket !

    Queen.   No more !

    Ham. A king of shreds and patches,—

Enter Ghost.

Save me, and hover o'er me with your wings,
You heavenly guards ! What would your gracious figure ?

    Queen. Alas, he's mad !

    Ham. Do you not come your tardy son to chide,
That, lapsed in time and passion, lets go by
The important acting of your dread command ?
O, say !

    Ghost. Do not forget : this visitation
Is but to whet thy almost blunted purpose.
But, look, amazement on thy mother sits :
O, step between her and her fighting soul :
Conceit in weakest bodies strongest works :
Speak to her, Hamlet.

    Ham.   How is it with you, lady ?

    Queen. Alas, how is 't with you,
That you do bend your eye on vacancy
And with the incorporal air do hold discourse ?
Forth at your eyes your spirits wildly peep ;
And, as the sleeping soldiers in the alarm,
Your bedded hair, like life in excrements,

Start up, and stand an end. O gentle son,
Upon the heat and flame of thy distemper
Sprinkle cool patience. Whereon do you look?

Ham. On him, on him! Look you, how pale he glares
His form and cause conjoin'd, preaching to stones,
Would make them capable. Do not look upon me;
Lest with this piteous action you convert
My stern effects: then what I have to do
Will want true colour; tears perchance for blood.

Queen. To whom do you speak this?

Ham. Do you see nothing there?

Queen. Nothing at all; yet all that is I see.

Ham. Nor did you nothing hear?

Queen. No, nothing but ourselves.

Ham. Why, look you there! look, how it steals away!
My father, in his habit as he lived!
Look, where he goes, even now, out at the portal! [*Exit Ghost.*

Queen. This is the very coinage of your brain:
This bodiless creation ecstasy
Is very cunning in.

Ham. Ecstasy!
My pulse, as yours, doth temperately keep time,
And makes as healthful music: it is not madness
That I have utter'd: bring me to the test,
And I the matter will re-word; which madness
Would gambol from. Mother, for love of grace,
Lay not that flattering unction to your soul,
That not your trespass, but my madness speaks:
It will but skin and film the ulcerous place,
Whilst rank corruption, mining all within,
Infects unseen. Confess yourself to heaven;
Repent what's past; avoid what is to come;
And do not spread the compost on the weeds,
To make them ranker. Forgive me this my virtue;
For in the fatness of these pursy times
Virtue itself of vice must pardon beg,

Yea, curb and woo for leave to do him good.

   Queen. O Hamlet, thou hast cleft my heart in twain.

   Ham. O, throw away the worser part of it,

And live the purer with the other half. . . .

   Queen.   What shall I do ?

   Ham. Not this, by no means, that I bid you do :

Let the bloat king tempt you again to bed ;

Pinch wanton on your cheek ; call you his mouse ;

And let him, for a pair of reechy kisses,

Or paddling in your neck with his damn'd fingers,

Make you to ravel all this matter out,

That I essentially am not in madness,

But mad in craft. . . .

   Queen. Be thou assured, if words be made of breath,

And breath of life, I have no life to breathe

What thou hast said to me.

   Ham. I must to England ; you know that ?

   Queen.   Alack,

I had forgot : 'tis so concluded on.

   Ham. There's letters seal'd : and my two schoolfellows,

Whom I will trust as I will adders fang'd,

They bear the mandate ; they must sweep my way,

And marshal me to knavery. Let it work ;

For 'tis the sport to have the engineer

Hoist with his own petar : and 't shall go hard

But I will delve one yard below their mines,

And blow them at the moon : O, 'tis most sweet,

When in one line two crafts directly meet.

This man shall set me packing :

I'll lug the guts into the neighbour room.

Mother, good night. Indeed this counsellor

Is now most still, most secret and most grave,

Who was in life a foolish prating knave.

Come, sir, to draw toward an end with you.

Good night, mother.

                        ACT III, Scene iv, ll. 8-158, 180-188, 196-217

Hamlet. How all occasions do inform against me,
And spur my dull revenge ! What is a man,
If his chief good and market of his time
Be but to sleep and feed ? a beast, no more.
Sure, he that made us with such large discourse,
Looking before and after, gave us not
That capability and god-like reason
To fust in us unused. Now, whether it be
Bestial oblivion, or some craven scruple
Of thinking too precisely on the event,
A thought which, quarter'd, hath but one part wisdom
And ever three parts coward, I do not know
Why yet I live to say ' This thing's to do ; '
Sith I have cause and will and strength and means
To do 't. Examples gross as earth exhort me :
Witness this army of such mass and charge
Led by a delicate and tender prince,
Whose spirit with divine ambition puff'd
Makes mouths at the invisible event,
Exposing what is mortal and unsure
To all that fortune, death and danger dare,
Even for an egg-shell. Rightly to be great
Is not to stir without great argument,
But greatly to find quarrel in a straw
When honour's at the stake. How stand I then,
That have a father kill'd, a mother stain'd,
Excitements of my reason and my blood,
And let all sleep ? while, to my shame, I see
The imminent death of twenty thousand men,
That, for a fantasy and trick of fame,
Go to their graves like beds, fight for a plot
Whereon the numbers cannot try the cause,
Which is not tomb enough and continent
To hide the slain ?

ACT IV, Scene iv, ll. 32-65

Elsinore. A room in the castle.

Enter QUEEN, HORATIO, *and a* Gentleman.

Queen. I will not speak with her.

Gent. She is importunate, indeed distract :
Her mood will needs be pitied.

Queen.   What would she have ?

Gent. She speaks much of her father ; says she hears
There's tricks i' the world ; and hems, and beats her heart ;
Spurns enviously at straws ; speaks things in doubt,
That carry but half sense : her speech is nothing,
Yet the unshaped use of it doth move
The hearers to collection ; they aim at it,
And botch the words up fit to their own thoughts ;
Which, as her winks, and nods, and gestures yield them,
Indeed would make one think there might be thought,
Though nothing sure, yet much unhappily.

Hor. 'Twere good she were spoken with ; for she may strew
Dangerous conjectures in ill-breeding minds.

Queen. Let her come in.   [*Exit Horatio.*
To my sick soul, as sin's true nature is,
Each toy seems prologue to some great amiss :
So full of artless jealousy is guilt,
It spills itself in fearing to be spilt.

Re-enter HORATIO, *with* OPHELIA.

Oph. Where is the beauteous majesty of Denmark ?

Queen. How now, Ophelia !

Oph. [*Sings*] How should I your true love know
                    From another one ?
             By his cockle hat and staff,
                    And his sandal shoon.

Queen. Alas, sweet lady, what imports this song ?

Oph. Say you ? nay, pray you, mark.
[*Sings*]   He is dead and gone, lady,
                    He is dead and gone ;

At his head a grass-green turf,
　　At his heels a stone.

Queen. Nay, but, Ophelia,——

Oph. Pray you, mark.

[*Sings*] White his shroud as the mountain snow,——

Enter KING.

Queen. Alas, look here, my lord.

Oph. [*Sings*] Larded with sweet flowers;
　　Which bewept to the grave did go
　　　With true-love showers.

King. How do you, pretty lady?

Oph. Well, God 'ild you! They say the owl was a baker's daughter. Lord, we know what we are, but know not what we may be. God be at your table!

King. Conceit upon her father.

Oph. Pray you, let's have no words of this; but when they ask you what it means, say you this:

[*Sings*.]　　To-morrow is Saint Valentine's day,
　　　All in the morning betime,
　　And I a maid at your window,
　　　To be your Valentine.
　Then up he rose, and donn'd his clothes,
　　　And dupp'd the chamber-door;
　　Let in the maid, that out a maid
　　　Never departed more.

King. Pretty Ophelia!

Oph. Indeed, la, without an oath, I'll make an end on 't

[*Sings*]　　By Gis and by Saint Charity,
　　　Alack, and fie for shame!
　　Young men will do 't, if they come to 't;
　　　By cock, they are to blame.
　　Quoth she, before you tumbled me,
　　　You promised me to wed.
　　So would I ha' done, by yonder sun,
　　　And thou hadst not come to my bed.

363

King. How long hath she been thus?

Oph. I hope all will be well. We must be patient: but I cannot choose but weep, to think they should lay him i' the cold ground. My brother shall know of it: and so I thank you for your good counsel. Come, my coach! Good night, ladies; good night, sweet ladies; good night, good night.

                                     [Exit. . . .

                                     [A noise within.

Queen.   Alack, what noise is this? . . .

King. The doors are broke.   *[Noise within.*

       Enter LAERTES, *armed;* Danes *following.*

Laer. Where is this king? Sirs, stand you all without.

Danes. No, let's come in.

Laer.   I pray you, give me leave.

Danes. We will, we will.

               [They retire without the door. . . .

King.   What is the cause, Laertes,
That thy rebellion looks so giant-like?
Let him go, Gertrude; do not fear our person:
There's such divinity doth hedge a king
That treason can but peep to what it would,
Acts little of his will. . . .

Danes. [*Within*]   Let her come in.

Laer. How now! what noise is that?

           Re-enter OPHELIA.

O heat, dry up my brains! tears seven times salt,
Burn out the sense and virtue of mine eye!
By heaven, thy madness shall be paid by weight,
Till our scale turn the beam. O rose of May!
Dear maid, kind sister, sweet Ophelia!
O heavens! is't possible, a young maid's wits
Should be as mortal as an old man's life?
Nature is fine in love, and where 'tis fine,
It sends some precious instance of itself
After the thing it loves.

Oph. [*Sings*]

    They bore him barefaced on the bier;

    Hey non nonny, nonny, hey nonny;

    And in his grave rain'd many a tear:—

Fare you well, my dove!

Laer. Hadst thou thy wits, and didst persuade revenge.
It could not move thus.

Oph. [*Sings*] You must sing a-down a-down,

    An you call him a-down-a.

O, how the wheel becomes it! It is the false steward, that
stole his master's daughter.

Laer. This nothing's more than matter.

Oph. There's rosemary, that's for remembrance; pray,
love, remember: and there is pansies, that's for thoughts.

Laer. A document in madness, thoughts and remembrance
fitted.

Oph. There's fennel for you, and columbines: there's rue for
you; and here's some for me: we may call it herb-grace o' Sun-
days: O, you must wear your rue with a difference. There's
a daisy: I would give you some violets, but they withered all
when my father died: they say he made a good end,—

[*Sings*] For bonny sweet Robin is all my joy.

Laer. Thought and affliction, passion, hell itself,
She turns to favour and to prettiness.

Oph. [*Sings*] And will he not come again?

    And will he not come again?

      No, no, he is dead:

      Go to thy death-bed:

    He never will come again.

    His beard was as white as snow,

    All flaxen was his poll:

      He is gone, he is gone,

      And we cast away moan:

    God ha' mercy on his soul!

And of all Christian souls, I pray God. God be wi' ye.

ACT IV, Scene v, ll. 1-74, 96, 111-114, 120-5, 152-200

Enter QUEEN.

King.   How now, sweet queen !

Queen. One woe doth tread upon another's heel,
So fast they follow : your sister's drown'd, Laertes.

Laertes. Drown'd ! O, where ?

Queen. There is a willow grows aslant a brook,
That shows his hoar leaves in the glassy stream ;
There with fantastic garlands did she come
Of crow-flowers, nettles, daisies, and long purples
That liberal shepherds give a grosser name,
But our cold maids do dead men's fingers call them :
There, on the pendent boughs her coronet weeds
Clambering to hang, an envious sliver broke ;
When down her weedy trophies and herself
Fell in the weeping brook. Her clothes spread wide ;
And, mermaid-like, awhile they bore her up :
Which time she chanted snatches of old tunes ;
As one incapable of her own distress,
Or like a creature native and indued
Unto that element : but long it could not be
Till that her garments, heavy with their drink,
Pull'd the poor wretch from her melodious lay
To muddy death.

Laer.   Alas, then, she is drown'd ?

Queen. Drown'd, drown'd.

ACT IV, Scene vii, ll. 163-185

A churchyard.

Enter two Clowns, *with spades*, &c.

First Clo. Is she to be buried in Christian burial that
wilfully seeks her own salvation ?

Sec. Clo. I tell thee she is : and therefore make her grave
straight : the crowner hath sat on her, and finds it Christian
burial.

First Clo. How can that be, unless she drowned herself in
her own defence ?

Sec. Clo. Why, 'tis found so.

First Clo. It must be ' se offendendo ; ' it cannot be else. For here lies the point : if I drown myself wittingly, it argues an act : and an act hath three branches ; it is, to act, to do, and to perform : argal, she drowned herself wittingly.

Sec Clo. Nay, but hear you, goodman delver,—

First Clo. Give me leave. Here lies the water ; good : here stands the man ; good : if the man go to this water, and drown himself, it is, will he, nill he, he goes,—mark you that ; but if the water come to him and drown him, he drowns not himself : argal, he that is not guilty of his own death shortens not his own life.

Sec. Clo. But is this law ?

First Clo. Ay, marry, is 't ; crowner's quest law.

Sec. Clo. Will you ha' the truth on't ? If this had not been a gentlewoman, she should have been buried out o' Christian burial.

First Clo. Why, there thou say'st : and the more pity that great folk should have countenance in this world to drown or hang themselves, more than their even Christian. Come, my spade. There is no ancient gentlemen but gardeners, ditchers, and grave-makers : they hold up Adam's profession.

Sec. Clo. Was he a gentleman ?

First Clo. A' was the first that ever bore arms.

Sec. Clo. Why, he had none.

First Clo. What, art a heathen ? How dost thou understand the Scripture ? The Scripture says ' Adam digged : ' could he dig without arms ? . . .

Enter HAMLET *and* HORATIO, *at a distance.*

[*Clown digs, and sings.*

In youth, when I did love, did love,
  Methought it was very sweet,
To contract, O, the time, for, ah, my behove,
  O, methought, there was nothing meet.

Ham. Has this fellow no feeling of his business, that he sings at grave-making ?

Hor. Custom hath made it in him a property of easiness.

Ham. 'Tis e'en so : the hand of little employment hath the daintier sense.

First Clo. [*Sings*]

> But age, with his stealing steps,
>   Hath claw'd me in his clutch,
> And hath shipped me intil the land,
>   As if I had never been such.

[*Throws up a skull.*

Ham. That skull had a tongue in it, and could sing once : how the knave jowls it to the ground, as if it were Cain's jawbone, that did the first murder ! It might be the pate of a politician, which this ass now o'er-reaches ; one that would circumvent God, might it not ?

Hor. It might, my lord.

Ham. Or of a courtier ; which could say ' Good morrow, sweet lord ! How dost thou, good lord ? ' This might be my lord such-a-one, that praised my lord such-a-one's horse, when he meant to beg it ; might it not ?

Hor. Ay, my lord.

Ham. Why, e'en so : and now my Lady Worm's ; chapless, and knocked about the mazzard with a sexton's spade : here's fine revolution, an we had the trick to see't. Did these bones cost no more the breeding, but to play at loggats with 'em ? mine ache to think on't.

First Clo. [*Sings*]

> A pick-axe, and a spade, a spade,
>   For and a shrouding sheet :
> O, a pit of clay for to be made
>   For such a guest is meet.

[*Throws up another skull.*

Ham. There's another : why may not that be the skull of a lawyer ? Where be his quiddities now, his quillets, his cases, his tenures, and his tricks ? why does he suffer this rude knave now to knock him about the sconce with a dirty shovel, and will not tell him of his action of battery ? Hum ! This fellow might be in 's time a great buyer of land, with his statutes, his recognizances, his fines, his double vouchers, his recoveries : is this the fine of his fines, and the recovery of his recoveries, to have his fine pate full of fine dirt ? will his vouchers vouch him no more of his purchases, and double ones too, than the length and breadth of a pair of indentures ? The very conveyances of his lands will hardly lie in this box ; and must the inheritor himself have no more, ha ?

Hor. Not a jot more, my lord.

Ham. Is not parchment made of sheep-skins ?

Hor. Ay, my lord, and of calf-skins too.

Ham. They are sheep and calves which seek out assurance in that. I will speak to this fellow. Whose grave's this, sirrah ?

First Clo. Mine, sir.

[*Sings*]   O, a pit of clay for to be made
                 For such a guest is meet.

Ham. I think it be thine, indeed ; for thou liest in't.

First Clo. You lie out on 't, sir, and therefore it is not yours : for my part, I do not lie in 't, and yet it is mine.

Ham. Thou dost lie in 't, to be in 't and say it is thine : 'tis for the dead, not for the quick ; therefore thou liest.

First Clo. 'Tis a quick lie, sir ; 'twill away again, from me to you.

Ham. What man dost thou dig it for ?

First Clo. For no man, sir.

Ham. What woman, then ?

First Clo. For none, neither.

Ham. Who is to be buried in 't ?

First Clo. One that was a woman, sir ; but, rest her soul, she's dead.

Ham. How absolute the knave is ! we must speak by the card, or equivocation will undo us. By the Lord, Horatio, these three years I have taken a note of it ; the age is grown so picked that the toe of the peasant comes so near the heel of the courtier, he galls his kibe. How long hast thou been a grave-maker?

First Clo. Of all the days i' the year, I came to 't that day that our last king Hamlet overcame Fortinbras.

Ham. How long is that since?

First Clo. Cannot you tell that? every fool can tell that: it was the very day that young Hamlet was born; he that is mad, and sent into England.

Ham. Ay, marry, why was he sent into England?

First Clo. Why, because he was mad: he shall recover his wits there; or, if he do not, it's no great matter there.

Ham. Why?

First Clo. 'Twill not be seen in him there; there the men are as mad as he.

Ham. How came he mad?

First Clo. Very strangely, they say.

Ham. How strangely?

First Clo. Faith, e'en with losing his wits.

Ham. Upon what ground?

First Clo. Why, here in Denmark: I have been sexton here, man and boy, thirty years.

Ham. How long will a man lie i' the earth ere he rot?

First Clo. I' faith, if he be not rotten before he die—as we have many pocky corses now-a-days, that will scarce hold the laying in—he will last you some eight year or nine year: a tanner will last you nine year.

Ham. Why he more than another.

First Clo. Why, sir, his hide is so tanned with his trade, that he will keep out water a great while; and your water is a sore decayer of your whoreson dead body. Here's a skull now; this skull has lain in the earth three and twenty years.

Ham. Whose was it?

First Clo. A whoreson mad fellow's it was: whose do you think it was?

Ham. Nay, I know not.

First Clo. A pestilence on him for a mad rogue! a' poured

a flagon of Rhenish on my head once. This same skull, sir,
was Yorick's skull, the king's jester.

Ham. This ?

First Clo. E'en that.

Ham. Let me see. [*Takes the skull.*] Alas, poor Yorick !
I knew him, Horatio : a fellow of infinite jest, of most excellent
fancy : he hath borne me on his back a thousand times ; and
now, how abhorred in my imagination it is ! my gorge rises
at it. Here hung those lips that I have kissed I know not how
oft. Where be your gibes now ? your gambols ? your songs ?
your flashes of merriment, that were wont to set the table on
a roar ? Not one now, to mock your own grinning ? quite
chap-fallen ? Now get you to my lady's chamber, and tell her,
let her paint an inch thick, to this favour she must come ;
make her laugh at that. Prithee, Horatio, tell me one thing.

Hor. What's that, my lord ?

Ham. Dost thou think Alexander looked o' this fashion i'
the earth ?

Hor. E'en so.

Ham. And smelt so ? pah !   [*Puts down the skull.*

Hor. E'en so, my lord.

Ham. To what base uses we may return, Horatio ! Why
may not imagination trace the noble dust of Alexander, till he
find it stopping a bung-hole ?

Hor. 'Twere to consider too curiously, to consider so.

Ham. No, faith, not a jot ; but to follow him thither with
modesty enough, and likelihood to lead it : as thus : Alexander
died, Alexander was buried, Alexander returneth into dust ;
the dust is earth ; of earth we make loam ; and why of that
loam, whereto he was converted, might they not stop a beer-
barrel ?

Imperious Caesar, dead and turn'd to clay,
Might stop a hole to keep the wind away :
O, that that earth, which kept the world in awe,
Should patch a wall to expel the winter's flaw !
But soft ! but soft ! aside : here comes the king.

Enter Priests, *&c. in procession; the Corpse of* OPHELIA,
LAERTES *and* Mourners *following;* KING, QUEEN, *their
trains, &c.*

The queen, the courtiers : who is this they follow ?
And with such maimed rites ? This doth betoken
The corse they follow did with desperate hand
Fordo its own life : 'twas of some estate.
Couch we awhile, and mark.   [*Retiring with Horatio.*

 Laer. What ceremony else ?

 Ham.   That is Laertes,
A very noble youth : mark.

 Laer. What ceremony else ?

 First Priest. Her obsequies have been as far enlarged
As we have warrantise : her death was doubtful ;
And, but that great command o'ersways the order,
She should in ground unsanctified have lodged
Till the last trumpet ; for charitable prayers,
Shards, flints and pebbles should be thrown on her :
Yet here she is allow'd her virgin crants,
Her maiden strewments and the bringing home
Of bell and burial.

 Laer. Must there no more be done ?

 First Priest.   No more be done :
We should profane the service of the dead
To sing a requiem and such rest to her
As to peace-parted souls.

 Laer.   Lay her i' the earth :
And from her fair and unpolluted flesh
May violets spring ! I tell thee, churlish priest,
A ministering angel shall my sister be,
When thou liest howling.

 Ham.   What, the fair Ophelia !

 Queen. Sweets to the sweet : farewell !

          [*Scattering flowers.*

I hoped thou shouldst have been my Hamlet's wife ;

I thought thy bride-bed to have deck'd, sweet maid,
And not have strew'd thy grave.

   Laer.   O, treble woe
Fall ten times treble on that cursed head,
Whose wicked deed thy most ingenious sense
Deprived thee of ! Hold off the earth awhile,
Till I have caught her once more in mine arms :

                                 [Leaps into the grave.
Now pile your dust upon the quick and dead,
Till of this flat a mountain you have made,
To o'ertop old Pelion, or the skyish head
Of blue Olympus.

   Ham. [*Advancing*] What is he whose grief
Bears such an emphasis ? whose phrase of sorrow
Conjures the wandering stars, and makes them stand
Like wonder-wounded hearers ? This is I,
Hamlet the Dane.   *[Leaps into the grave.*

   Laer.   The devil take thy soul !

                        [Grappling with him.
   Ham. Thou pray'st not well.
I prithee, take thy fingers from my throat ;
For, though I am not splenitive and rash,
Yet have I something in me dangerous,
Which let thy wiseness fear : hold off thy hand.

   King. Pluck them asunder.

   Queen.   Hamlet, Hamlet !

   All. Gentlemen,—

   Hor.   Good my lord, be quiet.

   [*The Attendants part them, and they come out of the grave.*
   Ham. Why, I will fight with him upon this theme
Until my eyelids will not longer wag.

   Queen. O my son, what theme ?

   Ham. I loved Ophelia : forty thousand brothers
Could not, with all their quantity of love,
Make up my sum. What wilt thou do for her ?

   King. O, he is mad, Laertes.

Queen. For love of God, forbear him.

Ham. 'Swounds, show me what thou'lt do :
Woo't weep ? woo't fight ? woo't fast ? woo't tear thyself ?
Woo't drink up eisel ? eat a crocodile ?
I'll do't. Dost thou come here to whine ?
To outface me with leaping in her grave ?
Be buried quick with her, and so will I :
And, if thou prate of mountains, let them throw
Millions of acres on us, till our ground,
Singeing his pate against the burning zone,
Make Ossa like a wart ! Nay, an thou'lt mouth,
I'll rant as well as thou.

    Queen.   This is mere madness :
And thus awhile the fit will work on him ;
Anon, as patient as the female dove,
When that her golden couplets are disclosed,
His silence will sit drooping.

    Ham.   Hear you, sir ;
What is the reason that you use me thus ?
I loved you ever : but it is no matter ;
Let Hercules himself do what he may,
The cat will mew and dog will have his day.

                        ACT V, Scene i, ll. 1-42, 69-315

A hall in the castle.

Enter HAMLET, HORATIO *and* OSRIC.

Osr. Your lordship is right welcome back to Denmark.

Ham. I humbly thank you, sir. Dost know this water-fly ?

Hor. No, my good lord.

Ham. Thy state is the more gracious ; for 'tis a vice to know him. He hath much land, and fertile : let a beast be lord of beasts, and his crib shall stand at the king's mess : 'tis a chough ; but, as I say, spacious in the possession of dirt.

Osr. Sweet lord, if your lordship were at leisure, I should impart a thing to you from his majesty.

Ham. I will receive it, sir, with all diligence of spirit. Put your bonnet to his right use; 'tis for the head.

Osr. I thank your lordship, it is very hot.

Ham. No, believe me, 'tis very cold; the wind is northerly.

Osr. It is indifferent cold, my lord, indeed.

Ham. But yet methinks it is very sultry and hot for my complexion.

Osr. Exceedingly, my lord; it is very sultry,—as 'twere,—I cannot tell how. But, my lord, his majesty bade me signify to you that he has laid a great wager on your head: sir, this is the matter,—

Ham. I beseech you, remember—

[*Hamlet moves him to put on his hat.*

Osr. Nay, good my lord; for mine ease, in good faith. Sir, here is newly come to court Laertes; believe me, an absolute gentleman, full of most excellent differences, of very soft society and great showing: indeed, to speak feelingly of him, he is the card or calendar of gentry, for you shall find in him the continent of what part a gentleman would see.

Ham. Sir, his definement suffers no perdition in you; though, I know, to divide him inventorially would dizzy the arithmetic of memory, and yet but yaw neither, in respect of his quick sail. But, in the verity of extolment, I take him to be a soul of great article; and his infusion of such dearth and rareness, as, to make true diction of him, his semblable is his mirror, and who else would trace him, his umbrage, nothing more.

Osr. Your lordship speaks most infallibly of him.

Ham. The concernancy, sir? why do we wrap the gentleman in our more rawer breath?

Osr. Sir?

Hor. Is 't not possible to understand in another tongue? You will do 't, sir, really.

Ham. What imports the nomination of this gentleman?

Osr. Of Laertes?

Hor. His purse is empty already; all 's golden words are spent.

Ham. Of him, sir.

Osr. I know you are not ignorant—

Ham. I would you did, sir; yet, in faith, if you did, it would not much approve me. Well, sir?

Osr. You are not ignorant of what excellence Laertes is—

Ham. I dare not confess that, lest I should compare with him in excellence; but, to know a man well, were to know himself.

Osr. I mean, sir, for his weapon; but in the imputation laid on him by them, in his meed he's unfellowed.

Ham. What's his weapon?

Osr. Rapier and dagger.

Ham. That's two of his weapons: but, well.

Osr. The king, sir, hath wagered with him six Barbary horses: against the which he has imponed, as I take it, six French rapiers and poniards, with their assigns, as girdle, hangers, and so: three of the carriages, in faith, are very dear to fancy, very responsive to the hilts, most delicate carriages, and of very liberal conceit.

Ham. What call you the carriages?

Hor. I knew you must be edified by the margent ere you had done.

Osr. The carriages, sir, are the hangers.

Ham. The phrase would be more german to the matter, if we could carry cannon by our sides: I would it might be hangers till then. But, on: six Barbary horses against six French swords, their assigns, and three liberal-conceited carriages; that's the French bet against the Danish. Why is this 'imponed,' as you call it?

Osr. The king, sir, hath laid, that in a dozen passes between yourself and him, he shall not exceed you three hits: he hath laid on twelve for nine; and it would come to immediate trial, if your lordship would vouchsafe the answer.

Ham. How if I answer 'no'?

Osr. I mean, my lord, the opposition of your person in trial.

Ham. Sir, I will walk here in the hall : if it please his majesty, 'tis the breathing time of day with me ; let the foils be brought, the gentleman willing, and the king hold his purpose, I will win for him an I can ; if not, I will gain nothing but my shame and the odd hits. . . .

Enter KING, QUEEN, LAERTES, Lords, *and* Attendants
with foils, &c.

King. Set me the stoups of wine upon that table.
If Hamlet give the first or second hit,
Or quit in answer of the third exchange,
Let all the battlements their ordnance fire ;
The king shall drink to Hamlet's better breath ;
And in the cup an union shall he throw,
Richer than that which four successive kings
In Denmark's crown have worn. Give me the cups ;
And let the kettle to the trumpet speak,
The trumpet to the cannoneer without,
The cannons to the heavens, the heavens to earth,
' Now the king drinks to Hamlet.' Come, begin :
And you, the judges, bear a wary eye. . . .
Our son shall win.

Queen.   He's fat, and scant of breath.
Here, Hamlet, take my napkin, rub thy brows :
The queen carouses to thy fortune, Hamlet.

Ham. Good madam !

King.   Gertrude, do not drink.

Queen. I will, my lord ; I pray you, pardon me.

King. [*Aside*] It is the poison'd cup : it is too late. . . .

Laer. Have at you now !

[*Laertes wounds Hamlet ; then, in scuffling, they change rapiers,
and Hamlet wounds Laertes.*

King.   Part them ; they are incensed.

Ham. Nay, come, again.   [*The Queen falls.*

Osr.   Look to the queen there, ho !

Hor. They bleed on both sides. How is it, my lord ?

Osr. How is't, Laertes?

Laer. Why, as a woodcock to mine own springe, Osric;
I am justly kill'd with mine own treachery.

Ham. How does the queen?

King.   She swounds to see them bleed.

Queen. No, no, the drink, the drink,—O my dear Hamlet,—
The drink, the drink! I am poison'd.   [*Dies.*

Ham. O villany! Ho! let the door be lock'd: Treachery!
Seek it out.

Laer. It is here, Hamlet: Hamlet, thou art slain;
No medicine in the world can do thee good;
In thee there is not half an hour of life;
The treacherous instrument is in thy hand,
Unbated and envenom'd: the foul practice
Hath turn'd itself on me; lo, here I lie,
Never to rise again: thy mother's poison'd:
I can no more: the king, the king's to blame.

Ham. The point!—envenom'd too!
Then, venom, to thy work.   [*Stabs the King.*

All. Treason! treason!

King. O, yet defend me, friends; I am but hurt.

Ham. Here, thou incestuous, murderous, damned Dane,
Drink off this potion. Is thy union here?
Follow my mother.   [*King dies.*

Laer.   He is justly served;
It is a poison temper'd by himself.
Exchange forgiveness with me, noble Hamlet:
Mine and my father's death come not upon thee,
Nor thine on me!   [*Dies.*

Ham. Heaven make thee free of it! I follow thee.
I am dead, Horatio. Wretched queen, adieu!
You that look pale and tremble at this chance,
That are but mutes or audience to this act,
Had I but time—as this fell sergeant, death,
Is strict in his arrest—O, I could tell you—
But let it be. Horatio, I am dead;

Thou livest; report me and my cause aright
To the unsatisfied.

Hor.   Never believe it :
I am more an antique Roman than a Dane :
Here's yet some liquor left.

Ham.   As thou'rt a man,
Give me the cup : let go ; by heaven, I'll have't.
O good Horatio, what a wounded name,
Things standing thus unknown, shall live behind me !
If thou didst ever hold me in thy heart,
Absent thee from felicity awhile,
And in this harsh world draw thy breath in pain,
To tell my story.   [*March afar off, and shot within.*
                    What warlike noise is this ?

Osr. Young Fortinbras, with conquest come from Poland,
To the ambassadors of England gives
This warlike volley.

Ham.   O, I die, Horatio ;
The potent poison quite o'er-crows my spirit :
I cannot live to hear the news from England ;
But I do prophesy the election lights
On Fortinbras : he has my dying voice ;
So tell him, with the occurrents, more and less,
Which have solicited. The rest is silence.   [*Dies.*

Hor. Now cracks a noble heart. Good night, sweet prince ;
And flights of angels sing thee to thy rest !
Why does the drum come hither ?   [*March within.*

Enter FORTINBRAS, *the* English Ambassadors, *and others.*

Fort. Where is this sight ?

Hor.   What is it ye would see ?
If aught of woe or wonder, cease your search.

Fort. This quarry cries on havoc. O proud death,
What feast is toward in thine eternal cell,
That thou so many princes at a shot
So bloodily hast struck ? . . .

Hor. Since, so jump upon this bloody question,
You from the Polack wars, and you from England,
Are here arrived, give order that these bodies
High on a stage be placed to the view;
And let me speak to the yet unknowing world
How these things came about: so shall you hear
Of carnal, bloody, and unnatural acts,
Of accidental judgements, casual slaughters,
Of deaths put on by cunning and forced cause,
And, in this upshot, purposes mistook
Fall'n on the inventors' heads: all this can I
Truly deliver.
    Fort.   Let us haste to hear it,
And call the noblest to the audience.
For me, with sorrow I embrace my fortune:
I have some rights of memory in this kingdom,
Which now to claim my vantage doth invite me.
    Hor. Of that I shall have also cause to speak,
And from his mouth whose voice will draw on more:
But let this same be presently perform'd,
Even while men's minds are wild; lest more mischance,
On plots and errors, happen.
    Fort.   Let four captains
Bear Hamlet, like a soldier, to the stage;
For he was likely, had he been put on,
To have proved most royally: and, for his passage,
The soldiers' music and the rites of war
Speak loudly for him.
             ACT V, Scene ii, ll. 81-185, 278-290, 298-303, 312-378, 386-411

Troilus and Cressida

Troy. Before Priam's palace.

Enter TROILUS *armed, and* PANDARUS.

Tro. Call here my varlet; I'll unarm again :
Why should I war without the walls of Troy,
That find such cruel battle here within ?
Each Trojan that is master of his heart,
Let him to field ; Troilus, alas ! hath none.

Pan. Will this gear ne'er be mended ?

Tro. The Greeks are strong and skilful to their strength,
Fierce to their skill and to their fierceness valiant ;
But I am weaker than a woman's tear,
Tamer than sleep, fonder than ignorance,
Less valiant than the virgin in the night
And skilless as unpractised infancy.

Pan. Well, I have told you enough of this : for my part, I'll
not meddle nor make no further. He that will have a cake out
of the wheat must needs tarry the grinding.

Tro. Have I not tarried ?

Pan. Ay, the grinding ; but you must tarry the bolting.

Tro. Have I not tarried ?

Pan. Ay, the bolting, but you must tarry the leavening.

Tro. Still have I tarried.

Pan. Ay, to the leavening ; but here's yet in the word
' hereafter ' the kneading, the making of the cake, the heating
of the oven and the baking ; nay, you must stay the cooling
too, or you may chance to burn your lips.

Tro. Patience herself, what goddess e'er she be,
Doth lesser blench at sufferance than I do.
At Priam's royal table do I sit ;
And when fair Cressid comes into my thoughts,—
So, traitor ! ' When she comes ! ' When is she thence ?

Pan. Well, she looked yesternight fairer than ever I saw
her look, or any woman else.

Tro. I was about to tell thee :—when my heart,
As wedged with a sigh, would rive in twain,
Lest Hector or my father should perceive me,
I have, as when the sun doth light a storm,
Buried this sigh in wrinkle of a smile. . . .

Pan. An her hair were not somewhat darker than Helen's—
well, go to—there were no more comparison between the
women : but, for my part, she is my kinswoman ; I would
not, as they term it, praise her : but I would somebody had
heard her talk yesterday, as I did. I will not dispraise your
sister Cassandra's wit, but—

Tro. O Pandarus ! I tell thee, Pandarus,—
When I do tell thee, there my hopes lie drown'd,
Reply not in how many fathoms deep
They lie indrench'd. I tell thee I am mad
In Cressid's love : thou answer'st ' she is fair ; '
Pour'st in the open ulcer of my heart
Her eyes, her hair, her cheek, her gait, her voice,
Handlest in thy discourse, O, that her hand,
In whose comparison all whites are ink,
Writing their own reproach, to whose soft seizure
The cygnet's down is harsh and spirit of sense
Hard as the palm of ploughman : this thou tell'st me,
As true thou tell'st me, when I say I love her ;
But, saying thus, instead of oil and balm,
Thou lay'st in every gash that love hath given me
The knife that made it.

Pan. I speak no more than truth.

Tro. Thou dost not speak so much.

Pan. Faith, I'll not meddle in't. Let her be as she is : if
she be fair, 'tis the better for her ; an she be not, she has the
mends in her own hands.

Tro. Good Pandarus, how now, Pandarus !

Pan. I have had my labour for my travail ; ill-thought on
of her and ill-thought on of you ; gone between and between
but small thanks for my labour.

Tro. What, art thou angry, Pandarus? what, with me?

Pan. Because she's kin to me, therefore she's not so fair as
Helen : an she were not kin to me, she would be as fair on
Friday as Helen is on Sunday. But what care I? I care not
an she were a black-a-moor; 'tis all one to me.

Tro. Say I she is not fair? . . .

Pan. Pray you, speak no more to me : I will leave all as I
found it, and there an end.   [*Exit Pandarus. An alarum.*

Tro. Peace, you ungracious clamours! peace, rude sounds!
Fools on both sides! Helen must needs be fair,
When with your blood you daily paint her thus.
I cannot fight upon this argument;
It is too starved a subject for my sword.
But Pandarus,—O gods, how do you plague me!
I cannot come to Cressid but by Pandar;
And he's as tetchy to be woo'd to woo,
As she is stubborn-chaste against all suit.
Tell me, Apollo, for thy Daphne's love,
What Cressid is, what Pandar, and what we?
Her bed is India; there she lies, a pearl :
Between our Ilium and where she resides,
Let it be call'd the wild and wandering flood,
Ourself the merchant, and this sailing Pandar
Our doubtful hope, our convoy and our bark.

ACT I, Scene i, ll. 1-38, 41-81, 90-107

Things won are done; joy's soul lies in the doing.

ACT I, Scene ii, l. 312

Trumpet, blow loud,
Send thy brass voice through all these lazy tents.

ACT I, Scene iii, ll. 256-257

There is seen
The baby figure of the giant mass
Of things to come at large.

ACT I, Scene iii, ll. 344-346

You are for dreams and slumbers, brother priest.

ACT II, Scene ii, l. 37

Troilus. We turn not back the silks upon the merchant,
When we have soil'd them, nor the remainder viands
We do not throw in unrespective sieve,
Because we now are full. It was thought meet
Paris should do some vengeance on the Greeks:
Your breath of full consent bellied his sails;
The seas and winds, old wranglers, took a truce
And did him service: he touch'd the ports desired,
And for an old aunt whom the Greeks held captive,
He brought a Grecian queen, whose youth and freshness
Wrinkles Apollo's, and makes stale the morning.
Why keep we her? the Grecians keep our aunt:
Is she worth keeping? why, she is a pearl,
Whose price hath launch'd above a thousand ships,
And turn'd crown'd kings to merchants.
If you'll avouch 'twas wisdom Paris went—
As you must needs, for you all cried ' Go, go,'—
If you'll confess he brought home noble prize—
As you must needs, for you all clapp'd your hands,
And cried ' Inestimable ! '—why do you now
The issue of your proper wisdoms rate,
And do a deed that fortune never did,
Beggar the estimation which you prized
Richer than sea and land ? O, theft most base,
That we have stol'n what we do fear to keep ! . . .
She is a theme of honour and renown,
A spur to valiant and magnanimous deeds,
Whose present courage may beat down our foes,
And fame in time to come canonize us ;
For, I presume, brave Hector would not lose
So rich advantage of a promised glory
As smiles upon the forehead of this action
For the wide world's revenue.

ACT II, Scene ii, 69-93, 199-206

Ajax. Why should a man be proud? How doth pride grow? I know not what pride is.

Agamemnon. Your mind is the clearer, Ajax, and your virtues the fairer. He that is proud eats up himself: pride is his own glass, his own trumpet, his own chronicle; and whatever praises itself but in the deed, devours the deed in the praise.

Ajax. I do hate a proud man, as I hate the engendering of toads.

Nestor. Yet he loves himself: is't not strange?   [*Aside.*

ACT II, Scene iii, ll. 161-171

There is no tarrying here; the hart Achilles
Keeps thicket.

ACT II, Scene iii, ll. 269-270

The mortal Venus, the heart-blood of beauty, love's invisible soul.

ACT III, Scene i, l. 34-35

Fair thoughts be your fair pillow!

ACT III, Scene i, l. 49

Sweet Helen, I must woo you
To help unarm our Hector: his stubborn buckles,
With these your white enchanting fingers touch'd,
Shall more obey than to the edge of steel
Or force of Greekish sinews; you shall do more
Than all the island kings,—disarm great Hector.

ACT III, Scene i, ll. 162-167

Pandarus. Have you seen my cousin?

Troilus. No, Pandarus: I stalk about her door,
Like a strange soul upon the Stygian banks
Staying for waftage. O, be thou my Charon,
And give me swift transportance to those fields
Where I may wallow in the lily-beds
Proposed for the deserver! O gentle Pandarus,

From Cupid's shoulder pluck his painted wings,
And fly with me tô Cressid !
    Pan. Walk here i' the orchard, I'll bring her straight.
                                [Exit.

    Tro. I am giddy ; expectation whirls me round.
The imaginary relish is so sweet
That it enchants my sense : what will it be,
When that the watery palate tastes indeed
Love's thrice repured nectar ? death, I fear me,
Swooning destruction, or some joy too fine,
Too subtle-potent, tuned too sharp in sweetness,
For the capacity of my ruder powers :
I fear it much ; and I do fear besides,
That I shall lose distinction in my joys ;
As doth a battle, when they charge on heaps
The enemy flying.
                  Re-enter PANDARUS.

    Pan. She's making her ready, she'll come straight : you
must be witty now. She does so blush, and fetches her wind
so short, as if she were frayed with a sprite : I'll fetch her. It
is the prettiest villain : she fetches her breath as short as a
new-ta'en sparrow.   *[Exit.*
    Tro. Even such a passion doth embrace my bosom :
My heart beats thicker than a feverous pulse ;
And all my powers do their bestowing lose,
Like vassalage at unawares encountering
The eye of majesty.
                            ACT III, Scene ii, ll. 8-41

    Cressida. Prince Troilus, I have loved you night and day
For many weary months.
    Troilus. Why was my Cressid then so hard to win ?
    Cres. Hard to seem won : but I was won, my lord,
With the first glance that ever—pardon me—
If I confess much, you will play the tyrant.
I love you now ; but not, till now, so much
But I might master it : in faith, I lie ;

My thoughts were like unbridled children, grown
Too headstrong for their mother. See, we fools !
Why have I blabb'd ? who shall be true to us,
When we are so unsecret to ourselves ?
But, though I loved you well, I woo'd you not ;
And yet, good faith, I wish'd myself a man,
Or that we women had men's privilege
Of speaking first. Sweet, bid me hold my tongue,
For in this rapture I shall surely speak
The thing I shall repent. See, see, your silence,
Cunning in dumbness, from my weakness draws
My very soul of counsel ! stop my mouth.

 Tro. And shall, albeit sweet music issues thence.

 Pan. Pretty, i' faith.

 Cres. My lord, I do beseech you, pardon me ;
'Twas not my purpose, thus to beg a kiss :
I am ashamed. O heavens ! what have I done ?
For this time will I take my leave, my lord.

 Tro. Your leave, sweet Cressid !

 Pan. Leave ! an you take leave till to-morrow morning,—

 Cres. Pray you, content you.

 Tro.   What offends you, lady ?

 Cres. Sir, mine own company.

 Tro.   You cannot shun
Yourself.

 Cres. Let me go and try :
I have a kind of self resides with you ;
But an unkind self, that itself will leave,
To be another's fool. I would be gone :
Where is my wit ? I know not what I speak.

 Tro. Well know they what they speak that speak so
   wisely.

 Cres. Perchance, my lord, I show more craft than love ;
And fell so roundly to a large confession,
To angle for your thoughts : but you are wise,
Or else you love not, for to be wise and love

Exceeds man's might ; that dwells with gods above.

Tro. O that I thought it could be in a woman—
As, if it can, I will presume in you—
To feed for aye her lamp and flames of love ;
To keep her constancy in plight and youth,
Outliving beauty's outward, with a mind
That doth renew swifter than blood decays !
Or that persuasion could but thus convince me,
That my integrity and truth to you
Might be affronted with the match and weight
Of such a winnow'd purity in love ;
How were I then uplifted ! but, alas !
I am as true as truth's simplicity
And simpler than the infancy of truth.

Cres. In that I'll war with you.

Tro.   O virtuous fight,
When right with right wars who shall be most right !
True swains in love shall in the world to come
Approve their truths by Troilus : when their rhymes,
Full of protest, of oath and big compare,
Want similes, truth tired with iteration,
As true as steel, as plantage to the moon,
As sun to day, as turtle to her mate,
As iron to adamant, as earth to the centre,
Yet, after all comparisons of truth,
As truth's authentic author to be cited,
' As true as Troilus ' shall crown up the verse,
And sanctify the numbers.

Cres.   Prophet may you be !
If I be false, or swerve a hair from truth,
When time is old and hath forgot itself,
When waterdrops have worn the stones of Troy,
And blind oblivion swallow'd cities up,
And mighty states characterless are grated
To dusty nothing, yet let memory,
From false to false, among false maids in love,

Upbraid my falsehood! when they've said ' as false
As air, as water, wind, or sandy earth,
As fox to lamb, as wolf to heifer's calf,
Pard to the hind, or stepdame to her son,'
' Yea,' let them say, to stick the heart of falsehood,
' As false as Cressid.'

 Pan. Go to, a bargain made : seal it, seal it; I'll be the
witness. Here I hold your hand, here my cousin's. If ever
you prove false one to another, since I have taken such pains to
bring you together, let all pitiful goers-between be called to
the world's end after my name ; call them all Pandars ; let all
constant men be Troiluses, all false women Cressids, and all
brokers-between Pandars! say, amen.

 Tro. Amen.

 Cres. Amen.

 Pan. Amen. Whereupon I will show you a chamber with
a bed ; which bed, because it shall not speak of your pretty
encounters, press it to death : away!

ACT III, Scene ii, ll. 122-218

The Grecian camp. Before Achilles' tent.

Enter AGAMEMNON, ULYSSES, NESTOR, AJAX, MENELAUS,
ACHILLES *and* PATROCLUS.

 Ulyss. Achilles stands i' the entrance of his tent :
Please it our general to pass strangely by him,
As if he were forgot ; and, princes all,
Lay negligent and loose regard upon him :
I will come last. . . .

 Achil. What, comes the general to speak with me ?
You know my mind, I'll fight no more 'gainst Troy.

 Agam. What says Achilles ? would he aught with us ?

 Nest. Would you, my lord, aught with the general ?

 Achil. No.

 Nest. Nothing, my lord.

 Agam. The better. [*Exeunt Agamemnon and Nestor.*

 Achil. Good day, good day.

Men. How do you ? how do you ?   [*Exit.*
Achil. What, does the cuckold scorn me ?
Ajax. How now, Patroclus !
Achil. Good morrow, Ajax.
Ajax. Ha ?
Achil. Good morrow.
Ajax. Ay, and good next day too.   [*Exit.*
Achil. What mean these fellows ? Know they not
     Achilles ?
Patr. They pass by strangely : they were used to bend,
To send their smiles before them to Achilles ;
To come as humbly as they used to creep
To holy altars.
     Achil.   What, am I poor of late ?
'Tis certain, greatness, once fall'n out with fortune,
Must fall out with men too : what the declined is
He shall as soon read in the eyes of others
As feel in his own fall ; for men, like butterflies,
Show not their mealy wings but to the summer. . . .
Here is Ulysses :
I'll interrupt his reading.
How now, Ulysses !
     Ulyss.   Now, great Thetis' son !
Achil. What are you reading ?
     Ulyss.   A strange fellow here
Writes me : ' That man, how dearly ever parted,
How much in having, or without or in,
Cannot make boast to have that which he hath,
Nor feels not what he owes, but by reflection ;
As when his virtues shining upon others
Heat them and they retort that heat again
To the first giver.'
     Achil.   This is not strange, Ulysses.
The beauty that is borne here in the face
The bearer knows not, but commends itself
To others' eyes ; nor doth the eye itself,

That most pure spirit of sense, behold itself,
Not going from itself; but eye to eye opposed
Salutes each other with each other's form;
For speculation turns not to itself,
Till it hath travell'd and is mirror'd there
Where it may see itself. This is not strange at all.

Ulyss. I do not strain at the position,—
It is familiar,—but at the author's drift;
Who, in his circumstance, expressly proves
That no man is the lord of any thing,
Though in and of him there be much consisting,
Till he communicate his parts to others;
Nor doth he of himself know them for aught
Till he behold them form'd in the applause
Where they're extended; who, like an arch, reverberates
The voice again, or, like a gate of steel
Fronting the sun, receives and renders back
His figure and his heat. I was much wrapt in this;
And apprehended here immediately
The unknown Ajax.
Heavens, what a man is there! a very horse,
That has he knows not what. Nature, what things there are
Most abject in regard and dear in use!
What things again most dear in the esteem
And poor in worth! Now shall we see to-morrow—
An act that very chance doth throw upon him—
Ajax renown'd. O heavens, what some men do,
While some men leave to do!
How some men creep in skittish fortune's hall,
Whiles others play the idiots in her eyes!
How one man eats into another's pride,
While pride is fasting in his wantonness!
To see these Grecian lords!—why, even already
They clap the lubber Ajax on the shoulder,
As if his foot were on brave Hector's breast
And great Troy shrieking.

Achil. I do believe it ; for they pass'd by me
As misers do by beggars, neither gave to me
Good word nor look : what, are my deeds forgot ?

Ulyss. Time hath, my lord, a wallet at his back,
Wherein he puts alms for oblivion,
A great-sized monster of ingratitudes :
Those scraps are good deeds past ; which are devour'd
As fast as they are made, forgot as soon
As done : perseverance, dear my lord,
Keeps honour bright : to have done is to hang
Quite out of fashion, like a rusty mail
In monumental mockery. . . .
For time is like a fashionable host
That slightly shakes his parting guest by the hand,
And with his arms outstretch'd, as he would fly,
Grasps in the comer : welcome ever smiles,
And farewell goes out sighing. O, let not virtue seek
Remuneration for the thing it was ;
For beauty, wit,
High birth, vigour of bone, desert in service,
Love, friendship, charity, are subjects all
To envious and calumniating time.
One touch of nature makes the whole world kin,
That all with one consent praise new-born gawds,
Though they are made and moulded of things past,
And give to dust that is a little gilt
More laud than gilt o'er-dusted.
The present eye praises the present object.

ACT III, Scene iii, ll. 38-42, 55-79, 92-153, 165-180

My mind is troubled, like a fountain stirr'd ;
And I myself see not the bottom of it.

ACT III, Scene iii, ll. 311-312

Court of Pandarus' house.

Enter TROILUS *and* CRESSIDA.

Tro. Dear, trouble not yourself : the morn is cold.

Cres. Then, sweet my lord, I'll call mine uncle down ;
He shall unbolt the gates.

Tro.   Trouble him not ;
To bed, to bed : sleep kill those pretty eyes,
And give as soft attachment to thy senses
As infants' empty of all thought !

Cres.   Good morrow, then.

Tro. I prithee now, to bed.

Cres.   Are you a-weary of me ?

Tro. O Cressida ! but that the busy day,
Waked by the lark, hath roused the ribald crows,
And dreaming night will hide our joys no longer,
I would not from thee.

Cres.   Night hath been too brief.

Tro. Beshrew the witch ! with venomous wights she stays
As tediously as hell, but flies the grasps of love
With wings more momentary-swift than thought.
You will catch cold, and curse me.

Cres.   Prithee, tarry :
You men will never tarry.
O foolish Cressid ! I might have still held off,
And then you would have tarried. Hark ! there's one up.

Pan. [*Within*] What, 's all the doors open here ?

Tro. It is your uncle.

Cres. A pestilence on him ! now will he be mocking :
I shall have such a life !

                             ACT IV, Scene ii, ll. 1-22

Pandarus' house.

Enter PANDARUS *and* CRESSIDA.

Pan. Here, here, here he comes.

Enter TROILUS.

Ah, sweet ducks !

Cres. O Troilus ! Troilus !   [*Embracing him.*

Pan. What a pair of spectacles is here ! Let me embrace too.
O heart,' as the goodly saying is,

393

' ——O heart, heavy heart,
      Why sigh'st thou without breaking?'

where he answers again,

' Because thou canst not ease thy smart
      By friendship nor by speaking.'

There was never a truer rhyme. Let us cast away nothing
for we may live to have need of such a verse: we see it, we
see it. How now, lambs?

    Tro. Cressid, I love thee in so strain'd a purity,
That the bless'd gods, as angry with my fancy,
More bright in zeal than the devotion which
Cold lips blow to their deities, take thee from me.

    Cres. Have the gods envy?

    Pan. Ay, ay, ay, ay; 'tis too plain a case.

    Cres. And is it true that I must go from Troy?

    Tro. A hateful truth.

    Cres.   What, and from Troilus too?

    Tro. From Troy and Troilus.

    Cres.   Is it possible?

    Tro. And suddenly; where injury of chance
Puts back leave-taking, justles roughly by
All time of pause, rudely beguiles our lips
Of all rejoindure, forcibly prevents
Our lock'd embrasures, strangles our dear vows
Even in the birth of our own labouring breath:
We two, that with so many thousand sighs
Did buy each other, must poorly sell ourselves
With the rude brevity and discharge of one.
Injurious time now with a robber's haste
Crams his rich thievery up, he knows not how:
As many farewells as be stars in heaven,
With distinct breath and consign'd kisses to them,
He fumbles up into a loose adieu,
And scants us with a single famish'd kiss,
Distasted with the salt of broken tears.

    Æne. [*Within*] My lord, is the lady ready?

Tro. Hark ! you are call'd : some say the Genius so
Cries ' come ' to him that instantly must die.
Bid them have patience ; she shall come anon.

Pan. Where are my tears ? rain, to lay this wind, or my
heart will be blown up by the root.   [*Exit.*

Cres. I must then to the Grecians ?

Tro.   No remedy.

Cres. A woful Cressid 'mongst the merry Greeks !
When shall we see again ?

Tro. Hear me, my love : be thou but true of heart,—

Cres. I true ! how now ! what wicked deem is this ?

Tro. Nay, we must use expostulation kindly,
For it is parting from us :
I speak not ' be thou true,' as fearing thee,
For I will throw my glove to Death himself,
That there's no maculation in thy heart :
But ' be thou true,' say I, to fashion in
My sequent protestation ; be thou true,
And I will see thee.

Cres. O, you shall be exposed, my lord, to dangers
As infinite as imminent ! but I'll be true.

Tro. And I'll grow friend with danger. Wear this sleeve.

Cres. And you this glove. When shall I see you ?

Tro. I will corrupt the Grecian sentinels,
To give thee nightly visitation.
But yet be true.

Cres.   O heavens ! ' be true ' again !

Tro. Hear why I speak it, love :
The Grecian youths are full of quality ;
They're loving, well composed with gifts of nature,
Flowing and swelling o'er with arts and exercise :
How novelty may move, and parts with person,
Alas, a kind of godly jealousy—
Which, I beseech you, call a virtuous sin—
Makes me afeard.

Cres.   O heavens ! you love me not.

Tro. Die I a villain, then !
In this I do not call your faith in question
So mainly as my merit : I cannot sing,
Nor heel the high lavolt, nor sweeten talk,
Nor play at subtle games ; fair virtues all,
To which the Grecians are most prompt and pregnant :
But I can tell that in each grace of these
There lurks a still and dumb-discoursive devil
That tempts most cunningly : but be not tempted.
   Cres. Do you think I will ?
   Tro. No.
But something may be done that we will not :
And sometimes we are devils to ourselves,
When we will tempt the frailty of our powers,
Presuming on their changeful potency.
   Æne. [*Within*] Nay, good my lord,—
   Tro.   Come, kiss ; and let us part. . . .
   Cres. My lord, will you be true ?

                   Act IV, Scene iv, ll. 11-100, 103

   Diomedes. Lady, a word : I'll bring you to your father.
                    [*Exit with Cressida.*

   Nestor. A woman of quick sense.
   Ulysses.   Fie, fie upon her !
There's language in her eye, her cheek, her lip,
Nay, her foot speaks ; her wanton spirits look out
At every joint and motive of her body.
O, these encounterers, so glib of tongue,
That give accosting welcome ere it comes,
And wide unclasp the tables of their thoughts
To every ticklish reader ! set them down
For sluttish spoils of opportunity
And daughters of the game.

                   Act IV, Scene v, ll. 53-63

The youngest son of Priam, a true knight,
Not yet mature, yet matchless, firm of word,

Speaking in deeds and deedless in his tongue ;
Not soon provoked nor being provoked soon calm'd ;
His heart and hand both open and both free ;
For what he has he gives, what thinks he shows ;
Yet gives he not till judgement guide his bounty,
Nor dignifies an impair thought with breath ;
Manly as Hector, but more dangerous ;
For Hector in his blaze of wrath subscribes
To tender objects, but he in heat of action
Is more vindicative than jealous love :
They call him Troilus, and on him erect
A second hope, as fairly built as Hector.
Thus says Æneas ; one that knows the youth
Even to his inches, and with private soul
Did in great Ilion thus translate him to me.

ACT IV, Scene v, ll. 96-112

Agamemnon. Worthy of arms ! as welcome as to one
That would be rid of such an enemy ;
But that's no welcome : understand more clear,
What's past and what's to come is strew'd with husks
And formless ruin of oblivion ;
But in this extant moment, faith and troth,
Strain'd purely from all hollow bias-drawing,
Bids thee, with most divine integrity,
From heart of very heart, great Hector, welcome.

ACT IV, Scene v, ll. 163-171

Let me embrace thee, good old chronicle,
That hast so long walk'd hand in hand with time :
Most reverend Nestor, I am glad to clasp thee.

ACT IV, Scene v, ll. 202-204

Ulysses. I wonder now how yonder city stands
When we have here her base and pillar by us.
   Hector. I know your favour, Lord Ulysses, well.
Ah, sir, there's many a Greek and Trojan dead,

397

Since first I saw yourself and Diomed
In Ilion, on your Greekish embassy.

Ulyss. Sir, I foretold you then what would ensue :
My prophecy is but half his journey yet ;
For yonder walls, that pertly front your town,
Yond towers, whose wanton tops do buss the clouds,
Must kiss their own feet.

Hect.   I must not believe you :
There they stand yet, and modestly I think,
The fall of every Phrygian stone will cost
A drop of Grecian blood : the end crowns all,
And that old common arbitrator, Time
Will one day end it.

ACT IV, Scene v, ll. 210-226

Thersites. Here's Agamemnon, an honest fellow enough,
and one that loves quails ; but he has not so much brain as
ear-wax : and the goodly transformation of Jupiter there, his
brother, the bull,—the primitive statue, and oblique memorial
of cuckolds ; a thrifty shoeing-horn in a chain, hanging at his
brother's leg,—to what form but that he is, should wit larded
with malice and malice forced with wit turn him to ? To an
ass, were nothing ; he is both ass and ox : to an ox, were
nothing ; he is both ox and ass. To be a dog, a mule, a cat, a
fitchew, a toad, a lizard, an owl, a puttock, or a herring without
a roe, I would not care ; but to be Menelaus ! I would conspire
against destiny. Ask me not what I would be, if I were not
Thersites : for I care not to be the louse of a lazar, so I were
not Menelaus. Hoy-day ! spirits and fires !

ACT V, Scene i, ll. 56-73

The Grecian Camp.   Before Calchas' tent.

Enter DIOMEDES.

Dio. What, are you up here, ho ? speak.
Cal. [*Within*] Who calls ?
Dio. Diomed. Calchas, I think. Where's your daughter ?

Cal. [*Within*] She comes to you.

Enter TROILUS *and* ULYSSES, *at a distance; after*
them, THERISTES.

Ulyss. Stand where the torch may not discover us.

Enter CRESSIDA.

Tro. Cressid comes forth to him.

Dio.   How now, my charge !

Cres. Now, my sweet guardian ! Hark, a word with you.

[*Whispers.*

Tro. Yea, so familiar !

Ulyss. She will sing any man at first sight.

Ther. And any man may sing her, if he can take her cliff ;
she's noted.

Dio. Will you remember ?

Cres. Remember ! yes.

Dio. Nay, but do, then ;
And let your mind be coupled with your words.

Tro. What should she remember ?

Ulyss. List.

Cres. Sweet honey Greek, tempt me no more to folly.

Ther. Roguery !

Dio. Nay, then,——

Cres. I'll tell you what,——

Dio. Foh, foh ! come, tell a pin : you are forsworn.

Cres. In faith, I cannot : what would you have me do ?

Ther. A juggling trick,—to be secretly open.

Dio. What did you swear you would bestow on me ?

Cres. I prithee, do not hold me to mine oath ;
Bid me do any thing but that, sweet Greek.

Dio. Good night.

Tro. Hold, patience !

Ulyss. How now, Trojan !

Cres. Diomed,——

Dio. No, no, good night : I'll be your fool no more.

Tro. Thy better must.

Cres. Hark, one word in your ear.

Tro. O plague and madness!

Ulyss. You are moved, prince; let us depart, I pray you,
Lest your displeasure should enlarge itself
To wrathful terms: this place is dangerous;
The time right deadly; I beseech you, go.

Tro. Behold, I pray you!

Ulyss. Nay, good my lord, go off:
You flow to great distraction; come, my lord.

Tro. I pray thee, stay.

Ulyss. You have not patience; come.

Tro. I pray you, stay; by hell and all hell's torments,
I will not speak a word!

Dio. And so, good night.

Cres. Nay, but you part in anger.

Tro. Doth that grieve thee?
O wither'd truth!

Ulyss. Why, how now, lord!

Tro. By Jove,
I will be patient.

Cres. Guardian!—why, Greek!

Dio. Foh, foh! adieu; you palter.

Cres. In faith, I do not: come hither once again.

Ulyss. You shake, my lord, at something: will you go?
You will break out.

Tro. She strokes his cheek!

Ulyss. Come, come.

Tro. Nay, stay; by Jove, I will not speak a word:
There is between my will and all offences
A guard of patience: stay a little while.

Ther. How the devil Luxury, with his fat rump and potato-
finger, tickles these together! Fry, lechery, fry!

Dio. But will you, then?

Cres. In faith, I will, la; never trust me else.

Dio. Give me some token for the surety of it.

Cres. I'll fetch you one.

Ulyss. You have sworn patience.

Tro.   Fear me not, sweet lord ;
I will not be myself, nor have cognition
Of what I feel : I am all patience.

Re-enter CRESSIDA.

Ther. Now the pledge ; now, now, now !

Cres. Here, Diomed, keep this sleeve.

Tro. O beauty ! where is thy faith ?

Ulyss.   My lord,—

Tro. I will be patient ; outwardly I will.

Cres. You look upon that sleeve ; behold it well.
He loved me—O false wench !—Give 't me again.

Dio. Whose was 't ?

Cres. It is no matter, now I have 't again.
I will not meet with you to-morrow night :
I prithee, Diomed, visit me no more.

Ther. Now she sharpens : well said, whetstone !

Dio. I shall have it.

Cres.   What, this ?

Dio.   Ay, that.

Cres. O, all you gods ! O pretty, pretty pledge !
Thy master now lies thinking in his bed
Of thee and me, and sighs, and takes my glove,
And gives memorial dainty kisses to it,
As I kiss thee. Nay, do not snatch it from me ;
He that takes that doth take my heart withal.

Dio. I had your heart before, this follows it.

Tro. I did swear patience.

Cres. You shall not have it, Diomed ; faith, you shall not ;
I'll give you something else.

Dio. I will have this : whose was it ?

Cres.   It is no matter.

Dio. Come, tell me whose it was.

Cres. 'Twas one's that loved me better than you will.
But, now you have it, take it.

Dio.   Whose was it?

Cres. By all Diana's waiting-women yond,
And by herself, I will not tell you whose.

Dio. To-morrow will I wear it on my helm,
And grieve his spirit that dares not challenge it.

Tro. Wert thou the devil, and worest it on thy horn,
It should be challenged.

Cres. Well, well, 'tis done, 'tis past : and yet it is not ;
I will not keep my word.

Dio.   Why, then, farewell ;
Thou never shalt mock Diomed again.

Cres. You shall not go : one cannot speak a word,
But it straight starts you.

Dio.   I do not like this fooling.

Ther. Nor I, by Pluto : but that that likes not you pleases
me best.

Dio. What, shall I come ? the hour ?

Cres. Ay, come :—O Jove !—do come :—I shall be plagued.

Dio. Farewell till then.

Cres.   Good night : I prithee, come.
                                        [*Exit Diomedes.*

Troilus, farewell ! one eye yet looks on thee ;
But with my heart the other eye doth see.
Ah, poor our sex ! this fault in us I find,
The error of our eye directs our mind :
What error leads must err ; O, then conclude
Minds sway'd by eyes are full of turpitude.   [*Exit.*

Ther. A proof of strength she could not publish more,
Unless she said ' My mind is now turn'd whore.'

Ulyss. All's done, my lord.

Tro.   It is.

Ulyss.   Why stay we, then ?

Tro. To make a recordation to my soul
Of every syllable that here was spoke.
But if I tell how these two did co-act,
Shall I not lie in publishing a truth ?

402

Sith yet there is a credence in my heart,
An esperance so obstinately strong,
That doth invert the attest of eyes and ears,
As if those organs had deceptious functions,
Created only to calumniate.
Was Cressid here?

 Ulyss.   I cannot conjure, Trojan.

 Tro. She was not, sure.

 Ulyss.   Most sure she was.

 Tro. Why, my negation hath no taste of madness.

 Ulyss. Nor mine, my lord : Cressid was here but now.

 Tro. Let it not be believed for womanhood !
Think, we had mothers ; do not give advantage
To stubborn critics, apt, without a theme,
For depravation, to square the general sex
By Cressid's rule : rather think this not Cressid.

 Ulyss. What hath she done, prince, that can soil our
  mothers ?

 Tro. Nothing at all, unless that this were she.

 Ther. Will he swagger himself out on's own eyes ?

 Tro. This she ? no, this is Diomed's Cressida :
If beauty have a soul, this is not she ;
If souls guide vows, if vows be sanctimonies,
If sanctimony be the gods' delight,
If there be rule in unity itself,
This is not she. O madness of discourse,
That cause sets up with and against itself !
Bi-fold authority ! where reason can revolt
Without perdition, and loss assume all reason
Without revolt : this is, and is not, Cressid.
Within my soul there doth conduce a fight
Of this strange nature that a thing inseparate
Divides more wider than the sky and earth,
And yet the spacious breadth of this division
Admits no orifex for a point as subtle
As Ariachne's broken woof to enter.

Instance, O instance ! strong as Pluto's gates ;
Cressid is mine, tied with the bonds of heaven :
Instance, O instance ! strong as heaven itself ;
The bonds of heaven are slipp'd, dissolved, and loosed ;
And with another knot, five-finger-tied,
The fractions of her faith, orts of her love,
The fragments, scraps, the bits and greasy relics
Of her o'er-eaten faith, are bound to Diomed.

Ulyss. May worthy Troilus be half attach'd
With that which here his passion doth express ?

Tro. Ay, Greek ; and that shall be divulged well
In characters as red as Mars his heart
Inflamed with Venus : never did young man fancy
With so eternal and so fix'd a soul.
Hark, Greek : as much as I do Cressid love,
So much by weight hate I her Diomed :
That sleeve is mine that he'll bear on his helm ;
Were it a casque composed by Vulcan's skill,
My sword should bite it : not the dreadful spout
Which shipmen do the hurricano call,
Constringed in mass by the almighty sun,
Shall dizzy with more clamour Neptune's ear
In his descent than shall my prompted sword
Falling on Diomed.

Ther. He'll tickle it for his concupy.

Tro. O Cressid ! O false Cressid ! false, false, false !
Let all untruths stand by thy stained name,
And they'll seem glorious.

Ulyss.   O, contain yourself ;
Your passion draws ears hither.

Enter ÆNEAS.

Æne. I have been seeking you this hour, my lord :
Hector, by this, is arming him in Troy ;
Ajax, your guard, stays to conduct you home.

Tro. Have with you, prince, My courteous lord, adieu.

Farewell, revolted fair ! and, Diomed,
Stand fast, and wear a castle on thy head !
   Ulyss. I'll bring you to the gates.
   Tro. Accept distracted thanks.

           [*Exeunt Troilus, Æneas, and Ulysses.*
   Ther. Would I could meet that rogue Diomed ! I would
croak like a raven ; I would bode, I would bode. Patroclus
will give me any thing for the intelligence of this whore : the
parrot will not do more for an almond than he for a commodious
drab. Lechery, lechery ; still, wars and lechery ; nothing else
holds fashion : a burning devil take them !

Act V, Scene ii, ll. 1-197

Even in the fan and wind of your fair sword.

Act V, Scene iii, l. 41.

All's Well that Ends Well

'Twere all one

That I should love a bright particular star.

Act I, Scene i, ll. 96-97

Was this fair face the cause, quoth she,
Why the Grecians sacked Troy ?

Act I, Scene iii, ll. 74-75

Countess.   What, pale again ?
My fear hath catch'd your fondness : now I see
The mystery of your loneliness, and find
Your salt tears' head : now to all sense 'tis gross
You love my son ; invention is ashamed,
Against the proclamation of thy passion,
To say thou dost not : therefore tell me true ;
But tell me then, 'tis so ; for, look, thy cheeks
Confess it, th' one to th' other ; and thine eyes
See it so grossly shown in thy behaviours

405

That in their kind they speak it : only sin
And hellish obstinacy tie thy tongue,
That truth should be suspected. Speak, is 't so ?
If it be so, you have wound a goodly clew ;
If it be not, forswear 't : howe'er, I charge thee,
As heaven shall work in me for thine avail,
To tell me truly.

   Helena.   Good madam, pardon me !

 Count. Do you love my son ?

 Hel.   Your pardon, noble mistress !

 Count. Love you my son ?

 Hel.   Do not you love him, madam ?

 Count. Go not about ; my love hath in 't a bond,
The state of your affection ; for your passions
Have to the full appeach'd.

 Hel.   Then, I confess,
Here on my knee, before high heaven and you,
That before you, and next unto high heaven,
I love your son.
My friends were poor, but honest ; so 's my love :
Be not offended ; for it hurts not him
That he is loved of me : I follow him not
By any token of presumptuous suit ;
Nor would I have him till I do deserve him ;
Yet never know how that desert should be.
I know I love in vain, strive against hope ;
Yet in this captious and intenible sieve
I still pour in the waters of my love
And lack not to lose still : thus, Indian-like,
Religious in mine error, I adore
The sun, that looks upon his worshipper,
But knows of him no more. My dearest madam,
Let not your hate encounter with my love
For loving where you do : but if yourself,
Whose aged honour cites a virtuous youth,
Did ever in so true a flame of liking

Wish chastely and love dearly, that your Dian
Was both herself and love ; O, then, give pity
To her, whose state is such that cannot choose
But lend and give where she is sure to lose ;
That seeks not to find that her search implies,
But riddle-like lives sweetly where she dies !

Act I, Scene iii, ll. 175-223

Parolles. What the devil should move me to undertake the recovery of this drum, being not ignorant of the impossibility, and knowing I had no such purpose ? I must give myself some hurts, and say I got them in exploit : yet slight ones will not carry it ; they will say, ' Came you off with so little ? ' and great ones I dare not give. Wherefore, what's the instance ? Tongue, I must put you into a butter-woman's mouth and buy myself another of Bajazet's mule, if you prattle me into these perils.

Second Lord. Is it possible he should know what he is, and be that he is ?

Act IV, Scene i, ll. 37-49

But, fair soul,
In your fine frame hath love no quality ?

Act IV, Scene ii, ll. 3-4

Parolles. If my heart were great,
'Twould burst at this. Captain I'll be no more ;
But I will eat and drink, and sleep as soft
As captain shall : simply the thing I am
Shall make me live.

Act IV, Scene iii, ll. 366-370

All is whole ;
Not one word more of the consumed time.
Let's take the instant by the forward top ;
For we are old, and on our quick'st decrees
The inaudible and noiseless foot of Time
Steals ere we can effect them.

Act V, Scene iii, ll. 37-42

407

P

Measure for Measure

Duke. Spirits are not finely touch'd
But to fine issues, nor Nature never lends
The smallest scruple of her excellence
But, like a thrifty goddess, she determines
Herself the glory of a creditor,
Both thanks and use. But I do bend my speech
To one that can my part in him advertise ;
Hold therefore, Angelo :——
In our remove be thou at full ourself ;
Mortality and mercy in Vienna
Live in thy tongue and heart.

Act I, Scene i, ll. 36-46

Our natures do pursue,
Like rats that ravin down their proper bane,
A thirsty evil ; and when we drink we die.

Act I, Scene ii, ll. 132-134

Lucio [*to Claudio*]. Thy head stands so tickle on thy
shoulders that a milkmaid, if she be in love, may sigh it off.

Act I, Scene ii, ll. 176-178

My holy sir, none better knows than you
How I have ever loved the life removed
And held in idle price to haunt assemblies
Where youth, and cost, and witless bravery keeps.

Act I, Scene iii, ll. 7-10

A nunnery.

Lucio. Gentle and fair, your brother kindly greets you :
Not to be weary with you, he's in prison.
Isabella. Woe me ! for what ?
Lucio. For that which, if myself might be his judge
He should receive his punishment in thanks :
He hath got his friend with child.

408

Isab. Sir, make me not your story.

Lucio.   It is true.
I would not—though 'tis my familiar sin
With maids to seem the lapwing and to jest,
Tongue far from heart—play with all virgins so :
I hold you as a thing ensky'd and sainted,
By your renouncement an immortal spirit,
And to be talk'd with in sincerity,
As with a saint. . . .

                              All hope is gone,
Unless you have the grace by your fair prayer
To soften Angelo. . . .

Isab. I'll see what I can do.

                                        ACT I, Scene iv, ll. 24-37, 68-70, 84

To PROVOST *and* ANGELO *enter* ISABELLA *and* LUCIO.

Provost.   God save your honour !

Angelo. Stay a little while. [*To Isab.*] You're welcome :
    what's your will ?

Isab. I am a woeful suitor to your honour,
Please but your honour hear me.

Ang.   Well ; what's your suit ?

Isab. There is a vice that most I do abhor,
And most desire should meet the blow of justice ;
For which I would not plead, but that I must ;
For which I must not plead, but that I am
At war 'twixt will and will not.

Ang.   Well ; the matter ?

Isab. I have a brother is condemn'd to die :
I do beseech you, let it be his fault,
And not my brother.

Prov. [*Aside*] Heaven give thee moving graces !

Ang. Condemn the fault, and not the actor of it ?
Why, every fault's condemn'd ere it be done :
Mine were the very cipher of a function,
To fine the faults whose fine stands in record,

And let go by the actor.

    Isab.   O just but severe law !
I had a brother, then. Heaven keep your honour !

    Lucio. [*Aside to Isab.*] Give 't not o'er so: to him again,
    entreat him ;
Kneel down before him, hang upon his gown :
You are too cold ; if you should need a pin,
You could not with more tame a tongue desire it :
To him, I say !

    Isab. Must he needs die ?

    Ang.   Maiden, no remedy.

    Isab. Yes ; I do think that you might pardon him,
And neither heaven nor man grieve at the mercy.

    Ang. I will not do 't.

    Isab.   But can you, if you would ?

    Ang. Look, what I will not, that I cannot do.

    Isab. But might you do 't, and do the world no wrong,
If so your heart were touch'd with that remorse
As mine is to him ?

    Ang.   He's sentenced ; 'tis too late.

    Lucio. [*Aside to Isab.*] You are too cold.

    Isab. Too late ? why, no ; I, that do speak a word,
May call it back again. Well, believe this,
No ceremony that to great ones 'longs,
Not the king's crown, nor the deputed sword,
The marshal's truncheon, nor the judge's robe,
Become them with one half so good a grace
As mercy does.
If he had been as you and you as he,
You would have slipt like him ; but he, like you,
Would not have been so stern.

    Ang.   Pray you, be gone.

    Isab. I would to heaven I had your potency,
And you were Isabel ! should it then be thus ?
No ; I would tell what 'twere to be a judge,
And what a prisoner.

Lucio. [*Aside to Isab*.] Ay, touch him; there's the vein.

Ang. Your brother is a forfeit of the law,
And you but waste your words.

Isab.   Alas, alas!
Why, all the souls that were were forfeit once;
And He that might the vantage best have took
Found out the remedy. How would you be,
If He, which is the top of judgement, should
But judge you as you are? O, think on that;
And mercy then will breathe within your lips,
Like man new made.

Ang.   Be you content, fair maid;
It is the law, not I condemn your brother:
Were he my kinsman, brother, or my son,
It should be thus with him: he must die to-morrow.

Isab. To-morrow! O, that's sudden! Spare him, spare
    him!
He's not prepared for death. Even for our kitchens
We kill the fowl of season: shall we serve heaven
With less respect than we do minister
To our gross selves? Good, good my lord, bethink you;
Who is it that hath died for this offence?
There's many have committed it.

Lucio.   [*Aside to Isab*.]   Ay, well said.

Ang. The law hath not been dead, though it hath slept:
Those many had not dared to do that evil,
If the first that did the edict infringe
Had answer'd for his deed: now 'tis awake,
Takes note of what is done; and, like a prophet,
Looks in a glass, that shows what future evils,
Either new, or by remissness new-conceived,
And so in progress to be hatch'd and born,
Are now to have no successive degrees,
But, ere they live, to end.

Isab.   Yet show some pity.

Ang. I show it most of all when I show justice;

For then I pity those I do not know,
Which a dismiss'd offence would after gall ;
And do him right that, answering one foul wrong,
Lives not to act another. Be satisfied ;
Your brother dies to-morrow ; be content.

Isab. So you must be the first that gives this sentence,
And he that suffers. O, it is excellent
To have a giant's strength ; but it is tyrannous
To use it like a giant.

Lucio. [*Aside to Isab.*] That's well said.

Isab. Could great men thunder
As Jove himself does, Jove would ne'er be quiet,
For every pelting, petty officer
Would use his heaven for thunder ;
Nothing but thunder ! Merciful Heaven,
Thou rather with thy sharp and sulphurous bolt
Split'st the unwedgeable and gnarled oak
Than the soft myrtle : but man, proud man,
Drest in a little brief authority,
Most ignorant of what he 's most assured,
His glassy essence, like an angry ape,
Plays such fantastic tricks before high heaven
As make the angels weep ; who, with our spleens,
Would all themselves laugh mortal.

Lucio. [*Aside to Isab.*] O, to him, to him, wench ! he will
relent ;
He's coming ; I perceive't.

Prov. [*Aside*] Pray heaven she win him !

Isab. We cannot weigh our brother with ourself :
Great men may jest with saints ; 'tis wit in them,
But in the less foul profanation.

Lucio. Thou 'rt i' the right, girl ; more o' that.

Isab. That in the captain 's but a choleric word,
Which in the soldier is flat blasphemy.

Lucio. [*Aside to Isab.*] Art avised o' that ? more on't.

Ang. Why do you put these sayings upon me ?

Isab. Because authority, though it err like others,
Hath yet a kind of medicine in itself,
That skins the vice o' the top. Go to your bosom ;
Knock there, and ask your heart what it doth know
That's like my brother's fault : if it confess
A natural guiltiness such as is his,
Let it not sound a thought upon your tongue
Against my brother's life.

Ang.   [*Aside*] She speaks, and 'tis
Such sense, that my sense breeds with it. Fare you well.

Isab. Gentle my lord, turn back.

Ang. I will bethink me : come again to-morrow.

Isab. Hark how I'll bribe you : good my lord, turn back.

Ang. How ! bribe me ?

Isab. Ay, with such gifts that heaven shall share with
    you.

Lucio. [*Aside to Isab.*] You had marr'd all else.

Isab. Not with fond shekels of the tested gold,
Or stones whose rates are either rich or poor
As fancy values them ; but with true prayers
That shall be up at heaven and enter there
Ere sun-rise, prayers from preserved souls,
From fasting maids whose minds are dedicate
To nothing temporal.

Ang.   Well ; come to me to-morrow.

Lucio. [*Aside to Isab.*] Go to ; 'tis well ; away !

Isab. Heaven keep your honour safe !

Ang.   [*Aside*] Amen :
For I am that way going to temptation,
Where prayers cross.

Isab.   At what hour to-morrow
Shall I attend your lordship ?

Ang.   At any time 'fore noon.

Isab. 'Save your honour !

                        [*Exeunt Isabella, Lucio, and Provost.*

Ang.   From thee, even from thy virtue !

What's this, what's this ? Is this her fault or mine ?
The tempter or the tempted, who sins most ?
Ha !
Not she ; nor doth she tempt : but it is I
That, lying by the violet in the sun,
Do as the carrion does, not as the flower,
Corrupt with virtuous season. Can it be
That modesty may more betray our sense
Than woman's lightness ? Having waste ground enough,
Shall we desire to raze the sanctuary
And pitch our evils there ? O, fie, fie, fie !
What dost thou, or what art thou, Angelo ?
Dost thou desire her foully for those things
That make her good ? O, let her brother live :
Thieves for their robbery have authority
When judges steal themselves. What, do I love her,
That I desire to hear her speak again,
And feast upon her eyes ? What is 't I dream on ?
O cunning enemy, that, to catch a saint,
With saints dost bait thy hook ! Most dangerous
Is that temptation that doth goad us on
To sin in loving virtue : never could the strumpet,
With all her double vigour, art and nature,
Once stir my temper ; but this virtuous maid
Subdues me quite. Ever till now,
When men were fond, I smiled and wonder'd how.

ACT II, Scene ii, ll. 25-187

A room in a prison.

Enter, severally, DUKE *disguised as a friar, and* PROVOST.
Duke. Hail to you, provost ! so I think you are.
Prov. I am the provost. What's your will, good friar ?
Duke. Bound by my charity and my blest order,
I come to visit the afflicted spirits
Here in the prison. Do me the common right
To let me see them and to make me know

The nature of their crimes, that I may minister
To them accordingly.

    Prov. I would do more than that, if more were needful.

Enter JULIET.

Look, here comes one : a gentlewoman of mine,
Who, falling in the flaws of her own youth,
Hath blister'd her report : she is with child ;
And he that got it, sentenced ; a young man
More fit to do another such offence
Than die for this.

    Duke. When must he die ?

    Prov.   As I do think, to-morrow.
I have provided for you : stay awhile,   [*To Juliet.*
And you shall be conducted.

    Duke. Repent you, fair one, of the sin you carry ?

    Jul. I do ; and bear the shame most patiently.

    Duke. I'll teach you how you shall arraign your conscience,
And try your penitence, if it be sound,
Or hollowly put on.

    Jul.   I'll gladly learn.

    Duke. Love you the man that wrong'd you ?

    Jul. Yes, as I love the woman that wrong'd him.

    Duke. So then it seems your most offenceful act
Was mutually committed ?

    Jul.   Mutually.

    Duke. Then was your sin of heavier kind than his.

    Jul. I do confess it, and repent it, father.

    Duke. 'Tis meet so, daughter : but lest you do repent,
As that the sin hath brought you to this shame,
Which sorrow is always towards ourselves, not heaven,
Showing we would not spare heaven as we love it,
But as we stand in fear,—

    Jul. I do repent me, as it is an evil,
And take the shame with joy.

    Duke.   There rest.

415

Your partner, as I hear, must die to-morrow,
And I am going with instruction to him.
Grace go with you, Benedicite!   [*Exit.*

    Jul. Must die to-morrow! O injurious love,
That respites me a life, whose very comfort
Is still a dying horror!
    Prov.   'Tis pity of him.   [*Exeunt.*
ACT II, Scene iii, ll. 1-42

A room in the prison.

Enter DUKE *disguised as before,* CLAUDIO, *and* PROVOST.

    Duke. So then you hope of pardon from Lord Angelo?
    Claud. The miserable have no other medicine
But only hope:
I've hope to live, and am prepared to die.
    Duke. Be absolute for death; either death or life
Shall thereby be the sweeter. Reason thus with life:
If I do lose thee, I do lose a thing
That none but fools would keep: a breath thou art,
Servile to all the skyey influences,
That dost this habitation, where thou keep'st,
Hourly afflict: merely, thou art death's fool;
For him thou labour'st by thy flight to shun
And yet runn'st toward him still. Thou art not noble;
For all the accommodations that thou bear'st
Are nursed by baseness. Thou 'rt by no means valiant;
For thou dost fear the soft and tender fork
Of a poor worm. Thy best of rest is sleep,
And that thou oft provokest; yet grossly fear'st
Thy death, which is no more. Thou art not thyself;
For thou exist'st on many a thousand grains
That issue out of dust. Happy thou art not;
For what thou hast not, still thou strivest to get,
And what thou hast, forget'st. Thou art not certain;
For thy complexion shifts to strange effects,
After the moon. If thou art rich, thou'rt poor;

416

For, like an ass whose back with ingots bows,
Thou bear'st thy heavy riches but a journey,
And death unloads thee. Friend hast thou none ;
For thine own bowels, which do call thee sire,
The mere effusion of thy proper loins,
Do curse the gout, serpigo, and the rheum,
For ending thee no sooner. Thou hast nor youth nor age,
But, as it were, an after-dinner's sleep,
Dreaming on both ; for all thy blessed youth
Becomes as aged, and doth beg the alms
Of palsied eld ; and when thou art old and rich,
Thou hast neither heat, affection, limb, nor beauty,
To make thy riches pleasant. What's yet in this
That bears the name of life ? Yet in this life
Lie hid moe thousand deaths : yet death we fear,
That makes these odds all even.

  Claud.   I humbly thank you.
To sue to live, I find I seek to die ;
And, seeking death, find life : let it come on.

  Isab. [*Within*] What, ho ! Peace here ; grace and good
  company !

  Prov. Who's there ? come in : the wish deserves a welcome.

  Duke. Dear sir, ere long I'll visit you again.

  Claud. Most holy sir, I thank you.

Enter ISABELLA.

  Isab. My business is a word or two with Claudio.

  Prov. And very welcome. Look, signior, here's your
  sister.

  Duke. Provost, a word with you.

  Prov. As many as you please.

  Duke. Bring me to hear them speak, where I may be con-
cealed.   [*Exeunt Duke and Provost.*

  Claud. Now, sister, what's the comfort ?

  Isab.   Why,

As all comforts are ; most good, most good indeed.
Lord Angelo, having affairs to heaven,
Intends you for his swift ambassador,
Where you shall be an everlasting leiger :
Therefore your best appointment make with speed ;
To-morrow you set on.

 Claud.   Is there no remedy ?

 Isab. None, but such remedy as, to save a head,
To cleave a heart in twain.

 Claud.   But is there any ?

 Isab. Yes, brother, you may live :
There is a devilish mercy in the judge,
If you'll implore it, that will free your life,
But fetter you till death.

 Claud.   Perpetual durance ?

 Isab. Ay, just ; perpetual durance, a restraint,
Though all the world's vastidity you had,
To a determined scope.

 Claud.   But in what nature ?

 Isab. In such a one as, you consenting to 't,
Would bark your honour from that trunk you bear,
And leave you naked.

 Claud.   Let me know the point.

 Isab. O, I do fear thee, Claudio ; and I quake,
Lest thou a feverous life shouldst entertain,
And six or seven winters more respect
Than a perpetual honour. Darest thou die ?
The sense of death is most in apprehension ;
And the poor beetle, that we tread upon,
In corporal sufferance finds a pang as great
As when a giant dies.

 Claud.   Why give you me this shame ?
Think you I can a resolution fetch
From flowery tenderness ? If I must die,
I will encounter darkness as a bride,
And hug it in mine arms.

Isab. There spake my brother ; there my father's grave
Did utter forth a voice. Yes, thou must die :
Thou art too noble to conserve a life
In base appliances. This outward-sainted deputy,
Whose settled visage and deliberate word
Nips youth i' the head and follies doth emmew
As falcon doth the fowl, is yet a devil ;
His filth within being cast, he would appear
A pond as deep as hell.

    Claud.   The prenzie Angelo !

    Isab. O, 'tis the cunning livery of hell,
The damned'st body to invest and cover
In prenzie guards ! Dost thou think, Claudio ?
If I would yield him my virginity,
Thou mightst be freed.

    Claud.   O heavens ! it cannot be.

    Isab. Yes, he would give 't thee, from this rank offence,
So to offend him still. This night's the time
That I should do what I abhor to name,
Or else thou diest to-morrow.

    Claud.   Thou shalt not do 't.

    Isab. O, were it but my life,
I'ld throw it down for your deliverance
As frankly as a pin.

    Claud.   Thanks, dear Isabel.

    Isab. Be ready, Claudio, for your death to-morrow.

    Claud. Yes. Has he affections in him,
That thus can make him bite the law by the nose,
When he would force it ? Sure, it is no sin ;
Or of the deadly seven it is the least.

    Isab. Which is the least ?

    Claud. If it were damnable, he being so wise,
Why would he for the momentary trick
Be perdurably fined ? O Isabel !

    Isab. What says my brother ?

    Claud.   Death is a fearful thing.

Isab. And shamed life a hateful.

Claud. Ay, but to die, and go we know not where ;
To lie in cold obstruction and to rot ;
This sensible warm motion to become
A kneaded clod ; and the delighted spirit
To bathe in fiery floods, or to reside
In thrilling region of thick-ribbed ice ;
To be imprison'd in the viewless winds,
And blown with restless violence round about
The pendent world ; or to be worse than worst
Of those that lawless and incertain thought
Imagine howling : 'tis too horrible !
The weariest and most loathed worldly life
That age, ache, penury and imprisonment
Can lay on nature is a paradise
To what we fear of death.

Isab. Alas, alas !

Claud. Sweet sister, let me live :
What sin you do to save a brother's life,
Nature dispenses with the deed so far
That it becomes a virtue.

Isab. O you beast !
O faithless coward ! O dishonest wretch !
Wilt thou be made a man out of my vice ?
Is 't not a kind of incest, to take life
From thine own sister's shame ? What should I think ?
Heaven shield my mother play'd my father fair !
For such a warped slip of wilderness
Ne'er issued from his blood. Take my defiance !
Die, perish ! Might but my bending down
Reprieve thee from thy fate, it should proceed :
I'll pray a thousand prayers for thy death,
No word to save thee.

Claud. Nay, hear me, Isabel.

Isab. O, fie, fie, fie !
Thy sin's not accidental, but a trade.

Mercy to thee would prove itself a bawd :
'Tis best that thou diest quickly.

 Claud.   O hear me, Isabella !

ACT III, Scene i, ll. 1-151

I will presently to Saint Luke's : there, at the moated grange, resides this dejected Mariana.

ACT III, Scene i, ll. 276-278

The moated grange at ST LUKE'S.

Enter MARIANA *and a* BOY.

BOY *sings*.

Take, O, take those lips away,
 That so sweetly were forsworn ;
And those eyes, the break of day,
 Lights that do mislead the morn :
But my kisses bring again, bring again ;
Seals of love, but sealed in vain, sealed in vain.

Mari. Break off thy song, and haste thee quick away.

ACT IV, Scene i, ll. 1-7

A room in the prison.

Enter PROVOST *and* POMPEY.

Prov. Come, sir, leave me your snatches, and yield me a direct answer. To-morrow morning are to die Claudio and Barnardine. Here is in our prison a common executioner, who in his office lacks a helper : if you will take it on you to assist him, it shall redeem you from your gyves ; if not, you shall have your full time of imprisonment and your deliverance with an unpitied whipping, for you have been a notorious bawd.

Pom. Sir, I have been an unlawful bawd time out of mind ; but yet I will be content to be a lawful hangman. I would be glad to receive some instruction from my fellow partner.

Prov. What, ho ! Abhorson ! Where's Abhorson, there ?

Enter ABHORSON.

Abhor. Do you call, sir ?

421

Prov. Sirrah, here's a fellow will help you to-morrow in your execution. If you think it meet, compound with him by the year, and let him abide here with you ; if not, use him for the present and dismiss him. He cannot plead his estimation with you ; he hath been a bawd.

Abhor. A bawd, sir ? fie upon him ! he will discredit our mystery. . . .

Enter DUKE *disguised as before.*

Duke. What is that Barnardine who is to be executed in the afternoon ?

Prov. A Bohemian born, but here nursed up and bred ; one that is a prisoner nine years old.

Duke. How came it that the absent duke had not either delivered him to his liberty or executed him ? I have heard it was ever his manner to do so.

Prov. His friends still wrought reprieves for him : and, indeed, his fact, till now in the government of Lord Angelo, came not to an undoubtful proof.

Duke. It is now apparent ?

Prov. Most manifest, and not denied by himself.

Duke. Hath he borne himself penitently in prison ? how seems he to be touched ?

Prov. A man that apprehends death no more dreadfully but as a drunken sleep ; careless, reckless, and fearless of what's past, present, or to come ; insensible of mortality, and desperately mortal.

Duke. He wants advice.

Prov. He will hear none : he hath evermore had the liberty of the prison ; give him leave to escape hence, he would not : drunk many times a day, if not many days entirely drunk. We have very oft awaked him, as if to carry him to execution, and showed him a seeming warrant for it : it hath not moved him at all.

ACT IV, Scene ii, ll. 6-30, 132-161

Look, the unfolding star calls up the shepherd.

ACT IV, Scene ii, l. 219

Another room in the prison.

Enter POMPEY.

Pom. I am as well acquainted here as I was in our house of profession : one would think it were Mistress Overdone's own house, for here be many of her old customers. . . .

Enter ABHORSON.

Abhor. Sirrah, bring Barnardine hither.

Pom. Master Barnardine ! you must rise and be hanged, Master Barnardine !

Abhor. What, ho, Barnardine !

Bar. [*Within*] A pox o' your throats ! Who makes that noise there ? What are you ?

Pom. Your friends, sir ; the hangman. You must be so good, sir, to rise and be put to death.

Bar. [*Within*] Away, you rogue, away ! I am sleepy.

Abhor. Tell him he must awake, and that quickly too.

Pom. Pray, Master Barnardine, awake till you are executed, and sleep afterwards.

Abhor. Go in to him, and fetch him out.

Pom. He is coming, sir, he is coming ; I hear his straw rustle.

Abhor. Is the axe upon the block, sirrah ?

Pom. Very ready, sir.

Enter BARNARDINE.

Bar. How now, Abhorson ? what's the news with you ?

Abhor. Truly, sir, I would desire you to clap into your prayers ; for, look you, the warrant's come.

Bar. You rogue, I have been drinking all night ; I am not fitted for 't.

Pom. O, the better, sir ; for he that drinks all night, and is hanged betimes in the morning, may sleep the sounder all the next day.

Abhor. Look you, sir; here comes your ghostly father: do we jest now, think you?

Enter DUKE *disguised as before.*

Duke. Sir, induced by my charity, and hearing how hastily you are to depart, I am come to advise you, comfort you and pray with you.

Bar. Friar, not I: I have been drinking hard all night, and I will have more time to prepare me, or they shall beat out my brains with billets: I will not consent to die this day, that's certain.

Duke. O, sir, you must: and therefore I beseech you
Look forward on the journey you shall go.

Bar. I swear I will not die to-day for any man's persuasion.

Duke. But hear you.

Bar. Not a word: if you have any thing to say to me, come to my ward; for thence will not I to-day.

ACT IV, Scene iii, ll. 1-4, 22-67

Lucio. They say the duke will be here to-morrow. By my troth, Isabel, I loved thy brother: if the old fantastical duke of dark corners had been at home, he had lived. [*Exit Isabella.*

Duke. Sir, the duke is marvellous little beholding to your reports; but the best is, he lives not in them.

Lucio. Friar, thou knowest not the duke so well as I do: he's a better woodman than thou takest him for.

Duke. Well, you'll answer this one day. Fare ye well.

Lucio. Nay, tarry; I'll go along with thee: I can tell thee pretty tales of the duke.

Duke. You have told me too many of him already, sir, if they be true; if not true, none were enough.

Lucio. I was once before him for getting a wench with child.

Duke. Did you such a thing?

Lucio. Yes, marry, did I: but I was fain to forswear it; they would else have married me to the rotten medlar.

Duke. Sir, your company is fairer than honest. Rest you well.

Lucio. By my troth, I'll go with thee to the lane's end : if bawdy talk offend you, we'll have very little of it. Nay, friar, I am a kind of burr ; I shall stick.

ACT IV, Scene iii, ll. 161-190

Isabella. Is it not strange and strange ?
Duke.   Nay, it is ten times strange.

ACT V, Scene i, l. 42

Let the devil
Be sometime honour'd for his burning throne !

ACT V, Scene i, ll. 294-295

Duke [disguised].   My business in this state
Made me a looker on here in Vienna,
Where I have seen corruption boil and bubble
Till it o'er-run the stew ; laws for all faults,
But faults so countenanced, that the strong statutes
Stand like the forfeits in a barber's shop,
As much in mock as mark.
    Escalus. Slander to the state ! Away with him to
        prison ! . . .
    Lucio. Come, sir ; come, sir ; come, sir ; foh, sir ! Why,
you bald-pated, lying rascal, you must be hooded, must you ?
Show your knave's visage, with a pox to you ! show your
sheep-biting face, and be hanged an hour ! Will't not off ?
        [*Pulls off the friar's hood, and discovers the Duke.*
    Duke. Thou art the first knave that e'er madest a duke.

ACT V, Scene i, ll. 318-325, 355-361

AFTERNOON

PART II
OTHELLO
MACBETH
KING LEAR

Othello, the Moor of Venice

Keep up your bright swords, for the dew will rust them.

Act I, Scene ii, l. 59

Othello. Most potent, grave, and reverend signiors,
My very noble and approved good masters,
That I have ta'en away this old man's daughter,
It is most true ; true, I have married her :
The very head and front of my offending
Hath this extent, no more. Rude am I in my speech,
And little bless'd with the soft phrase of peace ;
For since these arms of mine had seven years' pith,
Till now some nine moons wasted, they have used
Their dearest action in the tented field,
And little of this great world can I speak,
More than pertains to feats of broil and battle,
And therefore little shall I grace my cause
In speaking for myself. Yet, by your gracious patience,
I will a round unvarnish'd tale deliver
Of my whole course of love ; what drugs, what charms,
What conjuration and what mighty magic,
For such proceeding I am charged withal,
I won his daughter.
Brabantio.   A maiden never bold ;
Of spirit so still and quiet, that her motion
Blush'd at herself. . . .
Oth. Her father loved me ; oft invited me ;
Still question'd me the story of my life,
From year to year, the battles, sieges, fortunes,
That I have pass'd.
I ran it through, even from my boyish days,
To the very moment that he bade me tell it ;
Wherein I spake of most disastrous chances,
Of moving accidents by flood and field,

429

Of hair-breadth scapes i' the imminent deadly breach,
Of being taken by the insolent foe
And sold to slavery, of my redemption thence
And portance in my travels' history :
Wherein of antres vast and deserts idle,
Rough quarries, rocks and hills whose heads touch heaven,
It was my hint to speak,—such was the process ;
And of the Cannibals that each other eat,
The Anthropophagi and men whose heads
Do grow beneath their shoulders. This to hear
Would Desdemona seriously incline :
But still the house-affairs would draw her thence :
Which ever as she could with haste dispatch,
She 'ld come again, and with a greedy ear
Devour up my discourse : which I observing,
Took once a pliant hour, and found good means
To draw from her a prayer of earnest heart
That I would all my pilgrimage dilate,
Whereof by parcels she had something heard,
But not intentively : I did consent,
And often did beguile her of her tears,
When I did speak of some distressful stroke
That my youth suffer'd. My story being done,
She gave me for my pains a world of sighs :
She swore, in faith, 'twas strange, 'twas passing strange,
'Twas pitiful, 'twas wondrous pitiful :
She wish'd she had not heard it, yet she wish'd
That heaven had made her such a man : she thank'd me,
And bade me, if I had a friend that loved her,
I should but teach him how to tell my story,
And that would woo her. Upon this hint I spake :
She loved me for the dangers I had pass'd,
And I loved her that she did pity them.
This only is the witchcraft I have used :
Here comes the lady ; let her witness it.

ACT I, Scene iii, ll. 76-96, 128-170

Desdemona. Dear lords, if I be left behind,
A moth of peace, and he go to the war,
The rites for which I love him are bereft me,
And I a heavy interim shall support
By his dear absence. Let me go with him.

ACT I, Scene iii, ll. 256-260

Othello. O my fair warrior !
Desdemona.   My dear Othello !
Oth. It gives me wonder great as my content
To see you here before me. O my soul's joy !
If after every tempest come such calms,
May the winds blow till they have waken'd death !
And let the labouring bark climb hills of seas
Olympus-high and duck again as low
As hell's from heaven ! If it were now to die,
'Twere now to be most happy ; for, I fear,
My soul hath her content so absolute
That not another comfort like to this
Succeeds in unknown fate.
Des.   The heavens forbid
But that our loves and comforts should increase,
Even as our days do grow !
Oth.   Amen to that, sweet powers !
I cannot speak enough of this content ;
It stops me here ; it is too much of joy :
And this, and this, the greatest discords be [*Kissing her.*
That e'er our hearts shall make !

ACT II, Scene i, ll. 184-201

Silence that dreadful bell : it frights the isle
From her propriety.

ACT II, Scene iii, ll. 175-176

The garden of the castle.

. . . [*Exeunt Desdemona and Emilia.*
Othello. Excellent wretch ! Perdition catch my soul,

431

But I do love thee ! and when I love thee not,
Chaos is come again.

    Iago. My noble lord,—

    Oth.   What dost thou say, Iago ?

    Iago. Did Michael Cassio, when you woo'd my lady,
Know of your love ?

    Oth. He did, from first to last : why dost thou ask ?

    Iago. But for a satisfaction of my thought ;
No further harm.

    Oth.   Why of thy thought, Iago ?

    Iago. I did not think he had been acquainted with her.

    Oth. O, yes ; and went between us very oft.

    Iago. Indeed !

    Oth. Indeed ! ay, indeed : discern'st thou aught in that ?
Is he not honest ?

    Iago.   Honest, my lord !

    Oth.   Honest ! ay, honest.

    Iago. My lord, for aught I know.

    Oth. What dost thou think ?

    Iago.   Think, my lord !

    Oth.   Think, my lord !
By heaven, he echoes me,
As if there were some monster in his thought
Too hideous to be shown.   Thou dost mean something :
I heard thee say even now, thou likedst not that,
When Cassio left my wife : what didst not like ?
And when I told thee he was of my counsel
In my whole course of wooing, thou criedst ' Indeed ! '
And didst contract and purse thy brow together
As if thou then hadst shut up in thy brain
Some horrible conceit : if thou dost love me,
Show me thy thought.

    Iago. My lord, you know I love you.

    Oth.   I think thou dost ;
And, for I know thou 'rt full of love and honesty,
And weigh'st thy words before thou givest them breath,

Therefore these stops of thine fright me the more :
For such things in a false disloyal knave
Are tricks of custom, but in a man that's just
They are close delations, working from the heart
That passion cannot rule.

    Iago.   For Michael Cassio,
I dare be sworn I think that he is honest.

    Oth. I think so too.

    Iago.   Men should be what they seem ;
Or those that be not, would they might seem none !

    Oth. Certain, men should be what they seem.

    Iago. Why, then, I think Cassio's an honest man.

    Oth. Nay, yet there's more in this :
I prithee, speak to me as to thy thinkings,
As thou dost ruminate, and give thy worst of thoughts
The worst of words.

    Iago.   Good my lord, pardon me :
Though I am bound to every act of duty,
I am not bound to that all slaves are free to.
Utter my thoughts ? Why, say they are vile and false ;
As where's that palace whereinto foul things
Sometimes intrude not ? who has a breast so pure,
But some uncleanly apprehensions
Keep leets and law-days and in session sit
With meditations lawful ?

    Oth. Thou dost conspire against thy friend, Iago,
If thou but think'st him wrong'd and makest his ear
A stranger to thy thoughts.

    Iago.   I do beseech you—
Though I perchance am vicious in my guess,
As, I confess, it is my nature's plague
To spy into abuses, and oft my jealousy
Shapes faults that are not—that your wisdom yet,
From one that so imperfectly conceits,
Would take no notice, nor build yourself a trouble
Out of his scattering and unsure observance.

It were not for your quiet nor your good,
Nor for my manhood, honesty, or wisdom,
To let you know my thoughts.

    Oth.   What dost thou mean ?

    Iago. Good name in man and woman, dear my lord,
Is the immediate jewel of their souls :
Who steals my purse steals trash ; 'tis something, nothing ;
'Twas mine, 'tis his, and has been slave to thousands ;
But he that filches from me my good name
Robs me of that which not enriches him
And makes me poor indeed.

    Oth. By heaven, I'll know thy thoughts.

    Iago. You cannot, if my heart were in your hand ;
Nor shall not, whilst 'tis in my custody.

    Oth. Ha !

    Iago.   O, beware, my lord, of jealousy ;
It is the green-eyed monster which doth mock
The meat it feeds on : that cuckold lives in bliss
Who, certain of his fate, loves not his wronger ;
But, O, what damned minutes tells he o'er
Who dotes, yet doubts, suspects, yet strongly loves !

    Oth. O misery !

    Iago. Poor and content is rich and rich enough,
But riches fineless is as poor as winter
To him that ever fears he shall be poor.
Good heaven, the souls of all my tribe defend
From jealousy !

    Oth.   Why, why is this ?
Think'st thou I'ld make a life of jealousy,
To follow still the changes of the moon
With fresh suspicions ? No ; to be once in doubt
Is once to be resolved : exchange me for a goat,
When I shall turn the business of my soul
To such exsufflicate and blown surmises,
Matching thy inference. 'Tis not to make me jealous
To say my wife is fair, feeds well, loves company,

434

Is free of speech, sings, plays and dances well ;
Where virtue is, these are more virtuous :
Nor from mine own weak merits will I draw
The smallest fear or doubt of her revolt ;
For she had eyes, and chose me. No, Iago ;
I'll see before I doubt ; when I doubt, prove ;
And on the proof, there is no more but this,—
Away at once with love or jealousy !

    Iago. I am glad of it ; for now I shall have reason
To show the love and duty that I bear you
With franker spirit : therefore, as I am bound,
Receive it from me. I speak not yet of proof.
Look to your wife ; observe her well with Cassio ;
Wear your eye thus, not jealous nor secure :
I would not have your free and noble nature,
Out of self-bounty, be abused ; look to 't
I know our country disposition well ;
In Venice they do let heaven see the pranks
They dare not show their husbands ; their best conscience
Is not to leave 't undone, but keep 't unknown.

    Oth. Dost thou say so ?

    Iago. She did deceive her father, marrying you ;
And when she seem'd to shake and fear your looks,
She loved them most.

    Oth.   And so she did.

    Iago.   Why, go to then ;
She that, so young, could give out such a seeming,
To seel her father's eyes up close as oak—
He thought 'twas witchcraft—but I am much to blame ;
I humbly do beseech you of your pardon
For too much loving you.

    Oth.   I am bound to thee for ever

    Iago. I see this hath a little dash'd your spirits.

    Oth. Not a jot, not a jot.

    Iago.   I' faith, I fear it has.
I hope you will consider what is spoke

Comes from my love. But I do see you're moved:
I am to pray you not to strain my speech
To grosser issues nor to larger reach
Than to suspicion.

    Oth. I will not.

    Iago.   Should you do so, my lord,
My speech should fall into such vile success
As my thoughts aim not at. Cassio's my worthy friend—
My lord, I see you're moved.

    Oth.   No, not much moved:
I do not think but Desdemona's honest.

    Iago. Long live she so! and long live you to think so!

    Oth. And yet, how nature erring from itself,—

    Iago. Ay, there's the point: as—to be bold with you—
Not to affect many proposed matches
Of her own clime, complexion, and degree,
Whereto we see in all things nature tends—
Foh! one may smell in such a will most rank,
Foul disproportion, thoughts unnatural.
But pardon me; I do not in position
Distinctly speak of her; though I may fear
Her will, recoiling to her better judgement,
May fall to match you with her country forms
And happily repent.

    Oth.   Farewell, farewell:
If more thou dost perceive, let me know more;
Set on thy wife to observe: leave me, Iago.

    Iago. [*Going*] My lord, I take my leave.

    Oth. Why did I marry? This honest creature doubtless
Sees and knows more, much more, than he unfolds.

    Iago. [*Returning*] My lord, I would I might entreat your
      honour
To scan this thing no further; leave it to time:
Though it be fit that Cassio have his place,
For, sure, he fills it up with great ability,
Yet, if you please to hold him off awhile,

You shall by that perceive him and his means:
Note, if your lady strain his entertainment
With any strong or vehement importunity;
Much will be seen in that. In the mean time,
Let me be thought too busy in my fears—
As worthy cause I have to fear I am—
And hold her free, I do beseech your honour.

    Oth. Fear not my government.

    Iago. I once more take my leave.   *[Exit.*

    Oth. This fellow's of exceeding honesty,
And knows all qualities, with a learned spirit,
Of human dealings. If I do prove her haggard,
Though that her jesses were my dear heart-strings,
I 'ld whistle her off and let her down the wind,
To prey at fortune. Haply, for I am black
And have not those soft parts of conversation
That chamberers have, or for I am declined
Into the vale of years,—yet that's not much—
She's gone. I am abused; and my relief
Must be to loathe her. O curse of marriage,
That we can call these delicate creatures ours,
And not their appetites! I had rather be a toad,
And live upon the vapour of a dungeon,
Than keep a corner in the thing I love
For others' uses. Yet, 'tis the plague of great ones;
Prerogatived are they less than the base;
'Tis destiny unshunnable, like death:
Even then this forked plague is fated to us
When we do quicken. Desdemona comes:

    Re-enter DESDEMONA *and* EMILIA.

If she be false, O, then heaven mocks itself!
I'll not believe 't. . . .

    Iago. I will in Cassio's lodging lose this napkin,
And let him find it. Trifles light as air
Are to the jealous confirmations strong

As proofs of holy writ: this may do something.
The Moor already changes with my poison:
Dangerous conceits are, in their natures, poisons,
Which at the first are scarce found to distaste,
But with a little act upon the blood,
Burn like the mines of sulphur. I did say so:
Look, where he comes!

Re-enter OTHELLO.

                     Not poppy, nor mandragora,
Nor all the drowsy syrups of the world,
Shall ever medicine thee to that sweet sleep
Which thou owedst yesterday.

    Oth.   Ha! ha! false to me?
    Iago. Why, how now, general! no more of that.
    Oth. Avaunt! be gone! thou hast set me on the rack:
I swear 'tis better to be much abused
Than but to know 't a little.

    Iago.   How now, my lord!
    Oth. What sense had I of her stol'n hours of lust?
I saw 't not, thought it not, it harm'd not me:
I slept the next night well, was free and merry;
I found not Cassio's kisses on her lips:
He that is robb'd, not wanting what is stol'n,
Let him not know 't, and he's not robb'd at all.

    Iago. I am sorry to hear this.
    Oth. I had been happy, if the general camp,
Pioners and all, had tasted her sweet body,
So I had nothing known. O, now, for ever
Farewell the tranquil mind! farewell content!
Farewell the plumed troop, and the big wars,
That make ambition virtue! O, farewell!
Farewell the neighing steed, and the shrill trump,
The spirit-stirring drum, the ear-piercing fife,
The royal banner, and all quality,
Pride, pomp and circumstance of glorious war!
And, O you mortal engines, whose rude throats

The immortal Jove's dread clamours counterfeit,
Farewell! Othello's occupation's gone!

Iago. Is 't possible, my lord?

Oth. Villain, be sure thou prove my love a whore,
Be sure of it; give me the ocular proof;
Or, by the worth of man's eternal soul,
Thou hadst been better have been born a dog
Than answer my waked wrath!

Iago.   Is 't come to this?

Oth. Make me to see 't; or, at the least, so prove it,
That the probation bear no hinge nor loop
To hang a doubt on; or woe upon thy life!

Iago. My noble lord,—

Oth. If thou dost slander her and torture me,
Never pray more; abandon all remorse;
On horror's head horrors accumulate;
Do deeds to make heaven weep, all earth amazed;
For nothing canst thou to damnation add
Greater than that.

Iago.   O grace! O heaven forgive me!
Are you a man? have you a soul or sense?
God be wi' you; take mine office. O wretched fool,
That livest to make thine honesty a vice!
O monstrous world! Take note, take note, O world,
To be direct and honest is not safe.
I thank you for this profit; and from hence
I'll love no friend, sith love breeds such offence.

Oth. Nay, stay: thou shouldst be honest.

Iago. I should be wise, for honesty's a fool
And loses that it works for.

Oth.   By the world,
I think my wife be honest and think she is not;
I think that thou art just and think thou art not.
I'll have some proof. Her name, that was as fresh
As Dian's visage, is now begrimed and black
As mine own face. If there be cords, or knives,

Poison, or fire, or suffocating streams,
I'll not endure it. Would I were satisfied !

Iago. I see, sir, you are eaten up with passion :
I do repent me that I put it to you.
You would be satisfied ?

  Oth.   Would ! nay, I will.

Iago. And may : but, how ? how satisfied, my lord ?
Would you, the supervisor, grossly gape on—
Behold her topp'd ?

  Oth.   Death and damnation ! O !

Iago. It were a tedious difficulty, I think,
To bring them to that prospect : damn them then,
If ever mortal eyes do see them bolster
More than their own ! What then ? how then ?
What shall I say ? Where's satisfaction ?
It is impossible you should see this,
Were they as prime as goats, as hot as monkeys,
As salt as wolves in pride, and fools as gross
As ignorance made drunk. But yet, I say,
If imputation and strong circumstances,
Which lead directly to the door of truth,
Will give you satisfaction, you may have 't.

  Oth. Give me a living reason she's disloyal.

Iago. I do not like the office :
But, sith I am enter'd in this cause so far,
Prick'd to 't by foolish honesty and love,
I will go on. I lay with Cassio lately ;
And, being troubled with a raging tooth,
I could not sleep.
There are a kind of men so loose of soul,
That in their sleeps will mutter their affairs :
One of this kind is Cassio :
In sleep I heard him say ' Sweet Desdemona,
Let us be wary, let us hide our loves ; '
And then, sir, would he gripe and wring my hand,
Cry ' O sweet creature ! ' and then kiss me hard,

As if he pluck'd up kisses by the roots
That grew upon my lips : then laid his leg
Over my thigh, and sigh'd, and kiss'd ; and then
Cried ' Cursed fate that gave thee to the Moor ! '

Oth. O monstrous ! monstrous !

Iago.   Nay, this was but his dream.

Oth. But this denoted a foregone conclusion :
'Tis a shrewd doubt, though it be but a dream.

Iago. And this may help to thicken other proofs
That do demonstrate thinly.

Oth.   I'll tear her all to pieces.

Iago. Nay, but be wise : yet we see nothing done ;
She may be honest yet. Tell me but this,
Have you not sometimes seen a handkerchief
Spotted with strawberries in your wife's hand ?

Oth. I gave her such a one ; 'twas my first gift.

Iago. I know not that : but such a handkerchief—
I am sure it was your wife's—did I to-day
See Cassio wipe his beard with.

Oth.   If it be that,—

Iago. If it be that, or any that was hers,
It speaks against her with the other proofs.

Oth. O, that the slave had forty thousand lives !
One is too poor, too weak for my revenge.
Now do I see 'tis true. Look here, Iago ;
All my fond love thus do I blow to heaven.
'Tis gone.
Arise, black vengeance, from thy hollow cell !
Yield up, O love, thy crown and hearted throne
To tyrannous hate ! Swell, bosom, with thy fraught,
For 'tis of aspics' tongues !

Iago.   Yet be content.

Oth. O, blood, blood, blood !

Iago. Patience, I say ; your mind perhaps, may change.

Oth. Never, Iago. Like to the Pontic sea,
Whose icy current and compulsive course

Ne'er feels retiring ebb, but keeps due on
To the Propontic and the Hellespont,
Even so my bloody thoughts, with violent pace,
Shall ne'er look back, ne'er ebb to humble love,
Till that a capable and wide revenge
Swallow them up. Now, by yond marble heaven,
[*Kneels*] In the due reverence of a sacred vow
I here engage my words.

  Iago.   Do not rise yet.
[*Kneels*] Witness, you ever-burning lights above,
You elements that clip us round about,
Witness that here Iago doth give up
The execution of his wit, hands, heart,
To wrong'd Othello's service ! Let him command,
And to obey shall be in me remorse,
What bloody business ever.

  Oth.   I greet thy love,
Not with vain thanks, but with acceptance bounteous,
And will upon the instant put thee to 't :
Within these three days let me hear thee say
That Cassio 's not alive.

  Iago. My friend is dead ; 'tis done at your request :
But let her live.

  Oth.   Damn her, lewd minx ! O, damn her !
Come, go with me apart ; I will withdraw,
To furnish me with some swift means of death
For the fair devil. Now art thou my lieutenant.

  Iago. I am your own for ever.   [*Exeunt.*
       ACT III, Scene iii, ll. 90-279, 321-479

Before the castle.

Enter DESDEMONA, EMILIA.

  Des. Where should I lose that handkerchief, Emilia ?
  Emil. I know not, madam.
  Des. Believe me, I had rather have lost my purse
Full of crusadoes : and, but my noble Moor

Is true of mind and made of no such baseness
As jealous creatures are, it were enough
To put him to ill thinking.

    Emil. Is he not jealous?

    Des. Who, he? I think the sun where he was born
Drew all such humours from him.

    Emil. Look, where he comes.

    Des. I will not leave him now till Cassio
Be call'd to him.

Enter OTHELLO.

    How is't with you, my lord?

    Oth. Well, my good lady. [*Aside*] O, hardness to dis-
semble!—

How do you, Desdemona?

    Des. Well, my good lord.

    Oth. Give me your hand: this hand is moist, my lady.

    Des. It yet hath felt no age nor known no sorrow.

    Oth. This argues fruitfulness and liberal heart:
Hot, hot, and moist: this hand of yours requires
A sequester from liberty, fasting and prayer,
Much castigation, exercise devout;
For here's a young and sweating devil here,
That commonly rebels. 'Tis a good hand,
A frank one.

    Des. You may, indeed, say so;
For 'twas that hand that gave away my heart.

    Oth. A liberal hand: the hearts of old gave hands;
But our new heraldry is hands, not hearts.

    Des. I cannot speak of this. Come now, your promise.

    Oth. What promise, chuck?

    Des. I have sent to bid Cassio come speak with you.

    Oth. I have a salt and sorry rheum offends me;
Lend me thy handkerchief.

    Des. Here, my lord.

    Oth. That which I gave you.

    Des. I have it not about me.

Oth. Not?

Des. No, indeed, my lord.

Oth. That is a fault.
That handkerchief
Did an Egyptian to my mother give;
She was a charmer, and could almost read
The thoughts of people: she told her, while she kept it,
'Twould make her amiable and subdue my father
Entirely to her love, but if she lost it
Or made a gift of it, my father's eye
Should hold her loathed and his spirits should hunt
After new fancies: she, dying, gave it me;
And bid me, when my fate would have me wive,
To give it her. I did so: and take heed on't;
Make it a darling like your precious eye;
To lose 't or give 't away were such perdition
As nothing else could match.

Des. Is't possible?

Oth. 'Tis true: there's magic in the web of it:
A sibyl, that had number'd in the world
The sun to course two hundred compasses,
In her prophetic fury sew'd the work;
The worms were hallow'd that did breed the silk;
And it was dyed in mummy which the skilful
Conserved of maidens' hearts.

Des. Indeed! is't true?

Oth. Most veritable; therefore look to't well.

Des. Then would to God that I had never seen't!

Oth. Ha! wherefore?

Des. Why do you speak so startingly and rash?

Oth. Is't lost? is't gone? speak, is it out o' the way?

Des. Heaven bless us!

Oth. Say you?

Des. It is not lost; but what an if it were?

Oth. How!

Des. I say, it is not lost.

Oth. Fetch't, let me see't.

Des. Why, so I can, sir, but I will not now.
This is a trick to put me from my suit:
Pray you, let Cassio be received again.

Oth. Fetch me the handkerchief: my mind misgives.

Des. Come, come;
You'll never meet a more sufficient man.

Oth. The handkerchief!

Des. I pray, talk me of Cassio.

Oth. The handkerchief!

Des. A man that all his time
Hath founded his good fortunes on your love,
Shared dangers with you,—

Oth. The handkerchief!

Des. In sooth, you are to blame.

Oth. Away! [*Exit.*

Emil. Is not this man jealous?

Des. I ne'er saw this before.
Sure, there's some wonder in this handkerchief:
I am most unhappy in the loss of it.

Emil. 'Tis not a year or two shows us a man:
They are all but stomachs, and we all but food;
They eat us hungerly, and when they are full,
They belch us.

ACT III, Scene iv, ll. 23-106

Cyprus. Before the castle.

Enter OTHELLO *and* IAGO.

Iago. Will you think so?

Oth. Think so, Iago!

Iago. What,
To kiss in private?

Oth. An unauthorized kiss.

Iago. Or to be naked with her friend in bed
An hour or more, not meaning any harm?

Oth. Naked in bed, Iago, and not mean harm!

445

It is hypocrisy against the devil :
They that mean virtuously, and yet do so,
The devil their virtue tempts, and they tempt heaven.

Iago. So they do nothing, 'tis a venial slip :
But if I give my wife a handkerchief,—

Oth. What then ?

Iago. Why, then, 'tis hers, my lord ; and, being hers,
She may, I think, bestow't on any man.

Oth. She is protectress of her honour too :
May she give that ?

Iago. Her honour is an essence that's not seen ;
They have it very oft that have it not :
But, for the handkerchief,—

Oth. By heaven, I would most gladly have forgot it.
Thou said'st—O, it comes o'er my memory,
As doth the raven o'er the infected house,
Boding to all—he had my handkerchief.

Iago. Ay, what of that ?

Oth. That's not so good now.

Iago. What,
If I had said I had seen him do you wrong ?
Or heard him say,—as knaves be such abroad,
Who having, by their own importunate suit,
Or voluntary dotage of some mistress,
Convinced or supplied them, cannot choose
But they must blab—

Oth. Hath he said any thing ?

Iago. He hath, my lord ; but be you well assured,
No more than he'll unswear.

Oth. What hath he said ?

Iago. 'Faith, that he did—I know not what he did.

Oth. What ? what ?

Iago. Lie—

Oth. With her ?

Iago. With her, on her ; what you will.

Oth. Lie with her ! lie on her ! We say lie on her, when

they belie her. Lie with her! that's fulsome.—Handkerchief
—confessions—handkerchief !—To confess, and be hanged for
his labour ;—first, to be hanged, and then to confess.—I
tremble at it. Nature would not invest herself in such shadow-
ing passion without some instruction. It is not words that
shake me thus. Pish ! Noses, ears, and lips.—Is't possible ?—
Confess—handkerchief !—O devil !   [*Falls in a trance.*

Iago. Work on,
My medicine, work ! Thus credulous fools are caught ;
And many worthy and chaste dames even thus,
All guiltless, meet reproach. What, ho ! my lord !
My lord, I say ! Othello !

Enter CASSIO.

How now, Cassio !

Cas. What's the matter ?

Iago. My lord is fall'n into an epilepsy :
This is his second fit ; he had one yesterday.

Cas. Rub him about the temples.

Iago.   No, forbear ;
The lethargy must have his quiet course :
If not, he foams at mouth and by and by
Breaks out to savage madness. Look, he stirs :
Do you withdraw yourself a little while,
He will recover straight : when he is gone,
I would on great occasion speak with you.   [*Exit Cassio.*
How is it, general ? have you not hurt your head ?

Oth. Dost thou mock me ?

Iago.   I mock you ! no, by heaven.
Would you would bear your fortune like a man !

Oth. A horned man's a monster and a beast.

Iago.   There's many a beast then in a populous city,
And many a civil monster.

Oth. Did he confess it ?

Iago.   Good sir, be a man ;
Think every bearded fellow that's but yoked

May draw with you : there's millions now alive
That nightly lie in those unproper beds
Which they dare swear peculiar : your case is better.
O, 'tis the spite of hell, the fiend's arch-mock,
To lip a wanton in a secure couch,
And to suppose her chaste ! No, let me know ;
And knowing what I am, I know what she shall be.

    Oth. O, thou art wise ; 'tis certain.

    Iago.   Stand you awhile apart ;
Confine yourself but in a patient list.
Whilst you were here o'erwhelmed with your grief—
A passion most unsuiting such a man—
Cassio came hither : I shifted him away,
And laid good 'scuse upon your ecstasy,
Bade him anon return and here speak with me ;
The which he promised. Do but encave yourself,
And mark the fleers, the gibes, and notable scorns,
That dwell in every region of his face ;
For I will make him tell the tale anew,
Where, how, how oft, how long ago, and when
He hath, and is again to cope your wife :
I say, but mark his gesture. Marry, patience ;
Or I shall say you are all in all in spleen,
And nothing of a man.

    Oth.   Dost thou hear, Iago ?
I will be found most cunning in my patience ;
But—dost thou hear ?—most bloody.

    Iago.   That's not amiss ;
But yet keep time in all. Will you withdraw ? [*Othello retires.*
Now will I question Cassio of Bianca,
A housewife that by selling her desires
Buys herself bread and clothes : it is a creature
That dotes on Cassio ; as 'tis the strumpet's plague
To beguile many and be beguiled by one :
He, when he hears of her, cannot refrain
From the excess of laughter. Here he comes :

Re-enter CASSIO.

As he shall smile, Othello shall go mad ;
And his unbookish jealousy must construe
Poor Cassio's smiles, gestures and light behaviour,
Quite in the wrong. How do you now, lieutenant ?

Cas. The worser that you give me the addition
Whose want even kills me.

Iago. Ply Desdemona well, and you are sure on't.
[*Speaking lower*] Now, if this suit lay in Bianca's power,
How quickly should you speed !

Cas.   Alas, poor caitiff !

Oth. Look, how he laughs already !

Iago. I never knew woman love man so.

Cas. Alas, poor rogue ! I think, i' faith, she loves me.

Oth. Now he denies it faintly, and laughs it out.

Iago. Do you hear, Cassio ?

Oth.   Now he importunes him
To tell it o'er : go to ; well said, well said.

Iago. She gives it out that you shall marry her :
Do you intend it ?

Cas. Ha, ha, ha !

Oth. Do you triumph, Roman ? do you triumph ?

Cas. I marry her ! what ? a customer ! Prithee, bear
some charity to my wit ; do not think it so unwholesome.
Ha, ha, ha !

Oth. So, so, so, so : they laugh that win.

Iago. 'Faith, the cry goes that you shall marry her.

Cas. Prithee, say true.

Iago. I am a very villain else.

Oth. Have you scored me ? Well.

Cas. This is the monkey's own giving out : she is persuaded I will marry her, out of her own love and flattery, not
out of my promise.

Oth. Iago beckons me ; now he begins the story.

Cas. She was here even now ; she haunts me in every
place. I was the other day talking on the sea-bank with

certain Venetians; and thither comes the bauble, and, by this hand, she falls me thus about my neck—

Oth. Crying 'O dear Cassio!' as it were: his gesture imports it.

Cas. So hangs, and lolls, and weeps upon me; so hales, and pulls me: ha, ha, ha!

Oth. Now he tells how she plucked him to my chamber. O, I see that nose of yours, but not that dog I shall throw it to.

Cas. Well, I must leave her company.

Iago. Before me! look, where she comes.

Cas. 'Tis such another fitchew! marry, a perfumed one.

Enter BIANCA.

What do you mean by this haunting of me?

Bian. Let the devil and his dam haunt you! What did you mean by that same handkerchief you gave me even now? I was a fine fool to take it. I must take out the work?—A likely piece of work, that you should find it in your chamber, and not know who left it there! This is some minx's token, and I must take out the work? There; give it your hobby-horse: wheresoever you had it, I'll take out no work on't.

Cas. How now, my sweet Bianca! how now! how now!

Oth. By heaven, that should be my handkerchief!

Bian. An you'll come to supper to-night, you may; an you will not, come when you are next prepared for.   [*Exit.*

Iago. After her, after her.

Cas. 'Faith, I must; she'll rail in the street else.

Iago. Will you sup there?

Cas. 'Faith, I intend so.

Iago. Well, I may chance to see you; for I would very fain speak with you.

Cas. Prithee, come; will you?

Iago. Go to; say no more.   [*Exit Cassio.*

Oth. [*Advancing*] How shall I murder him, Iago?

Iago. Did you perceive how he laughed at his vice?

Oth. O Iago!

Iago. And did you see the handkerchief?

Oth. Was that mine?

Iago. Yours, by this hand: and to see how he prizes the foolish woman your wife! she gave it him, and he hath given it his whore.

Oth. I would have him nine years a-killing. A fine woman! a fair woman! a sweet woman!

Iago. Nay, you must forget that.

Oth. Ay, let her rot, and perish, and be damned to-night; for she shall not live: no, my heart is turned to stone; I strike it, and it hurts my hand. O, the world hath not a sweeter creature: she might lie by an emperor's side and command him tasks.

Iago. Nay, that's not your way.

Oth. Hang her! I do but say what she is: so delicate with her needle: an admirable musician: O! she will sing the savageness out of a bear: of so high and plenteous wit and invention:——

Iago. She's the worse for all this.

Oth. O, a thousand thousand times: and then, of so gentle a condition!

Iago. Ay, too gentle.

Oth. Nay, that's certain: but yet the pity of it, Iago! O Iago, the pity of it, Iago!

Iago. If you are so fond over her iniquity, give her patent to offend; for, if it touch not you, it comes near nobody.

Oth. I will chop her into messes: cuckold me!

Iago. O, 'tis foul in her.

Oth. With mine officer!

Iago. That's fouler.

Oth. Get me some poison, Iago; this night: I'll not expostulate with her, lest her body and beauty unprovide my mind again: this night, Iago.

Iago. Do it not with poison, strangle her in her bed, even the bed she hath contaminated.

Oth. Good, good: the justice of it pleases: very good.

Iago. And for Cassio, let me be his undertaker : you shall hear more by midnight.

Oth. Excellent good. [*A trumpet within.*] What trumpet is that same ?

Iago. Something from Venice, sure. 'Tis Lodovico Come from the duke ; and, see, your wife is with him.

Enter LODOVICO, DESDEMONA, *and* Attendants.

Lod. Save you, worthy general !

Oth.   With all my heart, sir.

Lod. The duke and senators of Venice greet you.

[*Gives him a letter.*

Oth. I kiss the instrument of their pleasures.

[*Opens the letter, and reads.*

Des. And what's the news, good cousin Lodovico ?

Iago. I am very glad to see you, signior ;
Welcome to Cyprus.

Lod. I thank you. How does Lieutenant Cassio ?

Iago. Lives, sir.

Des. Cousin, there's fall'n between him and my lord
An unkind breach : but you shall make all well.

Oth. Are you sure of that ?

Des. My lord ?

Oth. [*Reads*] ' This fail you not to do, as you will— '

Lod. He did not call ; he's busy in the paper. Is there division 'twixt my lord and Cassio ?

Des. A most unhappy one : I would do much
To atone them, for the love I bear to Cassio.

Oth. Fire and brimstone !

Des.   My lord ?

Oth.   Are you wise ?

Des. What, is he angry ?

Lod.   May be the letter moved him ;
For, as I think, they do command him home,
Deputing Cassio in his government.

Des. Trust me, I am glad on't.

Oth.   Indeed !

Des.   My lord ?

Oth. I am glad to see you mad.

Des.   Why, sweet Othello,—

Oth. [*Striking her*] Devil !

Des. I have not deserved this.

Lod. My lord, this would not be believed in Venice,
Though I should swear I saw't : 'tis very much :
Make her amends ; she weeps.

Oth.   O devil, devil !
If that the earth could teem with woman's tears,
Each drop she falls would prove a crocodile.
Out of my sight !

Des.   I will not stay to offend you.   [*Going.*

Lod. Truly, an obedient lady :
I do beseech your lordship, call her back.

Oth. Mistress !

Des.   My lord ?

Oth.   What would you with her, sir ?

Lod. Who, I, my lord ?

Oth. Ay ; you did wish that I would make her turn :
Sir, she can turn, and turn, and yet go on,
And turn again ; and she can weep, sir, weep ;
And she's obedient, as you say, obedient,
Very obedient. Proceed you in your tears.
Concerning this, sir,—O well-painted passion !—
I am commanded home. Get you away ;
I'll send for you anon. Sir, I obey the mandate,
And will return to Venice. Hence, avaunt ! [*Exit Desdemona.*
Cassio shall have my place. And, sir, to-night,
I do entreat that we may sup together :
You are welcome, sir, to Cyprus.—Goats and monkeys !
                                                    [*Exit.*

Lod. Is this the noble Moor whom our full senate
Call all in all sufficient ? Is this the nature
Whom passion could not shake ? whose solid virtue

The shot of accident, nor dart of chance,
Could neither graze nor pierce?

Iago. He is much changed.

ACT IV, Scene i, ll. 1-279

A room in the castle.

Desdemona. My lord, what is your will?

Othello. Pray, chuck, come hither.

Des. What is your pleasure?

Oth. Let me see your eyes;
Look in my face.

Des. What horrible fancy's this?

Oth. [*To Emilia*] Some of your function, mistress;
Leave procreants alone and shut the door;
Cough, or cry 'hem,' if any body come:
Your mystery, your mystery: nay, dispatch. [*Exit Emilia.*

Des. Upon my knees, what doth your speech import?
I understand a fury in your words,
But not the words.

Oth. Why, what art thou?

Des. Your wife, my lord; your true
And loyal wife.

Oth. Come, swear it, damn thyself;
Lest, being like one of heaven, the devils themselves
Should fear to seize thee: therefore be double damn'd:
Swear thou art honest.

Des. Heaven doth truly know it.

Oth. Heaven truly knows that thou art false as hell.

Des. To whom, my lord? with whom? how am I false?

Oth. O Desdemona! away! away! away!

Des. Alas the heavy day! Why do you weep?
Am I the motive of these tears, my lord?
If haply you my father do suspect
An instrument of this your calling back,
Lay not your blame on me: if you have lost him,
Why, I have lost him too.

Oth.   Had it pleased heaven
To try me with affliction ; had they rain'd
All kind of sores and shames on my bare head,
Steep'd me in poverty to the very lips,
Given to captivity me and my utmost hopes,
I should have found in some place of my soul
A drop of patience : but, alas, to make me
A fixed figure for the time of scorn
To point his slow unmoving finger at !
Yet could I bear that too ; well, very well :
But there, where I have garner'd up my heart,
Where either I must live, or bear no life ;
The fountain from the which my current runs,
Or else dries up ; to be discarded thence !
Or keep it as a cistern for foul toads
To knot and gender in ! Turn thy complexion there,
Patience, thou young and rose-lipp'd cherubin,—
Ay, there, look grim as hell !

Des. I hope my noble lord esteems me honest.

Oth. O, ay ; as summer flies are in the shambles,
That quicken even with blowing. O thou weed,
Who art so lovely fair and smell'st so sweet
That the sense aches at thee, would thou hadst ne'er been
    born !

Des. Alas, what ignorant sin have I committed ?

Oth. Was this fair paper, this most goodly book,
Made to write ' whore ' upon ? What committed !
Committed ! O thou public commoner !
I should make very forges of my cheeks,
That would to cinders burn up modesty,
Did I but speak thy deeds. What committed !
Heaven stops the nose at it and the moon winks,
The bawdy wind that kisses all it meets
Is hush'd within the hollow mine of earth,
And will not hear it. What committed !
Impudent strumpet !

Des.   By heaven, you do me wrong.

Oth. Are not you a strumpet?

Des.   No, as I am a Christian:
If to preserve this vessel for my lord
From any other foul unlawful touch
Be not to be a strumpet, I am none.

Oth. What, not a whore?

Des.   No, as I shall be saved.

Oth. Is't possible?

Des. O, heaven forgive us!

Oth.   I cry you mercy, then:
I took you for that cunning whore of Venice
That married with Othello. [*Raising his voice*] You,
    mistress,
That have the office opposite to Saint Peter
And keep the gate of hell!

Re-enter EMILIA.

                    You, you, ay, you!
We have done our course; there's money for your pains:
I pray you, turn the key and keep our counsel.   [*Exit.*

Emil. Alas, what does this gentleman conceive?
How do you, madam? how do you, my good lady?

Des. 'Faith, half asleep.

Emil. Good madam, what's the matter with my lord?

Des. With who?

Emil. Why, with my lord, madam.

Des. Who is thy lord?

Emil.   He that is yours, sweet lady.

Des. I have none: do not talk to me, Emilia;
I cannot weep; nor answer have I none,
But what should go by water. Prithee, to-night
Lay on my bed my wedding sheets: remember;
And call thy husband hither.

Emil.   Here's a change indeed! [*Exit.*

Des. 'Tis meet I should be used so, very meet.

How have I been behaved, that he might stick
The small'st opinion on my least misuse ?

Re-enter EMILIA *with* IAGO.

Iago. What is your pleasure, madam ? How is't with
you ?

Des. I cannot tell. Those that do teach young babes
Do it with gentle means and easy tasks :
He might have chid me so ; for, in good faith,
I am a child to chiding.

Iago.   What's the matter, lady ?

Emil. Alas, Iago, my lord hath so bewhored her,
Thrown such despite and heavy terms upon her,
As true hearts cannot bear.

Des. Am I that name, Iago ?

Iago.   What name, fair lady ?

Des. Such as she says my lord did say I was.

Emil. He call'd her whore : a beggar in his drink
Could not have laid such terms upon his callat.

Iago. Why did he so ?

Des. I do not know ; I am sure I am none such.

Iago. Do not weep, do not weep. Alas the day !

Emil. Hath she forsook so many noble matches,
Her father and her country and her friends,
To be call'd whore ? would it not make one weep ?

Des. It is my wretched fortune.

Iago.   Beshrew him for't !
How comes this trick upon him ?

Des.   Nay, heaven doth know.

Emil. I will be hang'd, if some eternal villain,
Some busy and insinuating rogue,
Some cogging, cozening slave, to get some office,
Have not devised this slander ; I'll be hang'd else.

Iago. Fie, there is no such man ; it is impossible.

Des. If any such there be, heaven pardon him !

Emil. A halter pardon him ! and hell gnaw his bones !

Why should he call her whore ? who keeps her company ?
What place ? what time ? what form ? what likelihood ?
The Moor's abused by some most villanous knave,
Some base notorious knave, some scurvy fellow.
O heaven, that such companions thou'ldst unfold,
And put in every honest hand a whip
To lash the rascals naked through the world
Even from the east to the west !

    Iago.   Speak within door.

    Emil. O, fie upon them ! Some such squire he was
That turn'd your wit the seamy side without,
And made you to suspect me with the Moor.

    Iago. You are a fool ; go to.

    Des.   O good Iago,
What shall I do to win my lord again ?
Good friend, go to him ; for, by this light of heaven,
I know not how I lost him. Here I kneel :
If e'er my will did trespass 'gainst his love,
Either in discourse of thought or actual deed,
Or that mine eyes, mine ears, or any sense,
Delighted them in any other form ;
Or that I do not yet, and ever did,
And ever will—though he do shake me off
To beggarly divorcement—love him dearly,
Comfort forswear me ! Unkindness may do much ;
And his unkindness may defeat my life,
But never taint my love. I cannot say ' whore : '
It does abhor me now I speak the word ;
To do the act that might the addition earn
Not the world's mass of vanity could make me.

    Iago. I pray you, be content ; 'tis but his humour :
The business of the state does him offence,
And he does chide with you.

    Des. If 'twere no other,—

    Iago.   'Tis but so, I warrant.
                            [Trumpets within.

Hark, how these instruments summon to supper !
The messengers of Venice stay the meat :
Go in, and weep not ; all things shall be well.

Act IV, Scene ii, ll. 24-171

Another room in the castle.

Emilia. How goes it now ? he looks gentler than he did.

Desdemona. He says he will return incontinent :
He hath commanded me to go to bed,
And bade me to dismiss you.

 Emil.   Dismiss me !

 Des. It was his bidding ; therefore, good Emilia,
Give me my nightly wearing, and adieu :
We must not now displease him.

 Emil. I would you had never seen him !

 Des. So would not I : my love doth so approve him,
That even his stubbornness, his checks, his frowns,—
Prithee, unpin me,—have grace and favour in them.

 Emil. I have laid those sheets you bade me on the bed.

 Des. All's one. Good faith, how foolish are our minds !
If I do die before thee, prithee, shroud me
In one of those same sheets.

 Emil.   Come, come, you talk.

 Des. My mother had a maid call'd Barbara :
She was in love, and he she loved proved mad
And did forsake her : she had a song of ' willow ; '
An old thing 'twas, but it express'd her fortune,
And she died singing it : that song to-night
Will not go from my mind ; I have much to do,
But to go hang my head all at one side,
And sing it like poor Barbara. Prithee, dispatch.

 Emil. Shall I go fetch your night-gown ?

 Des.   No, unpin me here.
This Lodovico is a proper man.

 Emil. A very handsome man.

 Des. He speaks well.

459

Emil. I know a lady in Venice would have walked barefoot
to Palestine for a touch of his nether lip.

 Des. [*Singing*] The poor soul sat sighing by a sycamore tree,
  Sing all a green willow ;
 Her hand on her bosom, her head on her knee,
  Sing willow, willow, willow :
 The fresh streams ran by her, and murmur'd her moans ;
  Sing willow, willow, willow ;
 Her salt tears fell from her, and soften'd the stones ;—
Lay by these :—
[*Singing*] Sing willow, willow, willow ;
Prithee, hie thee ; he'll come anon :—
[*Singing*] Sing all a green willow must be my garland.
 Let nobody blame him ; his scorn I approve,—
Nay, that's not next.—Hark ! who is't that knocks ?

 Emil. It's the wind.

 Des. [*Singing*] I call'd my love false love ; but what said he
 then ?
   Sing willow, willow, willow :
If I court moe women, you'll couch with moe men.—
So, get thee gone ; good night. Mine eyes do itch ;
Doth that bode weeping ?

 Emil.   'Tis neither here nor there.

 Des. I have heard it said so. O, these men, these men !
Dost thou in conscience think,—tell me, Emilia,—
That there be women do abuse their husbands
In such gross kind ?

 Emil.   There be some such, no question.

 Des. Wouldst thou do such a deed for all the world ?

 Emil. Why, would not you ?

 Des.   No, by this heavenly light !

 Emil. Nor I neither by this heavenly light ;
I might do't as well i' the dark.

 Des. Wouldst thou do such a deed for all the world ?

 Emil. The world's a huge thing : it is a great price
For a small vice.

Des. In troth, I think thou wouldst not.

Emil. In troth, I think I should ; and undo't when I had done. Marry, I would not do such a thing for a joint-ring nor for measures of lawn, nor for gowns, petticoats, nor caps nor any petty exhibition ; but, for the whole world,—why, who would not make her husband a cuckold to make him a monarch ? I should venture purgatory for't.

Des. Beshrew me, if I would do such a wrong
For the whole world.

Emil. Why, the wrong is but a wrong i' the world ; and having the world for your labour, 'tis a wrong in your own world, and you might quickly make it right.

Des. I do not think there is any such woman.

Emil. Yes, a dozen ; and as many to the vantage as would store the world they played for.
But I do think it is their husbands' faults
If wives do fall : say that they slack their duties,
And pour our treasures into foreign laps,
Or else break out in peevish jealousies,
Throwing restraint upon us ; or say they strike us,
Or scant our former having in despite ;
Why, we have galls, and though we have some grace,
Yet have we some revenge. Let husbands know
Their wives have sense like them : they see and smell
And have their palates both for sweet and sour,
As husbands have. What is it that they do
When they change us for others ? Is it sport ?
I think it is : and doth affection breed it ?
I think it doth : is't frailty that thus errs ?
It is so too : and have not we affections,
Desires for sport, and frailty, as men have ?
Then let them use us well : else let them know,
The ills we do, their ills instruct us so.

Des. Good night, good night.

ACT IV, Scene iii, ll. 11-105

461

He hath a daily beauty in his life
That makes me ugly.

ACT V, Scene i, ll. 18-19

A bedchamber in the castle : DESDEMONA *in bed asleep ;*
a light burning.

Enter OTHELLO.

Oth. It is the cause, it is the cause, my soul,—
Let me not name it to you, you chaste stars !—
It is the cause. Yet I'll not shed her blood ;
Nor scar that whiter skin of hers than snow,
And smooth as monumental alabaster.
Yet she must die, else she'll betray more men.
Put out the light, and then put out the light :
If I quench thee, thou flaming minister,
I can again thy former light restore,
Should I repent me : but once put out thy light,
Thou cunning'st pattern of excelling nature,
I know not where is that Promethean heat
That can thy light relume. When I have pluck'd the rose,
I cannot give it vital growth again,
It musts needs wither : I'll smell it on the tree.

[Kissing her.

Ah, balmy breath, that dost almost persuade
Justice to break her sword ! One more, one more.
Be thus when thou art dead, and I will kill thee,
And love thee after. One more, and this the last :
So sweet was ne'er so fatal. I must weep,
But they are cruel tears : this sorrow's heavenly ;
It strikes where it doth love. She wakes.

    Des. Who's there ? Othello ?

    Oth.   Ay, Desdemona.

    Des. Will you come to bed, my lord ?

    Oth. Have you pray'd to-night, Desdemona ?

    Des.   Ay, my lord.

    Oth. If you bethink yourself of any crime

462

Unreconciled as yet to heaven and grace,
Solicit for it straight.

    Des. Alas, my lord, what do you mean by that?

    Oth. Well, do it, and be brief; I will walk by:
I would not kill thy unprepared spirit;
No; heaven forfend! I would not kill thy soul.

    Des. Talk you of killing?

    Oth.   Ay, I do.

    Des.   Then heaven
Have mercy on me!

    Oth.   Amen, with all my heart!

    Des. If you say so, I hope you will not kill me.

    Oth. Hum!

    Des. And yet I fear you; for you are fatal then
When your eyes roll so: why I should fear I know not,
Since guiltiness I know not; but yet I feel I fear.

    Oth. Think on thy sins.

    Des.   They are loves I bear to you.

    Oth. Ay, and for that thou diest.

    Des. That death's unnatural that kills for loving.
Alas, why gnaw you so your nether lip?
Some bloody passion shakes your very frame:
These are portents; but yet I hope, I hope,
They do not point on me.

    Oth.   Peace, and be still!

    Des. I will so. What's the matter?

    Oth. That handkerchief which I so loved and gave thee
Thou gavest to Cassio.

    Des.   No, by my life and soul!
Send for the man, and ask him.

    Oth.   Sweet soul, take heed,
Take heed of perjury; thou art on thy death-bed.

    Des. Ay, but not yet to die.

    Oth.   Yes, presently:
Therefore confess thee freely of thy sin;
For to deny each article with oath

Cannot remove nor choke the strong conception
That I do groan withal.   Thou art to die.

   Des. Then Lord have mercy on me !

   Oth.   I say, amen.

   Des. And have you mercy too ! I never did
Offend you in my life ; never loved Cassio
But with such general warranty of heaven
As I might love ; I never gave him token.

   Oth. By heaven, I saw my handkerchief in's hand.
O perjured woman ! thou dost stone my heart,
And makest me call what I intend to do
A murder, which I thought a sacrifice :
I saw the handkerchief.

   Des.   He found it then ;
I never gave it him : send for him hither ;
Let him confess a truth.

   Oth.   He hath confess'd.

   Des. What, my lord ?

   Oth. That he hath used thee.

   Des.   How ? unlawfully ?

   Oth.   Ay.

   Des. He will not say so.

   Oth.   No, his mouth is stopp'd ;
Honest Iago hath ta'en order for't.

   Des. O ! my fear interprets : what, is he dead ?

   Oth. Had all his hairs been lives, my great revenge
Had stomach for them all.

   Des. Alas ! he is betray'd and I undone.

   Oth. Out, strumpet ! weep'st thou for him to my face ?

   Des. O, banish me, my lord, but kill me not !

   Oth. Down, strumpet !

   Des. Kill me to-morrow : let me live to-night !

   Oth. Nay, if you strive,—

   Des. But half an hour !

   Oth.   Being done, there is no pause.

   Des. But while I say one prayer !

Oth. It is too late.

[*He stifles her.*

Emil. [*Within*] My lord, my lord! what, ho! my lord,
my lord!

Oth. What noise is this? Not dead? not yet quite dead?
I that am cruel am yet merciful;
I would not have thee linger in thy pain:
So, so.

Emil. [*Within*] What, ho! my lord, my lord!

Oth. Who's there?

Emil. [*Within*] O, good my lord, I would speak a word with
you!

Oth. Yes: 'tis Emilia. By and by. She's dead.
'Tis like she comes to speak of Cassio's death.—
The noise was here. Ha! no more moving?
Still as the grave. Shall she come in? were't good?—
I think she stirs again:—no. What's best to do?
If she come in, she'll sure speak to my wife:
My wife? my wife? what wife! I have no wife.
O, insupportable! O heavy hour!
Methinks it should be now a huge eclipse
Of sun and moon, and that the affrighted globe
Should yawn at alteration.

Emil. [*Within*] I do beseech you
That I may speak with you, O, good my lord!

Oth. I had forgot thee: O, come in, Emilia:
Soft; by and by. Let me the curtains draw.
Where art thou? [*Unlocks the door.*

Enter EMILIA.

What's the matter with thee now?

Emil. O, my good lord, yonder's foul murders done!

Oth. What, now?

Emil. But now, my lord.

Oth. It is the very error of the moon;
She comes more nearer earth than she was wont,
And makes men mad.

Emil. Cassio, my lord, hath kill'd a young Venetian
Call'd Roderigo.

Oth. Roderigo kill'd !
And Cassio kill'd !

Emil. No, Cassio is not kill'd.

Oth. Not Cassio kill'd ! then murder's out of tune,
And sweet revenge grows harsh.

Des. O, falsely, falsely murder'd !

Emil. Alas, what cry is that ?

Oth. That ! what ?

Emil. Out, and alas ! that was my lady's voice.
Help ! help, ho ! help ! O lady, speak again !
Sweet Desdemona ! O sweet mistress, speak !

Des. A guiltless death I die.

Emil. O, who hath done this deed ?

Des. Nobody ; I myself. Farewell :
Commend me to my kind lord : O, farewell ! [*Dies.*

Oth. Why, how should she be murder'd ?

Emil. Alas, who knows ?

Oth. You heard her say herself, it was not I.

Emil. She said so : I must needs report the truth.

Oth. She's, like a liar, gone to burning hell :
'Twas I that kill'd her.

Emil. O, the more angel she,
And you the blacker devil !

Oth. She turn'd to folly, and she was a whore.

Emil. Thou dost belie her, and thou art a devil.

Oth. She was false as water.

Emil. Thou art rash as fire, to say
That she was false : O, she was heavenly true !

Oth. Cassio did top her ! ask thy husband else.
O, I were damn'd beneath all depth in hell,
But that I did proceed upon just grounds
To this extremity. Thy husband knew it all.

Emil. My husband !

Oth. Thy husband.

Emil. That she was false to wedlock?

Oth. Ay, with Cassio. Nay, had she been true,
If heaven would make me such another world
Of one entire and perfect chrysolite,
I'ld not have sold her for it.

Emil. My husband!

Oth.   Ay, 'twas he that told me first:
An honest man he is, and hates the slime
That sticks on filthy deeds.

Emil.   My husband!

Oth. What needs this iteration, woman? I say thy husband.

Emil. O mistress, villany hath made mocks with love!
My husband say that she was false!

Oth.   He, woman;
I say thy husband: dost understand the word?
My friend, thy husband, honest, honest Iago.

Emil. If he say so, may his pernicious soul
Rot half a grain a day! he lies to the heart:
She was too fond of her most filthy bargain.

Oth. Ha!

Emil. Do thy worst:
This deed of thine is no more worthy heaven
Than thou wast worthy her.

Oth.   Peace, you were best.

Emil. Thou hast not half that power to do me harm
As I have to be hurt. O gull! O dolt!
As ignorant as dirt! thou hast done a deed—
I care not for thy sword; I'll make thee known,
Though I lost twenty lives.—Help! help, ho! help!
The Moor hath kill'd my mistress! Murder! murder!

Enter MONTANO, GRATIANO, IAGO, *and others.*

Mon. What is the matter? How now, general!

Emil. O, are you come, Iago? you have done well,
That men must lay their murders on your neck.

Gra. What is the matter?

Emil. Disprove this villain, if thou be'st a man :
He says thou told'st him that his wife was false :
I know thou didst not, thou'rt not such a villain :
Speak, for my heart is full.

Iago. I told him what I thought, and told no more
Than what he found himself was apt and true.

Emil. But did you ever tell him she was false ?

Iago. I did.

Emil. You told a lie ; an odious, damned lie ;
Upon my soul, a lie, a wicked lie.
She false with Cassio !—did you say with Cassio ?

Iago. With Cassio, mistress. Go to, charm your tongue.

Emil. I will not charm my tongue ; I am bound to speak :
My mistress here lies murder'd in her bed,—

All. O heavens forfend !

Emil. And your reports have set the murder on.

Oth. Nay, stare not, masters : it is true, indeed.

Gra. 'Tis a strange truth.

Mon. O monstrous act !

Emil.   Villany, villany, villany !
I think upon't, I think : I smell't : O villany !—
I thought so then :—I'll kill myself for grief :—
O villany, villany !

Iago. What, are you mad ? I charge you, get you home.

Emil. Good gentlemen, let me have leave to speak :
'Tis proper I obey him, but not now.
Perchance, Iago, I will ne'er go home.

Oth. O ! O ! O !   [*He falls on the bed.*

Emil.   Nay, lay thee down and roar ;
For thou hast kill'd the sweetest innocent
That e'er did lift up eye.

Oth.   [*Rising*] O, she was foul !
I scarce did know you, uncle : there lies your niece,
Whose breath, indeed, these hands have newly stopp'd :
I know this act shows horrible and grim.

Gra. Poor Desdemona ! I am glad thy father's dead :

468

Thy match was mortal to him, and pure grief
Shore his old thread in twain : did he live now,
This sight would make him do a desperate turn,
Yea, curse his better angel from his side,
And fall to reprobation.

   Oth. 'Tis pitiful ; but yet Iago knows
That she with Cassio hath the act of shame
A thousand times committed ; Cassio confess'd it :
And she did gratify his amorous works
With that recognizance and pledge of love
Which I first gave her ; I saw it in his hand :
It was a handkerchief, an antique token
My father gave my mother.

   Emil. O heaven ! O heavenly powers !

   Iago. Come, hold your peace.

   Emil.   'Twill out, 'twill out : I peace !
No, I will speak as liberal as the north :
Let heaven and men and devils, let them all,
All, all, cry shame against me, yet I'll speak.

   Iago. Be wise, and get you home.

   Emil.   I will not.

                    [*Iago offers to stab Emilia.*

   Gra.   Fie !
Your sword upon a woman ?

   Emil. O thou dull Moor ! that handkerchief thou speak'st
    of
I found by fortune and did give my husband ;
For often, with a solemn earnestness,
More than indeed belong'd to such a trifle,
He begg'd of me to steal it.

   Iago.   Villanous whore !

   Emil. She give it Cassio ! no, alas ! I found it,
And I did give't my husband.

   Iago.   Filth, thou liest !

   Emil. By heaven, I do not, I do not, gentlemen.
O murderous coxcomb ! what should such a fool

Do with so good a woman ?

Oth.   Are there no stones in heaven
But what serve for the thunder ?—Precious villain !

                [He runs at Iago : Iago, from behind,
                      stabs Emilia, and exit.

   Gra. The woman falls ; sure, he hath kill'd his wife.

   Emil. Ay, ay : O, lay me by my mistress' side.

   Gra. He's gone, but his wife's kill'd.

   Mon. 'Tis a notorious villain. Take you this weapon,
Which I have here recover'd from the Moor :
Come, guard the door without ; let him not pass,
But kill him rather. I'll after that same villain,
For 'tis a damned slave.   *[Exeunt Montano and Gratiano.*

   Oth.   I am not valiant neither,
But every puny whipster gets my sword :
But why should honour outlive honesty ?
Let it go all.

   Emil.   What did thy song bode, lady ?
Hark, canst thou hear me ? I will play the swan,
And die in music. *[Singing]* Willow, willow, willow.—
Moor, she was chaste ; she loved thee, cruel Moor ;
So come my soul to bliss, as I speak true ;
So speaking as I think, I die, I die.   *[Dies.*

   Oth. I have another weapon in this chamber ;
It is a sword of Spain, the ice-brook's temper :—
O, here it is. Uncle, I must come forth.

   Gra. *[Within]* If thou attempt it, it will cost thee dear :
Thou hast no weapon, and perforce must suffer.

   Oth. Look in upon me then and speak with me,
Or, naked as I am, I will assault thee.

Re-enter GRATIANO.

   Gra. What is the matter ?

   Oth.   Behold, I have a weapon ;
A better never did itself sustain
Upon a soldier's thigh : I have seen the day,

That, with this little arm and this good sword,
I have made my way through more impediments
Than twenty times your stop : but, O vain boast !
Who can control his fate ? 'tis not so now.
Be not afraid, though you do see me weapon'd ;
Here is my journey's end, here is my butt,
And very sea-mark of my utmost sail.
Do you go back dismay'd ? 'tis a lost fear ;
Man but a rush against Othello's breast,
And he retires. Where should Othello go ?
Now, how dost thou look now ? O ill-starr'd wench !
Pale as thy smock ! when we shall meet at compt,
This look of thine will hurl my soul from heaven,
And fiends will snatch at it. Cold, cold, my girl !
Even like thy chastity. O cursed slave !
Whip me, ye devils,
From the possession of this heavenly sight !
Blow me about in winds ! roast me in sulphur !
Wash me in steep-down gulfs of liquid fire !
O Desdemona ! Desdemona ! dead !
Oh ! Oh ! Oh !

Enter LODOVICO, MONTANO, CASSIO *carried in a chair,
and* Officers *with* IAGO, *prisoner.*

Lod. Where is this rash and most unfortunate man ?
Oth. That's he that was Othello : here I am.
Lod. Where is that viper ? bring the villain forth.
Oth. I look down towards his feet ; but that's a fable.
If that thou be'st a devil, I cannot kill thee. [*Wounds Iago.*
Lod. Wrench his sword from him.
Iago. I bleed, sir ; but not kill'd.
Oth. I am not sorry neither : I'ld have thee live ;
For, in my sense, 'tis happiness to die.
Lod. O thou Othello, that wert once so good,
Fall'n in the practice of a damned slave,
What shall be said to thee ?

Oth.   Why, any thing :
An honourable murderer, if you will ;
For nought I did in hate, but all in honour.

Lod. This wretch hath part confess'd his villany :
Did you and he consent in Cassio's death ?

Oth. Ay.

Cas. Dear general, I never gave you cause.

Oth. I do believe it, and I ask you pardon.
Will you, I pray, demand that demi-devil
Why he hath thus ensnared my soul and body ?

Iago. Demand me nothing : what you know, you know :
From this time forth I never will speak word.

Lod. What, not to pray ?

Gra.   Torments will ope your lips.

Oth. Well, thou dost best.

Lod. Sir, you shall understand what hath befall'n,
Which, as I think, you know not. Here is a letter
Found in the pocket of the slain Roderigo ;
And here another : the one of them imports
The death of Cassio to be undertook
By Roderigo.

Oth.   O villain !

Cas.   Most heathenish and most gross !

Lod. Now here's another discontented paper,
Found in his pocket too ; and this, it seems,
Roderigo meant to have sent this damned villain ;
But that belike Iago in the interim
Came in and satisfied him.

Oth.   O the pernicious caitiff !
How came you, Cassio, by that handkerchief
That was my wife's ?

Cas.   I found it in my chamber :
And he himself confess'd but even now
That there he dropp'd it for a special purpose
Which wrought to his desire.

Oth.   O fool ! fool ! fool !

Cas. There is besides in Roderigo's letter,
How he upbraids Iago, that he made him
Brave me upon the watch ; whereon it came
That I was cast : and even but now he spake,
After long seeming dead, Iago hurt him,
Iago set him on.

    Lod. You must forsake this room, and go with us :
Your power and your command is taken off,
And Cassio rules in Cyprus. For this slave,
If there be any cunning cruelty
That can torment him much and hold him long,
It shall be his. You shall close prisoner rest,
Till that the nature of your fault be known
To the Venetian state. Come, bring him away.

    Oth. Soft you ; a word or two before you go.
I have done the state some service, and they know't.
No more of that. I pray you, in your letters,
When you shall these unlucky deeds relate,
Speak of me as I am ; nothing extenuate,
Nor set down aught in malice : then must you speak
Of one that loved not wisely but too well ;
Of one not easily jealous, but being wrought
Perplex'd in the extreme ; of one whose hand,
Like the base Indian, threw a pearl away
Richer than all his tribe ; of one whose subdued eyes,
Albeit unused to the melting mood,
Drop tears as fast as the Arabian trees
Their medicinal gum. Set you down this ;
And say besides, that in Aleppo once,
Where a malignant and a turban'd Turk
Beat a Venetian and traduced the state,
I took by the throat the circumcised dog,
And smote him, thus.   *[Stabs himself.*

    Lod. O bloody period !

    Gra.   All that's spoke is marr'd.

    Oth. I kiss'd thee ere I kill'd thee : no way but this ;

Killing myself, to die upon a kiss.

[*Falls on the bed, and dies*.

   Cas. This did I fear, but thought he had no weapon ;
For he was great of heart.

   Lod.   [*To Iago*] O Spartan dog,
More fell than anguish, hunger, or the sea !
Look on the tragic loading of this bed ;
This is thy work : the object poisons sight ;
Let it be hid.

ACT V, Scene ii, ll. 1-365

Macbeth

A desert place.

Thunder and lightning.   Enter three Witches.

   First Witch. When shall we three meet again
In thunder, lightning, or in rain ?

   Sec. Witch. When the hurlyburly's done,
When the battle's lost and won.

   Third Witch. That will be ere the set of sun.

   First Witch. Where the place ?

   Sec. Witch.   Upon the heath.

   Third Witch. There to meet with Macbeth.

   First Witch. I come, Graymalkin !

   Sec. Witch. Paddock calls.

   Third Witch. Anon.

   All. Fair is foul, and foul is fair :
Hover through the fog and filthy air.   [*Exeunt*.

ACT I, Scene i, ll. 1-12

A heath near Forres.

To the three Witches *enter* MACBETH *and* BANQUO.

   Macb. So foul and fair a day I have not seen.

   Ban. How far is't call'd to Forres ? What are these
So wither'd and so wild in their attire,

474

That look not like the inhabitants o' the earth,
And yet are on't? Live you? or are you aught
That man may question? You seem to understand me,
By each at once her choppy finger laying
Upon her skinny lips: you should be women,
And yet your beards forbid me to interpret
That you are so.

    Macb.   Speak, if you can: what are you?
    First Witch. All hail, Macbeth! hail to thee, thane of
      Glamis!
    Sec. Witch. All hail, Macbeth! hail to thee, thane of
      Cawdor!
    Third Witch. All hail, Macbeth, thou shalt be king here-
      after!
    Ban. Good sir, why do you start; and seem to fear
Things that do sound so fair? I' the name of truth,
Are ye fantastical, or that indeed
Which outwardly ye show? My noble partner
You greet with present grace and great prediction
Of noble having and of royal hope,
That he seems rapt withal: to me you speak not.
If you can look into the seeds of time,
And say which grain will grow and which will not,
Speak then to me, who neither beg nor fear
Your favours nor your hate.

    First Witch. Hail!
    Sec. Witch. Hail!
    Third Witch. Hail!
    First Witch. Lesser than Macbeth, and greater.
    Sec. Witch. Not so happy, yet much happier.
    Third Witch. Thou shalt get kings, though thou be none:
So all hail, Macbeth and Banquo!
    First Witch. Banquo and Macbeth, all hail!
    Macb. Stay, you imperfect speakers, tell me more:
By Sinel's death I know I am thane of Glamis;
But how of Cawdor? the thane of Cawdor lives,

A prosperous gentleman ; and to be king
Stands not within the prospect of belief,
No more than to be Cawdor. Say from whence
You owe this strange intelligence ? or why
Upon this blasted heath you stop our way
With such prophetic greeting ? Speak, I charge you.

[*Witches vanish.*

   Ban. The earth hath bubbles, as the water has,
And these are of them. Whither are they vanish'd ?
   Macb. Into the air ; and what seem'd corporal melted
As breath into the wind. Would they had stay'd !
   Ban. Were such things here as we do speak about ?
Or have we eaten on the insane root
That takes the reason prisoner ?
   Macb. Your children shall be kings.
   Ban.   You shall be king.
   Macb. And thane of Cawdor too : went it not so ?
   Ban. To the selfsame tune and words.

ACT I, Scene iii, ll. 38-88

   Macbeth   [*Aside*] Two truths are told,
As happy prologues to the swelling act
Of the imperial theme.—I thank you, gentlemen.
[*Aside*] This supernatural soliciting
Cannot be ill, cannot be good : if ill,
Why hath it given me earnest of success,
Commencing in a truth ? I am thane of Cawdor :
If good, why do I yield to that suggestion
Whose horrid image doth unfix my hair
And make my seated heart knock at my ribs,
Against the use of nature ? Present fears
Are less than horrible imaginings :
My thought, whose murder yet is but fantastical,
Shakes so my single state of man that function
Is smother'd in surmise, and nothing is
But what is not.

476

Banquo.   Look, how our partner's rapt.

Macb. [*Aside*] If chance will have me king, why, chance
    may crown me,
Without my stir.

Ban.   New honours come upon him,
Like our strange garments, cleave not to their mould
But with the aid of use.

Macb.   [*Aside*] Come what come may,
Time and the hour runs through the roughest day.

Ban. Worthy Macbeth, we stay upon your leisure.

Macb. Give me your favour : my dull brain was wrought
With things forgotten. Kind gentlemen, your pains
Are register'd where every day I turn
The leaf to read them. Let us toward the king.
Think upon what hath chanced, and, at more time,
The interim having weigh'd it, let us speak
Our free hearts each to other.

Ban.   Very gladly.

Macb. Till then, enough. Come, friends.

Act I, Scene iii, ll. 127-156

Malcolm.   Nothing in his life
Became him like the leaving it ; he died
As one that had been studied in his death
To throw away the dearest thing he owed,
As 'twere a careless trifle.

Duncan.   There's no art
To find the mind's construction in the face :
He was a gentleman on whom I built
An absolute trust.   Act I, Scene iv, ll. 7-14

Inverness. Macbeth's castle.

Enter Lady Macbeth, *reading a letter.*

Lady M. ' They met me in the day of success ; and I have
learned by the perfectest report, they have more in them than
mortal knowledge. When I burned in desire to question them

477

further, they made themselves air, into which they vanished. Whiles I stood rapt in the wonder of it, came missives from the king, who all-hailed me " Thane of Cawdor ; " by which title, before, these weird sisters saluted me, and referred me to the coming on of time, with " Hail, king that shalt be ! " This have I thought good to deliver thee, my dearest partner of greatness, that thou mightst not lose the dues of rejoicing, by being ignorant of what greatness is promised thee. Lay it to thy heart, and farewell.'

Glamis thou art, and Cawdor ; and shalt be
What thou art promised : yet do I fear thy nature ;
It is too full o' the milk of human kindness
To catch the nearest way : thou wouldst be great ;
Art not without ambition, but without
The illness should attend it : what thou wouldst highly,
That wouldst thou holily ; wouldst not play false,
And yet wouldst wrongly win : thou'ldst have, great Glamis,
That which cries ' Thus thou must do, if thou have it ;
And that which rather thou dost fear to do
Than wishest should be undone.' Hie thee hither,
That I may pour my spirits in thine ear ;
And chastise with the valour of my tongue
All that impedes thee from the golden round,
Which fate and metaphysical aid doth seem
To have thee crown'd withal.

Enter a Messenger.

What is your tidings ?

Mess. The king comes here to-night.

Lady M. Thou'rt mad to say it :
Is not thy master with him ? who, were 't so,
Would have inform'd for preparation.

Mess. So please you, it is true : our thane is coming :
One of my fellows had the speed of him,
Who, almost dead for breath, had scarcely more
Than would make up his message.

Lady M.   Give him tending;
He brings great news.   [*Exit Messenger.*
                    The raven himself is hoarse
That croaks the fatal entrance of Duncan
Under my battlements. Come, you spirits
That tend on mortal thoughts, unsex me here,
And fill me from the crown to the toe top-full
Of direst cruelty! make thick my blood;
Stop up the access and passage to remorse,
That no compunctious visitings of nature
Shake my fell purpose, nor keep peace between
The effect and it! Come to my woman's breasts,
And take my milk for gall, you murdering ministers,
Wherever in your sightless substances
You wait on nature's mischief! Come, thick night,
And pall thee in the dunnest smoke of hell,
That my keen knife see not the wound it makes,
Nor heaven peep through the blanket of the dark,
To cry ' Hold, hold ! '

                    Enter MACBETH.

                    Great Glamis ! worthy Cawdor !
Greater than both, by the all-hail hereafter !
Thy letters have transported me beyond
This ignorant present, and I feel now
The future in the instant.
    Macb.   My dearest love,
Duncan comes here to-night.
    Lady M.   And when goes hence?
    Macb. To-morrow, as he purposes.
    Lady M.   O, never
Shall sun that morrow see !
Your face, my thane, is as a book where men
May read strange matters. To beguile the time,
Look like the time; bear welcome in your eye,
Your hand, your tongue: look like the innocent flower,

But be the serpent under't.   He that's coming
Must be provided for : and you shall put
This night's great business into my dispatch ;
Which shall to all our nights and days to come
Give solely sovereign sway and masterdom.

   Macb. We will speak further.

   Lady M.   Only look up clear ;
To alter favour ever is to fear :
Leave all the rest to me.

Act I, Scene v, ll. 1-74

Before Macbeth's castle.

   Duncan. This castle hath a pleasant seat ; the air
Nimbly and sweetly recommends itself
Unto our gentle senses.

   Banquo.   This guest of summer,
The temple-haunting martlet, does approve,
By his loved mansionry, that the heaven's breath
Smells wooingly here : no jutty, frieze,
Buttress, nor coign of vantage, but this bird
Hath made his pendent bed and procreant cradle :
Where they most breed and haunt, I have observed,
The air is delicate.

Act I, Scene vi, ll. 1-10

Macbeth's castle.

Hautboys and torches.   Enter a Sewer, *and divers* Servants
   with dishes and service, and pass over the stage.   Then enter
   Macbeth.

   Macb. If it were done when 'tis done, then 'twere well
It were done quickly : if the assassination
Could trammel up the consequence, and catch
With his surcease success ; that but this blow
Might be the be-all and the end-all here,
But here, upon this bank and shoal of time,
We'ld jump the life to come.   But in these cases
We still have judgement here ; that we but teach

480

Bloody instructions, which, being taught, return
To plague the inventor : this even-handed justice
Commends the ingredients of our poison'd chalice
To our own lips. He's here in double trust ;
First, as I am his kinsman and his subject,
Strong both against the deed ; then, as his host,
Who should against his murderer shut the door,
Not bear the knife myself. Besides, this Duncan
Hath borne his faculties so meek, hath been
So clear in his great office, that his virtues
Will plead like angels, trumpet-tongued, against
The deep damnation of his taking-off ;
And pity, like a naked new-born babe,
Striding the blast, or heaven's cherubim, horsed
Upon the sightless couriers of the air,
Shall blow the horrid deed in every eye,
That tears shall drown the wind. I have no spur
To prick the sides of my intent, but only
Vaulting ambition, which o'erleaps itself
And falls on the other.

Enter LADY MACBETH.

How now ! what news ?

Lady M. He has almost supp'd : why have you left the
   chamber ?

Macb. Hath he ask'd for me ?

Lady M.   Know you not he has ?

Macb. We will proceed no further in this business :
He hath honour'd me of late ; and I have bought
Golden opinions from all sorts of people,
Which would be worn now in their newest gloss,
Not cast aside so soon.

Lady M.   Was the hope drunk
Wherein you dress'd yourself ? hath it slept since ?
And wakes it now, to look so green and pale
At what it did so freely ? From this time

Such I account thy love. Art thou afeard
To be the same in thine own act and valour
As thou art in desire? Wouldst thou have that
Which thou esteem'st the ornament of life,
And live a coward in thine own esteem,
Letting ' I dare not ' wait upon ' I would,'
Like the poor cat i' the adage?

  Macb.   Prithee, peace:
I dare do all that may become a man;
Who dares do more is none.

  Lady M.   What beast was't, then,
That made you break this enterprise to me?
When you durst do it, then you were a man;
And, to be more than what you were, you would
Be so much more the man. Nor time nor place
Did then adhere, and yet you would make both:
They have made themselves, and that their fitness now
Does unmake you. I have given suck, and know
How tender 'tis to love the babe that milks me:
I would, while it was smiling in my face,
Have pluck'd my nipple from his boneless gums,
And dash'd the brains out, had I so sworn as you
Have done to this.

  Macb.   If we should fail?

  Lady M.   We fail!
But screw your courage to the sticking-place,
And we'll not fail. When Duncan is asleep—
Whereto the rather shall his day's hard journey
Soundly invite him—his two chamberlains
Will I with wine and wassail so convince
That memory, the warder of the brain,
Shall be a fume, and the receipt of reason
A limbeck only: when in swinish sleep
Their drenched natures lie as in a death,
What cannot you and I perform upon
The unguarded Duncan? what not put upon

His spongy officers, who shall bear the guilt
Of our great quell?

Macb.   Bring forth men-children only;
For thy undaunted mettle should compose
Nothing but males. Will it not be received,
When we have mark'd with blood those sleepy two
Of his own chamber and used their very daggers,
That they have done't?

Lady M.   Who dares receive it other,
As we shall make our grief and clamour roar
Upon his death?

Macb.   I am settled, and bend up
Each corporal agent to this terrible feat.

ACT I, Scene vii, ll. 1-80

Court of Macbeth's castle.

Enter BANQUO, *and* FLEANCE *bearing a torch before him.*

Ban. How goes the night, boy?

Fle. The moon is down; I have not heard the clock.

Ban. And she goes down at twelve.

Fle.   I take't, 'tis later, sir.

Ban. Hold, take my sword. There's husbandry in heaven;
Their candles are all out. Take thee that too.
A heavy summons lies like lead upon me,
And yet I would not sleep: merciful powers,
Restrain in me the cursed thoughts that nature
Gives way to in repose!

Enter MACBETH, *and a* Servant *with a torch.*

                    Give me my sword.
Who's there?

Macb. A friend.

Ban. What, sir, not yet at rest? The king's a-bed:
He hath been in unusual pleasure, and
Sent forth great largess to your offices.
This diamond he greets your wife withal,

483

By the name of most kind hostess ; and shut up
In measureless content.

 Macb.   Being unprepared,
Our will became the servant to defect ;
Which else should free have wrought.

 Ban.   All's well.
I dreamt last night of the three weird sisters :
To you they have show'd some truth.

 Macb.   I think not of them :
Yet, when we can entreat an hour to serve,
We would spend it in some words upon that business,
If you would grant the time.

 Ban.   At your kind'st leisure.

 Macb. If you shall cleave to my consent, when 'tis,
It shall make honour for you.

 Ban.   So I lose none
In seeking to augment it, but still keep
My bosom franchised and allegiance clear,
I shall be counsell'd.

 Macb.   Good repose the while !

 Ban. Thanks, sir : the like to you !

        [*Exeunt Banquo and Fleance.*

 Macb. Go bid thy mistress, when my drink is ready,
She strike upon the bell. Get thee to bed. [*Exit Servant*
Is this a dagger which I see before me,
The handle toward my hand ? Come, let me clutch thee.
I have thee not, and yet I see thee still.
Art thou not, fatal vision, sensible
To feeling as to sight ? or art thou but
A dagger of the mind, a false creation,
Proceeding from the heat-oppressed brain ?
I see thee yet, in form as palpable
As this which now I draw.
Thou marshall'st me the way that I was going ;
And such an instrument I was to use.
Mine eyes are made the fools o' the other senses,

Or else worth all the rest; I see thee still,
And on thy blade and dudgeon gouts of blood,
Which was not so before. There's no such thing:
It is the bloody business which informs
Thus to mine eyes. Now o'er the one half-world
Nature seems dead, and wicked dreams abuse
The curtain'd sleep; witchcraft celebrates
Pale Hecate's offerings, and wither'd murder,
Alarum'd by his sentinel, the wolf,
Whose howl's his watch, thus with his stealthy pace,
With Tarquin's ravishing strides, towards his design
Moves like a ghost. Thou sure and firm-set earth,
Hear not my steps, which way they walk, for fear
Thy very stones prate of my whereabout,
And take the present horror from the time,
Which now suits with it. Whiles I threat, he lives:
Words to the heat of deeds too cold breath gives. [*A bell rings.*
I go, and it is done; the bell invites me.
Hear it not, Duncan; for it is a knell
That summons thee to heaven or to hell.

Act II, Scene i, ll. 1-64

Court of Macbeth's castle.

Enter Lady Macbeth.

Lady M. That which hath made them drunk hath made
me bold ·
What hath quench'd them hath given me fire. Hark! Peace!
It was the owl that shriek'd, the fatal bellman,
Which gives the stern'st good-night. He is about it:
The doors are open; and the surfeited grooms
Do mock their charge with snores: I have drugg'd their
possets,
That death and nature do contend about them,
Whether they live or die.

Macb. [*Within*] Who's there? what, ho!

Lady M. Alack, I am afraid they have awaked,

485

And 'tis not done.   The attempt and not the deed
Confounds us.   Hark ! I laid their daggers ready ;
He could not miss 'em.   Had he not resembled
My father as he slept, I had done't.

Enter MACBETH.

My husband !

Macb. I have done the deed.   Didst thou not hear a
    noise ?

Lady M. I heard the owl scream and the crickets cry.
Did not you speak ?

Macb.   When ?

Lady M.   Now.

Macb.   As I descended ?

Lady M. Ay.

Macb. Hark !
Who lies i' the second chamber ?

Lady M.   Donalbain.

Macb. This is a sorry sight.   [*Looking on his hands*.

Lady M. A foolish thought, to say a sorry sight.

Macb. There's one did laugh in's sleep, and one cried
    ' Murder ! '
That they did wake each other : I stood and heard them :
But they did say their prayers, and address'd them
Again to sleep.

Lady M.   There are two lodged together.

Macb. One cried ' God bless us ! ' and ' Amen ' the other ;
As they had seen me with these hangman's hands.
Listening their fear, I could not say ' Amen,'
When they did say ' God bless us ! '

Lady M.   Consider it not so deeply.

Macb. But wherefore could not I pronounce ' Amen ' ?
I had most need of blessing, and ' Amen '
Stuck in my throat.

Lady M.   These deeds must not be thought
After these ways ; so, it will make us mad.

Macb. Methought I heard a voice cry ' Sleep no more !
Macbeth does murder sleep,' the innocent sleep,
Sleep that knits up the ravell'd sleave of care,
The death of each day's life, sore labour's bath,
Balm of hurt minds, great nature's second course,
Chief nourisher in life's feast,—

  Lady M.   What do you mean ?

  Macb. Still it cried ' Sleep no more ! ' to all the house :
' Glamis hath murder'd sleep, and therefore Cawdor
Shall sleep no more ; Macbeth shall sleep no more.'

  Lady M. Who was it that thus cried ? Why, worthy thane,
You do unbend your noble strength, to think
So brainsickly of things. Go get some water,
And wash this filthy witness from your hand.
Why did you bring these daggers from the place ?
They must lie there : go carry them ; and smear
The sleepy grooms with blood.

  Macb.   I'll go no more :
I am afraid to think what I have done ;
Look on't again I dare not.

  Lady M.   Infirm of purpose !
Give me the daggers : the sleeping and the dead
Are but as pictures : 'tis the eye of childhood
That fears a painted devil. If he do bleed,
I'll gild the faces of the grooms withal ;
For it must seem their guilt.   [*Exit. Knocking within*

  Macb.   Whence is that knocking ?
How is't with me, when every noise appals me ?
What hands are here ? ha ! they pluck out mine eyes.
Will all great Neptune's ocean wash this blood
Clean from my hand ? No, this my hand will rather
The multitudinous seas incarnadine,
Making the green one red.

     Re-enter LADY MACBETH.

  Lady M. My hands are of your colour ; but I shame

To wear a heart so white. [*Knocking within.*] I hear a
  knocking
At the south entry: retire we to our chamber:
A little water clears us of this deed:
How easy is it, then! Your constancy
Hath left you unattended. [*Knocking within.*] Hark! more
  knocking.
Get on your nightgown, lest occasion call us,
And show us to be watchers. Be not lost
So poorly in your thoughts.
  Macb. To know my deed, 'twere best not know myself.
                                                  [*Knocking within.*
Wake Duncan with thy knocking! I would thou couldst!

ACT II, Scene ii, ll. 1-74

Court of Macbeth's castle.

Knocking within. Enter a Porter.

Porter. Here's a knocking indeed! If a man were porter of
hell-gate, he should have old turning the key. [*Knocking
within.*] Knock, knock, knock! Who's there, i' the name of
Beelzebub? Here's a farmer, that hanged himself on the
expectation of plenty: come in time; have napkins enow
about you; here you'll sweat for't. [*Knocking within.*]
Knock, knock! Who's there, in the other devil's name?
Faith, here's an equivocator, that could swear in both the
scales against either scale; who committed treason enough
for God's sake, yet could not equivocate to heaven: O, come
in, equivocator. [*Knocking within.*] Knock, knock, knock!
Who's there? Faith, here's an English tailor come hither, for
stealing out of a French hose: come in, tailor; here you may
roast your goose. [*Knocking within.*] Knock, knock; never
at quiet! What are you? But this place is too cold for hell.
I'll devil-porter it no further: I had thought to have let in
some of all professions that go the primrose way to the everlasting bonfire. [*Knocking within.*] Anon, anon! I pray you,
remember the porter.   [*Opens the gate.*

ACT II, Scene iii, ll. 1-25

488

Lennox. The night has been unruly : where we lay,
Our chimneys were blown down ; and, as they say,
Lamentings heard i' the air ; strange screams of death,
And prophesying with accents terrible
Of dire combustion and confused events
New hatch'd to the woeful time : the obscure bird
Clamour'd the livelong night : some say, the earth
Was feverous and did shake.

    Macbeth.   'Twas a rough night.

    Len. My young remembrance cannot parallel
A fellow to it.

Enter MACDUFF.

    Macd. O horror, horror, horror ! Tongue nor heart
Cannot conceive nor name thee !

    Macb.⎱
    Len. ⎰   What's the matter ?

    Macd. Confusion now hath made his masterpiece !
Most sacrilegious murder hath broke ope
The Lord's anointed temple, and stole thence
The life o' the building !

    Macb.   What is't you say ? the life ?

    Len. Mean you his majesty ?

    Macd. Approach the chamber, and destroy your sight
With a new Gorgon : do not bid me speak ;
See, and then speak yourselves. [*Exeunt Macbeth and Lennox.*
                        Awake, awake !
Ring the alarum-bell. Murder and treason !
Banquo and Donalbain ! Malcolm ! awake !
Shake off this downy sleep, death's counterfeit,
And look on death itself ! up, up, and see
The great doom's image ! Malcolm ! Banquo !
As from your graves rise up, and walk like sprites,
To countenance this horror ! Ring the bell.   [*Bell rings.*

Enter LADY MACBETH.

    Lady M. What's the business,

489

That such a hideous trumpet calls to parley
The sleepers of the house ?   speak, speak !
 Macd.   O gentle lady,
'Tis not for you to hear what I can speak :
The repetition, in a woman's ear,
Would murder as it fell.

     Re-enter BANQUO.

      O Banquo, Banquo,
Our royal master's murder'd !
 Lady M.   Woe, alas !
What, in our house ?
 Ban.   Too cruel any where.
Dear Duff, I prithee, contradict thyself,
And say it is not so.

   Re-enter MACBETH *and* LENNOX, *with* ROSS.

 Macb. Had I but died an hour before this chance,
I had lived a blessed time ; for, from this instant,
There's nothing serious in mortality :
All is but toys : renown and grace is dead ;
The wine of life is drawn, and the mere lees
Is left this vault to brag of.
       ACT II, Scene iii, ll. 59-101

    Outside Macbeth's castle.

    Enter ROSS *and an* old Man.

 Old M. Threescore and ten I can remember well :
Within the volume of which time I have seen
Hours dreadful and things strange ; but this sore night
Hath trifled former knowings.
 Ross.   Ah, good father,
Thou seest, the heavens, as troubled with man's act,
Threaten his bloody stage : by the clock, 'tis day,
And yet dark night strangles the travelling lamp :
Is't night's predominance, or the day's shame,

That darkness does the face of earth entomb,
When living light should kiss it?

   Old M.   'Tis unnatural,
Even like the deed that's done. On Tuesday last,
A falcon, towering in her pride of place,
Was by a mousing owl hawk'd at and kill'd.

   Ross. And Duncan's horses—a thing most strange and
      certain—
Beauteous and swift, the minions of their race,
Turn'd wild in nature, broke their stalls, flung out,
Contending 'gainst obedience, as they would make
War with mankind.

   Old M.   'Tis said they eat each other.

   Ross. They did so, to the amazement of mine eyes
That look'd upon't.

                             Act II, Scene iv, ll. 1-20

   Macbeth.   To be thus is nothing;
But to be safely thus.—Our fears in Banquo
Stick deep; and in his royalty of nature
Reigns that which would be fear'd: 'tis much he dares;
And, to that dauntless temper of his mind,
He hath a wisdom that doth guide his valour
To act in safety. There is none but he
Whose being I do fear: and, under him,
My Genius is rebuked; as, it is said,
Mark Antony's was by Caesar. He chid the sisters
When first they put the name of king upon me,
And bade them speak to him: then prophet-like
They hail'd him father to a line of kings:
Upon my head they placed a fruitless crown,
And put a barren sceptre in my gripe,
Thence to be wrench'd with an unlineal hand,
No son of mine succeeding. If't be so,
For Banquo's issue have I filed my mind;
For them the gracious Duncan have I murder'd;

Put rancours in the vessel of my peace
Only for them ; and mine eternal jewel
Given to the common enemy of man,
To make them kings, the seed of Banquo kings !
Rather than so, come fate into the list,
And champion me to the utterance !

ACT III, Scene i, ll. 48-72

    Lady Macbeth. How now, my lord ! why do you keep
    alone,
Of sorriest fancies your companions making,
Using those thoughts which should indeed have died
With them they think on ? Things without all remedy
Should be without regard : what's done is done.
    Macbeth. We have scotch'd the snake, not kill'd it :
She'll close and be herself, whilst our poor malice
Remains in danger of her former tooth.
But let the frame of things disjoint, both the worlds suffer,
Ere we will eat our meal in fear and sleep
In the affliction of these terrible dreams
That shake us nightly : better be with the dead,
Whom we, to gain our peace, have sent to peace,
Than on the torture of the mind to lie
In restless ecstasy. Duncan is in his grave ;
After life's fitful fever he sleeps well ;
Treason has done his worst : nor steel, nor poison,
Malice domestic, foreign levy, nothing,
Can touch him further.
    Lady M.   Come on ;
Gentle my lord, sleek o'er your rugged looks ;
Be bright and jovial among your guests to-night.
    Macb. So shall I, love ; and so, I pray, be you :
Let your remembrance apply to Banquo ;
Present him eminence, both with eye and tongue :
Unsafe the while, that we
Must lave our honours in these flattering streams,

And make our faces vizards to our hearts,
Disguising what they are.

    Lady M.   You must leave this.

    Macb. O, full of scorpions is my mind, dear wife !
Thou know'st that Banquo, and his Fleance, lives.

    Lady M. But in them nature's copy's not eterne.

    Macb. There's comfort yet ; they are assailable ;
Then be thou jocund : ere the bat hath flown
His cloister'd flight, ere to black Hecate's summons
The shard-borne beetle with his drowsy hums
Hath rung night's yawning peal, there shall be done
A deed of dreadful note.

    Lady M.   What's to be done ?

    Macb. Be innocent of the knowledge, dearest chuck,
Till thou applaud the deed. Come, seeling night,
Scarf up the tender eye of pitiful day ;
And with thy bloody and invisible hand
Cancel and tear to pieces that great bond
Which keeps me pale ! Light thickens ; and the crow
Makes wing to the rooky wood :
Good things of day begin to droop and drowse ;
Whiles night's black agents to their preys do rouse.
Thou marvell'st at my words : but hold thee still :
Things bad begun make strong themselves by ill.
So, prithee, go with me.

                                    Act III, Scene ii, ll. 8-56

A park near the palace.

Enter three Murderers.

    First Mur. But who did bid thee join with us ?

    Third Mur.   Macbeth.

    Sec. Mur. He needs not our mistrust, since he delivers
Our offices and what we have to do
To the direction just.

    First Mur.   Then stand with us.
The west yet glimmers with some streaks of day :

Now spurs the lated traveller apace
To gain the timely inn ; and near approaches
The subject of our watch.

Third Mur.   Hark ! I hear horses.

Ban. [*Within*] Give us a light there, ho !

Sec. Mur.   Then 'tis he : the rest
That are within the note of expectation
Already are i' the court.

First Mur.   His horses go about.

Third Mur. Almost a mile : but he does usually,
So all men do, from hence to the palace gate
Make it their walk.

Sec. Mur.   A light, a light !

   Enter BANQUO, *and* FLEANCE *with a torch.*

Third Mur.   'Tis he.

First Mur. Stand to't.

Ban. It will be rain to-night.

First Mur.   Let it come down.

         [*They set upon Banquo.*

Ban. O, treachery ! Fly, good Fleance, fly, fly, fly !
Thou mayst revenge. O slave !

        [*Dies. Fleance escapes.*

Third Mur. Who did strike out the light ?

First Mur.   Was't not the way ?

Third Mur. There's but one down ; the son is fled.

Sec. Mur.   We have lost
Best half of our affair.

First Mur. Well, let's away, and say how much is done.

       ACT III, Scene iii, ll. 1-22

   The same. Hall in the palace.

 A banquet prepared. Enter MACBETH, LADY MACBETH,
   ROSS, LENNOX, Lords, *and Attendants.*

Macb. You know your own degrees ; sit down : at first
And last the hearty welcome.

Lords.   Thanks to your majesty.

Macb. Ourself will mingle with society,
And play the humble host.
Our hostess keeps her state, but in best time
We will require her welcome.

Lady M. Pronounce it for me, sir, to all our friends ;
For my heart speaks they are welcome.

First Murderer *appears at the door.*

Macb. See, they encounter thee with their hearts' thanks.
Both sides are even : here I'll sit i' the midst :
Be large in mirth ; anon we'll drink a measure
The table round. [*Approaching the door.*] There's blood
    upon thy face.

Mur. 'Tis Banquo's then.

Macb. 'Tis better thee without than he within.
Is he dispatch'd ?

Mur. My lord, his throat is cut ; that I did for him.

Macb. Thou art the best o' the cut-throats : yet he's good
That did the like for Fleance : if thou didst it,
Thou art the nonpareil.

Mur.   Most royal sir,
Fleance is 'scaped.

Macb. Then comes my fit again : I had else been perfect,
Whole as the marble, founded as the rock,
As broad and general as the casing air :
But now I am cabin'd, cribb'd, confined, bound in
To saucy doubts and fears. But Banquo's safe ?

Mur. Ay, my good lord : safe in a ditch he bides,
With twenty trenched gashes on his head ;
The least a death to nature.

Macb.   Thanks for that :
There the grown serpent lies ; the worm that's fled
Hath nature that in time will venom breed,
No teeth for the present. Get thee gone : to-morrow
We'll hear, ourselves, again.   [*Exit Murderer.*

495

Lady M.　　　　　　　　My royal lord,
You do not give the cheer : the feast is sold
That is not often vouch'd, while 'tis a-making,
'Tis given with welcome : to feed were best at home ;
From thence the sauce to meat is ceremony ;
Meeting were bare without it.

Macb.　　　　　　　　　Sweet remembrancer !
Now, good digestion wait on appetite,
And health on both !

Len.　　　　　　　May't please your highness sit.

　　[The ghost of Banquo enters, and sits in Macbeth's place.

Macb. Here had we now our country's honour roof'd,
Were the graced person of our Banquo present ;
Who may I rather challenge for unkindness
Than pity for mischance !

Ross.　　　　　　　　His absence, sir,
Lays blame upon his promise. Please't your highness
To grace us with your royal company.

Macb. The table's full.

Len.　　　　　　Here is a place reserved, sir.

Macb. Where ?

Len. Here, my good lord. What is't that moves your
　highness ?

Macb. Which of you have done this ?

Lords.　　　　　　　　What, my good lord ?

Macb. Thou canst not say I did it : never shake
Thy gory locks at me.

Ross. Gentlemen, rise : his highness is not well.

Lady M. Sit, worthy friends : my lord is often thus,
And hath been from his youth : pray you, keep seat ;
The fit is momentary ; upon a thought
He will again be well : if much you note him,
You shall offend him and extend his passion :
Feed, and regard him not. Are you a man ?

Macb. Ay, and a bold one, that dare look on that
Which might appal the devil.

Lady M.   O proper stuff !
This is the very painting of your fear :
This is the air-drawn dagger, which, you said,
Led you to Duncan. O, these flaws and starts,
Impostors to true fear, would well become
A woman's story at a winter's fire,
Authorized by her grandam. Shame itself !
Why do you make such faces ? When all's done,
You look but on a stool.

   Macb. Prithee, see there ! behold ! look ! lo ! how say
    you ?
Why, what care I ? If thou canst nod, speak too.
If charnel-houses and our graves must send
Those that we bury back, our monuments
Shall be the maws of kites.   [*Ghost vanishes.*

   Lady M.   What, quite unmann'd in folly ?
   Macb. If I stand here, I saw him.
   Lady M.   Fie, for shame !
   Macb. Blood hath been shed ere now, i' the olden time,
Ere human statute purged the gentle weal ;
Ay, and since too, murders have been perform'd
Too terrible for the ear : the times have been,
That, when the brains were out, the man would die,
And there an end ; but now they rise again,
With twenty mortal murders on their crowns,
And push us from our stools : this is more strange
Than such a murder is.

   Lady M.   My worthy lord,
Your noble friends do lack you.

   Macb.   I do forget.
Do not muse at me, my most worthy friends ;
I have a strange infirmity, which is nothing
To those that know me. Come, love and health to all ;
Then I'll sit down. Give me some wine ; fill full.
I drink to the general joy o' the whole table,
And to our dear friend Banquo, whom we miss ;

Would he were here ! to all, and him, we thirst,
And all to all.

    Lords.   Our duties, and the pledge.

Re-enter Ghost.

    Macb. Avaunt ! and quit my sight ! let the earth hide
    thee !
Thy bones are marrowless, thy blood is cold ;
Thou hast no speculation in those eyes
Which thou dost glare with !

    Lady M.   Think of this, good peers,
But as a thing of custom : 'tis no other ;
Only it spoils the pleasure of the time.

    Macb. What man dare, I dare :
Approach thou like the rugged Russian bear,
The arm'd rhinoceros, or the Hyrcan tiger ;
Take any shape but that, and my firm nerves
Shall never tremble : or be alive again,
And dare me to the desert with thy sword ;
If trembling I inhabit then, protest me
The baby of a girl. Hence, horrible shadow !
Unreal mockery, hence !   [*Ghost vanishes.*
           Why, so : being gone,
I am a man again. Pray you, sit still.

    Lady M. You have displaced the mirth, broke the good
    meeting,
With most admired disorder.

    Macb.   Can such things be,
And overcome us like a summer's cloud,
Without our special wonder ? You make me strange
Even to the disposition that I owe,
When now I think you can behold such sights,
And keep the natural ruby of your cheeks,
When mine is blanch'd with fear.

    Ross.   What sights, my lord ?

    Lady M. I pray you, speak not ; he grows worse and worse ;

Question enrages him. At once, good night :
Stand not upon the order of your going,
But go at once.

   Len.   Good night ; and better health
Attend his majesty !

   Lady M.   A kind good night to all !

                  [Exeunt all but Macbeth and Lady M.

   Macb. It will have blood ; they say, blood will have blood :
Stones have been known to move and trees to speak ;
Augurs and understood relations have
By magot-pies and choughs and rooks brought forth
The secret'st man of blood. What is the night ?

   Lady M. Almost at odds with morning, which is which.

   Macb. How say'st thou, that Macduff denies his person
At our great bidding ?

   Lady M.   Did you send to him, sir ?

   Macb. I hear it by the way ; but I will send :
There's not a one of them but in his house
I keep a servant fee'd. I will to-morrow,
And betimes I will, to the weird sisters :
More shall they speak ; for now I am bent to know,
By the worst means, the worst. For mine own good,
All causes shall give way : I am in blood
Stepp'd in so far that, should I wade no more,
Returning were as tedious as go o'er :
Strange things I have in head, that will to hand ;
Which must be acted ere they may be scann'd.

   Lady M. You lack the season of all natures, sleep.

   Macb. Come, we'll to sleep. My strange and self-abuse
Is the initiate fear that wants hard use :
We are yet but young in deed.

                        Act III, Scene iv, ll. 1-144

A cavern. In the middle, a boiling cauldron.

Thunder. Enter the three Witches.

First Witch. Thrice the brinded cat hath mew'd.

Sec. Witch. Thrice and once the hedge-pig whined.

Third Witch. Harpier cries 'Tis time, 'tis time.

First Witch. Round about the cauldron go ;
In the poison'd entrails throw.
Toad, that under cold stone
Days and nights has thirty one
Swelter'd venom sleeping got,
Boil thou first i' the charmed pot.

All. Double, double toil and trouble ;
Fire burn and cauldron bubble.

Sec. Witch. Fillet of a fenny snake,
In the cauldron boil and bake ;
Eye of newt and toe of frog,
Wool of bat and tongue of dog,
Adder's fork and blind-worm's sting,
Lizard's leg and howlet's wing,
For a charm of powerful trouble,
Like a hell-broth boil and bubble.

All. Double, double toil and trouble ;
Fire burn and cauldron bubble.

Third Witch. Scale of dragon, tooth of wolf,
Witches' mummy, maw and gulf
Of the ravin'd salt-sea shark,
Root of hemlock digg'd i' the dark,
Liver of blaspheming Jew,
Gall of goat, and slips of yew
Sliver'd in the moon's eclipse,
Nose of Turk and Tartar's lips,
Finger of birth-strangled babe
Ditch-deliver'd by a drab,
Make the gruel thick and slab :
Add thereto a tiger's chaudron,
For the ingredients of our cauldron.

All. Double, double toil and trouble ;
Fire burn and cauldron bubble.

Sec. Witch. Cool it with a baboon's blood,

Then the charm is firm and good. . . .
By the pricking of my thumbs,
Something wicked this way comes. . . .

Enter MACBETH.

Macb. How now, you secret, black, and midnight hags !
What is't you do ?
 All.   A deed without a name.
 Macb. I conjure you, by that which you profess,
Howe'er you come to know it, answer me :
Though you untie the winds and let them fight
Against the churches ; though the yesty waves
Confound and swallow navigation up ;
Though bladed corn be lodged and trees blown down ;
Though castles topple on their warders' heads ;
Though palaces and pyramids do slope
Their heads to their foundations ; though the treasure
Of nature's germens tumble all together,
Even till destruction sicken ; answer me
To what I ask you.
 First Witch. Speak.
 Sec. Witch.   Demand.
 Third Witch.   We'll answer.
 First Witch. Say, if thou'dst rather hear it from our
  mouths,
Or from our masters ?
 Macb.   Call 'em ; let me see 'em.
 First Witch. Pour in sow's blood, that hath eaten
Her nine farrow ; grease that's sweaten
From the murderer's gibbet throw
Into the flame.
 All.   Come, high or low ;
Thyself and office deftly show !

  Thunder. *First* Apparition : *an armed Head.*

 Macb. Tell me, thou unknown power,—
 First Witch.   He knows thy thought :

Hear his speech, but say thou nought.

First App. Macbeth! Macbeth! Macbeth! beware
Macduff;

Beware the thane of Fife. Dismiss me. Enough. [*Descends.*

Macb. Whate'er thou art, for thy good caution, thanks;
Thou hast harp'd my fear aright: but one word more,—

First Witch. He will not be commanded: here's another,
More potent than the first.

Thunder. Second Apparition: *a bloody Child.*

Sec. App. Macbeth! Macbeth! Macbeth!

Macb. Had I three ears, I'ld hear thee.

Sec. App. Be bloody, bold, and resolute; laugh to scorn
The power of man, for none of woman born
Shall harm Macbeth.   [*Descends.*

Macb. Then live, Macduff: what need I fear of thee?
But yet I'll make assurance double sure,
And take a bond of fate: thou shalt not live;
That I may tell pale-hearted fear it lies,
And sleep in spite of thunder.

Thunder. Third Apparition: *a Child crowned, with a
tree in his hand.*

What is this
That rises like the issue of a king,
And wears upon his baby-brow the round
And top of sovereignty?

All.   Listen, but speak not to't.

Third App. Be lion-mettled, proud; and take no care
Who chafes, who frets, or where conspirers are:
Macbeth shall never vanquish'd be until
Great Birnam wood to high Dunsinane hill
Shall come against him.   [*Descends.*

Macb.   That will never be:
Who can impress the forest, bid the tree
Unfix his earth-bound root? Sweet bodements! good!
Rebellion's head, rise never till the wood

Of Birnam rise, and our high-placed Macbeth
Shall live the lease of nature, pay his breath
To time and mortal custom. Yet my heart
Throbs to know one thing : tell me, if your art
Can tell so much : shall Banquo's issue ever
Reign in this kingdom ?

    All.   Seek to know no more.

    Macb. I will be satisfied : deny me this,
And an eternal curse fall on you ! Let me know.
Why sinks that cauldron ? and what noise is this ? [*Hautboys.*

    First Witch. Show !

    Sec. Witch. Show !

    Third Witch. Show !

    All. Show his eyes, and grieve his heart ;
Come like shadows, so depart !

A show of Eight Kings, *the last with a glass in his hand;
Banquo's Ghost following.*

    Macb. Thou art too like the spirit of Banquo ; down !
Thy crown does sear mine eye-balls. And thy hair,
Thou other gold-bound brow, is like the first.
A third is like the former. Filthy hags !
Why do you show me this ? A fourth ! Start, eyes !
What, will the line stretch out to the crack of doom ?
Another yet ! A seventh ! I'll see no more :
And yet the eighth appears, who bears a glass
Which shows me many more ; and some I see
That two-fold balls and treble sceptres carry :
Horrible sight ! Now, I see, 'tis true ;
For the blood-bolter'd Banquo smiles upon me,
And points at them for his.   [*Apparitions vanish.*] . . .
          [*Music. The Witches dance, and then vanish.*

    Macb. Where are they ? Gone ? Let this pernicious
      hour
Stand aye accursed in the calendar !
Come in, without there !

Enter LENNOX.

Len.   What's your grace's will ?

Macb. Saw you the weird sisters ?

Len.   No, my lord.

Macb. Came they not by you ?

Len.   No, indeed, my lord.

Macb. Infected be the air whereon they ride ;
And damn'd all those that trust them ! I did hear
The galloping of horse : who was't came by ?

Len. 'Tis two or three, my lord, that bring you word
Macduff is fled to England.

Macb.   Fled to England !

Len. Ay, my good lord.

Macb. Time, thou anticipatest my dread exploits :
The flighty purpose never is o'ertook
Unless the deed go with it : from this moment
The very firstlings of my heart shall be
The firstlings of my hand. And even now,
To crown my thoughts with acts, be it thought and done :
The castle of Macduff I will surprise ;
Seize upon Fife ; give to the edge o' the sword
His wife, his babes, and all unfortunate souls
That trace him in his line. No boasting like a fool :
This deed I'll do before this purpose cool.
But not more sights !—Where are these gentlemen ?
Come, bring me where they are.

                    ACT IV, Scene i, ll. 1-38, 44-45, 48-124, 133-156

Angels are bright still, though the brightest fell.

                                ACT IV, Scene iii, l. 22

Macduff.   How does my wife ?

Ross. Why, well.

Macd.   And all my children ?

Ross.   Well too.

Macd. The tyrant has not batter'd at their peace ?

Ross. No ; they were well at peace when I did leave 'em.

Macd. Be not a niggard of your speech : how goes't ? . . .

Ross.   I have words
That would be howl'd out in the desert air,
Where hearing should not latch them.

Macd.   What concern they ?
The general cause ? or is it a fee-grief
Due to some single breast ?

Ross.   No mind that's honest
But in it shares some woe ; though the main part
Pertains to you alone.

Macd.   If it be mine,
Keep it not from me, quickly let me have it.

Ross. Let not your ears despise my tongue for ever,
Which shall possess them with the heaviest sound
That ever yet they heard.

Macd.   Hum ! I guess at it.

Ross. Your castle is surprised ; your wife and babes
Savagely slaughter'd : to relate the manner,
Were, on the quarry of these murder'd deer,
To add the death of you.

Mal.   Merciful heaven !
What, man ! ne'er pull your hat upon your brows ;
Give sorrow words : the grief that does not speak
Whispers the o'er-fraught heart and bids it break.

Macd. My children too ?

Ross.   Wife, children, servants, all
That could be found.

Macd.   And I must be from thence !
My wife kill'd too ?

Ross.   I have said.

Mal.   Be comforted :
Let's make us medicines of our great revenge,
To cure this deadly grief.

Macd. He has no children. All my pretty ones ?
Did you say all ? O hell-kite ! All ?

What, all my pretty chickens and their dam
At one fell swoop ?

 Mal. Dispute it like a man.

 Macd.   I shall do so ;
But I must also feel it as a man :
I cannot but remember such things were,
That were most precious to me.

         Act IV, Scene iii, ll. 176-180, 193-223

       Macbeth

Is ripe for shaking, and the powers above
Put on their instruments. Act IV, Scene iii, ll. 237-239

  Dunsinane. Ante-room in the castle.

 Enter a Doctor of Physic *and a* Waiting-Gentlewoman.

 Doct. I have two nights watched with you, but can perceive no truth in your report. When was it she last walked ?

 Gent. Since his majesty went into the field, I have seen her rise from her bed, throw her nightgown upon her, unlock her closet, take forth paper, fold it, write upon't, read it, afterwards seal it, and again return to bed ; yet all this while in a most fast sleep.

 Doct. A great perturbation in nature, to receive at once the benefit of sleep, and do the effects of watching ! In this slumbery agitation, besides her walking and other actual performances, what, at any time, have you heard her say ?

 Gent. That, sir, which I will not report after her.

 Doct. You may to me : and 'tis most meet you should.

 Gent. Neither to you nor any one ; having no witness to confirm my speech.

   Enter Lady MACBETH, *with a taper.*

Lo you, here she comes ! This is her very guise ; and, upon my life, fast asleep. Observe her ; stand close.

 Doct. How came she by that light ?

 Gent. Why, it stood by her : she has light by her continually ; 'tis her command.

Doct. You see, her eyes are open.

Gent. Ay, but their sense is shut.

Doct. What is it she does now? Look, how she rubs her hands.

Gent. It is an accustomed action with her, to seem thus washing her hands: I have known her continue in this a quarter of an hour.

Lady M. Yet here's a spot.

Doct. Hark! she speaks: I will set down what comes from her, to satisfy my remembrance the more strongly.

Lady M. Out, damned spot! out, I say!—One: two: why, then 'tis time to do't.—Hell is murky!—Fie, my lord, fie! a soldier, and afeard? What need we fear who knows it, when none can call our power to account?—Yet who would have thought the old man to have had so much blood in him.

Doct. Do you mark that?

Lady M. The thane of Fife had a wife: where is she now? —What, will these hands ne'er be clean?—No more o' that, my lord, no more o' that: you mar all with this starting.

Doct. Go to, go to; you have known what you should not.

Gent. She has spoke what she should not, I am sure of that: heaven knows what she has known.

Lady M. Here's the smell of the blood still: all the perfumes of Arabia will not sweeten this little hand. Oh, oh, oh!

Doct. What a sigh is there! The heart is sorely charged.

Gent. I would not have such a heart in my bosom for the dignity of the whole body.

Doct. Well, well, well,—

Gent. Pray God it be, sir.

Doct. This disease is beyond my practice: yet I have known those which have walked in their sleep who have died holily in their beds.

Lady M. Wash your hands, put on your nightgown; look not so pale.—I tell you yet again, Banquo's buried; he cannot come out on's grave.

Doct. Even so?

Lady M. To bed, to bed! there's knocking at the gate:
come, come, come, come, give me your hand. What's done
cannot be undone.—To bed, to bed, to bed!   [*Exit.*

Doct. Will she go now to bed?

Gent. Directly.

Doct. Foul whisperings are abroad: unnatural deeds
Do breed unnatural troubles: infected minds
To their deaf pillows will discharge their secrets:
More needs she the divine than the physician.
God, God forgive us all! Look after her;
Remove from her the means of all annoyance,
And still keep eyes upon her. So, good night:
My mind she has mated, and amazed my sight.
I think, but dare not speak.

Gent.   Good night, good doctor.

ACT V, Scene i, ll. 1-87

Now does he feel
His secret murders sticking on his hands;
Now minutely revolts upbraid his faith-breach;
Those he commands move only in command,
Nothing in love: now does he feel his title
Hang loose about him, like a giant's robe
Upon a dwarfish thief.   ACT V, Scene ii, ll. 16-22

Dunsinane. A room in the castle.

To MACBETH, Doctor, *and* Attendants *enter a* Servant.

Macb. The devil damn thee black, thou cream-faced loon!
Where got'st thou that goose look?

Serv. There is ten thousand—

Macb.   Geese, villain?

Serv.   Soldiers, sir.

Macb. Go prick thy face, and over-red thy fear,
Thou lily-liver'd boy. What soldiers, patch?
Death of thy soul! those linen cheeks of thine
Are counsellors to fear. What soldiers, wheyface?

508

Serv. The English force, so please you.

Macb. Take thy face hence.   [*Exit Servant.*

           Seyton !—I am sick at heart,
When I behold—Seyton, I say !—This push
Will cheer me ever, or disseat me now.
I have lived long enough : my way of life
Is fall'n into the sear, the yellow leaf ;
And that which should accompany old age,
As honour, love, obedience, troops of friends,
I must not look to have ; but, in their stead,
Curses, not loud but deep, mouth-honour, breath,
Which the poor heart would fain deny, and dare not.
Seyton !

Enter SEYTON.

Sey. What is your gracious pleasure ?

Macb.   What news more ?

Sey. All is confirm'd, my lord, which was reported.

Macb. I'll fight till from my bones my flesh be hack'd.
Give me my armour.

Sey.   'Tis not needed yet.

Macb. I'll put it on.
Send out moe horses ; skirr the country round ;
Hang those that talk of fear. Give me mine armour.
How does your patient, doctor ?

Doct.   Not so sick, my lord,
As she is troubled with thick-coming fancies,
That keep her from her rest.

Macb.   Cure her of that.
Canst thou not minister to a mind diseased,
Pluck from the memory a rooted sorrow,
Raze out the written troubles of the brain
And with some sweet oblivious antidote
Cleanse the stuff'd bosom of that perilous stuff
Which weighs upon the heart ?

Doct.   Therein the patient
Must minister to himself.

Macb. Throw physic to the dogs; I'll none of it.
Come, put mine armour on; give me my staff.
Seyton, send out. Doctor, the thanes fly from me.
Come, sir, dispatch. If thou couldst, doctor, cast
The water of my land, find her disease,
And purge it to a sound and pristine health,
I would applaud thee to the very echo,
That should applaud again.—Pull't off, I say.—
What rhubarb, cyme, or what purgative drug,
Would scour these English hence?

ACT V, Scene iii, ll. 11-56

Dunsinane. Within the castle.

Enter MACBETH, SEYTON, *and* Soldiers, *with drum and colours.*

Macb. Hang out our banners on the outward walls;
The cry is still ' They come : ' our castle's strength
Will laugh a siege to scorn : here let them lie
Till famine and the ague eat them up :
Were they not forced with those that should be ours,
We might have met them dareful, beard to beard,
And beat them backward home.   [*A cry of women within.*
                                        What is that noise?

Sey. It is the cry of women, my good lord.   [*Exit.*

Macb. I have almost forgot the taste of fears :
The time has been, my senses would have cool'd
To hear a night-shriek ; and my fell of hair
Would at a dismal treatise rouse and stir
As life were in't : I have supp'd full with horrors ;
Direness, familiar to my slaughterous thoughts,
Cannot once start me.

Re-enter SEYTON.

                        Wherefore was that cry?
Sey. The queen, my lord, is dead.
Macb. She should have died hereafter ;

510

There would have been a time for such a word.
To-morrow, and to-morrow, and to-morrow,
Creeps in this petty pace from day to day
To the last syllable of recorded time,
And all our yesterdays have lighted fools
The way to dusty death.   Out, out, brief candle !
Life's but a walking shadow, a poor player
That struts and frets his hour upon the stage
And then is heard no more : it is a tale
Told by an idiot, full of sound and fury,
Signifying nothing.   ACT V, Scene v, ll. 1-28

Another part of the field.

Enter MACBETH.

Macb. Why should I play the Roman fool, and die
On mine own sword ? whiles I see lives, the gashes
Do better upon them. ·

Enter MACDUFF.

Macd.   Turn, hell-hound, turn !
Macb. Of all men else I have avoided thee :
But get thee back ; my soul is too much charged
With blood of thine already.
Macd.   I have no words :
My voice is in my sword : thou bloodier villain
Than terms can give thee out !   [*They fight.*
Macb.   Thou losest labour :
As easy mayst thou the intrenchant air
With thy keen sword impress as make me bleed :
Let fall thy blade on vulnerable crests ;
I bear a charmed life, which must not yield
To one of woman born.
Macd.   Despair thy charm ;
And let the angel whom thou still hast served
Tell thee, Macduff was from his mother's womb
Untimely ripp'd.
Macb. Accursed be that tongue that tells me so,

For it hath cow'd my better part of man !
And be these juggling fiends no more believed,
That palter with us in a double sense ;
That keep the word of promise to our ear,
And break it to our hope.   I'll not fight with thee.
    Macd. Then yield thee, coward,
And live to be the show and gaze o' the time :
We'll have thee, as our rarer monsters are,
Painted upon a pole, and underwrit,
' Here may you see the tyrant.'
    Macb.   I will not yield,
To kiss the ground before young Malcolm's feet,
And to be baited with the rabble's curse.
Though Birnam wood be come to Dunsinane,
And thou opposed, being of no woman born,
Yet I will try the last.   Before my body
I throw my warlike shield.   Lay on, Macduff,
And damn'd be him that first cries ' Hold, enough ! '
                         [Exeunt, fighting.   Alarums.
                             ACT V, Scene viii, ll. 1-34

    Ross. Your son, my lord, has paid a soldier's debt. . . .
    Siward.   Why then, God's soldier be he !
                         ACT V, Scene viii, ll. 39, 47

King Lear

    Cordelia. [*Aside*] What shall Cordelia do ? Love, and be
    silent.
    Lear. Of all these bounds, even from this line to this,
With shadowy forests and with champains rich'd,
With plenteous rivers and wide-skirted meads,
We make thee lady : to thine and Albany's issue
Be this perpetual. . . .

                              Now, our joy,
Although the last, not least ; to whose young love
The vines of France and milk of Burgundy
Strive to be interess'd ; what can you say to draw
A third more opulent than your sisters ? Speak.

Cor. Nothing, my lord.

Lear. Nothing !

Cor. Nothing.

Lear. Nothing will come of nothing : speak again.

Cor. Unhappy that I am, I cannot heave
My heart into my mouth : I love your majesty
According to my bond ; nor more nor less.

Lear. How, how, Cordelia ! mend your speech a little,
Lest it may mar your fortunes.

Cor.   Good my lord,
You have begot me, bred me, loved me : I
Return those duties back as are right fit,
Obey you, love you, and most honour you.
Why have my sisters husbands, if they say
They love you all ? Haply, when I shall wed,
That lord whose hand must take my plight shall carry
Half my love with him, half my care and duty :
Sure, I shall never marry like my sisters,
To love my father all.

Lear. But goes thy heart with this ?

Cor.   Ay, good my lord.

Lear. So young, and so untender ?

Cor. So young, my lord, and true.

Lear. Let it be so ; thy truth, then, be thy dower :
For, by the sacred radiance of the sun,
The mysteries of Hecate, and the night ;
By all the operation of the orbs
From whom we do exist, and cease to be ;
Here I disclaim all my paternal care,
Propinquity and property of blood,
And as a stranger to my heart and me

Hold thee, from this, for ever. The barbarous Scythian,
Or he that makes his generation messes
To gorge his appetite, shall to my bosom
Be as well neighbour'd, pitied, and relieved,
As thou my sometime daughter.

  Kent.   Good my liege,—

  Lear. Peace, Kent !
Come not between the dragon and his wrath. . . .
The bow is bent and drawn, make from the shaft. . . .

  France. Fairest Cordelia, that art most rich, being poor ;
Most choice, forsaken ; and most loved, despised !
Thee and thy virtues here I seize upon :
Be it lawful I take up what's cast away.

         Act I, Scene i, ll. 63-68, 84-124, 145, 253-256

  Lear. What art thou ?

  Kent (*disguised*). A very honest-hearted fellow, and as
poor as the king.

  Lear. If thou be as poor for a subject as he is for a king,
thou art poor enough. What wouldst thou ?

  Kent. Service.

  Lear. Who wouldst thou serve ?

  Kent. You.

  Lear. Dost thou know me, fellow ?

  Kent. No, sir ; but you have that in your countenance
which I would fain call master.

  Lear. What's that ?

  Kent. Authority.   Act I, Scene iv, ll. 19-32

  Lear. Now, my friendly knave, I thank thee : there's
earnest of thy service.   [*Giving Kent money*.

       Enter Fool.

  Fool. Let me hire him too : here's my coxcomb.

          [*Offering Kent his cap*.

  Lear. How now, my pretty knave ! how dost thou ?

  Fool. Sirrah, you were best take my coxcomb.

Kent. Why, fool?

Fool. Why, for taking one's part that's out of favour : nay, an thou canst not smile as the wind sits, thou'lt catch cold shortly : there, take my coxcomb : why, this fellow has banished two on's daughters, and did the third a blessing against his will ; if thou follow him, thou must needs wear my coxcomb. How now, nuncle ! Would I had two coxcombs and two daughters !

Lear. Why, my boy ?

Fool. If I gave them all my living, I'ld keep my coxcombs myself. There's mine ; beg another of thy daughters.

Lear. Take heed, sirrah ; the whip.

Fool. Truth's a dog must to kennel ; he must be whipped out, when Lady the brach may stand by the fire and stink. . . .

Dost thou know the difference, my boy, between a bitter fool and a sweet fool ?

Lear. No, lad ; teach me.

Fool.   That lord that counsell'd thee
          To give away thy land,
       Come place him here by me,
          Do thou for him stand :
       The sweet and bitter fool
          Will presently appear ;
       The one in motley here,
          The other found out there.

Lear. Dost thou call me fool, boy ?

Fool. All thy other titles thou hast given away ; that thou wast born with.

Kent. This is not altogether fool, my lord.

Fool. No, faith, lords and great men will not let me ; if I had a monopoly out, they would have part on't : and ladies too, they will not let me have all fool to myself ; they'll be snatching. Give me an egg, nuncle, and I'll give thee two crowns.

Lear. What two crowns shall they be ?

Fool. Why, after I have cut the egg i' the middle, and eat up the meat, the two crowns of the egg. When thou clovest thy crown i' the middle, and gavest away both parts, thou borest thy ass on thy back o'er the dirt : thou hadst little wit in thy bald crown, when thou gavest thy golden one away. If I speak like myself in this, let him be whipped that first finds it so.

[*Singing*]   Fools had ne'er less wit in a year ;
                For wise men are grown foppish,
            They know not how their wits to wear,
                Their manners are so apish.

Lear. When were you wont to be so full of songs, sirrah ?

Fool. I have used it, nuncle, ever since thou madest thy daughters thy mothers : for when thou gavest them the rod, and put'st down thine own breeches,

[*Singing*]   Then they for sudden joy did weep,
                And I for sorrow sung,
            That such a king should play bo-peep,
                And go the fools among.

Prithee, nuncle, keep a schoolmaster that can teach thy fool to lie : I would fain learn to lie.

Lear. An you lie, sirrah, we'll have you whipped.

Fool. I marvel what kin thou and thy daughters are : they'll have me whipped for speaking true, thou'lt have me whipped for lying ; and sometimes I am whipped for holding my peace. I had rather be any kind o' thing than a fool : and yet I would not be thee, nuncle ; thou hast pared thy wit o' both sides, and left nothing i' the middle : here comes one o' the parings.

Enter GONERIL. . . .

Lear. Your name, fair gentlewoman ?

Gon. This admiration, sir, is much o' the savour
Of other your new pranks. I do beseech you
To understand my purposes aright :
As you are old and reverend, you should be wise.
Here do you keep a hundred knights and squires ;

516

Men so disorder'd, so debosh'd and bold,
That this our court, infected with their manners,
Shows like a riotous inn : epicurism and lust
Make it more like a tavern or a brothel
Than a graced palace. The shame itself doth speak
For instant remedy : be then desired
By her, that else will take the thing she begs,
A little to disquantity your train ;
And the remainder, that shall still depend,
To be such men as may besort your age,
And know themselves and you.

    Lear.   Darkness and devils !
Saddle my horses ; call my train together.
Degenerate bastard ! I'll not trouble thee :
Yet have I left a daughter.

    Gon. You strike my people ; and your disorder'd rabble
Make servants of their betters.

                 Enter ALBANY.

    Lear. Woe, that too late repents,—[*To Alb*.]
      O, sir, are you come ?
Is it your will ? Speak, sir. Prepare my horses.
Ingratitude, thou marble-hearted fiend,
More hideous when thou show'st thee in a child
Than the sea-monster !

    Alb.   Pray, sir, be patient.

    Lear. [*To Gon*.] Detested kite ! thou liest :
My train are men of choice and rarest parts,
That all particulars of duty know,
And in the most exact regard support
The worships of their name. O most small fault,
How ugly didst thou in Cordelia show !
That, like an engine, wrench'd my frame of nature
From the fix'd place ; drew from my heart all love,
And added to the gall. O Lear, Lear, Lear !
Beat at this gate, that let thy folly in,   [*Striking his head*.

And thy dear judgement out! Go, go, my people.

    Alb. My lord, I am guiltless, as I am ignorant
Of what hath moved you.

    Lear.   It may be so, my lord.
Hear, nature, hear; dear goddess, hear!
Suspend thy purpose, if thou didst intend
To make this creature fruitful!
Into her womb convey sterility!
Dry up in her the organs of increase;
And from her derogate body never spring
A babe to honour her! If she must teem,
Create her child of spleen; that it may live,
And be a thwart disnatured torment to her!
Let it stamp wrinkles in her brow of youth;
With cadent tears fret channels in her cheeks;
Turn all her mother's pains and benefits
To laughter and contempt; that she may feel
How sharper than a serpent's tooth it is
To have a thankless child! Away, away!   [*Exit.*

    Alb. Now, gods that we adore, whereof comes this?

    Gon. Never afflict yourself to know the cause;
But let his disposition have that scope
That dotage gives it.

                Re-enter LEAR.

    Lear. What, fifty of my followers at a clap!
Within a fortnight!

    Alb.   What's the matter, sir?

    Lear. I'll tell thee: [*To Gon.*] Life and death! I am
      ashamed
That thou hast power to shake my manhood thus;
That these hot tears, which break from me perforce,
Should make thee worth them. Blasts and fogs upon thee!
The untented woundings of a father's curse
Pierce every sense about thee! Old fond eyes,
Beweep this cause again, I'll pluck ye out,
And cast you, with the waters that you lose,

518

To temper clay. Yea, is it come to this?
Let it be so: yet have I left a daughter,
Who, I am sure, is kind and comfortable:
When she shall hear this of thee, with her nails
She'll flay thy wolvish visage. Thou shalt find
That I'll resume the shape which thou dost think
I have cast off for ever: thou shalt, I warrant thee.

ACT I, Scene iv, ll. 102-126, 151-206, 257-332

Fool. Canst tell how an oyster makes his shell?

Lear. No.

Fool. Nor I neither; but I can tell why a snail has a house.

Lear. Why?

Fool. Why, to put his head in; not to give it away to his daughters, and leave his horns without a case.

Lear. I will forget my nature. So kind a father! Be my horses ready?

Fool. Thy asses are gone about 'em. The reason why the seven stars are no more than seven is a pretty reason.

Lear. Because they are not eight?

Fool. Yes, indeed: thou wouldst made a good fool.

Lear. To take't again perforce! Monster ingratitude!

Fool. If thou wert my fool, nuncle, I'ld have thee beaten for being old before thy time.

Lear. How's that?

Fool. Thou shouldst not have been old till thou hadst been wise.

Lear. O, let me not be mad, not mad, sweet heaven!
Keep me in temper: I would not be mad!

ACT I, Scene v, ll. 26-51

Regan. How dost, my lord?

Gloucester. O, madam, my old heart is crack'd, it's crack'd!

ACT II, Scene i, ll. 91-92

Lear. O, how this mother swells up toward my heart!
Hysterica passio, down, thou climbing sorrow,
Thy element's below! Where is this daughter?

ACT II, Scene iv, ll. 56-58

Lear. Death on my state ! wherefore
                    [*Looking on Kent in the stocks.*
Should he sit here ?   This act persuades me
That this remotion of the duke and her
Is practice only.   Give me my servant forth.
Go tell the duke and's wife I'ld speak with them,
Now, presently : bid them come forth and hear me,
Or at their chamber-door I'll beat the drum
Till it cry sleep to death.

Glou. I would have all well betwixt you.   [*Exit.*

Lear. O me, my heart, my rising heart ! but, down !

Fool. Cry to it, nuncle, as the cockney did to the eels when she put 'em i' the paste alive ; she knapped 'em o' the cox-combs with a stick, and cried ' Down, wantons, down ! ' 'Twas her brother that, in pure kindness to his horse, buttered his hay.

Enter CORNWALL, REGAN, GLOUCESTER, *and* Servants.

Lear. Good morrow to you both.

Corn.   Hail to your grace !
                            [*Kent is set at liberty.*

Reg. I am glad to see your highness.

Lear. Regan, I think you are ; I know what reason
I have to think so : if thou shouldst not be glad,
I would divorce me from thy mother's tomb,
Sepulchring an adultress. [*To Kent*] O, are you free ?
Some other time for that.   Beloved Regan,
Thy sister's naught : O Regan, she hath tied
Sharp-tooth'd unkindness, like a vulture, here :
                            [*Points to his heart.*
I can scarce speak to thee ; thou'lt not believe
With how depraved a quality—O Regan !

Reg. I pray you, sir, take patience : I have hope
You less know how to value her desert
Than she to scant her duty.

Lear.   Say, how is that ?

Reg. I cannot think my sister in the least
Would fail her obligation : if, sir, perchance
She have restrain'd the riots of your followers,
'Tis on such ground, and to such wholesome end,
As clears her from all blame.

    Lear. My curses on her !

    Reg.   O, sir, you are old ;
Nature in you stands on the very verge
Of her confine : you should be ruled and led
By some discretion, that discerns your state
Better than you yourself. Therefore, I pray you,
That to our sister you do make return ;
Say you have wrong'd her, sir.

    Lear.   Ask her forgiveness ?
Do you but mark how this becomes the house :
' Dear daughter, I confess that I am old ;   [*Kneeling.*
Age is unnecessary : on my knees I beg
That you'll vouchsafe me raiment, bed, and food.'

    Reg. Good sir, no more ; these are unsightly tricks :
Return you to my sister.

    Lear.   [*Rising*] Never, Regan :
She hath abated me of half my train ;
Look'd black upon me ; struck me with her tongue,
Most serpent-like, upon the very heart :
All the stored vengeances of heaven fall
On her ingrateful top ! Strike her young bones,
You taking airs, with lameness !

    Corn.   Fie, sir, fie !

    Lear. You nimble lightnings, dart your blinding flames
Into her scornful eyes ! Infect her beauty,
You fen-suck'd fogs, drawn by the powerful sun,
To fall and blast her pride !

    Reg. O the blest gods ! so will you wish on me,
When the rash mood is on.

    Lear. No, Regan, thou shalt never have my curse :
Thy tender-hefted nature shall not give

Thee o'er to harshness : her eyes are fierce ; but thine
Do comfort and not burn. 'Tis not in thee
To grudge my pleasures, to cut off my train,
To bandy hasty words, to scant my sizes,
And in conclusion to oppose the bolt
Against my coming in : thou better know'st
The offices of nature, bond of childhood,
Effects of courtesy, dues of gratitude ;
Thy half o' the kingdom hast thou not forgot,
Wherein I thee endow'd.

  Reg.   Good sir, to the purpose.
  Lear. Who put my man i' the stocks ?   [*Tucket within.*
  Corn.   What trumpet's that ?
  Reg. I know't, my sister's : this approves her letter,
That she would soon be here.

Enter OSWALD.

             Is your lady come ?
  Lear. This is a slave, whose easy-borrow'd pride
Dwells in the fickle grace of her he follows.
Out, varlet, from my sight !
  Corn.   What means your grace ?
  Lear. Who stock'd my servant ? Regan, I have good
   hope
Thou didst not know on't. Who comes here ? O heavens,

Enter GONERIL.

If you do love old men, if your sweet sway
Allow obedience, if yourselves are old,
Make it your cause ; send down, and take my part !
[*To Gon.*] Art not ashamed to look upon this beard ?
O Regan, wilt thou take her by the hand ?
  Gon. Why not by the hand, sir ? How have I offended ?
All's not offence that indiscretion finds
And dotage terms so.
  Lear.   O sides, you are too tough ;

522

Will you yet hold? How came my man i' the stocks?

Corn. I set him there, sir : but his own disorders
Deserved much less advancement.

Lear.   You ! did you ?

Reg. I pray you, father, being weak, seem so.
If, till the expiration of your month,
You will return and sojourn with my sister,
Dismissing half your train, come then to me :
I am now from home, and out of that provision
Which shall be needful for your entertainment.

Lear. Return to her, and fifty men dismiss'd ?
No, rather I abjure all roofs, and choose
To wage against the enmity o' the air ;
To be a comrade with the wolf and owl,—
Necessity's sharp pinch ! Return with her ?
Why, the hot-blooded France, that dowerless took
Our youngest born, I could as well be brought
To knee his throne, and, squire-like, pension beg
To keep base life afoot. Return with her ?
Persuade me rather to be slave and sumpter
To this detested groom.   [*Pointing at Oswald.*

Gon.   At your choice, sir.

Lear. I prithee, daughter, do not make me mad :
I will not trouble thee, my child ; farewell :
We'll no more meet, no more see one another :
But yet thou art my flesh, my blood, my daughter ;
Or rather a disease that's in my flesh,
Which I must needs call mine : thou art a boil,
A plague-sore, an embossed carbuncle,
In my corrupted blood. But I'll not chide thee ;
Let shame come when it will, I do not call it :
I do not bid the thunder-bearer shoot,
Nor tell tales of thee to high-judging Jove :
Mend when thou canst ; be better at thy leisure :
I can be patient ; I can stay with Regan,
I and my hundred knights.

Reg.   Not altogether so :
I look'd not for you yet, nor am provided
For your fit welcome. . . .

    Lear. I gave you all—

    Reg.   And in good time you gave it.

    Lear. Made you my guardians, my depositaries ;
But kept a reservation to be follow'd
With such a number. What, must I come to you
With five and twenty, Regan ? said you so ?

    Reg. And speak't again, my lord ; no more with me.

    Lear. Those wicked creatures yet do look well-favour'd,
When others are more wicked ; not being the worst
Stands in some rank of praise. [*To Gon.*] I'll go with thee :
Thy fifty yet doth double five-and-twenty,
And thou art twice her love.

    Gon.   Hear me, my lord :
What need you five and twenty, ten, or five,
To follow in a house where twice so many
Have a command to tend you ?

    Reg.   What need one ?

    Lear. O, reason not the need : our basest beggars
Are in the poorest thing superfluous :
Allow not nature more than nature needs,
Man's life's as cheap as beast's : thou art a lady ;
If only to go warm were gorgeous,
Why, nature needs not what thou gorgeous wear'st,
Which scarcely keeps thee warm. But, for true need,—
You heavens, give me that patience, patience I need !
You see me here, you gods, a poor old man,
As full of grief as age ; wretched in both !
If it be you that stir these daughters' hearts
Against their father, fool me not so much
To bear it tamely ; touch me with noble anger,
And let not women's weapons, water-drops,
Stain my man's cheeks ! No, you unnatural hags,
I will have such revenges on you both,

That all the world shall—I will do such things,—
What they are, yet I know not; but they shall be
The terrors of the earth. You think I'll weep;
No, I'll not weep:
I have full cause of weeping; but this heart
Shall break into a hundred thousand flaws,
Or ere I'll weep. O fool, I shall go mad!

> [*Exeunt Lear, Gloucester, Kent, and Fool. Storm and tempest. . . .*

Re-enter GLOUCESTER.

Glou. Alack, the night comes on, and the bleak winds
Do sorely ruffle; for many miles about
There's scarce a bush.

Reg.   O, sir, to wilful men,
The injuries that they themselves procure
Must be their schoolmasters. Shut up your doors:
He is attended with a desperate train;
And what they may incense him to, being apt
To have his ear abused, wisdom bids fear.

Corn. Shut up your doors, my lord; 'tis a wild night:
My Regan counsels well: come out o' the storm.

ACT II, Scene iv, ll. 113-236, 253-289, 303-310

A heath.

Storm still. Enter KENT *and a* Gentleman, *meeting.*

Kent. Who's there, besides foul weather?
Gent. One minded like the weather, most unquietly.
Kent. I know you. Where's the king?
Gent. Contending with the fretful element;
Bids the wind blow the earth into the sea,
Or swell the curled waters 'bove the main,
That things might change or cease; tears his white hair,
Which the impetuous blasts, with eyeless rage,
Catch in their fury, and make nothing of;
Strives in his little world of man to out-scorn
The to-and-fro-conflicting wind and rain.

This night, wherein the cub-drawn bear would couch,
The lion and the belly-pinched wolf
Keep their fur dry, unbonneted he runs,
And bids what will take all.

    Kent.   But who is with him?

    Gent. None but the fool; who labours to outjest
His heart-struck injuries.   Act III, Scene i, ll. 1-17

Another part of the heath. Storm still.

Enter Lear *and* Fool.

    Lear. Blow, winds, and crack your cheeks! rage! blow!
You cataracts and hurricanoes, spout,
Till you have drench'd our steeples, drown'd the cocks!
You sulphurous and thought-executing fires,
Vaunt-couriers to oak-cleaving thunderbolts,
Singe my white head! And thou, all-shaking thunder,
Smite flat the thick rotundity o' the world!
Crack nature's moulds, all germens spill at once,
That make ingrateful man!

    Fool. O nuncle, court holy-water in a dry house is better
than this rain-water out o' door. Good nuncle, in, and ask
thy daughters' blessing: here's a night pities neither wise
man nor fool.

    Lear. Rumble thy bellyful! Spit, fire! spout, rain!
Nor rain, wind, thunder, fire, are my daughters:
I tax not you, you elements, with unkindness;
I never gave you kingdom, call'd you children,
You owe me no subscription: then let fall
Your horrible pleasure; here I stand, your slave,
A poor, infirm, weak, and despised old man:
But yet I call you servile ministers,
That have with two pernicious daughters join'd
Your high engender'd battles 'gainst a head
So old and white as this. O! O! 'tis foul!

    Fool. He that has a house to put's head in has a good head-
piece.

> The cod-piece that will house
> > Before the head has any,
> The head and he shall louse ;
> > So beggars marry many.
> The man that makes his toe
> > What he his heart should make
> Shall of a corn cry woe,
> > And turn his sleep to wake.

For there was never yet fair woman but she made mouths in a glass.

Lear. No, I will be the pattern of all patience ; I will say nothing.

Enter KENT.

Kent. Who's there ?

Fool. Marry, here's grace and a cod-piece ; that's a wise man and a fool.

Kent. Alas, sir, are you here ? things that love night
Love not such nights as these ; the wrathful skies
Gallow the very wanderers of the dark,
And make them keep their caves : since I was man,
Such sheets of fire, such bursts of horrid thunder,
Such groans of roaring wind and rain, I never
Remember to have heard : man's nature cannot carry
The affliction nor the fear.

Lear. Let the great gods,
That keep this dreadful pother o'er our heads,
Find out their enemies now. Tremble, thou wretch,
That hast within thee undivulged crimes,
Unwhipp'd of justice : hide thee, thou bloody hand ;
Thou perjured, and thou simular man of virtue
That art incestuous : caitiff, to pieces shake,
That under covert and convenient seeming
Hast practised on man's life : close pent-up guilts,
Rive your concealing continents, and cry
These dreadful summoners grace. I am a man
More sinn'd against than sinning.

Kent.   Alack, bare-headed !
Gracious my lord, hard by here is a hovel ;
Some friendship will it lend you 'gainst the tempest :
Repose you there ; while I to this hard house—
More harder than the stones whereof 'tis raised ;
Which even but now, demanding after you,
Denied me to come in—return, and force
Their scanted courtesy.
    Lear.   My wits begin to turn.
Come on, my boy : how dost, my boy ? art cold ?
I am cold myself.   Where is this straw, my fellow ?
The art of our necessities is strange,
That can make vile things precious.   Come, your hovel.
Poor fool and knave, I have one part in my heart
That's sorry yet for thee.
    Fool. [*Singing*] He that has and a little tiny wit,—
            With hey, ho, the wind and the rain,—
        Must make content with his fortunes fit,
            For the rain it raineth every day.
    Lear. True, my good boy.   Come, bring us to this hovel.
                            [*Exeunt Lear and Kent.*
    Fool. This is a brave night to cool a courtezan.
                            ACT III, Scene ii, ll. 1-79

                    The heath.   Before a hovel.

                Enter LEAR, KENT, *and* Fool.

    Kent. Here is the place, my lord ; good my lord, enter :
The tyranny of the open night's too rough
For nature to endure.   [*Storm still.*
    Lear.   Let me alone.
    Kent. Good my lord, enter here.
    Lear.   Wilt break my heart ?
    Kent. I had rather break mine own.   Good my lord, enter.
    Lear. Thou think'st 'tis much that this contentious storm
Invades us to the skin : so 'tis to thee ;
But where the greater malady is fix'd,

The lesser is scarce felt. Thou'ldst shun a bear ;
But if thy flight lay toward the raging sea,
Thou'ldst meet the bear i' the mouth. When the mind's
    free,
The body's delicate : the tempest in my mind
Doth from my senses take all feeling else
Save what beats there. Filial ingratitude !
Is it not as this mouth should tear this hand
For lifting food to't ? But I will punish home :
No, I will weep no more. In such a night
To shut me out ! Pour on ; I will endure.
In such a night as this ! O Regan, Goneril !
Your old kind father, whose frank heart gave all,—
O, that way madness lies ; let me shun that ;
No more of that.

    Kent.   Good my lord, enter here.

    Lear. Prithee, go in thyself ; seek thine own ease :
This tempest will not give me leave to ponder
On things would hurt me more. But I'll go in.
[*To the Fool*] In, boy ; go first. You houseless poverty,—
Nay, get thee in. I'll pray, and then I'll sleep. [*Fool goes in.*
Poor naked wretches, wheresoe'er you are,
That bide the pelting of this pitiless storm,
How shall your houseless heads and unfed sides,
Your loop'd and window'd raggedness, defend you
From seasons such as these ? O, I have ta'en
Too little care of this ! Take physic, pomp ;
Expose thyself to feel what wretches feel,
That thou mayst shake the superflux to them,
And show the heavens more just.

    Edg. [*Within*] Fathom and half, fathom and half ! Poor
Tom !   [*The Fool runs out from the hovel.*

    Fool. Come not in here, nuncle, here's a spirit. Help me,
help me !

    Kent. Give me thy hand. Who's there ?

    Fool. A spirit, a spirit : he says his name's poor Tom.

Kent. What art thou that dost grumble there i' the straw ?
Come forth.

Enter EDGAR *disguised as a madman.*

Edg. Away ! the foul fiend follows me !
Through the sharp hawthorn blows the cold wind.
Hum ! go to thy cold bed, and warm thee.

Lear. Hast thou given all to thy two daughters ?
And art thou come to this ?

Edg. Who gives any thing to poor Tom ? whom the foul
fiend hath led through fire and through flame, and through
ford and whirlipool, o'er bog and quagmire ; that hath laid
knives under his pillow, and halters in his pew ; set ratsbane
by his porridge ; made him proud of heart, to ride on a bay
trotting-horse over four-inched bridges, to course his own
shadow for a traitor. Bless thy five wits ! Tom's a-cold,—
O, do de, do de, do de. Bless thee from whirlwinds, star-
blasting, and taking ! Do poor Tom some charity, whom the
foul fiend vexes : there could I have him now,—and there,—
and there again, and there. [*Storm still.*

Lear. What, have his daughters brought him to this pass ?
Couldst thou save nothing ? Didst thou give them all ?

Fool. Nay, he reserved a blanket, else we had been all
shamed.

Lear. Now, all the plagues that in the pendulous air
Hang fated o'er men's faults light on thy daughters !

Kent. He hath no daughters, sir.

Lear. Death, traitor ! nothing could have subdued nature
To such a lowness but his unkind daughters.
Is it the fashion, that discarded fathers
Should have thus little mercy on their flesh ?
Judicious punishment ! 'twas this flesh begot
Those pelican daughters.

Edg. Pillicock sat on Pillicock-hill :
Halloo, halloo, loo, loo !

Fool. This cold night will turn us all to fools and madmen.

Edg. Take heed o' the foul fiend : obey thy parents ; keep thy word justly ; swear not ; commit not with man's sworn spouse ; set not thy sweet heart on proud array. Tom's a-cold.

Lear. What hast thou been ?

Edg. A serving-man, proud in heart and mind ; that curled my hair ; wore gloves in my cap ; served the lust of my mistress' heart, and did the act of darkness with her ; swore as many oaths as I spake words, and broke them in the sweet face of heaven : one that slept in the contriving of lust, and waked to do it : wine loved I deeply, dice dearly ; and in woman out-paramoured the Turk : false of heart, light of ear, bloody of hand ; hog in sloth, fox in stealth, wolf in greediness, dog in madness, lion in prey. Let not the creaking of shoes nor the rustling of silks betray thy poor heart to woman : keep thy foot out of brothels, thy hand out of plackets, thy pen from lenders' books, and defy the foul fiend.
Still through the hawthorn blows the cold wind :
Says suum, mun, ha, no, nonny.
Dolphin my boy, my boy, sessa ! let him trot by. [*Storm still.*

Lear. Why, thou wert better in thy grave than to answer with thy uncovered body this extremity of the skies. Is man no more than this ? Consider him well. Thou owest the worm no silk, the beast no hide, the sheep no wool, the cat no perfume. Ha ! here's three on's are sophisticated ! Thou art the thing itself : unaccommodated man is no more but such a poor, bare, forked animal as thou art. Off, off, you lendings ! come, unbutton here. [*Tearing off his clothes.*

Fool. Prithee, nuncle, be contented ; 'tis a naughty night to swim in. Now a little fire in a wild field were like an old lecher's heart ; a small spark, all the rest on's body cold. Look, here comes a walking fire.

Enter GLOUCESTER, *with a torch.*

Edg. This is the foul fiend Flibbertigibbet : he begins at curfew, and walks till the first cock ; he gives the web and the

531

pin, squints the eye, and makes the hare-lip; mildews the white wheat, and hurts the poor creature of earth.

S. Withold footed thrice the old;

He met the night-mare, and her nine-fold;

Bid her alight,

And her troth plight,

And, aroint thee, witch, aroint thee!

Kent. How fares your grace?

Lear. What's he?

Kent. Who's there? What is't you seek?

Glou. What are you there? Your names?

Edg. Poor Tom; that eats the swimming frog, the toad, the tadpole, the wall-newt and the water; that in the fury of his heart, when the foul fiend rages, eats cow-dung for sallets; swallows the old rat and the ditch-dog; drinks the green mantle of the standing pool; who is whipped from tithing to tithing, and stock-punished, and imprisoned; who hath had three suits to his back, six shirts to his body, horse to ride, and weapon to wear;

But mice and rats, and such small deer,

Have been Tom's food for seven long year.

Beware my follower. Peace, Smulkin; peace, thou fiend!

Glou. What, hath your grace no better company?

Edg. The prince of darkness is a gentleman: Modo he's call'd, and Mahu.

Glou. Our flesh and blood is grown so vile, my lord, That it doth hate what gets it.

Edg. Poor Tom's a-cold.

Glou. Go in with me: my duty cannot suffer To obey in all your daughters' hard commands: Though their injunction be to bar my doors, And let this tyrannous night take hold upon you, Yet have I ventured to come seek you out, And bring you where both fire and food is ready.

Lear. First let me talk with this philosopher. What is the cause of thunder?

Kent. Good my lord, take his offer ; go into the house.

Lear. I'll talk a word with this same learned Theban.
What is your study ?

Edg. How to prevent the fiend, and to kill vermin.

Lear. Let me ask you one word in private.

Kent. Importune him once more to go, my lord ;
His wits begin to unsettle.

Glou.   Canst thou blame him ?

                                      [*Storm still.*

His daughters seek his death : ah, that good Kent !
He said it would be thus, poor banish'd man !
Thou say'st the king grows mad ; I'll tell thee, friend,
I am almost mad myself : I had a son,
Now outlaw'd from my blood ; he sought my life,
But lately, very late : I loved him, friend ;
No father his son dearer : truth to tell thee,
The grief hath crazed my wits. What a night's this !
I do beseech your grace,—

Lear.   O, cry you mercy, sir.
Noble philosopher, your company.

Edg. Tom's a-cold.

Glou. In, fellow, there, into the hovel : keep thee warm.

Lear. Come, let's in all.

Kent.   This way, my lord.

Lear.   With him ;
I will keep still with my philosopher.

Kent. Good my lord, soothe him ; let him take the fellow.

Glou. Take him you on.

Kent. Sirrah, come on ; go along with us.

Lear. Come, good Athenian.

Glou. No words, no words : hush.

Edg. Child Rowland to the dark tower came,
            His word was still,—Fie, foh, and fum,
        I smell the blood of a British man.

                              ACT III, Scene iv, ll. 1-189

533

A chamber in a farmhouse adjoining the castle.

Enter GLOUCESTER, LEAR, KENT, Fool, *and* EDGAR.

Glou. Here is better than the open air; take it thankfully. I will piece out the comfort with what addition I can: I will not be long from you.

Kent. All the power of his wits have given way to his impatience: the gods reward your kindness! [*Exit Gloucester.*

Edg. Fraretto calls me; and tells me Nero is an angler in the lake of darkness. Pray, innocent, and beware the foul fiend.

Fool. Prithee, nuncle, tell me whether a madman be a gentleman or a yeoman?

Lear. A king, a king!

Fool. No, he's a yeoman that has a gentleman to his son; for he's a mad yeoman that sees his son a gentleman before him.

Lear. To have a thousand with red burning spits
Come hissing in upon 'em,—

Edg. The foul fiend bites my back.

Fool. He's mad that trusts in the tameness of a wolf, a horse's health, a boy's love, or a whore's oath.

Lear. It shall be done; I will arraign them straight.
[*To Edgar*] Come, sit thou here, most learned justicer;
[*To the Fool*] Thou, sapient sir, sit here. Now, you she foxes!

Edg. Look, where he stands and glares! Wantest thou eyes at trial, madam?
        Come o'er the bourn, Bessy, to me,—

Fool.   Her boat hath a leak,
            And she must not speak
        Why she dares not come over to thee.

Edg. The foul fiend haunts poor Tom in the voice of a nightingale. Hopdance cries in Tom's belly for two white herring. Croak not, black angel; I have no food for thee.

Kent. How do you, sir? Stand you not so amazed:
Will you lie down and rest upon the cushions?

Lear. I'll see their trial first. Bring in the evidence.

[To Edgar] Thou robed man of justice, take thy place ;
[To the Fool] And thou, his yoke-fellow of equity,
Bench by his side : *[To Kent]* you are o' the commission,
Sit you too.

    Edg. Let us deal justly.

           Sleepest or wakest thou, jolly shepherd ?
             Thy sheep be in the corn ;
        And for one blast of thy minikin mouth,
             Thy sheep shall take no harm.
Pur ! the cat is gray.

    Lear. Arraign her first ; 'tis Goneril. I here take my oath
before this honourable assembly, she kicked the poor king her
father.

    Fool. Come hither, mistress. Is your name Goneril ?

    Lear. She cannot deny it.

    Fool. Cry you mercy, I took you for a joint-stool.

    Lear. And here's another, whose warp'd looks proclaim
What store her heart is made on. Stop her there !
Arms, arms, sword, fire ! Corruption in the place !
False justicer, why hast thou let her 'scape ?

    Edg. Bless thy five wits !

    Kent. O pity ! Sir, where is the patience now,
That you so oft have boasted to retain ?

    Edg. *[Aside]* My tears begin to take his part so much,
They'll mar my counterfeiting.

    Lear. The little dogs and all,
Tray, Blanch, and Sweet-heart, see, they bark at me.

    Edg. Tom will throw his head at them. Avaunt, you curs !
        Be thy mouth or black or white,
        Tooth that poisons if it bite ;
        Mastiff, greyhound, mongrel grim,
        Hound or spaniel, brach or lym,
        Or bobtail tike or trundle-tail,
        Tom will make them weep and wail :
        For, with throwing thus my head,
        Dogs leap the hatch, and all are fled.

Do de, de, de. Sessa! Come, march to wakes and fairs and
market-towns. Poor Tom, thy horn is dry.

Lear. Then let them anatomize Regan; see what breeds
about her heart. Is there any cause in nature that makes
these hard hearts? [*To Edgar*] You, sir, I entertain for one
of my hundred; only I do not like the fashion of your garments: you will say they are Persian attire; but let them be
changed.

Kent. Now, good my lord, lie here and rest awhile.

Lear. Make no noise, make no noise; draw the curtains:
so, so, so. We'll go to supper i' the morning. So, so, so.

Fool. And I'll go to bed at noon.

ACT III, Scene vi, ll. 1-92

The sea, with such a storm as his bare head
In hell-black night endured, would have buoy'd up,
And quench'd the stelled fires:
Yet, poor old heart, he holp the heavens to rain.
If wolves had at thy gate howl'd that stern time,
Thou shouldst have said 'Good porter, turn the key,'
All cruels else subscribed.

ACT III, Scene vii, ll. 59-65

Gloucester.   Is it a beggar-man?

Old Man. Madman and beggar too.

Glouc. He has some reason, else he could not beg.
I' the last night's storm I such a fellow saw;
Which made me think a man a worm: my son
Came then into my mind; and yet my mind
Was then scarce friends with him: I have heard more since.
As flies to wanton boys, are we to the gods,
They kill us for their sport. . . .

Dost thou know Dover?

Edgar. Ay, master.

Glou. There is a cliff, whose high and bending head
Looks fearfully in the confined deep:
Bring me but to the very brim of it,

536

And I'll repair the misery thou dost bear
With something rich about me : from that place
I shall no leading need.
    Edg.   Give me thy arm :
Poor Tom shall lead thee.
                   ACT IV, Scene i, ll. 31-38, 74-82

                  O Goneril !
You are not worth the dust which the rude wind
Blows in your face.   ACT IV, Scene ii, ll. 29-30

    Cordelia. Alack, 'tis he : why, he was met even now
As mad as the vex'd sea ; singing aloud ;
Crown'd with rank fumiter and furrow-weeds,
With bur-docks, hemlock, nettles, cuckoo-flowers,
Darnel, and all the idle weeds that grow
In our sustaining corn.
                   ACT IV, Scene iv, ll. 1-6

       Fields near Dover.

    Enter GLOUCESTER, *and* EDGAR *dressed like a peasant.*
    Glou. When shall we come to the top of that same hill ?
    Edg. You do climb up it now : look, how we labour.
    Glou. Methinks the ground is even.
    Edg.   Horrible steep.
Hark, do you hear the sea ?
    Glou.   No, truly.
    Edg. Why, then, your other senses grow imperfect
By your eyes' anguish.
    Glou.   So may it be, indeed :
Methinks thy voice is alter'd ; and thou speak'st
In better phrase and matter than thou didst.
    Edg. You're much deceived : in nothing am I changed
But in my garments.
    Glou.   Methinks you're better spoken.
    Edg. Come on, sir ; here's the place : stand still. How
       fearful
And dizzy 'tis, to cast one's eyes so low !

The crows and choughs that wing the midway air
Show scarce so gross as beetles : half way down
Hangs one that gathers samphire, dreadful trade !
Methinks he seems no bigger than his head :
The fishermen, that walk upon the beach,
Appear like mice ; and yond tall anchoring bark,
Diminish'd to her cock ; her cock, a buoy
Almost too small for sight : the murmuring surge,
That on the unnumber'd idle pebbles chafes,
Cannot be heard so high. I'll look no more ;
Lest my brain turn, and the deficient sight
Topple down headlong.

    Glou.   Set me where you stand.

    Edg. Give me your hand : you are now within a foot
Of the extreme verge : for all beneath the moon
Would I not leap upright.

    Glou.   Let go my hand.
Here, friend, 's another purse ; in it a jewel
Well worth a poor man's taking : fairies and gods
Prosper it with thee ! Go thou farther off ;
Bid me farewell, and let me hear thee going.

    Edg. Now fare you well, good sir.

    Glou.   With all my heart.

    Edg. Why I do trifle thus with his despair
Is done to cure it.

    Glou. [*Kneeling*] O you mighty gods !
This world I do renounce, and, in your sights,
Shake patiently my great affliction off :
If I could bear it longer, and not fall
To quarrel with your great opposeless wills,
My snuff and loathed part of nature should
Burn itself out. If Edgar live, O, bless him !
Now, fellow, fare thee well.   [*He falls forward.*

    Edg.   Gone, sir : farewell.
And yet I know not how conceit may rob
The treasury of life, when life itself

Yields to the theft : had he been where he thought,
By this, had thought been past. Alive or dead ?
Ho, you sir ! friend ! Hear you, sir ! speak !
Thus might he pass indeed : yet he revives.
What are you, sir ?

Glou.   Away, and let me die.

Edg. Hadst thou been aught but gossamer, feathers, air,
So many fathom down precipitating,
Thou'dst shiver'd like an egg : but thou dost breathe ;
Hast heavy substance ; bleed'st not ; speak'st ; art sound.
Ten masts at each make not the altitude
Which thou hast perpendicularly fell :
Thy life's a miracle. Speak yet again.

Glou. But have I fall'n, or no ?

Edg. From the dread summit of this chalky bourn.
Look up a-height ; the shrill-gorged lark so far
Cannot be seen or heard : do but look up.

Glou. Alack, I have no eyes.
Is wretchedness deprived that benefit,
To end itself by death ? 'Twas yet some comfort,
When misery could beguile the tyrant's rage,
And frustrate his proud will.

Edg.   Give me your arm :
Up : so. How is't ? Feel you your legs ? You stand.

Glou. Too well, too well.

Edg.   This is above all strangeness.
Upon the crown o' the cliff, what thing was that
Which parted from you ?

Glou.   A poor unfortunate beggar.

Edg. As I stood here below, methought his eyes
Were two full moons ; he had a thousand noses,
Horns whelk'd and waved like the enridged sea :
It was some fiend ; therefore, thou happy father,
Think that the clearest gods, who make them honours
Of men's impossibilities, have preserved thee.

Glou. I do remember now : henceforth I'll bear

Affliction till it do cry out itself
' Enough, enough,' and die. That thing you speak of,
I took it for a man ; often 'twould say
' The fiend, the fiend : ' he led me to that place.

    Edg. Bear free and patient thoughts. But who comes
      here ?

    Enter LEAR, *fantastically dressed with wild flowers.*
The safer sense will ne'er accommodate
His master thus.

    Lear. No, they cannot touch me for coining ; I am the
king himself.

    Edg. O thou side-piercing sight !

    Lear. Nature's above art in that respect. There's your
press-money. That fellow handles his bow like a crow-
keeper : draw me a clothier's yard. Look, look, a mouse !
Peace, peace ; this piece of toasted cheese will do't. There's
my gauntlet ; I'll prove it on a giant. Bring up the brown
bills. O, well flown, bird ! i' the clout, i' the clout : hewgh !
Give the word.

    Edg. Sweet marjoram.

    Lear. Pass.

    Glou. I know that voice.

    Lear. Ha ! Goneril, with a white beard ! They flattered
me like a dog ; and told me I had white hairs in my beard ere
the black ones were there. To say ' ay ' and ' no ' to every
thing that I said !—' Ay ' and ' no ' too was no good divinity.
When the rain came to wet me once, and the wind to make me
chatter ; when the thunder would not peace at my bidding ;
there I found 'em, there I smelt 'em out. Go to, they are not
men o' their words : they told me I was every thing ; 'tis a
lie, I am not ague-proof.

    Glou. The trick of that voice I do well remember :
Is't not the king ?

    Lear.   Ay, every inch a king :
When I do stare, see how the subject quakes.

I pardon that man's life. What was thy cause?
Adultery?
Thou shalt not die: die for adultery! No:
The wren goes to't, and the small gilded fly
Does lecher in my sight.
Let copulation thrive; for Gloucester's bastard son
Was kinder to his father than my daughters
Got 'tween the lawful sheets.
To't, luxury, pell-mell! for I lack soldiers.
Behòld yond simpering dame,
Whose face between her forks presages snow;
That minces virtue, and does shake the head
To hear of pleasure's name;
The fitchew, nor the soiled horse, goes to't
With a more riotous appetite.
Down from the waist they are Centaurs,
Though women all above:
But to the girdle do the gods inherit,
Beneath is all the fiends';
There's hell, there's darkness, there's the sulphurous pit,
Burning, scalding, stench, consumption; fie, fie, fie! pah,
pah! Give me an ounce of civet, good apothecary, to sweeten
my imagination: there's money for thee.

Glou. O, let me kiss that hand!

Lear. Let me wipe it first; it smells of mortality.

Glou. O ruin'd piece of nature! This great world
Shall so wear out to nought. Dost thou know me?

Lear. I remember thine eyes well enough. Dost thou
squiny at me? No, do thy worst, blind Cupid; I'll not love.
Read thou this challenge; mark but the penning of it.

Glou. Were all the letters suns, I could not see one.

Edg. I would not take this from report; it is,
And my heart breaks at it.

Lear. Read.

Glou. What, with the case of eyes?

Lear. O, ho, are you there with me? No eyes in your head,

nor no money in your purse? Your eyes are in a heavy case, your purse in a light: yet you see how this world goes.

Glou. I see it feelingly.

Lear. What, art mad? A man may see how this world goes with no eyes. Look with thine ears: see how yond justice rails upon yond simple thief. Hark, in thine ear: change places; and, handy-dandy, which is the justice, which is the thief? Thou hast seen a farmer's dog bark at a beggar?

Glou. Ay, sir.

Lear. And the creature run from the cur? There thou mightst behold the great image of authority: a dog's obeyed in office.

Thou rascal beadle, hold thy bloody hand!
Why dost thou lash that whore? Strip thine own back;
Thou hotly lust'st to use her in that kind
For which thou whipp'st her. The usurer hangs the cozener.
Through tatter'd clothes small vices do appear;
Robes and furr'd gowns hide all. Plate sin with gold,
And the strong lance of justice hurtless breaks;
Arm it in rags, a pigmy's straw does pierce it.
None does offend, none, I say, none; I'll able 'em:
Take that of me, my friend, who have the power
To seal the accuser's lips. Get thee glass eyes;
And, like a scurvy politician, seem
To see the things thou dost not. Now, now, now, now:
Pull off my boots: harder, harder: so.

Edg. O, matter and impertinency mix'd!
Reason in madness!

Lear. If thou wilt weep my fortunes, take my eyes.
I know thee well enough; thy name is Gloucester:
Thou must be patient; we came crying hither:
Thou know'st, the first time that we smell the air,
We wawl and cry. I will preach to thee: mark.

Glou. Alack, alack the day!

Lear. When we are born, we cry that we are come
To this great stage of fools: this' a good block;

It were a delicate stratagem, to shoe
A troop of horse with felt : I'll put't in proof ;
And when I have stol'n upon these sons-in-law,
Then, kill, kill, kill, kill, kill, kill !

Enter a Gentleman, *with* Attendants.

Gent. O, here he is : lay hand upon him. Sir,
Your most dear daughter—

Lear. No rescue ? What, a prisoner ? I am even
The natural fool of fortune. Use me well ;
You shall have ransom. Let me have surgeons ;
I am cut to the brains.

Gent.   You shall have any thing.

Lear. No seconds ? all myself ?
Why, this would make a man a man of salt,
To use his eyes for garden water-pots,
Ay, and laying autumn's dust.

Gent.   Good sir,—

Lear. I will die bravely, like a bridegroom. What !
I will be jovial : come, come ; I am a king,
My masters, know you that.

Gent. You are a royal one, and we obey you.

Lear. Then there's life in't. Nay, if you get it, you shall
get it with running. Sa, sa, sa, sa.

[*Exit running ; Attendants follow.*
ACT IV, Scene vi, ll. 1-207

A tent in the French camp. LEAR *on a bed asleep, soft music
playing ;* Gentleman, *and others attending.*

Enter CORDELIA, KENT, *and* Doctor.

Cordelia. How does the king ?

Doct. Madam, sleeps still.

Cor. O you kind gods,
Cure this great breach in his abused nature !
The untuned and jarring senses, O, wind up
Of this child-changed father !

Doct.   So please your majesty
That we may wake the king : he hath slept long.

Cor. Be govern'd by your knowledge, and proceed
I' the sway of your own will. Is he array'd ?

Gent. Ay, madam ; in the heaviness of his sleep
We put fresh garments on him.

Doct. Be by, good madam, when we do awake him ;
I doubt not of his temperance.

Cor.   Very well.

Doct. Please you, draw near. Louder the music there !

Cor. O my dear father ! Restoration hang
Thy medicine on my lips ; and let this kiss
Repair those violent harms that my two sisters
Have in thy reverence made !

Kent.   Kind and dear princess !

Cor. Had you not been their father, these white flakes
Had challenged pity of them. Was this a face
To be opposed against the warring winds ?
To stand against the deep dread-bolted thunder ?
In the most terrible and nimble stroke
Of quick, cross lightning ? to watch—poor perdu !—
With this thin helm ? Mine enemy's dog,
Though he had bit me, should have stood that night
Against my fire ; and wast thou fain, poor father,
To hovel thee with swine, and rogues forlorn,
In short and musty straw ? Alack, alack !
'Tis wonder that thy life and wits at once
Had not concluded all. He wakes ; speak to him.

Doct. Madam, do you ; 'tis fittest.

Cor. How does my royal lord ? How fares your majesty ?

Lear. You do me wrong to take me out o' the grave :
Thou art a soul in bliss ; but I am bound
Upon a wheel of fire, that mine own tears
Do scald like molten lead.

Cor.   Sir, do you know me ?

Lear. You are a spirit, I know : when did you die ?

Cor. Still, still, far wide !

Doct. He's scarce awake : let him alone awhile.

Lear. Where have I been ?   Where am I ?   Fair daylight ?
I am mightily abused.   I should e'en die with pity,
To see another thus.   I know not what to say.
I will not swear these are my hands : let's see ;
I feel this pin prick.   Would I were assured
Of my condition !

  Cor.   O, look upon me, sir,
And hold your hands in benediction o'er me :
No, sir, you must not kneel.

    Lear.   Pray, do not mock me :
I am a very foolish fond old man,
Fourscore and upward, not an hour more nor less ;
And, to deal plainly,
I fear I am not in my perfect mind.
Methinks I should know you, and know this man ;
Yet I am doubtful : for I am mainly ignorant
What place this is ;   and all the skill I have
Remembers not these garments ;   nor I know not
Where I did lodge last night.   Do not laugh at me ;
For, as I am a man, I think this lady
To be my child Cordelia.

    Cor.   And so I am, I am.

    Lear. Be your tears wet ?   yes, 'faith.   I pray, weep
      not :
If you have poison for me, I will drink it.
I know you do not love me ;   for your sisters
Have, as I do remember, done me wrong :
You have some cause, they have not.

    Cor.   No cause, no cause.

    Lear. Am I in France ?

    Kent.   In your own kingdom, sir.

    Lear. Do not abuse me.

    Doct. Be comforted, good madam : the great rage,
You see, is kill'd in him : and yet it is danger

To make him even o'er the time he has lost.
Desire him to go in ; trouble him no more
Till further settling.

    Cor. Will't please your highness walk ?

    Lear.   You must bear with me :
Pray you now, forget and forgive : I am old and foolish.

                         Act IV, Scene vii, ll. 12-85

    Edg. Away, old man ; give me thy hand ; away !
King Lear hath lost, he and his daughter ta'en :
Give me thy hand ; come on.

    Glou. No farther, sir ; a man may rot even here.

    Edg. What, in ill thoughts again ? Men must endure
Their going hence, even as their coming hither :
Ripeness is all.   Act V, Scene ii, ll. 5-11

The British camp near Dover.

Enter, in conquest, with drum and colours, EDMUND ; LEAR
    and CORDELIA, *prisoners ;* Captain, Soldiers, &c.

    Edm. Some officers take them away : good guard,
Until their greater pleasures first be known
That are to censure them.

    Cor.   We are not the first
Who, with best meaning, have incurr'd the worst.
For thee, oppressed king, am I cast down ;
Myself could else out-frown false fortune's frown.
Shall we not see these daughters and these sisters ?

    Lear. No, no, no, no ! Come, let's away to prison :
We two alone will sing like birds i' the cage :
When thou dost ask me blessing, I'll kneel down,
And ask of thee forgiveness : so we'll live,
And pray, and sing, and tell old tales, and laugh
At gilded butterflies, and hear poor rogues
Talk of court news ; and we'll talk with them too,
Who loses and who wins ; who's in, who's out ;
And take upon's the mystery of things,
As if we were God's spies : and we'll wear out,

In a wall'd prison, packs and sects of great ones,
That ebb and flow by the moon.
    Edm.   Take them away.
    Lear. Upon such sacrifices, my Cordelia,
The gods themselves throw incense. Have I caught thee?
He that parts us shall bring a brand from heaven,
And fire us hence like foxes. Wipe thine eyes;
The good-years shall devour them, flesh and fell,
Ere they shall make us weep: we'll see 'em starve first.
Come.   *[Exeunt Lear and Cordelia, guarded.*
                      Act V, Scene iii, ll. 1-26

The gods are just, and of our pleasant vices
Make instruments to plague us:
The dark and vicious place where thee he got
Cost him his eyes.   Act V, Scene iii, ll. 170-173

    Enter LEAR, *with* CORDELIA *dead in his arms;* EDGAR,
        Captain, *and others following.*

    Lear. Howl, howl, howl, howl! O, you are men of
    stones:
Had I your tongues and eyes, I'ld use them so
That heaven's vault should crack. She's gone for ever!
I know when one is dead, and when one lives;
She's dead as earth. Lend me a looking-glass;
If that her breath will mist or stain the stone,
Why, then she lives.
    Kent.   Is this the promised end?
    Edg. Or image of that horror?
    Albany.   Fall, and cease!
    Lear. This feather stirs; she lives! if it be so,
It is a chance which does redeem all sorrows
That ever I have felt.
    Kent. [Kneeling] O my good master!
    Lear. Prithee, away.
    Edg.   'Tis noble Kent, your friend.
    Lear. A plague upon you, murderers, traitors all!

I might have saved her; now she's gone for ever!
Cordelia, Cordelia! stay a little. Ha!
What is't thou say'st? Her voice was ever soft,
Gentle, and low, an excellent thing in woman.
I kill'd the slave that was a-hanging thee.

    Capt. 'Tis true, my lords, he did.

    Lear.   Did I not, fellow?
I have seen the day, with my good biting falchion
I would have made them skip: I am old now,
And these same crosses spoil me. Who are you?
Mine eyes are not o' the best: I'll tell you straight.

    Kent. If fortune brag of two she loved and hated,
One of them we behold.

    Lear. This is a dull sight. Are you not Kent?

    Kent.   The same.
Your servant Kent. Where is your servant Caius?

    Lear. He's a good fellow, I can tell you that;
He'll strike, and quickly too: he's dead and rotten.

    Kent. No, my good lord; I am the very man,—

    Lear. I'll see that straight.

    Kent. That, from your first of difference and decay,
Have follow'd your sad steps.

    Lear.   You are welcome hither.

    Kent. Nor no man else: all's cheerless, dark, and deadly.
Your eldest daughters have fordone themselves,
And desperately are dead.

    Lear.   Ay, so I think.

    Alb. He knows not what he says: and vain it is
That we present us to him.

    Edg.   Very bootless.

                 Enter a Captain.

    Capt. Edmund is dead, my lord.

    Alb.   That's but a trifle here.
Your lords and noble friends, know our intent.
What comfort to this great decay may come

Shall be applied : for us, we will resign,
During the life of this old majesty,
To him our absolute power : [*To Edgar and Kent*] you, to
    your rights ;
With boot, and such addition as your honours
Have more than merited. All friends shall taste
The wages of their virtue, and all foes
The cup of their deservings. O, see, see !
    Lear. And my poor fool is hang'd ! No, no, no life !
Why should a dog, a horse, a rat, have life,
And thou no breath at all ? Thou'lt come no more,
Never, never, never, never, never !
Pray you, undo this button : thank you, sir.
Do you see this ? Look on her, look, look, her lips,
Look there, look there !   [*Dies*.
    Edg.   He faints ! My lord, my lord !
    Kent. Break, heart ; I prithee, break !
    Edg.   Look up, my lord.
    Kent. Vex not his ghost : O, let him pass ! he hates him
    much
That would upon the rack of this tough world
Stretch him out longer.
                          Act V, Scene iii, ll. 257-315

AFTERNOON

PART III

ANTONY AND CLEOPATRA
CORIOLANUS
TIMON OF ATHENS

Antony and Cleopatra

Alexandria.   A room in Cleopatra's palace.

Enter DEMETRIUS *and* PHILO.

Phi. Nay, but this dotage of our general's
O'erflows the measure : those his goodly eyes,
That o'er the files and musters of the war
Have glow'd like plated Mars, now bend, now turn,
The office and devotion of their view
Upon a tawny front : his captain's heart,
Which in the scuffles of great fights hath burst
The buckles on his breast, reneges all temper,
And is become the bellows and the fan
To cool a gipsy's lust.

Flourish.   Enter ANTONY, CLEOPATRA, *her Ladies, the Train, with Eunuchs fanning her.*

                              Look, where they come :
Take but good note, and you shall see in him
The triple pillar of the world transform'd
Into a strumpet's fool : behold and see.

Cleo. If it be love indeed, tell me how much.

Ant. There's beggary in the love that can be reckon'd.

Cleo. I'll set a bourn how far to be beloved.

Ant. Then must thou needs find out new heaven, new earth.

Enter an Attendant.

Att. News, my good lord, from Rome.

Ant.   Grates me : the sum.

Cleo. Nay, hear them, Antony. . . .

Ant. Let Rome in Tiber melt, and the wide arch
Of the ranged empire fall !   Here is my space.
Kingdoms are clay : our dungy earth alike

Feeds beast as man : the nobleness of life
Is to do thus ; when such a mutual pair   *[Embracing.*
And such a twain can do't, in which I bind,
On pain of punishment, the world to weet
We stand up peerless.

    Cleo.   Excellent falsehood !
Why did he marry Fulvia, and not love her ?
I'll seem the fool I am not ; Antony
Will be himself.

    Ant.   But stirr'd by Cleopatra.
Now, for the love of Love and her soft hours,
Let's not confound the time with conference harsh :
There's not a minute of our lives should stretch
Without some pleasure now. What sport to-night ?

    Cleo. Hear the ambassadors.

    Ant.   Fie, wrangling queen !
Whom every thing becomes, to chide, to laugh,
To weep ; whose every passion fully strives
To make itself, in thee, fair and admired !
No messenger, but thine ; and all alone
To-night we'll wander through the streets and note
The qualities of people. Come, my queen ;
Last night you did desire it : speak not to us.

                        Act I, Scene i, ll. 1-19, 33-55

    Enobarbus. Cleopatra, catching but the least noise of this, dies instantly ; I have seen her die twenty times upon far poorer moment : I do think there is mettle in death, which commits some loving act upon her, she hath such a celerity in dying.

    Antony. She is cunning past man's thought.

                        Act I, Scene ii, ll. 144-150

Eternity was in our lips and eyes.

                           Act I, Scene iii, l. 35

This common body,
Like to a vagabond flag upon the stream,

Goes to and back, lackeying the varying tide,
To rot itself with motion.   ACT I, Scene iv, ll. 44-47

Alexandria.   Cleopatra's palace.

Enter CLEOPATRA, CHARMIAN, IRAS, *and* MARDIAN.

Cleo. Charmian !
Char. Madam ?
Cleo. Ha, ha !
Give me to drink mandragora.
Char.   Why, madam ?
Cleo. That I might sleep out this great gap of time
My Antony is away.
Char.   You think of him too much.
Cleo. O, 'tis treason !
Char.   Madam, I trust, not so. . . .
Cleo.   O Charmian,
Where think'st thou he is now ?   Stands he, or sits he ?
Or does he walk ? or is he on his horse ?
O happy horse, to bear the weight of Antony !
Do bravely, horse ! for wot'st thou whom thou movest ?
The demi-Atlas of this earth, the arm
And burgonet of men.   He's speaking now,
Or murmuring ' Where's my serpent of old Nile ? '
For so he calls me : now I feed myself
With most delicious poison.   Think on me,
That am with Phoebus' amorous pinches black,
And wrinkled deep in time ?   Broad-fronted Caesar,
When thou wast here above the ground, I was
A morsel for a monarch : and great Pompey
Would stand and make his eyes grow in my brow ;
There would he anchor his aspect and die
With looking on his life.

Enter ALEXAS.

Alex.   Sovereign of Egypt, hail !
Cleo. How much unlike art thou Mark Antony !

Yet, coming from him, that great medicine hath
With his tinct gilded thee.
How goes it with my brave Mark Antony?

Alex. Last thing he did, dear queen,
He kiss'd,—the last of many doubled kisses,—
This orient pearl. His speech sticks in my heart.

Cleo. Mine ear must pluck it thence.

Alex.   'Good friend,' quoth he,
'Say, the firm Roman to great Egypt sends
This treasure of an oyster; at whose foot,
To mend the petty present, I will piece
Her opulent throne with kingdoms; all the east,
Say thou, shall call her mistress.' So he nodded,
And soberly did mount an arm-gaunt steed,
Who neigh'd so high, that what I would have spoke
Was beastly dumb'd by him.

Cleo.   What, was he sad or merry?

Alex. Like to the time o' the year between the extremes
Of hot and cold, he was nor sad nor merry.

Cleo. O well-divided disposition! Note him,
Note him, good Charmian, 'tis the man; but note him:
He was not sad, for he would shine on those
That make their looks by his; he was not merry,
Which seem'd to tell them his remembrance lay
In Egypt with his joy; but between both:
O heavenly mingle! Be'st thou sad or merry,
The violence of either thee becomes,
So does it no man else. Met'st thou my posts?

Alex. Ay, madam, twenty several messengers:
Why do you send so thick?

Cleo.   Who's born that day
When I forget to send to Antony,
Shall die a beggar. Ink and paper, Charmian.
Welcome, my good Alexas. Did I, Charmian,
Ever love Caesar so?

Char.   O that brave Caesar!

Cleo. Be choked with such another emphasis !
Say, the brave Antony.
 Char.   The valiant Caesar !
 Cleo. By Isis, I will give thee bloody teeth,
If thou with Caesar paragon again
My man of men.
 Char.   By your most gracious pardon,
I sing but after you.
 Cleo.   My salad days,
When I was green in judgement : cold in blood,
To say as I said then ! But, come, away ;
Get me ink and paper :
He shall have every day a several greeting,
Or I'll unpeople Egypt.   [*Exeunt.*
          ACT I, Scene v, ll. 1-7, 18-78

 Enobarbus. When she first met Mark Antony, she pursed
up his heart, upon the river of Cydnus.
 Agrippa. There she appeared indeed ; or my reporter
devised well for her.
 Eno. I will tell you.
The barge she sat in, like a burnish'd throne,
Burn'd on the water : the poop was beaten gold ;
Purple the sails, and so perfumed that
The winds were love-sick with them ; the oars were silver,
Which to the tune of flutes kept stroke, and made
The water which they beat to follow faster,
As amorous of their strokes. For her own person,
It beggar'd all description : she did lie
In her pavilion—cloth-of-gold of tissue—
O'er-picturing that Venus where we see
The fancy outwork nature : on each side her
Stood pretty dimpled boys, like smiling Cupids,
With divers-colour'd fans, whose wind did seem
To glow the delicate cheeks which they did cool,
And what they undid did.

Agr.   O, rare for Antony!

Eno. Her gentlewomen, like the Nereides,
So many mermaids, tended her i' the eyes,
And made their bends adornings : at the helm
A seeming mermaid steers : the silken tackle
Swell with the touches of those flower-soft hands,
That yarely frame the office. From the barge
A strange invisible perfume hits the sense
Of the adjacent wharfs. The city cast
Her people out upon her ; and Antony,
Enthroned i' the market-place, did sit alone,
Whistling to the air ; which, but for vacancy,
Had gone to gaze on Cleopatra too
And made a gap in nature.

Agr.   Rare Egyptian!

Eno. Upon her landing, Antony sent to her,
Invited her to supper : she replied,
It should be better he became her guest ;
Which she entreated : our courteous Antony,
Whom ne'er the word of ' No ' woman heard speak,
Being barber'd ten times o'er, goes to the feast,
And for his ordinary pays his heart
For what his eyes eat only.

Agr.   Royal wench!

She made great Caesar lay his sword to bed :
He ploughed her, and she cropp'd.

Eno.   I saw her once
Hop forty paces through the public street ;
And having lost her breath, she spoke, and panted,
That she did make defect perfection,
And, breathless, power breathe forth.

Mecaenas. Now Antony must leave her utterly.

Eno. Never ; he will not :
Age cannot wither her, nor custom stale
Her infinite variety : other women cloy
The appetites they feed : but she makes hungry

Where most she satisfies : for vilest things
Become themselves in her ; that the holy priests
Bless her when she is riggish.

ACT II, Scene ii, ll. 191-245

Alexandria. Cleopatra's palace.

Enter CLEOPATRA, CHARMIAN, IRAS, and ALEXAS.

Cleo. Give me some music ; music, moody food
Of us that trade in love.

Attend.   The music, ho !

Enter MARDIAN the Eunuch.

Cleo. Let it alone ; let's to billiards : come, Charmian.

Char. My arm is sore ; best play with Mardian.

Cleo. As well a woman with an eunuch play'd
As with a woman. Come, you'll play with me, sir ?

Mar. As well as I can, madam.

Cleo. And when good will is show'd, though't come too
    short,
The actor may plead pardon. I'll none now :
Give me mine angle ; we'll to the river : there,
My music playing far off, I will betray
Tawny-finn'd fishes ; my bended hook shall pierce
Their slimy jaws ; and, as I draw them up,
I'll think them every one an Antony,
And say ' Ah, ha ! you're caught.'

Char.   'Twas merry when
You wager'd on your angling ; when your diver
Did hang a salt-fish on his hook, which he
With fervency drew up.

Cleo.   That time,—O times !—
I laugh'd him out of patience ; and that night
I laugh'd him into patience : and next morn,
Ere the ninth hour, I drunk him to his bed ;
Then put my tires and mantles on him, whilst
I wore his sword Philippan.

ACT II, Scene v, ll. 1-23

559

> Pity me, Charmian,
> But do not speak to me.
>
> ACT II, Scene v, 118-119

> Come, thou monarch of the vine,
> Plumpy Bacchus with pink eyne !
> In thy fats our cares be drown'd,
> With thy grapes our hairs be crown'd :
> Cup us, till the world go round,
> Cup us, till the world go round !
>
> ACT II, Scene vii, ll. 120-125

The April's in her eyes : it is love's spring,
And these the showers to bring it on.

ACT III, Scene ii, ll. 43-44

Her tongue will not obey her heart, nor can
Her heart inform her tongue,—the swan's down-feather,
That stands upon the swell at full of tide,
And neither way inclines.   ACT III, Scene ii, ll. 47-50

But let determined things to destiny
Hold unbewail'd their way.

ACT III, Scene vi, ll. 84-85

Alarum. Enter ENOBARBUS.

Eno. Naught, naught, all naught ! I can behold no
    longer :
The Antoniad, the Egyptian admiral,
With all their sixty, fly and turn the rudder :
To see't mine eyes are blasted.

Enter SCARUS.

Scar.   Gods and goddesses,
All the whole synod of them !
    Eno.   What's thy passion ?
    Scar. The greater cantle of the world is lost
With very ignorance ; we have kiss'd away
Kingdoms and provinces.

560

Eno.   How appears the fight?

Scar. On our side like the token'd pestilence,
Where death is sure. Yon ribaudred nag of Egypt,—
Whom leprosy o'ertake!—i' the midst o' the fight,
When vantage like a pair of twins appear'd,
Both as the same, or rather ours the elder,
The breese upon her, like a cow in June,
Hoists sails and flies.

Eno. That I beheld:
Mine eyes did sicken at the sight, and could not
Endure a further view.

Scar.   She once being loof'd,
The noble ruin of her magic, Antony,
Claps on his sea-wing, and, like a doting mallard,
Leaving the fight in height, flies after her:
I never saw an action of such shame;
Experience, manhood, honour, ne'er before
Did violate so itself.   Act III, Scene x, ll. 1-24

Alexandria. Cleopatra's palace.

Eros.   Sir, the queen.

Antony. O, whither hast thou led me, Egypt? See,
How I convey my shame out of thine eyes
By looking back what I have left behind
'Stroy'd in dishonour.

Cleopatra.   O my lord, my lord,
Forgive my fearful sails! I little thought
You would have follow'd.

Ant.   Egypt, thou knew'st too well
My heart was to thy rudder tied by the strings,
And thou shouldst tow me after: o'er my spirit
Thy full supremacy thou knew'st, and that
Thy beck might from the bidding of the gods
Command me.

Cleo.   O, my pardon!

Ant.   Now I must
To the young man send humble treaties, dodge

561

And palter in the shifts of lowness; who
With half the bulk o' the world play'd as I pleased,
Making and marring fortunes. You did know
How much you were my conqueror; and that
My sword, made weak by my affection, would
Obey it on all cause.

    Cleo.   Pardon, pardon!

    Ant. Fall not a tear, I say; one of them rates
All that is won and lost: give me a kiss;
Even this repays me.   Act III, Scene xi, ll. 50-71

Egypt. Caesar's camp.

Enter Caesar, Dolabella, *with others.*

    Caes. Let him appear that's come from Antony.
Know you him?

    Dol.   Caesar, 'tis his schoolmaster:
An argument that he is pluck'd, when hither
He sends so poor a pinion of his wing,
Which had superfluous kings for messengers
Not many moons gone by.

Enter Euphronius, *ambassador from Antony.*

    Caes.   Approach, and speak.

    Euph. Such as I am, I come from Antony:
I was of late as petty to his ends
As is the morn-dew on the myrtle-leaf
To his grand sea.   Act III, Scene xii, ll. 1-10

Against the blown rose may they stop their nose
That kneel'd unto the buds.

                Act III, Scene xiii, ll. 39-40

    Antony. I will be treble-sinew'd, hearted, breathed,
And fight maliciously: for when mine hours
Were nice and lucky, men did ransom lives
Of me for jests; but now I'll set my teeth,
And send to darkness all that stop me. Come,

Let's have one other gaudy night : call to me
All my sad captains ; fill our bowls once more ;
Let's mock the midnight bell.

    Cleopatra.   It is my birth-day :
I had thought to have held it poor ; but, since my lord
Is Antony again, I will be Cleopatra.

Act III, Scene xiii, ll. 178-187

The same. Before the palace.

Enter two Soldiers to their guard.

First Sold. Brother, good night : to-morrow is the day.
Sec. Sold. It will determine one way : fare you well.
Heard you of nothing strange about the streets ?
First Sold. Nothing. What news ?
Sec. Sold. Belike 'tis but a rumour. Good night to
    you.
First Sold. Well, sir, good night.

Enter two other Soldiers.

Sec. Sold. Soldiers, have careful watch.
Third Sold. And you. Good night, good night.

        [*They place themselves in every corner of the stage.*
Fourth Sold. Here we : and if to-morrow
Our navy thrive, I have an absolute hope
Our landmen will stand up.
    Third Sold.   'Tis a brave army,
And full of purpose.

        [*Music of the hautboys as under the stage.*
Fourth Sold.   Peace ! what noise ?
First Sold.   List ! list !
Sec. Sold. Hark !
First Sold.   Music i' the air.
Third Sold.   Under the earth.
Fourth Sold. It signs well, does it not ?
Third Sold.   No.
First Sold.   Peace, I say !

563

What should this mean?

Sec. Sold. 'Tis the god Hercules, whom Antony loved,
Now leaves him.

First Sold. Walk; let's see if other watchmen
Do hear what we do?   [*They advance to another post.*

Sec. Sold.   How now, masters!

All.   [*Speaking together*] How now!
How now! do you hear this?

First Sold.   Ay; is't not strange?

Third Sold. Do you hear, masters? do you hear?

First Sold. Follow the noise so far as we have quarter;
Let's see how it will give off.

All.   Content. 'Tis strange.

                              [*Exeunt.*

                        ACT IV, Scene iii, ll. 1-23

The same. A room in the palace.

Enter ANTONY *and* CLEOPATRA, CHARMIAN, *and
others attending.*

Ant. Eros! mine armour, Eros!

Cleo.   Sleep a little.

Ant. No, my chuck. Eros, come; mine armour, Eros!

Enter EROS *with armour.*

Come, good fellow, put mine iron on:
If fortune be not ours to-day, it is
Because we brave her: come.

Cleo.   Nay, I'll help too.
What's this for?

Ant.   Ah, let be, let be! thou art
The armourer of my heart: false, false; this, this.

Cleo. Sooth, la, I'll help: thus it must be.

Ant.   Well, well;
We shall thrive now. Seest thou, my good fellow?
Go put on thy defences.

Eros.   Briefly, sir.

Cleo. Is not this buckled well ?
Ant.   Rarely, rarely :
He that unbuckles this, till we do please
To daff't for our repose, shall hear a storm.
Thou fumblest, Eros ; and my queen's a squire
More tight at this than thou : dispatch. O love,
That thou couldst see my wars to-day, and knew'st
The royal occupation ! thou shouldst see
A workman in't.   ACT IV, Scene iv, ll. 1-18

Antony. Give me thy hand ;

Enter CLEOPATRA, *attended.*

To this great fairy I'll commend thy acts,
Make her thanks bless thee. [*To Cleo.*] O thou day o' the
          world,
Chain mine arm'd neck ; leap thou, attire and all,
Through proof of harness to my heart, and there
Ride on the pants triumphing !
    Cleo.   Lord of lords !
O infinite virtue, comest thou smiling from
The world's great snare uncaught ?
    Ant.   My nightingale,
We have beat them to their beds. What, girl ! though
          grey
Do something mingle with our younger brown, yet ha' we
A brain that nourishes our nerves, and can
Get goal for goal of youth. Behold this man ;
Commend unto his lips thy favouring hand :
Kiss it, my warrior : he hath fought to-day
As if a god, in hate of mankind, had
Destroy'd in such a shape.
    Cleo.   I'll give thee, friend,
An armour all of gold ; it was a king's.
    Ant. He has deserved it, were it carbuncled
Like holy Phoebus' car. Give me thy hand :
Through Alexandria make a jolly march ;

565

Bear our hack'd targets like the men that owe them :
Had our great palace the capacity
To camp this host, we all would sup together,
And drink carouses to the next day's fate,
Which promises royal peril. Trumpeters,
With brazen din blast you the city's ear ;
Make mingle with our rattling tabourines ;
That heaven and earth may strike their sounds together,
Applauding our approach.   ACT IV, Scene viii, ll. 11-39

Enter ENOBARBUS.

Eno.   O, bear me witness, night,—
Third Sold. What man is this ?
Sec. Sold.   Stand close, and list him.
Eno. Be witness to me, O thou blessed moon,
When men revolted shall upon record
Bear hateful memory, poor Enobarbus did
Before thy face repent !
First Sold.   Enobarbus !
Third Sold.   Peace !
Hark further.
Eno. O sovereign mistress of true melancholy,
The poisonous damp of night dispunge upon me,
That life, a very rebel to my will,
May hang no longer on me : throw my heart
Against the flint and hardness of my fault ;
Which, being dried with grief, will break to powder,
And finish all foul thoughts. O Antony,
Nobler than my revolt is infamous,
Forgive me in thine own particular ;
But let the world rank me in register
A master-leaver and a fugitive :
O Antony ! O Antony !   [*Dies.*
                                    ACT IV, Scene ix, ll. 5-23

Scarus.   Swallows have built
In Cleopatra's sails their nests : the augurers

566

Say they know not, they cannot tell; look grimly,
And dare not speak their knowledge. Antony
Is valiant, and dejected; and, by starts,
His fretted fortunes give him hope, and fear,
Of what he has, and has not.

[Alarum afar off, as at a sea-fight.

Enter ANTONY.

Ant.   All is lost;
This foul Egyptian hath betrayed me:
My fleet hath yielded to the foe; and yonder
They cast their caps up and carouse together
Like friends long lost. Triple-turn'd whore! 'tis thou
Hast sold me to this novice; and my heart
Makes only wars on thee. Bid them all fly;
For when I am revenged upon my charm,
I have done all. Bid them all fly; begone. *[Exit Scarus.*
O sun, thy uprise shall I see no more:
Fortune and Antony part here; even here
Do we shake hands. All come to this? The hearts
That spaniel'd me at heels, to whom I gave
Their wishes, do discandy, melt their sweets
On blossoming Caesar; and this pine is bark'd,
That overtopp'd them all. Betray'd I am:
O this false soul of Egypt! this grave charm,—
Whose eye beck'd forth my wars, and call'd them home;
Whose bosom was my crownet, my chief end,—
Like a right gipsy, hath, at fast and loose,
Beguiled me to the very heart of loss.
What, Eros, Eros!

Enter CLEOPATRA.

                                        Ah, thou spell! Avaunt!
Cleo. Why is my lord enraged against his love?
Ant. Vanish, or I shall give thee thy deserving,
And blemish Caesar's triumph. Let him take thee,
And hoist thee up to the shouting plebeians:

Follow his chariot, like the greatest spot
Of all thy sex; most monster-like, be shown
For poor'st diminutives, for doits; and let
Patient Octavia plough thy visage up
With her prepared nails.   [*Exit Cleopatra.*

               'Tis well thou'rt gone,
If it be well to live; but better 'twere
Thou fell'st into my fury, for one death
Might have prevented many.   Eros, ho!
The shirt of Nessus is upon me: teach me,
Alcides, thou mine ancestor, thy rage:
Let me lodge Lichas on the horns o' the moon;
And with those hands, that grasp'd the heaviest club,
Subdue my worthiest self.   The witch shall die:
To the young Roman boy she hath sold me, and I fall
Under this plot; she dies for't.   Eros, ho!

                             ACT IV, Scene xii, ll. 3-49

Alexandria.   Cleopatra's palace.

Enter ANTONY *and* EROS.

Ant. Eros, thou yet behold'st me?

Eros.   Ay, noble lord.

Ant. Sometimes we see a cloud that's dragonish;
A vapour sometime like a bear or lion,
A tower'd citadel, a pendent rock,
A forked mountain, or blue promontory
With trees upon't, that nod unto the world,
And mock our eyes with air: thou hast seen these
    signs;
They are black vesper's pageants.

Eros.   Ay, my lord.

Ant. That which is now a horse, even with a thought
The rack dislimns, and makes it indistinct,
As water is in water.

Eros.   It does, my lord.

Ant. My good knave Eros, now thy captain is

Even such a body : here I am Antony :
Yet cannot hold this visible shape, my knave.
I made these wars for Egypt : and the queen,—
Whose heart I thought I had, for she had mine ;
Which whilst it was mine had annex'd unto't
A million more, now lost,—she, Eros, has
Pack'd cards with Caesar, and false-play'd my glory
Unto an enemy's triumph.
Nay, weep not, gentle Eros ; there is left us
Ourselves to end ourselves.

Enter MARDIAN.

       O, thy vile lady !
She has robb'd me of my sword.

 Mar.   No, Antony ;
My mistress loved thee, and her fortunes mingled
With thine entirely.

 Ant.   Hence, saucy eunuch ; peace !
She hath betray'd me and shall die the death.

 Mar. Death of one person can be paid but once,
And that she has discharged : what thou wouldst do
Is done unto thy hand : the last she spake
Was ' Antony ! most noble Antony ! '
Then in the midst a tearing groan did break
The name of Antony ; it was divided
Between her heart and lips : she render'd life,
Thy name so buried in her.

 Ant.   Dead, then ?

 Mar.   Dead.

 Ant. Unarm, Eros ; the long day's task is done,
And we must sleep. [*To Mar.*] That thou depart'st hence
  safe,
Does pay thy labour richly ; go.   [*Exit Mardian.*
         Off, pluck off :
The seven-fold shield of Ajax cannot keep
The battery from my heart. O, cleave, my sides !

Heart, once be stronger than thy continent,
Crack thy frail case ! Apace, Eros, apace.
No more a soldier : bruised pieces, go ;
You have been nobly borne. From me awhile. [*Exit Eros.*
I will o'ertake thee, Cleopatra, and
Weep for my pardon. So it must be, for now
All length is torture : since the torch is out,
Lie down, and stray no farther : now all labour
Mars what it does ; yea, very force entangles
Itself with strength : seal then, and all is done.
Eros !—I come, my queen :—Eros !—Stay for me :
Where souls do couch on flowers, we'll hand in hand,
And with our sprightly port make the ghosts gaze :
Dido and her Æneas shall want troops,
And all the haunt be ours. Come, Eros, Eros !

Re-enter EROS.

Eros. What would my lord ?
    Ant.   Since Cleopatra died,
I have lived in such dishonour, that the gods
Detest my baseness. I, that with my sword
Quarter'd the world, and o'er green Neptune's back
With ships made cities, condemn myself to lack
The courage of a woman ; less noble mind
Than she which by her death our Caesar tells
' I am conqueror of myself.' Thou art sworn, Eros,
That, when the exigent should come, which now
Is come indeed, when I should see behind me
The inevitable prosecution of
Disgrace and horror, that, on my command,
Thou then wouldst kill me : do't ; the time is come :
Thou strikest not me, 'tis Caesar thou defeat'st.
Put colour in thy cheek.
    Eros.   The gods withhold me !
Shall I do that which all the Parthian darts,
Though enemy, lost aim, and could not ?

Ant.   Eros,
Wouldst thou be window'd in great Rome and see
Thy master thus with pleach'd arms, bending down
His corrigible neck, his face subdued
To penetrative shame, whilst the wheel'd seat
Of fortunate Caesar, drawn before him, branded
His baseness that ensued ?

    Eros.   I would not see't.

    Ant. Come, then ; for with a wound I must be cured.
Draw that thy honest sword, which thou hast worn
Most useful for thy country.

    Eros.   O, sir, pardon me !

    Ant. When I did make thee free, sworest thou not then
To do this when I bade thee ? Do it at once ;
Or thy precedent services are all
But accidents unpurposed. Draw, and come.

    Eros. Turn from me, then, that noble countenance,
Wherein the worship of the whole world lies.

    Ant. Lo thee !   [*Turning from him.*

    Eros. My sword is drawn.

    Ant.   Then let it do at once
The thing why thou hast drawn it.

    Eros.   My dear master,
My captain, and my emperor, let me say,
Before I strike this bloody stroke, farewell.

    Ant. 'Tis said, man ; and farewell.

    Eros. Farewell, great chief. Shall I strike now ?

    Ant.   Now, Eros.

    Eros. Why, there then : thus I do escape the sorrow
Of Antony's death.   [*Kills himself.*

    Ant.   Thrice-nobler than myself !
Thou teachest me, O valiant Eros, what
I should, and thou couldst not. My queen and Eros
Have by their brave instruction got upon me
A nobleness in record : but I will be
A bridegroom in my death, and run into't

As to a lover's bed. Come, then ; and, Eros,
Thy master dies thy scholar : to do thus

                             [Falling on his sword.

I learn'd of thee. How ! not dead ? not dead ?
The guard, ho ! O, dispatch me !

          Enter DERCETAS *and* Guard.

First Guard.   What's the noise ?

Ant. I have done my work ill, friends : O, make an end
Of what I have begun.

Sec. Guard.   The star is fall'n.

First Guard. And time is at his period.

All.   Alas, and woe !

Ant. Let him that loves me strike me dead.

First Guard.   Not I.

Sec. Guard. Nor I.

Third Guard. Nor any one. . . .

Ant. Bear me, good friends, where Cleopatra bides ;
'Tis the last service that I shall command you.

First Guard. Woe, woe are we, sir, you may not live to
    wear
All your true followers out.

All.   Most heavy day !

Ant. Nay, good my fellows, do not please sharp fate
To grace it with your sorrows : bid that welcome
Which comes to punish us, and we punish it
Seeming to bear it lightly. Take me up :
I have led you oft : carry me now, good friends,
And have my thanks for all.   *[Exeunt, bearing Antony.*

               ACT IV, Scene xiv, ll. 1-110, 131-140

        Alexandria. A monument.

   Enter CLEOPATRA, *and her maids aloft, with*
         CHARMIAN *and* IRAS.

Cleo. O Charmian, I will never go from hence.

Char. Be comforted, dear madam.

Cleo.   No, I will not:

All strange and terrible events are welcome,
But comforts we despise; our size of sorrow,
Proportion'd to our cause, must be as great
As that which makes it.

Enter, below, DIOMEDES.

How now! is he dead?
Dio. His death's upon him, but not dead.
Look out o' the other side your monument;
His guard have brought him thither.

Enter, below, ANTONY, *borne by the* Guard.

Cleo.   O sun,
Burn the great sphere thou movest in! darkling stand
The varying star o' the world. O Antony,
Antony, Antony! Help, Charmian, help, Iras, help;
Help, friends below; let's draw him hither.
Ant.   Peace!
Not Caesar's valour hath o'erthrown Antony,
But Antony's hath triumph'd on itself.
Cleo. So it should be, that none but Antony
Should conquer Antony; but woe 'tis so!
Ant. I am dying, Egypt, dying; only
I here importune death awhile, until
Of many thousand kisses the poor last
I lay upon thy lips.
Cleo.   I dare not, dear,—
Dear my lord, pardon,—I dare not,
Lest I be taken: not the imperious show
Of the full-fortuned Caesar ever shall
Be brooch'd with me; if knife, drugs, serpents, have
Edge, sting, or operation, I am safe:
Your wife Octavia, with her modest eyes
And still conclusion, shall acquire no honour
Demuring upon me. But come, come, Antony,—
Help me, my women,—we must draw thee up:
Assist, good friends.

Ant.   O, quick, or I am gone.

Cleo. Here's sport indeed ! How heavy weighs my lord !
Our strength is all gone into heaviness,
That makes the weight : had I great Juno's power,
The strong-wing'd Mercury should fetch thee up,
And set thee by Jove's side. Yet come a little,—
Wishers were ever fools,—O, come, come, come ;

            [*They heave Antony aloft to Cleopatra.*

And welcome, welcome ! die where thou hast lived :
Quicken with kissing : had my lips that power,
Thus would I wear them out.

    All.   A heavy sight !

Ant. I am dying, Egypt, dying :
Give me some wine, and let me speak a little.

Cleo. No, let me speak ; and let me rail so high,
That the false housewife Fortune break her wheel,
Provoked by my offence.

    Ant.   One word, sweet queen :
Of Caesar seek your honour, with your safety. O !

Cleo. They do not go together.

    Ant.   Gentle, hear me :
None about Caesar trust but Proculeius.

Cleo. My resolution and my hands I'll trust ;
None about Caesar.

Ant. The miserable change now at my end
Lament nor sorrow at ; but please your thoughts
In feeding them with those my former fortunes
Wherein I lived, the greatest prince o' the world,
The noblest ; and do now not basely die,
Not cowardly put off my helmet to
My countryman,—a Roman by a Roman
Valiantly vanquish'd. Now my spirit is going ;
I can no more.

Cleo.   Noblest of men, woo't die ?
Hast thou no care of me ? shall I abide
In this dull world, which in thy absence is

No better than a sty ?   O, see, my women,   [*Antony dies.*
The crown o' the earth doth melt.   My lord !
O, wither'd is the garland of the war,
The soldier's pole is fall'n : young boys and girls
Are level now with men ; the odds is gone,
And there is nothing left remarkable
Beneath the visiting moon.   [*Faints.*
  Char.   O, quietness, lady !
  Iras. She is dead too, our sovereign.
  Char.   Lady !
  Iras.   Madam !
  Char. O madam, madam, madam !
  Iras.   Royal Egypt,
Empress !
  Char. Peace, peace, Iras !
  Cleo. No more, but e'en a woman, and commanded
By such poor passion as the maid that milks
And does the meanest chares.   It were for me
To throw my sceptre at the injurious gods ;
To tell them that this world did equal theirs
Till they had stol'n our jewel.   All's but naught ;
Patience is sottish, and impatience does
Become a dog that's mad : then is it sin
To rush into the secret house of death,
Ere death dare come to us ?   How do you, women ?
What, what ! good cheer ! Why, how now, Charmian !
My noble girls ! Ah, women, women, look,
Our lamp is spent, it's out !   Good sirs, take heart :
We'll bury him ; and then, what's brave, what's noble,
Let's do it after the high Roman fashion,
And make death proud to take us.   Come, away :
This case of that huge spirit now is cold :
Ah, women, women ! come ; we have no friend
But resolution, and the briefest end.
    [*Exeunt ; those above bearing off Antony's body.*
          ACT IV, Scene xv, ll. 1-91

Caesar.   What is't thou say'st ?

Dercetas. I say, O Caesar, Antony is dead.

Caes. The breaking of so great a thing should make
A greater crack : the round world
Should have shook lions into civil streets,
And citizens to their dens : the death of Antony
Is not a single doom ; in the name lay
A moiety of the world.

Der.   He is dead, Caesar ;
Not by a public minister of justice,
Nor by a hired knife ; but that self hand,
Which writ his honour in the acts it did,
Hath, with the courage which the heart did lend it,
Splitted the heart. This is his sword ;
I robb'd his wound of it ; behold it stain'd
With his most noble blood.

Caes.   Look you sad, friends ?
The gods rebuke me, but it is tidings
To wash the eyes of kings.

Agrippa.   And strange it is,
That nature must compel us to lament
Our most persisted deeds.

Mecaenas.   His taints and honours
Waged equal with him.

Agr.   A rarer spirit never
Did steer humanity : but you, gods, will give us
Some faults to make us men. Caesar is touch'd.

Mec. When such a spacious mirror's set before him,
He needs must see himself.

Caes.   O Antony !
I have follow'd thee to this ; but we do lance
Diseases in our bodies : I must perforce
Have shown to thee such a declining day,
Or look on thine ; we could not stall together
In the whole world : but yet let me lament,
With tears as sovereign as the blood of hearts,

That thou, my brother, my competitor
In top of all design, my mate in empire,
Friend and companion in the front of war,
The arm of mine own body, and the heart
Where mine his thoughts did kindle,—that our stars,
Unreconciliable, should divide
Our equalness to this. Hear me, good friends,—
But I will tell you at some meeter season.

ACT V, Scene i, ll. 12-49

Alexandria. A room in the monument.

Enter CLEOPATRA, CHARMIAN, *and* IRAS.

Cleo. My desolation does begin to make
A better life. 'Tis paltry to be Caesar;
Not being Fortune, he's but Fortune's knave,
A minister of her will: and it is great
To do that thing that ends all other deeds;
Which shackles accidents and bolts up change;
Which sleeps, and never palates more the dug,
The beggar's nurse and Caesar's. . . .

[*Here Proculeius and two of the Guard ascend the monument by a ladder placed against a window, and, having descended, come behind Cleopatra. Some of the Guard unbar and open the gates.*

Gal. [*To Proculeius and the Guard*] Guard her till Caesar come. [*Exit.*

Iras. Royal queen!

Char. O Cleopatra! thou art taken, queen.

Cleo. Quick, quick, good hands. [*Drawing a dagger.*
Pro. Hold, worthy lady, hold:
[*Seizes and disarms her.*

Do not yourself such wrong, who are in this
Relieved, but not betray'd.

Cleo. What, of death too,
That rids our dogs of languish?

Pro. Cleopatra,

577

Do not abuse my master's bounty by
The undoing of yourself: let the world see
His nobleness well acted, which your death
Will never let come forth.

    Cleo.   Where art thou, death?
Come hither, come! come, come, and take a queen
Worth many babes and beggars!

    Pro.   O, temperance, lady!

    Cleo. Sir, I will eat no meat, I'll not drink, sir;
If idle talk will once be necessary,
I'll not sleep neither: this mortal house I'll ruin,
Do Caesar what he can. Know, sir, that I
Will not wait pinion'd at your master's court;
Nor once be chastised with the sober eye
Of dull Octavia. Shall they hoist me up
And show me to the shouting varletry
Of censuring Rome? Rather a ditch in Egypt
Be gentle grave unto me! rather on Nilus' mud
Lay me stark naked, and let the water-flies
Blow me into abhorring! rather make
My country's high pyramides my gibbet,
And hang me up in chains! . . .

Enter DOLABELLA.

    Dol. Most noble empress, you have heard of me?

    Cleo. I cannot tell.

    Dol.   Assuredly you know me.

    Cleo. No matter, sir, what I have heard or known.
You laugh when boys or women tell their dreams;
Is't not your trick?

    Dol.   I understand not, madam.

    Cleo. I dream'd there was an Emperor Antony:
O, such another sleep, that I might see
But such another man!

    Dol.   If it might please ye,—

    Cleo. His face was as the heavens; and therein stuck

A sun and moon, which kept their course, and lighted
The little O, the earth.

    Dol.   Most sovereign creature,—

    Cleo. His legs bestrid the ocean : his rear'd arm
Crested the world : his voice was propertied
As all the tuned spheres, and that to friends ;
But when he meant to quail and shake the orb,
He was as rattling thunder. For his bounty,
There was no winter in't ; an autumn 'twas
That grew the more by reaping : his delights
Were dolphin-like ; they show'd his back above
The element they lived in : in his livery
Walk'd crowns and crownets ; realms and islands were
As plates dropp'd from his pocket.

    Dol.   Cleopatra !

    Cleo. Think you there was, or might be, such a man
As this I dream'd of ?

    Dol.   Gentle madam, no.

    Cleo. You lie, up to the hearing of the gods.
But, if there be, or ever were, one such,
It's past the size of dreaming : nature wants stuff
To vie strange forms with fancy ; yet, to imagine
An Antony, were nature's piece 'gainst fancy,
Condemning shadows quite. . . .

    Enter CAESAR, GALLUS, PROCULEIUS, MECAENAS,
      SELEUCUS, *and others of his train.* . . .

    Caesar. Make not your thoughts your prisons : no, dear
      queen ;
For we intend so to dispose you as
Yourself shall give us counsel. Feed, and sleep :
Our care and pity is so much upon you,
That we remain your friend ; and so, adieu.

    Cleo. My master, and my lord !

    Caes. Not so. Adieu. [*Flourish. Exeunt Caesar and his train.*

    Cleo. He words me, girls, he words me, that I should not

Be noble to myself : but, hark thee, Charmian.

[*Whispers Charmian.*

Iras. Finish, good lady ; the bright day is done,
And we are for the dark. . . .

Cleo.   Now, Iras, what think'st thou ?
Thou, an Egyptian puppet, shalt be shown
In Rome, as well as I : mechanic slaves
With greasy aprons, rules, and hammers, shall
Uplift us to the view ; in their thick breaths,
Rank of gross diet, shall we be enclouded,
And forced to drink their vapour.

Iras.   The gods forbid !

Cleo. Nay, 'tis most certain, Iras : saucy lictors
Will catch at us, like strumpets ; and scald rhymers
Ballad us out o' tune : the quick comedians
Extemporally will stage us, and present
Our Alexandrian revels ; Antony
Shall be brought drunken forth, and I shall see
Some squeaking Cleopatra boy my greatness
I' the posture of a whore.

Iras.   O the good gods !

Cleo. Nay, that's certain.

Iras. I'll never see't ; for, I am sure, my nails
Are stronger than mine eyes.

Cleo.   Why, that's the way
To fool their preparation, and to conquer
Their most absurd intents.

Re-enter CHARMIAN.

       Now, Charmian !
Show me, my women, like a queen : go fetch
My best attires : I am again for Cydnus,
To meet Mark Antony : sirrah Iras, go.
Now, noble Charmian, we'll dispatch indeed ;
And, when thou hast done this chare, I'll give thee leave
To play till doomsday. Bring our crown and all.
Wherefore's this noise ?   [*Exit Iras. A noise within.*

Enter a Guardsman.

Guard. Here is a rural fellow
That will not be denied your highness' presence:
He brings you figs.

Cleo. Let him come in. [*Exit Guardsman.*
What poor an instrument
May do a noble deed! he brings me liberty.
My resolution's placed, and I have nothing
Of woman in me: now from head to foot
I am marble-constant; now the fleeting moon
No planet is of mine.

Re-enter Guardsman, *with* Clown *bringing in a basket.*

Guard. This is the man.

Cleo. Avoid, and leave him. [*Exit Guardsman.*
Hast thou the pretty worm of Nilus there,
That kills and pains not?

Clown. Truly, I have him: but I would not be the party
that should desire you to touch him, for his biting is immortal;
those that do die of it do seldom or never recover.

Cleo. Rememberest thou any that have died on't?

Clown. Very many, men and women too. I heard of one
of them no longer than yesterday: a very honest woman, but
something given to lie; as a woman should not do, but in the
way of honesty: how she died of the biting of it, what pain
she felt: truly, she makes a very good report o' the worm;
but he that will believe all that they say, shall never be saved
by half that they do: but this is most fallible, the worm's an
odd worm.

Cleo. Get thee hence; farewell.

Clown. I wish you all joy of the worm.
[*Setting down his basket.*

Cleo. Farewell.

Clown. You must think this, look you, that the worm will
do his kind.

Cleo. Ay, ay; farewell.

Clown. Look you, the worm is not to be trusted but in the

keeping of wise people ; for, indeed, there is no goodness in the worm.

Cleo. Take thou no care ; it shall be heeded.

Clown. Very good. Give it nothing, I pray you, for it is not worth the feeding.

Cleo. Will it eat me ?

Clown. You must not think I am so simple but I know the devil himself will not eat a woman : I know that a woman is a dish for the gods, if the devil dress her not. But, truly, these same whoreson devils do the gods great harm in their women ; for in every ten that they make, the devils mar five.

Cleo. Well, get thee gone ; farewell.

Clown. Yes, forsooth : I wish you joy o' the worm. [*Exit.*

Re-enter IRAS *with a robe, crown, &c.*

Cleo. Give me my robe, put on my crown ; I have
Immortal longings in me : now no more
The juice of Egypt's grape shall moist this lip :
Yare, yare, good Iras ; quick. Methinks I hear
Antony call ; I see him rouse himself
To praise my noble act ; I hear him mock
The luck of Caesar, which the gods give men
To excuse their after wrath : husband, I come :
Now to that name my courage prove my title !
I am fire and air ; my other elements
I give to baser life. So ; have you done ?
Come then, and take the last warmth of my lips.
Farewell, kind Charmian ; Iras, long farewell.

                    [*Kisses them. Iras falls and dies.*
Have I the aspic in my lips ? Dost fall ?
If thou and nature can so gently part,
The stroke of death is as a lover's pinch,
Which hurts, and is desired. Dost thou lie still ?
If thus thou vanishest, thou tell'st the world
It is not worth leave-taking.

Char. Dissolve, thick cloud, and rain ; that I may say,

The gods themselves do weep !
 Cleo.   This proves me base :
If she first meet the curled Antony,
He'll make demand of her, and spend that kiss
Which is my heaven to have. Come, thou mortal wretch,
     [*To an asp, which she applies to her breast.*
With thy sharp teeth this knot intrinsicate
Of life at once untie : poor venomous fool,
Be angry, and dispatch. O, couldst thou speak,
That I might hear thee call great Caesar ass
Unpolicied !
 Char. O eastern star !
 Cleo.   Peace, peace !
Dost thou not see my baby at my breast,
That sucks the nurse asleep ?
 Char.   O, break ! O, break !
 Cleo. As sweet as balm, as soft as air, as gentle,—
O Antony !—Nay, I will take thee too :
     [*Applying another asp to her arm.*
What should I stay—   [*Dies.*
 Char. In this vile world ? So, fare thee well.
Now boast thee, death, in thy possession lies
A lass unparallel'd. Downy windows, close ;
And golden Phoebus never be beheld
Of eyes again so royal ! Your crown's awry ;
I'll mend it, and then play.

     Enter the Guard, *rushing in.*
 First Guard. Where is the queen ?
 Char.   Speak softly, wake her not.
 First Guard. Caesar hath sent—
 Char.   Too slow a messenger.
     [*Applies an asp.*
O, come apace, dispatch ! I partly feel thee.
 First Guard. Approach, ho ! All's not well : Caesar's
  beguiled.
 Sec. Guard. There's Dolabella sent from Caesar ; call him.

First Guard. What work is here! Charmian, is this well
    done?

Char. It is well done, and fitting for a princess
Descended of so many royal kings.
Ah, soldier!   [*Dies.*

                Re-enter DOLABELLA.

Dol. How goes it here?
Sec. Guard.   All dead.
Dol.   Caesar, thy thoughts
Touch their effects in this: thyself art coming
To see perform'd the dreaded act which thou
So sought'st to hinder.

         [*Within* ' A way there, a way for Caesar!'

    Re-enter CAESAR *and all his train, marching.*

Dol. O sir, you are too sure an augerer;
That you did fear is done.
Caes.   Bravest at the last,
She levell'd at our purposes, and, being royal,
Took her own way. The manner of their deaths?
I do not see them bleed.
Dol.   Who was last with them?
First Guard. A simple countryman, that brought her figs:
This was his basket.
Caes.   Poison'd, then.
First Guard.   O Caesar,
This Charmian lived but now; she stood and spake:
I found her trimming up the diadem
On her dead mistress; tremblingly she stood
And on the sudden dropp'd.
Caes.   O noble weakness!
If they had swallow'd poison, 'twould appear
By external swelling: but she looks like sleep,
As she would catch another Antony
In her strong toil of grace.

     ACT V, Scene ii, ll. 1-8, 36-62, 71-100, 185-194, 207-351

Coriolanus

To break the heart of generosity,
And make bold power look pale—they threw their caps
As they would hang them on the horns o' the moon,
Shouting their emulation.   ACT I, Scene i, ll. 215-218

Rome. A room in Marcius' house.

Enter VOLUMNIA *and* VIRGILIA : *they set them down
on two low stools, and sew.*

Enter VALERIA, *with an* Usher *and* Gentlewoman.

Val. My ladies both, good day to you.

Vol. Sweet madam.

Vir. I am glad to see your ladyship.

Val. How do you both ? you are manifest house-keepers. What are you sewing here ? A fine spot, in good faith. How does your little son ?

Vir. I thank your ladyship ; well, good madam.

Vol. He had rather see the swords, and hear a drum, than look upon his schoolmaster.

Val. O' my word, the father's son : I'll swear, 'tis a very pretty boy. O' my troth, I looked upon him o' Wednesday half an hour together : has such a confirmed countenance. I saw him run after a gilded butterfly ; and when he caught it, he let it go again ; and after it again ; and over and over he comes, and up again ; catched it again ; or whether his fall enraged him, or how 'twas, he did so set his teeth and tear it ; O, I warrant, how he mammocked it !

Vol. One on's father's moods.

Val. Indeed, la, 'tis a noble child.

Vir. A crack, madam.

Val. Come, lay aside your stitchery ; I must have you play the idle huswife with me this afternoon.

Vir. No, good madam ; I will not out of doors.

Val. Not out of doors !

585

Vol. She shall, she shall.

Vir. Indeed, no, by your patience ; I'll not over the threshold till my lord return from the wars.

Val. Fie, you confine yourself most unreasonably : come, you must go visit the good lady that lies in.

Vir. I will wish her speedy strength, and visit her with my prayers ; but I cannot go thither.

Vol. Why, I pray you ?

Vir. 'Tis not to save labour, nor that I want love.

Val. You would be another Penelope : yet, they say, all the yarn she spun in Ulysses' absence did but fill Ithaca full of moths. Come ; I would your cambric were sensible as your finger, that you might leave pricking it for pity. Come, you shall go with us.

Vir. No, good madam, pardon me ; indeed, I will not forth.

Val. In truth, la, go with me ; and I'll tell you excellent news of your husband.

Vir. O, good madam, there can be none yet.

Val. Verily, I do not jest with you ; there came news from him last night.

Vir. Indeed, madam ?

Val. In earnest, it's true ; I heard a senator speak it. Thus it is : the Volsces have an army forth ; against whom Cominius the general is gone, with one part of our Roman power : your lord and Titus Lartius are set down before their city Corioli ; they nothing doubt prevailing and to make it brief .wars. This is true, on mine honour ; and so, I pray, go with us.

Vir. Give me excuse, good madam ; I will obey you in every thing hereafter.

Vol. Let her alone, lady : as she is now, she will but disease our better mirth.

Val. In troth, I think she would. Fare you well, then. Come, good sweet lady. Prithee, Virgilia, turn thy solemness out o' door, and go along with us.

Vir. No, at a word, madam; indeed, I must not. I wish
you much mirth.

Val. Well, then, farewell.

ACT I, Scene iii, ll. 51-124

Marcius.   Come I too late?

Cominius. Ay, if you come not in the blood of others,
But mantled in your own.

Mar.   O, let me clip ye
In arms as sound as when I woo'd, in heart
As merry as when our nuptial day was done,
And tapers burn'd to bedward!

ACT I, Scene vi, ll. 27-32

Coriolanus.   My gracious silence, hail!
Wouldst thou have laugh'd had I come coffin'd home,
That weep'st to see me triumph? Ah, my dear,
Such eyes the widows in Corioli wear,
And mothers that lack sons.

ACT II, Scene i, ll. 192-196

                Alone he enter'd
The mortal gate of the city, which he painted
With shunless destiny; aidless came off,
And with a sudden re-inforcement struck
Corioli like a planet.

ACT II, Scene ii, ll. 114-118

          Custom calls me to't:
What custom wills, in all things should we do't,
The dust on antique time would lie unswept,
And mountainous error be too highly heapt
For truth to o'er-peer.

ACT II, Scene iii, ll. 124-128

His nature is too noble for the world:
He would not flatter Neptune for his trident,
Or Jove for's power to thunder. His heart's his
   mouth ·
What his breast forges, that his tongue must vent;

587

And, being angry, does forget that ever
He heard the name of death.

ACT III, Scene i, ll. 255-260

> Despising,
> For you, the city, thus I turn my back:
> There is a world elsewhere.

ACT III, Scene iii, ll. 133-135

> I go alone,
> Like to a lonely dragon, that his fen
> Makes fear'd and talk'd of more than seen.

ACT IV, Scene i, ll. 29-31

Antium.   A hall in Aufidius's house.

Third Servingman. Where dwellest thou?
Coriolanus. Under the canopy.
Third Serv. Under the canopy!
Cor. Ay.
Third Serv. Where's that?
Cor. I' the city of kites and crows.
Third Serv. I' the city of kites and crows! What an ass it
is! Then thou dwellest with daws too?
Cor. No, I serve not thy master.
Third Serv. How, sir! do you meddle with my master?
Cor. Ay; 'tis an honester service than to meddle with thy
mistress.
Thou pratest, and pratest; serve with thy trencher, hence!
                    [*Beats him away.   Exit third Servingman.*

Enter AUFIDIUS *with the second* Servingman.

Auf. Where is this fellow?
Sec. Serv. Here, sir: I'ld have beaten him like a dog, but
for disturbing the lords within.   [*Retires.*
Auf. Whence comest thou; what wouldst thou? thy name?
Why speak'st not? speak, man: what's thy name?
Cor. If, Tullus,   [*Unmuffling.*
Not yet thou knowest me, and, seeing me, dost not

588

Think me for the man I am, necessity
Commands me name myself.

   Auf.   What is thy name?

   Cor. A name unmusical to the Volscians' ears,
And harsh in sound to thine.

   Auf.   Say, what's thy name?
Thou hast a grim appearance, and thy face
Bears a command in't; though thy tackle's torn,
Thou show'st a noble vessel: what's thy name?

   Cor. Prepare thy brow to frown: know'st thou me yet?

   Auf. I know thee not: thy name?

   Cor. My name is Caius Marcius, who hath done
To thee particularly and to all the Volsces
Great hurt and mischief; thereto witness may
My surname, Coriolanus: the painful service,
The extreme dangers and the drops of blood
Shed for my thankless country are requited
But with that surname; a good memory,
And witness of the malice and displeasure
Which thou shouldst bear me: only that name remains;
The cruelty and envy of the people,
Permitted by our dastard nobles, who
Have all forsook me, hath devour'd the rest;
And suffer'd me by the voice of slaves to be
Whoop'd out of Rome. Now this extremity
Hath brought me to thy hearth; not out of hope—
Mistake me not—to save my life, for if
I had fear'd death, of all the men i' the world
I would have 'voided thee, but in mere spite,
To be full quit of those my banishers,
Stand I before thee here. Then if thou hast
A heart of wreak in thee, that wilt revenge
Thine own particular wrongs and stop those maims
Of shame seen through thy country, speed thee straight,
And make my misery serve thy turn: so use it
That my revengeful services may prove

As benefits to thee, for I will fight
Against my canker'd country with the spleen
Of all the under fiends. But if so be
Thou darest not this and that to prove more fortunes
Thou'rt tired, then, in a word, I also am
Longer to live most weary, and present
My throat to thee and to thy ancient malice ;
Which not to cut would show thee but a fool,
Since I have ever follow'd thee with hate,
Drawn tuns of blood out of thy country's breast,
And cannot live but to thy shame, unless
It be to do thee service.

    Auf.   O Marcius, Marcius !
Each word thou hast spoke hath weeded from my heart
A root of ancient envy. If Jupiter
Should from yond cloud speak divine things,
And say ' Tis true,' I'ld not believe them more
Than thee, all noble Marcius. Let me twine
Mine arms about that body, where against
My grained ash an hundred times hath broke,
And scarr'd the moon with splinters : here I clip
The anvil of my sword, and do contest
As hotly and as nobly with thy love
As ever in ambitious strength I did
Contend against thy valour. Know thou first,
I loved the maid I married ; never man
Sigh'd truer breath ; but that I see thee here,
Thou noble thing ! more dances my rapt heart
Than when I first my wedded mistress saw
Bestride my threshold. Why, thou Mars ! I tell thee,
We have a power on foot ; and I had purpose
Once more to hew thy target from thy brawn,
Or lose mine arm for't : thou hast beat me out
Twelve several times, and I have nightly since
Dreamt of encounters 'twixt thyself and me ;
We have been down together in my sleep,

Unbuckling helms, fisting each other's throat,
And waked half dead with nothing. Worthy Marcius,
Had we no quarrel else to Rome, but that
Thou art thence banish'd, we would muster all
From twelve to seventy, and pouring war
Into the bowels of ungrateful Rome,
Like a bold flood o'er-bear. O, come, go in,
And take our friendly senators by the hands;
Who now are here, taking their leaves of me,
Who am prepared against your territories.
Though not for Rome itself.

  Cor.   You bless me, gods!

  Auf. Therefore, most absolute sir, if thou wilt have
The leading of thine own revenges, take
The one half of my commission; and set down—
As best thou art experienced, since thou know'st
Thy country's strength and weakness,—thine own ways;
Whether to knock against the gates of Rome,
Or rudely visit them in parts remote,
To fright them, ere destroy. But come in:
Let me commend thee first to those that shall
Say yea to thy desires. A thousand welcomes!
And more a friend than e'er an enemy;
Yet, Marcius, that was much. Your hand: most welcome!

    [*Exeunt Coriolanus and Aufidius. The two Servingmen
       come forward.*

  First Serv. Here's a strange alteration!

  Sec. Serv. By my hand, I had thought to have strucken
him with a cudgel; and yet my mind gave me his clothes
made a false report of him.

  First Serv. What an arm he has! he turned me about with
his finger and his thumb, as one would set up a top.

  Sec. Serv. Nay, I knew by his face that there was something in him: he had, sir, a kind of face, methought,—I
cannot tell how to term it.

  First Serv. He had so; looking as it were—would I were

hanged, but I thought there was more in him than I could think.

Sec. Serv. So did I, I'll be sworn : he is simply the rarest man i' the world.

First Serv. I think he is : but a greater soldier than he, you wot one.

Sec. Serv. Who, my master?

First Serv. Nay, it's no matter for that.

Sec. Serv. Worth six on him.

First Serv. Nay, not so neither : but I take him to be the greater soldier.

Sec. Serv. Faith, look you, one cannot tell how to say that : for the defence of a town, our general is excellent.

First Serv. Ay, and for an assault too.

Re-enter third Servingman.

Third Serv. O slaves, I can tell you news,—news, you rascals!

First and Sec. Serv. What, what, what? let's partake.

Third Serv. I would not be a Roman, of all nations; I had as lieve be a condemned man.

First and Sec. Serv. Wherefore? wherefore?

Third Serv. Why, here's he that was wont to thwack our general, Caius Marcius.

First Serv. Why do you say 'thwack our general'?

Third Serv. I do not say 'thwack our general'; but he was always good enough for him.

Sec. Serv. Come, we are fellows and friends : he was ever too hard for him; I have heard him say so himself.

First Serv. He was too hard for him directly, to say the troth on't : before Corioli he scotched him and notched him like a carbonado.

Sec. Serv. An he had been cannibally given, he might have broiled and eaten him too.

First Serv. But, more of thy news?

Third Serv. Why, he is so made on here within, as if he

were son and heir to Mars; set at upper end o' the table;
no question asked him by any of the senators, but they stand
bald before him: our general himself makes a mistress of
him; sanctifies himself with's hand and turns up the white o'
the eye to his discourse. But the bottom of the news is, our
general is cut i' the middle and but one half of what he was
yesterday; for the other has half, by the entreaty and grant
of the whole table. He'll go, he says, and sowl the porter of
Rome gates by the ears: he will mow all down before him,
and leave his passage polled.

Sec. Serv. And he's as like to do't as any man I can imagine.

Third Serv. Do't! he will do't; for, look you, sir, he has
as many friends as enemies; which friends, sir, as it were,
durst not, look you, sir, show themselves, as we term it, his
friends whilst he's in directitude.

First Serv. Directitude! what's that?

Third Serv. But when they shall see, sir, his crest up again,
and the man in blood, they will out of their burrows, like
conies after rain, and revel all with him.

First Serv. But when goes this forward?

Third Serv. To-morrow; to-day; presently; you shall
have the drum struck up this afternoon: 'tis, as it were, a
parcel of their feast, and to be executed ere they wipe their lips.

Sec. Serv. Why, then we shall have a stirring world again.
This peace is nothing, but to rust iron, increase tailors, and
breed ballad-makers.

First Serv. Let me have war, say I; it exceeds peace as
far as day does night; it's spritely, waking, audible, and full
of vent. Peace is a very apoplexy, lethargy; mulled, deaf,
sleepy, insensible; a getter of more bastard children than
war's a destroyer of men.

Sec. Serv. 'Tis so: and as war, in some sort, may be said
to be a ravisher, so it cannot be denied but peace is a great
maker of cuckolds.

First Serv. Ay, and it makes men hate one another.

Third Serv. Reason; because they then less need one

another. The wars for my money. I hope to see Romans as
cheap as Volscians. They are rising, they are rising.

 All. In, in, in, in !   Act IV, Scene v, ll. 40-251

 Menenius.   Pray now, your news ?
You have made fair work, I fear me.—Pray, your news ?—
If Marcius should be join'd with Volscians,—

 Cominius.   If !
He is their god : he leads them like a thing
Made by some other deity than nature,
That shapes man better ; and they follow him,
Against us brats, with no less confidence
Than boys pursuing summer butterflies,
Or butchers killing flies.

 Men.   You have made good work,
You and your apron-men ; you that stood so much
Upon the voice of occupation and
The breath of garlic-eaters !

 Com.   He will shake
Your Rome about your ears.

 Men.   As Hercules
Did shake down mellow fruit. You have made fair work ! . . .

 Citizens. Faith, we hear fearful news.

 First Cit.   For mine own part,
When I said, banish him, I said, 'twas pity.

 Sec. Cit. And so did I.

 Third Cit. And so did I ; and, to say the truth, so did
very many of us : that we did, we did for the best ; and
though we willingly consented to his banishment, yet it was
against our will.   Act IV, Scene vi, ll. 87-100, 139-146

           O, a kiss
Long as my exile, sweet as my revenge !

             Act V, Scene iii, ll. 44-45

 Coriolanus.   What is this ?
Your knees to me ? to your corrected son ?

Then let the pebbles on the hungry beach
Fillip the stars ; then let the mutinous winds
Strike the proud cedars 'gainst the fiery sun ;
Murdering impossibility, to make
What cannot be, slight work.

    Volumnia.   Thou art my warrior ;
I holp to frame thee.   Do you know this lady ?

    Cor. The noble sister of Publicola,
The moon of Rome, chaste as the icicle
That's curdied by the frost from purest snow
And hangs on Dian's temple : dear Valeria !

    Vol. This is a poor epitome of yours,
Which by the interpretation of full time
May show like all yourself.

    Cor.   The god of soldiers,
With the consent of supreme Jove, inform
Thy thoughts with nobleness ; that thou mayst prove
To shame unvulnerable, and stick i' the wars
Like a great sea-mark, standing every flaw,
And saving those that eye thee !
                                   Act V, Scene iii, ll. 56-75

Ne'er through an arch so hurried the blown tide,
As the recomforted through the gates.   Why, hark you !

        [Trumpets ; hautboys ; drums beat ; all together.
The trumpets, sackbuts, psalteries and fifes,
Tabors and cymbals and the shouting Romans,
Make the sun dance.
                                   Act V, Scene iv, ll. 50-54

          Antium.   A public place.

    To TULLUS AUFIDIUS, *with* Attendants, *and three or
four* Conspirators,

    Enter CORIOLANUS, *marching with drum and colours ;
Commoners being with him.*

    Cor.   We have made peace
With no less honour to the Antiates
Than shame to the Romans : and we here deliver,

Subscribed by the consuls and patricians,
Together with the seal o' the senate, what
We have compounded on.

  Auf.   Read it not, noble lords;
But tell the traitor, in the high'st degree
He hath abused your powers.

  Cor. Traitor! how now!

  Auf.   Ay, traitor, Marcius!

  Cor.   Marcius!

  Auf. Ay, Marcius, Caius Marcius: dost thou think
I'll grace thee with that robbery, thy stol'n name
Coriolanus in Corioli?
You lords and heads o' the state, perfidiously
He has betray'd your business, and given up,
For certain drops of salt, your city Rome,
I say 'your city,' to his wife and mother;
Breaking his oath and resolution like
A twist of rotten silk, never admitting
Counsel o' the war, but at his nurse's tears
He whined and roar'd away your victory,
That pages blush'd at him and men of heart
Look'd wondering each at other.

  Cor.   Hear'st thou, Mars?

  Auf. Name not the god, thou boy of tears!

  Cor.   Ha!

  Auf. No more.

  Cor. Measureless liar, thou hast made my heart
Too great for what contains it. Boy! O slave!
Pardon me, lords, 'tis the first time that ever
I was forced to scold. Your judgements, my grave
    lords,
Must give this cur the lie: and his own notion—
Who wears my stripes impress'd upon him; that
Must bear my beating to his grave—shall join
To thrust the lie unto him.

  First Lord. Peace, both, and hear me speak.

Cor. Cut me to pieces, Volsces ; men and lads,
Stain all your edges on me. Boy ! false hound !
If you have writ your annals true, 'tis there,
That, like an eagle in a dove-cote, I
Flutter'd your Volscians in Corioli :
Alóne I did it. Boy !

Act V, Scene vi, ll. 79-117

Timon of Athens

I do fear,
When every feather sticks in his own wing,
Lord Timon will be left a naked gull,
Which flashes now a phoenix.

Act II, Scene i, ll. 29-32

When every room
Hath blazed with lights and bray'd with minstrelsy.

Act II, Scene ii, ll. 169-170

Piety, and fear,
Religion to the gods, peace, justice, truth,
Domestic awe, night-rest, and neighbourhood,

Act IV, Scene i, ll. 15-17

Leak'd is our bark,
And we, poor mates, stand on the dying deck,
Hearing the surges threat : we must all part
Into this sea of air.

Act IV, Scene ii, ll. 19-22

Timon. Put up thy gold : go on,—here's gold,—go on ;
Be as a planetary plague, when Jove
Will o'er some high-viced city hang his poison
In the sick air : let not thy sword skip one :
Pity not honour'd age for his white beard ;
He is an usurer : strike me the counterfeit matron ;

597

It is her habit only that is honest,
Herself's a bawd : let not the virgin's cheek
Make soft thy trenchant sword ; for those milk-paps,
That through the window-bars bore at men's eyes,
Are not within the leaf of pity writ,
But set them down horrible traitors : spare not the babe,
Whose dimpled smiles from fools exhaust their mercy ;
Think it a bastard, whom the oracle
Hath doubtfully pronounced thy throat shall cut,
And mince it sans remorse : swear against objects ;
Put armour on thine ears and on thine eyes ;
Whose proof, nor yells of mothers, maids, nor babes,
Nor sight of priests in holy vestments bleeding,
Shall pierce a jot. There's gold to pay thy soldiers :
Make large confusion ; and, thy fury spent,
Confounded be thyself ! Speak not, be gone.

ACT IV, Scene iii, ll. 107-128

Timon.   Common mother, thou,
                              [*Digging.*

Whose womb unmeasurable, and infinite breast,
Teems, and feeds all ; whose self-same mettle,
Whereof thy proud child, arrogant man, is puff'd,
Engenders the black toad and adder blue,
The gilded newt and eyeless venom'd worm,
With all the abhorred births below crisp heaven
Whereon Hyperion's quickening fire doth shine ;
Yield him, who all thy human sons doth hate,
From forth thy plenteous bosom, one poor root !
Ensear thy fertile and conceptious womb,
Let it no more bring out ingrateful man !
Go great with tigers, dragons, wolves, and bears ;
Teem with new monsters, whom thy upward face
Hath to the marbled mansion all above
Never presented !—O, a root,—dear thanks !—
Dry up thy marrows, vines, and plough-torn leas ;

Whereof ingrateful man, with liquorish draughts
And morsels unctuous, greases his pure mind,
That from it all consideration slips !

ACT IV, Scene iii, ll. 177-196

Apemantus. Thou hast cast away thyself, being like thy-
self ;
A madman so long, now a fool. What, think'st
That the bleak air, thy boisterous chamberlain,
Will put thy shirt on warm ? will these moss'd trees,
That have outlived the eagle, page thy heels,
And skip where thou point'st out ? will the cold brook,
Candied with ice, caudle thy morning taste,
To cure thy o'er-night's surfeit ?

ACT IV, Scene iii, ll. 220-227

Timon.   But myself,
Who had the world as my confectionary,
The mouths, the tongues, the eyes and hearts of men
At duty, more than I could frame employment,
That numberless upon me stuck as leaves
Do on the oak, have with one winter's brush
Fell from their boughs and left me open, bare
For every storm that blows.

ACT IV, Scene iii, ll. 259-266

Timon. Then, Timon, presently prepare thy grave ;
Lie where the light foam of the sea may beat
Thy grave-stone daily.

ACT IV, Scene iii, ll. 378-380

Timon. [*To the gold*] O thou sweet king-killer, and dear
divorce
'Twixt natural son and sire ! thou bright defiler
Of Hymen's purest bed ! thou valiant Mars !
Thou ever young, fresh, loved and delicate wooer,
Whose blush doth thaw the consecrated snow
That lies on Dian's lap !

ACT IV, Scene iii, ll. 382-387

Timon. I'll example you with thievery :
The sun's a thief, and with his great attraction
Robs the vast sea ; the moon's an arrant thief,
And her pale fire she snatches from the sun :
The sea's a thief, whose liquid surge resolves
The moon into salt tears.

ACT IV, Scene iii, ll. 438-443

Timon. Why, I was writing of my epitaph ;
It will be seen to-morrow : my long sickness
Of health and living now begins to mend,
And nothing brings me all things. . . .
Come not to me again : but say to Athens,
Timon hath made his everlasting mansion
Upon the beached verge of the salt flood ;
Who once a day with his embossed froth
The turbulent surge shall cover.

ACT V, Scene i, ll. 188-191, 217-221

Before the walls of Athens.

Trumpets sound. Enter ALCIBIADES *with his powers.*

Alcib. Sound to this coward and lascivious town
Our terrible approach.   *[A parley sounded.*

ACT V, Scene iv, ll. 1-2

Soldier. My noble general, Timon is dead ;
Entomb'd upon the very hem o' the sea. . . .
Alcibiades. Though thou abhorr'dst in us our human
    griefs,
Scorn'dst our brain's flow and those our droplets which
From niggard nature fall, yet rich conceit
Taught thee to make vast Neptune weep for aye
On thy low grave, on faults forgiven.

ACT V, Scene iv, ll. 65-66, 75-79

SUNSET

PERICLES

CYMBELINE

THE WINTER'S TALE

THE TWO NOBLE KINSMEN

HENRY VIII

THE TEMPEST

Pericles

Enter PERICLES, *on shipboard.*

Per. Thou god of this great vast, rebuke these surges,
Which wash both heaven and hell ; and thou, that hast
Upon the winds command, bind them in brass,
Having call'd them from the deep ! O, still
Thy deafening, dreadful thunders ; gently quench
Thy nimble, sulphurous flashes ! O, how, Lychorida,
How does my queen ? Thou stormest venomously ;
Wilt thou spit all thyself ? The seaman's whistle
Is as a whisper in the ears of death,
Unheard.   ACT III, Scene i, ll. 1-10

Pericles. A terrible childbed hast thou had, my dear ;
No light, no fire : the unfriendly elements
Forgot thee utterly ; nor have I time
To give thee hallow'd to thy grave, but straight
Must cast thee, scarcely coffin'd, in the ooze ;
Where, for a monument upon thy bones,
And e'er-remaining lamps, the belching whale
And humming water must o'erwhelm thy corpse,
Lying with simple shells.   ACT III, Scene i, ll. 57-65

Cerimon. Gentlemen,
This queen will live : nature awakes ; a warmth
Breathes out of her : she hath not been entranced
Above five hours : see how she gins to blow
Into life's flower again !
    First Gent.   The heavens,
Through you, increase our wonder and set up
Your fame for ever.
        Cer.   She is alive ; behold,

603

Her eyelids, cases to those heavenly jewels
Which Pericles hath lost,
Begin to part their fringes of bright gold ;
The diamonds of a most praised water
Do appear, to make the world twice rich. Live,
And make us weep to hear your fate, fair creature,
Rare as you seem to be.   [*She moves.*

    Thaisa.   O dear Diana,
Where am I ? Where's my lord ? What world is this ?
                        ACT III, Scene ii, ll. 92-106

       Enter MARINA, *with a basket of flowers.*

    Mar. No, I will rob Tellus of her weed,
To strew thy green with flowers : the yellows, blues,
The purple violets, and marigolds,
Shall as a carpet hang upon thy grave,
While summer-days do last. Ay me ! poor maid,
Born in a tempest, when my mother died,
This world to me is like a lasting storm,
Whirring me from my friends.   ACT IV, Scene i, ll. 14-21

                    Thou dost look
Like Patience gazing on kings' graves, and smiling
Extremity out of act.   ACT V, Scene i, ll. 138-140

Cymbeline

A room in Cymbeline's palace.

Enter IMOGEN *and* PISANIO.

    Imo. I would thou grew'st unto the shores o' the haven,
And question'dst every sail : if he should write,
And I not have it, 'twere a paper lost,
As offer'd mercy is. What was the last

That he spake to thee?

    Pis.   It was his queen, his queen!

    Imo. Then waved his handkerchief?

    Pis.   And kiss'd it, madam.

    Imo. Senseless linen! happier therein than I!

And that was all?

    Pis.   No, madam; for so long

As he could make me with this eye or ear

Distinguish him from others, he did keep

The deck, with glove, or hat, or handkerchief,

Still waving, as the fits and stirs of's mind

Could best express how slow his soul sail'd on,

How swift his ship.

    Imo.   Thou shouldst have made him

As little as a crow, or less, ere left

To after-eye him.

    Pis.   Madam, so I did.

    Imo. I would have broke mine eye-strings; crack'd them,

   but

To look upon him, till the diminution

Of space had pointed him sharp as my needle,

Nay, follow'd him, till he had melted from

The smallness of a gnat to air, and then

Have turn'd mine eye and wept. But, good Pisanio,

When shall we hear from him?

    Pis.   Be assured, madam,

With his next vantage.

    Imo. I did not take my leave of him, but had

Most pretty things to say: ere I could tell him

How I would think on him at certain hours

Such thoughts and such, or I could make him swear

The shes of Italy should not betray

Mine interest and his honour, or have charged him

At the sixth hour of morn, at noon, at midnight

To encounter me with orisons, for then

I am in heaven for him; or ere I could

Give him that parting kiss which I had set
Betwixt two charming words, comes in my father
And like the tyrannous breathing of the north
Shakes all our buds from growing.
ACT I, Scene iii, ll. 1-37

While yet the dew's on ground, gather those flowers.
ACT I, Scene v, l. 1

She is alone the Arabian bird.
ACT I, Scene vi, l. 17

What, are men mad? Hath nature given them eyes
To see this vaulted arch, and the rich crop
Of sea and land, which can distinguish 'twixt
The fiery orbs above and the twinn'd stones
Upon the number'd beach? and can we not
Partition make with spectacles so precious
'Twixt fair and foul?
ACT I, Scene vi, ll. 32-38

> *Imogen's bedchamber in Cymbeline's palace: a trunk
> in one corner of it.*
>
> IMOGEN *in bed, reading; a* Lady *attending.*

Imo. Who's there? my woman Helen?
Lady. Please you, madam.
Imo. What hour is it?
Lady. Almost midnight, madam.
Imo. I have read three hours then: mine eyes are weak:
Fold down the leaf where I have left: to bed:
Take not away the taper, leave it burning;
And if thou canst awake by four o' the clock,
I prithee, call me. Sleep hath seized me wholly. [*Exit Lady.*
To your protection I commend me, gods.
From fairies and the tempters of the night
Guard me, beseech ye.
[Sleeps. Iachimo comes from the trunk.
Iach. The crickets sing, and man's o'er-labour'd sense

Repairs itself by rest. Our Tarquin thus
Did softly press the rushes, ere he waken'd
The chastity he wounded. Cytherea,
How bravely thou becomest thy bed, fresh lily,
And whiter than the sheets ! That I might touch !
But kiss ; one kiss ! Rubies unparagon'd,
How dearly they do't ! 'Tis her breathing that
Perfumes the chamber thus : the flame o' the taper
Bows toward her, and would under-peep her lids,
To see the enclosed lights, now canopied
Under these windows, white and azure laced
With blue of heaven's own tinct. But my design,
To note the chamber : I will write all down :
Such and such pictures ; there the window ; such
The adornment of her bed ; the arras ; figures,
Why, such and such ; and the contents o' the story.
Ah, but some natural notes about her body,
Above ten thousand meaner moveables
Would testify, to enrich mine inventory.
O sleep, thou ape of death, lie dull upon her !
And be her sense but as a monument,
Thus in a chapel lying ! Come off, come off :
                              [*Taking off her bracelet.*
As slippery as the Gordian knot was hard !
'Tis mine ; and this will witness outwardly,
As strongly as the conscience does within,
To the madding of her lord. On her left breast
A mole cinque-spotted, like the crimson drops
I' the bottom of a cowslip : here's a voucher,
Stronger than ever law could make : this secret
Will force him think I have pick'd the lock and ta'en
The treasure of her honour. No more. To what end ?
Why should I write this down, that's riveted,
Screw'd to my memory ? She hath been reading late
The tale of Tereus ; here the leaf's turn'd down
Where Philomel gave up. I have enough :

To the trunk again, and shut the spring of it.
Swift, swift, you dragons of the night, that dawning
May bare the raven's eye ! I lodge in fear ;
Though this a heavenly angel, hell is here.   [*Clock strikes.*
One, two, three : time, time !

                    [*Goes into the trunk.   The scene closes.*
                    ACT II, Scene ii, ll. 1-51

    Hark, hark ! the lark at heaven's gate sings,
        And Phoebus 'gins arise,
    His steeds to water at those springs
        On chaliced flowers that lies ;
    And winking Mary-buds begin
        To ope their golden eyes :
    With every thing that pretty is,
        My lady sweet, arise :
            Arise, arise.
                            ACT II, Scene iii, ll. 22-30

The swiftest harts have posted you by land ;
And winds of all the corners kiss'd your sails,
To make your vessel nimble.
                            ACT II, Scene iv, ll. 27-29

    Iachimo.   First, her bedchamber,—
Where, I confess, I slept not, but profess
Had that was well worth watching—it was hang'd
With tapestry of silk and silver ; the story
Proud Cleopatra, when she met her Roman,
And Cydnus swell'd above the banks, or for
The press of boats or pride : a piece of work
So bravely done, so rich, that it did strive
In workmanship and value ; which I wonder'd
Could be so rarely and exactly wrought,
Since the true life on't was—
    Posthumus.   This is true ;
And this you might have heard of here, by me,
Or by some other.

Iach.   More particulars
Must justify my knowledge.
    Post.   So they must,
  Or do your honour injury.
    Iach.   The chimney
Is south the chamber, and the chimney-piece
Chaste Dian bathing : never saw I figures
So likely to report themselves : the cutter
Was as another nature, dumb ; outwent her,
Motion and breath left out.
    Post.   This is a thing
  Which you might from relation likewise reap,
Being, as it is, much spoke of.
    Iach.   The roof o' the chamber
With golden cherubins is fretted : her andirons—
I had forgot them—were two winking Cupids
Of silver, each on one foot standing, nicely
Depending on their brands.   ACT II, Scene iv, ll. 66-91

                    I thought her
As chaste as unsunned snow.
                        .   ACT II, Scene v, ll. 12-13

                Remember, sir, my liege,
  The kings your ancestors, together with
  The natural bravery of your isle, which stands
  As Neptune's park, ribbed and paled in
  With rocks unscaleable and roaring waters,
  With sands that will not bear your enemies' boats,
  But suck them up to the topmast. A kind of conquest
  Caesar made here ; but made not here his brag
  Of ' Came ' and ' saw ' and ' overcame : ' with shame—
  The first that ever touch'd him—he was carried
  From off our coast, twice beaten ; and his shipping—
  Poor ignorant baubles !—on our terrible seas,
  Like egg-shells moved upon their surges, crack'd

                    609

As easily 'gainst our rocks : for joy whereof
The famed Cassibelan, who was once at point—
O giglot fortune !—to master Caesar's sword,
Made Lud's town with rejoicing fires bright
And Britons strut with courage.

Act III, Scene i, ll. 16-33

Wales : a mountainous country with a cave.

Enter, from the cave, Belarius ; Guiderius, *and*
Arviragus *following.*

Bel. A goodly day not to keep house, with such
Whose roof's as low as ours ! Stoop, boys ; this gate
Instructs you how to adore the heavens and bows you
To a morning's holy office : the gates of monarchs
Are arch'd so high that giants may jet through
And keep their impious turbans on, without
Good morrow to the sun. Hail, thou fair heaven !
We house i' the rock, yet use thee not so hardly
As prouder livers do.

 Gui.   Hail, heaven !

 Arv.   Hail, heaven !

 Bel. Now for our mountain sport : up to yond hill ;
Your legs are young ; I'll tread these flats. Consider,
When you above perceive me like a crow,
That it is place which lessens and sets off :
And you may then revolve what tales I have told you
Of courts, of princes, of the tricks in war :
This service is not service, so being done,
But being so allow'd : to apprehend thus,
Draws us a profit from all things we see ;
And often, to our comfort, shall we find
The sharded beetle in a safer hold
Than is the full-wing'd eagle. O, this life
Is nobler than attending for a check,
Richer than doing nothing for a bauble,
Prouder than rustling in unpaid-for silk :

610

Such gain the cap of him that makes 'em fine,
Yet keeps his book uncross'd : no life to ours.

Gui. Out of your proof you speak : we, poor unfledged,
Have never wing'd from view o' the nest, nor know not
What air's from home. Haply this life is best,
If quiet life be best ; sweeter to you
That have a sharper known ; well corresponding
With your stiff age : but unto us it is
A cell of ignorance ; travelling a-bed ;
A prison for a debtor, that not dares
To stride a limit.

Arv.　　　　　What should we speak of
When we are old as you ? when we shall hear
The rain and wind beat dark December, how,
In this our pinching cave, shall we discourse
The freezing hours away ? We have seen nothing ;
We are beastly, subtle as the fox for prey,
Like warlike as the wolf for what we eat ;
Our valour is to chase what flies ; our cage
We make a quire, as doth the prison'd bird,
And sing our bondage freely.

Bel.　　　　　　How you speak !
Did you but know the city's usuries
And felt them knowingly ; the art o' the court,
As hard to leave as keep ; whose top to climb
Is certain falling, or so slippery that
The fear's as bad as falling ; the toil o' the war,
A pain that only seems to seek out danger
I' the name of fame and honour ; which dies i' the search,
And hath as oft a slanderous epitaph
As record of fair act ; nay, many times,
Doth ill deserve by doing well ; what's worse,
Must court'sy at the censure :—O boys, this story
The world may read in me : my body's mark'd
With Roman swords, and my report was once
First with the best of note : Cymbeline loved me,

And when a soldier was the theme, my name
Was not far off : then was I as a tree
Whose boughs did bend with fruit : but in one night,
A storm or robbery, call it what you will,
Shook down my mellow hangings, nay, my leaves,
And left me bare to weather. . . .

                      [Exeunt Guiderius and Arviragus.

How hard it is to hide the sparks of nature !
These boys know little they are sons to the king ;
Nor Cymbeline dreams that they are alive.
They think they are mine ; and though train'd up thus meanly
I' the cave wherein they bow, their thoughts do hit
The roofs of palaces, and nature prompts them
In simple and low things to prince it much
Beyond the trick of others. This Polydore,
The heir of Cymbeline and Britain, who
The king his father call'd Guiderius,—Jove !
When on my three-foot stool I sit and tell
The warlike feats I have done, his spirits fly out
Into my story : say ' Thus mine enemy fell,
And thus I set my foot on's neck ; ' even then
The princely blood flows in his cheek, he sweats,
Strains his young nerves and puts himself in posture
That acts my words. The younger brother, Cadwal,
Once Arviragus, in as like a figure,
Strikes life into my speech and shows much more
His own conceiving.

                             Act III, Scene iii, ll. 1-64, 79-98

Pisanio. What shall I need to draw my sword ? the paper
Hath cut her throat already. No, 'tis slander,
Whose edge is sharper than the sword, whose tongue
Outvenoms all the worms of Nile, whose breath
Rides on the posting winds and doth belie
All corners of the world : kings, queens and states,
Maids, matrons, nay, the secrets of the grave
This viperous slander enters. What cheer, madam ?

Imogen. False to his bed ! What is it to be false ?
To lie in watch there and to think on him ?
To weep 'twixt clock and clock ? if sleep charge nature,
To break it with a fearful dream of him
And cry myself awake ? that's false to's bed, is it ? . . .
                              Look !
I draw the sword myself : take it, and hit
The innocent mansion of my love, my heart :
Fear not ; 'tis empty of all things but grief :
Thy master is not there, who was indeed
The riches of it : do his bidding ; strike.

                              ACT III, Scene iv, ll. 34-46, 68-73

Hath Britain all the sun that shines ? Day, night,
Are they not but in Britain ? I' the world's volume
Our Britain seems as of it, but not in't ;
In a great pool a swan's nest.

                              ACT III, Scene iv, ll. 139-142

Belarius.   O thou goddess,
Thou divine Nature, how thyself thou blazon'st
In these two princely boys ! They are as gentle
As zephyrs blowing below the violet,
Not wagging his sweet head ; and yet as rough,
Their royal blood enchafed, as the rudest wind,
That by the top doth take the mountain pine,
And make him stoop to the vale. 'Tis wonder
That an invisible instinct should frame them
To royalty unlearn'd, honour untaught,
Civility not seen from other, valour
That wildly grows in them.

                              ACT IV, Scene ii, ll. 169-180

Enter ARVIRAGUS, *with* IMOGEN, *as dead, bearing her
in his arms.*

Arv.   The bird is dead
That we have made so much on. I had rather

Have skipp'd from sixteen years of age to sixty,
To have turn'd my leaping-time into a crutch,
Than have seen this.

   Guiderius.   O sweetest, fairest lily !
My brother wears thee not the one half so well
As when thou grew'st thyself. . . .

   Arv.   With fairest flowers
Whilst summer lasts and I live here, Fidele,
I'll sweeten thy sad grave : thou shalt not lack
The flower that's like thy face, pale primrose, nor
The azured harebell, like thy veins, no, nor
The leaf of eglantine, whom not to slander,
Out-sweeten'd not thy breath : the ruddock would,
With charitable bill,—O bill, sore-shaming
Those rich-left heirs that let their fathers lie
Without a monument !—bring thee all this ;
Yea, and furr'd moss besides, when flowers are none,
To winter-ground thy corse.

   Gui.   Prithee, have done ;
And do not play in wench-like words with that
Which is so serious. Let us bury him,
And not protract with admiration what
Is now due debt. To the grave !

   Arv.   Say, where shall's lay him ?
   Gui. By good Euriphile, our mother.
   Arv.   Be't so :
And let us, Polydore, though now our voices
Have got the mannish crack, sing him to the ground,
As once our mother. . . .

   Gui. Cadwal,
I cannot sing : I'll weep, and word it with thee ;
For notes of sorrow out of tune are worse
Than priests and fanes that lie.

   Arv.   We'll speak it then. . . .
   Gui.   Fear no more the heat o' the sun,
          Nor the furious winter's rages ;

   Thou thy worldly task hast done,
    Home art gone, and ta'en thy wages:
   Golden lads and girls all must,
    As chimney-sweepers, come to dust.

Arv. Fear no more the frown o' the great;
    Thou art past the tyrant's stroke;
   Care no more to clothe and eat;
    To thee the reed is as the oak:
   The sceptre, learning, physic, must
   All follow this, and come to dust.

Gui. Fear no more the lightning-flash,
Arv.   Nor the all-dreaded thunder-stone;
Gui. Fear not slander, censure rash;
Arv.   Thou hast finish'd joy and moan:
Both. All lovers young, all lovers must
   Consign to thee, and come to dust.

Gui. No exorciser harm thee!
Arv. Nor no witchcraft charm thee!
Gui. Ghost unlaid forbear thee!
Arv. Nothing ill come near thee!
Both. Quiet consummation have;
   And renowned be thy grave!

  Re-enter BELARIUS, *with the body of* CLOTEN.

Gui. We have done our obsequies: come, lay him down.
Bel. Here's a few flowers; but 'bout midnight, more:
The herbs that have on them cold dew o' the night
Are strewings fitt'st for graves. Upon their faces.
You were as flowers, now wither'd: even so
These herblets shall, which we upon you strew.
Come on, away: apart upon our knees.
The ground that gave them first has them again:
Their pleasures here are past, so is their pain.
     [*Exeunt Belarius, Guiderius, and Arviragus*

Imo. [*Awakening*] Yes, sir, to Milford-Haven; which is
 the way ?—
I thank you.—By yond bush ?—Pray, how far thither ?
'Ods pittikins ! can it be six mile yet ?—
I have gone all night. 'Faith, I'll lie down and sleep.
But, soft ! no bedfellow !—O gods and goddesses !

         [*Seeing the body of Cloten.*

These flowers are like the pleasures of the world ;
This bloody man, the care on't. I hope I dream ;
For so I thought I was a cave-keeper,
And cook to honest creatures : but 'tis not so ;
'Twas but a bolt of nothing, shot at nothing,
Which the brain makes of fumes : our very eyes
Are sometimes like our judgements, blind. Good faith,
I tremble still with fear : but if there be
Yet left in heaven as small a drop of pity
As a wren's eye, fear'd gods, a part of it !
The dream's here still : even when I wake, it is
Without me, as within me ; not imagined, felt.

    Act IV, Scene ii, ll. 197-203, 218-237, 239-242, 258-307

 Imogen. I'll follow, sir. But first, an't please the
  gods,
I'll hide my master from the flies, as deep
As these poor pickaxes can dig ; and when
With wild wood-leaves and weeds I ha' strew'd his grave,
And on it said a century of prayers,
Such as I can, twice o'er, I'll weep and sigh ;
And leaving so his service, follow you,
So please you entertain me.
 Lucius.   Ay, good youth ;
And rather father thee than master thee.
My friends,
The boy hath taught us manly duties : let us
Find out the prettiest daisied plot we can,
And make him with our pikes and partisans

A grave : come, arm him. Boy, he is preferr'd
By thee to us, and he shall be interr'd
As soldiers can.
                              ACT IV, Scene ii, ll. 387-402

I, in mine own woe charm'd,
Could not find death where I did hear him groan,
Nor feel him where he struck : being an ugly monster,
'Tis strange he hides him in fresh cups, soft beds,
Sweet words ; or hath more ministers than we
That draw his knives i' the war.
                              ACT V, Scene iii, ll. 68-73

Be not with mortal accidents opprest.
                              ACT V, Scene iv, l. 99

    Imogen. Why did you throw your wedded lady from you ?
Think that you are upon a rock ; and now
Throw me again.   [*Embracing him.*
    Posthumus.   Hang there like fruit, my soul,
Till the tree die !
                              ACT V, Scene v, ll. 261-264

The Winter's Tale

Nine changes of the watery star. . . .
                              ACT I, Scene ii, l. 1

    Hermione gives her hand to Polixenes.
    Leontes.   [*Aside*] Too hot, too hot !
To mingle friendship far is mingling bloods.
I have tremor cordis on me : my heart dances ;
But not for joy ; not joy.
                              ACT I, Scene ii, ll. 108-111

    Hermione. What wisdom stirs amongst you ? Come, sir,
      now
I am for you again : pray you, sit by us,
And tell's a tale.

617

Mamillius.   Merry or sad shall't be?

Her. As merry as you will.

Mam. A sad tale's best for winter: I have one
Of sprites and goblins.

Her.   Let's have that, good sir.
Come on, sit down: come on, and do your best
To frighten me with your sprites; you're powerful at it.

Mam. There was a man—

Her.   Nay, come, sit down; then on.

Mam. Dwelt by a churchyard: I will tell it softly;
Yond crickets shall not hear it.

Her.   Come on, then,
And give't me in mine ear.   ACT II, Scene i, ll. 21-32

A sea-port in Sicilia.

Enter CLEOMENES *and* DION.

Cleo. The climate's delicate, the air most sweet,
Fertile the isle, the temple much surpassing
The common praise it bears. . . .

Dion.   O, the sacrifice!
How ceremonious, solemn and unearthly
It was i' the offering!   ACT III, Scene i, ll. 1-3, 6-8

A thousand knees
Ten thousand years together, naked, fasting,
Upon a barren mountain, and still winter
In storm perpetual, could not move the gods
To look that way thou wert.

ACT III, Scene ii, ll. 211-215

Clown. I have seen two such sights, by sea and by land!
but I am not to say it is a sea, for it is now the sky: betwixt
the firmament and it you cannot thrust a bodkin's point.

Shepherd. Why, boy, how is it?

Clo. I would you did but see how it chafes, how it rages,
how it takes up the shore! but that's not to the point. O, the

most piteous cry of the poor souls ! sometimes to see 'em, and not to see 'em ; now the ship boring the moon with her main-mast, and anon swallowed with yest and froth, as you'ld thrust a cork into a hogshead. And then for the land-service, to see how the bear tore out his shoulder-bone ; how he cried to me for help and said his name was Antigonus, a nobleman. But to make an end of the ship, to see how the sea flap-dragoned it : but, first, how the poor souls roared, and the sea mocked them ; and how the poor gentleman roared and the bear mocked him, both roaring louder than the sea or weather.

Shep. Name of mercy, when was this, boy ?

Clo. Now, now : I have not winked since I saw these sights : the men are not yet cold under water, nor the bear half dined on the gentleman : he's at it now.

Act III, Scene iii, ll. 84-109

A road near the Shepherd's *cottage.*

Enter Autolycus, *singing.*

When daffodils begin to peer,
  With heigh ! the doxy over the dale,
Why, then comes in the sweet o' the year ;
  For the red blood reigns in the winter's pale.

The white sheet bleaching on the hedge,
  With heigh ! the sweet birds, O, how they sing !
Doth set my pugging tooth on edge ;
  For a quart of ale is a dish for a king.

The lark, that tirra-lyra chants,
  With heigh ! with heigh ! the thrush and the jay,
Are summer songs for me and my aunts,
  While we lie tumbling in the hay.

I have served Prince Florizel and in my time wore three pile ; but now I am out of service :

But shall I go mourn for that, my dear ?
  The pale moon shines by night :

And when I wander here and there,
    I then do most go right.

If tinkers may have leave to live,
    And bear the sow-skin budget,
Then my account I well may give,
    And in the stocks avouch it.

My traffic is sheets ; when the kite builds, look to lesser linen.
My father named me Autolycus ; who being, as I am, littered
under Mercury, was likewise a snapper-up of unconsidered
trifles. With die and drab I purchased this caparison, and
my revenue is the silly cheat. Gallows and knock are too
powerful on the highway : beating and hanging are terrors to
me : for the life to come, I sleep out the thought of it. A
prize ! a prize !

Enter Clown.

Clo. Let me see : every 'leven wether tods ; every tod
yields pound and odd shilling ; fifteen hundred shorn, what
comes the wool to ?

Aut. [*Aside*] If the springe hold, the cock's mine.

Clo. I cannot do't without counters. Let me see ; what
am I to buy for our sheep-shearing feast ? Three pound of
sugar, five pound of currants, rice,—what will this sister of
mine do with rice ? But my father hath made her mistress of
the feast, and she lays it on. She hath made me four and
twenty nosegays for the shearers, three-man-song-men all,
and very good ones ; but they are most of them means and
bases ; but one puritan amongst them, and he sings psalms to
hornpipes. I must have saffron to colour the warden pies ;
mace ; dates ?—none, that's out of my note ; nutmegs, seven ;
a race or two of ginger, but that I may beg ; four pound of
prunes, and as many of raisins o' the sun.

Aut. O that ever I was born !   [*Grovelling on the ground.*

Clo. I' the name of me—

Aut. O, help me, help me ! pluck but off these rags ; and
then, death, death !

620

Clo. Alack, poor soul! thou hast need of more rags to lay on thee, rather than have these off.

Aut. O sir, the loathsomeness of them offends me more than the stripes I have received, which are mighty ones and millions.

Clo. Alas, poor man! a million of beating may come to a great matter.

Aut. I am robbed, sir, and beaten; my money and apparel ta'en from me, and these detestable things put upon me.

Clo. What, by a horseman, or a footman?

Aut. A footman, sweet sir, a footman.

Clo. Indeed, he should be a footman by the garments he has left with thee: if this be a horseman's coat, it hath seen very hot service. Lend me thy hand, I'll help thee: come, lend me thy hand.

Aut. O, good sir, tenderly, O!

Clo. Alas, poor soul!

Aut. O, good sir, softly, good sir! I fear, sir, my shoulder-blade is out.

Clo. How now! canst stand?

Aut. [*Picking his pocket*] Softly, dear sir; good sir, softly. You ha' done me a charitable office.

Clo. Dost lack any money? I have a little money for thee.

Aut. No, good sweet sir; no, I beseech you, sir: I have a kinsman not past three quarters of a mile hence, unto whom I was going; I shall there have money, or any thing I want; offer me no money, I pray you; that kills my heart.

Clo. What manner of fellow was he that robbed you?

Aut. A fellow, sir, that I have known to go about with troll-my-dames: I knew him once a servant of the prince: I cannot tell, good sir, for which of his virtues it was, but he was certainly whipped out of the court.

Clo. His vices, you would say; there's no virtue whipped out of the court: they cherish it to make it stay there; and yet it will no more but abide.

Aut. Vices, I would say, sir. I know this man well: he

hath been since an ape-bearer; then a process-server, a bailiff; then he compassed a motion of the Prodigal Son, and married a tinker's wife within a mile where my land and living lies; and, having flown over many knavish professions, he settled only in rogue: some call him Autolycus.

Clo. Out upon him! prig, for my life, prig: he haunts wakes, fairs and bear-baitings.

Aut. Very true, sir; he, sir, he; that's the rogue that put me into this apparel.

Clo. Not a more cowardly rogue in all Bohemia: if you had but looked big and spit at him, he'ld have run.

Aut. I must confess to you, sir, I am no fighter: I am false of heart that way; and that he knew, I warrant him.

Clo. How do you now?

Aut. Sweet sir, much better than I was; I can stand and walk: I will even take my leave of you, and pace softly towards my kinsman's.

Clo. Shall I bring thee on the way?

Aut. No, good-faced sir; no, sweet sir.

Clo. Then fare thee well: I must go buy spices for our sheep-shearing.

Aut. Prosper you, sweet sir! [*Exit Clown.*] Your purse is not hot enough to purchase your spice. I'll be with you at your sheep-shearing too: if I make not this cheat bring out another and the shearers prove sheep, let me be unrolled and my name put in the book of virtue!

[*Sings*]   Jog on, jog on, the foot-path way,
          And merrily hent the stile-a:
          A merry heart goes all the day,
          Your sad tires in a mile-a.   [*Exit.*

ACT IV, Scene iii, ll. 1-135

The Shepherd's *cottage.*

Enter FLORIZEL *and* PERDITA.

Flo. These your unusual weeds to each part of you
Do give a life: no shepherdess, but Flora

622

Peering in April's front. This your sheep-shearing
Is as a meeting of the petty gods,
And you the queen on't.

 Per.   Sir, my gracious lord,
To chide at your extremes it not becomes me :
O, pardon, that I name them ! Your high self,
The gracious mark o' the land, you have obscured
With a swain's wearing, and me, poor lowly maid,
Most goddess-like prank'd up : but that our feasts
In every mess have folly and the feeders
Digest it with a custom, I should blush
To see you so attired, sworn, I think,
To show myself a glass.

 Flo.   I bless the time
When my good falcon made her flight across
Thy father's ground.

 Per.   Now Jove afford you cause !
To me the difference forges dread ; your greatness
Hath not been used to fear. Even now I tremble
To think your father, by some accident,
Should pass this way as you did : O, the Fates !
How would he look, to see his work so noble
Vilely bound up ? What would he say ? Or how
Should I, in these my borrow'd flaunts, behold
The sternness of his presence ?

 Flo.   Apprehend
Nothing but jollity. The gods themselves,
Humbling their deities to love, have taken
The shapes of beasts upon them : Jupiter
Became a bull, and bellow'd ; the green Neptune
A ram, and bleated ; and the fire-robed god,
Golden Apollo, a poor humble swain,
As I seem now. Their transformations
Were never for a piece of beauty rarer,
Nor in a way so chaste, since my desires
Run not before mine honour, nor my lusts

Burn hotter than my faith.

    Per.   O, but, sir,
Your resolution cannot hold, when 'tis
Opposed, as it must be, by the power of the king :
One of these two must be necessities,
Which then will speak, that you must change this purpose,
Or I my life.

    Flo.   Thou dearest Perdita,
With these forced thoughts, I prithee, darken not
The mirth o' the feast. Or I'll be thine, my fair,
Or not my father's. For I cannot be
Mine own, nor any thing to any, if
I be not thine. To this I am most constant,
Though destiny say no. Be merry, gentle ;
Strangle such thoughts as these with any thing
That you behold the while. Your guests are coming :
Lift up your countenance, as it were the day
Of celebration of that nuptial which
We two have sworn shall come.

    Per.   O lady Fortune,
Stand you auspicious !

    Flo.   See, your guests approach :
Address yourself to entertain them sprightly,
And let's be red with mirth.

    Enter Shepherd, Clown, MOPSA, DORCAS, *and others,*
        with POLIXENES *and* CAMILLO *disguised.*

    Shep. Fie, daughter ! when my old wife lived, upon
This day she was both pantler, butler, cook,
Both dame and servant ; welcomed all, served all ;
Would sing her song and dance her turn ; now here,
At upper end o' the table, now i' the middle ;
On his shoulder, and his ; her face o' fire
With labour and the thing she took to quench it,
She would to each one sip. You are retired,
As if you were a feasted one and not

The hostess of the meeting : pray you, bid
These unknown friends to's welcome ; for it is
A way to make us better friends, more known.
Come, quench your blushes and present yourself
That which you are, mistress o' the feast : come on,
And bid us welcome to your sheep-shearing,
As your good flock shall prosper.

   Per.   [*To Pol.*] Sir, welcome :
It is my father's will I should take on me
The hostess-ship o' the day. [*To Cam.*] You're welcome, sir.
Give me those flowers there, Dorcas. Reverend sirs,
For you there's rosemary and rue ; these keep
Seeming and savour all the winter long :
Grace and remembrance be to you both,
And welcome to our shearing !

   Pol.   Shepherdess,—
A fair one are you—well you fit our ages
With flowers of winter.

   Per.   Sir, the year growing ancient,
Not yet on summer's death, nor on the birth
Of trembling winter, the fairest flowers o' the season
Are our carnations and streak'd gillyvors,
Which some call nature's bastards : of that kind
Our rustic garden's barren ; and I care not
To get slips of them.

   Pol.   Wherefore, gentle maiden,
Do you neglect them ?

   Per.   For I have heard it said
There is an art which in their piedness shares
With great creating nature.

   Pol.   Say there be ;
Yet nature is made better by no mean
But nature makes that mean : so, over that art
Which you say adds to nature, is an art
That nature makes. You see, sweet maid, we marry
A gentler scion to the wildest stock,

And make conceive a bark of baser kind
By bud of nobler race : this is an art
Which does mend nature, change it rather, but
The art itself is nature.

    Per   So it is.

    Pol. Then make your garden rich in gillyvors,
And do not call them bastards.

    Per.   I'll not put
The dibble in earth to set one slip of them ;
No more than were I painted I would wish
This youth should say 'twere well and only therefore
Desire to breed by me. Here's flowers for you ;
Hot lavender, mints, savory, marjoram ;
The marigold, that goes to bed wi' the sun
And with him rises weeping : these are flowers
Of middle summer, and I think they are given
To men of middle age. You're very welcome.

    Cam. I should leave grazing, were I of your flock,
And only live by gazing.

    Per.   Out, alas !
You'ld be so lean, that blasts of January
Would blow you through and through. Now, my fair'st
    friend,
I would I had some flowers o' the spring that might
Become your time of day ; and yours, and yours,
That wear upon your virgin branches yet
Your maidenheads growing : O Proserpina,
For the flowers now, that frighted thou let'st fall
From Dis's waggon ! daffodils,
That come before the swallow dares, and take
The winds of March with beauty ; violets dim,
But sweeter than the lids of Juno's eyes
Or Cytherea's breath ; pale primroses,
That die unmarried, ere they can behold
Bright Phoebus in his strength—a malady
Most incident to maids ; bold oxlips and

The crown imperial ; lilies of all kinds,
The flower-de-luce being one ! O, these I lack,
To make you garlands of, and my sweet friend,
To strew him o'er and o'er !

   Flo.   What, like a corse ?

   Per. No, like a bank for love to lie and play on ;
Not like a corse ; or if, not to be buried,
But quick and in mine arms. Come, take your flowers :
Methinks I play as I have seen them do
In Whitsun pastorals : sure this robe of mine
Does change my disposition.

   Flo.   What you do
Still betters what is done. When you speak, sweet,
I'ld have you do it ever : when you sing,
I'ld have you buy and sell so, so give alms,
Pray so ; and, for the ordering your affairs,
To sing them too : when you do dance, I wish you
A wave o' the sea, that you might ever do
Nothing but that ; move still, still so,
And own no other function : each your doing,
So singular in each particular,
Crowns what you are doing in the present deed,
That all your acts are queens.

   Per.   O Doricles,
Your praises are too large : but that your youth,
And the true blood which peepeth fairly through 't,
Do plainly give you out an unstain'd shepherd,
With wisdom I might fear, my Doricles,
You woo'd me the false way.

   Flo.   I think you have
As little skill to fear as I have purpose
To put you to 't. But come ; our dance, I pray :
Your hand, my Perdita : so turtles pair,
That never mean to part.

   Per.   I'll swear for 'em.

   Pol. This is the prettiest low-born lass that ever

Ran on the green-sward : nothing she does or seems
But smacks of something greater than herself,
Too noble for this place.

  Cam.   He tells her something
That makes her blood look out : good sooth, she is
The queen of curds and cream.

  Clo.   Come on, strike up !

  Dor. Mopsa must be your mistress : marry, garlic,
To mend her kissing with !

  Mop.   Now, in good time !

  Clo. Not a word, a word ; we stand upon our manners.
Come, strike up ! !

    [*Music. Here a dance of Shepherds and Shepherdesses.*

  Pol. Pray, good shepherd, what fair swain is this
Which dances with your daughter ?

  Shep. They call him Doricles ; and boasts himself
To have a worthy feeding : but I have it
Upon his own report and I believe it ;
He looks like sooth. He says he loves my daughter :
I think so too ; for never gazed the moon
Upon the water as he'll stand and read
As 'twere my daughter's eyes : and, to be plain,
I think there is not half a kiss to choose
Who loves another best.

  Pol.   She dances featly.

  Shep. So she does any thing ; though I report it,
That should be silent : if young Doricles
Do light upon her, she shall bring him that
Which he not dreams of.

       Enter Servant.

  Serv. O master, if you did but hear the pedlar at the door,
you would never dance again after a tabor and pipe ; no, the
bagpipe could not move you : he sings several tunes faster
than you'll tell money ; he utters them as he had eaten ballads
and all men's ears grew to his tunes.

  Clo. He could never come better ; he shall come in. I

love a ballad but even too well, if it be doleful matter
merrily set down, or a very pleasant thing indeed and sung
lamentably.

Serv. He hath songs for man or woman, of all sizes;
no milliner can so fit his customers with gloves: he has the
prettiest love-songs for maids; so without bawdry, which
is strange; with such delicate burthens of dildos and fadings,
'jump her and thump her;' and where some stretch-mouthed
rascal would, as it were, mean mischief and break a foul gap
into the matter, he makes the maid to answer 'Whoop, do me
no harm, good man;' puts him off, slights him, with 'Whoop,
do me no harm, good man.'

Pol. This is a brave fellow.

Clo. Believe me, thou talkest of an admirable conceited
fellow. Has he any unbraided wares?

Serv. He hath ribbons of all the colours i' the rainbow;
points more than all the lawyers in Bohemia can learnedly
handle, though they come to him by the gross: inkles, cad-
disses, cambrics, lawns: why, he sings 'em over as they were
gods or goddesses; you would think a smock were a she-
angel, he so chants to the sleeve-hand and the work about the
square on't.

Clo. Prithee bring him in; and let him approach singing.

Per. Forewarn him that he use no scurrilous words in's
tunes.   [*Exit Servant.*

Clo. You have of these pedlars, that have more in them than
you'ld think, sister.

Per. Ay, good brother, or go about to think.

> *Enter* AUTOLYCUS, *singing.*
>   Lawn as white as driven snow;
>   Cyprus black as e'er was crow;
>   Gloves as sweet as damask roses;
>   Masks for faces and for noses;
>   Bugle bracelet, necklace amber,
>   Perfume for a lady's chamber;

> Golden quoifs and stomachers,
> For my lads to give their dears :
> Pins and poking-sticks of steel,
> What maids lack from head to heel :
> Come buy of me, come ; come buy, come buy ;
> Buy, lads, or else your lasses cry :
> Come buy.

Clo. If I were not in love with Mopsa, thou shouldst take no money of me ; but being enthralled as I am, it will also be the bondage of certain ribbons and gloves.

Mop. I was promised them against the feast ; but they come not too late now.

Dor. He hath promised you more than that, or there be liars.

Mop. He hath paid you all he promised you : may be, he has paid you more, which will shame you to give him again.

Clo. Is there no manners left among maids ? will they wear their plackets where they should bear their faces ? Is there not milking-time, when you are going to bed, or kiln-hole, to whistle off these secrets, but you must be tittle-tattling before all our guests ? 'tis well they are whispering : clamour your tongues, and not a word more.

Mop. I have done. Come, you promised me a tawdry-lace and a pair of sweet gloves.

Clo. Have I not told thee how I was cozened by the way and lost all my money ?

Aut. And indeed, sir, there are cozeners abroad ; therefore it behoves men to be wary.

Clo. Fear not thou, man, thou shalt lose nothing here.

Aut. I hope so, sir ; for I have about me many parcels of charge.

Clo. What hast here ? ballads ?

Mop. Pray now, buy some : I love a ballad in print o' life, for then we are sure they are true.

Aut. Here's one to a very doleful tune, how a usurer's wife was brought to bed of twenty money-bags at a burthen and how she longed to eat adders' heads and toads carbonadoed.

Mop. Is it true, think you ?

Aut. Very true, and but a month old.

Dor. Bless me from marrying a usurer !

Aut. Here's the midwife's name to't, one Mistress Tale-porter, and five or six honest wives that were present. Why should I carry lies abroad ?

Mop. Pray you now, buy it.

Clo. Come on, lay it by : and let's first see moe ballads ; we'll buy the other things anon.

Aut. Here's another ballad of a fish, that appeared upon the coast on Wednesday the fourscore of April, forty thousand fathom above water, and sung this ballad against the hard hearts of maids : it was thought she was a woman and was turned into a cold fish for she would not exchange flesh with one that loved her : the ballad is very pitiful and as true.

Dor. Is it true too, think you ?

Aut. Five justices' hands at it, and witnesses more than my pack will hold.

Clo. Lay it by too : another.

Aut. This is a merry ballad, but a very pretty one.

Mop. Let's have some merry ones.

Aut. Why, this is a passing merry one and goes to the tune of ' Two maids wooing a man : ' there's scarce a maid westward but she sings it ; 'tis in request, I can tell you.

Mop. We can both sing it : if thou'lt bear a part, thou shalt hear ; 'tis in three parts.

Dor. We had the tune on't a month ago.

Aut. I can bear my part ; you must know 'tis my occupa-tion ; have at it with you.

SONG.

A.   Get you hence, for I must go

        Where it fits not you to know.

D. Whither ? *M.* O, whither ? *D.* Whither ?

M.   It becomes thy oath full well,

        Thou to me thy secrets tell.

D. Me, too, let me go thither.

631

Y

M.	Or thou goest to the grange or mill.
D.	If to either, thou dost ill.

A. Neither. *D.* What, neither ? *A.* Neither.

D.	Thou hast sworn my love to be.
M.	Thou hast sworn it more to me :
	Then whither goest ? say, whither ?

Clo. We'll have this song out anon by ourselves : my father and the gentlemen are in sad talk, and we'll not trouble them. Come, bring away thy pack after me. Wenches, I'll buy for you both. Pedlar, let's have the first choice. Follow me, girls.   [*Exit with Dorcas and Mopsa.*

Aut. And you shall pay well for 'em.   [*Follows singing.*

<blockquote>

Will you buy any tape,

   Or lace for your cape,

My dainty duck, my dear-a ?

   Any silk, any thread,

   Any toys for your head,

Of the new'st and finest, finest wear-a ?

   Come to the pedlar ;

   Money's a medler,

That doth utter all men's ware-a.   [*Exit.*

</blockquote>

Re-enter Servant.

Serv. Master, there is three carters, three shepherds, three neat-herds, three swine-herds, that have made themselves all men of hair, they call themselves Saltiers, and they have a dance which the wenches say is a gallimaufry of gambols, because they are not in't ; but they themselves are o' the mind, if it be not too rough for some that know little but bowling, it will please plentifully.

Shep. Away ! we'll none on't : here has been too much homely foolery already. I know, sir, we weary you.

Pol. You weary those that refresh us : pray, let's see these four threes of herdsmen.

Serv. One three of them, by their own report, sir, hath

danced before the king ; and not the worst of the three but
jumps twelve foot and a half by the squier.

Shep. Leave your prating : since these good men are
pleased, let them come in ; but quickly now.

Serv. Why, they stay at door, sir.   [*Exit.*

Here a dance of twelve Satyrs.

Pol. O, father, you'll know more of that hereafter.
[*To Cam.*] Is it not too far gone ? 'Tis time to part them.
He's simple and tells much. [*To Flor.*] How now, fair
    shepherd !
Your heart is full of something that does take
Your mind from feasting. Sooth, when I was young
And handed love as you do, I was wont
To load my she with knacks : I would have ransack'd
The pedlar's silken treasury and have pour'd it
To her acceptance ; you have let him go
And nothing marted with him. If your lass
Interpretation should abuse and call this
Your lack of love or bounty, you were straited
For a reply, at least if you make a care
Of happy holding her.

Flo.   Old sir, I know
She prizes not such trifles as these are :
The gifts she looks from me are pack'd and lock'd
Up in my heart ; which I have given already,
But not deliver'd. O, hear me breathe my life
Before this ancient sir, who, it should seem,
Hath sometime loved ! I take thy hand, this hand,
As soft as dove's down and as white as it,
Or Ethiopian's tooth, or the fann'd snow that's
    bolted
By the northern blasts twice o'er.

Pol.   What follows this ?
How prettily the young swain seems to wash
The hand was fair before ! I have put you out :

But to your protestation; let me hear
What you profess.

    Flo.   Do, and be witness to't.

    Pol. And this my neighbour too?

    Flo.   And he, and more
Than he, and men, the earth, the heavens, and all:
That, were I crown'd the most imperial monarch,
Thereof most worthy, were I the fairest youth
That ever made eye swerve, had force and knowledge
More than was ever man's, I would not prize them
Without her love; for her employ them all;
Commend them and condemn them to her service
Or to their own perdition.

    Pol.   Fairly offer'd.

    Cam. This shows a sound affection.

    Shep.   But, my daughter,
Say you the like to him?

    Per.   I cannot speak
So well, nothing so well; no, nor mean better:
By the pattern of mine own thoughts I cut out
The purity of his.

    Shep.   Take hands, a bargain!
And, friends unknown, you shall bear witness to't:
I give my daughter to him, and will make
Her portion equal his.

    Flo.   O, that must be
I' the virtue of your daughter: one being dead,
I shall have more than you can dream of yet;
Enough then for your wonder. But, come on,
Contract us 'fore these witnesses.

    Shep.   Come, your hand;
And, daughter, yours.

    Pol.   Soft, swain, awhile, beseech you;
Have you a father?

    Flo.   I have: but what of him?

    Pol. Knows he of this?

Flo.   He neither does nor shall.

Pol. Methinks a father
Is at the nuptial of his son a guest
That best becomes the table. Pray you once more,
Is not your father grown incapable
Of reasonable affairs ? is he not stupid
With age and altering rheums ? can he speak ? hear ?
Know man from man ? dispute his own estate ?
Lies he not bed-rid ? and again does nothing
But what he did being childish ?

Flo.   No, good sir ;
He has his health and ampler strength indeed
Than most have of his age.

Pol.   By my white beard,
You offer him, if this be so, a wrong
Something unfilial : reason my son
Should choose himself a wife, but as good reason
The father, all whose joy is nothing else
But fair posterity, should hold some counsel
In such a business.

Flo.   I yield all this ;
But for some other reasons, my grave sir,
Which 'tis not fit you know, I not acquaint
My father of this business.

Pol.   Let him know't.

Flo. He shall not.

Pol.   Prithee, let him.

Flo.   No, he must not.

Shep. Let him, my son : he shall not need to grieve
At knowing of thy choice.

Flo.   Come, come, he must not.
Mark our contract.

Pol.   Mark your divorce, young sir,

                              [*Discovering himself.*

Whom son I dare not call ; thou art too base
To be acknowledged : thou a sceptre's heir,

That thus affect'st a sheep-hook ! Thou old traitor,
I am sorry that by hanging thee I can
But shorten thy life one week. And thou, fresh piece
Of excellent witchcraft, who of force must know
The royal fool thou copest with,—

   Shep.   O, my heart !

   Pol. I'll have thy beauty scratch'd with briers, and made
More homely than thy state. For thee, fond boy,
If I may ever know thou dost but sigh
That thou no more shalt see this knack, as never
I mean thou shalt, we'll bar thee from succession ;
Not hold thee of our blood, no, not our kin,
Far than Deucalion off : mark thou my words :
Follow us to the court. Thou churl, for this time,
Though full of our displeasure, yet we free thee
From the dead blow of it. And you, enchantment,—
Worthy enough a herdsman ; yea, him too,
That makes himself, but for our honour therein,
Unworthy thee,—if ever henceforth thou
These rural latches to his entrance open,
Or hoop his body more with thy embraces,
I will devise a death as cruel for thee
As thou art tender to't.   *[Exit.*

   Per.   Even here undone !
I was not much afeard ; for once or twice
I was about to speak and tell him plainly,
The selfsame sun that shines upon his court
Hides not his visage from our cottage but
Looks on alike. Will't please you, sir, be gone ?
I told you what would come of this : beseech you,
Of your own state take care : this dream of mine,—
Being now awake, I'll queen it no inch farther,
But milk my ewes and weep.

   Cam.   Why, how now, father !
Speak ere thou diest.

   Shep.   I cannot speak, nor think,

Nor dare to know that which I know. O sir!
You have undone a man of fourscore three,
That thought to fill his grave in quiet, yea,
To die upon the bed my father died,
To lie close by his honest bones : but now
Some hangman must put on my shroud and lay me
Where no priest shovels in dust. O cursed wretch,
That knew'st this was the prince, and wouldst adventure
To mingle faith with him! Undone! undone!
If I might die within this hour, I have lived
To die when I desire.   [*Exit.*

  Flo.   Why look you so upon me?
I am but sorry, not afeard ; delay'd,
But nothing alter'd : what I was, I am ;
More straining on for plucking back, not following
My leash unwillingly.

  Cam.   Gracious my lord,
You know your father's temper : at this time
He will allow no speech, which I do guess
You do not purpose to him ; and as hardly
Will he endure your sight as yet, I fear :
Then, till the fury of his highness settle,
Come not before him.

  Flo.   I not purpose it.
I think, Camillo?

  Cam.   Even he, my lord.

  Per. How often have I told you 'twould be thus!
How often said, my dignity would last
But till 'twere known!

  Flo.   It cannot fail but by
The violation of my faith ; and then
Let nature crush the sides o' the earth together
And mar the seeds within! Lift up thy looks :
From my succession wipe me, father ; I
Am heir to my affection.

  Cam.   Be advised.

Flo. I am, and by my fancy : if my reason
Will thereto be obedient, I have reason ;
If not, my senses, better pleased with madness
Do bid it welcome.

 Cam.   This is desperate, sir.

 Flo. So call it : but it does fulfil my vow ;
I needs must think it honesty. Camillo,
Not for Bohemia, nor the pomp that may
Be thereat glean'd, for all the sun sees or
The close earth wombs or the profound sea hides
In unknown fathoms, will I break my oath
To this my fair beloved.   Act IV, Scene iv, ll. 1-502

       A cause more promising
Than a wild dedication of yourselves
To unpath'd waters, undream'd shores.

        Act IV, Scene iv, ll. 575-577

 Paulina. Were I the ghost that walk'd, I'ld bid you mark
Her eye, and tell me for what dull part in't
You chose her.

 Leontes.   Stars, stars,
And all eyes else dead coals ! Act V, Scene i, ll. 63-65, 67-68

       I, an old turtle,
Will wing me to some wither'd bough and there
My mate, that's never to be found again,
Lament till I am lost.

        Act V, Scene iii, ll. 132-135

The Two Noble Kinsmen

Roses their sharp spines being gone,
Not royal in their smells alone,
But in their hue,

Maiden-pinks, of odour faint,
Daisies smell-less, yet most quaint,
And sweet thyme true.

Primrose first-born child of Ver,
Merry springtime's harbinger,
With her bells dim.
Oxlips in their cradles growing,
Marigolds on death-beds blowing,
Larks-heels trim.

All dear nature's children sweet,
Lie 'fore bride and bridegroom's feet,
Blessing their sense.
Not an angel of the air,
Bird melodious, or bird fair,
Is absent hence.

The crow, the slanderous cuckoo, nor
The boding raven, nor chough hoar
Nor chatt'ring pie,
May on our bridehouse perch or sing,
Or with them any discord bring,
But from it fly.

ACT I, Scene i, ll. 1-24

Urns and odours bring away,
Vapours, sighs, darken the day;
Our dole more deadly looks than dying:
Balms, and gums, and heavy cheers,
Sacred vials fill'd with tears,
And clamours, through the wild air flying:

Come all sad and solemn shows,
That are quick-eyed pleasure's foes;
We convent nought else but woes.
We convent nought else but woes.

ACT I, Scene v, ll. 1-10

Oh great corrector of enormous times,
Shaker of o'er rank states, thou grand decider
Of dusty, and old titles, that heal'st the blood
Of the earth when it is sick, and cur'st the world
O' th' pleuresy of people. . . .

ACT V, Scene i, ll. 62-66

The Famous History of the Life of

King Henry the Eighth

An ante-chamber of the Queen's *apartments.*

Enter ANNE BULLEN *and an Old* Lady.

Anne. Not for that neither: here's the pang that pinches:
His highness having lived so long with her, and she
So good a lady that no tongue could ever
Pronounce dishonour of her; by my life,
She never knew harm-doing: O, now, after
So many courses of the sun enthroned,
Still growing in a majesty and pomp, the which
To leave a thousand-fold more bitter than
'Tis sweet at first to acquire,—after this process,
To give her the avaunt! it is a pity
Would move a monster.

    Old L.   Hearts of most hard temper
Melt and lament for her.

    Anne.   O, God's will! much better
She ne'er had known pomp: though't be temporal,
Yet, if that quarrel, fortune, do divorce
It from the bearer, 'tis a sufferance panging
As soul and body's severing.

    Old L.   Alas, poor lady!
She's a stranger now again.

    Anne.   So much the more
Must pity drop upon her. Verily,

640

I swear, 'tis better to be lowly born,
And range with humble livers in content,
Than to be perk'd up in a glistering grief,
And wear a golden sorrow.

  Old L.   Our content
Is our best having.

  Anne.   By my troth and maidenhead,
I would not be a queen.

  Old L.   Beshrew me, I would,
And venture maidenhead for't; and so would you,
For all this spice of your hypocrisy:
You, that have so fair parts of woman on you,
Have too a woman's heart; which ever yet
Affected eminence, wealth, sovereignty;
Which, to say sooth, are blessings; and which gifts,
Saving your mincing, the capacity
Of your soft cheveril conscience would receive,
If you might please to stretch it.

  Anne.   Nay, good troth.

  Old L. Yes, troth, and troth; you would not be a queen?

  Anne. No, not for all the riches under heaven.

  Old L. 'Tis strange: a three-pence bow'd would hire me,
Old as I am, to queen it: but, I pray you,
What think you of a duchess? have you limbs
To bear that load of title?

  Anne.   No, in truth.

  Old L. Then you are weakly made: pluck off a little;
I would not be a young count in your way,
For more than blushing comes to: if your back
Cannot vouchsafe this burthen, 'tis too weak
Ever to get a boy.

  Anne.   How you do talk!
I swear again, I would not be a queen
For all the world.

  Old L.   In faith, for little England
You'ld venture an emballing: I myself

Would for Carnarvonshire, although there long'd
No more to the crown but that. Lo, who comes here?

Enter the LORD CHAMBERLAIN.

Cham. Good morrow, ladies. What were't worth to know
The secret of your conference?

Anne. My good lord,
Not your demand; it values not your asking:
Our mistress' sorrows we were pitying.

Cham. It was a gentle business, and becoming
The action of good women: there is hope
All will be well.

Anne. Now, I pray God, amen!

Cham. You bear a gentle mind, and heavenly blessings
Follow such creatures. That you may, fair lady,
Perceive I speak sincerely, and high note's
Ta'en of your many virtues, the king's majesty
Commends his good opinion of you, and
Does purpose honour to you no less flowing
Than Marchioness of Pembroke; to which title
A thousand pound a year, annual support,
Out of his grace he adds.

Anne. I do not know
What kind of my obedience I should tender;
More than my all is nothing: nor my prayers
Are not words duly hallow'd, nor my wishes
More worth than empty vanities; yet prayers and wishes
Are all I can return. Beseech your lordship,
Vouchsafe to speak my thanks and my obedience,
As from a blushing handmaid, to his highness;
Whose health and royalty I pray for.

Cham. Lady,
I shall not fail to approve the fair conceit
The king hath of you. [*Aside*] I have perused her well;
Beauty and honour in her are so mingled
That they have caught the king: and who knows yet

But from this lady may proceed a gem
To lighten all this isle ? I'll to the king,
And say I spoke with you.   [*Exit Lord Chamberlain.*
   Anne.   My honour'd lord.
   Old L. Why, this it is ; see, see !
I have been begging sixteen years in court,
Am yet a courtier beggarly, nor could
Come pat betwixt too early and too late
For any suit of pounds ; and you, O fate !
A very fresh-fish here—fie, fie, fie upon
This compell'd fortune !—have your mouth fill'd up
Before you open it.
   Anne.   This is strange to me.
   Old L. How tastes it ? is it bitter ? forty pence, no.
There was a lady once, 'tis an old story,
That would not be a queen, that would she not,
For all the mud in Egypt : have you heard it ?
   Anne. Come, you are pleasant.
   Old L.   With your theme, I could
O'ermount the lark. The Marchioness of Pembroke !
A thousand pounds a year for pure respect !
No other obligation ! By my life,
That promises moe thousands : honour's train
Is longer than his foreskirt. By this time
I know your back will bear a duchess : say,
Are you not stronger than you were ?
   Anne.   Good lady,
Make yourself mirth with your particular fancy,
And leave me out on't. Would I had no being,
If this salute my blood a jot : it faints me,
To think what follows.
The queen is comfortless, and we forgetful
In our long absence : pray, do not deliver
What here you've heard to her.
   Old L.   What do you think me ?
                    Act II, Scene iii, ll. 1-108

Orpheus with his lute made trees,
And the mountain tops that freeze,
  Bow themselves when he did sing:
To his music plants and flowers
Ever sprung; as sun and showers
  There had made a lasting spring.

Every thing that heard him play,
Even the billows of the sea,
  Hung their heads, and then lay by.
In sweet music is such art,
Killing care and grief of heart
  Fall asleep, or hearing, die.

ACT III, Scene i, ll. 3-14

Wolsey.   What should this mean?
What sudden anger's this? how have I reap'd it?
He parted frowning from me, as if ruin
    Leap'd from his eyes. . . .
I have touch'd the highest point of all my greatness;
And, from that full meridian of my glory,
I haste now to my setting: I shall fall
Like a bright exhalation in the evening,
And no man see me more. . . .
Farewell! a long farewell, to all my greatness!
This is the state of man: to-day he puts forth
The tender leaves of hopes; to-morrow blossoms,
And bears his blushing honours thick upon him;
The third day comes a frost, a killing frost,
And, when he thinks, good easy man, full surely
His greatness is a-ripening, nips his root,
And then he falls, as I do. I have ventured,
Like little wanton boys that swim on bladders,
This many summers in a sea of glory,
But far beyond my depth: my high-blown pride
At length broke under me and now has left me,
Weary and old with service, to the mercy

644

Of a rude stream, that must for ever hide me.
Vain pomp and glory of this world, I hate ye :
I feel my heart new open'd. O, how wretched
Is that poor man that hangs on princes' favours !
There is, betwixt that smile we would aspire to,
That sweet aspect of princes, and their ruin,
More pangs and fears than wars or women have :
And when he falls, he falls like Lucifer,
Never to hope again. . . .
O Cromwell, Cromwell !
Had I but served my God with half the zeal
I served my king, he would not in mine age
Have left me naked to mine enemies.

ACT III, Scene ii, ll. 203-206, 223-227, 351-372, 454-457

The Tempest

Now would I give a thousand furlongs of sea for an acre
of barren ground, long heath, brown furze, any thing. The
wills above be done ! but I would fain die a dry death.

ACT I, Scene i, ll. 68-71

The island. Before PROSPERO'S *cell.*

Enter PROSPERO *and* MIRANDA.

Mir. If by your art, my dearest father, you have
Put the wild waters in this roar, allay them.
The sky, it seems, would pour down stinking pitch,
But that the sea, mounting to the welkin's cheek,
Dashes the fire out. O, I have suffered
With those that I saw suffer : a brave vessel,
Who had, no doubt, some noble creature in her,
Dash'd all to pieces. O, the cry did knock
Against my very heart. Poor souls, they perish'd.
Had I been any god of power, I would

645

Have sunk the sea within the earth or ere
It should the good ship so have swallow'd and
The fraughting souls within her.

    Pros.   Be collected :
No more amazement : tell your piteous heart
There's no harm done.

    Mir.   O, woe the day !

    Pros.   No harm.
I have done nothing but in care of thee,
Of thee, my dear one, thee, my daughter, who
Art ignorant of what thou art, nought knowing
Of whence I am, nor that I am more better
Than Prospero, master of a full poor cell,
And thy no greater father.

    Mir.   More to know
Did never meddle with my thoughts.

    Pros.   'Tis time
I should inform thee farther. Lend thy hand,
And pluck my magic garment from me. So :

                        [Lays down his mantle.
Lie there, my art. Wipe thou thine eyes ; have comfort.
The direful spectacle of the wreck, which touch'd
The very virtue of compassion in thee,
I have with such provision in mine art
So safely ordered that there is no soul—
No, not so much perdition as an hair
Betid to any creature in the vessel
Which thou heard'st cry, which thou saw'st sink. Sit down ;
For thou must now know farther.

    Mir.   You have often
Begun to tell me what I am, but stopp'd
And left me to a bootless inquisition,
Concluding ' Stay : not yet.'

    Pros.   The hour's now come ;
The very minute bids thee ope thine ear ;
Obey and be attentive. Canst thou remember

A time before we came unto this cell?
I do not think thou canst, for then thou wast not
Out three years old.

    Mir.   Certainly, sir, I can.

    Pros. By what? by any other house or person?
Of any thing the image tell me that
Hath kept with thy remembrance.

    Mir.   'Tis far off
And rather like a dream that an assurance
That my remembrance warrants. Had I not
Four or five women once that tended me?

    Pros. Thou hadst, and more, Miranda. But how is it
That this lives in thy mind? What seest thou else
In the dark backward and abysm of time? . . .

             They hurried us aboard a bark,
Bore us some leagues to sea; where they prepared
A rotten carcass of a boat, not rigg'd,
Nor tackle, sail, nor mast; the very rats
Instinctively have quit it: there they hoist us,
To cry to the sea that roar'd to us, to sigh
To the winds whose pity, sighing back again,
Did us but loving wrong.

    Mir.   Alack, what trouble
Was I then to you!

    Pros.   O, a cherubin
Thou wast that did preserve me. . . .

                      [*Resumes his mantle.*
Sit still, and hear the last of our sea-sorrow.
Here in this island we arrived; and here
Have I, thy schoolmaster, made thee more profit
Than other princesses can that have more time
For vainer hours and tutors not so careful.

    Mir. Heavens thank you for't! And now, I pray you, sir,
For still 'tis beating in my mind, your reason
For raising this sea-storm?

    Pros.   Know thus far forth.

By accident most strange, bountiful Fortune,
Now my dear lady, hath mine enemies
Brought to this shore ; and by my prescience
I find my zenith doth depend upon
A most auspicious star, whose influence
If now I court not but omit, my fortunes
Will ever after droop.   Here cease more questions :
Thou art inclined to sleep ; 'tis a good dulness,
And give it way : I know thou canst not choose.

           [Miranda sleeps.
Come away, servant, come.   I am ready now.
Approach, my Ariel, come.

Enter ARIEL.

 Ari. All hail, great master ! grave sir, hail ! I come
To answer thy best pleasure ; be't to fly,
To swim, to dive into the fire, to ride
On the curl'd clouds, to thy strong bidding task
Ariel and all his quality.
 Pros.   Hast thou, spirit,
Perform'd to point the tempest that I bade thee ?
 Ari. To every article.
I boarded the king's ship ; now on the beak,
Now in the waist, the deck, in every cabin,
I flamed amazement. . . .
       Safely in harbour
Is the king's ship ; in the deep nook, where once
Thou call'dst me up at midnight to fetch dew
From the still-vex'd Bermoothes, there she's hid. . . .
 Is there more toil ?   Since thou dost give me pains,
Let me remember thee what thou hast promised,
Which is not yet perform'd me.
 Pros.   How now ?   moody ?
What is't thou canst demand ?
 Ari.   My liberty.
 Pros. Before the time be out ?   no more !

Ari.   I prithee,
Remember I have done thee worthy service ;
Told thee no lies, made thee no mistakings, served
Without or grudge or grumblings : thou didst promise
To bate me a full year.

Pros.   Dost thou forget
From what a torment I did free thee ?

Ari.   No.

Pros. Thou dost, and think'st it much to tread the ooze
Of the salt deep,
To run upon the sharp wind of the north,
To do me business in the veins o' the earth
When it is baked with frost. . . .

Ari.   Pardon, master ;
I will be correspondent to command
And do my spiriting gently.

Pros.   Do so, and after two days
I will discharge thee.

Ari.   That's my noble master !
What shall I do ? say what ; what shall I do ?

Pros. Go make thyself like a nymph o' the sea.

ACT I, Scene ii, ll. 1-50, 144-153, 170-198,
226-229, 242-256, 296-301

Caliban. As wicked dew as e'er my mother brush'd
With raven's feather from unwholesome fen
Drop on you both ! a south-west blow on ye
And blister you all o'er !

Prospero. For this, be sure, to-night thou shalt have cramps,
Side-stitches that shall pen thy breath up ; urchins
Shall, for that vast of night that they may work,
All exercise on thee ; thou shalt be pinch'd
As thick as honeycomb, each pinch more stinging
Than bees that made 'em.

Cal.   I must eat my dinner.
This island's mine, by Sycorax my mother,
Which thou takest from me. When thou camest first,

649

Thou strokedst me and madest much of me, wouldst give me
Water with berries in't, and teach me how
To name the bigger light, and how the less,
That burn by day and night : and then I loved thee
And show'd thee all the qualities o' the isle,
The fresh springs, brine-pits, barren place and fertile :
Cursed be I that did so ! All the charms
Of Sycorax, toads, beetles, bats, light on you !
For I am all the subjects that you have,
Which first was mine own king : and here you sty me
In this hard rock, whiles you do keep from me
The rest o' the island. . . .

  Pros.   Thou didst seek to violate
The honour of my child.

  Cal. O ho, O ho ! would't had been done !

ACT I, Scene ii, ll. 321-344, 347-349

   To PROSPERO *and* MIRANDA *enter* ARIEL,
    invisible, playing and singing ;
     FERDINAND *following.*

      ARIEL'S *song.*

   Come unto these yellow sands,
    And then take hands :
   Courtsied when you have and kiss'd
    The wild waves whist,
   Foot it featly here and there ;
   And, sweet sprites, the burthen bear.

Burthen [*dispersedly*]. Hark, hark !

         Bow-wow.
   The watch-dogs bark :
         Bow-wow.

Ari.   Hark, hark ! I hear
   The strain of strutting chanticleer
   Cry, Cock-a-diddle-dow.

  Fer. Where should this music be ? i' the air or the earth ?
It sounds no more : and, sure, it waits upon
Some god o' the island. Sitting on a bank,

Weeping again the king my father's wreck,
This music crept by me upon the waters,
Allaying both their fury and my passion
With its sweet air : thence I have follow'd it,
Or it hath drawn me rather. But 'tis gone.
No, it begins again.

ARIEL *sings*.

Full fathom five thy father lies ;
 Of his bones are coral made ;
Those are pearls that were his eyes :
 Nothing of him that doth fade
But doth suffer a sea-change
Into something rich and strange.
Sea-nymphs hourly ring his knell :

Burthen. Ding-dong.

Ari. Hark ! now I hear them,—Ding-dong, bell.

Fer. The ditty does remember my drown'd father.
This is no mortal business, nor no sound
That the earth owes. I hear it now above me.

Prospero. The fringed curtains of thine eye advance
And say what thou seest yond.

Miranda.   What is't ? a spirit ?
Lord, how it looks about ! Believe me, sir,
It carries a brave form. But 'tis a spirit.

Pros. No, wench ; it eats and sleeps and hath such senses
As we have, such. This gallant which thou seest
Was in the wreck ; and, but he's something stain'd
With grief that's beauty's canker, thou mightst call him
A goodly person : he hath lost his fellows
And strays about to find 'em.

Mir.   I might call him
A thing divine, for nothing natural
I ever saw so noble.

Pros. [*Aside*] It goes on, I see,
As my soul prompts it. Spirit, fine spirit ! I'll free thee
Within two days for this.

651

Fer.   Most sure, the goddess
On whom these airs attend ! Vouchsafe my prayer
May know if you remain upon this island ;
And that you will some good instruction give
How I may bear me here : my prime request,
Which I do last pronounce, is, O you wonder !
If you be maid or no ?

    Mir.   No wonder, sir ;
But certainly a maid.

    Fer.   My language ! heavens !
I am the best of them that speak this speech,
Were I but where 'tis spoken.

    Pros.   How ? the best ?
What wert thou, if the King of Naples heard thee ?

    Fer. A single thing, as I am now, that wonders
To hear thee speak of Naples.   He does hear me ;
And that he does I weep : myself am Naples,
Who with mine eyes, never since at ebb, beheld
The king my father wreck'd.

    Mir.   Alack, for mercy !

    Fer. Yes, faith, and all his lords ; the Duke of Milan
And his brave son being twain.

    Pros.   [*Aside*] The Duke of Milan
And his more braver daughter could control thee,
If now 'twere fit to do't.   At the first sight
They have changed eyes.   Delicate Ariel,
I'll set thee free for this. [*To Fer.*] A word, good sir ;
I fear you have done yourself some wrong : a word.

    Mir. Why speaks my father so ungently ?   This
Is the third man that e'er I saw, the first
That e'er I sigh'd for : pity move my father
To be inclined my way !

    Fer.   O, if a virgin,
And your affection not gone forth, I'll make you
The queen of Naples.

    Pros.   Soft, sir ! one word more.

[*Aside*] They are both in either's powers; but this swift
    business
I must uneasy make, lest too light winning
Make the prize light. [*To Fer.*] One word more; I charge
    thee
That thou attend me: thou dost here usurp
The name thou owest not; and hast put thyself
Upon this island as a spy, to win it
From me, the lord on't.

    Fer.   No, as I am a man.

    Mir. There's nothing ill can dwell in such a temple:
If the ill spirit have so fair a house,
Good things will strive to dwell with't.

    Pros.   Follow me.
Speak not you for him; he's a traitor. Come;
I'll manacle thy neck and feet together:
Sea-water shalt thou drink; thy food shall be
The fresh-brook muscles, wither'd roots and husks
Wherein the acorn cradled. Follow.

    Fer.   No;
I will resist such entertainment till
Mine enemy has more power.

                  [*Draws, and is charmed from moving.*

    Mir.   O dear father,
Make not too rash a trial of him, for
He's gentle and not fearful.

    Pros.   What? I say,
My foot my tutor? Put thy sword up, traitor;
Who makest a show but darest not strike, thy conscience
Is so possess'd with guilt: come from thy ward,
For I can here disarm thee with this stick
And make thy weapon drop.

    Mir.   Beseech you, father.

    Pros. Hence! hang not on my garments.

    Mir.   Sir, have pity;
I'll be his surety.

Pros.   Silence ! one word more
Shall make me chide thee, if not hate thee. What !
An advocate for an impostor ! hush !
Thou think'st there is no more such shapes as he,
Having seen but him and Caliban : foolish wench !
To the most of men this is a Caliban
And they to him are angels.

    Mir.   My affections
Are then most humble ; I have no ambition
To see a goodlier man.

    Pros.   Come on ; obey :
Thy nerves are in their infancy again
And have no vigour in them.

    Fer.   So they are ;
My spirits, as in a dream, are all bound up.
My father's loss, the weakness which I feel,
The wreck of all my friends, nor this man's threats,
To whom I am subdued, are but light to me,
Might I but through my prison once a day
Behold this maid : all corners else o' the earth
Let liberty make use of ; space enough
Have I in such a prison.

    Pros. [*Aside*] It works. [*To Fer.*] Come on.
Thou hast done well, fine Ariel ! [*To Fer.*] Follow me.
[*To Ari.*] Hark what thou else shalt do me.

    Mir.   Be of comfort ;
My father's of a better nature, sir,
Than he appears by speech : this is unwonted
Which now came from him.

    Pros.   Thou shalt be as free
As mountain winds : but then exactly do
All points of my command.

    Ari.   To the syllable.

    Pros. Come, follow. Speak not for him.

ACT I, Scene ii, ll. 376-501

Another part of the island.

Enter CALIBAN *with a burden of wood. A noise of
thunder heard.*

Cal. All the infections that the sun sucks up
From bogs, fens, flats, on Prosper fall and make him
By inch-meal a disease ! His spirits hear me
And yet I needs must curse. But they'll nor pinch,
Fright me with urchin-shows, pitch me i' the mire,
Nor lead me, like a firebrand, in the dark
Out of my way, unless he bid 'em ; but
For every trifle are they set upon me ;
Sometimes like apes that mow and chatter at me
And after bite me, then like hedgehogs which
Lie tumbling in my barefoot way and mount
Their pricks at my footfall ; sometime am I
All wound with adders who with cloven tongues
Do hiss me into madness.

Enter TRINCULO.

Lo, now, lo !
Here comes a spirit of his, and to torment me
For bringing wood in slowly. I'll fall flat ;
Perchance he will not mind me.

Trin. Here's neither bush nor shrub, to bear off any weather
at all, and another storm brewing ; I hear it sing i' the wind :
yond same black cloud, yond huge one, looks like a foul
bombard that would shed his liquor. If it should thunder as it
did before, I know not where to hide my head : yond same
cloud cannot choose but fall by pailfuls. What have we here ?
a man or a fish ? dead or alive ? A fish : he smells like a fish ;
a very ancient and fish-like smell ; a kind of not of the newest
Poor-John. A strange fish ! Were I in England now, as once
I was, and had but this fish painted, not a holiday fool there
but would give a piece of silver : there would this monster
make a man ; any strange beast there makes a man : when
they will not give a doit to relieve a lame beggar, they will lay

out ten to see a dead Indian. Legged like a man! and his
fins like arms! Warm o' my troth! I do now let loose my
opinion; hold it no longer: this is no fish, but an islander,
that hath lately suffered by a thunderbolt. [*Thunder.*] Alas,
the storm is come again! my best way is to creep under
his gaberdine: there is no other shelter hereabout: misery
acquaints a man with strange bed-fellows. I will here shroud
till the dregs of the storm be past.

Enter STEPHANO, *singing: a bottle in his hand.*

Ste.   I shall no more to sea, to sea,
                  Here shall I die ashore—

This is a very scurvy tune to sing at a man's funeral: well,
here's my comfort.   [*Drinks.*
[*Sings.*

          The master, the swabber, the boatswain and I,
                  The gunner and his mate
      Loved Mall, Meg and Marian and Margery,
              But none of us cared for Kate;
              For she had a tongue with a tang,
              Would cry to a sailor, Go hang!
      She loved not the savour of tar nor of pitch,
      Yet a tailor might scratch her where'er she did itch:
              Then to sea, boys, and let her go hang!

This is a scurvy tune too: but here's my comfort.   [*Drinks.*

Cal. Do not torment me: Oh!

Ste. What's the matter? Have we devils here? Do you
put tricks upon's with savages and men of Ind, ha? I have not
'scaped drowning to be afeard now of your four legs; for it
hath been said, As proper a man as ever went on four legs
cannot make him give ground; and it shall be said so again
while Stephano breathes at nostrils.

Cal. The spirit torments me; Oh!

Ste. This is some monster of the isle with four legs, who
hath got, as I take it, an ague. Where the devil should he
learn our language? I will give him some relief, if it be but

for that. If I can recover him and keep him tame and get to Naples with him, he's a present for any emperor that ever trod on neat's-leather.

Cal. Do not torment me, prithee; I'll bring my wood home faster.

Ste. He's in his fit now and does not talk after the wisest. He shall taste of my bottle: if he have never drunk wine afore, it will go near to remove his fit. If I can recover him and keep him tame, I will not take too much for him; he shall pay for him that hath him, and that soundly.

Cal. Thou dost me yet but little hurt; thou wilt anon, I know it by thy trembling: now Prosper works upon thee.

Ste. Come on your ways; open your mouth; here is that which will give language to you, cat: open your mouth; this will shake your shaking, I can tell you, and that soundly: you cannot tell who's your friend: open your chaps again.

Trin. I should know that voice: it should be—but he is drowned; and these are devils: O defend me!

Ste. Four legs and two voices: a most delicate monster! His forward voice now is to speak well of his friend; his backward voice is to utter foul speeches and to detract. If all the wine in my bottle will recover him, I will help his ague. Come. Amen! I will pour some in thy other mouth.

Trin. Stephano!

Ste. Doth thy other mouth call me? Mercy, mercy! This is a devil, and no monster: I will leave him; I have no long spoon.

Trin. Stephano! If thou beest Stephano, touch me and speak to me; for I am Trinculo—be not afeard—thy good friend Trinculo.

Ste. If thou beest Trinculo, come forth: I'll pull thee by the lesser legs: if any be Trinculo's legs, these are they. Thou art very Trinculo indeed! How camest thou to be the siege of this moon-calf? can he vent Trinculos?

Trin. I took him to be killed with a thunderstroke. But art thou not drowned, Stephano? I hope now thou art not drowned. Is the storm overblown? I hid me under the dead moon-calf's gaberdine for fear of the storm. And art thou living, Stephano? O Stephano, two Neapolitans 'scaped!

Ste. Prithee, do not turn me about; my stomach is not constant.

Cal. [*Aside*] These be fine things, and if they be not sprites. That's a brave god and bears celestial liquor.
I will kneel to him.

Ste. How didst thou 'scape? How camest thou hither? swear by this bottle how thou camest hither. I escaped upon a butt of sack which the sailors heaved o'erboard, by this bottle! which I made of the bark of a tree with mine own hands since I was cast ashore.

Cal. I'll swear upon that bottle to be thy true subject; for the liquor is not earthly.

Ste. Here; swear then how thou escapedst.

Trin. Swum ashore, man, like a duck: I can swim like a duck, I'll be sworn.

Ste. Here, kiss the book. Though thou canst swim like a duck, thou art made like a goose.

Trin. O Stephano, hast any more of this?

Ste. The whole butt, man: my cellar is in a rock by the sea-side where my wine is hid. How now, moon-calf! how does thine ague?

Cal. Hast thou not dropp'd from heaven?

Ste. Out o' the moon, I do assure thee: I was the man i' the moon when time was.

Cal. I have seen thee in her and I do adore thee:
My mistress show'd me thee and thy dog and thy bush.

Ste. Come, swear to that; kiss the book: I will furnish it anon with new contents: swear.

Trin. By this good light, this is a very shallow monster! I afeard of him! A very weak monster! The man i' the moon! A most poor credulous monster! Well drawn, monster, in good sooth!

Cal. I'll show thee every fertile inch o' th' island;

And I will kiss thy foot : I prithee, be my god.

Trin. By this light, a most perfidious and drunken monster ! when's god's asleep, he'll rob his bottle.

Cal. I'll kiss thy foot ; I'll swear myself thy subject.

Ste. Come on then ; down, and swear.

Trin. I shall laugh myself to death at this puppy-headed monster. A most scurvy monster ! I could find in my heart to beat him,—

Ste. Come, kiss.

Trin. But that the poor monster's in drink : an abominable monster !

Cal. I'll show thee the best springs ; I'll pluck thee
    berries ;
I'll fish for thee and get thee wood enough.
A plague upon the tyrant that I serve !
I'll bear him no more sticks, but follow thee,
Thou wondrous man.

Trin. A most ridiculous monster, to make a wonder of a poor drunkard !

Cal. I prithee, let me bring thee where crabs grow ;
And I with my long nails will dig thee pig-nuts ;
Show thee a jay's nest and instruct thee how
To snare the nimble marmoset ; I'll bring thee
To clustering filberts and sometimes I'll get thee
Young scamels from the rock. Wilt thou go with me ?

Ste. I prithee now, lead the way without any more talking. Trinculo, the king and all our company else being drowned, we will inherit here : here ; bear my bottle : fellow Trinculo, we'll fill him by and by again.

Cal. [*Sings drunkenly*]

    Farewell, master ; farewell, farewell !

Trin. A howling monster ; a drunken monster !

Cal.   No more dams I'll make for fish ;
        Nor fetch in firing
        At requiring ;

> Nor scrape trencher, nor wash dish :
> 'Ban, 'Ban, Cacaliban
> Has a new master : get a new man.

Freedom, hey-day! hey-day, freedom! freedom, hey-day, freedom!

Ste. O brave monster! Lead the way.

ACT II, Scene ii, ll. 1-192

Before PROSPERO'S *cell.*

To FERDINAND, *bearing a log, enter* MIRANDA ;
and PROSPERO *at a distance, unseen.*

Mir.　　　　　　　　Alas, now, pray you,
Work not so hard : I would the lightning had
Burnt up those logs that you are enjoin'd to pile !
Pray, set it down and rest you : when this burns,
'Twill weep for having wearied you. My father
Is hard at study ; pray now, rest yourself ;
He's safe for these three hours.

Fer.　　　　　　　　O most dear mistress,
The sun will set before I shall discharge
What I must strive to do.

Mir.　　　　　　　　If you'll sit down,
I'll bear your logs the while : pray, give me that ;
I'll carry it to the pile.

Fer.　　　　　　　　No, precious creature ;
I had rather crack my sinews, break my back,
Than you should such dishonour undergo,
While I sit lazy by.

Mir.　　　　　　It would become me
As well as it does you : and I should do it
With much more ease ; for my good will is to it,
And yours it is against.

Pros.　　　　　　Poor worm, thou art infected !
This visitation shows it.

Mir.　　　　　You look wearily.

660

Fer. No, noble mistress ; 'tis fresh morning with me
When you are by at night. I do beseech you—
Chiefly that I might set it in my prayers—
What is your name ?
   Mir.   Miranda.—O my father,
I have broke your hest to say so !
   Fer.   Admired Miranda !
Indeed the top of admiration ! worth
What's dearest to the world ! Full many a lady
I have eyed with best regard and many a time
The harmony of their tongues hath into bondage
Brought my too diligent ear : for several virtues
Have I liked several women ; never any
With so full soul, but some defect in her
Did quarrel with the noblest grace she owed
And put it to the foil : but you, O you,
So perfect and so peerless, are created
Of every creature's best !
   Mir.   I do not know
One of my sex ; no woman's face remember,
Save, from my glass, mine own ; nor have I seen
More that I may call men than you, good friend,
And my dear father : how features are abroad,
I am skilless of ; but, by my modesty,
The jewel in my dower, I would not wish
Any companion in the world but you,
Nor can imagination form a shape,
Besides yourself, to like of. But I prattle
Something too wildly and my father's precepts
I therein do forget.
   Fer.   I am in my condition
A prince, Miranda ; I do think, a king ;
I would, not so !—and would no more endure
This wooden slavery than to suffer
The flesh-fly blow my mouth. Hear my soul speak :
The very instant that I saw you, did

My heart fly to your service ; there resides,
To make me slave to it ; and for your sake
Am I this patient log-man.

    Mir.   Do you love me ?

    Fer. O heaven, O earth, bear witness to this sound
And crown what I profess with kind event
If I speak true ! if hollowly, invert
What best is boded me to mischief ! I
Beyond all limit of what else i' the world
Do love, prize, honour you.

    Mir.   I am a fool
To weep at what I am glad of.

    Pros.   Fair encounter
Of two most rare affections ! Heavens rain grace
On that which breeds between 'em !

    Fer.   Wherefore weep you ?

    Mir. At mine unworthiness that dare not offer
What I desire to give, and much less take
What I shall die to want. But this is trifling ;
And all the more it seeks to hide itself,
The bigger bulk it shows. Hence, bashful cunning !
And prompt me, plain and holy innocence !
I am your wife, if you will marry me ;
If not, I'll die your maid : to be your fellow
You may deny me ; but I'll be your servant,
Whether you will or no.

    Fer.   My mistress, dearest ;
And I thus humble ever.

    Mir.   My husband, then ?

    Fer. Ay, with a heart as willing
As bondage e'er of freedom : here's my hand.

    Mir. And mine, with my heart in't : and now farewell
Till half an hour hence.

    Fer.   A thousand thousand !

                    [Exeunt Fer. and Mir. severally

    Pros. So glad of this as they I cannot be,

Who are surprised withal; but my rejoicing
At nothing can be more.

Act III, Scene i, ll. 15-94

Another part of the island.

Enter CALIBAN, STEPHANO, and TRINCULO.

Ste. Tell not me; when the butt is out, we will drink water; not a drop before: therefore bear up, and board 'em. Servant-monster, drink to me.

Trin. Servant-monster! the folly of this island! They say there's but five upon this isle: we are three of them; if th' other two be brained like us, the state totters.

Ste. Drink, servant-monster, when I bid thee: thy eyes are almost set in thy head.

Trin. Where should they be set else? he were a brave monster indeed, if they were set in his tail.

Ste. My man-monster hath drown'd his tongue in sack: for my part, the sea cannot drown me; I swam, ere I could recover the shore, five and thirty leagues off and on. By this light, thou shalt be my lieutenant, monster, or my standard.

Trin. Your lieutenant, if you list; he's no standard.

Ste. We'll not run, Monsieur Monster.

Trin. Nor go neither; but you'll lie like dogs and yet say nothing neither.

Ste. Moon-calf, speak once in thy life, if thou beest a good moon-calf.

Cal. How does thy honour? Let me lick thy shoe. I'll not serve him; he is not valiant.

Trin. Thou liest, most ignorant monster: I am in case to justle a constable. Why, thou deboshed fish, thou, was there ever man a coward that hath drunk so much sack as I to-day? Wilt thou tell a monstrous lie, being but half a fish and half a monster?

Cal. Lo, how he mocks me! wilt thou let him, my lord?

Trin. 'Lord' quoth he! That a monster should be such a natural!

Cal. Lo, lo, again! bite him to death, I prithee.

663

z

Ste. Trinculo, keep a good tongue in your head: if you prove a mutineer,—the next tree! The poor monster's my subject and he shall not suffer indignity.

Cal. I thank my noble lord. Wilt thou be pleased to hearken once again to the suit I made to thee?

Ste. Marry, will I: kneel and repeat it; I will stand, and so shall Trinculo.

Enter ARIEL, *invisible.*

Cal. As I told thee before, I am subject to a tyrant, a sorcerer, that by his cunning hath cheated me of the island.

Ari. Thou liest.

Cal. Thou liest, thou jesting monkey, thou: I would my valiant master would destroy thee! I do not lie.

Ste. Trinculo, if you trouble him any more in's tale, by this hand, I will supplant some of your teeth.

Trin. Why, I said nothing.

Ste. Mum, then, and no more. Proceed.

Cal. I say, by sorcery he got this isle;
From me he got it. If thy greatness will
Revenge it on him,—for I know thou darest,
But this thing dare not,—

Ste. That's most certain.

Cal. Thou shalt be lord of it and I'll serve thee.

Ste. How now shall this be compassed? Canst thou bring me to the party?

Cal. Yea, yea, my lord: I'll yield him thee asleep,
Where thou mayst knock a nail into his head.

Ari. Thou liest; thou canst not.

Cal. What a pied ninny's this! Thou scurvy patch!
I do beseech thy greatness, give him blows
And take his bottle from him: when that's gone
He shall drink nought but brine; for I'll not show him
Where the quick freshes are.

Ste. Trinculo, run into no further danger: interrupt the monster one word further, and, by this hand, I'll turn my mercy out o' doors and make a stock-fish of thee.

Trin. Why, what did I ? I did nothing. I'll go farther off.

Ste. Didst thou not say he lied ?

Ari. Thou liest.

Ste. Do I so ? take thou that. [*Beats Trin.*] As you like this, give me the lie another time.

Trin. I did not give the lie. Out o' your wits and hearing too ? A pox o' your bottle ! this can sack and drinking do. A murrain on your monster, and the devil take your fingers !

Cal. Ha, ha, ha !

Ste. Now, forward with your tale. Prithee, stand farther off.

Cal. Beat him enough : after a little time
I'll beat him too.

Ste.   Stand farther. Come, proceed.

Cal. Why, as I told thee, 'tis a custom with him,
I' the' afternoon to sleep : there thou mayst brain him,
Having first seized his books, or with a log
Batter his skull, or paunch him with a stake,
Or cut his wezand with thy knife. . . .

Thou makest me merry ; I am full of pleasure :
Let us be jocund : will you troll the catch
You taught me but while-ere ?

Ste. At thy request, monster, I will do reason, any reason.
Come on, Trinculo, let us sing.   [*Sings.*

> Flout 'em and scout 'em
> And scout 'em and flout 'em ;
> Thought is free.

Cal. That's not the tune.

                [*Ariel plays the tune on a tabor and pipe.*

Ste. What is this same ?

Trin. This is the tune of our catch, played by the picture of Nobody.

Ste. If thou beest a man, show thyself in thy likeness : if thou beest a devil, take't as thou list.

Trin. O, forgive me my sins !

Ste. He that dies pays all debts : I defy thee. Mercy upon us !

Cal. Art thou afeard ?

Ste. No, monster, not I.

Cal. Be not afeard ; the isle is full of noises,
Sounds and sweet airs, that give delight and hurt not.
Sometimes a thousand twangling instruments
Will hum about mine ears, and sometimes voices
That, if I then had waked after long sleep,
Will make me sleep again : and then, in dreaming,
The clouds methought would open and show riches
Ready to drop upon me, that, when I waked,
I cried to dream again.

 Ste. This will prove a brave kingdom to me, where I shall
have my music for nothing.

 Cal. When Prospero is destroyed.

 Ste. That shall be by and by : I remember the story.

 Trin. The sound is going away ; let's follow it, and after
do our work.

 Ste. Lead, monster ; we'll follow. I would I could see
this taborer ; he lays it on.

 Trin. Wilt come ? I'll follow, Stephano.

ACT III, Scene ii, ll. 1-99, 125-161

The never-surfeited sea.

ACT III, Scene iii, l. 55

Nothing but heart-sorrow

And a clear life ensuing.

ACT III, Scene iii, ll. 81-82

O, it is monstrous, monstrous !

Methought the billows spoke and told me of it ;
The winds did sing it to me, and the thunder,
That deep and dreadful organ-pipe, pronounced
The name of Prosper : it did bass my trespass.
Therefore my son i' the ooze is bedded, and
I'll seek him deeper than e'er plummet sounded
And with him there lie mudded.

ACT III, Scene iii, ll. 95-102

As I hope

For quiet days, fair issue and long life.

ACT IV, Scene i, ll. 23-24

Ariel. Before you can say ' come ' and ' go,'
  And breathe twice and cry ' so, so,'
  Each one, tripping on his toe,
  Will be here with mop and mow.
  Do you love me, master ? nó ?
Prospero. Dearly, my delicate Ariel.

ACT IV, Scene i, ll. 44-49

Iris. Ceres, most bounteous lady, thy rich leas
Of wheat, rye, barley, vetches, oats and pease ;
Thy turfy mountains, where live nibbling sheep,
And flat meads thatch'd with stover, them to keep ;
Thy banks with pioned and twilled brims,
Which spongy April at thy hest betrims,
To make cold nymphs chaste crowns ; and thy broom-
    groves,
Whose shadow the dismissed bachelor loves,
Being lass-lorn ; thy pole-clipt vineyard ;
And thy sea-marge, sterile and rocky-hard,
Where thou thyself dost air ;—the queen o' the sky,
Whose watery arch and messenger am I,
Bids thee leave these, and with her sovereign grace,
Here on this grass-plot, in this very place,
To come and sport : her peacocks fly amain :
Approach, rich Ceres, her to entertain.

Enter CERES.

Cer. Hail, many-colour'd messenger, that ne'er
Dost disobey the wife of Jupiter ;
Who with thy saffron wings upon my flowers
Diffusest honey-drops, refreshing showers,
And with each end of thy blue bow dost crown
My bosky acres and my unshrubb'd down,

667

Rich scarf to my proud earth ; why hath thy queen
Summon'd me hither, to this short-grass'd green ?

ACT IV, Scene i, ll. 60-83

Iris. You sunburnt sicklemen, of August weary,
Come hither from the furrow and be merry :
Make holiday ; your rye-straw hats put on
And these fresh nymphs encounter every one
In country footing. . . .

*Enter certain Reapers, properly habited : they join with the
Nymphs in a graceful dance ; towards the end whereof
PROSPERO starts suddenly, and speaks ; after which,
to a strange, hollow, and confused noise, they heavily
vanish. . . .*

Pros. You do look, my son, in a moved sort,
As if you were dismay'd : be cheerful, sir.
Our revels now are ended. These our actors,
As I foretold you, were all spirits and
Are melted into air, into thin air :
And, like the baseless fabric of this vision,
The cloud-capp'd towers, the gorgeous palaces,
The solemn temples, the great globe itself,
Yea, all which it inherit, shall dissolve
And, like this insubstantial pageant faded,
Leave not a rack behind. We are such stuff
As dreams are made on, and our little life
Is rounded with a sleep. Sir, I am vex'd ;
Bear with my weakness ; my old brain is troubled :
Be not disturb'd with my infirmity :
If you be pleased, retire into my cell
And there repose : a turn or two I'll walk,
To still my beating mind.
    Ferdinand. Miranda.   We wish your peace.

ACT IV, Scene i, ll. 134-138, 146-163

Pray you, tread softly, that the blind mole may not
Hear a foot fall.

ACT IV, Scene i, ll. 194-195

Before PROSPERO'S *cell.*

Enter PROSPERO *in his magic robes, and* ARIEL.

Pros. Now does my project gather to a head :
My charms crack not ; my spirits obey ; and time
Goes upright with his carriage. How's the day ?

Ari. On the sixth hour ; at which time, my lord,
You said our work should cease.

Pros.   I did say so,
When first I raised the tempest. Say, my spirit,
How fares the king and's followers ?

Ari.   Confined together
In the same fashion as you gave in charge,
Just as you left them ; all prisoners, sir,
In the line-grove which weather-fends your cell ;
They cannot budge till your release. The king,
His brother and yours, abide all three distracted
And the remainder mourning over them,
Brimful of sorrow and dismay ; but chiefly
Him that you term'd, sir, ' The good old lord, Gonzalo ; '
His tears run down his beard, like winter's drops
From eaves of reeds. Your charm so strongly works 'em
That if you now beheld them, your affections
Would become tender.

Pros.   Dost thou think so, spirit ?

Ari. Mine would, sir, were I human.

Pros.   And mine shall.
Hast thou, which art but air, a touch, a feeling
Of their afflictions, and shall not myself,
One of their kind, that relish all as sharply,
Passion as they, be kindlier moved than thou art ?
Though with their high wrongs I am struck to the quick,
Yet with my nobler reason 'gainst my fury
Do I take part : the rarer action is
In virtue than in vengeance : they being penitent,
The sole drift of my purpose doth extend

669

Not a frown further. Go release them, Ariel :
My charms I'll break, their senses I'll restore,
And they shall be themselves.

    Ari.   I'll fetch them, sir.   [*Exit*

    Pros. Ye elves of hills, brooks, standing lakes and groves,
And ye that on the sands with printless foot
Do chase the ebbing Neptune and do fly him
When he comes back ; you demi-puppets that
By moonshine do the green sour ringlets make,
Whereof the ewe not bites, and you whose pastime
Is to make midnight mushrooms, that rejoice
To hear the solemn curfew ; by whose aid,
Weak masters though ye be, I have bedimm'd
The noontide sun, call'd forth the mutinous winds,
And 'twixt the green sea and the azured vault
Set roaring war : to the dread rattling thunder
Have I given fire and rifted Jove's stout oak
With his own bolt ; the strong-based promontory
Have I made shake and by the spurs pluck'd up
The pine and cedar : graves at my command
Have waked their sleepers, oped, and let 'em forth
By my so potent art. But this rough magic
I here abjure, and, when I have required
Some heavenly music, which even now I do,
To work mine end upon their senses that
This airy charm is for, I'll break my staff,
Bury it certain fathoms in the earth,
And deeper than did ever plummet sound
I'll drown my book.   [*Solemn music.*

      Re-enter ARIEL *before : then* ALONSO, *with a frantic
      gesture, attended by* GONZALO ; SEBASTIAN *and*
      ANTONIO *in like manner, attended by* ADRIAN *and*
      FRANCISCO : *they all enter the circle which* PROSPERO
      had made, and there stand charmed ; which PROSPERO
      observing, speaks :

A solemn air and the best comforter
To an unsettled fancy cure thy brains,
Now useless, boil'd within thy skull! There stand,
For you are spell-stopp'd.
Holy Gonzalo, honourable man,
Mine eyes, even sociable to the show of thine,
Fall fellowly drops. The charm dissolves apace,
And as the morning steals upon the night,
Melting the darkness, so their rising senses
Begin to chase the ignorant fumes that mantle
Their clearer reason. . . .
                                   Their understanding
Begins to swell, and the approaching tide
Will shortly fill the reasonable shore
That now lies foul and muddy. Not one of them
That yet looks on me, or would know me: Ariel,
Fetch me the hat and rapier in my cell:
I will discase me, and myself present
As I was sometime Milan: quickly, spirit;
Thou shalt ere long be free.

> ARIEL *sings and helps to attire him.*
>
> Where the bee sucks, there suck I:
> In a cowslip's bell I lie;
> There I couch when owls do cry.
> On the bat's back I do fly
> After summer merrily.
> Merrily, merrily shall I live now
> Under the blossom that hangs on the bough.

Pros. Why, that's my dainty Ariel! I shall miss thee;
But yet thou shalt have freedom: so, so, so. . . .
Ari. I drink the air before me, and return.

ACT V, Scene i, ll. 1-68, 79-96, 102

Miranda.   O, wonder!
How many goodly creatures are there here!

How beauteous mankind is ! O brave new world,
That has such people in't !.

    Prospero.   'Tis new to thee.

                        ACT V, Scene i, ll. 181-184

    Prospero   I'll deliver all ;
And promise you calm seas, auspicious gales
And sail so expeditious that shall catch
Your royal fleet far off. [*Aside to Ari.*] My Ariel, chick,
That is thy charge : then to the elements
Be free, and fare thou well !

                        ACT V, Scene i, ll. 313-318

POEMS

SONNETS
THE PHOENIX AND THE TURTLE

Sonnets

From fairest creatures we desire increase,
That thereby beauty's rose might never die.

I, ll. 1-2

Thou art thy mother's glass, and she in thee
Calls back the lovely April of her prime.

III, ll. 9-10

For never-resting time leads summer on
To hideous winter and confounds him there ;
Sap check'd with frost and lusty leaves quite gone,
Beauty o'ersnow'd and bareness every where :
Then, were not summer's distillation left,
A liquid prisoner pent in walls of glass,
Beauty's effect with beauty were bereft.

V, ll. 5-11

Yet mortal looks adore his beauty still,
Attending on his golden pilgrimage.

VII, ll. 7-8

Music to hear, why hear'st thou music sadly ?

VIII, l. 1

When lofty trees I see barren of leaves
Which erst from heat did canopy the herd,
And summer's green all girded up in sheaves
Borne on the bier with white and bristly beard,
Then of thy beauty do I question make,
That thou among the wastes of time must go.

XII, ll. 5-10

Against the stormy gusts of winter's day
And barren rage of death's eternal cold ?

XIII, ll. 11-12

675

Not from the stars do I my judgement pluck ;
And yet methinks I have astronomy.   XIV, ll. 1-2

When I consider every thing that grows
Holds in perfection but a little moment,
That this huge stage presenteth nought but shows
Whereon the stars in secret influence comment ;
When I perceive that men as plants increase,
Cheered and check'd even by the self-same sky,
Vaunt in their youthful sap, at height decrease,
And wear their brave state out of memory ;
Then the conceit of this inconstant stay
Sets you most rich in youth before my sight,
Where wasteful Time debateth with Decay,
To change your day of youth to sullied night ;
    And all in war with Time for love of you,
    As he takes from you, I engraft you new.   XV

Now stand you on the top of happy hours,
And many maiden gardens yet unset
With virtuous wish would bear your living flowers.
                        XVI, ll. 5-7

If I could write the beauty of your eyes
And in fresh numbers number all your graces,
The age to come would say ' This poet lies ;
Such heavenly touches ne'er touch'd earthly faces.
So should my papers yellow'd with their age
Be scorn'd like old men of less truth than tongue,
And your true rights be term'd a poet's rage
And stretched metre of an antique song.   XVII, ll. 5-12

Shall I compare thee to a summer's day ?
Thou art more lovely and more temperate :
Rough winds do shake the darling buds of May,
And summer's lease hath all too short a date :
Sometime too hot the eye of heaven shines,
And often is his gold complexion dimm'd ;

And every fair from fair sometime declines,
By chance or nature's changing course untrimm'd ;
But thy eternal summer shall not fade
Nor lose possession of that fair thou owest ;
Nor shall Death brag thou wander'st in his shade,
When in eternal lines to time thou growest :
   So long as men can breathe or eyes can see,
   So long lives this and this gives life to thee.

XVIII

Devouring Time, blunt thou the lion's paws . . .
And burn the long-lived phoenix in her blood ;
Make glad and sorry seasons as thou fleets,
And do whate'er thou wilt, swift-footed Time,
To the wide world and all her fading sweets ;
But I forbid thee one most heinous crime :
O, carve not with thy hours my love's fair brow,
Nor draw no lines there with thine antique pen.

XIX, ll. 1, 4-10

So is it not with me as with that Muse
Stirr'd by a painted beauty to his verse,
Who heaven itself for ornament doth use
And every fair with his fair doth rehearse ;
Making a couplement of proud compare,
With sun and moon, with earth and sea's rich gems,
With April's first-born flowers, and all things rare
That heaven's air in this huge rondure hems.
O, let me, true in love, but truly write,
And then believe me, my love is as fair
As any mother's child, though not so bright
As those gold candles fix'd in heaven's air.

XXI, ll. 1-12

As an unperfect actor on the stage
Who with his fear is put besides his part,
Or some fierce thing replete with too much rage,
Whose strength's abundance weakens his own heart,

677

So I, for fear of trust, forget to say
The perfect ceremony of love's rite.   XXIII, ll. 1-6

Great princes' favourites their fair leaves spread
But as the marigold at the sun's eye,
And in themselves their pride lies buried,
For at a frown they in their glory die.
The painful warrior famoused for fight,
After a thousand victories once foil'd,
Is from the book of honour razed quite,
And all the rest forgot for which he toil'd.

                                          XXV, ll. 5-12

Lord of my love, to whom in vassalage
Thy merit hath my duty strongly knit,
To thee I send this written embassage,
To witness duty, not to show my wit:
Duty so great, which wit so poor as mine
May make seem bare, in wanting words to show it . . .
Till whatsoever star that guides my moving
Points on me graciously with fair aspect
And puts apparel on my tatter'd loving,
To show me worthy of thy sweet respect.

                                    XXVI, ll. 1-6, 9-12

Weary with toil, I haste me to my bed,
The dear repose for limbs with travel tired;
But then begins a journey in my head,
To work my mind, when body's work's expired:
For then my thoughts, from far where I abide,
Intend a zealous pilgrimage to thee,
And keep my drooping eyelids open wide,
Looking on darkness which the blind do see:
Save that my soul's imaginary sight
Presents thy shadow to my sightless view,
Which, like a jewel hung in ghastly night,
Makes black night beauteous and her old face new.

                                         XXVII, ll. 1-12

When, in disgrace with fortune and men's eyes,
I all alone beweep my outcast state
And trouble deaf heaven with my bootless cries
And look upon myself and curse my fate,
Wishing me like to one more rich in hope,
Featured like him, like him with friends possess'd,
Desiring this man's art and that man's scope,
With what I most enjoy contented least;
Yet in these thoughts myself almost despising,
Haply I think on thee, and then my state,
Like to the lark at break of day arising
From sullen earth, sings hymns at heaven's gate;
    For thy sweet love remember'd such wealth brings
    That then I scorn to change my state with kings.

XXIX

When to the sessions of sweet silent thought
I summon up remembrance of things past,
I sigh the lack of many a thing I sought,
And with old woes new wail my dear time's waste:
Then can I drown an eye, unused to flow,
For precious friends hid in death's dateless night,
And weep afresh love's long since cancell'd woe,
And moan the expense of many a vanish'd sight:
Then can I grieve at grievances foregone,
And heavily from woe to woe tell o'er
The sad account of fore-bemoaned moan,
Which I new pay as if not paid before.
    But if the while I think on thee, dear friend,
    All losses are restored and sorrows end.

XXX

Thy bosom is endeared with all hearts,
Which I by lacking have supposed dead,
And there reigns love and all love's loving parts,
And all those friends which I thought buried.
How many a holy and obsequious tear
Hath dear religious love stol'n from mine eye

As interest of the dead, which now appear
But things removed that hidden in thee lie !
Thou art the grave where buried love doth live,
Hung with the trophies of my lovers gone,
Who all their parts of me to thee did give ;
That due of many now is thine alone :
    Their images I loved I view in thee,
    And thou, all they, hast all the all of me.

XXXI

If thou survive my well-contented day,
When that churl Death my bones with dust shall cover,
And shalt by fortune once more re-survey
These poor rude lines of thy deceased lover,
Compare them with the bettering of the time,
And though they be outstripp'd by every pen,
Reserve them for my love, not for their rhyme,
Exceeded by the height of happier men.
O, then vouchsafe me but this loving thought :
' Had my friend's Muse grown with this growing age,
A dearer birth than this his love had brought,
To march in ranks of better equipage :
    But since he died and poets better prove,
    Theirs for their style I'll read, his for his love.'

XXXII

Full many a glorious morning have I seen
Flatter the mountain-tops with sovereign eye,
Kissing with golden face the meadows green,
Gilding pale streams with heavenly alchemy ;
Anon permit the basest clouds to ride
With ugly rack on his celestial face,
And from the forlorn world his visage hide,
Stealing unseen to west with this disgrace :
Even so my sun one early morn did shine
With all-triumphant splendour on my brow ;
But out, alack ! he was but one hour mine ;
The region cloud hath mask'd him from me now.

Yet him for this my love no whit disdaineth;
Suns of the world may stain when heaven's sun staineth.
XXXIII

'Tis not enough that through the cloud thou break,
To dry the rain on my storm-beaten face.
XXXIV, ll. 5-6

Take all my loves, my love, yea, take them all;
What hast thou then more than thou hadst before? . . .
I do forgive thy robbery, gentle thief,
Although thou steal thee all my poverty.
XL, ll. 1-2, 9-10

So am I as the rich, whose blessed key
Can bring him to his sweet up-locked treasure,
The which he will not every hour survey,
For blunting the fine point of seldom pleasure.
Therefore are feasts so solemn and so rare,
Since, seldom coming, in the long year set,
Like stones of worth they thinly placed are,
Or captain jewels in the carcanet.
So is the time that keeps you as my chest,
Or as the wardrobe which the robe doth hide,
To make some special instant special blest,
By new unfolding his imprison'd pride.
LII, ll. 1-12

What is your substance, whereof are you made,
That millions of strange shadows on you tend?
LIII, ll. 1-2

The canker-blooms have full as deep a dye
As the perfumed tincture of the roses,
Hang on such thorns and play as wantonly
When summer's breath their masked buds discloses:
But, for their virtue only is their show,
They live unwoo'd and unrespected fade,
Die to themselves. Sweet roses do not so;
Of their sweet deaths are sweetest odours made:

And so of you, beauteous and lovely youth,
When that shall fade, my verse distills your truth.

LIV, ll. 5-14

Not marble, nor the gilded monuments
Of princes, shall outlive this powerful rhyme ; . . .
'Gainst death and all-oblivious enmity
Shall you pace forth.

LV, ll. 1-2, 9-10

Being your slave, what should I do but tend
Upon the hours and times of your desire ?
I have no precious time at all to spend,
Nor services to do, till you require.
Nor dare I chide the world-without-end hour
Whilst I, my sovereign, watch the clock for you.

LVII, ll. 1-6

Like as the waves make towards the pebbled shore,
So do our minutes hasten to their end ;
Each changing place with that which goes before,
In sequent toil all forwards do contend.
Nativity, once in the main of light,
Crawls to maturity, wherewith being crown'd,
Crooked eclipses 'gainst his glory fight,
And Time that gave doth now his gift confound.
Time doth transfix the flourish set on youth
And delves the parallels in beauty's brow,
Feeds on the rarities of nature's truth,
And nothing stands but for his scythe to mow :
    And yet to times in hope my verse shall stand,
    Praising thy worth, despite his cruel hand.

LX

Is it thy will thy image should keep open
My heavy eyelids to the weary night ?
Dost thou desire my slumbers should be broken,
While shadows like to thee do mock my sight ?

LXI, ll. 1-4

When I have seen by Time's fell hand defaced
The rich proud cost of outworn buried age;
When sometimes lofty towers I see down-razed
And brass eternal slave to mortal rage;
When I have seen the hungry ocean gain
Advantage on the kingdom of the shore. . . .

LXIV, ll. 1-6

Since brass, nor stone, nor earth, nor boundless sea,
But sad mortality o'er-sways their power,
How with this rage shall beauty hold a plea,
Whose action is no stronger than a flower?
O, how shall summer's honey breath hold out
Against the wreckful siege of battering days,
When rocks impregnable are not so stout,
Nor gates of steel so strong, but Time decays?
O fearful meditation! where, alack,
Shall Time's best jewel from Time's chest lie hid?
Or what strong hand can hold his swift foot back?
Or who his spoil of beauty can forbid?
 O, none, unless this miracle have might,
 That in black ink my love may still shine bright.

LXV

The golden tresses of the dead.

LXVIII, l. 5

No longer mourn for me when I am dead
Than you shall hear the surly sullen bell
Give warning to the world that I am fled
From this vile world, with vilest worms to dwell:
Nay, if you read this line, remember not
The hand that writ it; for I love you so
That I in your sweet thoughts would be forgot
If thinking on me then should make you woe.
O, if, I say, you look upon this verse
When I perhaps compounded am with clay,
Do not so much as my poor name rehearse,
But let your love even with my life decay,

683

Lest the wise world should look into your moan
And mock you with me after I am gone. LXXI

That time of year thou mayst in me behold
When yellow leaves, or none, or few, do hang
Upon those boughs which shake against the cold,
Bare ruin'd choirs, where late the sweet birds sang.
In me thou see'st the twilight of such day
As after sunset fadeth in the west,
Which by and by black night doth take away,
Death's second self, that seals up all in rest.
In me thou see'st the glowing of such fire
That on the ashes of his youth doth lie,
As the death-bed whereon it must expire
Consumed with that which it was nourish'd by.
  This thou perceivest, which makes thy love more strong,
  To love that well which thou must leave ere long.

LXXIII

So are you to my thoughts as food to life,
Or as sweet-season'd showers are to the ground.

LXXV, ll. 1-2

And precious phrase by all the Muses filed.

LXXXV, l. 4

Was it the proud full sail of his great verse.

LXXXVI, l. 1

That affable familiar ghost
Which nightly gulls him with intelligence.

LXXXVI, ll. 9-10

Farewell ! thou art too dear for my possessing.

LXXXVII, l. 1

Then hate me when thou wilt ; if ever, now ;
Now, while the world is bent my deeds to cross,
Join with the spite of fortune, make me bow,
And do not drop in for an after-loss :

Ah, do not, when my heart hath 'scaped this sorrow,
Come in the rearward of a conquer'd woe ;
Give not a windy night a rainy morrow,
To linger out a purposed overthrow.
If thou wilt leave me, do not leave me last,
When other petty griefs have done their spite,
But in the onset come ; so shall I taste
At first the very worst of fortune's might,
   And other strains of woe, which now seem woe,
   Compared with loss of thee will not seem so.   XC

The summer's flower is to the summer sweet,
Though to itself it only live and die.
                    XCIV, ll. 9-10

How like a winter hath my absence been
From thee, the pleasure of the fleeting year !
What freezings have I felt, what dark days seen !
What old December's bareness every where !
And yet this time removed was summer's time,
The teeming autumn, big with rich increase,
Bearing the wanton burden of the prime,
Like widow'd wombs after their lords' decease :
Yet this abundant issue seem'd to me
But hope of orphans and unfather'd fruit ;
For summer and his pleasures wait on thee,
And, thou away, the very birds are mute ;
   Or, if they sing, 'tis with so dull a cheer
   That leaves look pale, dreading the winter's near.
                    XCVII

From you have I been absent in the spring,
When proud-pied April dress'd in all his trim
Hath put a spirit of youth in every thing,
That heavy Saturn laugh'd and leap'd with him.
Yet nor the lays of birds nor the sweet smell
Of different flowers in odour and in hue
Could make me any summer's story tell,
Or from their proud lap pluck them where they grew ;

Nor did I wonder at the lily's white,
Nor praise the deep vermilion in the rose ;
They were but sweet, but figures of delight,
Drawn after you, you pattern of all those.
    Yet seem'd it winter still, and, you away,
    As with your shadow I with these did play.   XCVIII

The forward violet thus did I chide :
Sweet thief, whence didst thou steal thy sweet ? . . .
The lily I condemned for thy hand,
And buds of marjoram had stol'n thy hair :
The roses fearfully on thorns did stand,
One blushing shame, another white despair.
                          XCIX, ll. 1-2, 6-9

Our love was new and then but in the spring
When I was wont to greet it with my lays,
As Philomel in summer's front doth sing
And stops her pipe in growth of riper days :
Not that the summer is less pleasant now
Than when her mournful hymns did hush the night,
But that wild music burthens every bough
And sweets grown common lose their dear delight.
    Therefore like her I sometime hold my tongue,
    Because I would not dull you with my song.
                          CII, ll. 5-14

To me, fair friend, you never can be old,
For as you were when first your eye I eyed,
Such seems your beauty still. Three winters cold
Have from the forests shook three summers' pride,
Three beauteous springs to yellow autumn turn'd
In process of the seasons have I seen,
Three April perfumes in three hot Junes burn'd,
Since first I saw you fresh, which yet are green.
Ah ! yet doth beauty, like a dial-hand,
Steal from his figure and no pace perceived ;
So your sweet hue, which methinks still doth stand,
Hath motion and mine eye may be deceived :

For fear of which, hear this, thou age unbred ;
Ere you were born was beauty's summer dead.   CIV

When in the chronicle of wasted time
I see descriptions of the fairest wights,
And beauty making beautiful old rhyme
In praise of ladies dead and lovely knights,
Then, in the blazon of sweet beauty's best,
Of hand, of foot, of lip, of eye, of brow,
I see their antique pen would have express'd
Even such a beauty as you master now.
                         CVI, ll. 1-8

Not mine own fears, nor the prophetic soul
Of the wide world dreaming on things to come,
Can yet the lease of my true love control,
Supposed as forfeit to a confined doom.
The mortal moon hath her eclipse endured
And the sad augurs mock their own presage ;
Incertainties now crown themselves assured
And peace proclaims olives of endless age.
Now with the drops of this most balmy time
My love looks fresh, and Death to me subscribes,
Since, spite of him, I'll live in this poor rhyme,
While he insults o'er dull and speechless tribes :
   And thou in this shalt find thy monument,
   When tyrants' crests and tombs of brass are spent.
                         CVII

O, never say that I was false of heart.
                         CIX, l. 1

Most true it is that I have look'd on truth
Askance and strangely.
                         CX, ll. 5-6

Let me not to the marriage of true minds
Admit impediments. Love is not love
Which alters when it alteration finds,
Or bends with the remover to remove :

O, no! it is an ever-fixed mark
That looks on tempests and is never shaken;
It is the star to every wandering bark,
Whose worth's unknown, although his height be taken.
Love's not Time's fool, though rosy lips and cheeks
Within his bending sickle's compass come;
Love alters not with his brief hours and weeks,
But bears it out even to the edge of doom.
 If this be error and upon me proved,
 I never writ, nor no man ever loved. CXVI

What potions have I drunk of Siren tears,
Distill'd from limbecks foul as hell within.
           CXIX, ll. 1-2

No, it was builded far from accident.
           CXXIV, l. 5

O thou, my lovely boy, who in thy power
Dost hold Time's fickle glass, his sickle, hour.
           CXXVI, ll. 1-2

How oft, when thou, my music, music play'st.
           CXXVIII, l. 1

The expense of spirit in a waste of shame
Is lust in action; and till action, lust
Is perjured, murderous, bloody, full of blame,
Savage, extreme, rude, cruel, not to trust,
Enjoy'd no sooner but despised straight,
Past reason hunted, and no sooner had
Past reason hated, as a swallow'd bait
On purpose laid to make the taker mad;
Mad in pursuit and in possession so;
Had, having, and in quest to have, extreme;
A bliss in proof, and proved, a very woe;
Before, a joy proposed; behind, a dream.
 All this the world well knows; yet none knows well
 To shun the heaven that leads men to this hell. CXXIX

Nor that full star that ushers in the even.

CXXXII, l. 7

Tell me thou lovest elsewhere, but in my sight,
Dear heart, forbear to glance thine eye aside.

CXXXIX, ll. 5-6

Poor soul, the centre of my sinful earth,
Fool'd by these rebel powers that thee array,
Why dost thou pine within and suffer dearth,
Painting thy outward walls so costly gay?
Why so large cost, having so short a lease,
Dost thou upon thy fading mansion spend?
Shall worms, inheritors of this excess,
Eat up thy charge? is this thy body's end?
Then, soul, live thou upon thy servant's loss,
And let that pine to aggravate thy store;
Buy terms divine in selling hours of dross;
Within be fed, without be rich no more:
　So shalt thou feed on Death, that feeds on men,
　And Death once dead, there's no more dying then.

CXLVI

　　　O, how can Love's eye be true,
That is so vex'd with watching and with tears?

CXLVIII, ll. 9-10

Love is too young to know what conscience is.

CLI, l. 1

The Phoenix and the Turtle

Let the bird of loudest lay,
On the sole Arabian tree,
Herald sad and trumpet be,
To whose sound chaste wings obey.

But thou shrieking harbinger,
Foul precurrer of the fiend,
Augur of the fever's end,
To this troop come thou not near!

From this session interdict
Every fowl of tyrant wing,
Save the eagle, feather'd king :
Keep the obsequy so strict.

Let the priest in surplice white,
That defunctive music can,
Be the death-divining swan,
Lest the requiem lack his right.

And thou treble-dated crow,
That thy sable gender makest
With the breath thou givest and takest,
'Mongst our mourners shalt thou go.

Here the anthem doth commence :
Love and constancy is dead ;
Phoenix and the turtle fled
In a mutual flame from hence.

So they loved, as love in twain
Had the essence but in one ;
Two distincts, division none :
Number there in love was slain.

Hearts remote, yet not asunder ;
Distance, and no space was seen
'Twixt the turtle and his queen :
But in them it were a wonder.

So between them love did shine,
That the turtle saw his right
Flaming in the phoenix' sight ;
Either was the other's mine.

Property was thus appall'd,
That the self was not the same ;
Single nature's double name
Neither two not one was call'd.

Reason, in itself confounded,
Saw division grow together,
To themselves yet either neither,
Simple were so well compounded,

That it cried, How true a twain
Seemeth this concordant one !
Love hath reason, reason none,
If what parts can so remain.

Whereupon it made this threne
To the phoenix and the dove,
Co-supremes and stars of love,
As chorus to their tragic scene.

THRENOS.

Beauty, truth, and rarity,
Grace in all simplicity,
Here enclosed in cinders lie.

Death is now the phoenix' nest ;
And the turtle's loyal breast
To eternity doth rest,

Leaving no posterity :
'Twas not their infirmity,
It was married chastity.

Truth may seem, but cannot be ;
Beauty brag, but 'tis not she ;
Truth and beauty buried be.

To this urn let those repair
That are either true or fair ;
For these dead birds sigh a prayer.

APPENDIX

APPENDIX

I. THE DAWN

In this first section I include that element of Shakespeare's work which shows the first glimmering of his genius. This element is but a scanty one ; Shakespeare, till the age of about thirty, was an imitative writer ; he was learning his art, serving as an apprentice to Kyd and Marlowe, to Lyly, Greene, and other fashionable poets of the time ; he wrote as they wrote, and it is not possible to distinguish his verse from theirs by any very definite criterion of style. What does distinguish him from his contemporaries is his extraordinary versatility, his ease and flexibility in adapting himself to the various forms and conventions which were popular at the moment. He wrote two long amorous elegiac poems ; he composed four chronicle histories for the theatre in which he acted, or rather (as most believe) touched up or collaborated in them ; he wrote one of the tragedies of blood and horror which were so popular at the date, and a fantastic comedy in the style of Lyly, a pseudo-classic comedy adapted from Plautus ; he re-vamped the old farce of *The Taming of the Shrew* ; and, in *The Two Gentlemen of Verona*, he experimented in that popular form of romantic comedy which he was later on to bring to such perfection. What is remarkable in the early and immense output of this greatest of poets, is not the poetry, but rather the absence of any poetic vision, any magic of phrasing personal to himself. These nine plays, and two long poems,—all written at a time of life when many poets have produced some of their finest and most enduring achievement,—are characteristic of the age he lived in rather than of himself ; if he had died in his youth, like Keats or Shelley, he would have been remembered only as one of that dim galaxy of Elizabethan poets, and from his work, as from theirs, the careful anthologist could have but sifted out a few scanty grains of gold.

In these two poems and nine plays there is plenty of good Elizabethan verse and fine rhetoric to be found ; but this is not the gold we seek for. Grains of that gold however there are to be sifted out, lines here and there of magic verse, three lovely songs, and three great passages of poetry which no one but Shakespeare could have written,—Henry VI's daydream of a shepherd's life, Clarence's terrible dream, and Biron's speech on love—though this is regarded by some as an addition made to the play at a later date.

Still more unmistakably Shakespearean are the comic scenes of low life to be found in some of these early plays, Cade's boastings, the homely talk of the murderers of Clarence, the deception of Sly in *The Taming of the Shrew*, Launce's speeches about his dog in *The Two Gentlemen of Verona*, and the appearance of those simple souls, Holofernes the schoolmaster and Sir Nathaniel the curate, in *Love's Labour's Lost*.

Venus and Adonis and *The Rape of Lucrece*

These two uninspired, unimpassioned, pitilessly prolix poems, though little more than poetic exercises on given subjects, and attempts to retell two of Ovid's stories, rather indecent and rather absurd, in the elegiac Ovidian style, are nevertheless the most painstaking productions of his early period.

The merits, such as they are, of these two poems are an inexhaustible flow of words, a skill and polish of conscientious phrase-making, and an accurate external observation of detail. Hazlitt well describes them as ' a couple of ice-houses '. The description of the horse in *Venus and Adonis* (ll. 294-306) and that of the hunted hare (ll. 679-708) have often been picked out for admiration ; they are, as Hazlitt said of the lines about the horse, ' good, matter-of-fact poetry '.

Venus and Adonis, though greatly admired by Shakespeare's contemporaries, was blamed by some of them for its ' wantonness ', which has not indeed escaped the censure of later critics, who have regarded the theme, that of an amorous woman thrusting her favours on an unwilling youth, as repulsive in another sense. Shakespeare, perhaps owing to such criticisms, took the celebration of female chastity as the subject of his next poem ; his *Rape of Lucrece* won the approval of ' the wiser sort ' as a beautiful exposition of this theme. In this ' graver labour ' the Spenserian lyricism is largely replaced by rhetoric, and although the theme is more dramatic, and indeed a tragical one, the curious absence of any dramatic power or dramatic

696

characterization is perhaps what strikes us most in this work of one who was to become the greatest of dramatists. Tarquin's debates and vacillations have, as the editor of the Arden edition says, ' neither the purpose nor the effect of showing him a weak man struggling against passion, or hesitating between good and evil '; while the lengthy, laborious, high-conceited rhetorical railings against Night, Time, and Opportunity, into which Lucrece pedantically bursts immediately after she has been forced, are still more remote from dramatic reality and life. Though graver in purpose, *Lucrece* is less poetical than *Venus and Adonis*, and there are only a few lines to be sifted from it.

The *Henry VI* Plays

Although Shakespeare described *Venus and Adonis* as ' the first heir of my invention ', there is plenty of evidence to show that before 1592, the period of its composition, when owing to the Plague the theatres were closed, Shakespeare had already performed a good deal of theatrical work, both as an actor, and as a writer of new plays,—or at least as a reviser and patcher-up of old ones. In the three *Henry VI* plays are to be found the first evidences of his poetic and dramatic powers ; but in these long rambling histories the powers are not much in evidence. The plays are imitative plays, and show above all the influence, if not the collaboration or the actual hand of Marlowe, and to discriminate and sift out with any certainty the Shakespearean element is a task which has baffled all the critics. The Talbot scenes (IV, ii, and IV, vi) in *1 Henry VI*, are regarded by most as being of Shakespeare's composition ; the death of Cardinal Beaufort in the second of this trilogy (V, iii) was described by Hazlitt as a masterpiece, and, as a powerful first sketch of those unrepentant deaths of wicked men, has been singled out as a picture of despair and damnation in which Shakespeare gives the first evidence of his dramatic power ; while in the third play of the trilogy, the lament of young Clifford (*3 Henry VI*, V, i) is regarded as a passage of Shakespearean blank verse so mature in quality as to seem almost certainly an addition made by Shakespeare for some later revival of the play.

For my purpose I find nothing in the first (though probably not the first written) of these plays ; the ' mournful crocodile ' in the second part beguiled me with crocodilian tears; the strangely euphuistic sea-captain who steps ashore in Kent uttering 'a precious phrase by all the muses fil'd', and then vanishes for ever; Jack Cade becomes alive in his boasts, and Smith the weaver in one phrase of derisive comment; and in the third part, the pastoral daydream in which poor Henry VI indulges while the battle rages is the first long passage of Shakespeare's lovely lyric verse. A few other prints of Shakespeare's footsteps, a few lines and phrases which seem too good for any other hand than his, make up my scanty gleanings from these almost unreadable early plays.

Richard III

This play was written, Sir Edmund Chambers believes, in the winter or spring of 1592-93. It follows closely after the *Henry VI* plays, and shows an intimate connection with them, but surpasses the prototype, as Quincey Adams says, 'by giving to the episodic chronicle something of artistic unity and tragic effectiveness through the dominating figure of Richard, whose rise and fall constitute the proper movement of the plot, and whose character forms the central interest. Its immediate success with the public was astounding.'

The style of the play reveals the profound influence of Marlowe; it is indeed a fine performance on the brass, and whether Shakespeare wrote it has been questioned by many critics. But Clarence's dream could not have been written by any one else, and there are other touches of Shakespeare's hand,—lovely phrases here and there, and the talk of the Murderers is in the true vein of Shakespearean comedies.

Titus Andronicus

Shakespeare's next play was probably the *Comedy of Errors*, which Sir Edmund Chambers dates 1593. It is one of the least Shakespearean of the plays attributed to Shakespeare, and we can pass it over save for one line—

And Lapland sorcerers inhabit here.

IV, iii, l. 11.

Titus Andronicus follows, probably in the next year 1593-94. Shakespeare's authorship of this most horrible of Elizabethan plays has been doubted or denied by many critics. It is a tragedy of blood of the conventional Elizabethan type, and has been ascribed by various scholars to Kyd, Marlowe, Greene, Peele, or Lodge. Others have suggested that Shakespeare wrote it first as a poem; there are certainly lyrical touches in the sonorous rant, one of the most curious of which is the curious speech of Titus who, after murdering his enemies and making a pastry to be eaten of their blood and bones, becomes almost lachrymose over a fly that has been killed.

The Taming of the Shrew

This play, written perhaps in the same year as the preceding, is, like the *Comedy of Errors*, a boisterous farce, and the attribution to Shakespeare is considered doubtful by some critics. The induction, however, and the deception of Christopher Sly, is a genuine bit of Shakespearean comedy which no one else could have written.

The Two Gentlemen of Verona

In this play, ascribed by Chambers to 1594-95, Shakespeare made his first attempt to write one of those romantic comedies of which he was afterwards to become so incomparable a master. The total effect, however, is unplausible and unsatisfactory, although there are touches of lyric poetry in it, and one of Shakespeare's loveliest songs. There are gleams in it too of real life and observation, and Launce, though he has almost nothing to do with the plot, is perhaps the first of those low-life characters of amazing vitality and individuality which now begin to appear on Shakespeare's stage.

Love's Labour's Lost

This play is ascribed by Sir Edmund Chambers to the same year as the preceding, though some regard it as being Shakespeare's earliest play. It was printed in 1598 as being ' newly corrected and augmented by W. Shakespeare ', being thus the earliest play published with Shakespeare's name on the title.

The play is a light comedy written in the manner, then fashionable, of Lyly's court comedies, with the purpose of both mocking and exemplifying the linguistic affectations of the day. The euphuisms and affected phrases of the courtiers and above all of Armado, the pedantries of the schoolmaster Holofernes, and his foil, Sir Nathaniel the curate, are still amusing; the rustic pageant of the Nine Worthies is a bit of realistic humour, and Costard, in one speech, endows the poor curate with comic immortality. But it is in the songs that Shakespeare's genius shines most brightly,—in the songs, and in Biron's great speech on love, which, however, many regard as a later interpolation.

ACKNOWLEDGMENTS

The publishers gratefully acknowledge the permission granted to them by Macmillan & Company, Ltd., for the use, in compiling this anthology, of their Globe Edition of THE WORKS OF SHAKESPEARE. They also acknowledge the permission granted to them by Macmillan & Company, Ltd. and by The Macmillan Company of New York to print in the Introduction a quotation from SHAKESPEARE'S PROBLEM COMEDIES, by W. W. Lawrence. Quotations from Dr Mackail's STUDIES OF ENGLISH POETS and LECTURES ON POETRY are also printed in the Introduction, by permission of Longmans Green & Company, Ltd.